Bill Casey

D1533455

Business Driven Information Technology

Wendi Peck

Dave Fauth

Ray Zammuto

Barbara Bauer

Andrew Eiseman

GOODLUCK
IN THE NEW
JOB
Mark Endy [signature]

FOR PATTI —
ALL THE BEST
[signature]

BUSINESS DRIVEN INFORMATION

TECHNOLOGY *Answers to 100 Critical Questions for Every Manager*

David R. Laube

and Raymond F. Zammuto,

Editors

A joint project of the business community

and the faculty of the Business School

at the University of Colorado at Denver

STANFORD BUSINESS BOOKS
An Imprint of Stanford University Press
Stanford, California 2003

Stanford University Press
Stanford, California

© 2003 by the Board of Trustees of the Leland Stanford
Junior University. All rights reserved.

Text of Questions 24, 28, 66, 81, and 82 © by Accenture
LLP. Used with permission.

Printed in the United States of America on acid-free,
archival-quality paper

Library of Congress Cataloging-in-Publication Data

Business driven information technology : answers to
100 critical questions for every manager / edited by
David R. Laube and Raymond F. Zammuto.
    p.   cm.
   Includes bibliographical references and index.
   ISBN 0-8047-4943-4 (pbk. : alk. paper)
   1. Information technology—Management.   I. Laube,
David R. II. Zammuto, Raymond F.

HD30.2 .B734 2003
658.4′038—dc21

2003012489

Designed by Rob Ehle
Typeset by G & S Typesetters in 10/12 Minion
Original Printing 2003

Last figure below indicates year of this printing:
12 11 10 09 08 07 06 05 04 03

Special discounts for bulk quantities of Stanford
Business Books are available to corporations,
professional associations, and other organizations.
For details and discount information, contact the
special sales department of Stanford University Press.
Tel: (650) 736-1783, Fax: (650) 736-1784

Contents

List of Tables and Figures   xi

Preface   xiii

SECTION 1   IT and Strategy   1

1   How does information technology impact industries?   3

2   How has information technology changed the dynamics of competition
     within industries?   7

3   Why do some technological innovations create disruptive changes for
     industries while others do not?   10

4   What is a business-driven technology strategy?   14

5   Should a company be on the bleeding-, leading-, or following-edge
     of technology?   21

6   What are the benefits of mass customization?   25

7   Should a company consider interim or "throwaway" systems as part of
     its technology strategy?   30

SECTION 2   Information Technology   35

Architecture

8   What are the common IT architectures in use today?   39

9   What are the primary considerations for choosing an IT architecture?   42

10   How does an organization develop an architecture plan?   47

11   What are the basic concepts of client/server architecture?   51

12   What are the business implications of fat clients and thin clients?   54

13   What is middleware and the business implications of its use?   57

14   What are the benefits of eXtensible Markup Language (XML) and the
     barriers to its use?   62

15   What are Web services and their implications for an enterprise?   66

16   What are the advantages and disadvantages of a Windows-based versus
     a Unix-based software environment?   70

17 What are the business and technology reasons for choosing one Unix
    platform over another?   74

Applications

18 What are the characteristics of a transaction processing system?   79
19 What are the characteristics and benefits of a decision support system? 83
20 What are data warehouses and what are their benefits?   87
21 What is data mining and what are its uses?   91
22 What are the characteristics and benefits of group support systems?   95

Networks

23 What are the major hardware elements of a network and
    what is the role of each?   101
24 What are the most common types of data networks and their uses?   105
25 What are the differences between voice and data networks?   110
26 What are the implications of the Internet for business users?   114
27 What are the different broadband technologies and their uses?   117
28 What are the major wireless technology platforms?   121
29 How could the use of wireless devices transform how business is done? 126

Security

30 Why is security a major issue?   131
31 What does a firewall do?   135
32 What are viruses and how can an organization protect against them?   138
33 What are the major components of a disaster recovery plan?   142

SECTION 3   IT and E-business   **149**

34 What are the key components of an e-business strategy?   151
35 What kinds of revenue opportunities does e-business create?   155
36 What kinds of cost reduction opportunities does e-business offer?   159
37 What are the different types of business-to-business e-commerce models? 163
38 What are the differences among B2C e-business models?   167
39 What is the right mix of "bricks and clicks"?   171
40 How can a business learn more about its customers using IT?   174
41 What are the major privacy issues associated with e-business?   178
42 What are the uses of intranets, extranets, and portals?   182

43 What technical elements must be in place for a successful e-business
    implementation?   186

44 What are the primary issues involved with integrating front-end
    and back-end systems?   190

45 What e-business assumptions were proven wrong by the "dot.com crash"? 194

SECTION 4   IT and Organization   **199**

46 What impact does information technology have on an organization's
    ability to coordinate and control activities?   201

47 How does information technology affect communication,
    decision making, job design, and power within an organization?   205

48 What role does an organization's culture play in determining the
    benefits gained from new technologies?   208

49 How will other departments within your organization react to a
    technology project?   212

50 Why do customers and suppliers sometimes react negatively to an
    organization's IT projects?   216

51 What is knowledge management?   219

52 Does an e-learning strategy improve a company's training value?   223

53 What are the attributes of an effective relationship between an
    IT organization and the rest of the business?   228

54 Is a centralized or decentralized IT organization better?   233

55 How can the capability maturity model (CMM) be used to improve
    an IT organization's effectiveness?   237

56 How can an internal IT organization's success be measured?   242

57 What is the average tenure of a CIO and why?   246

SECTION 5   IT and Business Processes   **251**

58 Which is more important—business process or technology?   253

59 Why is it important to consider business process design when
    implementing a process technology?   256

60 How much transformation in business processes is needed or desirable? 260

61 When are radical changes in processes and technologies more
    desirable and effective than incremental changes?   265

62 What is an enterprise resource planning (ERP) system?   269

63 What risks does an organization face from an ERP implementation?   274

64 What are the challenges in using a vendor-supplied ERP system to
support redesigned business processes?   278

65 What is a customer relationship management (CRM) system?   282

66 What are the attributes of a good CRM system?   286

67 What are the key attributes of supply chain management (SCM) systems?   291

68 What are the key technology issues around SCM implementation?   294

69 What are the issues to consider when deciding to customize a
standard vendor application?   299

SECTION 6   IT and Resource Allocation   303

70 How does a company know how much it should spend on
information technology?   305

71 How should a company spend its money on technology?   309

72 Is it easier to justify a revenue-enhancing technology investment or one
that reduces costs?   312

73 Is revenue protection a valid justification for a technology investment?   315

74 Why is total cost of ownership (TCO) important?   319

75 Which is more important—the payback period for a project or its return
on investment? Are there other financial measures that should be considered
in evaluating a project?   322

76 How do you choose one technology project over another?   326

77 How will you know if the assumed benefits of a project have been realized? 331

78 What are the major components of a "build-or-buy" decision?   335

79 How do you select a vendor?   338

80 What are the advantages and disadvantages of using an application
service provider?   342

81 What purposes do different types of outsourcing relationships serve?   347

82 When should an organization consider outsourcing?   351

83 What are the considerations for outsourcing portions of your IT offshore? 355

84 When should an organization upgrade its software technologies?   359

SECTION 7   IT and Implementation   363

85 What are the risks associated with the business model of a project?   365

86 What are the risks associated with the implementation of a project?   369

87 What does technology implementation failure look like?   373

88 Why do so many technology implementations fail?   377

89 What are the key components of project management?   380

90 What are the key tools for managing a project?   385

91 What are the implications of Brooks's Law for staffing a technology project?   388

92 Why is it important to explicitly state the intended business result of an
    IT project? How should this be done?   392

93 What role does a project's sponsor need to play in the technology
    implementation process?   396

94 What questions does the project sponsor need to ask a project manager?   399

95 What role does a project's steering board need to play in the technology
    implementation process?   404

96 What are the key managerial authorities a project manager needs
    to succeed?   408

97 What are the keys to getting cross-functional work done?   412

98 What top ten actions can IT project managers take to increase the
    likelihood of implementation success?   415

99 Should you plan for failure?   418

100 How do you know when to kill a project?   421

SECTION 8   Resources   **425**

Appendix: Acronyms   475
Contributor Biographical Sketches   479
Index   495

Tables and Figures

Tables

Table 4.1	Business Strategies, Technology Initiatives, and Tactical Plans	18
Table 4.2	Current Business Situation vs. Future Technology-Enabled Vision	20
Table 5.1	Comparison of Bleeding-, Leading-, and Following-Edge Technology Factors	23
Table 5.2	Approach to Implementing Technology	24
Table 13.1	Middleware Categories	59
Table 23.1	Three Primary Types of Network Wiring	101
Table 23.2	Hardware and Cable Impacts on Transmission Speed	102
Table 33.1	Recovery Strategies	142
Table 39.1	Customer Types and Shopping Preferences	171
Table 52.1	E-learning Technologies	226
Table 60.1	Examples of Scale Options	261
Table 60.2	Example of the Scope and Magnitude of Transformation	262
Table 61.1	When to Implement Radical Changes	267
Table 64.1	Comparison of Competitive vs. Value-Oriented Companies	280
Table 70.1	IT Spending Percentages by Industry	306
Table 76.1	Sample Matrix—Project Alignment with Strategic Objectives	328
Table 76.2	Sample Matrix—Evaluate Financial Value of a Project	329
Table 76.3	Sample Matrix—Determining Project Risk	329
Table 76.4	Sample Matrix—Summary Evaluation of Proposed Projects	330
Table 90.1	Project Management Functions and Associated Tools	386
Table 90.2	Project Management Tool Features	387

Figures

Figure 1	Effective Technology Management	xv
Figure 4.1	Sample Porter 5-Forces Matrix	17
Figure 4.2	Sample SWOT Analysis	18
Figure 8.1	Architecture Overview	38
Figure 10.1	Example Systems Architecture Plan for Manufacturing Company	47
Figure 13.1	Diagram of Enterprise Application Integration (EAI)	57
Figure 14.1	Simple XML Document	61
Figure 17.1	Computing Platforms	73
Figure 24.1	Sample Network Architectures: LANS and WANS	105
Figure 24.2	Physical Network Topologies	106
Figure 26.1	Internet Architecture	113
Figure 30.1	Enterprise Security Architecture	131
Figure 34.1	Components of a Business Model	150
Figure 51.1	Interrelation of Knowledge Management Processes	221
Figure 53.1	Sample Balanced Scorecard for an IT Department	232
Figure 71.1	IT Spending Profile	312
Figure 83.1	Offshore Service Offering Spectrum	356
Figure 86.1	Levels of Project Risk	370
Figure 92.1	Good MOPs Enable Strategic Trade-Offs	394
Figure 96.1	Relationship between Project Manager Authorities and Project Success	409

Preface

In the twenty-first century, information technology (IT) is at the core of most business activities. It provides the foundation that enables today's business enterprises to function and flourish. So whether it is in procurement and production, manufacturing and maintenance, customer care and sales, communications and collaboration, tracking and measurement, or virtually any other business discipline, IT plays a critical role. With something so critical, one would think that the planning, integration, and implementation of IT in organizations would have a strong track record of success. Unfortunately, just the opposite is true. Many business professionals point to the use and deployment of IT as a point of weakness, not a point of strength, in their organizations. The reason for this is often that IT is being driven from a technical perspective, not from a business perspective.

This situation exists because many businesspeople see IT as being too complicated, too expensive, too risky, and too changeable. They don't take the time to understand the complex environment surrounding information technology management, and, for the most part, IT's impact on the enterprise remains poorly understood. Most businesspeople use technology on a daily basis and understand how specific technologies affect their ability to do their specific jobs. However, when it comes to the use of information technology to drive business value, many businesspeople do not participate fully in information technology decisions because of the complexities involved in choosing between competing projects, assessing project risk, and managing implementation, and because they often do not have the knowledge needed to understand what the technical teams are talking about. Poorly understood IT initiatives often end in failure. Sometimes the failure shows up when an IT project doesn't generate its promised financial benefits. Other times the technology doesn't work as promised or causes unintended problems within the organization's business processes, culture, or operations. In many cases, the failures are within the technology itself, and the resulting difficulties with its implementation result in projects that miss time and budget commitments.

But there is no need for failure to be so pervasive. A thorough knowledge of the key factors surrounding IT decisions can significantly reduce failure rates. But more important, when the managers of a business have a thorough knowledge of all aspects of information technology, they can ensure that there is an alignment of business and IT strategies, objectives, and activities. This book was written to help managers develop that knowledge and to help them understand the processes that allow business professionals to successfully drive the use of information technology in their organizations.

The idea for the book originally came when we were designing the foundation information technology class for the MBA curriculum at the University of Colorado at Denver. We wanted to create a class that would adequately prepare any MBA student to enter a world in which information technology plays a central role. We quickly realized that it needed to be focused not only on information technology itself, but also on the impact and implementation of information technology in an enterprise. We also realized that any course about information technology needed to strike a balance between practical experience and academic strength. So we framed the course and the book in the context of 100 questions that are critical for every manager. We then recruited a distinguished group of senior business leaders and faculty to answer those questions in a clear and concise way.

What Is Business Driven Information Technology?

When we talk about business driven information technology, we are really talking about aligning and managing four interrelated sets of activities within an organization. These activities are related to the strategic, financial, organizational, and technological systems of the firm. They are not separate or distinct, although they typically are treated as such in most books and articles about technology and technology management. For example, it is fairly easy to find books and articles on specific technologies (technological system), project management (organizational system), technology and innovation (strategic system), or technology investment (financial system). In reality, however, every technology project has to deal with all these systems simultaneously because they are closely interrelated. Most managers have expertise in one or two of these systems, but managing technology effectively requires the ability

Figure 1 Effective Technology Management

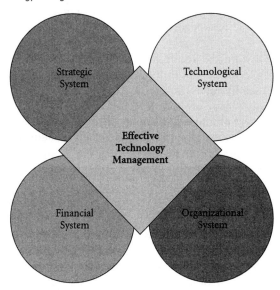

to align them and manage across their boundaries rather than solely within them. Literally, effective technology management means being able to manage at the intersection of these four systems, as illustrated in Figure 1.

Consider the following scenario: a company discovers that its major competitor is about to "go live" with a new supply chain management (SCM) system that will decrease its time from order to delivery by 50 percent while reducing costs; this is likely to result in the loss of several of the firm's major customers to the competitor (strategic system). Managers at the firm astutely realize that they have to close the gap quickly, so they launch a crash program to develop their own supply chain management system with their business partners. A vendor is selected based on a set of design criteria (technological system) and projected financial metrics (financial system) that indicate that the SCM investment will at least break even while protecting market share and margins. A project management team is assembled and charged with leading the required software development effort and implementing the system (organizational system).

A few months after the crash program's launch, the project team encounters "unforeseen" problems with the interfaces among the participating organizations' enterprise resource systems (technological system), and decides that their business processes have to be modified to fit the new SCM system (organizational system). These changes and the associated delay and escalating costs impact the project's financial metrics, increasing the projected payback period and decreasing the projected return on investment (financial system), which push the project's estimated returns into the red. Worse yet, projections indicate that the firm will lose one percent of its market share each month that the project is late, as its customers defect to its competitor (strategic system). How did they get into this situation? What could they have done to prevent it?

Situations like this are not uncommon. Decisions made at the outset of a project significantly affect a technology project's chances for success. Unless those early decisions take into account the interactions of all four systems, "unforeseen" problems are much more likely. And once a project is under way, an understanding of how changes made within one system ripple through to the others is extremely important. The answers to our 100 questions help readers understand the issues associated with all four systems and how they interact. Understanding these issues and interactions increases the chance that the initial project decisions and subsequent actions will reduce the number of "unforeseen" problems that doom many projects.

This book is divided into major sections that describe these four systems and their interactions. The first section, "IT and Strategy," focuses on the strategic system. It looks at how information technology has changed the competitive environments of many industries and, in turn, the strategic challenges that firms face. The answers to the questions in this section show why businesses need to carefully link technology investments to their corporate strategies through business-driven technology strategies. The answers also explore the strategic options that IT has created for firms, enabling them to deal with an ever-changing competitive landscape.

The "Information Technology" section focuses on the technological system and examines the underlying IT infrastructure of a firm. Its four parts examine specific issues related to architecture, applications, networks, and security. The answers are not intended to provide a mastery of this broad range of technical topics. Rather, they provide managers with an understanding of how different elements of technology work and fit together. And, by exploring the managerial issues associated with each topic, they provide a solid background that can be used to make informed business decisions.

The "IT and E-business" section first deals with the intersection of the technology and strategy systems, focusing on how the Internet has created new options for businesses to increase revenues and improve their responsiveness to customers while decreasing costs and extending their reach. Then, the answers review the requirements of making an e-business strategy work, such as the integration of front- and back-end systems, the technical elements that need to be in place, and privacy issues that need to be dealt with effectively.

The fourth section, "IT and Organization," looks at the organizational system; the interdependent relationship between information technology and an organization's structure, culture and people, stakeholder relations, and knowledge management. This section then examines the relationship between a firm's IT organization and the rest of the business. The answers show that an IT organization's ability to demonstrate alignment with the firm's strategy is key to its effective operation. Alignment requires the articulation of a business driven technology strategy and measurement systems that demonstrate this alignment.

The "IT and Business Processes" section focuses on the intersection of the organizational and technological systems. It opens with the perennial question of "Which is more important—business process or technology?"; the answers that follow explore this issue and its implications in some detail. The last part of this section examines three major processes and their associated technologies: enterprise resource planning (ERP), customer relationship management (CRM) and supply chain management (SCM) systems. The potential benefits of these systems are discussed, as are technical and organizational issues related to implementing them successfully.

The sixth section, "IT and Resource Allocation," focuses on the financial system, exploring issues related to technology investment. The answers in this section address questions such as how much a firm should invest in technology, how it should spend that money, what the relevant financial metrics are for evaluating projects, how it can choose among competing projects, and how it can determine if the benefits have been achieved.

The seventh section, "IT and Implementation," returns the discussion to the organizational system, examining issues related to the traditionally weakest area of IT management—that of project implementation. The section opens with a discussion of the risks inherent in project implementation. Most of the remaining answers then focus on how to manage projects to minimize these risks. They examine the requirements for effective project management and provide a wealth of information about managing the project management process. The final two questions close the circle by talking about what needs to be done when things go wrong. Should you plan for failure, and how do you know when to kill a project? While every manager hopes for success, failures are not uncommon, and knowing when to terminate a failing project saves time and money.

The answers to the questions are not meant to be complete treatises on a subject. They cover the basics and are short enough that the reader can absorb them quickly. Each answer contains a set of internal references to other questions, indicated by (Q##), that serve two purposes. First, they show readers where to find more information about a particular topic or issue within the 100 questions. Second, the internal references identify linkages among the four systems. When all the answers are considered in total, they constitute a strong body of very practical knowledge across a wide spectrum of technology topics. And, as a whole, they provide a comprehensive overview of what it means to "manage technology effectively."

The eighth and final section, "Resources," contains references to where further information can be found for each answer. "Web Resources" are portals where current information about a topic can be accessed. The "Articles" section directs readers to more focused discussions, and sometimes competing points of view. The "Books" section points to additional resources that can be accessed should more depth be desired.

The 100 Questions Project

Many books have stories behind them, and this one is no exception. This book is the result of a unique collaborative effort between the business community and the Business School at the University of Colorado at Denver, where it became known as the "100 Questions Project." Business executives, IT professionals, and faculty members volunteered to write the answers to the 100 Questions. The contributors and the editors have completed the project in support of the University of Colorado, and the book's royalties are being donated to the Business School.

We recruited an editorial team for the project that included three former CIOs—Barbara Bauer, Rina Delmonico, and Randy Weldon—two members of the CU-Denver Information Systems faculty—Jahangir Karimi and Dawn Gregg—and Sue Beers (TIA, Inc.). The editorial team set the direction for the answers, recruited authors, and reviewed and edited drafts for their content and compatibility with the project's editorial vision. Dawn Gregg also served in the role as the project's resource editor, researching and filling gaps in the resources. Sue Beers, our copy editor, undertook the enormous job of editing the answers into a coherent whole.

More than 60 business professionals and faculty members joined the project as authors. This group included more than 25 current or former CIOs, CEOs, COOs, and CTOs representing a broad range of firms, such as AT&T Broadband (now part of Comcast), Ball Corporation, Great-West Life & Annuity Insurance Company, J. D. Edwards, Johns Manville, MCDATA, Oppenheimer Funds, QSE Technologies, and SAIC, as well as partners from services firms such as Accenture LLP, Deloitte & Touche LLP, EDS, Executive Leadership Group, Fujitsu Consulting, Oracle Corporation, and PricewaterhouseCoopers LLP. As you'll see from the biographical sketches, the contributors draw upon many years of experience with information technology in formulating the answers. Over a ten-month period, they worked with the editorial team, writing and revising each answer. We appreciate the contributors' persistence. Our corporate and consulting contributors, in particular, had no idea what they were getting themselves into when they volunteered to participate in the project. Their diligence in producing their answers and their willingness to donate their royalties to the Business School is greatly appreciated.

In addition to the contributors, many other individuals lent their support to the project. Sueann Ambron, the dean of the Business School at the University of Colorado at Denver, was a consistent source of support and originally conceived the idea for this project. Christa Rabenold undertook the onerous task of formatting the answers' resources and endnotes. Ellen Metter, the campus business librarian, provided assistance to several of the contributors in researching their answers.

Several member of the business community who do not appear as authors also provided significant support to the project. We owe a special thanks to Daya Haddock and Cindy Gibson from TIA, Inc., for providing the resources for copyediting. Sharon Baake, Oracle Corporation, and Mike O'Hair and Joni Goheen, EDS, assisted us in lining up authors at critical points during the project. The board members of the Center for Information Technology Innovation at the University of Colorado at Denver provided extensive support in recruiting authors and developing the list of questions. We also want to thank Bill Hicks, who, while he was at Stanford University Press, recognized the potential of this book and got the process started that resulted in its publication. Finally, we thank our editorial team members for all their efforts. They have been an exceptional group of people with whom to work.

We hope that you find this book a valuable resource. You might read entire sections or multiple answers. Or perhaps you will focus on specific answers that pertain to a particular challenge you face. In any case, we believe it will give you a good foundation on the subject, whet your appetite for further exploration, and provide you with the tools to make business driven information technology a reality in your organization.

David R. Laube
Raymond F. Zammuto

Business Driven Information Technology

RAYMOND F. ZAMMUTO

SECTION 1 *IT and Strategy*

Information technology (IT) has had a profound effect on corporate strategy over the past three decades, changing the industry conditions in which businesses operate and the strategic options they can pursue. The "IT and Strategy" section in this book focuses on the impact of IT on industries and companies. Questions 1 and 2 explore how IT has changed the "rules of the game" in many industries and, in turn, the dynamics of competition within them. Question 3 examines why the impact of some new technologies is more profound than others, "disrupting" or creating fundamental changes in some industries while not in others. The conclusion that can be drawn from these answers is that IT has gone from being a tool to create competitive advantage to simply being the price of participation in many industries—something a business has to be good at in order to survive.

"Being good at IT" literally means using it to leverage a company's strategy regardless of strategic focus. Leveraging a company's strategy through IT means targeting technology investments to enhance specific strategic objectives. For example, if a firm's strategy is to be a low-cost producer, then its technology investments need to enhance its ability to lower costs. If its strategy is to differentiate itself from competitors by creating unique value for customers, its technology investments need to focus on making the firm more responsive to customers' needs and serving them. Thus, key to "being good at IT" is the ability to create a business driven technology strategy. Question 4 discusses the steps that a company needs to take to develop a business driven technology strategy that ensures that its IT investments and strategic direction are aligned.

Part of the formula in developing a business driven technology strategy is a company's overall technology orientation. Question 5 examines different orientations to technology, their benefits and drawbacks, and some of the conditions under which these different orientations are appropriate. At one end of the continuum is a "bleeding-edge" technology orientation, where a business adopts cutting-edge technologies to gain a competitive advantage by differentiating itself from its competitors. At the opposite end is a "following-edge" orientation, where technology is not an important factor in determining a business's competitive success. Most companies fall somewhere in between. Understanding a company's technology orientation is an important step in knowing what can and cannot be accomplished within the context of its technology strategy.

One of the new strategic options that IT has created for businesses is mass customization. Question 6 explains why mass customization is an appealing strategy. It provides the benefits of what were viewed as mutually exclusive strategies prior to the IT revolution: being a low-cost producer of standardized goods and services for the mass market, or being a differentiator that tailored its goods and services to specific market segments. Mass customization promises the economies of low-cost production coupled with the differentiator's responsiveness to specific customer needs. The answer also explains the difficulties in achieving the benefits of mass customization because it applies only in certain situations where specific market, organizational, and supply chain conditions are met.

Firms increasingly find themselves needing to respond rapidly to changing market conditions, time-limited windows of opportunity, regulatory mandates, and specific customer and organizational needs. Question 7, the final answer in this section, focuses on using IT to cope with rapid change through the use of "throwaway" or ad hoc systems as part of a company's technology strategy. While there is an appeal to quick responses for pressing needs, the answer shows that throwaway systems must be used cautiously because they can negatively impact the effectiveness of a company's overall technology strategy.

The message of this section is that technology has changed industries in ways that make sound strategies imperative. Information technology can play an important role in enhancing those strategies by making their execution faster, more efficient and effective, and more responsive to customer needs and market conditions. But unless a business's technology investments are carefully linked to its strategy, they are unlikely to lead to competitive success.

1. *How does information technology impact industries?*

RAYMOND F. ZAMMUTO

Information technology as we think of it today—computer-based systems—is a relatively new phenomenon in the history of business. Computer technology found its way into large firms, whose information processing needs had exceeded the capabilities of manual systems, during the 1950s. The introduction of IBM's System/360 in 1964 launched computers into the business mainstream, primarily by automating paper-intensive tasks such as transaction processing and record-keeping. The efficiencies generated by automation were compelling and thus began the massive wave of IT investment by business. By the end of 1999, the net stock of IT capital equipment approached $900 billion.[1]

Early analysts predicted that computers would revolutionize businesses and industries. However, until the early 1990s, studies of the economic impact of IT investment on industries revealed that it had not significantly affected industry productivity, raising questions as to whether the IT investments were paying off.[2] At the same time, some studies showed that significant gains were made by individual firms that invested heavily in IT.

CHANGING THE RULES OF THE GAME

While IT investment did not appear to affect the economic productivity of industries until the 1990s, earlier it did have a major impact on specific industries through

---

[1] Kevin J. Stiroh, "Investing in Information Technology: Productivity Payoffs for U.S. Industries," *Current Issues in Economics and Finance* 7.5 (2001): 1.

[2] Erik Brynjolfsson and Shinkyu Yang, "Information Technology and Productivity: A Review of the Literature," *Advances in Computers* 43 (1996): 179–214.

the actions of firms adopting IT as a competitive tool. Simply put, IT reshaped industries by changing the "rules of the game" as large firms discovered ways to leverage their strategies through its use.[3] Because the required investments were large and applications custom developed, firms making successful investments gained significant leads on their competitors through their accumulated IT experience and knowledge. In many cases, IT expertise itself became a source of competitive advantage.

Consider the case of the airline industry. American Airlines was the first airline to invest heavily in IT. Joined by IBM in a five-year development effort during the 1950s, American Airlines developed the first computerized customer reservation system, which eventually became the SABRE system. The original intent was to develop an inventory management system to reduce clerical costs. However, American Airlines discovered that information captured by the system was invaluable in managing passenger service levels and aircraft capacity, and for coordinating baggage handling, food, and fuel requirements. As American Airlines continued to experiment, it found new competitive uses of its IT, such as extending its reach into travel agents' offices in the 1970s, using the information to develop sophisticated pricing models after industry deregulation in 1978, and extending its expertise into new businesses such as IT consulting during the 1980s. The SABRE system itself became a significant source of revenues for AMR, American Airlines' parent corporation.[4]

American Airlines' successful IT investments changed the rules of competition in the airline industry. It forced other firms to respond to its strategy by developing their own IT capabilities, as did United Airlines with its Apollo reservation system, or by ceding industry leadership to the firms that could do so. The two firms that made the most successful IT investments, American Airlines and United Airlines, have held and traded the number 1 and 2 positions within the industry ever since. Similar stories are readily found in other industries. For example, Wal-Mart, which began investing heavily in a computerized logistics system during the 1970s, changed the retailing industry, as did Federal Express's (now known as FedEx) pioneering use of IT to increase reliability and customer service in the express transportation industry. Thus, while IT investment didn't show a discernable effect on industry-level productivity until the 1990s, it reshaped many industries by redefining what it meant to be competitive.

Increasing Productivity and Competition

The effect of IT on industries began to change in the late 1980s. Studies conducted in the early and mid-1990s revealed that IT investment was beginning to have a

---

[3] See, for example: F. Warren McFarland, "Information Technology Changes the Way You Compete," *Harvard Business Review* 62.3 (1984): 161–66.

[4] D. G. Copeland and J. L. McKenney, "Airline Reservation Systems: Lessons from History," *MIS Quarterly* 12.3 (1988): 353–70; James L. McKenney, Waves of Change: Business Evolution through Information Technology (Boston: HBSP, 1995) 98–140.

significant impact on the productivity of industries making heavy IT investments, not just selected firms within them. By the late 1990s there was no longer a question whether IT investments were paying off. For example, one study showed that industries experiencing the largest productivity gains in the late 1990s were those that were the most intensive IT users.[5] While there is no definitive evidence as to why productivity increases began to be observed at this time, there appear to be two major contributing factors: (1) advances in computer technology, and (2) the use of IT to integrate business operations.

1. Advances in Computer Technology   Continued development in computer technology made increasing computing power available at decreasing prices, reducing the cost barrier to IT investment. For example, a 1960s mainframe computer cost millions of dollars, had limited capabilities, and typically required the development of custom applications. In the case of American Airlines, it took 20 years of advances in computer technology and millions spent on software development before its original concept of a customer reservation system could be fully implemented. However, by 1990, the same computing power that cost millions in the 1960s could be purchased for a few thousand dollars, and many general off-the-shelf business applications could be purchased from vendors. By the late 1980s it became possible to do more with IT for a much smaller investment, making it possible for smaller firms within an industry to enable their strategies through the use of IT.

2. The Use of IT to Integrate Business Operations   The second factor is related to changes in how organizations use IT. Prior to the late 1980s, IT investment tended to create "islands of automation" where money was invested in departmental systems with little or no communication across them. These investments largely automated existing processes. In the late 1980s, organizations discovered that they could substantially improve the efficiency, speed, and flexibility of their operations by redesigning them along process lines, where both people and IT communicated across departmental boundaries, streamlining work flows and increasing employee productivity (**Q58**). By the mid-1990s, integrating operations across departments instead of automating within them had become an important theme in IT investment. With the introduction and widespread adoption of enterprise resource planning (ERP) systems (**Q62**), many organizations increased productivity and the speed and flexibility of their operations through a combination of restructuring and IT.

However, as more firms entered the world of IT-enabled operations, the ability to use IT as a source of sustainable competitive advantage decreased. In many industries, IT expertise in itself was no longer a source of competitive advantage because

[5] Stiroh, "Investing" 1–6. Kevin J. Stiroh, "Information Technology and the U.S. Productivity Revival: What Do the Industry Data Say?" *Federal Reserve Bank of New York Web Site*, Staff Report 115, 24 Jan. 2001, 11 Dec. 2002 <http://www.newyorkfed.org/rmaghome/staff_rp/2001/sr115.pdf>.

IT-based innovations could more easily be imitated. Consider the case of the express transportation industry, which FedEx pioneered through its use of information technology. Today FedEx and United Parcel Service (UPS) are in a tight competitive battle for industry leadership. Why? In large part because UPS spent about $1 billion per year through the 1990s to develop IT capabilities similar to FedEx's.[6] As more firms in an industry use IT to streamline their operations, the level of competition intensifies (**Q2**).

Investment in other types of applications during the late 1990s, such as supply chain management (**Q67**) and customer relationship management systems (**Q65**), coupled with the ability of the Internet to reduce the costs of communicating with customers, suppliers, and employees (**Q26**) have further enhanced the productivity effects of information technology on industries by reducing costs, increasing revenues, and increasing the speed of operations. Combined, these integrative systems have created new strategic options, such as the ability to closely tailor goods and services to specific consumer needs (mass customization, [**Q6**]), to know and target customers better (**Q65**), and to develop new channels of distribution (**Q35**).

Summary

IT reshaped many industries during the 1970s and 1980s by changing the "rules of the game." Once a firm successfully pioneered new strategic approaches to the use of information, other firms within its industry were forced to find a defensible niche, pioneer their own innovations, or follow the lead of the early mover. Large IT investments and experimentation allowed many early adopters to gain sustainable competitive advantages. However, during the 1990s, IT's impact on industries began to change. As the relative cost of IT decreased and more firms adopted vendor-provided applications, particularly those integrating operations, it became more difficult to gain a sustainable competitive advantage through IT investments. As Max Hopper, an American Airlines executive instrumental in the development of the SABRE system, wrote in 1990, "In this new era, information technology will be once more pervasive and less potent—table stakes for competition, but not a trump card for competitive success."[7] He was right. IT has simply become part of the price of participation.

---

[6] Brian O'Reilly, "They've Got Mail!" *Fortune* 7 Feb. 2000: 104.
[7] Max D. Hopper, "Rattling SABRE—New Ways to Compete on Information," *Harvard Business Review* 68.3 (1990): 2.

2. How has information technology changed the dynamics of competition within industries?

CHERI LINDEN

Information technology (IT) has changed the competitive dynamics of many industries by increasing the ease of manipulating information and moving it within organizations, as well as between them and their customers and suppliers. Michael Porter's research on IT and the Internet's impact on industry structure shows how his classic "five forces," which influence the level of competition within industries, change as a result of increased and less expensive flows of information.[1] These "five forces" are: (1) barriers to entry, (2) substitution threats, (3) the bargaining power of customers and (4) of suppliers, and (5) the intensity of rivalry. The overall impact, Porter concludes, is increased competition and a reduction in the extent to which firms can establish a sustainable advantage through operational efficiencies.

Increasing the Intensity of Rivalry

IT coupled with organizational restructuring has increased the efficiency of many businesses by reducing costs (**Q1**), often through vendor-provided ERP systems, (**Q62**). Early adopters of these systems gained short-term competitive advantages by becoming more efficient than their rivals. More efficient companies could lower prices while maintaining margins, squeezing the profitability of competitors if they attempted to compete on price. However, the widespread adoption of ERP systems meant that other, usually large, companies within their industries experienced similar gains.

This widespread adoption of ERP and other systems also increased the pace and intensity of industry competition as the flow of information within companies became more transparent. Markets could be monitored more closely and decisions made more quickly using decision support systems (**Q19**) and knowledge management practices (**Q51**). New products and services could be brought to market faster using IT-enabled development methods and flexible production and distribution technologies. Real-time information about sales improved sales forecasting, which, in turn, decreased procurement and logistics costs. Businesses slow to develop these capabilities were at a significant competitive disadvantage in that they could not maintain their margins in the face of decreasing prices, nor could they move as quickly as their competitors to respond to emerging threats or opportunities.

[1] Michael Porter, "Strategy and the Internet," *Harvard Business Review* 79.3 (2001): 67.

RESTRUCTURING SUPPLIER RELATIONSHIPS

Supply chain management (SCM) (Q67) technologies and the Internet have had a mixed effect on the relative bargaining power between companies and their suppliers. Early electronic data interchange (EDI) supply chain technologies were proprietary networks that increased the interdependence of businesses and their suppliers. Companies tied together in a supply chain network shared a common fate as changes in demand quickly rippled through a supply chain because it was relatively difficult for member firms to switch partners.

Later, Internet-based supply technologies (e.g., auctions and reverse auctions, vertical exchanges [Q36, Q37]) shifted the locus of bargaining power, depending on whether it was buyers or sellers consolidating volume. When purchasing was consolidated across companies, they gained bargaining power over suppliers, reducing their costs. In contrast, suppliers' pricing power increased when they consolidated their sales to businesses using the Internet, enabling them to maintain or raise prices. The Internet also can increase the power of suppliers by providing a channel to bypass traditional business partners and reach customers directly. As supply chain technologies continue to develop, particularly with the advent of Web services (Q15), the impact on the bargaining power of suppliers is likely to shift again as the costs of and technical barriers (Q68) to participating in supply chains decrease, reducing switching costs for both suppliers and businesses.

INCREASING NEW ENTRANT
AND SUBSTITUTION THREATS

The Internet reduces geographic barriers to market entry and reduces the need to build proprietary distribution channels. Increased numbers of competitors, coupled with consumers' increased ability to search for alternatives, heightens the intensity of rivalry within an industry and exerts downward pressures on pricing. In the banking industry, for example, the Internet has reduced geographic barriers to new entrants (i.e., other banks), as well as accelerated the blurring of the boundaries between the banking industry and the larger financial services industry. Besides extending the reach of banks not physically located in a geographic area, the Internet has exposed banks to increased competition with other types of financial service businesses (e.g., credit card companies, consumer finance firms, and mutual funds companies) for a share of consumer wealth.[2] As a result, consumers now have access to an enormous amount of information from a much broader range of financial service firms, allow-

---

[2] See, for example: Lloyd Darlington, "Banking without Boundaries," *Blueprint to the Digital Economy*, eds. Don Tapscott, Alex Lowry, and David Ticoll (New York: McGraw-Hill, 1998) 113–38.

ing them to shop for the services and prices that best fit their needs. The impact has been to increase the overall level of competition, which pressures businesses' margins.

INCREASING CONSUMER BARGAINING POWER

The Internet heightens the competitive impact of IT in many industries by increasing consumers' ability to access and search information, making it more transparent while decreasing its cost. Porter notes that the Internet has increased the power of buyers by enhancing their ability to compare products, service offerings, and prices across a greater range of providers. This increased transparency of information reduces switching costs by increasing consumers' ability to find and change providers of goods and services. In turn, consumer bargaining power increases, which exerts downward pressures on prices.

Consider the impact the Internet has had on the airline industry's marketing, pricing, and ticketing practices. With the advent of the Internet, new entrants (e.g., priceline.com, expedia.com, and travelocity.com) were launched to independently provide airline travel information providing customers real-time comparative pricing. Airlines first responded by creating company-sponsored Web sites to provide similar capabilities. Then a consortium of airlines created Orbitz.com as a joint-venture to compete against travel agents and the independent travel search engines for ticket sales. Orbitz was successful in reducing airline costs by diverting traffic from travel agents and the independent Web sites, reducing commissions paid (**Q36**). But it also had the unintended effect of reducing airline revenues because consumers had more fare alternatives presented to them in more usable ways. This has further commoditized air travel and increased competition by allowing people to choose easily among alternatives based on price.[3]

The overall impact of IT has been to increase the pace and intensity of competition in many industries, which tends to lower prices. However, the impact of technology on individual companies within an industry depends to a large extent on a company's ability to use it. For example, while technology has blurred the banking industry's traditional boundaries, thereby increasing the number of competitors that banks face, it has also increased their ability to reduce transaction costs, tailor services to their customers, and deliver services through new channels. Conducting transactions via the Internet significantly reduces costs for banks. A recent study shows that an Internet transaction costs a bank a penny compared to $.27 for an ATM transaction and $1.07 for a teller transaction.[4] The Internet also creates new distribution

[3] Saul Hansell, "Fare Idea Returns to Haunt Airlines," *New York Times on the Web* 27 Oct. 2002, 11 Dec. 2002 <http://www.nytimes.com/2002/10/27/business/yourmoney/27ORBI.html>.

[4] Stephanie Miles, "What's a Check?" *Wall Street Journal Online* 21 Oct. 2002, 11 Dec. 2002 <http://online.wsj.com/article_print/0,,SB1034890125612229148,00.html>.

channels that enable banks to serve their customers 24 hours a day, seven days a week, regardless of where that customer is located. Tools such as data mining (Q21) provide banks with the ability to more finely segment their markets, identify their most profitable customers, and tailor services to meet their specific needs.

CONCLUSION

Developing and pursuing a sound strategy is becoming increasingly critical as technology accelerates the pace and intensity of competition within industries. Strategies yield sustainable competitive advantage when they result in unique value for customers.[5] If a business can create unique value for customers through either the goods or services it produces or through how it delivers them, it is more likely to be able to maintain its margins in industries where the overall impact of technology has been to reduce prices. How a company uses IT can be an important factor in this equation. IT can leverage a company's strategy by reducing costs, increasing the speed of operations, better tailoring its offerings, and so on. But unless the use of IT is closely linked to a business's strategic objectives, it will result in wasted investments and a worsening competitive position, which is why a business driven technology strategy (Q4) is the best protection against wasted technology investments.

---

3. Why do some technological innovations create disruptive changes for industries while others do not?

RAYMOND F. ZAMMUTO AND JEFFREY R. NYSTROM

The term "disruptive technology" was popularized by Harvard Business School professor Clayton Christensen in his 1997 book, *The Innovator's Dilemma: When New Technologies Cause Great Companies to Fail*. Disruptive technologies create something new—whether they are new products, new services, or new ways of doing things—which usurp existing products, services or business models. Christensen's book has been very influential and is often cited as one of the intellectual justifications that fueled the Internet boom during the late 1990s.

---

[5] Michael Porter, "What Is Strategy?" *Harvard Business Review* 74.6 (1996): 61–78.

THE DYNAMICS OF DISRUPTION

When introduced, a new technology's goods and services typically do not attract much attention from an industry's incumbents or their mainstream customers. This is because they tend to be inferior to what is already available in terms of their overall performance, or the features they offer, compared to the established or "sustaining" technology's goods and services. Consider the personal computer during the late 1970s. Existing computer manufacturers, such as IBM, DEC, and Wang, and their customers, wrote it off as a toy, something of interest only to hobbyists, offered by unknown companies without established brands. However, new technologies often contain the seed of a new value proposition within them in that their goods and services are often cheaper, simpler, smaller, and more convenient to use.

The process by which a new technology's goods and services become disruptive is based on the premise that the rate of technological advance generally outpaces customers' abilities to use performance improvements. As incumbents improve the performance of their goods and services, they move upmarket to higher margin segments of the industry. In turn, this creates a vacuum in the market's less profitable segments. At the same time, performance improvements by innovating firms using the new technology enable them to better satisfy consumer needs and fill the vacuum at the market's low end. As the sustaining technology continues to improve, the incumbents' goods and services eventually overshoot their customers' needs for increased performance. Continuing improvements in the new technology, however, enable the innovators' goods and services to meet these customers' needs. As a result, the innovating firms move upmarket, eventually eroding demand for the incumbents' goods and services. When this happens, the new technology becomes disruptive and the industry's incumbents are unseated by the innovating firms.

This was exactly what happened to Digital Equipment Corporation (DEC), which was the innovator that developed and commercialized the minicomputer. DEC initially did not view the PC as a competitive threat but, with rapid improvements in performance, PCs were able to perform many of the functions of minicomputers. By the time DEC recognized the threat it was too late to respond and the company was acquired by a leading PC manufacturer, Compaq.

Why don't the established firms simply adopt the new technology? Christensen argues that leading firms fail to capitalize on new technologies for four reasons that are generally considered good management practice:

1. Leading firms listen carefully to their best customers who do not want the new technology because the new products are initially inferior to current products.

2. Leading firms carefully study market opportunities by measuring size and growth rates, but the markets created by new technologies are impossible to measure and difficult to predict.

3. Industry's leaders are large firms that pursue large markets. The embryonic markets for new technologies generally are not attractive because of their small size, which does not offer much opportunity for meaningful growth.

4. Corporate investment decisions focus on earning the best possible returns, while new technologies often result in less expensive products with lower margins.

As a result, it does not appear rational to pursue a new technology when a firm's sustaining technology offers better opportunities, at least in the short-run. By the time it is obvious that a firm's existing business has been undermined, it is usually too late to enter the market and regain industry leadership.

What Makes a New Technology Disruptive?

A key factor in whether a new technology becomes disruptive is the ability of innovating firms to establish a "value network" to support it. A value network is the constellation of firms—manufacturers, suppliers, distributors, other firms making complementary products, and so on—that create a market for the new technology's goods and services. The personal computer industry's value network included chipmakers, software firms, computer manufacturers, and retailers. During the early 1980s, a series of independent but mutually reinforcing actions by its members created a market for the personal computer. The introduction of the IBM PC provided a design standard leading to the rapid entry of clone manufacturers, whose lower prices increased demand. Microprocessor advances improved performance, and the development of applications software, such as spreadsheets and word processing programs, increased the range of practical applications for PCs. The result was that the PC market took off in the mid-1980s and, as noted earlier, PC manufacturers moved upmarket, taking away business from mainframe and minicomputer manufacturers whose late attempts to enter the PC market were generally unsuccessful.

However, establishing a value network around a new technology is not easy and many potentially disruptive technologies wither from a lack of a supporting infrastructure. The 2001–2002 implosion of the broadband industry is a case in point. Primary assumptions underlying the massive investments in broadband networks were that there would be rapid development of, and increasing demand for, bandwidth-hungry applications. The fact that many of the envisioned applications and demand for them never materialized has led to massive disruption in the industry.

Even when a value network can be established, creating a market for a new technology's products can be difficult, particularly if the rate of technological churn in an industry is high. Consider the case of wireless communications technology for personal communications and computing devices. One of the first technologies on the market was Bluetooth, a point-to-point wireless technology developed by Ericsson in 1995. Bluetooth was promoted as a disruptive technology that promised to provide a cheap and simple way to connect all types of electronic devices—phones, laptops, personal digital assistants, televisions, headsets, printers, camcorders. Realizing the key to establishing a market for the technology was the development of interoperability standards, Ericsson organized the Bluetooth Special Interest Group (SIG)[1] with several major companies, including 3Com, IBM, Intel, Lucent Technologies, Microsoft, Motorola, Nokia, and Toshiba, and invited virtually any firm interested in developing Bluetooth standards and applications to become "associate" members. By the end of 2001, the SIG totaled over 2,000 members.

Even though the value network had been established, the technology was still not successful. Bluetooth's 1998 launch was marred by interoperability problems that were not fixed until a later release in 2001. At the same time, WiFi (IEEE 802.111 wireless LAN) was rapidly gaining attention, with many industry observers predicting Bluetooth's demise. To complicate matters further, another disruptive contender known as ultrawideband wireless technology is awaiting U.S. Federal Communications Commission approval, and its proponents are sounding the death knell for both Bluetooth and WiFi. While wireless communications will eventually have a major and potentially disruptive impact on many industries, it is not likely to occur until a dominant design or technology standard emerges (**Q28, Q29**).

How Do You Recognize Disruptive Changes?

Obviously, identifying disruptive technologies with the 20/20 vision of hindsight is an easy proposition, but how do you do it in real-time for industries with significant technological churn? Andrew Grove, Intel's former chairman, offers some solid advice when he talks about strategic inflection points. A strategic inflection point is the point at which the old way of doing business in an industry disappears and a new one emerges. Disruptive technologies create strategic inflection points in industries, whether it be through the introduction of new products (the PC), new services (Internet-based discount brokerages), or new business models (Dell's "direct model"). Three of Grove's suggestions for recognizing disruptive changes are:[2]

1. Apply the "silver-bullet test." If you had one figurative bullet, for whom among your competitors would you save it? If the answer was clear in the past and not clear now, start looking around for a disruptive change.

2. Pay attention to warnings from people on the front line of your organization who are most likely to feel most vulnerable to changes in the market. Most often these people are middle managers and in your sales organization. If you hear

---

[1] *Bluetooth SIG, Inc. Member Web Site* <http://www.bluetooth.org>.

[2] Grove offers a number of additional suggestions in his book: Andrew S. Grove, *Only the Paranoid Survive* (New York: Currency Doubleday, 1996).

recurring themes in their warnings, it is time to pay serious attention and start looking around for a potential disruption.

3. Engage your customers and business partners in discussions about the direction your industry is taking. Disruptive changes can be more visible to people outside your organization than to those within.

Technology can indeed create disruptive change. The more you are aware of its potential and watch for it, the more likely you will be able to benefit from the change rather than be destroyed by it.

4. What is a business driven technology strategy?

RANDY WELDON

As competition within industries increases, the need for effective corporate strategies has become more important (Q1, Q2). Technology can play an important role in leveraging a firm's strategy by reducing costs, increasing the speed of operations, and enabling a firm to be more responsive to its customers. Unfortunately, many business people have been heard saying things such as, "We don't understand how this project fits into the overall direction of our business. Are we spending our limited funds on the right projects?" Or, "This is an IT (information technology) project. The IT department decides which technologies to implement without our input."

The above scenarios occur when technology strategy is driven by the IT department instead of being driven by the business. A few symptoms of this problem include:

- IT independently creates the technology strategy for the company and employees in other departments don't relate to it because they did not participate in creating it.

- IT, not the business, owns the projects and priorities.

- IT successes are described in IT terms rather than by the impact made on the business.

- Business (and often IT) people cannot articulate the technology strategy for the company, what projects are planned for the next few years, or how those projects help the business achieve its strategies.

How can we reverse this undesirable situation and create business driven technology strategies? Some companies, believing that technology is an important element of their strategy, hire a Chief Technical Officer (CTO) whose job is to develop that strategy.[1] However, despite the lofty title and job description, just designating someone to develop the plan rarely gets it done.

Characteristics of a Business Driven Technology Strategy

A technology strategy refers to how a company plans to use information technology to help achieve its strategic objectives. A successful technology strategy:

- starts with an understanding of the current systems architecture, quality of technical staff, vintage and effectiveness of existing systems, and current systems priorities,

- identifies the company's strategic objectives for the near future,

- describes a vision for how those objectives can be enabled through information technology,

- outlines the policies and high-level tactical plans for achieving that vision.

Performing the tasks described below will help build a solid business driven technology strategy.

Process to Achieve the Characteristics

Creating a business driven technology strategy requires IT members of the strategy development team to perform several tasks, including:

1. learning more about the business,

2. obtaining bottom-up input,

3. determining top-down direction,

4. creating a strategic technology vision and a plan to achieve it,

5. drafting a tactical implementation plan.

Learning the Business   To be credible with other departments, the IT team must learn and document relationships between the key business stakeholders, cross-functional processes, and process cycles in the company.

---

[1] The CTO can report to either the CIO (Chief Information Officer) or to another senior executive. In some companies, the top technology officer is called the CTO rather than the CIO, and there is only one individual fulfilling both functions.

- In addition to the project sponsor, key stakeholders might include:

  – customers

  – suppliers

  – employees

  – government agencies

  – investors

- Depending on the industry, cross-functional process groupings might include:

  – Customer-oriented processes (sometimes called CRM, or customer relationship management, activities such as sales and service [**Q65**])

  – Supplier-oriented processes (possibly including sourcing, procurement, contracting [**Q67**])

  – Enterprise resource planning processes (including sales and operations planning, order entry, and order fulfillment [**Q62**])

- Process cycles refer to how the key subprocesses relate to each other in terms of sequence of information and transactional flow.

Obtaining Bottom-Up Input   To gain an understanding of the business, IT members of the team should invite participation from department managers and subject matter experts in interviews, workshops, and other steps in the planning process. In addition, the business and IT people should discuss and document:

- business and technology trends in the industry,

- current or anticipated competitive threats and opportunities,

- ideas for using technology to serve customers better, create new markets, or improve processes.

Based on the output from this planning process, the joint business and IT group should identify, prioritize and document needs and opportunities for the coming years. This is not easy to accomplish since most organizations will want to assume unlimited funding for future systems projects. That is why guidance must come through the process described next.

Determining Top-Down Direction   Senior IT management should also meet with business executives to obtain high-level strategic planning goals and directions for the business. One objective for these sessions is to put boundaries around what otherwise could be an infinite number of directions for the technology strategy. Some sense of the willingness to invest in technology and the returns expected should also be obtained. Additional research insights may be gained from external groups such as Gartner Group, Forrester, or others.

4 ■━━━◀

Creating a Strategic Technology Vision   Armed with this top-down direction as well as the bottom-up input from the workshops, IT management can draft a business driven technology vision for the company and a plan to achieve that vision. The plan should have two main sections, a *strategic* plan (including the vision) and a *tactical implementation* plan.

The *strategic* section should demonstrate the business understanding gained in the earlier steps of the process including:

- An overview of the major business strategies and trends. Examples include:

  – lowest cost manufacturer

  – expansion into additional geographic areas

  – growth through mergers and acquisitions

- A Porter 5-Forces Matrix describing key business and technology forces (see simplified example in Figure 4.1).[2]

- A traditional SWOT (strengths, weaknesses, opportunities, and threats) diagram. Many entries will have technology implications (see simplified example in Figure 4.2).

At this point, it is essential that senior management be brought into the process. Some highly centralized companies have installed a technology review committee, whose job is to decide on technology priorities of the company. This group is often led by the CEO or COO. Other more decentralized companies allow these decisions to be made in individual business units. In either case, functional heads (marketing, operations, engineering, etc.) or heads of business units are usually members of the group. The buy-in of this group to the proposed vision will ensure that it is linked to the overall business strategy. Without such buy-in, the CIO or CTO must communicate the vision individually to key executives, leaving much room for misunderstanding between key business leaders.

Tactical Implementation Plan   The next step is to translate the strategic business drivers into a tactical list of technology and business process initiatives required to achieve the business objectives and the technology vision. An example initiative might be "Tie us closer to our customers by implementing a new customer relationship management system, including sales force automation, automated contracts and pricing, private portal/exchange, with an integrated call center."

A key part of the implementation plan is the resolution of conflicting technology

---

[2] Michael Porter, *Competitive Strategy: Techniques for Analyzing Industries and Competitors* (New York: Free Press, 1980).

Figure 4.1 Sample Porter 5-Forces Matrix

	Barriers to Entry + High capital requirements + Strong manufacturing expertise required + Overcapacity in industry	
Supplier Bargaining Power + Many potential sources of quality materials − We are small percentage of their sales	**Degree of Rivalry** − Many strong competitors − Strong price competition + Unique, custom value-add systems	**Customer Bargaining Power** − Many possible sources of products − Few large customers + Long-term contracts
	Threat of Substitution − Commodity products easily substituted + Specialty products patented, harder to copy	

(+) indicates a positive factor or force, while (−) indicates a negative force.

Figure 4.2 Sample SWOT Analysis

Strengths + Reputation for quality + Manufacturing expertise + Superior, custom systems differentiators	**Weaknesses** − Lack critical mass of factories over which to spread overhead costs − Limited pipeline of new products coming
Opportunities + Acquire small competitors in markets where we lack presence + License new products in short-run while building pipeline	**Threats** − Competitors buy small competitors before we do − Price war happens before we can build critical mass

(+) indicates a positive factor, while (−) indicates a negative factor.

Table 4.1 Business Strategies, Technology Initiatives, and Tactical Plans

Business Strategies and Objectives	Technology Initiatives	Tactical Plans
Geographic expansion and growth through acquisitions	Migrate to common ERP system (**Q62**) Develop rapid rollout team and process for new acquisitions; implement EAI integration middleware (**Q13**)	Starting now EAI in six months ERP in two years
Quality and manufacturing expertise	Publish standard operating procedures (SOPs) and best practices into content management system (CMS) (**Q52**) Make available to appropriate employees via intranet (Employee Portal) (**Q42**)	Starting now CMS in six months Portal in six months
Differentiate by understanding customers and being the easiest to do business with	Retain customer knowledge via CRM system (**Q65**) Share business information via private trading exchange (Customer Portal) (**Q37**)	Starting in one year CRM in phases over one and one-half years Exchange in six months

project priorities. To have a believable implementation plan, a short list (less than ten) of key initiatives must be prioritized, scheduled over the next few years (balancing limited people and financial resources), and supported by the necessary infrastructure, organization, and management processes. The best solution is to bring the short list of achievable projects to the technology review committee described above and allow them to approve the final decision. Not only does this further ensure the linkage of the final efforts to overall corporate strategies, but it usually results in at least one executive clearly being designated the sponsor for each project (**Q93**).

Based on the business drivers just described, major technology implications and related initiatives can be discerned, as shown in Table 4.1.

Then a series of graphics depicting the primary business stakeholders, processes, and cycles can be used to build a picture of how technology supports the business today, as well as a vision of how the picture could change in the future with new technology, greater integration and standardization, and other changes. Table 4.2 shows a simplified before-and-after picture for a manufacturing company.

Even at this early stage, management will want to understand the preliminary business case for each of the major initiatives. The IT planning team must work with

Table *4.2* Current Business Situation vs. Future Technology-Enabled Vision

Process Cycles	Current Situation	Future Vision
Purchasing	Three legacy purchasing systems across three divisions Distributed buying at 50 plant locations Not integrated with financial or manufacturing systems	One purchasing system within common integrated ERP system Consolidated buying across divisions and plants for like items Reduced costs using an eProcurement system
Manufacturing	Three legacy manufacturing systems across three divisions Difficulty sharing best practices verbally based on personal relationships, especially with many new plants acquired	Add newly acquired plants easily Migrate to best practices available through Intranet Integrate some new companies quickly using EAI software (**Q13**) without forcing costly migration to standard ERP system
Sales	Customer information kept in sales rep's personal files Sales orders taken over phone, fax, and EDI Account status given over phone	Customer information shared among all authorized personnel via CRM system Reduced sales order and account status costs by using the Internet
Logistics	Load tendering by calling multiple vendors over phone and fax Shipping status researched with multiple phone calls	Load tendering automated in transportation management system using the Internet Shipping status available to all over the Internet

the business managers to understand potential payback mechanisms including revenue enhancements, cost reductions, and process improvements. Then the team must develop time-phased approximations of expenses, capital expenditures, depreciation, lease payments, licenses, maintenance, consulting costs, internal personnel costs, and tax ramifications using net present value (NPV) or other return on investment (ROI) calculations (**Q74, Q72**). Tradeoffs between internal options and outsourcing options may also be involved (**Q81, Q82**).

IMPLICATIONS FOR MANAGERS

Business and IT managers should ensure that a technology strategy reflects business, technology, and the intersection between them. This will eliminate the risk that the technology strategy will not be sufficiently linked to the business. This also en-sures business buy-in for the plan, and increases the likelihood that the IT organiza-tion will be successful.

---

5. Should a company be on the bleeding-, leading-, or following-edge of technology?

MARK ENDRY

The decision on how aggressive to be with technology is difficult to make for some companies and natural for others. To arrive at the answer, one needs to under-stand how company strategy is supported by each option. Accurate analysis of the factors, followed by effective execution, can provide a competitive advantage for a company.

What Are the Different Types of Technologies?

For this discussion, there are four basic types of technologies:

1. following-edge technology

2. mainstream technology

3. leading-edge technology

4. bleeding-edge technology

These topics are discussed in more detail on this and the following page.

Following-Edge Technology   Following-edge technology works best for companies that require a stable, low-cost alternative. It is often used by firms in industries that do not depend heavily on technology or do not traditionally use technology as a dif-ferentiator. These technologies are proven and have been in production for some time, so service levels are more predictable. Changes are less frequent and new prob-lems are less likely to surface.

The lower cost of ownership for following-edge technologies may provide a com-petitive advantage.

Mainstream Technology   Mainstream technology is widely selected because it provides a stable solution with strong vendor support. Skilled resources are generally available to support the technology and training is easy to obtain to expand the support base. Mainstream technology regularly supports the standards that are in widespread use, facilitating the exchange of information between companies. Warranty support and maintenance contracts provide a regular flow of technology upgrades and patches, helping keep service levels stable.

Leading-Edge Technology   Leading-edge technology balances a reasonably predictable operating environment with solutions that can provide a competitive advantage. Companies employing leading-edge technology can take advantage of the price and performance gains available from the latest innovations in hardware and software. Leading-edge technology requires that a company be prepared for more frequent changes and those changes can increase costs. Companies should be prepared for a regular cycle of updates and patches that require testing and implementation, but the predictable cycle of releases provides time for planning and scheduling to minimize service interruptions.

Bleeding-Edge Technology   Bleeding-edge technology can be deployed to help a company stand out from its competitors. Early providers of e-procurement and online brokerage services demonstrated that bleeding-edge technology can create market opportunities that help first movers gain significant market share. Companies who aggressively use bleeding-edge technology tend to view technology as a differentiator. Companies using bleeding-edge technologies have to be prepared for some projects to fail, as the technologies do not always succeed. Companies should be prepared for frequent technology updates, some that may be needed immediately to keep production systems in operation. Support from vendors is typically minimal, given their own unfamiliarity with the new technology.

What Factors Should Be Considered?   A company should analyze several internal and external factors while making technology decisions. Careful alignment of the internal and external factors can differentiate a company from competitors.

Internal Factors   The internal factors to consider include company strategies such as:

- tolerance for risk,
- technology spending,
- service level requirements,
- vendor relationships.

A company's ability to attract and retain technology employees and/or the company's strategy to contract for or outsource technology work are also factors.

Table **5.1** *Comparison of Bleeding-, Leading-, and Following-Edge Technology Factors*

Factor	Bleeding	Leading	Mainstream	Following
Risk Tolerance	High	Medium	Low	Medium
Technology Spending	High	Medium	Medium-Low	Low
Service Interruption Tolerance	High	Medium	Low	Medium
Desire for Differentiation	High	Low	Low	Low
Impact on Sourcing Strategy	High	Medium	Low	Medium
Basis of Industry Differentiation	Technology	Technology	Cost	Cost
Rate of Industry Change	Rapid	Rapid	Stable	Stable
Industry Dependency on Technology	High	High	Low	Low

External Factors   External factors to consider include:

- the basis for differentiation in the industry or sector addressed by the company,
- the rate of industry change,
- the industry dependence on technology,
- specific vendor support that might be available for the industry.

How Do These Factors Map to Each Option?

Table 5.1 attempts to rate each factor against a particular technology approach. This generic table generalizes the rating of each factor to illustrate the considerations a company should make.

Does Bleeding-Edge Technology
Always Cost More?

Bleeding-edge technology can be cost effective. Depending on the technology, a company can achieve the cost savings and business process efficiencies that result in market differentiation. E-procurement is a good example (**Q79**). Early adopters not only reduced their procurement costs, but also achieved the prestige of being innovators in their markets.

Another example illustrates the value of early adopters within a single department. One IT group found that product development was always one step ahead of them on implementing new releases of desktop products. As soon as the beta version of a product was available on the Internet, product development would install it. This wreaked havoc with other products on the desktop, including virus scanners and network tools. Service outages increased, and IT wasted resources reacting to the resulting problems (Q84).

After weighing several options, the IT group decided to make this group their ally instead of their adversary. IT committed to having new releases of standard desktop products implemented across the enterprise within six months of the first customer ship date. To meet this goal, they asked the early adopters in the development group to help them troubleshoot new releases before implementing releases company-wide.

The first benefit of this approach was a reduction in service outages. As an early adopter of a new release, the IT group could act as a reference site for the desktop product vendor, who agreed to provide additional support in return. Once the program was fully implemented, the up-front costs of this aggressive approach were offset by a reduction in ongoing support costs.

KEY SUPPLIER RELATIONSHIPS ARE IMPORTANT, TOO

When making this decision, companies need to assess the relationships that they have with their key suppliers, as well as their approach to staffing their IT function. In particular, a company is much more likely to be successful deploying bleeding- or leading-edge technologies if it has a close relationship with its key suppliers and they are invested in making the company successful. Analogously, a company is much more likely to be successful deploying bleeding- or leading-edge technologies if the IT organization is staffed with highly skilled individuals who have a strong desire to continually learn new technologies.

IS THERE A SINGLE ANSWER FOR A COMPANY?

In many cases, the answer can differ by department, further complicating the decision. Consider the case of a company with two product lines:

- The legacy product line is expected to have a low cost of operation and does not require ongoing research and development. The department's goal is to "milk a cash cow" with minimal investment.

- The other product line offers customers new features and options, which require extensive research, development, testing and marketing.

Leading or bleeding-edge technology is likely to be too expensive for the legacy product line, but those technologies might be required for the other product line.

Table **5.2** Approach to Implementing Technology

Statement	% of Respondents
We like to be among the first to implement new technologies.	8%
We see ourselves as an early adopter, however we wait until we see the problems others have had with implementation.	40%
We adopt new technologies when we are confident that they have become mainstream and widely accepted.	44%
We are reluctant to go to new technologies and will generally do so only when necessary.	8%

Source: Ashton, Metzler & Associates and Key3Media Group, Inc., "Voice Over IP," Study, 6 May 2002.

How Do Companies Approach Technology?

Survey data show that relatively few companies are either truly bleeding-edge or laggards when it comes to the adoption of new technologies (Table 5.2). The bulk of companies are almost equally split into two camps relative to new technologies deployment. One camp likes to adopt a new technology only after the bleeding-edge adopters have exposed some of the major issues relative to the implementation of that technology. The second camp likes to wait until the technology has been in use for a while and the majority of issues have been resolved.

The decision to use bleeding-edge, leading-edge, or following-edge technologies needs to be a balanced one. The company's tolerance for risk, cost, and service interruption must be balanced with the potential value (both process efficiencies and market differentiation) each option affords.

6. *What are the benefits of mass customization?*

RAYMOND F. ZAMMUTO

Mass customization refers to the production of customized goods and services at the low costs associated with mass production. The term was coined by Stan Davis in his 1987 book, *Future Perfect*, and reflected the accelerating breakup of many mass markets. Marketing guru Regis McKenna notes that there were many leading brands in the early 1980s but "other" had become the leader in many product categories by the 2000.[1] In essence, consumer preferences shifted from "brand" in the 1980s to "choice" two decades later, reflecting increasing consumer demands for "what they want, when and where they want it."[2]

CUSTOMIZATION VS. MASS PRODUCTION

Mass customization captures the benefits of the two primary strategies open to organizations through the 1980s, *customization* and *mass production*. Customization was the earlier strategy of the two. All goods prior to the industrial revolution were, by definition, customized because they were manufactured on a craft basis. Craftsmen designed and handcrafted goods for individual consumers, making each item unique. The mechanization of production during the industrial revolution changed this because mechanized production required that goods be standardized (i.e., each unit produced was identical). Consumers benefited from lower prices because the efficiency of mass production lowered costs. For example, when Henry Ford began producing Model T's on assembly lines, the Ford Motor Company was able to lower the price of the Model T to consumers by 50 percent. At the same time, however, mass production reduced consumer choice. You could buy a Model T in any color as long as it was black.

Corporate strategy paralleled these methods of production. You could be a low-cost leader in an industry by mass producing standardized goods and services for the mass market, or you could differentiate your products by producing smaller quantities for specific, smaller (and usually premium) market segments. Michael Porter captured this distinction in his landmark 1980 book, *Competitive Strategy*, where the two primary generic strategies he described were cost leader vs. differentiator.[3]

MASS CUSTOMIZATION

Much as mechanization redefined production during the industrial revolution, the rise of information technology brought about fundamental changes to the production of goods and services during the 1980s. Programmable automation began replacing dedicated automation, which allowed changes in production to be made by modifying a system's software instead of scrapping and replacing dedicated

---

[1] Regis McKenna, *Total Access: Giving Customers What They Want in an Anytime, Anywhere World* (Boston: HBSP, 2002) 111.

[2] Brian Fitzgerald, "Mass Customization—At a Profit," *World Class Design to Manufacture* 43.1 (1995): 43.

[3] Michael Porter, *Competitive Strategy: Techniques for Analyzing Industries and Competitors* (New York: Free Press, 1980).

equipment that could manufacture only one specific item efficiently. Suddenly, economies of scope—the ability to efficiently and quickly produce any of a range of parts or services within a family—as opposed to economies of scale—the ability to efficiently produce a large volume of a single good or service—became a competitive possibility.[4]

In service operations, information technology advances created opportunities for the fast movement of information across historic functional boundaries streamlining operations, improving contact with customers, and creating whole new classes of value-adding services, which made it possible for service firms to differentiate their offerings across customer segments. Airlines, for example, identify and offer their high value customers—frequent fliers—special deals, discounts and additional services. Overall, advances in information technology make possible a new strategy where a firm can be simultaneously efficient and responsive in the design, production, and distribution of their goods and services, and can react quickly with greater flexibility as consumer demands and market conditions change.

In manufacturing industries, mass-customizing firms typically work with a set of modular designs or components that are modified according to customers preferences. Customers are presented with menus of choices, the final product reflecting the configuration they desire. Dell Computer is perhaps the most recognized example of this type of mass customizer. Dell Computer offers basic configurations that customers can modify by adding or subtracting components and specifying the type of component they desire, such as speed of the processor and size of the hard drive. Other mass customizers work from basic designs that are tailored to each specific consumer. Andersen Windows, for instance, offers basic window designs that are sized for each customer and customized with selected options.

Service customization, often in the form of value-adding services, is another form of mass customization. Amazon.com, for example, analyzes customer data using recommendation engines to suggest additional purchases based on past buying behavior. IT service providers, such as ASPs (**Q80**) are mass customizers in that they offer template-based application solutions to multiple clients that can be configured to each customer's needs.[5] Similarly, telecommunication firms are becoming mass customizers by packaging and pricing communications services into bundles targeted at different groups of consumers. Configuring the bundles is achieved by turning different services on or off through software, allowing these firms to offer each consumer exactly the package of services they want.

---

[4]M. Jelinek and J. D. Goldhar, "The Strategic Implications of the Factory of the Future," *MIT Sloan Management Review* 25.4 (1984): 29–37.

[5]Elena Christopher and Geraldine Cruz, *Mass Customization of IT and Business Services: Insights from the Automotive Industry*, Gartner, Inc., Dataquest Perspective ITSV-WW-DP-0135, 20 Sept. 2001.

WHY MASS CUSTOMIZATION IS HARD TO DO

While the benefits of mass customization are appealing, most organizations find it hard to do. There are three primary reasons for this:

1. customer demand

2. organizational capabilities

3. supply chain flexibility

Customer Demand   There is always a question of whether customization will increase the value of a good or service from the perspective of the customer. Gartner Research notes that only certain types of consumer products are amenable to mass customization—those where customers:

- desire to customize products to satisfy personal tastes or preferences,

- need to customize products for health or physiological needs,

- need to customize products for functionality.[6]

If there is potential demand, then there is a question of whether customers are willing to pay a premium and wait for the delivery of a good or service versus buying a standardized version immediately off-the-shelf at a lower price. Even within favorable product categories, it is likely that only a minority of consumers will value customization. In other words, while it may be technologically feasible to customize a good or service, there may not be a large enough market opportunity to make mass customization a profitable strategy.

Organizational Capabilities   Mass customization requires a higher degree of organizational flexibility than most organizations possess—particularly those that have been mass producers of goods and services. Historically, manufacturing and service organizations have been functionally organized with vertical flows of information and authority. Mass customization requires that information flow where it is needed quickly, regardless of who historically might have "owned" it. ERP and CRM systems can provide this type of information flow, but as is noted elsewhere in this volume (**Q63**, **Q64**), such systems are difficult to implement. Moreover, organizations need flexible cultures and structures that provide the authority needed by line personnel to respond quickly to varying customer needs, preferences, and demands (**Q48**). In other

---

[6] Hung LeHong, *CPG Industry: Will the Internet Bring Mass Customization?* Gartner, Inc., Commentary COM-13-5214, 23 May 2001.

words, the degree to which a firm can function as a mass customizer is directly related to the extent to which it has organizational and operational flexibility.

Supply Chain Flexibility   Mass customization also requires a flexible supply chain. Mass production is a push system, where firms produce a forecast and the suppliers provide inputs based on those forecasts. Inventories buffer the production system from demand variations, allowing the supply chain time to respond to changes in demand. In contrast, mass customization is a pull system, where goods and services are produced on demand. On one hand, costs are reduced by running "lean" systems with little or no inventory. On the other, little or no inventory means that the supply chain needs the ability to respond to demand changes in real-time. This requires that all the members of the supply chain have flexible operations and the ability to communicate with the mass-customizing firm quickly. Supply chain management systems (SCM) (**Q67**) can increase the speed of communication by integrating members' operations virtually, but, as is discussed elsewhere (**Q68**), these systems are difficult to implement successfully.[7]

IMPLICATIONS

Mass customization is an alluring strategy for many organizations. It can make them more responsive to the consumer, which can increase customer satisfaction and loyalty while increasing profit margins. However, achieving a successful mass customization strategy is difficult because it requires that:

- customization provides an attractive value proposition for consumers,

- the mass customizer is able to operate flexibly,

- the supply chain operates flexibly as well.

These last two points are where the technology comes in. Enterprise resource management systems (**Q62**), customer relationship management systems (**Q65**), and supply chain management systems (**Q66**) form the technological backbone that enables a mass customization strategy. If there is insufficient demand to make mass customization profitable or if these technologies cannot be successfully implemented (**Q78, Q79**), mass customization won't work.

---

[7] For an example of a flexible, integrated supply chain, see Joan Magretta, "The Power of Virtual Integration," *Harvard Business Review* 76.2 (1998): 72–84.

7. Should a company consider interim or "throwaway" systems as part of its technology strategy?

CHERYL L. WHITE AND THOMAS KIEFER

The theme of the 21st century is change. Building throwaway systems is one way to keep up with change. As information replaces commodities and materials as the primary product on the market, the need for instant access to useful and usable data grows exponentially. Unprecedented morphing in how businesses do business mandates an IT strategy that supports the development of interim and temporary IT solutions. The technical challenge is to remain abreast of the changing business environment without causing considerable harm to the user, the IT budget, and the IT systems portfolio.

Definition of Throwaway Systems

Throwaway systems can be understood as interim solutions built to solve specific and immediate business problems. Because the problems they are designed to address are typically urgent or short lived, throwaway systems tend to be punched out very quickly and often with less design, architecture, and development rigor than would normally be employed on IT systems targeted for long-term use. The end-state system can be a prototype, a "quick hit" created by a skunk works (or ad hoc) group, or any other integrated set of system components that work together well enough to temporarily deliver expanded business functionality at market speed. What separates throwaway systems from other IT solutions is the emphasis on interim or temporary use.

Why Companies Build Throwaway Systems

IT organizations invest in throwaway systems for a variety of reasons. In some cases, pressing business initiatives such as legal mandates may demand a rapid IT response. In other environments, competitive pressures may require immediate support of marketing or sales campaigns or the need to take advantage of a small window of market opportunity. Sometimes impatient users, unwilling to stand in line for new capability, will prevail upon management to trade features, functionality, and operating stability for speed of delivery. In other situations, a temporary solution is carved out to support clients until a fully featured system is constructed and released.

Benefits of Throwaway Systems

Throwaway systems can satisfy regulators, keep clients happy, or postpone large IT investments. Clearly, the primary benefit of throwaway systems is fast delivery. Secondary benefits include:

- rapid access to business information,

- the delivery of short-term solutions to pressing business problems or mandates,

- the creation of interim solutions when a rapidly evolving or volatile business environment precludes the design of the final systems solution.

Disadvantages of Throwaway Systems

However, a throwaway approach to systems development should be applied with caution. Often these systems lack solid architectures because of the speed at which they were designed and constructed, and they rarely integrate seamlessly into the applications suites they augment (**Q9**).

Because technical compromises have been made in the interest of time and effort, they may not be feature-rich. So in most organizations, the user's wish list continues to grow after the system is implemented. They want more and more features squeezed into the software: features that the designers never intended the software to accommodate; features that, if implemented, make the product unstable or unreliable (**Q69**); features that, if not implemented, jeopardize customer satisfaction.

Another frequent drawback of throwaway systems is that, because they were created for emergency problem solving, they are not designed to provide the throughput or response time required to support high traffic or hit volumes. This means they don't scale when the client wants the system expanded to serve a much larger user community. The good news to an IT organization is that its users are really pleased with the quick new system that serves the 100 person department. The bad news is when they want it immediately expanded to all 10,000 users in the division, sometimes it just can't technically be done (**Q86**).

And when, in the interest of delivery speed, the system is built using a development tool or operating platform different from the standard or legacy system architecture, the system will not integrate easily with other software used in the company. This hinders ready transfer of data between systems, hampers reuse, increases the possibility of data duplication, and serves to limit system transparency essential in net-enabled systems (**Q13**).

Few options exist for managing a system that is heavily encumbered with technical shortcomings. It can be enhanced on the existing platform, but that risks reinforcing the use of a poorly designed or fragile system—possibly allowing it to live with its inadequacies forever. It can be rebuilt entirely, requiring additional outlays in time and money, with equal or greater investment than that which was not feasible at the onset. Often the business case for a "rebuild" is not compelling since most of the business benefits have already been harvested by the use of the interim system. Finally, it can be shelved, as was the original intent, assuming its functionality has been replaced.

DEVELOPMENT APPROACHES
FOR THROWAWAY SYSTEMS

Ultimately the IT manager must trade off advantages and disadvantages. One way of doing this is to select a development approach that maximizes the advantages and minimizes the disadvantages of throwaway systems.

Although often maligned, development methodologies like Rapid Application Development (RAD), rapid prototyping, or Xtreme Programming (XP) are ideal for the rapid development of throwaway systems. These techniques follow the "build it, try it, fix it" approach and can be used to ensure that maximum business value is delivered in the shortest period of time, with the least amount of effort, operational instability, and technical risk in the finished product.

Another development approach for throwaway systems is to design and build system building blocks that hook together like "Legos." By keeping components small, generic, and plug-and-play, the upfront investment in business functionality remains modest compared to the monolithic architecture of the past. Modules develop rapidly, plug into the system infrastructure quickly with minimal operational impact, and can be discarded without regret when, as needs of the business evolve, they reach the end of their natural life. Properly designed, modular components have the added advantage of reuse. One module called by many functions eliminates redundant development and maintenance effort. Web services are starting to emerge as a major factor in this approach to systems development (**Q15**).

LESSONS LEARNED

Unfortunately, in most organizations, throwaway code is rarely thrown away. As a result, many companies have systems portfolios that contain a hodgepodge of "interim" systems that have taken up permanent residence. These systems are accompanied by high maintenance costs, inflexibility in the face of changing business needs, high operational risk, and, perhaps, a tenacious user community that will not part with them. If there is one lesson to be learned about the development of throwaway systems it is this: *include throwaway systems in the IT strategy cautiously and only after considering how these temporary systems will be designed, built, and thrown away.*

Ideally before embarking on an interim initiative, schedule a fully featured replacement system—one that is approved and funded—into the technologies work plan. Establish parameters for when the throwaway system will be discarded. Failing that, select an appropriate development methodology and invest up front in a robust design for the interim system that addresses system architecture and scalability issues. During the design phase, work through the implications that may occur if the system becomes a permanent fixture in the IT portfolio and define out-of-the-box mitigation strategies for those risks. Finally, understand that once implemented, the interim system may live forever, so build that contingency into the IT strategy in the planning phase.

SECTION 2 *Information Technology*

JAHANGIR KARIMI

Information technology (IT) has undergone rapid and fundamental changes since it was first introduced in organizations nearly 50 years ago. Building an IT infrastructure that supports existing business applications while remaining responsive to changes in IT is critical to the long-term competitiveness for many organizations. This is a difficult task not only because of the pace of change, but also because of the increasing breadth and depth of applications needing support. The intent of the IT section is to cover the basic issues of IT itself. So it starts with issues about IT architecture, applications, and networks. It then moves to coverage of essential components of IT infrastructure and finishes with a discussion of security, firewall, and disaster recovery issues that are associated with managing the IT environment.

ARCHITECTURE

A corporate IT architecture is essential for guiding application development, facilitating the integration and sharing of data, and identifying the major information categories and their relationships to business processes. The "Architecture" section focuses on the IT architectures that most companies implement in their business operations and points out the need for integration among them. Question 8 compares and contrasts centralized, distributed, and Web-based IT architectures. Question 9 examines important IT principles governing the selection of an appropriate IT architecture for an organization and identifies the important factors that need to be considered in developing one. Question 10 outlines the four tasks associated with the planning process for developing IT architectures and explains how to develop an architecture diagram.

In discussing the components of IT architecture, Question 11 starts by defining the roles of clients and servers and their evolution in supporting distributed, heterogeneous computing environments. Question 12 discusses the architectural and business trade-offs associated with using fat or thin client architectures, and points out four important criteria in the selection process.

Supporting heterogeneous distributed computing environments usually requires the use of middleware, which insulates developers from the complexities of dealing with multiple platforms and operating systems and speeds system development. Middleware increases portability, provides access to data in dissimilar databases, and supports development of open and flexible systems. Question 13 discusses four common categories of middleware and highlights the complexities associated with each. Questions 14 and 15 discuss two recent developments in Web-based middleware and highlight how XML and Web services can increase portability and connectivity of applications within and across companies and over the Web. Questions 16 and 17 deal with important developments in Windows-based and Unix-based application development environments, and discuss the business and technological reasons for selecting various platforms.

APPLICATIONS

The use of IT to support managerial decision making is rapidly increasing. Questions in the "Applications" section examine several important developments in management support systems (MSS). These systems are designed to aid managers in their decision making tasks and are essential, in many cases, for the operation of their businesses. Question 18 addresses the roles and common features of transaction processing systems (TPS). In Question 19, characteristics, major applications, and key benefits and challenges associated with the development and use of decision support systems (DSS) are discussed. A DSS attempts to improve the accuracy, timeliness, and quality of managerial decision making rather than emphasizing reduced costs.

The data needed for MSS and DSS applications are extracted from several sources and summarized in a variety of data warehouses and data marts. Question 20 highlights the differences between TPS databases and the data warehouses used for DSS. It further discusses the issues associated with selecting the appropriate type and technology for a data warehouse. It points out that the administration costs, and not the acquisition costs, are the major costs associated with implementing a data warehouse. Data-mining tools use the information contained in data warehouses to enable managers to develop insights into the operation of their businesses. Question 21 discusses the various uses of data-mining tools, suggests criteria for their evaluation, and highlights issues associated with their implementation and use.

Group support systems (GSS) are another form of MSS. They are specifically designed to support and enhance collaborative computing, group work, and other activities that normally occur at face-to-face meetings. Question 22 discusses the advantages and disadvantages of using a GSS and points out the various ways to bring GSS into a company.

NETWORKS

The "Network" section deals with the different types of networks common in today's IT environment. A reliable and robust network is a prerequisite to developing any distributed IT architecture. Question 23 discusses the physical network as a collection of communication links, cables, routers, and switching equipment. It distinguishes between various forms of network wiring or cabling in terms of their speed, capacity, and usage. Question 24 addresses various types of data networks, their architecture, and signaling methods. In Question 25, the differences between voice and data networks are highlighted. Although traditionally voice and data networks have been completely separate, the trend is to migrate more voice to data networks, and to address quality of service required by voice applications. Question 26 focuses on the network of all networks, the Internet, outlining the development of the Internet and discussing the role it plays in business.

The usability of a network is partially a function of bandwidth, or the capacity of the network to transmit data. Question 27 addresses the implications of broadband networks from both providers' and users' perspectives, and examines the different delivery mechanisms available today. Widespread access to high-bandwidth networks opens new network and computing capabilities for both corporate and home users.

Another development in networks is the availability of wireless technology platforms and their applications. Question 28 discusses wireless technologies. Issues associated with standards and the recent developments in wireless LANS and Personal Area Networks are discussed. Recent advances in wireless and portable devices and their impact on how business is conducted are addressed in Question 29.

SECURITY

As computer systems become more interconnected, security plays an increasingly important role in the management of the information resources of a company. Recent serious threats and legal responsibilities have many companies boosting their security chief to executive status. In addition, the increased reliance on the Internet as a business-to-business medium raises issues of how to incorporate customers and business partners into a company's security strategy. Question 30 discusses the importance of security not only for conducting business but also for doing it as efficiently as possible. It discusses the security architecture for an enterprise and the key decision drivers, policies, standards, and procedures for aligning a company's business vision with its IT security requirements. A firm's security architecture needs to provide a layered approach that enables the development of new ideas while protecting information assets of a company.

As part of the above layered approach, firewalls control the transfer of data between a company's network and an external network. Question 31 discusses the role of firewalls within a company's overall security architecture, and explains their benefits and limitations. But even with firewalls, viruses are still a problem. Question 32 describes viruses and explains various ways to protect systems against them. By understanding how viruses work, a company can put in place appropriate protection and recovery strategies to survive attacks.

As dependence on IT increases, so have economic vulnerabilities associated with downtime. Protection against viruses by itself is not enough to protect a company's assets when faced with a disaster or a crisis. The last question in this section, Question 33, outlines the major components of a disaster recovery plan along with various recovery strategies. Using multiple strategies for disaster recovery is becoming more common, as critical business processes are increasingly dependent on IT services.

A thorough understanding of this section will not provide a mastery of this broad range of technical topics, but it will provide a solid background that can be used to make informed business decisions.

8. *What are the common IT architectures in use today?*

WILLIAM WHITE AND DAWN GREGG

Information technology (IT) architectures consist of technology infrastructure and the models, policies, and plans for guiding its development. An IT architecture is used to convert business strategies into IT strategies, to develop a plan for a company's technology infrastructure, and to provide a framework for making technology decisions and resolving technological conflicts. Most companies implement different types of architectures depending on when and how the architecture becomes embedded in their business operations and how rapidly they can implement technological advances. For systems integration purposes, the common IT architectures depicted in Figure 8.1 are required to interoperate with each other as part of a larger corporate information system.

MAINFRAME ARCHITECTURE

The monolithic/mainframe architectures of the 1960s and 1970s comprised a single, physically large mainframe computer that was connected to numerous "dumb" terminals. The design of any software application architecture was based on the capabilities of the mainframe's operating system and available system components. The application design often included file access, primitive database capabilities, shared memory locations, etc. This design supported a large number of simultaneous users and high transaction volumes. Although these applications are less prevalent as they age, some large companies still run critical business applications that were built during this time.

Figure 8.1 Architecture Overview

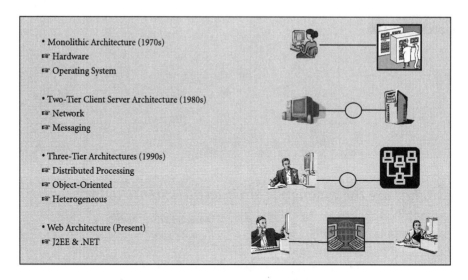

- Monolithic Architecture (1970s)
  ☞ Hardware
  ☞ Operating System

- Two-Tier Client Server Architecture (1980s)
  ☞ Network
  ☞ Messaging

- Three-Tier Architectures (1990s)
  ☞ Distributed Processing
  ☞ Object-Oriented
  ☞ Heterogeneous

- Web Architecture (Present)
  ☞ J2EE & .NET

TWO-TIER CLIENT/SERVER ARCHITECTURE

In the 1980s, distributed computing architectures began to be used. The first type of distributed architecture was the two-tier client/server architecture (**Q11**). In two-tier client/server architectures, the client is usually the user's desktop computer and the server is a more powerful machine that provides database services to many clients. The client/server software architecture is intended to improve *usability*, *flexibility*, and *interoperability* over monolithic architectures.[1]

The two-tier client/server architecture is used extensively for non-time-critical information processing applications like decision support systems (**Q19**). It is a good solution for distributed computing systems that need to support 12–100 simultaneous users. However, when the number of users exceeds 100, performance begins to deteriorate. In addition, most two-tier architectures limit interoperability because they implement complex processing logic (such as managing distributed database integrity) using proprietary DBMS (database management system) languages. Finally, most two-tier client/server systems provide limited flexibility in moving program functionality from one server to another.[2]

---

[1] Darleen Sadoski, "Client/Server Software Architectures—An Overview," *Carnegie Mellon Software Engineering Institute Web Site* 2 Aug. 1997, 3 Dec. 2002 <http://www.sei.cmu.edu/str/descriptions/clientserver.html>.

[2] Darleen Sadoski, "Two-Tier Software Architectures," *Carnegie Mellon Software Engineering Institute Web Site* 10 Jan. 1997, 3 Dec. 2002 <http://www.sei.cmu.edu/str/descriptions/twotier.html#512860>.

THREE-TIER CLIENT/SERVER ARCHITECTURES

In the 1990s, the industry introduced the three-tiered client/server model (sometimes called multitier model). In this model, a middle tier was added between the client user interface and the server databases. The middle tier is used to execute business logic and rules, and can accommodate hundreds of users by providing functions such as queuing, application execution, and database staging.[3] The functionality of the middle tier varies depending on the application domain (e.g., transaction processing monitors, message servers, or application servers, [**Q13**]). Three-tier architectures are used in distributed client/server environments which share resources, such as heterogeneous databases and processing rules.[4] The drawback to most of these architectures is they increased significantly the number of servers utilized by an application, thus increasing costs and complexities.

8 ━━━

WEB ARCHITECTURE

By the late 1990s, the organizations had to face the challenge of integrating the Internet into their systems architectures. IT organizations responded by applying classic architecture models to this new paradigm. Organizations that used multitier models tried to adapt the Web interface into the same client/server model. Older mainframe shops tried to interface a Web client to a monolithic architecture. These solutions were only partially successful. What was required from the computing industry was a new architecture that incorporated the prior architectural advances with the capabilities of the Internet.

To that end, two models have emerged, Sun's Java 2 Enterprise Edition (J2EE) and Microsoft's .NET. Both are complete application frameworks that leverage the Web infrastructure, but also allow the incorporation of older technology bases (e.g., legacy applications). These application architectures are being used in a new breed of applications that connect end users to distributed applications via intranets, extranets and the Internet (**Q26, Q42**).

.NET Application Architecture   The .NET Application Architecture views the application as a suite of services that are interconnected via a messaging service. The three principal sections of .NET are the Smart Client elements (targeted toward the Windows operating system), the XML Web Services (**Q14, Q15**), and the Server elements.

J2EE Application Architecture   The competing architectural framework is Sun's J2EE platform. The J2EE platform is intended to be a much broader framework that is not

---

[3] Darleen Sadoski, "Three-Tier Software Architectures," *Carnegie Mellon Software Engineering Institute Web Site* 26 Feb. 2000, 3 Dec. 2002 <http://www.sei.cmu.edu/str/descriptions/threetier .html#34492>.

[4] Sadoski, "Three-Tier."

platform dependent. J2EE defines standards and tools to access database management systems, via a middleware layer (Enterprise Java Beans) that provides transaction monitors, security, etc., to distributed applications (**Q13**).

CONCLUSION

Organizations today use a variety of IT architectures. Organizations still use monolithic mainframe architectures and client/server-based architectures for many of their information systems. However, the Internet has dramatically changed the way organizations use computers and Web application architectures will increasingly be adopted. The question organizations will face is which one to choose.

Both the .NET and J2EE architectures are remarkably similar. They both focus on support of various clients; both have a strong messaging connectivity capability and leverage the server side capabilities. Both have the ability to interface to legacy systems. The key criterion for most organizations is their existing infrastructure. In a heterogeneous environment, J2EE will provide the greatest range of flexibility. It has the greatest potential to support and leverage existing legacy applications. The .NET framework provides strong capabilities within the Microsoft family of products and also interfaces to other legacy systems. In either case, architectures within an organization gradually evolve over time. The changes are driven by the ability of those architectures to serve the business as well as the return on investment that can be generated by switching from one architecture to another. In the end, business value drives architecture decisions, as it should in all areas of IT.

---

9. What are the primary considerations for choosing an IT architecture?

STAN HUME

An information technology (IT) architecture is an extension and reflection of the organization's customer base, mission, strategy, structure, and culture. It is very similar to the architecture of a house. Just as the house's architecture reflects the tastes, ages, lifestyle, and needs of the owners, an IT architecture reflects the organization. Information architectures generally come about in one of two ways. Either they are planned and built from the ground up or they evolve, sometimes in an unfocused manner. In both cases, they tend to reflect the organization.

ARCHITECTURAL BACKGROUND

IT architecture is a set of policies and rules that govern the use of IT and plot a roadmap to the way business will be done in the future. It provides technical guidelines rather than rules for decision making. It has to cope with business uncertainty and technological change, making it one of the most difficult tasks to perform. A few decades ago, the IT architecture of an organization was very simple. Everything was contained in a single mainframe computer system. Users had access to the system through the "green screen" or "dumb" terminal (**Q12**) and the thought of linking one organization's private systems to another's was unthinkable. Small organizations that couldn't afford a mainframe were out of luck. In the past 25 years, the available options and external obligations have grown exponentially. Today, architectures are very complex, involving numerous technologies including mainframes, PCs, networks, servers, handheld devices, wireless devices, and the Internet. While this diversity has provided great opportunities for productivity, it has created a real challenge for IT organizations to support the environment in a cost effective manner.

IT PRINCIPLES AND ARCHITECTURAL COMPONENTS

IT architecture presents many difficult choices such as:

1. What data and applications must be company-wide and what should be managed locally?

2. What standards should be adopted or what vendors chosen?

3. What rules should govern the decisions?

4. What policies should guide the process?

To provide overall direction for an IT architecture, many organizations establish formal *IT principles* to define the rules of how the IT organization selects components in its architecture including:

- *Organization*—centralized, distributed, federated organizations (**Q54**)

- *Infrastructure*—connectivity needs among hardware, software, and communications components, for example, "We will only use common, mature technologies from established suppliers." (**Q79**)

- *Integration*—for example, "We will only integrate systems/applications using a particular technology or method." (**Q13**)

- *Applications*—for example, "We will buy rather than build." (**Q78**)

- *Data*—enterprise data plans need to be developed, for example, "We'll enter data once and share rather than enter the same data multiple times." (**Q20**)

A good architecture evolves over time and is documented and accessible to all managers in the business. It typically establishes standards for hardware, software, processes, and procedures in an effort to manage the diversity of the environment and keep costs down. An important part of IT architecture deals with distributing, using, and managing information to accomplish desired business strategy. Thus, IT architecture is as much a managerial issue as it is a technological one.

ORGANIZATION STRUCTURE

There is a very close linkage between the organization's structure and the IT architecture. This is best illustrated with a few examples. The IT architecture for a university that serves thousands of students who are generally located in a single campus environment would tend to focus on the functions that are provided to the students such as e-mail, registration, testing, library, and research, etc. Security would be of utmost importance so individuals can see only their information. Student-used systems would tend to be separated from administrative systems. Virtually every IT service would be centralized and managed from a single location.

A global manufacturing and sales organization, however, would have radically different systems to support its business. These systems might need to be multilingual and have differences by country due to cultural and legal requirements. They would then feed information to a central location for management reporting and financial accounting purposes. Rather than the centralized systems of a university, a global organization may have a decentralized architecture with interfaces and integration between the various business units (**Q54**).

Likewise, the IT architecture for a hospital, police department, bank, city government, online retailer, or overnight package service would reflect the function of the organization and would be heavily influenced by that organization's centralization / decentralization, the technical literacy of its user community, the speed that it has to operate, etc.

DEVELOPING AN IT ARCHITECTURE

What if an organization doesn't have an IT architecture? If the organization has systems, even two PCs with a network, it has a de facto architecture. If the architecture and systems are not meeting the needs of the organization, then one should document the current key systems, perform a gap analysis in light of the organization's vision and needs, and then develop the future architecture including defining the steps to getting there. Similarly, a new organization wishing to establish an IT architecture would define how its business processes should work and develop an architecture to match the business process needs (**Q10**).

CONSIDERATIONS IN CHOOSING AN ARCHITECTURE

An IT architecture is not created in a vacuum and an architecture that is appropriate for one organization likely would be inappropriate for another. Many factors must be considered in developing an IT architecture including:

- The core function of the organization, whether it is a business, hospital, government, university, etc., as discussed earlier.

- The overall organization's mission, goals, structure, geography, culture, and size. These factors impact architecture decisions such as languages, network structure, capacity, and centralized or decentralized systems.

- The user base and its technical literacy. The skills and knowledge of employees can affect the level of technology sophistication in an IT architecture. A complicated architecture that requires significant technical capability of a nontechnical user creates, rather than solves, a problem.

- How the organization changes over time. Factors such as rapid or slow growth, growth by acquisition, or regular business structure changes determine flexibility, sizing, and the centralized vs. decentralized decision.

- The competitive environment of the organization functions. Competitors' capabilities may dictate an organization's system requirements.

- Required core applications. The key core applications (billing, inventory, etc.) serve as the major building blocks for the architecture, so the architecture chosen for those big blocks impacts the smaller ones.

- What key data elements are needed and how the data should be organized and accessed. The determination of key data (customer, product, process, service, quality, etc.) and how it is organized, shared, and reported drives location, size, and integration requirements.

- Defined principles for applications, data, infrastructure, and integration. The "rules of the game" described earlier directly influence architecture decisions.

- Preparation for technology evolution. Today's architecture and technology decisions can directly impact an organization's ability to adopt tomorrow's technologies such as wireless and partner collaboration.

- The role of the Internet in the organization. How the Internet is used, whether it is for information dissemination, order processing, product distribution (e.g., software), customer service, etc., drives architecture, security, and integration decisions.

- The need for cooperation (integration) between trading partners (suppliers and customers). Proper architecture must be in place if B2B (business-to-business) capability is desired.

- The possible role of wireless devices (Web-enabled cell phones, PDAs). These devices create integration and security architecture needs.

- The relationship between computer systems and telephones (if any). Computer telephony integration (CTI) can be a key driver in customer service (call center) applications.

- Defined standards for hardware, software, and networks. Which building blocks are we allowed to use?

- Security. Having secure systems that are accessible both inside and outside a business drives many architecture decisions.

ARCHITECTURAL LEVELS

The final consideration in defining an IT architecture is what form it should take. An organization typically needs a multilevel architecture for each set of core applications, data, hardware, networks, etc. (**Q10**).

TECHNOLOGICAL CHANGE

The one constant in information technology is change. Technology is progressing at an ever-increasing rate. It was not long ago that the Internet really got rolling (circa 1995) and wireless devices came to be important in a business environment (circa 2000). IT architectures have been and will continue to be challenged to accommodate new technologies. Flexibility and planning are the keys to being able to do this. An organization with a monolithic legacy application environment, most likely will soon be challenged by the need to accommodate direct B2B transactions with their trading partners or constituents and to securely allow wireless transactions. This dictates that the IT architecture be multilevel and flexible.

SUMMARY

In summary, an organization's IT architecture should reflect the organization itself. The architecture should give the organization an expanded capability, provide the necessary services in a cost effective manner, and be flexible enough to accommodate organizational, environmental, and technological changes.

10. How does an organization develop an architecture plan?

THOMAS E. ANDREWS

Organizations rarely build IT environments from the ground up by following strict architectural guidelines (**Q9**) or working from a clear vision of the capabilities to be delivered. Rather, they inherit an existing environment and add features, functionality, and elements of technology one business request at a time without regard to a formal plan. Over time, some of the organization's key application vendors may mandate a different technology direction. Occasionally, executives will request a technology they read about in a trade publication that fits outside the current technology environment. Even internal IT employees may recommend technology directions that align with their skills or technology interests. Last, but not least, many business departments build or buy their own low-end solutions and demand that they be deployed throughout the company without regard to infrastructure capabilities or even ongoing support requirements.

How do IT leaders align and integrate the IT being used by their company so it:

- meets the needs of the business,

- is flexible and adaptable to future needs,

- is cost effective,

- follows a planned and guided approach,

- allows tactical solutions to satisfy strategic goals?

The solution to this problem is to develop a systems architecture plan. It is a process through which business strategies, principles, and guidelines determine how technologies can be blended together to satisfy those requirements. The goal of the systems architecture plan is to provide a framework identifying a target set of technology standards and processes to guide those involved in implementing, integrating, and managing IT. This framework should not only identify the technology (hardware, communications, database, and applications), it should also identify the processes, resources, policies, and systems management required to implement, support, and maintain it. While a systems architecture plan has a technology focus, its construction should be driven by the principles, values, and goals of the business.

Companies that follow a systems architecture plan generally improve interoperability among applications, allowing them to respond to business and technology changes more quickly and effectively. They can often reduce the diversity of technologies being used and ultimately reduce their support costs. More important, they usually are more closely aligned with the business. Now more than ever, companies are becoming more dependent upon the effective and efficient use of technology in their daily activities. The amount and complexity of technology used throughout companies is also growing significantly and will continue to grow unless attempts are made to manage its deployment.

What is needed to create a systems architecture plan? In simple terms, a system architecture plan requires six key elements. These elements are:

1. business vision, mission, and strategy

2. core business values and principles

3. business requirements (initiatives and user needs)

4. current IT portfolio

5. IT trends

6. logical technology map—architecture diagram

The first two elements are part of a firm's strategy, and the next three developed as part of its business driven technology strategy (Q4). The last element, the logical technology map or architecture diagram, is the focus of this answer.

Most companies are supporting multiple technology-based applications. They typically have applications hosted on mainframe, client/server, and/or Web environments. They probably have PCs and local area networks (LANs) supporting office automation and departmental systems. How can all these critical technology elements work together so that they satisfy current and future business objectives? How can IT organizations decide which technologies to use when faced with a specific business request? This is where a logical technology map or architecture diagram is important. An architecture diagram can help define what will be supported, how it will be supported (and funded), and what will not be supported. The diagram is a representation of all technology being used in the organization to deliver business-critical services.

One possible way to present an architecture diagram is in the form of a grid (see the manufacturing company example in Figure 10.1). This can be developed by first identifying the key services needed, who utilizes those services, and the types of technology needed to deliver them. Gradually, these services and technology lists should be grouped depending upon the investment and management principles being applied.

Those technologies and services having similar principles should be grouped together on common horizontal layers. These horizontal sections represent the management and investment strategy applied to that set of technologies. This mapping provides a means to visually understand the prioritized values or principles used in technology purchases and support efforts. Using the grid form of an architecture diagram, the horizontal tiers should be split between highly critical internal-focused, customer-focused, and non-production-focused technologies because the criteria used when investing in each are different. For most companies, these diagrams may

Figure 10.1 Example Systems Architecture Plan for Manufacturing Company

	Platforms and storage	Communi-cations	Data Mgmt	Application Development & packages	Enterprise Mgmt	Processes & staffing
Enterprise	Unix Enterprise Server	TCP/IP, VoIP	Common RDBMS, data dictionary	Consolidated Accounting, HR, e-mail, Portal	Backup/ Recovery, Systems Mgmt	Help Desk, Data Center, Methodology
Production Support	Unix Server		Common data-mining tools	MRP, DRP	Source Code mgmt	Business Analysts
Production Operations	Unix Servers Windows 2000 Server	100mb backbone, RF Protocol, Wireless		Inventory Mgmt, Process Monitoring	Predictive Maintenance	Product naming standards, SOPs
Container Manufac-turing	Standard PLCs	PLC Wireless Network Connections	SPC PLC Data Structures	SPC	Release control	PLC Maintenance Staff
Functional Workgroup	Windows NT Server, MS Office Server		Specific Workgroup Databases	Departmental Applications		
Individual	PCs, Thin Clients, Windows 2000, PDA	Employee high-speed home access	MS Access, MS Excel	MS Office, PC Level Applications	Desktop Mgmt	PC Support Staff
External	Browser interface	VPN, FTP			Directory Services	External Access Policy

(rows Production Support through Container Manufacturing grouped under **Manufacturing Operations**; Functional Workgroup through External grouped under **Ancillary Bus. Support**)

With permission of the TAM Group, Inc.

reflect three (3) horizontal tiers (enterprise, workgroup, and individual). The highest tier—enterprise—represents a class of technology, services, and support that:

- generally changes less often,
- has fewer technology components,
- receives significant management attention,
- is reused a number of times,
- has a higher price per component.

Solutions in the enterprise tier have a lower total cost of ownership because the investment values are generally focused primarily on cost and quality.

The vertical columns of the grid represent the entire IT landscape that is being managed. They include:

- platforms and storage,

- operating systems,

- data communications,

- applications development and packaged software,

- data management and structure,

- enterprise management, including security, and methods, processes, and skills.

Considering all seven areas during any new project presents a complete picture of what is needed to get the effort implemented, maintained, and supported. Without the overall perspective provided by an architecture diagram, the "total cost of ownership" (Q74) is difficult to understand. Many project plans only focus on implementation and do not identify the requirements for ongoing support, resources, and changes in policies and procedures.

When mapped correctly, the architecture diagram can be very helpful. It is best to create three different diagrams. One diagram should represent the current environment, one the future environment, and one those technology elements to be eliminated. Mapping the current environment allows a company to see where it has violated its principles in past technology decisions. Additionally, by mapping future technology components, a company can begin identifying future standards, determine what should become obsolete, and begin making tactical decisions that satisfy the long-term direction.

Finally, how is the architecture plan maintained? Chances are a company will never hit a state of architectural perfection; the architecture must be continually reviewed with each major technology initiative. The reality is that technologies change rapidly and vendors work hard to leverage new capabilities in their products. Companies also need to make architecture decisions when mergers and acquisitions occur because it is common for acquired companies to have a systems architecture that is different than that of the acquiring company.

Using the architecture diagram for all future projects helps a company to identify all the elements of technology needed, determine the level of robustness required, and look for opportunities for technology reuse. It offers a way to reduce the level of vendor bias that may occur within an IT organization. It allows a company to make tactical steps toward a strategic direction. Following a plan will help companies save money by not implementing dead-end solutions. It offers a method to align and integrate the information technology so that it not only meets the immediate needs of the business, but also so it can become flexible, cost effective, and follow a formal and planned approach.

---

11. What are the basic concepts of client/server architecture?

MARION K. JENKINS

A BRIEF HISTORY OF (COMPUTER) TIME

Client/server concepts have roots in early computer systems, so it is useful to briefly review the history of modern computing. Early computers (mainframes) were typically in a "glass room," with special power and air conditioning, and attended to by a priesthood of system programmers. Users typically shared a pool of "dumb" terminals and had to rely on centralized printing and storage resources. In this environment, the mainframe did all the processing, and users had no local computing horsepower.

In the late 1970s and early 1980s, smaller systems (minicomputers) were developed that required less power and air conditioning. Individual business unit owners wanted their own systems, more suited to their needs. Once a substantial number of applications were developed on these computers, inevitably other departments wanted access to them. Somewhat concurrently, Apple, IBM, and others developed the personal computer. Initially it seemed to have little application beyond that of the hobbyist. However, as powerful, shrink-wrapped applications were developed, and arcane operating systems such as MS-DOS were replaced by more user-friendly systems (e.g., Macintosh, Windows), users began to want to use PCs in the corporate computing environment. This allowed for a new army of computer users who cared little and understood even less about computer "systems." All they wanted was the latest software applications at their fingertips, but they needed the backup and redundant architecture that previously resided only in the glass room.

Concurrently, systems that were more scalable were introduced using common chip sets and operating systems, with features such as redundant power and multiple processors. They were far more powerful than "personal" computers—although they were based largely on the same architecture—but they were considerably smaller and less costly than mainframes or even minicomputers.

One last piece of technology was needed to make client/server architecture a reality. In the late 1970s, Xerox developed the standards and technology that we know today as Ethernet. This provided a standard means of linking together computers from different manufacturers and formed the basis for modern LANs and WANs (**Q24**).

At this point, all the pieces were in place to develop client/server systems:

- a strong business need for decentralized computing horsepower

- standard, powerful computers with user-friendly interfaces

- mature, shrink-wrapped user applications with widespread acceptance

- inexpensive, modular systems designed with enterprise-class architecture, such as power and network redundancy and file archiving network protocols to link them together

DEFINITION OF CLIENT AND SERVER

In the simplest sense, the client and server can be defined as follows:

- A *client* is an individual user's computer or a user application that does a certain amount of processing on its own. It also sends and receives requests to and from one or more servers for other processing and/or data.

- A *server* consists of one or more computers that receive and process requests from one or more client machines. A server is typically designed with some redundancy in power, network, computing, and file storage. However, a machine with dual processors is not necessarily a server. An individual workstation *can* function as a server.

Sometimes the term "server" or "client" may refer to the software rather than the computer. Thus, a "mail client" may refer to the mail software that resides on a client machine, rather than the machine itself.

THE EVOLUTION OF CLIENTS AND SERVERS

The earliest versions of client/server were merely shared files; when a user needed a file, it was copied from the server to the local machine. When finished, it was returned to the server. It was necessary to develop certain rules to handle conflict and synchronization issues. So as client/server systems evolved, they contained built-in synchronization and sharing engines. Client/server also embodies the concepts of user accounts and sharing of resources—the system must separate and keep track of different users' files and applications during a user session, then free up those resources for another user session.

As client/server applications evolved, the functionality of the application was separated logically into two parts: the processes requiring the majority of the computing horsepower were put on the server, and the user interface and less processor-intensive processes were put on the client.

CLIENT/SERVER EXAMPLES

A common client/server example is a *print server*. Most people have probably noticed a temporary lockup or slowdown when a document is printed on a stand-alone PC, especially if the document is complex. One can attach a printer to a PC and then share it with other users across the network. However, if everyone on the network simultaneously prints to that shared printer, it would likely lock up or even crash. Therefore, many times a machine is dedicated solely to handle printing—a print server. It "serves" print requests to all users, and off-loads this task from local machines. Another example is a *mail server* which functions much like a post office, receiving mail centrally and delivering individual messages to individual clients.

PUTTING IT ALL TOGETHER

In a small organization, a single server machine may serve more than one function, if the functions are simple enough. One or more applications may reside on a single server machine, with the server being divided into different "logical" partitions.

In a large corporate environment, there may be many servers for separate tasks. There is typically a primary domain controller (PDC), which authenticates users and controls access and log in to the computer system itself. There may be a mail server, which processes e-mail. There may also be a file server typically containing large disk drives and individual user directories to store user files in a uniform way. And there may be separate application servers for accounting, billing, customer care, Web, e-commerce, database, transaction, manufacturing, inventory, etc. They are typically linked together using integration software (frequently called *middleware* [Q13]) so that one can access many server applications from a single (client) machine, through a common interface, typically a browser.

Although client/server in its simplest form is two-tier (server and client), there are newer, more powerful architectures that are three-tier (where application logic lives in the middle-tier and it is separated from the data and user interface) or even n-tier (where there are several middle-tier components within a single business transaction) in nature. Sometimes client/server is referred to as distributed computing; they have the same basic concepts (Q8).

ADVANTAGES

There are many advantages to client/server architecture including that subsystems can be optimized for a particular set of applications. Systems can grow modularly, as different applications grow. Then more powerful subsystems can be installed without wasting resources on other applications. "Forklift upgrades," where an entire system is replaced, are theoretically kept to a minimum.

With most of the crucial applications and data residing on centralized machines, or clusters of machines, systems can be engineered to high standards of reliability and availability.

SUMMARY

Client/server architecture has become the dominant structure for corporate computing in both small and large organizations. It combines the best concepts of centralized, robust infrastructure with decentralized capability and control (Q54)—in other words, it gives both IT managers and end users what they want and need. If implemented properly, client/server architecture achieves the best balance between complexity, cost, and ease of use, with excellent scalability and reliability.

---

12. What are the business implications of fat clients and thin clients?

THOMAS E. ANDREWS

Many employees need access to a variety of computer-based applications to effectively complete their work. They also need a technical environment that is stable, reliable, cost effective, and well maintained. Two primary options to meet their needs include giving them a *fat client*, with strong local processing power, or a *thin client*, with a small amount of local processing power.

Before we discuss business issues involved in selecting the best option or combination of options, we must define these anthropomorphic terms.

FAT CLIENTS

Prior to the late 1970s, employees gained access to back-office computer applications through "dumb terminals," which were simple-minded TV-like devices connected to the central computer over the network. Around 1980, "personal computers" (PCs) were developed to allow greater office automation capabilities on the local desktop. As PCs grew more powerful, business application vendors began pushing some of their functionality from the mainframe out to the PC to take advantage of its additional processing power, thereby avoiding the need to send large amounts of data over the network. This style of application became known as a client/server application (**Q11**). Some client/server applications pushed so much functionality from the central computer-based application to the local PCs that the appetite for local computing power became more than an average desktop PC could provide. When more computing capability was added to the PCs, these more robust PCs with heavier functionality became known as "fat clients."

12 ▬

THIN CLIENTS

In recent years, the promise of high-speed, high-bandwidth access to applications from anywhere over the Web via an Internet browser or a very light front-end application has reversed the fat client trend back toward thin clients. In this scenario, most of the computing is performed on the central server, allowing the remote device to be much lighter weight in capability and cost. More and more software applications are being designed for thin client access by putting the presentation logic on the local thin client (with low network/computing demands), the business logic on a central application server (with high computing demands), and the data on a central database server (with high network demands). This offers application software vendors the ability to deliver their solutions over a wider range of access devices including regular PCs, inexpensive network PCs, simple thin client devices, Web access terminals, Palm or PDA wireless access devices, and cell phones (**Q29**).

DECISION CRITERIA FOR CHOOSING

Four key criteria for selecting fat or thin client devices include the company's IT standards, type of work being performed, distance and network bandwidth, and costs.

IT Standards   One factor when considering deployment of thin clients is the company's IT standards. Some companies mandate strong central control over what is allowed to be put on PCs (e.g., only company-provided applications). Other companies allow greater local control, even if it means higher costs. Points in favor of central control include ease of support when only known corporate applications are present on PCs, and enhanced security due to central backup and recovery processes.

Type of Work   What type of work does the employee do? Will the employee simply be entering transactions to perform a specific job function such as acknowledging receipts of supplier orders numerous times during the day? Repetitive, transaction-oriented work such as this is better suited for thin clients. In contrast, an employee who is extracting customer order forecasts, inventory status, and planned production schedules from multiple application systems and loading data into a spreadsheet to do some specialized production planning may benefit by having the data local on his or her fat client PC.

Distance and Bandwidth   Are users local to the application and do they have high bandwidth access, or are they remote users and have access to the application over a constrained bandwidth network? Fat clients are generally less responsive over such constrained networks since they are pulling down volumes of data to be processed by the business software that is running locally on the PC. Conversely, remote users with thin clients processing smaller amounts of data will generally get better response times. However, thin clients require a network connection and do not have the capability for much offline work.

Costs   Total costs of the two alternatives must be analyzed in terms of the following trade-offs:

- *Hardware costs*—Traditionally, fat client devices cost more than smaller, simpler, thin client devices, which usually do not have hard drives or powerful processors. Recently, however, PC prices have come down to a range closer to the thin client prices.

- *Development costs*—Many traditional software developers prefer to design fat client applications because it is harder and slower to design and develop distributed thin client applications where the presentation logic layer resides on the thin client and the data and application layers are located on central servers. However, in cases where applications are relatively volatile and require frequent changes, it is much easier to make such changes to thin client applications because the changes need only be made once centrally on the server and distributed automatically. This is especially true when data formats change. In that case, any data maintained locally must be converted to the new format before processing may continue. In addition, thin clients are well suited when centralized application integration support is required. Integration among multiple applications is implemented on the central server and then made available to all remote clients.

- *Local support costs*—When a fat client PC fails on the factory floor or at a remote facility, a local PC technician must spend significant time fixing it or replacing it with another expensive PC. Further complicating the support cost issue for many companies, especially large ones, is the fact that there is often a nonhomogeneous mix of PCs and software across the company.

Individual users may have loaded nonstandard software or drivers on their PCs and may be using more resources on those PCs than anyone realizes. PC technicians and help desk staff have a hard time troubleshooting problems when there are so many variations of fat clients in use. Conversely, when a thin client device fails in a remote location, anyone may quickly unplug the problem device and plug in a new, inexpensive replacement. No PC technicians are needed at the remote sites.

- *Central support cost*—Centrally, many more servers are required to support the thin clients, often in a ratio of approximately one server to thirty thin clients. Multiple highly paid systems administrators are required to manage the large number of central servers required to support a thousand or more users. Also, thin clients have a higher degree of reliance on both server and network availability, which may add costs.

- *Application deployment costs*—It should be easier and faster to deploy to a large number of users using a thin client architecture. Many vendor application software suites are currently designed as client/server applications. Using a thin client deployment should simplify the rollout of these applications since it may eliminate the need to upgrade existing PCs to suit a (fat) client/server environment. To gain the benefits of thin client implementations and support, yet retain the benefits of local processing capabilities and investments already in place, some companies are deploying thin client type applications on fat client PC devices.

13

THE FUTURE

The long-term trend is toward thin clients. Web-based applications will be the norm. Vendors will work to provide greater access using very-thin remote, wireless devices such as phones, PDAs, and pagers. Increased reliance on traditional networks and ultimately wireless networks will be managed. Each company should make the fat vs. thin client decision in an intentional fashion as part of its overall architecture and understand the implications of that decision.

---

13. What is middleware and what are the business implications of its use?

WILLIAM WHITE

Middleware is one of the most overused and least understood terms in IT. As Bill Gates testified recently in the Microsoft antitrust trial, "It's a term of such ambiguity, you wouldn't find me using it outside of the lawsuit." [1]

The objective of middleware is to allow communications between applications

[1] Joe Wilcox, "Gates Gamble Pays Off for Microsoft," *ZDNet* 23 Apr. 2002, 10 Dec. 2002 <http://news.zdnet.co.uk/story/0,,t272-s2108904,00.html>.

that were not originally designed to work with each other and may be running on different platforms. This is accomplished by removing selected tasks from an application and embedding them into separate modules or layers that are independent of the application and network location. The benefits to IT organizations are that middleware:

- allows the separation of business logic from the data, thus multiple applications can access common data;

- allows the separation of common business logic onto separate platforms, thus enabling network transparency;

- isolates the communication mechanisms between applications and data or applications and server-based modules.

Middleware has become very complex and sophisticated over the last 20 years; and in the last five years, its diversity has doubled as the Internet has moved to the forefront of application development.[2] Middleware is defined as software programs that provide an abstraction capability enabling applications to focus on the *business logic* vs. *how* and *where* underlying services are performed. For example, when an application issues an SQL statement requesting data from a database, the application does not need to know where the SQL call goes or how it is processed, only that it returned the requested data.

Why Embrace Middleware?

Given the complexity and variety of solutions offered by the vendor community, why should you embrace middleware? The world of IT mirrors the external world very closely in terms of the degree of interrelationships required between companies, organizations, and their systems. In that regard, you have to find ways for information and associated business processes to be compatible with each other. Systems become very complex and as new systems are added, they usually must speak to each other and operate seamlessly. When companies merge or acquire others, one of the biggest challenges is to integrate those disparate systems. Direct connections can be built between systems, but IT organizations rarely have the time to build custom linkages. The solution is—middleware.

Development teams have used middleware for years in various degrees—mostly in single applications—to reduce the amount of code and time invested to deliver the required business functionalities. Today, applications must be designed to facilitate rapid reorganization as a business shifts to address new markets, channels, and competition (**Q7**).

Middleware can be loosely segmented into four categories as shown in Figure 13.1.

---

[2] According to Gartner, the worldwide application integration, middleware, and portal markets will grow from $5.1 billion in 2001 to $10.5 billion by 2006 (*InternetWeek* 6/25/2002).

Figure 13.1 Diagram of Enterprise Application Integration (EAI)

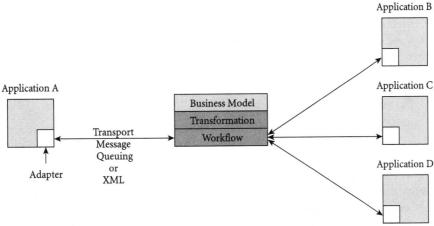

OBJECT- AND COMPONENT-ORIENTED MIDDLEWARE

The premise of J2EE, .NET, CORBA, and ORBs is to facilitate the reuse of components independent of the higher-level application. J2EE (Sun Microsystems) and .NET (Microsoft) are two complete platforms that provide an entire application architecture, *including* the middleware components, while CORBA and ORBs are architectures describing object-oriented process interactions over a network. Using prebuilt components has two benefits:

1. It drastically reduces development time by leveraging past projects and using code libraries.

2. It cuts time to market dramatically by developing reusable components.

Most IT shops today are moving away from pure object-oriented middleware due to significant implementation and manageability issues. More promising are Web services that are just starting to be implemented (**Q15**).

MESSAGE-ORIENTED MIDDLEWARE

Message-oriented middleware is one of the most commonly used middleware categories. In the first model, "publish and subscribe," an application can "publish" information, but it is up to the receiving application to "subscribe." In other words, a receiving application can be as simple as a warehouse reorder module that has subscribed to the warehouse inventory module and is interested in quantities on hand.

E-mail is a message-oriented middleware service. The e-mail application is only concerned with the message content and the delivery address. Middleware takes care of delivering the message. Models that are more sophisticated provide additional controls and capabilities. The second model is "message queuing" which is a much richer environment than regular e-mail. In this model, "messages" can be routed to multiple locations and the middleware can guarantee their delivery. In other words, the receiving application accepts the message and indicates that it is satisfactory. IBM's MQSeries is a prime example of such a product.

WEB-BASED MIDDLEWARE

The Web-based realm of browsers, Web servers, etc., is commonplace for all IT organizations and many applications now have a Web browser as their only user interface. The current trend is to use XML to move data between applications. XML is a language that defines a syntax and document organization for data, both containing human and machine-readable tag/value pairs (Q14). Many of the application integration middleware products use XML as the data exchange protocol; and in the B2B space, XML will be the dominant method of data exchange in the future, eventually replacing electronic data interchange (EDI). Web-based middleware is quickly evolving from its emerging new technology status, into a mainstream, complete application framework (Q14).

APPLICATION INTEGRATION MIDDLEWARE

This area has seen an explosion of growth over the last five years. Some of the different types of application integration middleware are discussed below.

Screen Scraping   This is one of the oldest and simplest forms of application integration. Simply, it is "reading" the character stream that is displayed on a terminal screen and using that information within the context of a separate application. Although this is widely used in many IT organizations because it can be implemented quickly, the big problem with screen scraping occurs when the "scraped" system changes, which renders the "reading" system inaccurate or unusable. Correcting this problem is costly.

Database Gateways   Database gateways act as interface translators that move data, SQL commands, and applications from one type of database to another. They must know the details (syntax, data format, data types, and catalog naming conventions) of the products to be accessed and synchronized with software releases of the data sources. The price of this accessibility is speed, because it is necessary to translate the

Table *13.1* Middleware Categories

Category	Examples
Object and Component Oriented Middleware	Component Object Model (COM) .NET **(Q8)** Java-based middleware (J2EE) **(Q8)** Common Object Request Broker Architecture (CORBA) Object Request Brokers (ORBs)
Message Oriented Middleware	publish and subscribe queuing systems
Web-based Middleware	Web browsers and their Web servers Hypertext Markup Language (HTML) **(Q26)** Extensible Markup Language (XML) **(Q4)**
Application Integration Middleware	Enterprise Application Integration (EAI) database gateways screen scraping

13 ━━

client request and the server results. The client, gateway, and server can reside on the same platform or different ones. This allows gateways to connect clients and servers running on dissimilar networks. They are ideally suited to bridge network protocols, such as TCP/IP, OSI, and SNA, while acting as the transportation interfaces for moving data among database platforms. Database gateways have the following functions: (1) accept statements specified by a well-defined grammar (usually SQL) from a client application, (2) translate the statements to a specific database format, (3) send the statements to be executed against the database, (4) translate the results back into a well-defined format, and (5) return the data and status information to the client.

Enterprise Application Integration (EAI)   EAI technologies are an amalgamation of communications/messaging, XML, data transformation, brokers, process models, and development frameworks. This "all-in-one" approach is usually provided by vendors who specialize in this particular technology. While the breadth of EAI technologies may appear to be daunting, the basic premise of this category is straightforward.

The high-level view of EAI is to enable a very intelligent layer of software to be the intermediary between dissimilar applications. For example, assume that a critical IT project will allow data to flow between two dissimilar manufacturing systems, such as SAP and Baan. Both of these packages are very complex and have a number of interfaces that can be utilized. However, the goal is to enable information flow between these two systems and allow for future interconnections. Therefore a more robust solution is often necessary, namely EAI.

SUMMARY

Do not be intimidated by the breadth and complexity of middleware. While this answer cannot cover all of the alternatives, most vendors do a very good job of describing the landscape. Invest time reading the whitepapers from vendors. What appear to be many divergent and competing technologies are variations on a theme. Discover the common themes and you have the keys to understanding.

14. What are the benefits of eXtensible Markup Language (XML) and the barriers to its use?

DAWN GREGG

XML stands for eXtensible Markup Language. It is much like HTML (Q26)—a markup language used by programmers for describing to a browser how data should be laid out on a screen. However, XML was designed to specify information *about* the data, not just how it should be displayed. Using XML, a system can recognize a string of numbers and text as an invoice or a set of images as pictures in a catalog.[1] The principle advantage of XML is that it supports user-defined tags (or descriptors) that allow both data and descriptive information about the data to be represented within a single text document. XML also organizes data and contains instructions for understanding that organization. One of its real advantages is that it can run on any platform with applications written in any computer language.[2] This has helped make XML a standard for data transmission and data manipulation over the Web.

XML allows the creation of "elements" that describe data precisely. It uses <tags> embedded in the data to identify where each element begins and ends. For example, Figure 14.1 shows a simple XML document that contains information related to a single product. In this example, the root element is "inventory" and the data for a single product is contained between the <product> and </product> markup tags. Individual characteristics of the product (such as its name and price) are specified using additional nested tags. This hierarchical structure is valuable in specifically iden-

[1] Beth Stackpole, "What Is XML?" *Darwinmag.com* 14 Feb. 2001, 3 Dec. 2002 <http://www.darwinmag.com/learn/curve/column.html?ArticleID=74>.

[2] Ron Gruner, "XML: Harnessing the Power for Your Investor Relations Web Site," *Strategic Investor Relations* 1.4 (2001): 43–49.

Figure 14.1 Simple XML Document

```
<?xml version="1.0"?>
<inventory>
  <product ID="1">
    <name>Malaysian Tea</name>
    <price>5.75</price>
    <size>22 oz.</size>
    <instock>35</instock>
  </product>
</inventory>
```

tifying a piece of data, allowing it to be selected, rearranged, or cut from one document and inserted into another.

Much of the flexibility of XML comes from the fact that the information elements are identified by special tags embedded in the data. This means that there is no need to specify ahead of time how long any piece of content will be, or in precisely what sequence the data will occur. This allows applications to tolerate variations in the data they receive because they can identify the information of interest to them.[3]

BENEFITS OF XML

Companies have begun to use XML for a wide variety of applications and have developed XML markup for describing specific types of data (for example, XBRL [Extensible Business Reporting Language] is used for financial data exchange).[4] XML is being adopted by organizations because it provides benefits over alternative data storage and transmission approaches.

XML enables a longer life span for information. XML data is plain text, and the XML markup is just plain text delimited by specific characters. Thus, XML gives organizations more freedom to use and reuse data without being tied to specific hardware or software.

XML has also gained a reputation in many industries as a favorable way to transfer structured data between applications.[5] The fact that XML is structured, flexible, and extensible provides many benefits to organizations that traditional Electronic

---

[3] Tommie Usdin and Tony Graham, "XML: Not a Silver Bullet, but a Great Pipe Wrench," *Standard View* 6.3 (1998): 127–32.

[4] *XBRL (Extensible Business Reporting Language) Web Site* n.d., 3 Dec. 2002 <http://www.xbrl.org>.

[5] Ron Dudley, "XML Standards Get Positive Response," *National Underwriter/Life & Health Financial Services* 106.20 (2002): 12.

Data Interchange (EDI) systems do not.[6] XML is just a data format, but the availability of XML standards and applications has allowed XML to become the principle enabling technology for business-to-business integration. Web services, for example, use special XML-based-documents called SOAP (Simple Object Access Protocol) envelopes to pass XML data between applications (**Q15**). Since XML is plain text, it can easily pass through firewalls and be read by applications, on any type of machine.

Finally, XML can be used to place data on the Web such that automated data classification tools can understand the data. The extensibility of XML allows individuals and groups to define a markup that allows for improved search engines that can match on tags as well as text content, and will support intelligent manipulation of the data by the client.[7] Another benefit of XML for Web data is that, in addition to improved searching, XML data can be transformed into browser readable HTML using a "stylesheet."[8]

BARRIERS TO XML ADOPTION

XML is a useful tool for storing and sharing data. However, it is not always the most appropriate tool for a given data-based application. There are three barriers or limiting factors that can determine if XML is appropriate for a given application.

First, XML is text based. This is convenient when it is necessary to share data between applications and machines. However, it is inefficient. Text-based data requires more memory for storage. In addition, the XML tags themselves add considerably to the amount of data that is transferred with an XML document. Thus, XML data puts a heavier load on computer networks by requiring them to transport and store larger volumes of data. In addition, text files are read differently than the binary files used in traditional database applications. Text files must be read in "sequence," that is, read line by line until the end of the file is reached. In contrast, binary files can allow programs to jump to a specific byte in the file providing "instant-access" to a desired set of data. Sequentially processing each line in XML files slows application programs, making XML much less efficient than a traditional database for accessing and manipulating large quantities of data.

A second barrier to XML adoption is that computer systems and databases contain data in incompatible formats. The binary files for one system cannot be read by a different type of system. One of the most time consuming challenges for software developers has been to exchange data between such systems. Converting the data to

---

[6] Electronic Data Interchange (EDI) provides a collection of standard message formats and an element dictionary allowing businesses to exchange data via an electronic messaging service.

[7] Usdin and Graham 127–32.

[8] eXtensible Stylesheet Language (XSL) is used to define how an XML file should be displayed by a browser. It can transform XML into HTML, filter and sort XML data, and format XML data, based on the data value.

XML can reduce this complexity and create data that can be read by different types of applications.[9] However, data compatibility is still an issue. For different programs to be able to communicate using XML, they need to understand what specific tags mean within the context of a given XML document (for example, in one system, price might be called <msrp> in another it could be <price>). If organizations plan on transferring data using XML, it is necessary to agree upon the set of tags that will be used. This creates issues when a transfer of data between organizations is desired. A purchaser may employ a system that defines tags in one way, but its supplier may have built its product catalogue with different definitions. So just because both organizations say that they are using XML doesn't meant that their systems can automatically communicate.

Finally, organizations already have made large investments in other data technologies. Converting existing data to XML can be slow and expensive. Many large organizations have invested millions of dollars in setting up networks that use EDI and are reluctant to abandon something that works well.[10]

Conclusion

XML is an enabling technology, not a solution to every data problem. It is ideal for the long-term storage of data where it will not be accessed frequently and where it may need to be read by a different machine or application than the one that originally stored the data. The text-based nature of XML data, its self-describing markup, and the availability of XML processors also makes XML a natural tool for machine-to-machine communication. Its heavy use in Web-based applications ensures that it will play an increasingly important role in how data is defined, stored, and shared.

[9] Jan Refsnes, "How Can XML Be Used?" *XMLFiles.com* 14 Aug. 2002, 3 Dec. 2002 <http://www.xmlfiles.com/xml/xml_usedfor.asp>.

[10] Amy Zuckerman, "EDI Is Tops but XML Is Coming Online," *World Trade* Aug. 2002: 16.

15. What are Web services and their implications for an enterprise?

DAVID R. LAUBE

In the world of IT, some product or idea is always going through the "hype cycle." Usually the promise is to revolutionize IT in some way. Some developments, such as the Internet or e-mail, live up to their billing. But, over time, most just find their proper place in the spectrum of IT tools and capabilities.[1] Web services seem to be one current area of IT buzz. They promise to connect IT platforms and computer users in automated and flexible ways and do amazing things in the area of cost and software development time. But with all the hype, it is sometimes difficult to determine the reality.

WHAT ARE WEB SERVICES?

Web services are self-contained business functions that can be accessed using standard Internet protocols. They are platform, language, and location independent. Like Legos, Web services are easily changeable building blocks used to create or integrate software.

Web services are similar to other distributed computing solutions that have been implemented in the past. What has created enormous interest is the ease of implementing them and their ability to be shared by virtually anyone because they are based on a set of standards. Although there are many standards, the three key ones are:

1. *SOAP* (Simple Object Access Protocol) — This is the mechanism used to pass data between Web services and their clients. It is based on XML, which is text based and infinitely portable (**Q14**).

2. *WSDL* (Web Services Description Language) — This is used to describe Web services so that other programs know how to communicate with them. This allows the automatic generation of the code for using a Web service. WSDL is also XML based.

3. *UDDI* (Universal Description, Discovery, and Integration) — This is an XML-enabled directory that allows anyone the ability to "look-up" the WSDL documents for Web services, making it much easier for anyone to find and use them.

[1] Examples include Object-Oriented Programming (OOP), Computer-Aided Software Engineering (CASE), Rapid Application Development (RAD) (**Q7**), Application Service Providers (ASPs) (**Q80**), and wireless devices (**Q29**).

THE PROMISE

The idea of easily built and sharable software modules has captivated the software industry and software vendors. Some believe it will be the way IT organizations can finally become cost effective and responsive.[2] Gartner has estimated that the use of Web services will result in a gain of as much as 25 percent in the efficiency of IT development.[3] Vendors are scrambling to "Web services enable" their existing product line and a whole new set of software capabilities and products are envisioned to spring from this new idea.

Outside the Firewall   Completely outside the firewall of companies, there is the battleground of Internet-based products and services. Here competitors such as Microsoft with their .NET software platform and the Liberty Alliance (a consortium of companies using Sun's J2EE platform [**Q8**]) battle for position as the lead software platform provider. Currently, when users of Microsoft's Hotmail (e-mail) service sign in, they are also signed in to a whole series of other services. The vision is that there will someday be a large "yellow pages–like" directory of Web services and, once signed in, consumers can have easy access to them. So there is a race to establish this directory once a critical mass of commercially viable Web services become available.

Some companies are already building Web services as commercial offerings that other companies can use in their business activities. Fidesic, for example, has built Web services that do electronic invoicing and payment processing. They offer these services to companies that want to streamline and reduce the costs of this process.[4] Other companies offer modules that calculate state and local taxes or run credit checks. With time, more and more companies will seize the opportunity to generate revenue by building and offering Web services.

Across the Firewall   In the B2C and B2B world (**Q37, Q38**) companies typically allow their customers or business partners across their firewall to access selected internal systems. In this environment, Web services, because they are easily accessed over the Web, are starting to flourish. For example, Ubid.com, an internet auction site, needed to expand the number of items available on their site. They built a set of Web services to handle functions such as "define a product," "add an auction," "update the auction," and "exchange auction fees." They then exposed these functions through Web services protocols. This allowed third party aggregators, who had other items for sale,

---

[2] Very early advocates of the benefits of Web services are John Hagel III and John Seely Brown, see John Hagel III and John Seely Brown. "Your Next IT Strategy," *Harvard Business Review* 79.9 (2001): 105–13

[3] Whit Andrews, *Web Services' First Payback: Internal AD Efficiency*, Gartner, Inc., Research Note SPA-14-3798, 24 Sept. 2001: 1.

[4] *Fidesic Corporation Web Site* <http://www.fidesic.com>.

to quickly link into Ubid's systems increasing Ubid's items for sale from 500,000 to over 2.5 million.[5] Another example is General Motors, who provides its dealers with a Web service that allows them to quickly find specific car models in the inventory of other dealers.[6]

It is anticipated that Web services could become the primary way B2B transactions are handled. Business partners will expose modules of their supply chain and procurement systems in the form of Web services and easily link them to transact business. B2C operations will be simplified as companies can make functions previously delivered over internal systems, like some customer service activities, easily available over the Web—enabling customer self-service. The key to the expansion of these activities is that these Web services can be built quickly and, with standard interfaces, can be offered easily over the Web.

Inside the Firewall   It is inside the firewall, the domain of internal systems, where Web services have really generated optimism.[7] That is because Web services have the potential to help solve the problem that haunts every CIO—systems integration. Making systems work together has always been difficult, particularly when most companies have systems using a variety of architectures, operating systems, hardware platforms, and communications protocols. Software budgets are drained when so much effort must be placed in integration.

How do Web services help? Because they are platform independent and use common Web protocols, software modules theoretically can be easily accessed. So if companies can build their business processes into these modules (Web services), then the common requirement to link them together is a relatively simple matter. Companies are moving rapidly in this direction.

- Home Depot, when launching a new point-of-sale (POS) system, created common functions such as price lookup, tax calculation, and return authorizations. They published them as Web services which allowed them to be used by all their ordering functions whether they were in stores, on their Web site, or for custom orders of home furnishings.[8]

- The Colorado Department of Agriculture developed Web services to integrate multiple systems that were used to track its captive deer and elk population. They reduced their reporting cycle from 3–4 weeks to real-time.[9]

[5] Matt Hicks, "Web Services Lead the Bidding," *eWeek* 11 Feb. 2002, 44 <http://www.eweek.com/article2/0,3959,3462,00.asp>

[6] Hagel and Seely Brown 110.

[7] Gartner estimates that more than 50 percent of organizations' first experience with Web services will be for internal applications (Andrews 1).

[8] Ann Bednarz, "The Home Depot's Latest Project: XML, Web Services," *Network World* 21 Jan. 2002 <http://www.nwfusion.com/news/2002/129295_01-21-2002.html>

[9] Debra Donston, "Web Services Rides Herd," *eWeek* 16 Sept. 2002, 43 <http://www.eweek.com/article2/0,3959,537454,00.asp>

• Merrill Lynch exposed a number of their internal systems capabilities as Web services. When they needed to integrate certain sets of business functionalities it cost them only $30,000 to do a job that previously would have cost $800,000.[10]

It is clear that the potential to significantly improve systems integration is one of the reasons why Web services are receiving so much attention.

15 ━━

THE PROBLEMS

Coupled with the promise of Web services are a number of problems that have yet to be overcome.

Standards   In order for Web services to work properly, they must completely interoperate and be platform independent. This requires Web services to follow a set of strict standards. Although the basic standards are in place, many detailed standards are unfinished. The major software vendors have stepped into this vacuum, offering their versions of software that try to anticipate an emerging standard. The result is that CIOs and CTOs are either forced to pick a vendor using a premature standard and risk future interoperability, or just delay the deployment of Web services until the standards settle down.

Security   Once a company allows customers or business partners through their firewall, security becomes a concern. Unfortunately, security is one area where Web services are particularly weak and standards for security are still being developed. In their absence, companies and vendors are employing temporary techniques to shore up the security around this technology. In addition, Web services are being applied to underlying applications that were developed originally for an internal environment and did not contain the security and controls necessary to provide safe access to outsiders. So CIOs may be reluctant to deploy Web services until these security issues are adequately addressed.

XML   The backbone of Web services is the sharing of data in XML format. But XML has its own share of problems (**Q14**). This includes problems associated with incompatible data definitions that could keep Web services from working properly between different corporate entities or departments. In addition, XML is a text format, which requires significantly more bandwidth to transmit compared to the binary data formats used by older systems. This can also slow the speed at which the services are executed, causing the application to fail the response time requirements of users, particularly in a large real-time environment. So the business case for wide-scale Web services deployment might also require upgrades to a company's infrastructure, severely cutting down on the project's ROI.

[10] Michael Vizard, "Web Services Are Delivering Savings," *Infoworld* 19 Aug. 2002: 8.

The Prognosis

Web services will certainly have an impact in IT environments in years ahead. Whether they will be the panacea some promise will depend on the ability of the vendors and the IT standards community to provide the framework that will give CIOs the confidence to deploy them. After that it will again be an ROI game. If Web services projects can generate proper returns to the business, they will see widespread deployment.

16. What are the advantages and disadvantages of a Windows-based versus a Unix-based software environment?

DAWN GREGG

Windows versus Unix—this is a debate that has captured the attention of the technology community for the last 15 years. It causes fierce arguments inside technology organizations whose employees are in both camps, and creates headlines in the technology community as the proponents of each side try to outmaneuver each other. One headline captures the fervor: "Montagues and Capulets, move over. Windows and Unix are today's fashionable feud. Feud, in fact, is too soft a word: This is war."[1]

How can managers choose between a Microsoft Windows® platform and one of the various Unix operating systems? Once you put aside the hype, as with most things, the answer depends on the particular software application and on the organization itself.

Operating System Selection

Windows is the most widely used operating system for personal computers and most organizations have no difficulty in selecting it for their desktop systems. Linux (an open source version of Unix [Q17]) is starting to emerge as a viable desktop alternative, but Windows still has the vast majority of market share. However, the selection of the operating system for an organization's servers is more difficult.

[1] Derek Slater, "Deciding Factors," *CIO.com* 1 Feb 2000, 18 Nov. 2002 <http://www.cio.com/archive/020100/index.html>.

Servers can run many different types of applications. These include Web and infrastructure applications, front-end applications, and enterprise critical applications.[2] Server platforms can support anywhere from just a few users to thousands. High-end servers (those priced over $100,000) generate 28 percent of the worldwide server revenue while low-end servers (those priced below $5000) generate 30 percent of worldwide server revenue.[3]

This variability in server functionality and price makes it difficult to make a "one-size-fits-all" approach for selecting servers for an organization. When doing so, IT managers often do not choose Windows or Unix exclusively, but instead choose Windows for some applications and Unix for others. Critical factors influencing this selection include the operating system's scalability, reliability, system management, and cost.

Scalability   Scalability is the ability of applications, operating systems, databases, and hardware/networks to grow over time as the business volumes grow without having to upgrade. It is the primary consideration for many high-end server applications. The system chosen must be capable of supporting the expected number of concurrent users without significantly degrading the performance of the server or causing it to crash. Historically, Windows platforms have only been able to support about one-third of the concurrent users that Unix platforms can support.[4] This has resulted in organizations choosing Unix as the high-end server platform to handle large corporate computing applications, such as tracking inventory, handling large volume Web sites, or managing bank accounts. The primary vendors of Unix platforms have been gradually increasing the scalability of their product offerings to the extent that large Unix servers are reaching the capability of what mainframes could accomplish only a few years ago.

Windows has also been "upscaling" its capabilities. Recently Windows placed fifth on the Transaction Performance Council's server performance ranking, a benchmarking metric traditionally dominated by Unix machines.[5] When combined with the fastest Intel-based processors, some analysts believe that the combination of experienced high-end server vendors and the demonstrated scalability of the latest versions of Windows could help Microsoft and Intel enter the high-end server market.[6]

Reliability   Reliability is also an important factor in server selection. Server reliability translates to high availability, which is essential for mission-critical applications.

[2] George Weiss, *Landscaping the Server Operating System Field*, Gartner, Inc., Market Analysis DF-16-0078, 30 May 2002: 1.

[3] Weiss 1.

[4] Slater.

[5] Stephen Shankland, "Windows Inches Up on Unix," *ZDNet* 10 Sept. 2002, 19 Nov. 2002 <http://zdnet.com.com/2100-1104-957226.html>.

[6] Paul McDougall, "Intel Demos Progress in High Performance Computing," *InformationWeek* 10 Sept. 2002, 19 Nov. 2002 <http://www.informationweek.com/story/IWK20020910S0003>.

When looking at system reliability, IT managers need to determine how much uptime is enough and how much they are willing to pay for it. Factors such as "failover" and quick restart and recovery without the loss of data or active transactions are important for some organizations. Unix servers have been operating in the more complex data centers for some time and have quite sophisticated capabilities in this area. But both operating systems are continuously improving and system reliabilities are likely to increase over the next few years.

System Management   There are substantial differences in the approach to system management between the Windows and Unix operating systems. Windows is designed for ease of use. Server administrators use graphical user interfaces (GUI) that are relatively easy to learn because they are based on the user interfaces used in all Windows systems.[7] Unix is designed for flexibility. Unix allows system administration tasks to be performed either using a graphical user interface at the command prompt or using scripting. Since Unix administration data is stored in text files instead of a database (like Microsoft), repetitive system administration tasks are fairly easy to automate.[8]

A major issue related to server system management is remote administration. Unix machines come with many tools that make remote management possible. Unix supports remote access at multiple levels, including the ability to login with a character session and by running GUI tools over the network. Windows does not come with any of these features.[9] However, it is possible to obtain significant remote management capabilities for Windows using add-on system administration tools.

Many enterprises manage hundreds of applications. The Windows-based applications are most likely running on dedicated servers resulting in large numbers of servers to manage. Although the early trend with Unix was for dedicated servers as well, recently corporations have been consolidating multiple individual Unix servers into a few large Unix machines. This substantially improves the manageability of the applications and reduces costs.

Cost   Most experts agree that the purchase costs for Windows machines can be significantly lower than that for a similar Unix machine. Windows is used on Intel-based hardware, which is significantly cheaper (both initial price and replacement parts) than the hardware used by most Unix machines.[10] However, Windows may not have

[7] "Comparing Microsoft Windows NT and UNIX System Management," Microsoft Corporation, White Paper, 1998: 4.

[8] Jon C. LeBlanc, *Migrate with Confidence from Microsoft Windows Servers to UNIX/Linux: Strategic Information for IT Executives and Managers*, White Paper, 29 Mar. 1999, 19 Nov. 1999 <http://www.cuug.ab.ca/~leblancj/nt_to_unix.html>.

[9] John Kirch, *Microsoft Windows NT Server 4.0 versus UNIX*, 7 Aug. 1999. 19 Nov. 2002 <http://kirch.net/unix-nt/>.

[10] Slater.

the low-cost hardware to themselves for long. Linux is emerging as a low-cost Unix-based alternative that is beginning to be used as a low-end operating system for file, print, and Web server applications (**Q17**).[11] The major Unix-based server vendors are investing heavily in Linux with the intention of also making Linux servers viable at the high end.

In addition, there are many costs associated with the selection and implementation of a computing platform. These include design costs, purchase costs, implementation costs, and maintenance costs (**Q17**).[12] In many server projects, the labor cost associated with designing, implementing, and maintaining the system represents the biggest and most important cost. Thus, analysts remain divided as to which platform is actually cheaper to own and operate.[13]

16 ■———◄

Conclusions and Predictions

Today, Unix and Windows share the server market, with Windows dominating in infrastructure servers and Unix dominating in enterprise critical servers. However, Gartner Group predicts, in the next five years the server landscape will shift dramatically. They predict Linux will begin to dominate the Web and infrastructure server domain, and Windows will gain a greater foothold in enterprise critical servers as well as gaining market share in other server application areas.[14] The next five years will be a period of intense competitive battles among server vendors.[15] In this battlefield, organizations will make their choice of server platform based on their specific circumstances as well as the strengths and weaknesses of those platforms at the time the decisions are made.

[11] Tony Smith, "Linux v. MS v. Unix—Who's Got the Big Mo?" *The Register* 25 June 2002, 21 Aug. 2002 <http://www.theregister.co.uk/content/61/25882.html>.

[12] William Stallings, *Computer Organization and Architecture: Designing for Performance*, 5th ed. (Upper Saddle River: Prentice Hall, 2000) 43–45.

[13] Slater.

[14] Slater.

[15] Slater.

17. What are the business and technology reasons for choosing one Unix platform over another?

DAWN GREGG

Computing platforms are the technological foundation on which your organization runs.[1] The selection of a computing platform is a subjective process that requires a method for comparing and choosing among hardware, operating system, software and vendor options.

EVALUATING PLATFORM OPTIONS

Computing platforms range from small, embedded systems, to PC clients, to large clusters of servers that operate together (Q11). Figure 17.1 illustrates where Linux and Unix systems fit into this picture.

Selecting a Linux or Unix server platform requires an organization to establish criteria for choosing among the available options. The weighting applied to an individual issue will depend on how the system is to be used (the application), on the makeup of the organization, and on how critical a given system is to the organization.

HARDWARE ISSUES

When assessing hardware, an organization needs to look at the systems it already has and determine how much additional capacity it may need. The hardware selected must have enough capacity to provide the desired performance. The hardware should also have a history of stability to ensure that it will have a minimum of downtime. Finally, the system needs to be flexible so it can continue to meet the needs of the organization as it grows.

Expected hardware performance can be compared using benchmarks performed by manufacturers or using comparisons made by independent consulting firms. Most hardware and software vendors have tools that allow a system to be sized based on anticipated usage patterns.

OPERATING SYSTEM ISSUES

UNIX   When choosing a Unix platform, one would think that operating system issues would be minimized. However, most hardware vendors offer their own version

---

[1] Ray Valdés, "The Perils of Platform Selection," *New Architect* (formerly *Web Techniques*) Mar. 2000, 21 Aug. 2002 <http://www.newarchitectmag.com/archives/2000/03/plat/>.

Figure 17.1 Computing Platforms

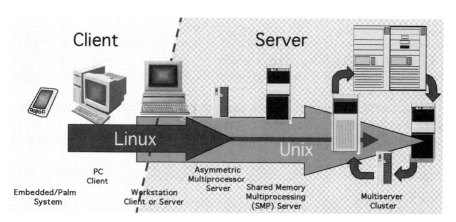

of Unix. While these different versions of Unix provide many of the same Unix fundamentals, they also have many functional differences including scalability, reliability, system management, Internet and Web application services, and directory and security services.[2]

Various consulting firms periodically do comparisons of the different Unix operating systems that can be used as a part of the operating system decision making process.[3, 4] However, having the current "best" version of Unix is not always the most important factor to consider when selecting a Unix operating system. In reality, the software application often determines the version of Unix that is selected. The different versions of Unix are not compatible with each other. This means all software needs to be recompiled (and possibly modified) on each different platform before it can be used on that type of system. This is a major expense for software providers and, as a result, some software providers only make their products available for one version of Unix.

Another consideration when selecting a Unix operating system is the organization's current systems and in-house expertise. In general, operating system environments that contain different versions of Unix are much harder to manage. It is often difficult for a system manager who is familiar with one type of Unix system to walk in and manage a Unix system from another manufacturer. Thus, once an organization has selected a specific hardware vendor, it is desirable to make future equipment purchases from the same manufacturer.

---

[2] "2002 UNIX Function Review," Report, *D. Brown Associates, Inc. Web Site* May 2002, 21 Aug. 2002 <http://www.dhbrown.com/dhbrown/02UnixFunRev.cfm>.

[3] Tony Iams, "2002 UNIX Function Review," *D.H. Brown Associates, Inc.* May 2002 <http://www.dhbrown.com>.

[4] "Vendor Ratings," *Gartner, Inc. Web Site* n.d., 21 Aug. 2002 <http://www.gartner.com/1_researchanalysis/vendor_rating/vr_main.html>.

Linux   In addition to Unix, there is Linux. Linux is an "open source" version of Unix that has traditionally been used as a client operating system or as a low-end operating system for file, print, and Web server applications.[5] However, Linux is beginning to be used more in critical enterprise-oriented applications. Linux has demonstrated its reliability to the point that businesses of all types and sizes have come to regard it as a viable alternative to proprietary Unix platforms. As a result, Linux is now the fastest growing operating system.[6]

Major software vendors are developing applications to run on Linux and developers are improving its stability and scalability. Linux can now be used to run server clusters and is capable of running a variety of mainstream business applications such as accounting, databases, and conferencing.[7]

Software Issues

Software selection also plays a major role in overall platform design. The types of software that are commonly part of a Unix platform include database server software, application server software, Web server software, file/print server software, firewall software, etc. Choosing the appropriate software for an organization's needs is critical to the overall platform performance (**Q13, Q18, Q19, Q20, Q22**).[8]

Viability Issues

The hardware and software components of platforms can be very complex. Many systems require consulting services, training, and technical support, both while the system is being implemented and after implementation to maintain the platform for the duration of its life. Thus, vendor support and service need to be major criteria in the platform selection process. This is one of the disadvantages of using Linux unless the company uses a version supported by the big hardware vendors.

Cost

The final criterion in platform selection is cost (**Q74**). There are many costs associated with the selection and implementation of a computing platform. These include:

[5] Tony Smith, "Linux v. MS v. Unix—Who's Got the Big Mo?" *The Register* 25 June 2002, 21 Aug. 2002 <http://www.theregister.co.uk/content/61/25882.html>.

[6] Mary Hubley and Nathan Muller, *Linux: What Major IT Vendors Are Doing*, Gartner, Inc., Technology Overview DPRO-90624, 9 Oct. 2002.

[7] Hubley and Muller.

[8] Nelson King, "Choosing an Internet Commerce Platform," *Computer Channel, Inc.* 1999 <http://www.compchannel.com>.

- *Design costs*—This is the estimated cost of designing the system, including the selection of all hardware and software components.

- *Purchase costs*—This consists of published prices for the hardware and software, and all items on the purchase contract.

- *Implementation costs*—This is a subjective number that requires the estimation of how long a project will take to get up and running—given the elements of the platform— and the staffing required. If different Unix systems are being used, this will include the costs to convert and port the software to the different systems.

- *Maintenance costs*—This number is the most often overlooked. It consists of the ongoing staff support and maintenance contract costs to keep the system up and running over the life of the system. It also includes costs to upgrade systems when new versions of the operating system or software are released.[9]

In most platform deployment projects, the labor cost associated with designing, implementing, and maintaining the system often represents the biggest and most important cost. If an organization is considering Linux as a cost-saving alternative, the following should be considered: (1) the skill levels of current IT staff, (2) the complexity of the applications, and (3) the amount and cost of migrating from a legacy environment, which may necessitate extra costs for consulting and integration services.[10]

Conclusion

The growing importance of total cost of ownership (TCO) (**Q74**) and system manageability for most enterprises makes the choice of the computing platform (and vendor) more critical than ever before.[11] A platform selection decision is often a long-term commitment for a business. Once an organization has committed to a given hardware vendor and software packages (and vendors), it is very difficult and costly to make major changes. When problems occur, organizations usually attempt to make the current system work instead of abandoning it.[12] Thus, the platform selection process should be viewed as a long-term strategic decision in which system reliability, scalability, and vendor viability are of paramount importance.

[9] Stallings 43–45.
[10] Hubley and Muller.
[11] Chris Goodhue and Tom Berg, *Getting a Grip on Hardware Management*, Gartner, Inc., Report R-140-120, 6 June 1997.
[12] Valdés.

18. What are the characteristics of a transaction processing system?

RINA DELMONICO

A transaction processing system (TPS) is an automated method of performing repeatable and consistent business activities, such as:

- billing for products or services,

- payroll,

- order entry and processing,

- warehousing, logistics, inventory replenishment,

- purchasing and return processing,

- manufacturing, tooling, building,

- product scheduling and delivery,

- monitoring of sales and commissions.

Transaction processing systems debuted in the late 1960s when businesses recognized the need for mechanisms that would reliably automate transactions. At that time, transaction processing systems were primarily implemented by organizations that handled large volumes of transactions due to the high cost of system development, implementation, and usage. Subsequently, these costs have dropped and off-the-shelf systems are now available. These systems come in a variety of formats and sizes, and transactions can be processed online, serially and relationally, using a variety of tools and equipment. Today, transaction processing systems are utilized in almost every industry regardless of transaction volume.

COMMON FEATURES OF A TPS

Regardless of the type of transaction processed, these systems share several important features in that they:

- automate day-to-day operational activities, increasing productivity and reducing cost,

- store distributed data and provide access to applications,

- maintain data integrity by ensuring a transaction is never incomplete and that data is never inconsistent between users,

- enable concurrent and independent processing of transactions,

- perform actions repetitively and consistently using stored data and functionality defined in an application such as:

  – reads

  – searches

  – writes

  – deletes

  – changes

  – converts

  – transfers

- ensure durability and timeliness so the system and data are available as and when they are needed.[1]

In a client/server environment, a transaction becomes the fundamental unit of recovery, consistency, and concurrency. This is important because in a simple debit-credit banking operation, for example, all credit transactions must succeed and any losses are unacceptable. The application must provide for the integrity expected in real-life business transactions. In addition, all participating applications must adhere to the transactional discipline to avoid corrupting an entire system. The application therefore needs to rely on the underlying system to help achieve this level of integrity without the need for huge development by the application developer.

---

[1] The issues are related to the ACID (Atomicity, Consistency, Isolation, and Durability) properties of transaction processing. See Robert Orfali, Dan Harkey, and Jeri Edwards, *Client/Server Survival Guide* (New York: Wiley, 1999) 320.

Measuring the Performance and Accuracy of a TPS

To prevent a transaction processing failure, it is critical to measure the performance and accuracy of a TPS's operation. The nature of transaction processing enables the measurement of the process itself as well as of specific data, including:

- cost per transaction,
- transaction volume per channel,
- time to market,
- inventory turns,
- sales cycle length,
- cost per employee,
- total cost of ownership (**Q74**).

Many of these measures are incorporated into transaction processing monitoring tools that manage the system as well as monitor transactions. Transaction processing monitors (TP monitors) specialize in managing transactions from their point of origin—typically on the client—across one or more servers, and then back to the originating client (Orfali et al., 1999).[2] When a transaction ends, the TP monitor ensures that all the systems involved in the transaction are left in a consistent state. In addition, TP monitors know how to run transactions, route them across systems, load-balance their execution, and restart them after failures. Simply put, they act as operating systems and provide information related to TPS performance. With TP monitors, the application programmers don't have to concern themselves with issues such as:

- concurrency,
- failures,
- broken connections,
- load balancing,
- the synchronization of resources across multiple platforms.

The Importance of a TPS

Here are three dramatic examples of how a business can be adversely affected if its transaction processing systems do not run smoothly:

[2] Orfali, Harkey, and Edwards 338.

- In 1999, eBay had three outages due to an unexpectedly high rate of growth and, as a result, their systems were shut down entirely for six hours. Their market capitalization dropped 10 percent for each of these outages.

- In 1994, after a series of outages, Cisco's reliance on their failing legacy systems resulted in a major, 48-hour shutdown. The inability to ship products and conduct business led them to implement Oracle's Enterprise Resource Planning (ERP) software to better manage their growing business.

- In 2000, UPS aired a television commercial that depicted the launching of a transactional dot.com Web site. As they became inundated with orders, the management team's feelings went from elation to panic as they were not prepared to handle the volume of orders they were now required to fulfill. This is an excellent example of poor transaction process planning.

These examples show that TPS failures are felt both internally and externally, often at a significant cost, and that they are critical to businesses that rely on them. Efficient transaction processing systems can streamline critical business processes while inefficient or faulty transaction processing systems can destroy a business. Thus, success depends on giving careful thought to scalability, growth rates, technology platforms, costs, and the ultimate importance of the IT infrastructure.

The Future of TPSs

Transaction processing will improve in the years to come. Increased cost effectiveness and reduced processing times will be part of the next wave of technological improvements. TPS tools will be able to:

- deploy applications on multiple servers,

- manage transactions that are distributed across them,

- perform some form of load-balancing,

- deploy software to clients and servers,

- manage multiserver, multicorporation environments.

The last point is particularly important because what started as transaction processing within organizations is rapidly shifting to the sharing of transaction information between organizations, which enables cross-organizational processes such as supply chain management (**Q67**). There will also be continued transaction productivity improvements for businesses through B2B-enabled business processes (**Q37**).

19. What are the characteristics and benefits of a decision support system?

STEVE KIEL

A *decision support system* (DSS) is an interactive and flexible computer-based system developed to support specific decision making processes. DSSs include systems for financial and sales analysis, executive information systems, as well as artificial neural networks designed to learn more about customer behavior. A DSS analyzes business data and presents it so that business decisions may be made more efficiently and effectively. Data sources for a DSS can be an *internal transaction processing system* (TPS) (**Q18**), a *data warehouse* (**Q20**), or external sources.

For a DSS to be useful, the decisions that are being supported must have a *measurable attribute* or *summary indicator*, such as total revenue or margin percentage that differentiates among alternative solutions. The process of developing those solutions, however, is outside the scope of a DSS. But once these attributes have been developed and the supporting information has been collected, a DSS creates its value by the ease and efficiency by which the alternatives can be evaluated.

CHARACTERISTICS OF A DSS

A DSS is composed of:

1. a data subsystem, which contains the data and is managed by a database management system,

2. a modeling subsystem consisting of the model base management system,

3. a communication subsystem, where the user can communicate with the DSS.

A DSS can provide support to all phases of the decision-making process and to all managerial levels—from individuals to groups and organizations. The data elements needed for DSS applications may be extracted from several sources and organized in a data warehouse. Regardless of how they are collected, the data elements must be validated and filtered. DSS is a user-oriented tool and many applications can be constructed by end users. End users access the data using different tools, depending on the reason for the access. For example, online analytical processing (OLAP) tools are used to generate queries, request ad hoc reports, conduct statistical analyses, and build DSS and multimedia applications.

These tools are used to perform:

1. sensitivity analyses to understand how a small change to a given input variable will affect the model's outputs,

2. what-if analyses to find out what impact a change in an input variable, assumption, or parameter value will have on the solution,

3. goal-seeking analyses to calculate the values of an input necessary to achieve a desired objective.

DIFFERENCES BETWEEN DSSs AND TPSs

A DSS is an *informational* application in contrast to an *operational* application that is developed to perform transaction processing. Most TPSs do not support the data content and organization requirements that are needed for DSS activities. For this reason, the DSS is most often supported in a separate environment, away from the TPS. There are several differences between DSSs and TPSs:

- *TPSs work with individual transactions.* DSSs queries work with large amounts of data. For example, a TPS would provide access to what John Smith purchased from store number 55 on May 5. In contrast, a DSS user might want to see the total sales for last year broken down by region and by product type.

- *TPSs must be updated in real-time.* Account balances need to be current and reflect the most recent transactions at all times. A DSS user works with high-level summary data. The decisions being made at that level are not affected by recent transactions.

- *A TPS data model is designed for efficient data entry.* Response times while customers are waiting are minimized. There is no manual data entry function with a DSS. The DSS structures are designed for efficient data retrieval.

- *TPS usage patterns are usually predictable.* The online users, such as order entry clerks, are processing transactions based on an established schedule. The bimonthly payroll run is an example of a batch process that is executed at the same time each month. DSS activity is often ad hoc and unpredictable. The quantity and content of the data required for today's analysis might be very different from what is required tomorrow.

DSS APPLICATIONS

A typical DSS application is financial analysis and reporting. Some solutions are commercially available "out of the box" and offer a complete application that provides financial reporting, analysis, budgeting, and planning. The general ledger system is usually the primary data source, but data can be input from other applications and external sources as well. A multidimensional data model is used to present data in the way that managers think about the data, and an extensive library of built-in functions helps users create forecasts and calculate performance ratios. Models are structured to give the users the ability to establish different detailed equations for particular types of organizations and scenarios. These applications minimize the effort required to load data, providing users more time to focus on qualitative analysis.

Another common DSS application is an *executive information system* (EIS). An EIS is designed to provide senior managers with access to information that is relevant to their decision making activities. The goal of an EIS is to collect and integrate internal and external data to be measured against key performance indicators (KPIs). It is typical for an EIS to provide features such as drill-down analysis, graphics, exception reporting, and the ability to highlight information that an executive feels is important. A common display format is a dashboard that shows red, yellow, and green lights to indicate the current status of each KPI. A dashboard created to present financial information would allow an executive to quickly review KPIs related to profitability, cash flow, cash positions, and asset management. An effective EIS is often the single location that can be used for immediate access to current financial and operational results. Of course, there are many other specific DSS applications. But they all focus around the objective of taking large amounts of data, and analyzing and presenting the data in a format useful for decision making.

Key Benefits and Challenges

Developing a DSS can be very costly. The integration of data from multiple sources, the development of a common understanding of data definitions, and cleansing data from systems with fewer controls all can cause a DSS project scope to expand quickly. Fortunately, there is also great benefit to be realized at the completion of the project that can offset the significant costs. Listed are some of the benefits of an effective DSS.

- The ability to analyze complex problems enables faster responses to unexpected situations.

- More objective decisions receive greater support and acceptance.

- The ability to integrate information sources can improve communication among business units. If business units have disparate systems, the only point of integration may be the DSS.

- Increased management team effectiveness as managers spend more time on analysis, planning, and implementation, and less time on data collecting, integration, and interpretation.

A few common development challenges can prevent an organization from realizing the benefits of a DSS. These development challenges are as follows:

- *Data elements are not understood.* When drawing data from disparate sources, data elements are sometimes transformed and renamed. Comprehensive documentation is needed to describe the meaning and origin of each of the data elements.

- *Reports are inconsistent.* If users have conflicting views about the definition of data elements, they may select different elements to create what they perceive as being the same report.

- *The current databases are "dirty."* Extra time should be included to develop documentation that describes the different data conditions and the appropriate steps for cleansing.

- *Users don't trust the reports.* If users do not trust the data elements or data integrity, they will not trust the reports that a DSS generates. Moreover, if IT develops a DSS system without user involvement, users may be unlikely to trust the results of the DSS analyses. Involving the users from the beginning will help create a sense of ownership, improve the level of support, and possibly identify desired measurements that are not currently available. It is best if these are identified in the beginning of the project rather than after implementation. Although these challenges are significant, they are common to DSS implementations and can be reduced through careful planning in the early stages of a DSS project.

What Works

Successful DSS development depends on understanding the requirements of the end user, having a clear description of the problems that the decisions are targeted at solving, having a detailed knowledge of the source data as well as, of course, the appropriate application of technology. A typical development project includes all of the phases of a standard development life cycle; analyze, design, build, test, and transition to production. After a DSS goes into production, it will require ongoing support and development resources as it evolves to meet changing requirements. Just as the business processes must adapt to the changing environment in which they operate, so must the DSS that supports these processes. The quality of a DSS is only as good as the business processes that it is designed to support, the level of understanding that the DSS designers have of those processes, and the quality of the data used for analysis.

20. What are data warehouses and what are their benefits?

GARY DODGE

A *data warehouse* is a storehouse of data built by an organization to be its long-term memory and a tool for strategic decision making. It is designed and built to supplement a business's transaction processing systems (TPS) (**Q18**), such as accounting, order management, human resources, manufacturing, etc., that are used to run its daily operations. The various TPSs often do not have common database structures because they can be purchased from multiple vendors and because their database designs are fundamentally driven by the procedural needs of each application. They are built for processing efficiency and to collect and manage data for each transaction area.

However, organizations have other needs as well. In addition to important tactical information such as, "How many controller boards do we have in stock?", there is a whole class of strategic questions that aren't generally part of a TPS application, such as, "Which supplier(s) should we be buying controller boards from?" or "What would be our product margins if we cut controller board costs by 15 percent?" Therefore, organizations that want the ability to analyze their corporate data for strategic decision making build comprehensive data warehouses to provide data for decision support applications (**Q19**) that answer these types of questions.

DATA WAREHOUSE CHARACTERISTICS

A number of years ago, Bill Inmon originally defined the concept of a data warehouse and described several key characteristics.[1]

Separate   Organizations usually separate their data warehouse environments from their many operational systems. This allows the data warehouse to be a world where spontaneous investigation of data is not just allowed but is encouraged. Most businesses don't want analysts making random inquiries into live production databases because of the risk that they could disrupt daily operations. Thus, a separate warehouse is built.

Subject-Oriented   The data warehouse is organized primarily around the data from a corporate perspective, not around the functional needs of a single application. For example, gathering all of the information about the *employee* subject area, might involve obtaining data from a variety of operational systems. Most data would likely come

[1] William H. Inmon, *Building the Data Warehouse*, 3rd ed. (New York: Wiley, 2002).

from the human resources systems, but some would come also from payroll, project accounting, and perhaps the sales compensation or order management systems. This would probably be the only place in the organization where all such employee data would be gathered.

Integrated   The data warehouse is designed to bring together and integrate data from many sources in order to provide a broader perspective of a problem. Combining data from various systems (as well as from external data sources) requires that the disparate data around a particular subject area is integrated. Sometimes there is a common key (such as a social security number) that conveniently ties all of these sources together. Frequently, however, this is not the case. Getting all the data about a customer, for example, might be quite difficult since different applications (and business units) within the same company might have many different definitions of a customer. In this all-too-common example, it isn't just a matter of *who* is in each unit's customer database, but also *what* customer information is maintained and *how* it is structured. Hence, integrating data from many sources is always the biggest and hardest task in building the data warehouse.

Nonvolatile   Nonvolatile means that data is maintained in the warehouse as it was originally created. Rather than update the warehouse data as operational changes occur, new data is added to the warehouse to record each change. A single record in the operational system may only "remember" the current status of an entity, such as inventory quantity on hand today. By contrast, the data warehouse would keep not only that data, but would add to the warehouse all the changes as they occur. This allows someone to see how frequently that particular item has changed status over the last month or year. Naturally this means that data warehouses can get quite large over time.

Accessible   The whole point of a data warehouse is to provide access to corporate data by knowledge workers. It is designed to be accessible on their own terms, regardless of their understanding of underlying data structures or the warehouse's physical implementation. It also allows the use of tools that permit an analyst to try various alternatives, apply value judgments to the results, and then try again.

Time-Variant   Information is entered into the data warehouse typically with some time attribute associated with it. The warehouse maintains a historical record that allows someone to look back and derive a "snapshot" of conditions at a previous point in time. It further allows analysts to evaluate the rate and magnitude of various changes over time.

Granular   Granularity refers to the level of detail held in the units of data stored in a data warehouse. There are four basic levels of detail in a typical data warehouse.

1. a current level of detail

2. an older level of detail (usually on alternate, bulk storage)

3. a level of lightly summarized data

4. a level of highly summarized data

As data ages, it passes from current detail to older detail. As the data is summarized, it passes from current detail to lightly summarized data, then from lightly summarized data to highly summarized data. Summaries may be refreshed manually or automatically by the database after loading new detailed data. Alternatively, some warehouses are built using "star schema" designs that allow detailed data to be dynamically and efficiently summarized when queried using varied dimensional criteria.[2]

The data warehouse's style of design, level of detail, and length of retention must be decided in a manner consistent with the company's willingness to invest in the technology resources to store and manipulate it. This allows analysts to dive as deeply into a subject as needed in order to come to important conclusions.

CHOOSING DATA WAREHOUSE TECHNOLOGY

Several architectural options for the data warehouse are possible. One is a centralized data warehouse that uses a single, large database to support all of the data loading and integration as well as the users' query activities. Some organizations choose to implement several smaller databases, called *data marts*, that each support a particular subject area or organizational unit, perhaps using highly summarized data. The risk of implementing multiple independent data marts is that it is very tempting to build them quickly without integrating them. This can result in the unfortunate situation where, for example, analysts from headquarters finance would present a report to senior management that would differ from a similar report prepared from a business unit's data mart. To avoid the uncomfortable argument over whose data is correct, organizations that use data marts should start with an integrated data warehouse that feeds data to the data marts. This preserves the consistency of data across the various data marts and provides additional detail or longer history in the warehouse when needed.

Another set of issues surround the selection of technology. One of the common problems in an initial data warehouse development effort is to overemphasize technology issues instead of the needs of a business (**Q4, Q58**). Fundamentally, there are many technology combinations that can successfully support a data warehouse. Without a good understanding of business concerns, it is very possible for technical staff

---

[2] Ralph Kimball, *Data Warehouse Toolkit*, 2nd ed. (New York: Wiley, 2002).

to select components that miss the actual target, being either too exotic or too basic. For instance, it is easy to be seduced by extremely expensive specialized architectures. It is just as easy, however, to assume that the warehouse will be able to use the same architecture that supports the rest of the business. An example is the organization that uses many small servers to run each internal application, but whose data warehousing needs quickly exceed the scalability of this platform (Q16).

Another aspect of technology that must be considered is that a data warehouse solution requires many different components. In addition to the database management system, tools will be needed for extracting, transforming, loading, and integrating data, for reporting and end user querying, for analytical processing, and perhaps for data mining (Q21).[3] Much of the technical complexity of a data warehouse is derived from the need to do "plumbing" to get these various tools to work well together without limiting the capabilities of one component in order to use it with another.

In the long run, the biggest cost of most data warehouses is not the hardware or the software components, but the total of various administration costs (Q74). These costs include the direct expense of administrators and administration-support tools. They also include less obvious indirect costs. Some routine administrative tasks such as loading or integrating data may consume large amounts of system resources during part of the day and prevent users from having access to the system. The opportunity costs of the system being unavailable do not become apparent until the warehouse becomes mission-critical to its users. Unfortunately, the cost of correcting the technology environment at that point is extremely high.

CONCLUSION

A successful data warehouse is the foundation of what is now generally referred to as *business intelligence*. The data warehouse, in itself, does not provide any direct benefit to an organization. The value comes when historical data can be integrated and analyzed easily, giving an organization the tools it needs to make informed strategic decisions.

[3] Carla Catalano, "OLAP (Online Analytical Processing)," *Computerworld.com* 30 Nov. 1998, 25 Nov. 2002 <http://www.computerworld.com/news/1998/story/0,11280,43438,00.html>; Stewart Deck, "Data Mining," *Computerworld.com* 29 Mar. 1999, 25 Nov. 2002 <http://www.computerworld.com/hardwaretopics/hardware/desktops/story/0,10801,43509,00.html>; Cathy Gagne, "Data Visualization," *Computerworld.com* 11 Oct. 1999, 25 Nov. 2002 <http://www.computerworld.com/softwaretopics/software/multimedia/story/0,10801,43536,00.html>; Amy Helen Johnson, "Data Warehouses," *Computerworld.com* 6 Dec. 1999, 25 Nov. 2002 <http://www.computerworld.com/databasetopics/data/story/0,10801,43544,00.html>; Marc Songini, "Collections of Data," *Computerworld.com* 15 Apr. 2002, 25 Nov. 2002 <http://www.computerworld.com/databasetopics/data/story/0,10801,70095,00.html>; Craig Stedman, "Metadata," *Computerworld.com* 18 Oct. 1999, 25 Nov. 2002 <http://www.computerworld.com/databasetopics/data/story/0,10801,43537,00.html>; Craig Stedman, "Object-Enabled Databases," *Computerworld.com* 9 Feb. 1998, 25 Nov. 2002 <http://www.computerworld.com/softwaretopics/software/apps/story/0,10801,43547,00.html>.

21. What is data mining and what are its uses?

MARK L. LABOVITZ

Data mining is a capability consisting of the hardware, software, "warmware" (skilled labor), and data to support the recognition of previously unknown but potentially useful relationships. It supports the transformation of data to information, knowledge and wisdom; a cycle that should take place in every organization. Companies are now using this capability to understand more about their customers, to design targeted sales and marketing campaigns, to predict what and how frequently customers will buy products, and to spot trends in customer preferences that lead to new product development. It is important to note that data mining is not software alone as some vendors would have clients believe. While software may play an important role, it is only in the context of clear objectives and careful thinking from business management along with the skill of the analyst that data mining ultimately leads to a success story rather than an embarrassing and costly failure.

Important Data-Mining Concepts

Any data-mining capability starts and ends with the business objectives and a design of the learning environment. A learning environment is a specific plan of discovery, which includes an operational or analysis-action plan to answer questions raised by pursuit of the business objectives. A partial list of questions commonly found in learning plans includes:

- Who are my customers and what do they look like? (profiling)

- Who are my most valuable customers? (determining customers' valuations, relationship discovery)

- What products or services are my most valuable customers likely to buy next? (likelihood)

- How should I segment my marketplace, or does my existing segmentation conform to my sales results? (market segmentation, relationship discovery, or likelihood)

- When should I contact a customer about a promotion or discount? How often and via what channel? Which products and Web site links should I include in e-mails to different customers? (optimizing customer contacts, explanatory behavior)

- Given a decision to perform a specific promotion or campaign, to whom should it be promoted? (scoring or ranking individuals in terms of their probability of behaving in a variety of predictable ways, likelihood)

The learning plan needs to be periodically updated as the environment changes and new insights are developed and deployed.

How Does Data Mining Work?

Data mining is a capability within the business intelligence system (BIS) of an organization's information system architecture. The purpose of the BIS is to support decision making through the analysis of data consolidated together from sources, which are either outside the organization or from internal transaction processing systems (TPS). The central data store of a BIS is the data warehouse or data marts.[1]

The source for the data is usually a data warehouse or series of data marts (**Q20**). However, knowledge workers and business analysts are interested in exploitable patterns or relationships in the data and not the specific values of any given set of data. The analyst uses the data to develop a generalization of the relationship (known as a *model*), which partially explains the data values being observed.

To achieve this, data-mining packages commonly found in the marketplace use methods from one or more of three approaches to analyze data. These approaches are:

1. *Statistical analysis*—based upon theories of distribution of errors or related probability laws.

2. *Data/knowledge discovery (KD)*—includes analysis and algorithms from pattern recognition, neural networks, and machine learning. (**Q51**)

3. *Specialized applications*—includes ANOVA/DOE (Analysis of Variance/Design of Experiments); the "meta-data" of statistics; Geographic Information Systems (GIS) and spatial analysis; and the analysis of unstructured data such as free text, graphical/visual, and audio data. Finally, visualization is used with other techniques or stand-alone.

KD and statistically based methods have not developed in complete isolation from one another. Many approaches which were originally statistically based have been augmented by KD methods and made more efficient and operationally feasible for use in business processes.

---

[1] Important, related issues are the movement, preparation, and maintenance of data when transferred from the TPS to the BIS as well as within the BIS. How an organization deals with these data issues will gate the quality of any data-mining results. The practices commonly used to deal with these issues include a number of fairly technical subjects, which when implemented consume a great deal of time and resources. These subjects are beyond the central focus of this answer.

EVALUATION CRITERIA

There are numerous data-mining software products available to organizations and they must evaluate them to fit their needs.[2] The following is a partial set of evaluation criteria to consider when purchasing data-mining software applications:

1. *User interface*—How is the user interface set up? Does the interface support generic data-mining analysis or does it adapt to a specific business's needs?

2. *End user functionality and access*—How easy is it for users to find and use previously created models/analyses? What support is provided for distribution of results? Can the tool be used to access and create models via the Web?

3. *Advanced analytical power*—What built-in support does the tool set provide for complex analysis? Does the tool set support analyses from all the business discovery classes? Are both statistically based and KD algorithms provided?

4. *Data transfer/ data store interface and file scoring*—Does the application perform file scoring and does it support selection and transfer of data between the analysis engine and the data store? How does the tool ensure that the data sources, models, reports, and metadata are all synchronized?

5. *Sampling*—What sort of sampling design schemas does the tool support and help implement?

6. *Data preprocessing and preparation*—What, if any, data preprocessing does the tool set support? Does it support variable transformation, recoding, and creation?

7. *Goodness of fit and validation*—Does the application provide comparison of models, modeling techniques, and analyses that aid in the selection of attributes most likely to solve a given business problem? What validation methodologies does the tool support?

8. *Customization*—What support is available to customize and develop applications? What can the tool do to support the implementation of models into the production environment?

9. *Availability of trained professionals*—How large and how experienced is the labor pool for professionals trained in the particular tool? Does the vendor have a certification program and how is that organized?

10. *Licensing and pricing*—What does the package cost, what is the total cost of ownership (**Q74**), and how is the system licensed—by server, by processors, by named seats, etc.

[2] "Software Suites for Data Mining and Knowledge Discovery," *KDNuggets Web Site* n.d. 12 Dec. 2002 <http://www.kdnuggets.com /software/suites.html>.

DATA-MINING ISSUES

There are several significant issues in implementing, using, and maintaining a data-mining capability that organizations need to address.

Understanding What You Are Getting   Buying a data-mining software engine is insufficient to realize an ongoing data-mining capability. The software engine is a tool kit. As such, prerequisite business plans, the internal IT infrastructure, and the craftsmen capable of using the tools must be secured and put into place.

Data Readiness for Analysis   Data-mining requires a consolidated, "de-duplicated" and cleaned data store to draw from. Seventy to 85 percent of the work in building models using data mining relates to the cleaning and preparation of data prior to a specific analysis.

Staffing   Data-mining software is not a replacement for skilled analysts. The algorithms used in data mining are quite powerful. If the users do not understand these issues or have access to knowledgeable staff, the results can be disastrous. The staff also needs to be committed to the effort. While the level of labor required to run a data-mining capability will vary with a number of factors, data mining is not a do-once-and-then-forget activity. Learnings are incremental and environments (internal and external) change; therefore learning is a constant and ongoing process and so is data mining. The ongoing use of a data-mining capability requires business analysis and data analysis skills.

Taking Action   Data mining is about acting upon the results and making changes. An important issue which must be addressed before undertaking the creation of a data-mining capability is the organization's ability to take the learnings, interpret the results, and make the recommended changes in the business and organization. The best use of data mining will challenge an organization's change management process.

Financial Considerations   There is a considerable danger of underestimating the costs of implementing, using, and maintaining a data-mining capability. As often occurs with other IT-enabled activities, the costs of integrating the data-mining engine and making it work in a specific environment are often underestimated by 50 percent or more. A frequently overlooked source of cost is the labor required to use and maintain the system. Data-mining software vendors have the tendency to make recommendations calling for fewer analysts of lower skill levels than will be actually required by the data-mining capability to meet company expectations. Finally, with respect to maintenance, the organization is not only faced with the maintenance activities typically associated with an IT system, but it also must expend resources to maintain other items such as models and data.

SUMMARY

Data mining is a data-driven capability for extracting patterns that can provide powerful answers to critical business questions. For companies willing to make the commitment to financial and technical resources, highly qualified analytical talent, the cleanup and maintenance of clean data, and the willingness to learn and act upon the results, data mining can provide a powerful competitive advantage.

22. What are the characteristics and benefits of group support systems?

JAHANGIR KARIMI

Groups make most major decisions in organizations. Solving complex problems requires that people work together, necessitating the formation of workgroups. A group support system (GSS) is a term describing any combination of hardware and software that enhances group work, and includes all forms of collaborative computing.[1] GSSs evolved after information technology researchers recognized that technology could be developed to support the many activities normally occurring at face-to-face meetings.

Most group work takes place in meetings. Despite the many criticisms of the effectiveness and efficiency of meetings, people still get together in groups to discuss issues and to work. Meetings can be effective despite the fact that up to 80 percent of what is discussed in a meeting is either forgotten or remembered incorrectly.[2]

[1] While communication primarily transmits information from a sender to a receiver, collaboration is much deeper. Collaboration conveys meaning or knowledge among group members. Material is actively worked upon during collaboration. Collaboration includes sharing documents, information, and knowledge. It includes activities such as brainstorming and voting. Collaboration implies people actively working together and requires collaborative computing support tools that build on communication methods. At the start of the 1990s, GSS was coined to replace group decision support system (GDSS) because researchers recognized that collaborative computing technologies were doing more than supporting decision making. They include electronic meeting systems and electronic conferencing systems.

[2] 3M Corporation's 3M Meeting Network (www.3m.com/meetingnetwork) and the Center for Rural Studies (crs.uvm.edu) have information, surveys, and tips about how to run a more effective meeting.

New tools are constantly evolving to support anytime/anyplace meetings. These computer-supported cooperative work systems are known as groupware. The major technology is called a GSS.

WHAT IS GROUPWARE?

Groupware refers to software products that provide collaborative support to groups. Groupware provides a mechanism for teams to share opinions, data, information, knowledge, and other resources. Most small group support emphasizes communication because small groups are generally formed to bring together people who need to communicate. Organizational systems focus more on coordination because coordinating the efforts of disparate groups is a major problem at the organizational level. Groupware typically contains capabilities for at least one of the following:

- electronic brainstorming

- electronic conferencing/meeting

- group scheduling

- calendaring

- planning

- conflict resolution

- model building

- videoconferencing

- electronic document sharing (e.g., screen sharing, whiteboards, or "liveboards")

- voting[3]

IMPLEMENTING A GSS

As with most systems, there are several ways to bring a GSS into a company:

- *Buy software packages and install them internally.* For organizations that anticipate very high usage of these features, this is often the preferred alternative. It can reduce the average cost of usage, and when incorporated into an employee portal (**Q42**), it can be

---

[3] For example, Lotus Notes/Domino Server was the first widely used groupware. Lotus Notes/Domino Server enables collaboration by letting users access and create shared information through specially programmed Notes documents. Many applications have been programmed (written) in Lotus Notes. This includes Learning Space, a courseware package for supporting distance learning.

conveniently accessible to many employees. One disadvantage of this approach is that not all the desired features are present in a single software package. This means that several packages need to be purchased, installed, and integrated, increasing the overall cost of the effort.

- *Buy the capabilities through an application services provider (ASP)* (**Q80**). This is frequently used for specific services such as e-mail. The advantage is that all of the operational issues are handled by the ASP and that costs are related to the volume of the services used. Particularly when GSSs are just being introduced, it is difficult to predict how much usage will occur. Therefore, a pricing model that keeps costs low during the initial introduction is desirable.

- *Use services provided by Web-based vendors* (**Q15**). In the GSS field, a number of companies now make these services available over the Web. For example, a company could hold a large sales meeting over the Web. The originating location would control the content and pace of the meeting, but anyone with a Web connection and a password could follow the presentation. As with an ASP, the operational issues of managing the application are handled by the vendor. The ubiquity of the Web means that participants do not need to be hooked into the corporate network—a significant advantage for travelers. Nevertheless, costs escalate as the services gain popularity and, at some point, it usually makes sense to bring the applications in-house.

Advantages and Disadvantages of a GSS

The goal of a GSS is to increase some of the benefits of collaboration and eliminate or reduce some of the process losses associated with working in groups.[4] A GSS reduces the process losses mentioned above by providing:

- alternative communication channels for the group, while permitting the group to work more efficiently and/or effectively with shared text, structured data, and graphics,

- process structuring for communication protocols and human roles (includes software support for a leadership or facilitation role),

- encouragement of the free exchange of ideas and opinions (e.g., anonymity),

- voting protocols to elicit the group's preference structure (e.g., one vote for preferred option, rating of each alternative, rank ordering of alternatives),

---

[4] Process losses include: (1) air time fragmentation, (2) concentration blocking, (3) attention blocking, (4) failure to remember, (5) conformance pressure, (6) evaluation apprehension, (7) free riding, (8) cognitive inertia (discussion moves along one train of thought without deviating), (9) socializing, (10) domination, (11) information overload, (12) coordination problems, (13) incomplete use of information, and (14) incomplete task analysis (Nunamaker et al., 1991).

- support for data collection, organization, filtering, formatting, feedback, and retrieval (generated or required by the group),

- availability of sophisticated decision aids in support of the group process (e.g., structural modeling, scaling methods, games and simulation, and statistical analysis and forecasting),

- synchronization of the communication process (e.g., who has read what, who has voted, when has a reasonable consensus been reached, when is there a new alternative to consider, where do disagreements exist, when to open or close an activity in the problem-solving process, etc.).

A GSS supports group processes including:

- brainstorming,

- list building,

- information gathering,

- voting,

- organizing,

- prioritizing,

- consensus building by:

    - electronic mail, messaging, and brainstorming tools,

    - idea generation systems and group outliner tools (for creating and commenting on multilevel lists),

    - coordination and topic commenter tools (for commenting on a list of topics),

    - workgroup project management and document interchange systems (for generating a list of ideas and supporting comments),

    - vote and negotiation support systems (for supporting consensus development),

    - information analysis, surveys, and modeling tools.[5]

GSSs have been successful because of their proven effectiveness in many organizations. When properly implemented, a GSS cuts costs, supports participants in making better decisions, and can substantially increase group productivity. However, for a GSS to succeed, it needs to be carefully implemented with adequate organizational support, executive sponsorship, proper design, and user involvement (Q86, Q93).

In addition to these traditional difficulties of implementing any system, GSSs

[5] Netscape Collabra Server, Microsoft NetMeeting, Novell GroupWise groupware, and Group-Systems (for Windows and the Web, GroupSystems.com) are examples of such tools.

sometimes have difficulty being approved in corporate approval processes. That is because the typical financial metrics used to prioritize systems projects (**Q75**) do not always apply to a GSS. It is difficult to quantify improved communication or better group productivity.

Even if a group can prove it is more productive, it is hard to determine how much is due to the system versus the extraordinary efforts of its members. So often, a GSS is implemented in an organization in order to cut costs such as travel expense. However, once its use becomes part of the culture of the organization, it can contribute greatly to the organization's effectiveness.

22

23. What are the major hardware elements of a network and what is the role of each?

DAWN GREGG

A computer network is "a collection of autonomous computers connected so they are capable of exchanging information."[1] At a minimum, every network includes:

- at least two computers,

- a network interface card on each computer (this allows the computer to talk to the network),

- a mechanism to connect the computers (usually a wire or cable, or hardware to allow a wireless connection),

- a network protocol such as TCP/IP, Novell, Ethertalk, or SNA (Systems Network Architecture).

Protocols are programs that are included within the operating system of most computers (e.g., Microsoft Windows 98, Windows NT, MAC O/S, Linux, or Unix). The network protocol provides a common language that allows different computers (or peripherals) to communicate with one another.

Most networks also contain a hub or switch that act as a connection point between the computers.[2] To understand the function of network components it is useful to understand the different types of networks and how they are interconnected (Q24).

[1] Andrew Tanenbaum, *Computer Networks*, 4th ed. (Upper Saddle River: Prentice Hall, 1996) 2.
[2] "The Building Blocks: Basic Components of Networks," *Cisco Web Site* n.d., 30 Aug. 2002 <http://www.cisco.com/warp/public/779/smbiz/netguide/i_bldg_blocks.html>.

Let's start by looking at the network hardware.

Network hardware allows computers to connect to a network and to connect different networks to one another. The five types of network hardware used in modern networks are:

1. network interface cards

2. hubs/repeaters

3. switches

4. routers

5. access points

Network Interface Cards   Network interface cards (NIC), or adapters, are required for a computer or peripheral device to connect to a network. NICs support specific network connections/speeds and cabling. High-speed connections require costlier NICs.

Hubs/Repeaters   Hubs connect multiple users to a single physical device, which connects to the network. Hubs forward any data packets (e.g., e-mail or word-processing documents) they receive from one workstation to all their remaining ports. All users connected to a single hub or stack of connected hubs are in the same "segment," sharing the hub bandwidth or data-carrying capacity.[3]

Switches   Switches are smarter than hubs and offer more dedicated bandwidth to users or groups of users. A switch forwards data packets only to the appropriate port for the intended recipient, based on information in each packet header.[4] Today, network designers are replacing hubs with switches to increase their network performance and bandwidth while protecting their existing wiring investments. (Note: these data switches are different from the switches used in voice networks [Q25]).

Routers   Routers are smarter than switches or hubs. They use a more complete packet *address* to determine the next location for the packet. Based on a network road map called a *routing table*, routers can help ensure that packets are traveling the most

---

[3] "The Building Blocks: Basic Components of Networks—Hubs," *Cisco Web Site* n.d., 30 Aug. 2002 <http://www.cisco.com/warp/public/779/smbiz/netguide/i4_hubs.html>.
[4] "The Building Blocks: Basic Components of Networks—Switches," *Cisco Web Site* n.d., 30 Aug. 2002 <http://www.cisco.com/warp/public/779/smbiz/netguide/i6_switches.html>.

Table 23.1 Three Primary Types of Network Wiring

Cable Type	Description	Used for . . .
Twisted Pair (Unshielded twisted pair (10Base-T))	2, 4, or 25 pairs of copper wires	Basic phone lines
Coaxial (10Base-5 cable) (10Base-2 cable)	Resembles round cable television wiring	Ethernet networks backbone media
Fiber Optic	Constructed of glass or plastic	Connections between "backbone" devices in larger networks

efficient paths to their destinations. If a link between two routers fails, the sending router can determine an alternate route to keep traffic moving.

Routers also provide links between networks that speak different languages. Routers are commonly used as *bridges* to connect local networks together or as *gateways* to connect LANs to wide area network (WAN) services (Q24).[5]

Access Points   Wireless networks utilize access points, which perform many of the same functions as a simple hub. Some access points also offer additional management and roaming functionality as well. Access points often act as a bridge between wireless networks to wired Ethernet or Fast Ethernet networks.[6]

NETWORK CABLING

The final component of a computer network is the network wiring or cabling. Wires are necessary to physically connect computers to the network (unless wireless NICs and access points are used). A summary of the three primary types of network wiring is shown in Table 23.1.[7]

Twisted Pair   Unshielded twisted pair (10Base-T) wiring is commonly made up of 2, 4, or 25 pairs of copper wires. This type of wiring is most common in homes and businesses. Often used for basic phone lines, unshielded twisted pair, called UTP

[5] "The Building Blocks: Basic Components of Networks—Routers," *Cisco Web Site* n.d., 30 Aug. 2002 <http://www.cisco.com/warp/public/779/smbiz/netguide/i7_routers.html>.
[6] "The Building Blocks: Basic Components of Networks—Access Points," *Cisco Web Site* n.d., 30 Aug. 2002 <http://www.cisco.com/warp/public/779/smbiz/netguide/i5_access.html>.
[7] "Cabletron Systems Cabling Guide," *Enterasys Web Site* 1996, 30 Aug. 2002 <http://www.enterasys.com/support/manuals/overview.html>.

Table *23.2* Hardware and Cable Impacts on Transmission Speed

System	Transmission Speed	Required Hardware
Traditional Ethernet	10 Mb	UTP Category 3 wiring or UTP Category 5 wiring
Fast Ethernet	100 Mb	Category 5 twisted pair 10/100 NIC cards
Gigabit Ethernet	up to 1000 Mbps	four-pair Category 5 UTP copper cable (up to 100 meters)
Fiber Distributed Data Interface (FDDI)	100 Mbps	fiber wiring hubs and switches different from Ethernet

Category 3, has been the standard for years. Recently, upgraded wiring called UTP Category 5 is available which meets current higher speed networking standards.

Coaxial Cable   This cable resembles round cable television wiring and is used exclusively in Ethernet networks. Thick coaxial cable (10Base-5 cable) is commonly used as a backbone media. Thin coaxial cable (10Base-2 cable) is a less shielded type of coaxial cabling. It is mostly found in homes and small offices.

Fiber Optics   Fiber optic cable is a high-performance media constructed of glass or plastic that uses pulses of light as a transmission method. Because fiber optics do not utilize electrical charges to pass data, they are free from the possibility of interference due to proximity to electrical fields. This cable is usually reserved for connections between "backbone" devices in larger networks. Fiber offers the highest bandwidth capacity and enables companies to connect their computers at extremely high speeds. However, fiber is the costliest of the wiring alternatives.

Table 23.2 shows some examples of the impact that hardware and cabling can have on transmission speed. The types of hardware and cable selected directly impact the transmission speed of the network. For example, traditional Ethernet systems can transmit 10 Mb of data per second and can operate on either UTP Category 3 or UTP Category 5. Fast Ethernet can transmit 10 times that but it requires Category 5 twisted pair wiring and 10/100 NIC cards.[8] Gigabit Ethernet operates at speeds up to 1000 Mbps. It uses four-pair Category 5 UTP copper cabling for distances up to 100 meters.[9] Implementation of Gigabit Ethernet requires new switches and NICs

[8] "The Building Blocks: Basic Components of Networks—Wiring and Cable," *Cisco Web Site* n.d., 30 Aug. 2002 <http://www.cisco.com/warp/public/779/smbiz/netguide/i2_wiring.html>.
[9] "Networking Basics," *3Com Corporation Web Site* n.d., 30 Aug. 2002 <http://www.3com.com/support/en_US/learning_center/read_more/basic.html>.

(network interface cards) and is relatively expensive. Fiber Distributed Data Interface (FDDI) is another technology, operating at 100 Mbps. FDDI requires different wiring (fiber) and different hubs and switches from Ethernet.[10]

CONCLUSION

Computer networks, from home networks to large WANs such as the Internet (Q26), utilize many of the same hardware components. Selecting the right hardware and cabling helps ensure a network provides the required data transmission speeds.

24

24. What are the most common types of data networks and their uses?

CHUCK MCGRATH

Today's most common data networks are composed of collections of computers and other information devices (e.g., printers, servers, scanners). These devices are linked to each other directly or indirectly through communications networks, using a standard common data language to share information and resources. Traditional data networks have employed dedicated direct or switched connections where circuits are solely used for the network. But today there is rapid evolution to nondedicated and nonswitched networks where data "packets" may take any number of routes from origin to destination rather than following a single path through the network (e.g., most Internet e-mail is carried over connectionless networks) (Q25).

NETWORK DIMENSIONS

Data networks used in organizations today are described along several dimensions.

- *Communication protocols*—These are the rules that allow different parts of the network to understand each other. Protocols define how data is to be formatted, how data integrity is maintained, and how data is transmitted between network nodes. Ethernet, HTTP, and TCP/IP are protocols common in data networks.

[10] "Network Technologies Overview," *Cisco Web Site* n.d., 30 Aug. 2002 <http://www.cisco .com/warp/public/779/smbiz/netguide/ii1_lan.html>.

- *Topology and design*—This refers to the road map of the network and details how key network components interconnect.

- *Addressing*—Network addressing is analogous to house street addressing or individual telephone numbering schemes. An address allows data to be directed to specific destinations in the data network. Each network node has a unique address.

- *Routing*—Network routing is similar to the process of delivering the mail. A special network device called a router determines the specific route for the data to take. How a path is determined and how the path is controlled are issues confronted in routing.

- *Switching* (**Q23**)—Short for port-switching, this is a method derived from traditional phone networks for forwarding information from one place to another based on fixed paths and synchronized time intervals. Switches are generally used to concentrate multiple local area networks (discussed later) onto a high-speed "backbone" that can be linked with other backbones in various ways.

- *Reliability*—Most data networks are subject to disruption so data integrity is a serious issue. Networks incorporate data error checking and error correction schemes to handle this issue. Reliability can also be provided by redundant connections between nodes.

- *Interoperability*—This refers to the degree that software and hardware from different vendors are able to communicate with each other.

- *Security*—Safeguarding information at all points in the network is the function of network security. This includes encryption for transmission security, firewalls for access security (**Q31**), and policies like password management. Security also includes physical security of the network hardware.

- *Standards*—Rules that promote interoperability, including hardware interfaces, communication protocols, and network architectures, are called network standards.

DATA NETWORK GEOGRAPHY

- *PAN* (Personal Area Network)—popular for home offices or personal use and typically supporting one or two computers and printers across the shared network

- *LAN* (Local Area Network)—generally within a single building and typically supporting a specific set of users connected to the network

- *MAN* (Metropolitan Area Network)—several LANs connected within a metropolitan area

- *WAN* (Wide Area Network)—includes larger geographic area and most likely some form of connection to a carrier network

Figure 24.1 Sample Network Architectures: LANs and WANs

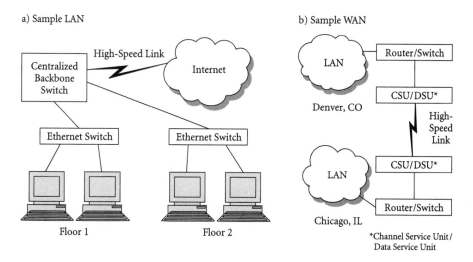

a) Sample LAN   b) Sample WAN

PHYSICAL TOPOLOGY

The physical topology of a network defines the way in which the computer nodes are connected (see Figure 24.2). Some types are:

- *Bus*—Each network node is connected to a common backbone line.
- *Star*—Each network node is connected via a central hub.
- *Ring*—Each network node is connected to a node on either side forming a loop.
- *Mesh*—Each network node is connected to every other node. Some mesh networks may have less redundancy in their connections. This topology is highly reliable but expensive due to the cost of linking all nodes redundantly.

NETWORK ARCHITECTURE

The manner in which the computers in the network are used in the network is called the architecture.[1] There are several architectures (**Q8**). The most common are:

- *Peer-to-peer*—This approach uses all elements on a network on an equal basis. There is no lead element or central hub.

---

[1] Douglas Comer, *Computer Networks and Internets*, 2nd ed. (Upper Saddle River: Prentice Hall, 1999).

*Figure **24.2** Physical Network Topologies*

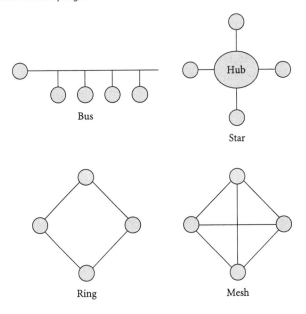

- *Client/server*—This paradigm calls for the client element to initiate communication with the server that waits passively until contacted (**Q11**).

- *Broadcast*—In this form of delivery, one copy of a packet is delivered to each computer on a network.

- *Multicast*—This is a form of addressing where a set of computers is assigned one address; a copy of any data sent to that address is delivered to each of the computers in the set. This is often used for audio or video conferences.

- *Unicast*—This is a form of packet delivery where each computer is assigned a unique address. When a packet is sent to a unicast address, one copy of the packet is delivered to the corresponding computer address. Unicast delivery is the most common type.

LOGICAL TOPOLOGY / SIGNALING METHOD

- *Circuit-based*—Connections in a communications network can be made in the traditional telephone model where a circuit is established (either temporarily during a call or permanently dedicated) regardless of the amount of traffic on the line (**Q25**). Circuit-based networks are more expensive since they require the full capacity to be available regardless of whether they are being used. They are more reliable, however, as a result.

- *Packet-switched*—Data is partitioned into packets. The packets have sequence numbers and addresses so they can be transmitted independently and may not all follow the same path through the network (**Q25**). This makes more efficient use of the network capacity. This in turn leads to lower costs for data transmission.

- *Frame relay*—This WAN packet-switching protocol provides multiple LAN-to-LAN connections across a single network connection. This feature provides significant savings on local circuit charges. Frame relay provides permanent virtual circuits (PVCs) between interconnected sites. PVCs are connection-oriented circuits like those in a circuit-switched network but frame relay allows them to be shared between multiple sites. The advantages are efficient use of bandwidth and reduction of cost.

- *ATM*—Asynchronous Transport Mode is a network environment that can be used to carry data, voice, and video separately and simultaneously over the same network path. Because it can offer guaranteed delivery of time-sensitive information, it is particularly suited for video transmission. It can be used in LANs, MANs, and WANs.

- *Ethernet* (10Base-T, 100Base-T, Gigabit)—Local area network protocols establishing standards for speed, cabling, collision detection, and other elements of data transmission.

  –10Base-T allows a transmission rate of 10 Mbps in a LAN environment.

  –100Base-T is a standard that allows transmission rates ten times faster than 10Base-T.

  –Gigabit Ethernet is ten times faster than 100Base-T but implementation requires new switches and NICs (network interface cards) in the PCs on the network and is relatively expensive.

Standards for 10 Gigabit, 40 Gigabit and 100 Gigabit Ethernet are being prepared and are expected to be available by 2010. This will allow Ethernet to move from the LAN to the MAN and then the WAN. As these protocols are developed, they will challenge Frame Relay and ATM as standards for the WAN. A single end-to-end network protocol will provide benefits of simplicity and improved performance in the network.

SUMMARY

Networks carry data across geographies and connect two or more computers. They differ primarily in the physical configuration of the network links (e.g., PAN, LAN, WAN), the speed at which they carry the data (e.g., Ethernet 10Base-T), the way the data is routed across the network elements (switched or nonswitched), and the format of the data as it is carried among those elements (Frame Relay, ATM, Ethernet protocols). The choice of which network to use in a specific application is based on a balanced consideration of the number of network elements to be connected, the distances and geography involved, and the volume of data and time frames for data delivery and the cost to provide service at desired levels of quality.

25. What are the differences between voice and data networks?

DAWN GREGG

Most organizations maintain separate networks to handle voice and data, because the requirements for transmitting voice and data are fundamentally different. Data is bursty and unpredictable whereas voice is delay sensitive. This has resulted in two completely different mechanisms for transmitting voice and data. Current telephone systems use *circuit switching* to guarantee delay-free high-quality voice transmission. Data networks use *packet switching* to optimize the data throughput (**Q24**).

VOICE NETWORKS

The public voice network, also known as the PSTN (public switched telephone network), uses a "circuit-switched" technology. When one party phones another, the call is set up by a series of switches. For example, to complete an international business phone call, a company's PBX (Private Branch Exchange) switches the call to the local exchange, which then switches it to a national exchange. From there, it goes to an international exchange, and then proceeds back down the network hierarchy until it reaches another PBX and, ultimately, the called party.[1] The paramount consideration in the design of traditional voice networks is reliability and continuity of connection. The PSTN establishes a continuous dedicated connection for the duration of the telephone call. This guarantees that every word arrives in the order it was spoken, without undue delays.

Switches are the core of any voice network; they are essentially large computers with network circuitry that can handle millions of calls. Local telephone companies deploy hundreds of these switches in central offices (COs) through which they route all telephone calls originating or terminating in an area. A subscription to local telephone service provides access to this giant network. Businesses can deploy small-scale switches (PBXs) to handle internal calls and to connect outgoing calls to the external telephone network.[2] Traditional phone sets are connected to the circuit-switched network with a pair of copper wires that transmit and receive the voice signal. Each call using the PSTN gets a dedicated 64 kbps link.[3]

The PSTN is used whenever someone accesses the Internet over a dial-up connection. The modem in their computer converts digital information into an analog

[1] Bob Emmerson, "Convergence: The Business Case for IP Telephony," White Paper, *Webtorials.Com*, Electronic Words, n.d.: 5, 3 Sept. 2002 <http://www.webtorials.com/main/resource/papers/emmerson/paper1/convergence.pdf>.

[2] Stephen Coates, "Linux Moves Slowly into Telephony," *Voice 2000: Supplement to Business Communications Review* Sept. 2000: 21.

[3] Emmerson 5.

signal that can be transmitted over the PSTN. Circuit switching ties up resources since the central exchanges and PBXs stay in the loop until after the call has been terminated.

DATA NETWORKS

The primary differences between a data network and a voice network are how resources are allocated and how information is routed. In a data environment, the data is not *switched*; it is *routed* by a computer system. IP (Internet Protocol) is the universal protocol that is used to route data on most data networks and on the Internet. When IP is used, the data stream is chopped into thousands of small packets, each with a unique number. Since these packets are then routed separately to the destination, packets can be lost, arrive at the final destination out-of-order, or arrive with mangled data. When this occurs, the receiving computer reorders the packets and requests that the sending computer resend any missing or defective ones.[4]

The hardware used in a data network is also different from what is used in voice networks. Data networks use routers, hubs, bridges, and gateways instead of switches. Instead of two copper wires, data network wiring (Ethernet) consists of four pairs of copper wires, which are twisted in pairs, to cancel out induced noise and balance the circuits (**Q23**).[5]

Packet switching enables efficient use of computing resources. Once a packet has been sent, part of the computing resource is free to handle another packet. This allows a data network to handle more than one simultaneous data transfer. In fact, they can handle many data transfers simultaneously since each packet of data has a unique identity. Packet switching is therefore more efficient than circuit switching and bandwidth requirements are drastically reduced.[6]

COMBINED DATA AND VOICE NETWORKS

One of the most widely used communications terms is *convergence*. In communications, it means transmitting voice, video, and data over the same network.[7]

The major drivers behind the movement toward convergence are:

1. *Flexibility*—Using data networks to transport voice gives companies the flexibility to deliver their voice traffic to virtually any location over any type of media.

[4] Andrew Tanenbaum, *Computer Networks*, 3rd ed. (Upper Saddle River: Prentice Hall, 1996) 150–51.

[5] *EtherLink III, Parallel Tasking, EISA and ISA Adapter Guide*, 3Com Corporation, 1992: Glossary, 6.

[6] Emmerson 6.

[7] Ian Angus, "Who Put the Con in Convergence?" *Business Communications Review*, Mar. 2002: 28.

2. *Lower cost of ownership*—Consolidating networks can save on communications costs, including reducing long-distance charges between offices and reducing administrative overhead.

3. *Corporate decentralization*—As companies decentralize their operations, they must find ways to deliver a uniform level of voice and data services to remote employees.

4. *Next-generation business applications*—Competitive pressures are forcing companies to deliver better services to customers, partners, and employees. Implementing next-generation applications depends upon convergence.[8]

In today's computing environment, convergence requires that voice be transmitted over an IP network. Using an IP (data) network to transmit voice is referred to as *Voice over IP* (VoIP). In VoIP, an analog voice signal is converted into a digital packet format, as used by the IP.

Every component of an enterprise network—from cabling and signaling protocols to switches and desktop devices—can affect the ability to run voice, video, and data over the same network.[9] The networks (LAN and WAN [**Q24**]) will be carrying additional traffic, so the infrastructure may need to be upgraded to handle it. In addition, the IP addressing scheme must be able to handle the new voice IP applications (e.g., IP-based interexchange carrier, long-distance service, IP-based local telephony).[10]

Quality of Service

IT professionals have been predicting convergence for a number of years. However, to date it has been difficult for data networks to provide the Quality of Service (QoS) required by voice applications. The QoS problem involves integrating delay-sensitive applications such as voice, audio, and video onto a single network with delay-insensitive applications such as e-mail, fax, and static file transfer. The principle QoS requirements that need to be met before convergence can occur are:[11]

- business-quality voice must be guaranteed (no jitter, loss, or delay),

- voice service must be reliable (99.9 percent up-time),

[8] Noemy Morris et al., "Voice Over IP: A Primer for Datacom Professionals," *Webtorials.Com*, MCK Communications, 2001: 3–4, 3 Sept. 2002 <http://www.webtorials.com/main/resource/papers/mck/paper1/4data/voip4data.pdf>.

[9] Steve Rigney, "Building an Integrated Network," *Voice 2000: Supplement to Business Communications Review* Sept. 2000: 14.

[10] Emmerson 13.

[11] Sandra L. Borthick, "QOS: Are We There Yet?" *Business Communications Review* Apr. 2000: 30.

- existing voice application investments, including voice mail and Automatic Call Distribution (ACD), must be preserved.[12]

These QoS concerns are being addressed. For example, most service level agreements (**Q54**) for packet networks now offer some measure of commitment for:

- availability,
- latency (the time it takes for data to travel from the sending computer to the receiving computer),
- jitter (variations in latency),
- packet loss,
- mean time to repair (MTTR).

In addition, most vendors of desktop devices for convergence (e.g., IP phones and videoconferencing) offer some level of QoS.[13] The Internet community has also developed the ReSerVation Protocol (RSVP) as part of a larger effort to enhance the Internet architecture with support for QoS.[14] Improvements in both QoS and in VoIP technology are continuously being made. Although adoption of the convergence model is still in its very early stages, the economic benefits will continuously drive movement in that direction.

CONCLUSION

Traditionally, voice and data networks have been completely separate. As technology progresses, the trend will be to migrate as much as possible to data networks. However, because of the huge investment in voice networks by the telecommunications industry as well as investments in their legacy PBXs by individual corporations, this migration will take some time. If the cost of providing VoIP and other enhanced services on the data networks drops significantly, this migration will likely accelerate.

---

[12] Rigney 17.
[13] Rigney 18.
[14] R. Braden, ed., et al., "Resource ReSerVation Protocol (RSVP): Version 1 Functional Specification," RFC 2205, *The Internet Engineering Task Force Web Site* Sept. 1997: 3, 30 Aug. 2002 <http://www.ietf.org/rfc/rfc2205.txt>.

26. *What are the implications of the Internet for business users?*

STEVEN WALCZAK

The Internet is a network of networks—where a network is a collection of computers that are connected through some telecommunications medium, such as wire, fiber optic cable, or satellite. In other words, it is like connecting together many networks to create a global communications network (**Q24**). Similar to its predecessors, the telegraph and telephone, the Internet is revolutionizing the way business is conducted in the Information Age.

A Short History

The idea of the Internet, then called ARPANET, was first published in 1967, though research on network technologies had been conducted at MIT and RAND since the early 1960s. ARPANET was implemented between 1969 and 1972 by the United States Defense Advanced Research Projects Agency (DARPA) with the goal of building a computer communications network that would be able to sustain partial system outages (at that time from perceived cold war threats). The first two networked computer systems were located at UCLA and Stanford University (SRI, Stanford Research Institute) with later connections coming from the University of California at Santa Barbara and the University of Utah. Original transmission speeds over the network infrastructure were approximately 50 Kbps (kilobits per second).

With the addition of the NSFNET to the Internet backbone (adding communication infrastructure) in 1986, the communication speeds of the Internet reached 45 Mbps (megabits per second). Additional pieces of the Internet backbone have been added periodically, such as NASA's NSINET, the Department of Energy's ESNET, and NORDUNET, one of Europe's major network backbones, which increase the reach and connectivity of the Internet.

The Internet Today

The Internet today includes universities, businesses, and individuals all over the world. Individuals and organizations may connect directly to the Internet by becoming an Internet node or can connect through an Internet service provider (ISP) such as Microsoft Network (MSN), AT&T, or AOL. Figure 26.1 shows how the Internet connects millions of computers over hundreds of thousands of networks, and tens of thousands of ISPs, using dozens of backbones and exchange ports.

Figure *26.1* Internet Architecture

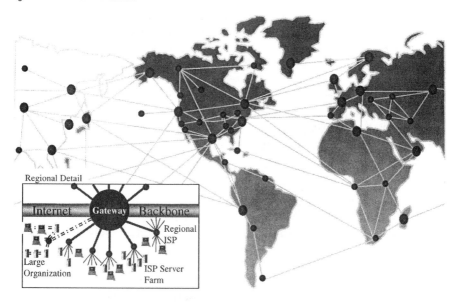

Regional Detail

Internet   Gateway   Backbone

Large
Organization

Regional
ISP

ISP Server
Farm

Many people view the Internet as being the World Wide Web (WWW), however, the Internet includes many distinct services, such as e-mail, chat, file transfer, and news groups. The World Wide Web does represent the Internet's fastest growing service. The WWW consists of primarily text-based documents that can contain graphics and active content like JavaScript, Flash animations, and audio, video, and Java applets. In the early days of the WWW, Web pages were usually static documents residing on a Web server. Today, many Web pages contain dynamic content that is generated from a database based on user requests. The majority of Web pages are written in HTML. HTML is a language that uses text "tags" to describe how a document should look when displayed by a browser. One of the features of HTML is that it allows hyperlinks to be embedded in a document. A hyperlink allows a user to click on a location within a Web page and be transferred to another location anywhere on the WWW.

The WWW is used to transfer documents residing on a Web server to a browser on someone's desktop. The browser and the Web server talk to each other using Hypertext Transfer Protocol (HTTP). The Internet uses the TCP (Transmission Control Protocol) and IP (Internet Protocol) communication protocols or TCP/IP (**Q25**). TCP/IP works by breaking a HTTP message up into uniform size pieces, which means that a larger message may necessitate several packets. Each packet contains data and is preceded by a header, with information about the source and destination address, error checking bits (checksums), identification, and other network communication information (**Q24**).

A second major service provided by the Internet is e-mail. E-mail allows anyone with an e-mail account to send an electronic message to anyone else in the world who also has an e-mail account. E-mail is the most widely used Internet application today. E-mail servers exchange messages using the Simple Mail Transfer Protocol (SMTP) which runs on top of the standard TCP/IP of the Internet.[1]

Other Internet services include FTP and news groups. The File Transfer Protocol (FTP) provides a standard way for computers to copy files between computers on the Internet. Usenet is a worldwide network of newsgroups (also called forums or message boards) on over 30,000 different topics. Newsgroups are names with a series of words and periods (for example, rec.pets.dogs.breeds).[2]

BUSINESS UTILIZATION OF THE INTERNET

What does the Internet network of networks using TCP/IP for data transmission mean to the business user? The Internet itself is a telecommunications infrastructure with over 200 million user accounts, with that number expected to grow to over 500 million user accounts by the year 2003 (http://www.datamonitor.com). The term "Internet" for most business professionals, however, means access to both the ever-growing number of users and also the ever-increasing quantity of information placed onto the Internet by those users. First, to use the Internet for any business reason, such as conducting e-commerce (**Q37**, **Q38**) or customer relationship management (CRM) (**Q40**) or just information access, your business must have computers and access to the Internet.

Gaining access may be done by either purchasing a direct connection (the fastest with respect to transmission speed) or gaining access through an Internet service provider company. The Internet backbones are commonly developed and supplied by national governments, but may be developed and maintained by private organizations. In the United States, the national Internet backbone or infrastructure is currently owned by large telecommunications providers, such as AT&T, Qwest, Sprint, Level3, and others, that lease their telecommunications connections to both national and local ISPs (internet service providers, such as MSN or AOL). ISPs lease access from national providers and provide direct Internet access to education and business customers. Gaining direct access normally involves leasing a high-speed telecommunications line and a router. This may cost several thousand dollars a year in monthly fees.

Small businesses and individuals typically gain access to the Internet through an ISP, such as AT&T or MSN. Internet service provider companies are middlemen between their customers and the Internet. Gaining access this way requires a com-

---

[1] "How Email Works," *LivingInternet Web Site* n.d., 15 Nov. 2002 <http://www.livinginternet.com/?e/ew.htm>.

[2] "Internet for Beginners," *About.com* n.d. 15 Nov. 2002 <http://netforbeginners.about.com/library/glossary>.

puter and modem (instead of a router) and will cost only several hundred dollars per year per user.

Finally, be aware that placing any information onto the Internet for transmission to another Internet node, such as e-mail, ftp, or file downloads from the WWW, is similar to broadcasting a message to the world. Individuals and organizations doing business on the Internet need to take care that private information transmitted via the Internet remains private. This can be accomplished using systems that encrypt the data transmitted between two computers (**Q30**).

CONCLUSION

The Internet is more than just a network. It is an information infrastructure that is changing industries and the ways in which organizations operate by increasing the availability and reducing the cost of disseminating information. It creates opportunities for firms to generate new revenues (**Q35**) and reduce costs (**Q36**). It enables organizations to increase the quality and level of communication with all its stakeholders, including its customers and employees (**Q40, Q42**). But the ability to use the Internet to leverage a business can only be realized within the context of a well-developed strategy (**Q34**) and organizations must understand the issues associated with its use (**Q41, Q43, Q44**) in order to employ it effectively.

---

27. What are the different broadband technologies and their uses?

JOSEPH BAGAN AND PHILIP WINTERBURN

Have you ever seen an MIS (management information system)? How about an ERP (enterprise resource planning) system? From time to time, acronyms and terms are coined without defining what the underlying proper noun really means. *Broadband* falls into such a category. Broadband is commonly used to refer to high-speed communications lines or services. It is a general term, frequently applied to anything that advances the notion of new content and services that travel faster than dial-up speed.[1]

[1] Dial-up speed refers to the speed attained through a standard POTS (plain old telephone service) line using a basic modem and is often referred to as narrowband. That speed, today, is limited

Because the term *broadband* is applied to both the services and the connection speed, it becomes a very confusing term. The Federal Communications Commission (FCC) has legally defined broadband as advanced telecommunications services achieving at least 200 Kbps (kilobits per second) in both directions.[2] (*Both directions* refers to the travel of the bits from the sending device to a receiving device and back, commonly referred to as *upstream* and *downstream*).

Delivery Mechanisms

There is a common misconception that broadband means high-speed delivery over the commercial cable network. This is not necessarily so. Today, there are a number of ways to deliver broadband speeds of 200+ Kbps to a home or business:

- cable
- digital subscriber line (DSL)
- satellite
- wireless
- direct connection
- high bandwidth

Cable

The advent of the cable modem and cable companies' significant investment in hybrid fiber coax (HFC) plants has enabled them to convert their one-way broadcast infrastructure to a bidirectional communications platform that can carry advanced services over the cable television lines. According to the FCC's report on the availability of advanced telecommunications capability services, cable accounts for 5.2 million of the total 9.6 million high-speed subscribers, as of June 30, 2001.[3]

---

to 56K or 56,000 bits per second and is frequently slower depending on the quality of the telephone line, modem capabilities, and other factors.

[2] Federal Communications Commission, *Deployment of Advanced Telecommunications Capability: Second Report*, Report, FCC 00-290 (Washington D.C.: Federal Communications Commission, Aug. 2000).

[3] Federal Communications Commission, *Deployment of Advanced Telecommunications Capability: Third Report*, Report, FCC 02-33 (Washington D.C.: Federal Communications Commission, Feb. 2002).

DSL

Carried over the POTS (plain old telephone service) copper wire network, DSL comes in many forms such as:

- SDSL (symmetric digital subscriber line)

- ADSL (asymmetric digital subscriber line)

- IDSL (ISDN digital subscriber line)

They all are marketed by local telephone companies under the banner of DSL. Customers are only capable of receiving this service if their location is within a certain distance from the telephone company's switching office (the central office or CO). The closer you are to the central office the faster the connection you can possibly obtain. The range for SDSL through IDSL varies by provider but is approximately 5,000 to 30,000 ft. from the central office. The distance from the central office, the actual speed (upstream and down) realized, and the quality of service are all factors to balance in delivering a DSL offering over POTS lines.

27

SATELLITE

Broadband satellite access can be either one-way or two-way. The one-way configuration uses a POTS line to connect for upstream traffic and downloads data directly from the satellite. So the satellite downloads are at high speed, but the uploads are limited by regular POTS speeds. The two-way configuration beams the upstream traffic directly to the satellite and requires different equipment than the one-way version. Broadband over satellite is available in any North American location with an unobstructed view of the southern sky. However, speeds are significantly slower than cable or DSL and they are subject to interference from weather conditions. Satellite providers are investing a significant amount of money on improving upstream traffic speeds in order to make their product offering more competitive with cable or DSL. This may be an area that will see significant innovation and improvement in the coming years.

WIRELESS

Mobile Wireless Mobile wireless services provided over cellular networks are not currently capable of delivering broadband speeds. New developments in wireless network technology are on the horizon that will greatly expand those speeds, but will require a significant investment on the part of the wireless providers. For this reason, provision of mobile broadband services will occur very gradually.

Fixed Wireless   Fixed wireless broadband requires the user to be in the line-of-sight of a tower or repeater. The transmission speeds can be affected by environmental conditions. This form of broadband service is not currently deployed very heavily. However, a new form of wireless capability, called WiFi (Wireless Fidelity) has started making significant inroads in the office-networking environment. Companies can deploy a wireless transmitter connected to the Internet or their corporate network. Anyone with a laptop and a wireless modem within range of a transmitter can connect to the network. In addition, another technology called Bluetooth is being used to connect PCs, printers, and other peripherals to the corporate LAN (local area network) using a different spectrum and technology than WiFi (**Q28**).

DIRECT CONNECTION

Broadband speeds can be obtained by purchasing high-speed circuits from the telephone company. These circuits are dedicated to single customers who connect directly with the service provider. Used mostly by businesses because of their high costs, such circuits are not normally referred to as broadband, even though they supply the same or higher speeds than broadband supplied by cable or DSL.

CHARACTERISTICS OF BROADBAND INTERNET ACCESS

Always On   The always-on connection changes the way residential users interact with the Internet and their computers. Historically, the delay incurred while waiting for a computer to be turned on, and then dialing into an Internet service provider (ISP) resulted in intermittent usage. Behaviors started to change as Internet service providers released fixed-price plans. However, with the advent of broadband and the capability for an always-on connection, a new evolution of Internet behavior is starting to emerge. Consumers are now leaving their computers turned on, with a browser page ready to use at a moment's notice. With the always-on connection in place, broadband providers are also beginning to see a change in the location of the computer, from office or den to living room and kitchen; and the usage patterns went from longer, single sessions to shorter, more frequent sessions.

High Bandwidth   For many, it is the ease of use, rapid downloads, and ready availability that has fueled the desire to acquire broadband access. However, it soon becomes apparent that the high bandwidth opens up other new capabilities:

- *Gaming*—The increase in bandwidth and the ability to stay connected for hours at a time has led to a significant increase in Internet gaming. Most action games require very rapid responses and interactions with the players.[4]

[4] Christine Chan and Maria Bumatay, "Broadband Net Surfing Accounts for More Than Half of All Time Spent Online, According to Nielsen//Netratings," Press Release, *Nielsen//*

- *Telecommuting*—Previously, home office users would have to suffer the slow speeds of dial-up or buy an expensive dedicated high-speed circuit. With broadband, they can now connect to office systems at speeds that are equivalent to their corporate LAN, making it much easier to conduct business from home.

- *Video conferencing*—With raised awareness over security concerns and travel restrictions, there has been an increase in Webcasting and video conferencing. Webcasts, or Web-based conferences, broadcast a presentation over the Internet that participants can watch while listening to the audio either through the Web or via a regular teleconference service. Video conferencing, though still in its early stages, will continue to gain on teleconferencing, given the human desire to interact visually as well as verbally. Both of these capabilities require broadband connections to operate effectively.

28 ▬

LOOKING AHEAD

As widespread access to broadband technology continues to grow, the competitive pressure to innovate applications that utilize this new platform will intensify. Personal video recorders (PVR) already have the capability to send recorded movies over a broadband connection to another PVR—a concept that is unthinkable over a narrowband connection. Leveraging the increased bandwidth to deliver new capabilities in movie delivery is currently being demonstrated in selected trial markets around the United States with interactive television and various forms of video on demand.

What will the "killer application" for broadband be? What will drive the consumer to obtain broadband access, aside from the convenience of the always-on connection and rapid download capabilities? All of this remains to be seen and adds to the excitement and intrigue of broadband.

---

28. What are the major wireless technology platforms?

JAMES D. COLLINS

The past ten years have seen an explosive growth in the number of providers of wireless telephone service and the number of people subscribing to these services.

Netratings Web Site, 5 Mar. 2002, 10 Sept. 2002 <http://www.nielsen-netratings.com/pr/pr_020305.pdf>.

Traditional mobile telephony is evolving rapidly and is enabling a host of new applications as the technology moves from first generation analog to second and third generation digital. In addition, the "no wires" paradigm can be seen in new wireless Local Area Network (LAN) and so-called Personal Area Network (PAN) technologies.

Mobile telephony (cellular telephony) offers customers the ability to use small compact telephone handsets operating on relatively low power from virtually any location. The secret of mobile telephony is the use of many linked *cell sites*. Each cell handles many calls but only over a small radius. As the customer moves between cells, the calls are automatically handed off from one cell to the next. By increasing the density of cells, greater and greater numbers of simultaneous users can be supported.

Mobile telephony emerged in cellular networks beginning in 1984, and through the early 1990s was based on analog transmission technologies. While analog cellular networks still exist, the industry has moved rapidly to a new generation of digital technologies. Compared to analog, these digital services offer greatly increased user capacity, fewer problems with noise and interference, and much better security. In addition, because they are digital, they allow new digital-based services including messaging, e-mail, Web browsing, and data transmission.

MOBILE TELEPHONY TECHNOLOGIES

There are three major digital Personal Communication System (PCS) technologies: TDMA, CDMA, and GSM. Each encodes the call into digital data packets (**Q24**). The encoding schemes vary and as a result these technologies are incompatible with one another.[1]

With the emergence of the Internet and high-speed broadband wired line access, wireless customers are demanding greater capabilities and speed from their wireless devices. To address these needs, wireless carriers are now building and deploying the next generations of wireless technology. These are the so-called 2.5G and 3G technologies, as they represent steps up from the current second generation (i.e., digital) 2G technologies. These technologies attempt to use available and newly allocated bandwidth more efficiently to allow higher transmission rates for each user.

- *2.5G*—In the near-term we are seeing "2.5G" technologies deployed. 2.5G are extensions of existing digital technologies and therefore can be deployed quickly and at reasonable cost. These 2.5G systems will allow customers to perform Web browsing,

[1] TDMA (Time Division Multiple Access) divides calls into time slices and interleaves slices from several calls together across time. CDMA (Code Division Multiple Access) divides a call into different frequency slices and interleaves slices from several calls together across the frequencies simultaneously. GSM (General System for Mobile Communications) uses a form of time division encoding similar to TDMA. In each case the phone reassembles the slices and the listener (for the most part) doesn't notice anything unusual about the call.

e-mail, and file transfers at rates meeting or exceeding those of dial-up lines (i.e., from approximately 56 Kbps up to 170 Kbps).

- *3G*—In the longer-term carriers will be deploying "3G" technologies. 3G is also known as "broadband wireless." 3G will deliver very high transmission rates that far exceed those of dial-up access and approach those of DSL and cable modems (i.e., in the range of up to 2 Mbps). 3G will enable video, high-speed Web browsing, and realistic transfers of very large files—all wirelessly.[2] 3G requires the use of a different radio spectrum. In Europe, service providers paid enormous amounts of money just to acquire the rights to the spectrum. Because of these high initial costs, the rollout of 3G networks is likely to take longer than initially anticipated.

28 ——

THE STANDARDS ISSUE

The single largest issue in global wireless communications is the lack of standards across and within countries. TDMA, CDMA, and GSM are mutually incompatible technologies. For example, a user with a TDMA phone cannot use it on CDMA or GSM networks. To make matters worse, the frequency ranges for these systems are different across the world. A GSM phone in the United States does not work on the GSM networks in Europe because of the different frequency ranges in use there.

To get around these issues most phone manufacturers now make dual or triple band phones. These phones operate on multiple frequency bands and in some cases even on different technologies. Care must be taken when acquiring such phones since some phones advertised as "dual band" merely function on analog and digital networks of the same technology. Unfortunately, even the 2.5G and 3G platforms being deployed still leave several competing, mutually incompatible standards in place both in the United States and globally. So the need for multimode devices will remain.

ENHANCED DIGITAL CAPABILITIES

Because it is digital, PCS offers several features in addition to simple voice phone calls. 2G subscribers can use Short Messaging Services (SMS). Short text messages of up to 160 characters can be digitally sent and received on the phones. This has turned these phones into text pager replacements. Users can also subscribe to a variety of messaging services that broadcast messages such as stock quotes, newsflashes, sports scores, etc. 2.5G and 3G operate at much higher data speeds and essentially have no limit on the length of messages sent or received. Customers using these systems can have full access to their e-mail as well as extended length text messages.

[2] There are three such technologies being developed: CDMA2000 Phase 2, EDGE (an improved GSM), and UMTS/WCDMA (a much faster version of GSM).

Another capability made possible is actual digital data transmission. 2G PCS phones can be used as modems when hooked to PCs. The phones operate at slow, but marginally useful, data rates of around 9.6 Kbps—which is slower than most dial-up lines. More recently, phones have been offered with Wireless Application Protocol (WAP) browser functions built in. This allows the phone itself to access the Internet and download files. WAP has nurtured the development of new devices and new enterprise applications for mobile workforces (**Q29**).

WIRELESS LANs AND PERSONAL AREA NETWORKS

WiFi.   The desire to be free from wires has led to wireless technology separate from the PCS industry. In particular, wireless LANs (WLANs) and so-called Wireless Personal Area Networks (WPANs) are emerging as strong contenders to traditional wire-based networks (**Q3**).

WiFi is effectively a wireless LAN (**Q24**) that uses a standard called 802.11 as defined by the Institute of Electrical and Electronics Engineers (IEEE). WiFi transmits its signals on a spectrum that hasn't been licensed to a specific service provider (cellular, PCS, and 3G operate on licensed spectra). The WiFi LAN consists of a wireless base station with a range of a few hundred feet connected directly to an Ethernet, DSL, cable modem, or other high-speed data network. PCs or PDAs with wireless adapter cards/boards connect to the base station. Transmission speeds will degrade based on quality of reception. Wireless networks found in airports are an example of WiFi. Commercial establishments, such as Starbucks and McDonalds, are making WiFi access available at hundreds of their locations, and other networks are proliferating rapidly.[3] These networks allow customers having laptop computers or PDAs equipped with wireless adapters to easily connect to the Internet while in their establishments. Unfortunately, although the wireless connection can be achieved, the actual connection to the Internet must occur through an internet service provider (ISP). Since there are many competing ISPs, individuals wanting wireless access to the Internet may have to navigate through a complicated process to utilize and pay for that Internet connection.

There are also known security issues with WiFi that make it problematic for use in a highly secure network. Anyone with a wireless card in his or her portable PC can cruise along a busy city street and look for spots where they acquire a signal. If proper security hasn't been implemented, this interloper can quickly be traveling on someone's corporate network. Web sites, seeking to help unauthorized people obtain free Internet access, have emerged, publishing these "hot spots" for all to see. This and other security issues are causing knowledgeable corporations to carefully control the use of WiFi.

[3] Ben Charny, "Starbucks Pours a Cup of Wireless," *ZDNet* 21 Aug. 2002, 30 Sept. 2002 <http://zdnet.com.com/2100-1106-954692.html>.

Assuming the security issues are resolved, WiFi wireless LANs offer great promise. They are relatively inexpensive to install and to maintain, as they have no fixed wiring infrastructure. New LAN users can be added easily to the network. They are also increasingly popular in home networks as individuals can wirelessly connect multiple home computers to one DSL or cable modem's Internet access point.

Complicating the WLAN picture, however, is that there are several WiFi standards (802.11a, 802.11b, and 802.11g) that operate at different spectra and at different speeds. The 802.11b standard has had the widest early deployment. It operates on the 2.4 Gigahertz spectrum which is the same spectrum used by many wireless phones. It has a maximum theoretical speed of 11 Mbps, although the practical expected speed is only 4–6 Mbps. The 802.11a standard, which operates at a different spectrum, is showing up in corporate network architectures because of its greater speeds (up to 54 Mbps) although over shorter distances. Unfortunately these two protocols are incompatible unless a vendor's product has been specifically designed to handle both. What may be more attractive is the 802.11g standard, which offers the same high speeds of 54 Mbps but operates on the same spectrum and is backwardly compatible with 802.11b. With WiFi's benefits, a business looking to deploy WLAN technology must weigh the risk of stranded investment in WiFi (such as its investment in 802.11b equipment) versus the risk and delay of newer standards that promise much greater speeds.

Bluetooth   Another recent wireless technology is known as Bluetooth. Bluetooth is a technology standard, supported by a consortium of major technology companies worldwide, for low-power, short-range data communications (Q3). It is designed to enable digital devices to communicate over short distances of up to several feet. Devices networked together in this way are known as personal area networks (PANs).

Typical Bluetooth applications will be those that eliminate the usual clutter of wires found on desks such as PC to printer connections. Other applications will include cell phone to PC connections, cell phone to point-of-sale device connections (e.g., Bluetooth equipped Coke machines), wireless microphone to cell phone connections, electronic security "keys," etc.

As a new technology, Bluetooth still has some issues. Compatibility and interference problems exist between WiFi and Bluetooth. As to market acceptance, Bluetooth is still trying to achieve enough critical mass where there are enough devices and applications available to justify an investment in it.

Wireless technologies are and will continue to be a driving force in the technology area. As the platforms improve, and standards stabilize, wireless technology will likely become a pervasive component of everyone's daily experience.

29. How could the use of wireless devices transform how business is done?

CARLOS E. C. SILVA AND PATRICIA M. WILKEY

Mobility is about eliminating boundaries. It is about extending access and enabling the sharing of information to anyone, anyplace, anytime. For the business executive, mobility is about a high return on investment. With the right mobile solution a business can empower customers, suppliers, employees, and a sales force to improve its competitive edge.

Key to the success of a mobile solution is a solid strategy that incorporates business process improvement. Wireless devices are becoming extensions of the traditional IT tools organizations use to perform tasks that once were restricted to wired devices. Any combination of Web-enabled cellular phones, pagers, personal digital assistants (PDAs) and wireless laptop computers are available to leverage in business-to-business (B2B), business-to-consumer (B2C), or business-to-employee (B2E) processes. As their use becomes pervasive, companies will see benefits in customer care and cost control. Mobile solutions are transforming how business is done because they provide new ways of reaching and serving customers.

In the last decade, many new applications have found their way into wireless devices. Mobile solutions can improve business operations in many ways by:

1. increasing productivity,

2. improving customer satisfaction and loyalty,

3. tightening security,

4. decreasing sales and service cycle times,

5. reducing costs.

INCREASING PRODUCTIVITY

Companies like UPS, FedEx, and Sears are using wireless devices to coordinate their deliveries, to guarantee efficiency on routing, to schedule services on demand, and to optimize inventory. With mobile terminals and applications an enterprise can now interconnect their whole value chain. Before the aid of wireless devices, drivers had to carry a paper route slip listing all their stops for pick up and delivery, and instructions for providing service. If a customer called to cancel, or a last minute order was placed, there was no way to easily modify the route. Wireless-integrated fulfillment systems now allow orders to be changed dynamically and routes adjusted according to the latest updates on the order system. These systems also track unauthorized stops, the duration of each stop, and any driver deviations from the optimized route.

Transit systems in metropolitan areas are experimenting with GPS-enabled devices that monitor the locations of buses at any given time. An automated phone system then provides callers with exact times when the bus will be at a certain stop. In case of delays due to weather, traffic, or accidents, users can be advised to take a different route, walk to a nearby stop, or simply leave home at the right time.

Improving Customer Satisfaction and Loyalty

Specialized maintenance companies are using wireless "add-ons" to increase the speed with which they respond to customer service needs. They have found that it is more efficient for the items being maintained to send wireless messages indicating when they need replenishment or maintenance, than it is to have service personnel poll them blindly. Some of the applications utilizing this approach are wireless notifications from printers needing toner, ATM machines needing money, vending machines needing replenishment, heavy-duty machinery needing replacement parts, industrial fuel tanks needing filling, and so on. In these situations, customers benefit because the machines never unexpectedly go out of service.

Delivering personalized user-specific content to the mobile user provides tremendous value among customers, suppliers, and vendors. Event metering and data tracking of digital information through applications allows immediate data intelligence capabilities for customer care relationships. Quicker information access provides competitive value in terms of convenience, speed, security, and quality of service. As EDS Chairman and CEO Dick Brown notes, "Mobility is not about technology—It's not about being wireless. It's about customers having the same experience anywhere they find themselves. It's a new level of freedom."

Tightening Security

Companies are adopting wireless technologies to improve security, too. To date, a broad range of wireless security applications have been developed. For example, security badges or "smart cards" can constantly transmit an employee's location inside buildings, automatically providing or restricting access to sensitive areas, unlocking doors, and logging location. Airports are already implementing these systems, and are now moving toward controlling luggage and cargo with similar technologies. At the same time public safety units are using real-time tracking to maintain an inventory of personnel in emergency situations.

Hazardous materials companies are adopting satellite-guided routing systems to keep trucks on predefined routes. Authorities are automatically notified if a truck drifts from its route or fails to make a checkpoint. As terrorist threats have increased, fleet management companies are equipping trucks, tractors, and trailers with devices that not only monitor and report their location, but also implement a "geo-fence." These devices allow for the definition of geographic areas, such as interstate and country borders or ports, where the risk of theft is high. A distress message is sent remotely to the base when an equipped vehicle approaches the boundaries of one of these areas. These systems also can restrict the use of equipment, such as to a designated construction site or only during "business hours." These applications can lower insurance costs and reduce the misuse of equipment.

Decreasing Sales and Service Cycle Time

B2C organizations are able to make use of wireless devices to push timely information. For example, along with Internet-enabled phones, it is expected that cars will be commonly equipped with wireless browsers in the future. In a pilot system in New York, retail and restaurant chains are advertising goods and services, when "in-cab" mobile browsers drive close to a point of sale. In the future, "in-car" browsers may make it possible to inform consumers of items on sale in a store, or the special in a restaurant, before they park their cars.

B2E data that is time sensitive is particularly amenable to wireless delivery. For example, sales force automation can play a key role to improving the operations of a business enterprise. In the past, companies often had separate sales forces and delivery teams. They can now combine these roles using wireless devices that enable their drivers to deliver, review, and take new orders on the customer site. With remote wireless access, a customer-facing employee can shorten the sales cycle resulting in quicker revenue generation.

Reducing Costs

In today's cost-conscious business environment, companies will consider technology investments if they can demonstrate reduced costs (Q72). Leveraging existing IT capabilities and investments is key. Implementing mobile applications or converting existing enterprise applications into wireless solutions aligned with reengineered business processes can yield quick returns on investment. For example, wireless local networks are extremely cost effective and easy to set up, especially when compared to the cost of rewiring workstations during employee moves.

Companies with large field forces are finding that they can save costs by providing their workers with secure access to information that was normally restricted to an office via paper or a desktop PC. For example, doctors can schedule appointments, review test results, and make diagnoses remotely. A sales representative can complete transactions, sell new services with access to a real-time product database, and troubleshoot issues while inventory and sales pipeline information is transmitted seamlessly and efficiently to corporate executives. An increase in the number of productive work hours can increase revenue generation by decreasing the number of sales visits it takes to close a deal. Additional cost containment can be realized by reducing the number of personnel required to support field forces.

The traditional "meter reading" job is another area where wireless technologies are generating efficiencies. More and more companies are finding that it is cost effective to gather its usage and billing information through wireless devices. Once the capital cost of wireless meters has been amortized, the ongoing labor savings can be significant.

29 ■————◄

THE OUTLOOK

While the early emphasis has been on wireless applications that improve service, responsiveness, and cost for companies, it is likely that new wireless solutions will focus on entirely new B2C services. Wireless location-based Internet applications are already starting to surface that provide customers information about the nearest coffee shop, notify a roadside service provider when a car breaks down, or track the location of children wearing security bracelets. When 3G telecommunication protocols emerge (Q28), multimedia applications will make streaming video, music on demand, and other broadband content services available. The result will be a whole new set of enterprises focused on delivering products and services through wireless technologies.

As wireless networks become more robust and provide greater capacity, the demand for new applications will increase as the use of wireless devices increases, making wireless devices a common feature of everyday life. Whether a user is at home, at work, or at play, information in the digital age will become a necessity, not just a "nice to have." As companies today are expected to have an Internet presence, they will be expected to have a wireless component to their services. Once that happens, we will be able to see the extent of the transformation that wireless technologies will bring.

30. Why is security a major issue?

ROB RUDLOFF AND TED V. SCHAEFER

Organizations increasingly rely on information systems to communicate, collaborate, and ultimately generate revenue. The logical boundaries between business units, partners, employees, and customers are becoming difficult to define as new Web, messaging, and remote access technologies make it easier and faster to share information. While sharing this information increases the speed of business, decreases costs, and allows many new ways of generating revenue, it also increases the risk that the confidentiality, integrity, and availability of information could be impacted. The impact to a business can be direct—such as having intellectual property compromised—or indirect—such as customers and business partners losing confidence and taking their business elsewhere.

The threat to information is not limited to outsiders, or hackers. In fact, the *2002 CSI/FBI Computer Crime and Security Survey* reports that 33 percent of respondents indicated security incidents originated within the enterprise.[1] *Insiders* are legitimate users that purposely or accidentally misused their access to the environment and caused some kind of business-affecting incident. This emphasizes the need for security to be applied throughout the environment, and not just to external access points. The boundary line between the Internet and internal networks is increasingly harder to define. The advent of Web portals for activities related to customer service, business-to-business applications, HR self-service applications, and others, allow users outside the network to access critical assets within the network (**Q42**). The challenge is building a security environment that allows appropriate access for authorized users, while still preventing and monitoring for unauthorized activity. The result is an environment

---

[1] "2002 CSI/FBI Computer Crime and Security Survey," *Computer Security Issues & Trends* 8.1 (2002).

that has to be protected regardless of the access point or method, while still allowing business to continue, and enabling authorized users to conduct business as efficiently as possible.

Security can be used to extend and support information sharing as well. A well-designed security architecture incorporates layers of protection for the environment, but includes a solid infrastructure that provides mechanisms to extend functionality. The protective layers combine security administration, controls, monitoring, detection, and response activities at multiple layers of the environment to control, detect and respond to incidents. The infrastructure focuses on standard approaches for authentication, authorization, administration, encryption, monitoring, and compliance that provide consistent integration and support for security.

An example of a standard approach to authentication might be a company that requires a username and password for authentication from the internal network but requires strong authentication using physical devices such as cards with magnetic strips (e.g., "hard tokens") when connecting from outside the network. Having this "standard approach" in place, documented, and enforced allows solution architects to focus on functionality instead of redesigning authentication requirements for every new solution. Similar approaches for authorization, administration, encryption, and monitoring and compliance increase the likelihood of consistently integrated security into the infrastructure.

The major components of a security architecture include a framework of support around a consistently applied model.[2] Figure 30.1 presents a starting place for defining a security architecture.

SUPPORT FRAMEWORK

The security vision and strategy, senior management committee, information security management structure, and training and awareness program provide the framework, or support structure, for the security architecture. Exclusion of any of these components weakens the model and can make it difficult to implement and enforce. The framework also helps deliver the message that security is pervasive throughout the enterprise—and not just a technical issue.

DECISION DRIVERS

The security approach within the framework is based on input from the business environment including the technology strategy and usage, business initiatives and processes, and threats and risk assessment. Without input from these three areas the

[2] Bruce Murphy, Rik Boren, and Steven Schlarman, "Enterprise Security Architecture," *Information Systems Security* 9.2 (2000).

Figure *30.1* Enterprise Security Architecture

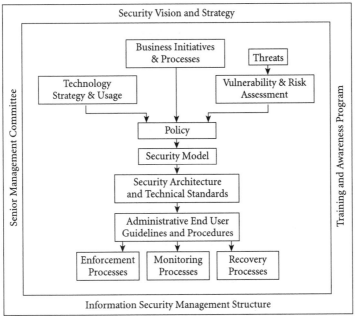

Reprinted with permission from Bruce Murphy, Rik Boren, and Steven Schlarman, "Enterprise Security Architecture," *Information Systems Security* 9.2 (2000): 20. Copyright CRC Press, Boca Raton, Florida.

security architecture will not be aligned with the overall vision for the business or the IT environment.

Technology strategy and usage provides the "IT vision" including what kind of systems, networks, applications, user interfaces, etc., to use. The security requirements for an enterprise moving toward a wireless network environment will differ significantly from a traditional "wired" network. The technology strategy and usage will also guide the type of security organization, skill sets required, and training required.

Business initiatives and processes are an equally critical element to appropriately integrate into the strategy. Security has to focus on appropriate protection of assets relative to their worth to the business—without fully understanding the business initiatives and processes, appropriate protection will be difficult to define, resources will be inefficiently allocated, and ultimately some assets will be overprotected and others underprotected.

The risk assessment component ensures that the security architecture is implemented on a risk-based approach—focusing on appropriate security to protect resources relative to their importance and the risk of compromise, destruction, or damage. Without a clear understanding of the business and technical environment, a risk assessment that represents the true environment will be difficult to achieve.

POLICIES, STANDARDS, AND PROCEDURES

Policies and standards form the basis for consistently implementing and enforcing security in the enterprise environment. Security policies should be based on the ISO 17799 standard.[3] The standard has received a great deal of international acceptance and is very important to consider if an organization conducts international business. The Security Model, Technical Standards, and Procedures should extend the policy from high-level statements to specific details about how/when/why/where security will be enforced. It is in this component of the security architecture where standards about authentication, authorization, administration, encryption, and monitoring and compliance must be established so they can be effectively enforced. While 100 percent security cannot be attained, the combination of security efforts around the areas discussed provides a layered security approach, appropriate for the resources protected. Applying resources where they will provide the greatest benefit, in that layered approach, will decrease the chances that security will be compromised, increase the chances that a compromise will be detected quickly, and ultimately reduce the chance of the organization being materially damaged by a compromise.

SECURITY OPERATIONS

Defining the enforcement, monitoring, and recovery processes establishes the approach for security operations. These processes will focus day-to-day activities around enforcing the security architecture. The security architecture should flow from top to bottom, so these processes are consistent throughout the architecture and represent the critical concerns of the enterprise. The consistent security flow from top to bottom ensures that everyone from the CEO to the technical network administrators understands why security measures are in place and how they play a part in the "big picture." Combining a standard framework approach to security with regular security reviews, security threat intelligence monitoring, and actively engaging security as a part of the design-build process will greatly enhance security across the organization.

CONCLUSION

The ultimate goal for any security architecture is to provide a risk-based approach to protecting information assets and a sound infrastructure that allows for innovation within a framework of controls. Following an enterprise security approach allows the security to be refined from strategic vision to specific operational processes

---

[3] *Information Technology—Code of Practice for Information Security Management*, International Organization for Standardization, Standard ISO/IEC 17799:2000, 2000.

as a part of the enterprise security architecture. The end result is a framework that provides a layered protection approach and an infrastructure that enables new ideas and developments.

31. What does a firewall do?

MIKE HAGER

31

Today our society increasingly relies on new information technologies and the Internet to:

- conduct business,

- manage industrial activities,

- engage in personal communications,

- perform scientific research.

While these technologies allow for enormous gains in efficiencies, they also create new vulnerabilities that can be exploited by those who would do us harm. The protection of our critical data in the Information Age has raised new challenges for us all.

The concept of protecting our valuables is not a new one developed for the technological age. In ancient times kings and noblemen designed their castles in such a way that a main entry point in and out controlled the access. We have all seen this depicted in pictures and movies, where to enter the castle you had to cross the drawbridge and your packages had to be inspected at a checkpoint. Your need to enter the castle was established and if you were approved, you were allowed to enter. When you departed the castle, you went through a similar process. To help provide protection for our corporate "castles" today, we utilize a tool to monitor traffic in and out of our networks. We call it a *firewall*. The goal of our firewalls today is one that we share with our ancient ancestors: keep the "bad guys" out and protect that which belongs to us.

In the not so distant past, the idea of having to protect our valuable networks and data from loss or compromise was not something that corporations had to deal with. Very few companies had computers and the thought of them communicating with each other, much less with employees and customers, was unheard of. Technology, the Internet, and our ability to communicate quickly and electronically has advanced at a phenomenal pace. In the midst of these new technological advancements and the creation of the new world of e-business, a new type of criminal, the *hacker*, has emerged. Just like the societies of the past, our new technology-based society is plagued with groups and individuals that want to utilize this technology to their advantage. They will do everything from the electronic equivalent of writing on other people's walls with spray paint, to stealing data or even shutting down the network or Web site. Some hackers just want to play with the technology and prove that they can break into your network, while others have a more sinister goal in mind. To help protect from these would be attackers, the "firewall" has emerged as one of the most critical tools needed to combat this new threat. So, what exactly is a firewall and how do we know if it is properly configured?

FIREWALL DESCRIPTION

A firewall is a combination of software and hardware that controls the transfer of data between the company's network and an external network. It therefore has the ability either to allow individuals in and out, or to block the flow of data into and out of a network. As in ancient days, the firewall effectively acts as a perimeter guard to provide the network with choke points through which all data must pass in order to enter or exit the corporate network.[1]

One common mistake companies make today is that they rely on the firewall as their only means of network protection. It is important to note that the firewall by itself does not represent a total security system. It is simply a tool to assist in the management of access into and out of the network. For it to be effective, a company must develop a comprehensive security policy and establish consistent security monitoring (Q30) which addresses security's major issues. Operating a firewall without a well-thought-out security policy is like driving in the dark with your headlights off. Eventually, you are going to crash.[2] *For a firewall to work, it must be a part of a consistent overall organizational security architecture.*[3]

Firewalls must be properly configured for them to be effective. To accomplish this, effective firewalls are designed to deny all inbound and outbound traffic with some exceptions. The exceptions are those that are specifically approved and authorized by the company's security policy (Q30). If the firewall rules are set to allow all traffic, nothing is protected. To help understand what rules are necessary, it is also necessary to understand exactly against what a firewall can and cannot protect.

---

[1] Matt Curtin and Marcus Ranum, "Internet Firewalls: Frequently Asked Questions, Rev. 10.0," *Interhack Web Site* 1 Dec. 2000, 31 July 2002 <http://www.interhack.net/pubs/fwfaq/>.

[2] Linda McCarthy, *Intranet Security, Stories from the Trenches* (Mountainview: Sun Microsystems, 1998) 131.

[3] Curtin and Ranum.

WHAT FIREWALLS CAN AND CANNOT DO

Some firewalls permit only e-mail traffic through them, thereby protecting the network only against attacks that target the e-mail service. Other firewalls provide a larger range of protections including protection from activities with known attack signatures. For example, a well-known attack signature is that of the "port map scan." Valid business users are assigned certain avenues within the firewall for their traffic to enter and exit. When the firewall rules are set up for that user, a port is assigned for their use. In addition to assigning the users to the port, the transmission protocol is also established. Certain ports are set to allow for a specific type of traffic, such as data transmissions utilizing File Transfer Protocol (FTP). For someone trying to break into the network, it is necessary to determine what ports are assigned to specific transmission protocols. To find this out, the interlopers conduct a scan of the firewall utilizing a software script or tool, commonly referred to as a scanner. From within the company, security personnel can review the logs of the firewall to learn if it has been receiving numerous port map scans from a specific Internet address. They then set up rules preventing transmissions to be received from that address thus blocking any attempt from that address to exploit any weaknesses in the firewall or network.

Other tools should also be utilized in conjunction with the firewall. Intrusion detection systems help identify invalid traffic and protocols and have extensive lists of known hacker signatures in their rule sets. They automatically block those signatures before they reach the firewall. Some companies set up "honey pots" which are servers that simulate real systems within the network but are not connected to any production system. When access to these systems is attempted, it is an indication that something improper is happening and triggers an investigation by security staff. However, these are only tools that help in protecting the network. The rules must be properly set based on the needs of the company and they must constantly be monitored to identify attacks on the network. The bottom line is that a properly configured and monitored firewall can prevent vandals from logging into machines on the network. In today's systems environment outsiders frequently must be allowed into internal networks in order to conduct approved business. The challenge in this case is to carefully manage these outsiders so they access only information to which they are entitled.[4]

WHAT IS MOST IMPORTANT?

The most important thing to do to ensure the protection of company networks and data is to *design a security strategy around multiple layers of protection*. The outside layer, commonly referred to as the gateway or perimeter layer, answers the

[4] PriceWaterhouseCoopers, *Risk Management Forecast 2001: Creating Trust in the E-Business World* (Jersey City: PriceWaterhouseCoopers, 2001) 6.

question "Can I come in?" That is primarily the role of the firewall. Other security must be in place on individual systems in order to control access only to authorized users.

Lastly, firewalls cannot protect a company against viruses (Q32) or encrypted data. This is why it is critical to have other tools *and* a strategy to deal with the encryption of data and how to design virus protection. The best approach for setting rules in a firewall is to work on the concept of blocking everything unless there is a valid business reason to allow the traffic, and then evaluate the effect that the rules have on network traffic. By doing so, you will ensure that the firewall is properly configured and is an integral part of company's security architecture.

INTERNAL SECURITY

As only *one* layer of a company's security, a firewall cannot really protect against traitors or incompetent individuals inside your corporate network. While industrial spies or internal employees intent on mischief could try to export information back out through the firewall, they are just as likely to export it through a telephone, fax machine, or portable media, such as diskettes and recordable CDs. Portable media are a far more likely means for information to leak from an organization than through a firewall. In addition, firewalls cannot protect a company against stupidity. Internal users sometimes reveal sensitive information over the telephone and are good targets for "social engineering" attackers who try to break in by completely bypassing the firewall. Before deciding whether this is a problem in your organization, ask yourself how much trouble a contractor has getting logged into the network or how much difficulty a user has getting a forgotten password reset. If the people on the help desk believe that every call is internal, it may be easy to gain unauthorized access.

---

32. What are viruses and how can an organization protect against them?

MIKE HAGER

One of the most dreaded messages IT managers can receive is news that a new computer virus has been discovered and is spreading its way around the world. Virus attacks are becoming more prevalent than ever before. Yearly thousands of people suffer often-irrecoverable damage to their systems and data. Yet many do not even know that they have been hit with a virus much less what they can do to avoid a recurrence. It is estimated that the worldwide impact of malicious code was $13.2 billion in the year 2001 alone, with the largest contributors being SirCam at $1.15 billion, Code Red (all variants) at $2.62 billion, and NIMDA at $635 million.[1]

When it comes to virus attacks, ignorance is certainly not bliss. Almost every computer user in the world has heard of computer viruses. Many even have had the misfortune of experiencing attacks firsthand either at the office or at home. So how do we protect ourselves against these dangerous attacks? The best possible weapon we have today in preventing a virus attack is knowledge. We need to understand how viruses enter and infect our computers and how they eventually spread and cause more damage. By doing so, we can deploy the methodology to inoculate our systems against these dangerous, often devastating programs.

32

What Is a Virus?

A computer virus is most often defined as "a malicious code or computer program." Computer viruses have been with us for some time; Fred Cohen first used the term "computer virus" in 1984. To a degree, a computer virus works almost like a biological virus because it gets onto a computer's hard disk without being invited or announcing its arrival. It lies in wait, later ambushing the computer when something innocent is done such as turning it on or opening a software application. It reproduces itself so it can secretly spread to other parts of the hard disk, to diskettes, or to other computers. In some cases, viruses may only print a nuisance message on the screen; but in other cases, they cause serious damage. One of the most destructive viruses was the "Love Bug" virus. It alone infected hundreds of thousands of computer systems and cost victims over $1 billion to eradicate.[2] For example, a virus can remove information from a hard drive. Since viruses are basically computer programs, they can be designed to accomplish anything any other computer program can do, without the owner's knowledge. Computer viruses cannot hurt any files they were not designed to attack. A virus designed for Microsoft's Outlook generally does not infect Qualcomm's Eudora, or other e-mail applications. Viruses cannot infect files on write-protected disks, and they cannot infect compressed files unless the files were infected before they were compressed. They can only take the action for which they were programmed.

[1] Beverly Waite, "Malicious Code Attacks Had $13.2 Billion Economic Impact in 2001," Press Release, *Computer Economics Web Site*, 4 Jan. 2002, 14 Aug. 2002 <http://www.computereconomics.com/article.cfm?id=133>.

[2] Paul Festa and Joe Wilcox, "Experts Estimate Damage in the Billions for Bug," *CNET* 5 May 2000, 14 Aug. 2002 <http://newscom.com/2100-1001-240112.html>.

Are There Different Kinds of Viruses?

One of the most dangerous aspects of computer viruses is that they are not all alike. A *worm* for instance is a program (usually stand-alone) that "worms" its way through either the computer's memory or a disk and alters data that it accesses. Worms burrow through and between networks and can change or overwrite data, corrupting as much as they can. They are very difficult to stop once launched since they can swiftly infect and destroy data.

A *trojan horse* is a program that attaches itself to seemingly innocent programs. Trojan horses do not necessarily replicate, but they open doors so that an attacker can enter undetected at a later date. *Logic* or *time bombs* are viruses that are activated or triggered after or during a certain event. Logic bombs usually lie in wait until you take a specific action. One of the best examples of a logic or time bomb is where a developer at one company felt that he was being worked out of his job. In his anger, he placed a logic bomb in the corporate computer systems. This would activate and begin deleting personnel files if his access was ever removed from the system.

How Do We Protect against Viruses?

Security Policy   To be able to develop a plan that can protect our systems against a virus attack there must be an effective security policy in place (**Q30**) that outlines a layered approach to stopping viruses from entering the system or network. Remember that a virus can do no damage unless it is inside the computer or network and an action has been taken to launch it. It is also important to note that no viruses will be found in the monitor, keyboard, and other attachments. They are only inside the network or in the computers themselves.

Educated Employees   The first step in preventing any virus attack is to understand how they work and then design a strategy to keep them out of your computer systems. The most critical part of this prevention process is to educate employees about viruses. While viruses can enter a company's computers in various ways, the majority of attacks occur through the simple action of opening an e-mail that initiates the program containing a virus. Educate employees to avoid opening any e-mail from anyone they do not personally know. Much of the effort in preventing a virus attack lies in understanding what these virus entry points are and how best to monitor and block possible intrusions.

Viruses enter a computer system through two main entry points, its disk drives and its network adapter cards. The drives may be any sort of storage media, such as a hard drive, diskette, CD, Zip, or Jaz. This makes any storage media that are inserted into these drives a possible source of virus infection. The most common network adapter card is a computer's network and/or modem card that connects the computer to the local intranet and/or the Internet. Viruses that enter through a network card are most likely disguised in the form of attachments in e-mails. These attachments are often program files or office documents containing macros (program code that launches other computer actions). Some Internet Web pages may also contain harmful programming codes that can transfer viruses or virus-like codes onto a computer system. A good security policy utilizes tools that prevent employees from accessing non-business-related Internet sites. Porn and hacker sites are notorious as Web sites where malicious codes reside, and it is easy to download a virus unknowingly from one of these sites. To guard systems against virus intrusion from these sources, many good antivirus programs allows users to completely scan all files read from disk drives or downloaded from the Internet.

Content Filtering   The next step is to ensure that you have multiple layers of protection on your home PC and your corporate systems. The deployment of a gateway content filtering tool for e-mail is a necessity. Content-filtering tools check all incoming and outbound e-mail for viruses and can prevent viruses from entering your systems. For home PCs, a personal firewall that restricts others from accessing the system without permission is recommended.

Antivirus Software   A second layer of virus protection must be deployed at the PC or workstation level. Install antivirus software on all computers and workstations. This software must be updated regularly to address newly discovered viruses so that a computer system is protected. For employees who do company work at home, their home machines also need to be protected with antivirus software, as do any laptop machines. While updating antivirus software can be automated within a company's network, laptop and home machines must be regularly updated by the employee. With new viruses being discovered daily, out-of-date antivirus software will provide little protection.

Screening at Entry Points   A third layer of protection addresses viruses that target the servers in the corporate network. In today's world of virtual private networks (VPN), extranets, and business-to-business connections, internal networks are extremely vulnerable to virus attack through a corporate network's many entry points. Consideration must be given to providing virus screening of all outside connections. When this is not possible from either a technological or budget prospective, there must be the capability to screen for viruses at the server level. Without this level of protection, an unknowing user of a VPN, for example, could place an infected file on an internal server and launch it where there is no protection. A firewall does not screen for viruses (Q31). Therefore, the key is to assess all entry points and make sure that they have the ability to screen for viruses.

The Vulnerability Gap

There is still one other extremely important thing to remember—the critical time between when new strains of virus are detected and when antivirus software venders develop a method of eradicating them. This is why it is important that corporate systems are backed up daily and critical files not stored on a network (such as a home PC) are placed on external disks. Should a destructive type of virus invade the network or home PC, sometimes the only way to eradicate the virus and bring the system back online is to recover your system to a date and time prior to becoming infected. It is for this reason that the practice of backing up everything daily is critical.

Viruses are the colds and flu of computer security: ubiquitous, at times—impossible to avoid despite the best efforts and often very costly to an organization's productivity.[3] While the environment that produces viruses is not going away, by taking the time to understand how they work and by putting in place appropriate protection and recovery strategies a company *can* survive a virus attack.

---

33. What are the major components of a disaster recovery plan?

DENISE BARNDT AND TED V. SCHAEFER

A disaster recovery (DR) plan is a combination of strategies, plans, and operational procedures that ensure the recovery and restoration of an organization's technology and telecommunications infrastructure in a crisis. The DR plan is one component of an overall business continuity plan that assists an organization with restoring normal business processes during crises.[1]

An enterprise has three principle levels of responsibility. Each level has a specific role in connection with an incident:

• Emergency management (tactical control)

• Crisis management (strategic direction)

---

[3] "Virus Information," *Computer Security Resource Center Web Site* 11 July 2002, 14 Aug. 2002 <http://csrc.nist.gov/virus/>.

[1] Charles V. Bagli, "Seeking Safety, Manhattan Firms Are Scattering," *The New York Times* 29 Jan. 2002, late ed.: A1+.

• Functional recovery

   – business processes—business continuity plans

   – technology processes—disaster recovery plans

The remainder of this answer concentrates on disaster recovery plans.

RECOVERY TIME OBJECTIVES AND
RECOVERY REQUIREMENTS

The *recovery time objective* is the negotiated acceptable interval for the recovery of business and IT functions following a disaster situation. *Recovery requirements* are the critical resources and system dependencies needed to recover business and IT functions within the recovery time objective. In order to decide which systems to restore and how quickly to restore them, the following questions must be answered:

1. What functions are critical to business operations and why?

2. What resources are required to support the critical business functions?

3. How long an interruption can these business functions withstand?

4. How much will it cost to establish a recovery capability that restores the critical resources in the required interval?

Senior management generally answers the first question. To answer the fourth question, IT and Facility Resource Owners can deliver strategy options and costs, based on the answers to questions 1 and 2. For example, a company could decide to restore billing and call centers within 24 hours, but wait and restore a weekly payroll system at week's end. Banks might require an ATM network to be restored in less than eight hours, but can wait several days for e-mail.

RECOVERY STRATEGIES

After the recovery time objectives and requirements have been defined, the recovery strategies can be analyzed and implementation decisions made. The recovery options for information technology include:

• developing an internal recovery capability,

• outsourcing recovery to a commercial provider,

• utilizing a hybrid of in-house and outsourced services.

A spectrum of approaches, starting with the most expensive, is presented in Table 33.1.

Table 33.1 Recovery Strategies

Option	Description	Notes
Hot Site	A fully equipped, operationally ready data center with hardware platforms available for almost immediate use.	This is the most expensive option, but the quickest to implement in an emergency.
Warm Site	A site that has mission critical data-processing capabilities for prioritized platforms, applications, data, and connectivity.	A warm site does not support all data-processing functions for the organization, only those deemed most important for recovery.
Cold Site	A location that is empty, but ready for computer equipment to be moved in.	A cold site is usually environmentally conditioned and can be readily wired for data communications.
Mobile Site	A portable recovery option that can be transported to the impacted location.	This option can support both information technology and an office environment.
"Buddy System" or *Reciprocal Site*	Two distant companies with similar equipment agree to use each other's data centers as recovery sites in case of a disaster.	This is a version of outsourcing.
Original Equipment Manufacturer (OEM) Insurance	A form of insurance guaranteeing that damaged computer equipment will be replaced with a system of equal or greater processing capacity within a specified period of time.	Offered by OEM or hardware companies, the insurance cost is usually six to eight percent of the monthly maintenance bill.
Quick Ship	A guaranteed rapid shipment of replacement as a recovery option.	Most third-party leasing vendors provide a service whereby customers pay a priority equipment search fee and the normal leading charges plus a premium when they request shipment.

DATA STORAGE RECOVERY STRATEGY

As part of a recovery strategy, off-site storage for data backups is needed so essential data files and application software can be restored. The creation of a data backup strategy includes the following:

1. What to back up—application software files, data files, security files, directory structures, etc.?

2. When to back up—hourly, daily, weekly, etc.?

3. What type of back up—full, incremental, differential, etc.?

Some of the solutions for off-site storage might be:

- *Off-site storage*—Depending on budget and geographic risks, physical off-site storage for tape or disk could be at a secure, climate-controlled, fireproof media vault at a storage facility, either internal to the organization or with a commercial media storage provider.

- *Electronic vaulting or advanced recovery services*—This approach involves sending data directly to a storage device at another location. The original media remains in the originating location. Again this option can be internal to the organization at an alternate or secondary data center or with a commercial provider.

The option finally chosen will depend on both budget and recovery time objectives as well as business recovery requirements.

PLAN DOCUMENTATION

After the recovery strategy is determined and implemented, the disaster recovery plan and supporting operational procedures must be documented. The plan should include:

- *Escalation and notification protocols*—These are usually linked to the organization's help desk and data center operations monitoring processes to provide early warning indicators of system and user problems. Escalations can reach the CEO in extreme circumstances.

- *Roles and responsibilities of the recovery team* (including recovery service providers and vendors)—This includes coordination with the business unit recovery and crisis management teams.

- *The restoration sequence for applications, platforms, and connectivity*

- *Detailed procedures for recovery of the applications, platforms, and connectivity*

• *Detailed procedures for restoration or return to normal operations* (if relocated to alternate processing facility or service provider).

TESTING AND MAINTENANCE

Testing a disaster recovery plan is crucial to its success. When organizations and systems change rapidly, plans need to be updated frequently. The IT organization must develop and follow a process that automatically updates and tests the plans in the normal course of business. If such activity is left for occasional attention or sporadic cleanup, other priorities will most likely interfere with testing and updating, dangerously leaving the organization exposed.

Testing should be conducted regularly to ensure that plans are valid and team members are familiar with the recovery procedures. Annual full-scale testing of the technology environment should be conducted, including end users as well as any critical third-party service providers. This type of testing requires extensive planning and coordination, and requires a high degree of resources in terms of people and budget.

Quarterly testing should also be conducted at the "component" level (i.e., specific portions of the plan). This can include testing the recovery team call-out procedures, data storage procedures, or a walk through of individual application or platform procedures.

CURRENT DEVELOPMENTS AND APPROACHES

Since September 11, 2001, everything related to disaster recovery is being reconsidered, such as the appropriate level of network protection, network location, inventory levels, and organizational priorities.[2] Since executives are now more willing to allocate resources to this area, companies have recalculated returns on security measures.

The most dominant recent developments in IT disaster recovery can be characterized as decentralization of workers, information technology infrastructure, network, and operations. This contrasts significantly with the earlier trend to centralize as much as possible in order to reduce overlapping locations and reduce costs.

Another change since September 11, 2001, is the new term "Distributed Headquarters."[3] Morgan Stanley, Goldman Sachs, American Express, Marsh & McLennan and others are moving (or have moved) complete departments and thousands of

[2] Gary A. Bolles and Terry A. Kirkpatrick, "Disaster Recovery," *CIO Insight Web Site* 10 Oct. 2001, 4 Feb. 4 2002 <http://www.cioinsight.com/print_article/0,3668,a%253D19552,00.asp>.

[3] Judith J. Johnson, "Disaster Recovery Planning with a Focus on Data Backup/Recovery," Paper, *SANS Institute Web Site* 26 Jan. 2001, 4 Feb. 2002 <http://rr.sans.org/incident/recovery .php>.

workers to new locations. "Across the board, not only companies directly affected by the attack, but also those in midtown [New York], are reviewing their location's strategies with a view towards decentralization and size reduction."[4] In addition to decentralization, companies such as Deutsche Bank and Instinet are planning to build backup operations as a part of a more general trend to move data centers and technical offices to a variety of sites.[5]

Another direction that decentralization has taken is the "work from home" approach. The dramatic improvement in remote networks is allowing more functions to be performed from home. Some companies have reported a lower turnover rate and a higher productivity rate after allowing a higher degree of telecommuting.[6] This allows a reduction in overall costs, even after including the additional expenditures on technology and networks.

With both social and economic consequences, companies must consider the tools and techniques required to manage the new structure in case of a disaster. Once a remote location has been established as an alternative headquarters, disaster management processes must be established. One solution establishes remote-access crisis management teams to restart the business process and the coordination of employees once disaster strikes.[7]

CONCLUSION

Disaster recovery is a living subject, depending on constantly changing assessments and technologies. To prevent disaster recovery programs from becoming obsolete, companies must commit to ongoing financial support to prepare for the unknown. The challenges facing IT departments today are expected to increase, since human nature and economic focused reasoning tend to have a negative correlation to spending as time goes by and costs accumulate. Disaster recovery plans in the past were relegated to the technical experts and received relatively little upper-management attention. But September 11, 2001, changed all that. Now, such plans are in the forefront of most companies' planning. By careful preparation and testing, these plans can ensure that business will continue through any crisis.

[4] Jerry Rothfeder, "Brave New World," *CIO Insight Web Site* 1 Nov. 2001, 4 Feb. 2002 <http://www.cioinsight.com/print_article/0,3668,a%253D18364,00.asp>.

[5] A.D. London, "Keeping the Distance," *Ma'ariv Web Site*, Israel, 2001, 29 Jan. 2002 <http://images.maariv.co.il/cache/ART216628.html>.

[6] John Girard, *Disaster Management Plan for Remote Access*, Gartner, Inc., Research Note TG-14-5458, 20 Sept. 2001.

[7] Robert M. Thomas, *Introduction to Local Area Networks*, 2nd ed. (San Francisco: Sybex, 1997); Kristin Noakes Fry and Trude Diamond, *Business Continuity and Disaster Recovery Planning and Management: Perspective*, Gartner, Inc., Technology Overview DPRO-100862, 8 Oct. 2001.

SECTION 3 *IT and E-business*

RANDY WELDON

We've all heard the saying, "e-business is *the* business." As the experience of the past few years has made abundantly clear, Internet-related strategies and technologies must be integrated with, not separated from, the rest of a company's business strategies and systems. Question 34 leads off this section explaining how to develop a credible e-business strategy to ensure commonality of purpose with the overall business. Rather than being about Web sites and banner advertisements, e-business is about optimizing business with partners across a company's value chain. The remainder of this section describes new opportunities, models, choices, and issues associated with conducting business over the Internet.

New Internet-enabled opportunities for most organizations take the form of revenue enhancements or cost reductions. As described in Question 35, companies became very excited in the late 1990s about the promises of new global markets and rapidly expanding revenues. Unfortunately these claims were overstated. Since then, businesses have learned how to use the Internet to realistically enhance revenue streams. New customers can be found and served over the Internet, especially in the cases of smaller or newer companies with limited physical reach. In addition, new businesses can be formed to bring exciting new electronic products and services to market. However, the largest opportunity for many traditional businesses manifests itself in increased business with existing customers.

Many companies realized they could easily experience direct benefits from the Internet through cost reduction opportunities as described in Question 36. Purchasing departments could achieve lower prices through simplified access to national volume contracts, standardized catalogs, and competition among more suppliers. In some cases, such as airline ticketing, middlemen can be cut out, thereby saving significant costs. Finally, the Internet provides a mechanism for streamlining business processes among business partners.

Most of the hype surrounding Internet-driven revenues seemed to relate to business-to-consumer (B2C) models examined in Question 37, simply because so many hundreds of millions of consumers now have direct access to businesses via the Internet. However, far larger dollar volumes are quietly flowing through the various business-to-business (B2B) models described in Question 38.

Similar hype abounded regarding the probability that pure-play Internet businesses, or "clicks," would make traditional "bricks" businesses obsolete. The dot.com crash of the late 1990s proved the hype wrong and many "clicks" have subsequently disappeared. But the experience of the past few years shows that the Internet is becoming a powerful way to expand the delivery of goods and services to customers through multiple channels. Question 39 explores the factors that determine the relative balance that businesses need to consider between "bricks and clicks."

In addition to generating hard benefits such as increased revenues and reduced costs, the Internet offers many less tangible but equally important opportunities. For example, Question 40 focuses on how companies can use Internet technologies to perform more effective, personalized, customized, and targeted marketing activities at lower cost. Needless to say, sales executives are excited about the possibilities of such "e-marketing" techniques. With this new access to personal or potentially sensitive information about customers comes significant new legal issues regarding privacy—a topic explored in Question 41.

E-business strategies and models must be executed in tangible ways. Some of the most common implementations include intranets for employees, extranets for external stakeholders such as customers and suppliers, and portals. The latter is a technique for aggregating information and functions in one place to simplify dealing with the overwhelming amount of information available on the Internet. Question 42 defines these terms and explains how they are used in businesses today. Question 43 adds that all of these implementations require some basic technical elements to succeed, notably a robust architecture and tools for handling security, personalization, content management, and interfaces with other corporate front-end, back-end, and desktop application systems. These issues and interfaces are critical to making an e-business initiative successful and are addressed in Question 44.

Finally, this section would not be complete without explaining the reasons for the devastating dot.com crash of 2000 and shortly thereafter, which is the topic addressed in Question 45. We have all learned from those mistaken assumptions!

E-business is here to stay. It is now a critical tool for most businesses. The elements of e-business, as described in this section, give the fundamentals of how to make e-business work in any enterprise.

34. What are the key components of an e-business strategy?

KIRK LOWERY

Over the past several years, business executives have searched for the e-business strategy that will leverage the power of the Internet to usher their business into a "new economy," one that delivers a quantum leap in revenue growth, cost efficiencies, competitive advantage, and market value. Despite significant investments, that quantum leap remains a dream for most companies. Many executives have become frustrated that their investments have not produced the results they expected and the dot.com crash has fueled skepticism about the value of the Internet to business (**Q45**). Like other technologies, the Internet is a tool, not a panacea. It is a global network (**Q26**) that, combined with a workable business model, offers opportunities to grow revenues, enhance customer relationships, streamline supply chains, reduce operating costs, and, in some cases, invent new businesses.

WHAT IS AN E-BUSINESS STRATEGY?

E-business is not about creating Web sites, it's about optimizing business across a business network. A business network is formed when partners work together to optimize their common value chain to the customer. Quite often, executives view an e-business strategy as something independent from their business model when, in fact, they are inseparable. The heart of a successful e-business strategy is a successful business model. E-business is the process of adapting and extending a business model to take advantage of the opportunities presented by the global network.

Innovative business leaders have successfully incorporated e-business into their business strategy in many ways. Before discussing key themes for success, it's helpful

Figure 34.1 Components of a Business Model

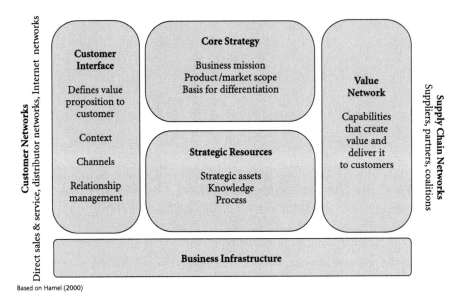

Based on Hamel (2000)

to have a common definition of a business model. Gary Hamel provides a simple, yet comprehensive definition (Figure 34.1) in his book *Leading the Revolution*: [1]

- A strong e-business strategy is dependent on a strong *core strategy*. Core strategy defines:

  – the basis on which a business chooses to compete,

  – its mission,

  – its mix of products and services,

  – the markets in which it competes,

  – its basis for differentiating from competitors.

- An e-business strategy can leverage existing *strategic resources* or create new ones. Strategic resources are the building blocks for a competitive advantage, such as:

  – Core competencies represent unique knowledge and capability.

  – Strategic assets are valuable tangible and intangible assets that contribute to advantage.

  – Core processes are unique activities or methodologies that enable the business to produce its output.

[1] Gary Hamel, *Leading the Revolution* (Boston: HBSP, 2000) 70 –91.

- *Customer interface* represents how a business manages relationships with its customers. Strengthening and differentiating the customer interface is an important aspect of an e-business strategy.

- *Value network* represents the suppliers, partners, and coalitions that complete the value chain. An e-business strategy enables all members of the value network to focus on their competencies, run their businesses more efficiently, and optimize common business processes.

- *Business infrastructure* represents the core processes, information systems, technology, and people needed to run the business (**Q43**).

E-business should leverage the strengths of a business model, accentuating differentiation and delivering efficiencies that result in greater competitiveness and profitability. E-business can be viewed in three dimensions, each of which is important to the whole:

1. E-business should focus on customer value and help differentiate customer relationships (**Q40**).

2. E-business should focus on those critical partners and suppliers that must work together to optimize the value chain to the customer.

3. E-business should deliver operational efficiencies that improve profitability and cash flow (**Q36**).

As a whole, e-business should integrate processes and technologies across the business network enabling all partners to focus on core competencies, serve customers better, run their businesses more efficiently, and jointly manage critical business processes. There are several key themes for developing a successful e-business strategy.

Focus on Customer Value

Business leaders are increasingly finding that their only source of sustainable competitive advantage comes through the experience they offer to their customers. The first step in forming a successful e-business strategy is developing a razor-sharp focus on customer needs and preferences. Customer value is a cornerstone of any successful e-business model. Focus e-business on the information and add value to the services that differentiate the business from its competitors (**Q40**).

Leverage Core Competencies

Executives are assessing their core competencies and choosing to automate (Q58) or outsource (Q82) noncore business functions. Others are leveraging their core competencies to create new businesses. For example, General Motors is outsourcing transportation and logistics functions to third-party logistics partners. Conversely, United Parcel Service (UPS) is leveraging its core competency in logistics to manage material flow and inventories for many global companies. The Internet provides the connectivity and information flow that enable business functions to be managed by partners. E-business should be used to leverage the core competencies of business partners and to build core competencies into new business opportunities.

Build Virtual Fulfillment Networks

E-business can enable a business to grow its brand by expanding product and service mix without a commensurate growth in physical infrastructure. A business that owns a trusted relationship with its customers is positioned to sell value-added products and services under its brand, and allows partners to fulfill those orders. At Cisco, for example, approximately 90 percent of its annual revenues are transacted with customers on the Internet. Half of those orders are never touched by a Cisco employee; they are passed on to partners in their business network for fulfillment.[2] A successful e-business strategy identifies opportunities to sell products and services that can be fulfilled by partners.

Differentiate through Customized Services

E-business innovators are leveraging intellectual capital to develop customized services that help differentiate their products. For example, a global engineering and construction company found that its real differentiation is not in its formidable ability to manage huge construction projects, but in the intellectual capital it has to optimize performance of the asset once it's in operation. Through customized services, they plan to use the Internet to make their intellectual capital available to customers for a fee. Packaging intellectual capital as customized services delivered over the Internet is another way of building a successful e-business strategy.

Streamline Business Infrastructure

Every business leader should be using the Internet to reinvent their cost structure (Q36). Global companies like General Electric, Alcoa, and Oracle have improved

[2] Grady Means and David Schneider, *MetaCapitalism: The E-Business Revolution and the Design of 21st Century Companies and Markets* (New York: Wiley, 2000) 22–26.

profit margins and cash flow by implementing Internet business processes that significantly cut operating costs. General Electric believes Internet business processes can improve operating margins by 50 percent.[3]

E-business can be used to improve access to information across the enterprise, to consolidate redundant business functions into global shared services, and to streamline processes through self-service capabilities. The payback is measured as improved visibility of global operations, lower operating costs, improved cash flow, and better service to business units.

Enable Internet Connectivity

In the future, competitive businesses will depend on the quality of information flow with customers, suppliers, business partners, and employees, each with different systems and devices. Successful companies will commit to Internet standards and implement a technology infrastructure that facilitates information flow inside and outside of the organization.

Conclusion

A successful e-business strategy is an extension of a successful business model that uses Internet technology to optimize relationships with customers, suppliers, partners, and employees. An e-business strategy should reflect a unique value proposition to customers and enable all partners to become more competitive and profitable. Success requires a continual process of planning and experimentation, learning from what other innovative companies are doing, and applying common themes for success.

---

35. What kinds of revenue opportunities does e-business create?

JAMES D. COLLINS

Much of the interest in e-business in the 1990s was driven by the belief that it would be the source of exciting new revenue opportunities both for existing businesses and for new start-up businesses. Both the business-to-consumer (B2C) and business-to-business (B2B) models (**Q37**, **Q38**) proliferated as traditional companies

[3] Howard Rudintsky, "Changing the Corporate DNA," *Forbes* 7 July 2000.

and new e-commerce companies entered the online marketplace. The revenue opportunities these models represent are almost endless. Nevertheless it is possible to understand them as falling into several broad categories driven by the nature of online commerce itself:

- Enhanced access to customers

- Enhanced sales to existing customers

- Electronically enabled products

ENHANCED ACCESS TO CUSTOMERS

A business, whether it is a B2C or B2B business, can increase its revenues by selling its products and services to a larger number of customers. A business is always looking for new sales channels, new geographies, and new customer segments as ways to access these new customers. E-business offers powerful new ways to reach them.

New Sales Channels   Online sales channels may take several forms. A common form of online channel is the online "shop." Within the online shop the customer may browse the company's products and services, learn more about them, understand options and features, and ultimately place an order. Even in cases where the order is not placed online, there is benefit to the company in having informed customers when they come in to a physical store to make the purchase. Some companies strive for a mix of "bricks and clicks" (**Q39**). According to J. Crew and others, buyers still want physical catalogs and stores in which to browse or see and touch certain items, but want the online channel to shop for greater information, greater selection, or other reasons at other times. The optimal solution according to Wal-Mart is "deep integration [of its online store] with the [physical] store."[1]

Many companies use this channel instead of having retail storefronts. Good examples are consumer electronics companies such as Sony or Palm. These companies typically have no dedicated retail storefronts and work through regular retail stores. But they also offer direct retail sales online (e.g., www.sonystyle.com or www.palm.com). This gives them access to customers that might not frequent those retail stores or who live in areas not served by a broad variety of retail establishments.

Extended Geographic Reach   Online commerce provides an easy way to penetrate a new geographic territory. Large, small, or specialized businesses can use their online sales sites to sell on a worldwide basis with little extra cost of doing so. This ability to

---

[1] Saul Hansell, "A Retailing Mix: On Internet, in Print and in Store," *New York Times on the Web* 14 Dec. 2002, 20 Dec. 2002 <http://www.nytimes.com/2002/12/14/technology/14ONLI .html?todaysheadlines>.

tap into expanded domestic or even international markets can be an immediate revenue boost to artists, jewelry makers, wineries, and the like, for initial orders and especially for reorders. As another example, the Hotel Gatti (www.hotel-gatti.com) is a small hotel in northern Italy that catered primarily to Italian travelers. By introducing its own Web site with English language options, it significantly extended its geographic reach. Now, at very little cost, the hotel communicates with and takes reservations from potential customers in the United States and other English-speaking countries. The bottom line is that e-business now allows any company to become a global one, regardless of its size.

New Customer Segments   Online commerce allows a business to identify and target customer segments that otherwise would be difficult or costly to serve. Several specialty automobile parts companies do significant business on-line with target customer segments. For example, 928 International, a company dealing exclusively in new and used maintenance and high-performance parts for the Porsche 928 automobile, has used its online shop (www.928intl.com) combined with selected advertising in specialist magazines to become the leading supplier of aftermarket parts for this specialty car.

A La Zing (www.alazing.com) is a small, specialized provider of foods. An interested customer segment can easily find A La Zing via any number of Web search engines. Once the customer is connected with the company, the company can easily maintain a relationship with that customer. A narrow segment of customers, such as those wanting Beef Stroganoff specialty foods, can find A La Zing via a Web search on "Beef Stroganoff." Once registered, the customer remains an easy target market for A La Zing in the future. It is unlikely that this segment would otherwise be large enough to support a regular retail presence. But when this business is aggregated through the Web, it can become a profitable niche.

Enhanced Sales to Existing Customers

Technology is enabling some sophisticated techniques that, when combined with electronic connectivity to the customer, allow a company to pull additional sales from their existing customer base. Customer relationship management (CRM) (Q65) and data mining systems (Q21) allow companies to not only target a broad range of customers with common buying characteristics, but to narrow the target down to the individual buyer. Targeted e-mail, for example, is far more effective than broadcast e-mail. Companies such as Amazon.com do an excellent job of suggesting choices based on past product purchases. In the B2B world, once the effort and expense has been expended to electronically connect companies, the convenience and efficiency of doing business together will enhance sales and make switching more difficult. So companies are anxious to establish the electronic bond that allows sophisticated interactions with their customers, enhancing the way they can serve them and ultimately providing a barrier to switching—all with the goal of getting more revenue from them.

ELECTRONICALLY ENABLED PRODUCTS

A major source of new revenues has come from digital products and services:

Digital Content   The Internet is especially well suited to the delivery of digital content to a customer. This content ranges across music, movies, photos, news and information, interactive multiplayer games, books, magazines, and almost anything else that can be digitized. Revenues may come from pay per use or subscriptions (such as Wall Street Journal, Lexis-Nexis). Purchase for download (such as software) is also another major revenue source that is likely to grow in the future. Downloadable entertainment (such as CDs, DVDs, and video games) has significant potential for revenues once copyright issues have been resolved. With broadband connectivity (Q27), a whole new world of revenue opportunities is appearing, just in the entertainment area alone.

Digital Services   Avoiding the copyright issues found with digital content, online digital services have proven to be a successful source of e-business revenues. For example, Kodak, as well as others, offers services that allow customers to deliver their electronic photos via the Internet and receive high-quality prints back via regular mail. Prices are highly competitive with local photo processors. Sites such as eBay and travel services such as Travelocity, Priceline.com, and others generate revenues by charging small commissions on each transaction. Similarly, a large number of online casinos (primarily based outside the United States) offer a full range of casino gambling to customers worldwide with the house in each case taking its usual share of the money wagered.

CONCLUSION

E-commerce offers a wide variety of new and expanded channels and other opportunities to grow revenues for a company. These companies can exploit the ubiquitous, global nature of the "World Wide Web" to access new customers in new markets almost as easily as they serve local customers. The very nature of the medium is well suited to creation and delivery of electronic products and services that simply don't exist outside the e-commerce arena (e.g., online gaming, music downloads, etc.). The challenge for e-businesses is to generate these revenues in an integrated fashion and turn those revenues into profits.

36. What kinds of cost reduction opportunities does e-business offer?

DAVID R. LAUBE

The advent of the Internet created a giant change in the way technology could impact business (**Q1**). Most of the focus was on business models that created new businesses and generated revenues in creative and exciting ways (**Q35, Q37**). In recent years, much of this excitement and promise gave way to reality as the fragility of many of those business models resulted in the dot.com crash (**Q45**). But rather than fade away like many other technology fads, the use of the Internet has quietly established itself as a real force for cost reduction inside many companies. It turns out that the use of e-business is changing the way companies do business with their customers and vendors, as well as how they handle their internal business processes. These cost reduction opportunities can be grouped into several major categories.

IMPROVE PRICING ON PURCHASED GOODS AND SERVICES

There are at least three good ways to reduce the cost of purchased goods and services:

1. *Increased scale*—Generally the more a company buys, the lower the price. This extends to the size of the supplier as well—if its size can generate savings that are passed through to customers.

2. *Increased competition*—When more people want to get into the business, they tend to shave their profit margins resulting in lower prices.

3. *Transparent information*—With transparent information, both the buyer and seller know all the facts and can make the best decisions for their companies.

E-business is ideally suited for an environment that produces all three characteristics. With auctions and reverse auctions, competition is rampant and the prices are available for all to see. People not otherwise able to participate as suppliers can see the opportunity and bid for the business, or offer their products for bid. This increases competition and increases the scale of the successful suppliers.

Industries are seeing the potential for combining their buying power into giant exchanges that utilize e-business technologies to generate enormous economies of scale (**Q37**). The auto industry, for example, has formed a business-to-business (B2B) exchange called Covisint. In 2001, General Motors conducted more than 600 auctions on the site worth $100 billion and saved three percent in its transaction costs for those deals.[1] In the same year, General Electric had a major e-business initiative designed to generate savings in excess of $600 million just in purchased products alone.[2] It is clear that much of the investment in e-business initiatives is focused in this area because the payoff is so high, particularly for companies that previously did not coordinate their purchasing or leverage their buying power.

ELIMINATE THE "MIDDLEMAN"

Many industries rely on intermediaries to sell their goods and services. Whether the intermediary is a retail store, a dealer, or an agent, the common characteristic is that the service provider or producer doesn't deal directly with the end customer. E-business is changing all that. Companies can now sell directly to their customers over the Web. In some industries, this is creating a tremendous opportunity to reduce costs. In the airline industry, for example, to move from a ticket sold through a travel agent to one sold over the Web, reduces the airline's cost of the ticket from $30 to $9.[3] It is the elimination of the compensation to that middle tier (the travel agent or the airline's own ticket agent) that largely drives this benefit. So any industry which has been shielded from direct contact with its customers can now establish an e-business connection with them and reduce costs. Companies will, however, need to balance the cost opportunity with the impact on their customers who might miss the contact, service, and convenience of that "middleman." They also need to consider the ramifications for their existing distribution system. Direct selling might alienate their existing resellers, dealers, or retailers and negatively impact their existing revenue stream.

STREAMLINE BUSINESS PROCESSES

E-business technology is allowing businesses to revolutionize the way they interact internally and with their vendors. The rise of supply chain management is designed to do just that, driven by opportunities to reduce costs (Q37, Q67). Companies that have automated their ordering processes with their vendors have generated visibility of inventories between themselves and their vendors and reduced order cycle time. All of this saves money. Building a tightly knit supply chain as well as its "build-to-order" e-business model, for example, has allowed Dell Computer Corp. to carry an inventory of only 5 days when its rivals need to carry 30 days or more.[4] The financial benefit allows Dell to be more aggressive in its pricing. General Motors is changing its process of designing cars by developing collaborative design capabilities with

[1] Derek Slater, "GM Shifts Gears," *CIO* 1 Apr. 2002: 53.
[2] "The Smart Businesses," *SmartBusiness* Sept. 2001: 72.
[3] Leo Mullin, interview with Martha MacCullum, *Morning Call*, CNBC, New York, 1 July 2002.
[4] Dick Hunter, interview, "How Dell Keeps from Stumbling," *BusinessWeek* 14 May 2001: 38B.

its vendors with a target to reduce design time by 50 percent or more. Daimler-Chrysler has formed an e-business group to do the same and has generated savings of 60 to 90 percent in certain steps of its design process.[5]

REDUCE IT COSTS

The technology underlying e-business and the Web is extending into IT itself with the use of Web architecture to significantly reduce the costs of designing, delivering, and operating IT systems.

The Corporate Intranet   Most corporations have built an internal Web, called an intranet (**Q42**), and are using it to significantly change the way internal business is conducted. Not only is it being used to improve communication through e-mail, instant messaging, information sharing, eliminating paperwork, etc., but the cost for IT to deliver and operate these services has reduced dramatically. That's because it is all on an easily maintainable common platform to which features can be easily added.[6]

Standardized Desktop Software and Connectivity   The common approach to creating a software application used to be to build the business functionality (general ledger, inventory management, etc.) and then build a specific user interface for each application. Users were then connected to the servers through direct connections, often over special purpose networks. Now, virtually every desktop has a browser. Users operate and navigate in that environment with ease. So software developers capitalize on that ubiquity by making all of their applications work in the context of the browser. Specific custom desktops are no longer necessary and training on how to navigate the desktop is minimal—saving considerable time and money. In addition, all desktops in an organization are usually connected to the intranet, eliminating custom networks. With ready-made desktops and connectivity, IT applications can now be delivered much faster and cheaper.

Web Services   One of the biggest problems in an IT organization is to integrate its disparate systems. Usually these systems are connected directly or through cumbersome middleware (**Q13**). Recently a new approach, called Web services, is emerging that allows systems to be integrated through the use of Web technology (**Q15**). Business functions can be encapsulated into software modules and moved around over the intranet so they can be reused by software throughout the company, reducing the

---

[5] Slater 54.
[6] James A. O'Brien, "US West Communications: The Business Value of a Corporate Intranet," *Management Information Systems: Managing Information Technology in the Internetworked Enterprise*, 4th ed. (Boston: Irwin/McGraw Hill, 1999) 350–52.

necessity to write programs for those functions in each application. This opportunity will likely accelerate as this technology advances.[7]

Reduce Infrastructure Investments

It is expensive for companies to maintain a physical presence that is convenient to all their customers. When expansion into a new geographic area is contemplated, the infrastructure of the buildings, the furnishings, the computers, and the network significantly raise the threshold of profitability. Some companies are finding that it is less risky to enter a geographic area with an e-business presence before they enter it physically. If their product or service is conducive to Web-based delivery (retail products, financial services, etc.), then they can wait until they have built up a customer base or a brand presence before spending the big dollars on physical locations.

Reduce Customer Service Costs

Many companies, particularly in service industries such as utilities (phone, power, cable), travel, financial services, etc., have established large call centers to provide service to their customers and to conduct business. These call centers, because of their high labor content, constitute a significant portion of their selling and service expense. With the advent of e-business, companies are trying to move as much customer contact time as possible from the live representative to the Web. Such things as billing inquiries, trouble reports, and simple orders from a catalog or price list are very easily handled in an electronic environment. The cost of a transaction handled in this way is over 50 percent less than if handled with a live person. By reducing the total number of calls into call centers, companies can redirect their savings into further technology investments or into profits.

Summary

More companies are unlocking the power of e-business to reduce costs. Here is where e-business investments can be calculated, tracked, and harvested, and it should be no surprise to see a significant movement of IT investment in that direction.

---

[7] John Hagel III and John Seely Brown, "Your Next IT Strategy," *Harvard Business Review* 79.9 (2001) 105–13.

37. What are the different types of business-to-business e-commerce models?

RANDY WELDON

When the dot.com bubble burst in 2000, people realized that not every Internet business model made sense (**Q45**). In many cases, there was no legitimate revenue equation or other business case justifying large investments in certain pure-play Internet or brick-and-mortar company Internet initiatives. Nevertheless, the amount of Internet-based business being conducted among traditional brick-and-mortar companies has been growing very rapidly, even as many Internet businesses have been sliding downhill. Explaining this phenomenon requires an understanding of:

- what business-to-business (B2B) e-commerce is,

- what the major types of B2B models are,

- when each model is the most appropriate.

BUSINESS-TO-BUSINESS (B2B) E-COMMERCE

B2B refers to one company transacting business with another over the Internet. Such basic buying and selling of goods and services (commerce) has been accomplished for many years over the phone, in person, via fax, through the mail, or using electronic data interchange (EDI). While added transactional efficiencies and cost savings may be gained from Internet-based commerce (**Q36**), the added value of the Internet comes from enhancing communications, adding revenue channels (**Q35**), and enabling greater collaboration.

There is no single B2B e-commerce model that works for all types of companies. In fact, most companies use a mix of models within their business. Many different conceptual frameworks for classifying these B2B models have been proposed.

In the earlier days of e-commerce, many Internet companies believed profitable business models could be based on simplistic solutions, such as:

- "disintermediation" (or bypassing) of traditional channels like wholesalers, distributors, and/or retail stores,

- transaction fees, often in excess of traditional EDI costs,

- auctions and reverse auctions where prices reach the lowest possible levels,

- convincing a critical mass of companies in an industry to join open, public marketplaces, where buyers could extract the lowest possible prices.

While there are specific circumstances where each of those solutions can be useful, many of them are based on invalid assumptions in the typical business world. For example:

- Many wholesalers and retailers are large and powerful, carry numerous items that any one supplier cannot provide, and maintain local warehouses with the ability to deliver critical or expensive items (e.g., prescription drugs) to local buyers (e.g., pharmacies) within a few hours. Hence, disintermediation is unlikely.[1]

- The ways companies make money in some industries are complex and drive behaviors that are difficult to automate or change quickly.

- Many companies are unwilling to be forced to sell or buy through an industry exchange which can add both an intermediary and extra costs.

- Most selling companies desire to maintain competitive advantages or relationships with customers, which public Internet marketplaces may reduce.

- Many companies have already invested in EDI solutions at low costs per transaction while Internet exchanges often charge higher transaction costs.

- Many companies already place or receive orders (or other data) computer-to-computer and do not want to manually enter or download on a Web site.

- Some companies have limited numbers of potential suppliers and/or customers within cost-effective shipping distances.

When B2B Works

In spite of the above, most companies are still very interested in conducting business with other companies over the Internet. Under certain circumstances, three general types of e-commerce models can make sense.

Public Marketplace and Exchange Models   Public marketplace and exchange models allow some companies to extend their reach to find new customer markets or supplier sources. Circumstances where these models apply are when:

- Companies in fragmented industries with large numbers of smaller potential buyers and/or sellers can benefit from participating in e-marketplaces or exchanges. Under these circumstances, companies can find new markets of prospective buyers or sellers of products or services more economically and easily than with traditional expensive advertising, exhibitions, mailings, etc. Examples might include wineries desiring to market their products nationally or even internationally to local outlets.

---

[1] Michael Hammer, "Out of the Box: The Myth of Disintermediation," *Information Week.com* 10 July 2000, 3 Dec. 2002 <http://www.informationweek.com/794/94uwmh.htm>.

Similar logic applies to companies selling or buying higher cost or unique items (or lower cost items with low shipping costs) in industries with global or geographically dispersed markets.

• Companies with large numbers of relatively commoditized products (such as office supplies, laboratory supplies, or repair parts) can benefit from publishing their catalogues in marketplaces or other places accessible from e-procurement systems like Ariba, SAP, or CommerceOne. Price, quality, and other attributes or contract terms still need to be negotiated securely. Grainger.com has been a leading example of this for several years.

• Companies that otherwise do not wish to participate in public marketplaces may still benefit from occasionally buying via reverse auctions or selling via auctions. This is true when a company has excess or dated goods (especially commoditized items) to sell, provided selling at auction prices does not cause the market for non-excess goods to drop. Makers of plastic bottles, for example, may benefit from buying commodity plastic resins via auctions.

The Gartner Group "anticipates three kinds marketplaces and exchanges to grow in use: (1) commodity marketplaces that support high-volume commodity trading of products, services, and financial instruments; (2) business services marketplaces targeting particular inter-enterprise processes, like financial services, logistics, and procurement; (3) Integration services marketplaces that help trading partners facilitate process-to-process integration." [2]

Private Exchange or Portal Models   Private exchange or portal models (Q42) enable companies to build on and protect revenues with existing and new customers. In a consolidated or consolidating industry, or in a mature industry, companies need to protect revenues and relationships, at a minimum. Adding value by connecting with existing customers via a private exchange or portal can differentiate a company from other relatively interchangeable suppliers. Private exchanges allow companies to send and receive customized inventory, order, payment, contract, pricing, specifications, and other information and applications to/from customers and suppliers. Wal-Mart announced that it would not participate in public exchanges in favor of its private exchange. Many other companies have reached the same conclusion.

Some industries have few potential suppliers and/or customers to do business with, and those companies can be very large and powerful. In those situations, it is likely that the large companies will use their leverage to encourage use of their own private exchanges to conduct business and share information in standardized ways. Such information often includes orders or releases against long-term contracts,

[2] "Power and Profit from E-Collaboration," *CIO.com* 1 May 2001, 3 Dec. 2002 <http://www.cio.com/sponsors/050101_sd_power.html>.

forecasts, and production schedules. For example, Anheuser-Busch Inc. requires suppliers and customers to connect with it via its Bud Exchange and Bud Net, respectively.

In some industries there are so-called market makers, channel masters, or other powerful companies (i.e., the "800 lb. gorillas"). These companies can also exert leverage and mandate use of their private exchanges. In the automotive industry, Covisint has attained significant, though not total, leverage (Q37).

It is possible in some industries for a public marketplace to be partitioned and secured in such a way as to look and act like a private exchange, though the options for adding custom, value-added differentiators are fewer and slower. Some public marketplace providers like FreeMarkets Inc. and VerticalNet Inc. have reinvented themselves as providers of private marketplace solutions.

Supply Chain Integration Models   Supply chain integration models promote the streamlining of business processes across the supply or distribution chains (Q36, Q67). Situations in which these types of models are likely to work well are:

- When using a public or private marketplace or exchange, the cost-saving opportunity exists for all parties to connect to the exchange once in a standardized way, rather than to build multiple, custom connections to all customers or suppliers. Sales- or purchasing-related processes like inventory control, order processing, invoicing, receivables/payables management, and payments handling can all be streamlined. This makes the most sense when these basic processes offer no special competitive advantage to a company.

- When a complex industry process involves multiple parties (such as reconciling disputed amounts related to "charge-backs" and rebates among manufacturers, wholesalers, buying groups, and pharmacies in the generic drug industry), the Internet can offer unique opportunities for streamlining. In those cases, common contract terms and pricing files can be maintained centrally and accessed by all parties anywhere in the process. This eliminates the primary reasons for the disputes such as timing differences and data entry errors in updating multiple independent files maintained separately. Similarly, packaging (can and bottle) manufacturers like Ball Corporation can coordinate all time-sensitive activities related to creating and approving graphics (labels, etc.) in one central place where all parties involved may access the status at any time.

In conclusion, not all Internet models make sense for all companies in all industries. However, there are workable B2B Internet models to fit almost any unique industry and company situation. Companies should seek out the options that fit them best.

38. What are the differences among B2C e-business models?

DAVID R. LAUBE

While the term e-commerce applies to all businesses conducted online, B2C refers to business-to-consumer business transactions. B2C models concentrate an enterprise's attention completely on its primary target—the consumer.

The real action started in the B2C marketplace when radical new business models enabled first-movers to grab market share in industries such as books (Amazon .com) and auctions (eBay). During the mid-1990s there was wild enthusiasm that B2C companies would take significant market share from traditional retailers and even dominate that space. Numerous B2C models emerged, but by the end of the 1990s many failed because their business model, financial, and consumer acceptance assumptions did not prove to be valid (**Q45**). Nonetheless, B2C business activities have continued, and as more is understood about which models still work, more and more successes are emerging.

Differences among B2C Models

Two key elements can be used to differentiate one B2C business model from another:

1. *Revenue streams*—how the proposed model generates revenue

2. *Margin opportunity*—how the proposed model generates profitability

Following is an analysis of generic forms of B2C models observable on the Web.[1]

Advertising Model

The advertising model is one of the earliest B2C models. The general premise is to provide content on the Web site that is of interest to viewers and drive "eyeballs" to the site. The Web site, much like a broadcaster, then charges to place advertising on the site.

Revenue Stream Revenue is generated by the sale of advertising. As with any advertising, the effectiveness of the Web site in attracting viewers who will respond to the ads impacts ad revenues and determines the attractiveness of this model.

[1] The framework of business models used here draws on an approach developed by Michael Rappa, "Business Models on the Web," <http://digitalenterprise.org/models/models.html>. This site is an excellent source of information about e-business models and this specific Web page includes links to more information on the B2C business models than is discussed here.

Margin Opportunity   The advertising model generates profits when the volume of viewer traffic is large or highly specialized. The more successful a Web site is in driving site usage, the more it can charge for the ads. This was originally thought to have the same margin potential as broadcast media such as TV or radio. Sluggish user responses to the ads have tempered the optimism somewhat, but advertisers are still exploring the potential of this medium.[2]

SUBSCRIPTION MODEL

Businesses with this model make content services (music, sports, video, information) available to members or visitors. These are not usually one-time purchases, but recurring services that the customer will use regularly. Included in this model would be Internet service providers like America Online or MSN who charge monthly fees for access to their sites and the Internet.

Revenue Stream   Users are charged a specific fee to get access to the content of the service. The amount of the fee is determined by the value of the content and the cost to obtain similar content elsewhere (i.e., an online magazine subscription price is likely to be less than the print subscription).

Margin Opportunity   To keep costs low, most sites try to repackage existing material for delivery over the Web. Major League Baseball (mlb.com), for example, broadcasts games using audio feeds that already exist. In some areas, like music broadcasting (listen.com), the costs are significantly less than if operating in a traditional radio or TV environment. For newspapers and magazines (wsj.com) they leverage content already prepared for their print products.

MERCHANT MODEL

This model includes the offering of wholesale and retail goods and services. In some cases, the goods and services may be unique to the Web site and not have a traditional "brick-and-mortar" storefront (**Q39**). Sometimes the product is in digital form (e.g., software) and can be distributed easily over the Web. The merchant model is the model most often associated with B2C.

Revenue Stream   Revenue is generated by selling goods and services over the Web site much like a retail store. The ability of the Web merchant to build a brand name impacts its ability to drive revenue since the key is the number of visitors who know

---

[2] New approaches to ad placement are showing some success. Search engines are now able to display ads related to the outcome of an individual's search, creating targeted ad opportunities.

about the Web site. Absent a strong brand, Web sites need to purchase priority positions on search engines, affiliate with a large commercial portal, or use other marketing tactics such as e-mail to generate visitors.

Margin Opportunity   Profitability in this model comes from one of three places.

1. *Large mass marketer*—If the company has chosen to be a large mass marketer and built a large infrastructure and distribution network, its only road to profitability is very large scale. These companies typically compete on price with other mass marketers and thus must generate large volumes to cover their infrastructure costs. Very few have achieved the scale necessary to be profitable.

2. *Affiliation with "bricks" retailers*—Companies with large retail store networks have added Web sites to enhance their sales opportunities. They typically already have strong distribution and purchasing capabilities and can leverage this as well as their existing brand name to their advantage on the Web site. With this shared overhead, they can be profitable at lower volumes than those using the strategy above.

3. *Niche retailers*—These companies sell products that are not readily available through traditional retail channels. They usually focus on specialty items or those that sell in small volumes. Because they don't compete with mass retailers on price, and their low volumes keep their overhead low, they can be profitable fairly quickly. Some might be able to minimize inventory costs by purchasing only what has already been sold to customers.

Brokerage Model

Brokers are market makers; they provide the mechanism to bring buyers and sellers together. Their product is, in effect, the intermediary service that either the buyer or the seller is willing to pay for. Examples include: orbitz.com, eBay.com, priceline.com, schwab.com, and many others.

Revenue Stream   Usually a broker charges a fee or commission for each transaction it enables.

Margin Opportunity   Profits are dependent on the infrastructure costs incurred to provide the electronic marketplace. Most companies must drive significant volume to cover those costs, so success usually is linked with strong market share in the segment being addressed.

Affiliate Model

In this model, the Web site provides links to other sites that are offering goods and services. It then receives a fee or commission from that Web site if the customer follows through with an order. Examples include cnet.com and bizrate.com.

Revenue Stream   There are two sources of revenue in this model. The first is the fee or commission earned for referring a customer to the merchant. The second is a placement fee that the Web site charges the merchant for a premium location on the Web page. For example, a merchant might pay to have its products shown first in a list of competitive alternatives.

Margin Opportunity   As with a sales commission, the Web site must perform to get paid. Business arrangements between the Web sites and the merchants can generate revenue based on "click-throughs" to the merchant site or revenue sharing on sales actually made. High traffic is key to the success of this model. The Web site must be sufficiently useful and generate enough value that people will use it rather than go directly to the merchant site. For this reason, these affiliate sites often offer price comparison services or offer expertise in a particular product or market niche.

Manufacturer Model

This model is used by companies who want to compress their distribution channel and use the Web to go directly to their customers. The objective is to cut distribution costs and build a direct relationship with their customers. This is often referred to as disintermediation (Q36). Companies such as Dell Computer Corporation for computer products and many of the airlines have rebuilt their entire business models based on this approach.

Revenue Stream   Revenue is generated from sales of the company's products or services.

Margin Opportunity   Profits in this model are largely driven by the ability of the company to cut its channel costs (distributors, retailers, agents, etc.). This can improve profit margins or allow companies to more aggressively price their products, thereby increasing market share.

Conclusion

The electronic marketplace is a dynamic, not static, area. E-commerce has not supplanted traditional channels; users have simply mixed and matched its capabilities to suit their personal needs. Nevertheless, B2C e-commerce is growing steadily with an increasing focus on adding value to products and services.[3] Despite the failure of many dot.coms (**Q45**), new players continue to emerge. B2C is here to stay and B2C models will continue to evolve as companies learn how to use this technology for competitive advantage.

39. What is the right mix of "bricks and clicks"?

CHERYL L. WHITE AND THOMAS KIEFER

The Web has ushered in a bright new world of boundless opportunities. With both a physical business environment (bricks) and a virtual environment (clicks) now possible, the question is not *whether* an organization should integrate the Internet into its brick-and-mortar business model, but *to what extent* Web-enabled technologies can add value to its existing physical business. The most effective solution is one that combines all traditional brick channels with new click channels so that a company can provide many access points for its customers. So whether customers call, write, e-mail, fax, or physically visit a company location, they can have a consistent high-quality business experience.

The Internet provides a way of doing business that is fast, cheap, and efficient compared to many brick-and-mortar methods. Three reasons stand out for why companies might want to transition all or part of an organization from a brick-and-mortar operation to one that is click-enabled: (1) building brand awareness, (2) building and keeping client relationships, and (3) reducing costs.

BUILDING BRAND AWARENESS

Imagine adding to an organization a storefront that is open 24 hours per day, 7 days per week and is accessible by potential consumers around the globe. Once inside, consumers can browse available products at their leisure, comparison shop, and check for special offers. They can find answers to questions or engage the company in conversation. While the consumer is browsing, the organization is watching the potential buyer closely, gathering data, and creating a profile of their habits. This rich

[3] Teri Robinson, "Report: Online Sales Spike, Led by Computers, Travel," *E-Commerce Times Web Site*, 19 Aug. 2002, 3 Dec. 2002 <http://www.ecommercetimes.com/perl/story/19079.html>.

data can be used to tailor a marketing approach to each type of consumer and create an attractive buying environment tailored to specific buyer personalities (**Q40**). These powerful new capabilities are compelling enough to drive organizations into a strategy that heavily utilizes clicks.

For some companies, a virtual storefront is the only means consumers have of entering the organization. These organizations are 100 percent clicks and the consumers' buying experience is entirely virtual. Their key to building brand awareness is to provide a product, service, or customer experience that is differentiated from their bricks-oriented competitors (**Q38**). Organizations catering to the time-honored brick-and-mortar buying customer, on the other hand, may find that their brand awareness is still dependent on their physical presence and a dramatic shift to virtual storefronts might be a high-risk strategy. These companies tend to follow the lead of companies like Target and Wal-Mart, who have eased into the virtual marketplace.

BUILDING AND KEEPING CLIENT RELATIONSHIPS

As many organizations have discovered, adding clicks to their brick-and-mortar presence can change the nature of the way they provide customer service. The frenetic pace of modern life means that consumers have increasingly high expectations about what they consider good customer service. Customers want their choice of products; they want access to information about them; they want help when they have questions; and they want to shop according to their schedule. In many circumstances, the addition of a virtual presence can accommodate these needs much more efficiently than with a bricks-based store. New technologies such as "chat" services or "push-to-talk" buttons on Web sites can connect customers to live service representatives immediately. So a combination of live and virtual customer interactions is now becoming commonplace, further enhancing that critical customer relationship.

Sometimes the nature of the product dictates which type of experience customers prefer. High-touch items like furniture are better sold in person while more generic items like books or CDs are easily sold over the Web. It also may be true that products could evolve from high to low touch over a period of time. For example, when booking a vacation cruise for the first time, customers may want to physically visit a travel agent who can describe the various types of vacation experiences and assist in the selection. The next time that same customer wants a cruise vacation, they may be knowledgeable enough that an interaction with a cruise line's Web site would be sufficient.

REDUCING COSTS

Many companies have chosen to use Web-based interactions with their customers as a means to reduce their costs (**Q36**). Particularly in service industries, it can

Table **39.1** *Customer Types and Shopping Preferences*

Clientele	Price Sensitivity	Loyalty	Balance of Bricks/Clicks
Patrons	High	Low	Clicks to reduce costs
Customers	Moderate	Moderate	Balance of bricks and clicks to deliver high value at minimum cost
Clients	Low, unless enticed by a special deal	High, as long as they receive good service	Bricks balanced with clicks for good service
Partners	Low, but will pay for extras	High, if service stays high	Bricks for the "high-touch" experience

Source: Based on McKenzie (2001).

be cheaper to service repetitive issues over the Web such as questions about billing or order status.

TAILORING A BALANCE OF BRICKS AND CLICKS

One way for an organization to understand the right balance of bricks and clicks is to focus on the nature of its customers. One approach developed by McKenzie is to consider that organizations have at least four types of clientele that he calls patrons, customers, clients, and partners as illustrated in Table 39.1.[1]

By properly understanding its customers and their characteristics, an organization can determine how best to serve them.

LEVERAGING A MIX OF BRICKS AND CLICKS

Companies are continuing to modify their positioning along the bricks-and-clicks spectrum. Many pure clicks companies, like Amazon.com, have added costly bricks (in the form of warehouses, etc.) in order to better satisfy the needs of their customers. Companies that once separated their Internet division from in-store shopping are now integrating them so that they can develop unified promotions, common inventory, and an integrated buying experience. On the other hand, others, like the airlines, are closing some of their travel offices and driving their customers to the Internet. Albertsons, Walgreens, and others are pioneering a "click-and-deliver" model that

[1] Ray McKenzie, *The Relationship Based Enterprise: Powering Business Success through Customer Relationship Management* (Montreal: McGraw-Hill Ryerson, 2001).

encourages in-store pickup of at-home purchases.[2] Other companies such as Circuit City, Sears, and Best Buy promote a "click-in-brick" approach that places Internet-linked kiosks within the store for consumer access to such services as bridal registries, information on out-of-stock items, and product location of items stocked in other stores. These approaches are designed to create a seamless shopping experience that adds "virtual square feet" without moving bricks.[3]

Ultimately, the right bricks-to-clicks ratio depends on the corporate business strategy. This strategy must consider the industry the company is in, the marketing model of its competition, and the mix of its consumer types. As the Internet matures and the buying consumer becomes more Internet literate, the right mix of bricks and clicks occurs when the organization reaches the desired depth of market penetration with a least-cost model for building brand awareness, managing the consumer relationships, and sustaining meaningful customer conversations.

---

40. How can a business learn more about its customers using IT?

MARY LEE STANSIFER AND RANDY WELDON

Making personal contacts and developing personal relationships have been and still are the mainstays of finding and retaining the most important customers in most industries. However, starting in the mid-1990s, sales executives grew excited about the "e-marketing" possibilities offered by several new information technologies. Such technologies promised to help companies connect more closely with their customers, find new customers, and increase sales and customer service; all at lower costs. First, these executives were exposed to new front-office customer relationship management (CRM) systems. (Q65, Q66).[1] They bought thousands of laptop PCs, handheld com-

---

[2] Nick Wingfiled, "Click and . . . Drive?" *Wall Street Journal* 15 July 2002, *Proquest*, Auraria Library, Denver, 10 Dec. 2002 <http://www.umi.com/pqdauto>.

[3] Ann Grimes, "What's in Store? *Wall Street Journal* 15 July 2002, *Proquest*, Auraria Library, Denver, 10 Dec. 2002 <http://www.umi.com/pqdauto>.

[1] Bryan Bergeron, *Essentials of CRM: A Guide to Customer Relationship Management* (New York: Wiley, 2002); Ginger Conlon, "No Turning Back," *Sales and Marketing Management* Dec. 1999: 50; Jill Dyché, *The CRM Handbook: A Business Guide to Customer Relationship Management* (Boston: Addison-Wesley, 2002); Andrew Fisher, "New Ways to Win Over Fickle Clients: In the Battle for

puters, and various wireless devices to help their field, sales, and service personnel capture and access key customer, marketing, and sales information. They also heard hype about a new, paradigm-shifting phenomenon called the Internet. All of these technologies promised to enable companies to reach more customers and learn more about them than ever before.

Successful E-marketing Approaches

Some of the promises offered by the new technologies have been fulfilled and some have not. Following are some of the major ways information technologies in general, and the Internet in particular, have successfully helped companies learn more about current or prospective customers.

Targeted Marketing   Traditional marketing approaches are becoming less and less effective. There are simply too many new product choices, too many companies trying to sell them, and too much resultant marketing "noise."[2] New, more targeted and effective techniques have recently been developed.

Market Analysis   Using "micromarketing databases," data warehouses (**Q20**), and data-mining tools and techniques (**Q21**), companies are analyzing customer data captured from multiple sources to define market segments. By using this information, companies can directly tailor marketing messages and campaigns to specific audiences who are most likely to be affected by those messages. Marketing dollars can be much more effectively spent on such targeted marketing. With the help of the Internet you can have an audience of one.[3] E*Trade, for example, has built a reputation for effective segmentation marketing based on analysis of data in its extremely large data warehouse.

Personalization and Customization   Companies are capturing information about specific customers' habits and preferences at all touch points, and are using that to present highly personalized marketing messages through telemarketers, mailings, e-mail, Internet, or other media. In the cases of e-mail and printed mail, companies often include hyperlinks or URLs to specific pages within the company's Web site to direct prospects to easily find information about the company's products or services.

Profits, Companies Are Turning to Customer Relationship Management (CRM) Systems," *The Financial Times* 17 Oct. 2001: 1.

[2] J. Patrick O'Halloran et al., "Insight Driven Marketing," Executive Summary, *Line 56 Media Web Site*, Accenture, 2001, 16 Sept. 2002 <http://www.line56.com/research/download/accenture_insight_driven.pdf>.

[3] Matt Haig, *The E-Marketing Handbook* (London: Kogan Page, 2001) 2.

E-mail also is quick, it is environmentally friendly, and you can generate a response rate better than direct mail.[4] In addition, companies are using modern portal software (Q42) to allow customers to customize the layout, content, and features of their personalized version of a company's Web site. In spite of all these efforts toward personalization through automation, a company must still understand the prospect's real needs and meet them, or the technology will fail.[5]

Understanding Customer Needs and Habits   Some sophisticated companies are employing "clickstream analysis," a new technology allowing them to analyze every keystroke prospective customers enter and determine where they went on a company's site, how much time they spent, and what they were most interested in. With this information, a company can proactively offer the customer more tailored products, services, or information to meet their specific needs. In the short-term, this process can require significant computer and people resources to analyze and act on the results.[6]

LOWER MARKETING AND SALES COST MODELS

Currently, companies acquire prospects through very inefficient processes such as paying vendors to provide contact and lead databases, or paying telemarketing firms or field sales forces to contact prospects via cold calls. More effective and lower cost marketing and sales models are being enabled by new information technologies.

Lead Generation   Companies are providing access to free, downloadable information over the Internet (e.g., white papers or other special deals prospective buyers want). To get the information the prospect wants, however, he or she must fill in some important contact and lead information first. This information goes directly into the company's CRM system, which is then forwarded to the appropriate account representatives or telemarketers who can follow up with calls and e-mails in less than a day. If you visit Web sites for sophisticated vendors such as Broadvision, Comergent, or Plumtree, you can download highly valuable research or other information at no cost. If you do, you can expect to receive a sales call within a day, and you will also start receiving e-mails regarding products, seminars, and other targeted sales information. This highly targeted process is much cheaper than traditional mass mailings or telemarketing calls.

Cross-Selling and Up-Selling   Cross-selling and up-selling are based on what prospective customers have entered in Google or Yahoo search engines, what parts of a

---

[4] Haig 93.

[5] O'Halloran et al.

[6] Shira Levine, "Clicking on the Customer: Clickstream Analysis Can Improve Website Marketing and Efficiency," *America's Network* 1 Apr. 2000: 86.

company's site they have looked at, or what products they ordered this time or in the past. A company can present the prospects with other products they may be interested in from their own and partners' catalogues. All of us have seen such targeted advertising when using the Internet to research books to buy on Barnes & Noble's site, find classmates for high school reunions, or meet similar needs.

Reduced Costs of Marketing Events   Many companies are using webcasts to conduct targeted, effective, and low-cost marketing events. Multiple targeted prospects are invited via e-mail and other means to attend a company's scheduled marketing event broadcast over the Web. Prospects listen on the phone and see presentations or other demonstrations over the Web. These events may focus on a product or on a topic of interest, but the vendor sponsors almost always get a brief chance to promote their company and demonstrate their products. In addition, one-on-one webcasts can be conducted directly with sales reps on a scheduled or unscheduled basis, or self-paced without sales reps. Sales reps talk to a prospect on the phone while directing them to a Web site where they can walk through a presentation over the Web at the same time. This technique saves travel time and costs, but can be somewhat less personal.

Access to Current, Low-Cost Marketing Collateral and Other Documentation   Sales people, distributors, and even customers can print the latest marketing collateral and other product documentation over the Internet from wherever they are, resulting in lower printing costs and enhanced accuracy and timeliness of information.

IMPLICATIONS

New technologies, such as the Internet, offer outstanding opportunities to gather information about customers needs and wants, offer value-add services beyond prior capabilities, and even generate new revenues. Nevertheless, while technology can help connect people and companies in new ways, it is not a panacea. Customers are people, and people fundamentally don't want a "relationship" with a machine. Personal relationships will continue to reign in many situations. Building relationships with customers allows a company to spend more time with more profitable loyal customers.[7]

True to human nature, marketing and sales contacts and related computer information files are often regarded by field sales people as personal assets, the basis of their initial value to prospective employers when they change jobs. Consequently, many sales people are reluctant to enter everything they know into company-owned CRM systems.

[7] James Barnes, *Secrets of Customer Relationship Management* (New York: McGraw-Hill, 2001) 34–37.

Despite these issues, it is clear that technology is now a driving force in the marketing strategy of most companies. With the proper balance between automated and personal contact, the whole marketing process can be much more effective and generate significant benefits to the companies willing to properly implement and leverage their technology investments.

41. What are the major privacy issues associated with e-business?

JACKY OORLOFF AND TED V. SCHAEFER

Privacy has become one of the key challenges facing any company active on the Internet. A major public policy issue of our time, privacy is at the epicenter of class action litigation, international regulation, FTC (Federal Trade Commission), and state Attorneys General inquiries. The negative press surrounding online information collection practices has also raised consumer concern about privacy. The privacy issues specific to e-business are only more complicated because of the truly global, borderless nature of the Internet. As a result, privacy advocates are closely monitoring online companies and are poised to attack whenever there is the appearance of any privacy related impropriety.

The presence of vocal advocates, media, and regulators increases the stakes for companies to protect their brand through solid privacy practices. Privacy impropriety can significantly damage a company's reputation in the eyes of one group of their major stakeholders, their customers.

In this highly charged environment, it is critically important that all organizations that collect consumer information online apply recognized best practices and industry standards to their business processes and to the development of technologies and business models.

WHAT IS PRIVACY?

One of the first challenges is the cultural, legal, and political variations in what the word "privacy" means. Privacy is a subjective concept and has different meanings to different individuals. Because of this, the very nature of managing this issue becomes complex, especially in the borderless, online realm. One generally accepted definition from a noted privacy academic defines privacy as, "The claim of individuals to determine when, how, and to what extent information about them is communicated to others."[1] However, even this definition will differ by country and by law.

PRIVACY DRIVERS

There are a number of drivers that make privacy an important consideration in any e-business initiative. Three of these are:

- building consumer trust

- global regulations governing privacy

- new technology

Let's look at each of these in more detail.

BUILDING CONSUMER TRUST

As companies expand their business into the online arena, privacy is a key consideration in building consumer trust. The Internet now makes it easier and more efficient to collect vast amounts of personal data, which was previously hindered by factors such as cost or inability to reach the end consumer. In doing this, however, consumer apprehension toward this new "e-world" has increased.

The one-to-one relationship the Internet facilitates has provided an unprecedented ability to collect individual information. While this provides unparalleled business opportunities, it also raises concerns. The ongoing media campaign regarding Internet privacy has pushed this issue to the forefront of the consumer's mind, making it a key inhibitor to increasing online transactions.

A recent study found 43 percent of Internet users believe businesses currently have no incentive to protect their privacy.[2] Given this heightened sensitivity, consumers are asking the questions: Who am I transacting with? How will my information be used? Will I receive unwanted solicitations? Is my credit card safe?

A simple, yet effective solution to help allay consumer fears is a company's privacy policy. An online policy is becoming a requisite for any Web site collecting an individual's information. Any company implementing an e-business solution should look closely at its information handling practices and outline this within the policy.

[1] Alan Westin, *Privacy and Freedom* (New York: Atheneum Publishers, 1967).
[2] Harris Interactive, *Consumer Privacy Attitudes and Behaviors Study Wave II*, Study for Privacy Leadership Initiative, 10 July 2001, 12 Aug 2002 <http://www.bbbonline.org/UnderstandingPrivacy/library/harris2-execsum.pdf>.

Following industry and regulatory guidance helps ensure the appropriate disclosures are included. However, posting a privacy policy is not enough.

Within the U.S., the FTC has recently reinforced its commitment to ensure compliance with the promises companies make.[3] As such, in this litigious environment, companies must ensure they "practice what they preach." In a complaint recently filed with the FTC, a U.S. media company was accused of selling a list of its customer e-mail addresses–something it promised not to do in the privacy policy posted on its Web site. Those who develop e-business initiatives need to be highly cognizant of the privacy disclosures made. Similarly, compliance obligations do not end at the Web site. Back-office procedures to support disclosures are a crucial component of managing privacy exposures. Another large U.S. company recently settled charges with the FTC because of an inadvertent release of customer e-mail addresses. The FTC charged the company's privacy promises were deceptive because the company failed to back them up with the appropriate security.

Global Regulations Governing Privacy

As companies build global Web sites, consolidate data centers, and integrate their customer strategies to meet global needs, e-business solutions need to address cross-border privacy rules in an unprecedented way. These requirements often add to the complexity of both policy design and ongoing compliance considerations.

Approaches to privacy regulation vary considerably across nations. Europe has long recognized an individual's right to privacy. As such, there exists robust, omnibus privacy legislation throughout this region. Following suit are Canada and many countries within the Asia-Pacific and Latin America regions. In contrast is the U.S., which has been focused on a broadly self-regulatory approach with limited, sectorial legislation addressing sensitive areas (financial and health information and children's privacy). A challenge for any company undertaking an e-business initiative is how to manage a global Web site while balancing these different legal requirements and consumer perspectives. How does a company develop a one-size-fits-all privacy policy and supporting practices? This challenge is further complicated because of the unresolved issues regarding online legal jurisdiction.

New Technology

New advances in technologies enabling both the collection and use of information have led to public discussions and attention on these practices. For example, Web

---

[3] Brian Krebs, "Online Privacy Policies Apply to Offline Data Practices – FTC," *Newsbytes* 10 Dec. 2001, *Lexis-Nexis,* Academic Universe, Auraria Library, Denver, 25 July 2002 <http://web .lexis-nexis.com/universe>.

bugs, Web site personalization, and cookies all provide innovative and extensive ways to collect and collate consumer information. Cookies, which are small text files placed on an individual's hard drive, have become commonplace with most Web sites. Primarily used for activities such as storing logon information and remembering user preferences, cookies have received criticism from privacy advocates. One major online advertiser recently suffered significant media and regulator backlash because of the widespread use of their cookies and the perception that it allowed the company to build detailed profiles of Web surfers.

The huge range of data collection technologies now in use across the Internet means that many companies are finding new and innovative ways to get to know their customers (**Q40**). However, this also exposes the company to additional risks because it may not be aware of the depth and breadth of information being collected. Many companies try managing this by communicating privacy requirements beyond the legal or marketing departments. The challenge of ensuring that a company is adhering to its stated privacy policy becomes even more difficult due to the rapid expansion of Web sites, development of new Web pages, and deployment of new technologies. For example, a large telecommunications company recently made changes to its Web site which inadvertently exposed its customers' account numbers in an easy to obtain format. This type of exposure can be minimized by implementing processes and controls to ensure Web site development complies with the company's privacy policy.

This is even more important when third-party companies are used to provide services such as Web development, metric reporting, or customer tracking. For example, a large online toy store came under fire for a tool used on their Web site to evaluate visitor behavior. The tool, which was provided by a third party, also collected detailed information about customer transactions as they shopped on the site. This information was collected directly by the third party and was not disclosed to the Web site's customers. Many other reported privacy breaches have come about, not because of the company's misuse of their customer's information, but due to misuse through third-party providers. A level of due diligence over the privacy and security of any third-party companies providing Web site functionality is important in reducing this risk.

CONCLUSION

Due to the large amount of personal data that can be collected and manipulated online, the need to allay consumer concerns surrounding Internet commerce, and the continuing media and regulatory scrutiny of this issue, many companies are establishing formal programs to address privacy. For example, large companies such as IBM, Hewlett Packard, Microsoft, Proctor & Gamble, and Eastman Kodak, have been proactive and outspoken in their efforts to develop programs to manage online privacy. This program starts with the creation of a robust online privacy policy that discloses the Web site's information handling practices and provides transparency into the company. This policy is only successful, however, if the necessary controls are in place, both on the Web site and behind the scenes, to support the disclosures made.

As such, the simple golden rule for managing e-business privacy concerns is, "Have good, transparent privacy policy disclosures that adequately reflect your business practices."

---

42. What are the uses of intranets, extranets, and portals?

RANDY WELDON

Many executives in nontechnology oriented companies are overwhelmed with new terminology when hearing or reading about Internet business opportunities. Some of them have a hard time relating to terms like *intranet, extranet,* and *portals.* For example, when business people are asked if they know what a portal is, they often say no, or at best, that it is one place where people can access various things on the Internet. However, when asked if they currently have a MyYahoo or MyMSN account, many of them say yes. They are primed to take the next step into business uses for such technologies.

INTRANETS, EXTRANETS, AND PORTALS

Before we can explain how to use the Internet to help with business processes, we must define a few key terms:

- intranet
- extranet
- portal

After we define each of these terms, we will look at the differences among them.

Intranet   An intranet is an internal Web site accessible over a company's private network. It is targeted at empowering employees and certain trusted partners to be more efficient at performing their jobs, managing their own work lives, and accessing knowledge when they need it. The intranet may also be accessible remotely over the Internet or via a private company network using the same security methods as external sites. Sometimes an intranet is also called an "employee portal," an "enterprise portal," or a "business-to-employee" (B2E) Web site.

Extranet An extranet is an external, secure Web site accessible over a wide area network (WAN). Such extranets (sometimes called "private exchanges" or "enterprise information portals" (EIP)) are targeted at key customers and partners (e.g., logistics partners, truck or rail carriers, etc.). Access from the outside requires strong security to not only protect company information assets such as confidential pricing or costs, but also to protect customer specific data such as sales forecasts, orders, and prices. An extranet often allows partners to enter or access authorized data within the company's back-office enterprise resource planning (ERP) systems (**Q62**).

Portal A portal is a window to everything an employee, customer, or external partner needs to conduct internal or external business efficiently and effectively with the company. Private portals connect a company with multiple customers or partners. Public portals (exchanges or marketplaces) connect multiple companies (including competitors) with multiple partners. Historically, public portals dealt with simple business activities such as catalogues, auctions, reverse auctions, and purchases involving standardized or commodity products. Emerging public marketplaces allow more sophisticated business interactions involving products with complex specifications, contract negotiations, and pricing.

42 ▬

USES OF INTRANETS, EXTRANETS, AND PORTALS

The intranet or employee portal is deployed over the company's secure internal network and is used by employees and other trusted partners. The extranet or partner portal is deployed over the secure external network and is used by customers, suppliers, or other partners. However, the security, content management, underlying portal administration and other features are increasingly based on the same tools and technologies as intranets and extranets. Intranets and extranets normally display content on Web pages in custom ways, whereas portals normally allow users to search for content in predefined categories and return it from the content management system to be presented in standardized ways.

Employee Portal Uses of an Intranet Originally, intranets were used primarily for departments to create Web pages so employees could link to simple functions and data sources, such as: news, weather, sports, stock prices, and commonly used forms (expense reports, purchase requisitions, etc.). Going forward, many intranets (called employee portals) will be deployed through portal software from vendors such as Plumtree, Epicentric, or others. Such employee portals will be used to aggregate all the business processes, applications, and knowledge sources applicable to an individual's job or a workgroup's collaboration. For example, J.D. Edwards, a large software company, has developed an award-winning intranet called the Knowledge Garden, which allows employees to publish and retrieve large amounts of knowledge-oriented content.[1]

Some other uses and functions of an employee portal are:

- single sign-on,

- personalization,

- customization of layout and content,

- authorized access based on employee roles or profiles,

- templates and content management,[2]

- common functions such as:

  - communications to/from executives,

  - collaboration among "communities of interest,"

  - general news,

  - specific news by industry, customer, competitor, supplier, etc.,

  - e-mail, calendar, address book,

  - forms and document management,

  - workflow applications,

  - stock portfolio,

  - company store,

  - employee want ads,

  - driving directions/maps.

Tools to Help Employees Manage Their Work Lives   Intranets (employee portals) can provide tools for employees to manage their work lives, such as:

- employee self-service access to view and change certain HR data (e.g., in employee database),

---

[1] "2002 J.D. Edwards Partner Programs," White Paper, *J.D. Edwards Web Site* [2001], 16 July 2002 <http://www.jdedwards.com/content/enUS/Partner-Partners/Partner%20Programs.pdf>.

[2] The IS (Information Services) department creates templates incorporating the approved look and feel, navigation and content management applications. This allows departments to author and publish their own "content" to Web pages, including text, graphics, documents, manuals, best practices, and standard operating procedures.

- job applicant tracking,

- annual benefits enrollment,

- manager self-service for performance reviews, etc.,

- travel and expense reporting tied to travel arrangements and company credit cards,

- simulations for retirement account options and growth.

Integration with Back-Office Applications   Back-office applications (e.g., SAP, Oracle, J.D. Edwards, PeopleSoft) can be integrated into the intranet or employee portal to enable employees to perform authorized job functions without signing in/out of the intranet (using single sign-on software). Integration is enabled via middleware (**Q13**) or a new technology called Web services (**Q15**) or other tools.

Knowledge Management   Knowledge Management (**Q51**) is made easier by using intranets to access:

- external and internal data sources for business intelligence,

- threaded discussions among communities of interest to promote innovation and knowledge sharing,

- management information for decision making,

- online learning and training (**Q52**),

- written and visual best practices at the point where work is performed.

Extranet, Partner Portal Uses   Early uses of extranets involved granting customers or partners secure access to company business data/activities such as catalogues, order entry, order status, and inventories.

Future extranets, in the form of private exchanges or portals, will allow customers or partners easy and secure access to integrated data or applications that the company chooses to "expose" to such partners through the portal or via Web services. Some of the objectives of an extranet or partner portal include:

- presenting a single face to the customer regardless of channel,

- providing one-stop shopping,

- enabling customer/partner self-service,[3]

- providing value-add applications and information,

---

[3] Self-service provides partners access to a company's extranet or portal to check inventory, order and shipping status, place orders, etc.

- streamlining business processes,

- enhancing communication and ties with partners,

- increasing the costs for customers to switch from your products/services to those from another provider.

Many companies are creating private exchanges or portals to connect with their known customers or suppliers to maintain control over relationships and retain or improve competitive advantage. The alternative is to participate in public exchanges or marketplaces along with competitors. The latter makes more sense when a company's participation is highly segregated and secure (mimicking a private exchange), a company's products are relatively standardized commodities, or the industry is highly fragmented and global suppliers and customers have a hard time finding each other.

Extranets also provide an excellent vehicle for collaboration such as dynamic, two-way sharing of information regarding product specifications, sales forecasts, production schedules, shipping optimization, inventory replenishment, etc.

SUMMARY

In summary, internal intranets can empower employees to perform their jobs more effectively by allowing them to create and retrieve knowledge easily. External extranets allow customers and other partners to connect with a company more easily, thereby increasing switching costs and reducing transactional costs. Either may be executed via Web pages or new portal technology tied to content management systems.

---

43. What technical elements must be in place for a successful e-business implementation?

RENÉ J. AERDTS AND WILLIAM H. PHIFER

Like any business strategy, successful implementation of an e-business strategy starts with a business plan, focusing on the products or services to be delivered and the delivery mechanisms. Regardless of whether the e-business strategy is part of a larger "bricks and clicks" approach or a "pure-play" (an Internet-only business interface) strategy, the underlying technology is crucial to the success of the complete enterprise. Inherently, e-business is not about either business or technology, but rather an integration of both (**Q36**). Therefore, the technology infrastructure, architecture, and standards must be clearly defined as prerequisites to e-business implementation. This architecture should address the applications and data interfaces, integration issues, and the technologies needed.

One of the key drivers toward a personalized e-business Web site experience is Right[6].[1] The Right[6] concept refers to providing the *right information* in the *right format* to the *right person* at the *right place* and the *right time* to take the *right action*. As such, the technologies deployed by an e-business not only interoperate with all other information systems, but at the same time enable the company's growth engine. Having the proper technical elements in place is essential to being able to deliver the Right[6] to the customer. The role of the IT department in an e-business strategy implementation is to provide Any[6]. The Any[6] concept refers to the capability to provide access to *any information* by *anyone, anywhere*, in *any format*, on *any device, anytime*—provided that the normal business constraints and security and privacy guidelines are adhered to.[2] It is important to note that Right[6] refers to the "push" and that Any[6] refers to the "pull" of information from an e-business.

43

THE PRESENT ENVIRONMENT

Currently, the following key components are required for a sustainable e-business environment:

- *Architecture*—The IT architecture (**Q8, Q44**) is at the core of the e-business, providing seamless integration between Web applications and the back-office systems. The architecture needs to be defined with the security, availability, reliability, scalability, and anticipated performance characteristics of the environment. The architecture design includes:

  – hardware and network platforms that are properly sized for growth

  – software such as database systems that provide the functionality and the integration with front and back-office systems

  – security

  – process and procedures

[1] Right[6] is an extension of the Right[5] concept used at EDS; see Jef Meerts, "Business Transformation in the Financial Industry: Principles for Surviving—and Thriving—in the Digital Economy," White Paper, *Electronic Data Systems Corporation Web Site* Mar. 2002, 18 Dec. 2002 <http://www.eds.com/thought/news_thought_bus_trans_financial.pdf>; Ian Miller, "It's What You Know That Counts," *Electronic Data Systems Corporation Web Site* Aug. 2000, 18 Dec. 2002 <http://www.eds.com/thought/en_news_thought_knowledge.pdf>.

[2] Any[6] is a concept used at EDS.

The software development environment and transportable language (usually Java in the case of Web-based development) as well as an integrated configuration management tool are also selected and appropriate standards defined. Most important, the architecture needs to be such that new technology can be inserted rapidly and without too much change to the environment to enable speed-to-market.

- *Tools*—Selection of the proper tools is an extremely important element in the success of an e-business. Tools need to be selected for content management (including documents, multimedia, manuals, etc.), customer/supplier/partner management, transactional management (orders, shipments, invoices, payments, etc.), and should include search engines and browsers. In addition to supporting individual technology components, these tools should enable a seamless view of the business. Finally, tools such as knowledge management systems (**Q51**) and trouble ticket systems are also necessary to support problem resolution.

- *Application interfaces*—All information technology systems need to communicate and interoperate to enable a seamless digital workflow from front-office to back-office without human intervention. The use of eXtensible Markup Language (XML) (**Q14**), which allows corporations to describe the content and context of data in a document, is emerging as the means for applications to share data. The successful e-business will have XML-enabled documents to allow for human-independent, document-to-document interaction. The use of middleware (**Q13**) will allow different applications to work together to present a seamless electronic experience for the customer.

- *Human interfaces*—The current (and future) e-business environment strives to achieve customer self-management. This can only be accomplished to its fullest extent through the implementation and deployment of intuitive and self-guiding customer interfaces. Customers should be able to navigate the Web sites easily without getting confused and should be able to complete their transactions with a minimal number of clicks. All Web site links should be operative and lead logically from one place to another. At the same time, it should be easy to interface with the help desk, customer relationship management tools, and self-help tools.

Additionally, the following technologies need to be incorporated at the core of the e-business effort:

- *Event-recognizing tools*—Business rules are a core competency of any business and the implementation or enforcement of these rules differs from company to company. The successful e-business deploys applications that allow the business to define important and critical business events with specific business rules that will be applied when these events are triggered within the system. For example, if an e-business system detects an order or a question being received by a new or prospective customer, then it should trigger messages to appropriate sales representatives for follow-up. It may also trigger sending e-mail or other messages to the new customers to inform them of related products or opportunities (i.e., cross-selling and up-selling opportunities). More important, these tools should recognize and report any exceptions, as these exceptions may be more important than the rules currently in place.

- *CRM*—The customer relationship management (CRM) (**Q65, Q66**) experience needs to be tailored to the environment being targeted, whether it is business-to-business (B2B) or business-to-consumer (B2C). The more that the e-business strategy focuses on being a "pure-play" as opposed to "bricks and clicks," the greater the reliance on electronic mechanisms to allow a client to communicate seamlessly with the organization. As a result, the CRM solution needs to integrate not only with the other information technology systems, but also with the phone systems, the Internet, and the paging systems. A successful e-business system integrates with all of a company's traditional information technology systems seamlessly.

Although the elements described above provide short- and medium-term technology areas to be addressed, medium- to long-term technology implementations include portals (**Q42**) clickstream analysis (**Q40**), front-end/back-end integration (**Q44**), and backup and recovery (**Q33**). The security (**Q30**) and privacy (**Q41**) issues are no different than those for any brick-and-mortar company.

43 ▬▬

THE FUTURE ENVIRONMENT

Each one of these technology areas is evolving rapidly, with new vendors and updated solutions coming to market almost on a daily basis. However, a glimpse of the future reveals some interesting and challenging times ahead.

Virtual Applications   Virtual applications relate to the concept of an application framework with "snap-in" applications that can be used in a plug-and-play manner to create new applications and services. The key enabler for these virtual applications is XML to link together the applications and services (**Q14**). One example is seen in the case of employee portal vendors that do not always create or sell all of the applications that a customer might want, such as customizable stock tickers and stock portfolio managers. Therefore, numerous third-party vendors sell "components," "modules," or "portlets" based on standards which can be easily plugged in to the main vendor's portal.

Customer Profiling   While the first implementation of this technology exists, the Holy Grail in the e-business environment includes the real-time profiling of clients. As clients browse through the portal, information is collected and analyzed in real-time. The result of this analysis is used to enhance the current client's session (**Q40**).

BSPs   As a progression from application service providers (ASPs) (**Q80**), the business service providers (BSPs) will provide a business function to an e-business such as providing enhanced application functionality and enhanced integration with other corporate (information technology) systems. Third-party logistics providers, for example, can operate a company's entire logistics function, including processes and systems.

Conclusion

It is not easy to successfully implement an e-business strategy. A critical part of the success lies in the technical elements. When they, along with the human elements and the business strategy itself, are properly in place, there is a much greater chance that the business endeavor will succeed.

---

44. What are the primary issues involved with integrating front-end and back-end systems?

JUDY SCOTT

Front-end systems are those systems which face toward the system's users, whether they are customers or employees. Back-end systems are those that provide the basic business functions such as financials, inventory, and manufacturing, which are often embedded in enterprise resource planning (ERP) systems (Q62). Integrating front-end and back-end systems is a major challenge and one of the largest budget items for CIOs.[1]

Need for Integration

Most companies are burdened with a complex mix of systems of varying vintages that are tenuously lashed together. Although many large companies have replaced hundreds of stand-alone systems with an ERP system, the promise of being able to function with just one system has never been fulfilled as companies rushed to add new systems to engage in e-business. Others add even more diverse systems when they undertake mergers and acquisitions. The result for most companies is multiple

---

[1] Tom Yager, "The Future of Application Integration," *InfoWorld Web Site*, 22 Feb. 2002, 5 Dec. 2002 <http://www.infoworld.com/articles/fe/xml/02/02/25/020225feintro.xml>.

systems on different hardware platforms, with different operating systems, using different databases, all with different data models, and different data definitions.

Into this difficult environment entered the e-business revolution. As Web sites proliferated in the second half of the 1990s, many organizations found that their new front-ends were independent from their back-office ERP system. Without the integration of front-end and enterprise systems, organizations had problems functioning effectively. For example, the lack of integration between online retailers' Web sites and their back-end enterprise systems manifested itself in poor customer service, fulfillment and distribution problems, failed and late deliveries, and lack of inventory control for online shopping. In 1999, when toys and other gifts did not arrive in time for Christmas, upset consumers initiated class action suits. Several on-line retailers, including CDnow, KBkids.com, and Toysrus.com, agreed to pay civil penalties totaling $1.5 million for variously failing to provide customers notice of delayed deliveries and continuing to promise prompt shipping despite backlogs."[2] Although most companies have solved these egregious problems, the fact remains that it is very difficult to integrate front-end and back-end systems. Executives who think that developing a good Web presence is simply a matter of quickly putting up a Web site will be disappointed in the result.

44 ▬

INTEGRATION ISSUES

Some of the integration issues that exist today are:

• *Getting data from the back-end to the front-end*—Organizations often underestimate the time, cost, and complexity to implement interfaces. Back-end systems have different definitions and layouts for similar sounding data elements, making it difficult to map them to the new front-end systems. Some systems do not expose their databases to the outside very easily, making it difficult to get the data for interfaces. Some newer back-end systems, such as ERP, have prebuilt application programming interfaces to enable connection at the application layer. Otherwise, integration needs to be at the database layer, and if that is not feasible, integration needs to be custom coded, requiring considerable time and cost.

• *Achieving speedy transactions through the firewall*—It is difficult and complex from a security and architectural standpoint to implement a Web system where people can access the back-end system processes and data through a firewall. Every transaction must pass through the firewall (both going to and coming from the back-end systems) (**Q30**). This introduces delay into the transaction, and can negatively impact the customer's experience.

---

[2] Amy Gunderson, "Toil and Trouble: Online Shopping Is Still a Muddle," *Fortune Web Site* 14 Aug. 2000, 5 Dec. 2002 <http://www.fortune.com/fortune/personalfortune/articles/0,15114,370204,00.html>.

- *Allowing only authorized users to access the back-end systems*—Many back-end systems were initially designed only for internal users. They often assume that all users are therefore authorized users. Controls over the initial access into these systems as well as controls over access to various components and data within the systems are often missing. When companies enter an e-business environment, they open up their back-end systems to customers entering through the Web. Significant effort and expense is required to provide the security adequate to protect the company's interests (**Q29**).

- *Dealing with competing sets of data sources*—Many organizations have implemented both an ERP system and a separate customer relationship management system (CRM). Both sets of systems are very comprehensive and create tightly linked databases of company information. Organizations need to determine which system will be the master and which will be the slave relative to customer data, sales data, pricing data, etc., for use in both the front- and back-end systems. This additionally raises issues such as data quality, its consistency and integrity.

- *Coping with inconsistent technology standards*—Technology standards in the e-business arena are still evolving. So it is most likely that no two companies communicate data in exactly the same way. Since most companies, of course, deal with many trading partners, each of whom may use their own variation on particular data definitions, it is extremely difficult to build a smoothly flowing set of transactions between trading partners in an e-business environment.

INTEGRATION SOLUTIONS

Some solutions that help resolve the previously discussed integration issues are:

- *Use prebuilt connectors*—An alternative that has become available is to purchase both the front-end as well as the back-end systems from a single enterprise software vendor. Most ERP vendors are rapidly providing Web capability as part of their overall product offerings. The disadvantage is that the ERP vendor may not have as much front-end functionality as best-of-breed software. Nevertheless, the integration provided by the vendor is a significant advantage. For companies that use multiple ERP vendors, several ERP business partners market ERP adaptors, which save deployment time by providing the code to integrate with a specified ERP system.

- *Utilize an EAI layer*—Enterprise Application Integration (EAI) software, (**Q13**), which is a middle layer of software that connects disparate systems, provides a vendor solution for integrating front-end e-commerce and back-end ERP systems.[3] EAI products promise an improvement over point-to-point integration, with increased flexibility, more maintainable solutions, and a faster return on investment. This is particularly

---

[3] Paul Korzeniowski, "EAI Tools Ease ERP Integration Woes," *eAI Journal Web Site* 1 Jan. 2000, 5 Dec. 2002 <http://www.eaijournal.com/Article.asp?ArticleID=153>.

true if the organization is integrating a number of different systems in an environment that is subject to frequent additions and changes. All the changes are done through the EAI layer, saving time and reducing complexity. For example, Toysrus.com formed a partnership with Amazon.com to manage its inventory and fulfillment.[4] Amazon.com used EAI software for integration, which let it see the inventory of its business partners in real-time. One risk with EAI, however, is when the ERP or Web systems vendors update their software, the EAI vendor often must also make changes so the interfaces will still work.

- *Start to deploy Web services*—Web services (**Q15**) is an emerging technology that provides some promise to solve the integration problem. Using tools supplied by a variety of vendors, companies can create software modules that run over Web protocols separately from the basic back-end systems. When the business functions are called for by the front-end system, they are provided over the Web rather than through the actual connection of the front-end to the back-end system. Quite a bit of sophisticated technology is necessary to make this approach work. Standards are still evolving as are the software development tools. But once this area matures, it is likely to provide significant relief in the quest for smooth systems integration.

- *Understand organizational considerations*—Despite the benefits of EAI software and Web services, there are technical, procedural, and cultural issues to address. An organization needs to know its processes before it integrates them (**Q58, Q59**). It must also be willing to change those processes, if necessary, to facilitate the systems integration plan. Business process modeling tools are available which help analysts cope with the complexity of concept integration. All this needs to take place before the technical tasks such as programming and customization are begun.

CONCLUSION

In summary, the primary issues involved with integrating front-end and ERP systems are both technical and organizational. Technical issues include weighing the advantages and disadvantages of alternative solutions and resolving data inconsistencies. Organizational issues such as resistance to change are typically associated with adoption of emerging technologies. Although standards are in a state of flux and the technologies are immature, they are rapidly evolving so organizations that are early adopters of the solutions may realize a competitive advantage.[5]

[4] Paul Kaihla, "Five Battle-Tested Rules of Online Retail," *Business 2.0 Web Site* April 2001, 5 Dec. 2002 <http://www.business2.com/articles/mag/0,1640,9599,FF.html>.
[5] Yager.

45. What e-business assumptions were proven wrong by the "dot.com crash"?

JUDY SCOTT

Although the dot.com crash during 2000–2001 was a shock to some, warning signs had been appearing for some time.[1] During the boom, it seemed that these start-ups could ignore traditional business principles (Q34). However, they made several financial, economic, consumer acceptance, and business model assumptions that have subsequently been proven wrong.[2]

FINANCIAL ASSUMPTIONS

Venture capital was plentiful and there was an assumption that availability would continue indefinitely.[3] Many companies raised significant cash in the public market but did not build business plans that brought them to a cash flow break-even point. When they needed additional funding, neither the public market nor the venture capital markets were willing to make new investments.

Some companies that were initially successful with high stock prices used their stock as currency to acquire other companies in an effort to build momentum to fuel future growth. But these other companies often had equally unsuccessful business models. The end result was that many companies vastly overpaid for such acquisitions. When they were later forced to write down these investments, it had a significantly negative impact on their financial condition.

ECONOMIC ASSUMPTIONS

There was an assumption that "getting big fast" was the highest priority. This assumption was based on what is known as the "theory of network externalities," which

---

[1] Timothy Hanrahan, "Dot.com Layoffs and Shutdowns," *The Wall Street Journal*, Rev., 28 Nov 2001, 31 July 2002 <http://interactive.wsj.com/public/resources/documents/dotcomlayoffs.htm>; Rachel Konrad, "End of the Beginning for Digital Economy," *CNET* 23 June 2000, 31 July 2002 <http://news.com.com/2009-1017-241989.html>; Peter Morville, "Lessons Learned from the Dot.Com Crash: A Passenger's Story," *Argus Center for Information Architechture* 12 Jan. 2001, 31 July 2002 <http://argus-acia.com/strange_connections/strange009.html>.

[2] Michael Porter, "Strategy and the Internet," *Harvard Business Review* 79.3 (2001): 63–78; Joan Magretta, "Why Business Models Matter," *Harvard Business Review* 80.5 (2002): 86–93.

[3] Krishna G. Palepu and Gillian Elcock, *The Role of Capital Market Intermediaries in the Dot.com Crash of 2000*, HBS Case 9-101-110, 7 June 2001.

explains that growth comes primarily from a "winner takes all" first-mover advantage.[4] As growth occurs and achieves a critical mass, it attracts more participants and becomes more valuable to the extent that other smaller networks cannot compete. This theory actually worked in the area of auctions as illustrated by the spectacular growth and dominance of eBay. On the other hand, there are many examples of dot.coms that erroneously tried to grow too fast, often when there was insufficient demand to justify their strategy. For example, Webvan—an online grocery provider—had overambitious plans for national expansion that were scaled back too late to prevent its demise.

A related assumption was that customers would be locked-in to their initial choice. Although some dot.coms such as Amazon.com have demonstrated strong customer loyalty and lock-in, generally consumers switch quite readily to competitors whose Web site is an easy click away. Despite personalization, lock-in is difficult for e-business because of the ease of clicking on another site and the availability of software agents that compare products.

Consumer Acceptance Assumptions

The gold rush mentality was also exemplified by the attitude of "build it and they will come." In the ensuing explosion of consumer Web sites, it became difficult to differentiate one from another. Without a recognized brand, companies had difficulties separating themselves from all the clutter. Consumers either could not find them or did not even know about them. And the cost and time necessary to build brand awareness proved to be insurmountable to most new market entrants.

Many dot.coms set up their businesses assuming that any type of product would sell on the Internet. Market research was either disregarded or ineffective. Start-ups assumed that consumers would instantly change their shopping habits for groceries, furniture, and a great variety of consumer products and services. They felt that the price and convenience advantages contemplated by their e-business storefronts would overcome any disadvantages consumers might have regarding their inability to see and touch the products. The reality was that products such as books, DVDs, and consumer electronic items, where a large inventory at competitive prices was crucial, seemed to sell well, but other "high-touch" products were not as successful.

In the case of groceries, for example, consumers were often hesitant to delegate the selection of fresh produce to others and were unwilling to pay delivery costs. For furniture, living.com and its competitors underestimated the risk that customers would be disappointed when they actually saw the product. The high cost of returns and the complexity and cost of delivering large, heavy products made this business segment unprofitable.

[4] R. Amit and C. Zott, "Value Creation in e-Business," *Strategic Management Journal* 22.6/7 (2001): 493–520.

In addition, many consumers hesitated purchasing something from someone unfamiliar to them; they wanted some assurance that they were dealing with a reputable party. eBay successfully addressed this issue by providing a feedback process where potential customers could see how previous customers rated sellers.

BUSINESS MODEL ASSUMPTIONS

In many business models, profitability was sacrificed for gains in market share. Free content or low prices were used to attract customers. The hope was that once a large enough market base was established, this base of business would cover their entire infrastructure and fixed costs. Any growth beyond that point was supposed to generate profitability. The reality was that few dot.coms ever reached that break-even point before they ran out of cash.

Another assumption was that "free" content would generate traffic to Web sites and would attract advertising dollars. The number of eyeballs became more important than revenues. This was paired with the assumption that Internet advertising would be effective. When certain types of advertising such as banner ads proved to be less successful than hoped, the dollars spent on these ads did not grow as anticipated. When combined with a general economic slowdown, online ad expenditures declined considerably, and business models that depended on online advertising became at risk.

A further faulty assumption was that the "cyberspace only" dot.coms would compete effectively against established retailers who could combine their Web sites with their physical stores. In addition to an established brand, the incumbent retailers found advantages in having both an electronic and a physical sales channel. Some customers wanted the ability to physically inspect the goods, interact with sales personnel, and return unsatisfactory merchandise. This gave the advantage to the "bricks and clicks" model (Q39).

In December 2001, at the International Conference on Information Systems, a debate titled "e-Business Autopsy" focused on some of the causes of the failures of e-business.[5] One of the items they pointed out contributing to the dot.com crash was the lack of understanding of the importance of a strong technical architecture. This was highlighted in the problems seen during the 1999 Christmas season when e-tailers failed to deliver toys and gifts in time, partly due to the lack of integration between their front-end and back-end systems (Q44). While good systems architecture and infrastructure are necessary, they are not sufficient for success. Dot.coms, such as living.com and Webvan, which had an over-reliance on technology, found that they

[5] Peter Weil et al., "E-Business Autopsy: What Have We Learned?" Panel Discussion Presentation, *Center for Information Systems Research Web Site* 19 Dec. 2001, 1 Aug. 2002 <http://web.mit.edu/cisr/www/ICIS_Panel_12-19-01_presentation.pdf>.

could not overcome the weaknesses of a poor business model.[6] The bad assumptions that caused the dot.com crash were not limited to the consumer side. Thousands of B2B (business-to-business) electronic marketplaces started-up based on the premise that participants would flock to them.[7] However, the entrepreneurs underestimated the reluctance of suppliers to participate.[8] Suppliers were concerned that their prices would be driven down to negligible margins. In addition, industry heavyweights, not wanting to pay transaction fees to intermediaries, formed consortiums to start their own e-marketplaces. The result is that most independent marketplaces have disappeared. The B2B marketplace will become dominated by large, industry-supported groups and individual companies that set up their own networks.

LESSONS LEARNED

In conclusion, there are several lessons learned from the dot.com crash:

- Companies should make wise use of their cash and never assume that future cash infusions will be available.

- "Get big fast" is a high-risk strategy if there is insufficient demand. Ineffective market research may incorrectly forecast strong demand. Consumers do not always accept new products and services quickly.

- Building brand awareness in e-business is just as difficult and expensive as in any retail endeavor.

- Profits do not always follow a first-mover advantage.[9]

- An offline presence has advantages, especially for "look-and-feel" products. Complementarities, such as brand and ease of returns, give "bricks and clicks" a competitive advantage over strictly online companies.

- Not every type of product is suitable for e-business. "Look-and-feel" products with variable quality need to be inexpensive.[10] Otherwise consumers won't be willing to risk purchasing them.

[6] Hal Berghel, "The Y2K E-Commerce Tumble," *Communications of the ACM* 44.8 (2001): 15–17.

[7] Richard Wise and David Morrison, "Beyond the Exchange: The Future of B2B," *Harvard Business Review* 78.6 (2000): 86–96.

[8] Lynda M. Applegate and Meredith Collura, *Ventro: Builder of B2B Businesses (Condensed)*, HBSP, HBS Case 9-801-274, 20 Dec. 2000.

[9] Peter Mellen, "The Myth of the Dot.Com Whiz Kids," *Georgetown Business* 13.2 (2001): 11.

[10] John M. de Figueiredo, "Finding Sustainable Profitability in Electronic Commerce," *MIT Sloan Management Review* 41.4 (2000): 41–52.

- The efficiencies of e-business may be countered by inefficiencies such as complex and expensive logistics for delivery and returns.

- "Over-reliance on technology cannot overcome the weaknesses of a bad business model."[11]

[11] Berghel 15–17.

SECTION 4 *IT and Organization*

BARBARA T. BAUER

Information technology is pervasive in organizations. Every department and unit in a business uses IT equipment and software, and every employee uses or is touched by it. Warehouse workers and retail clerks use sophisticated bar coding and handheld devices to track inventory shipments and sales. Data are collected and fed through the company to update all sorts of databases and applications such as procurement, order fulfillment and billing, accounting, financial, payroll, and personnel. The varieties of shared data and the applications involved are the circulation and metabolism of the business impacting everyone in the company from the night cleaning crew to the CEO.

An organization's structure and culture can either support or inhibit the use of information technology, determining the ability to use it and types of the benefits gained. The pervasive character of IT, along with its capabilities and the possible benefits, require careful, creative organizational planning and implementation. Because of the ubiquity of IT and because technology changes rapidly, careful consideration of the implications and interactions between information technology departments, company organizations, employees, customers, and external partners is a requirement for business success.

This section, "IT and Organization," addresses important organizational issues, starting with Question 46 on how IT affects an organization's ability to coordinate and control activities. Question 47 examines how IT alters other aspects of an organization's structure, such as communications, decision making, and power structures; and Question 48 discusses how an organization's culture can support or interfere with the effective use of IT. Knowing how to develop the right structure and encourage a positive culture is critical to success. Together, the answers to these three questions focus attention on the interrelationship between an organization's structure and culture and its ability to use IT effectively.

Technology projects do not take place within a vacuum. Questions 49 and 50 discuss how IT projects affect a technology's multiple stakeholders. Question 49 focuses on internal stakeholders, the other departments within an organization, while Question 50 examines how IT projects can affect two primary external stakeholders, customers and suppliers. The answers to these two questions show why not paying close attention to a project's stakeholders and their reactions to a project can lead to disaster.

Questions 51 and 52 focus on IT's role in capturing and sharing knowledge within an organization. Knowledge management, discussed in Question 51, is becoming a critical issue for companies, especially in rapidly changing industries where the ability to learn and act on those learnings makes a competitive difference. E-learning, as the answer to Question 52 shows, is emerging as the most flexible and cost-effective method for sharing knowledge and supporting continual learning.

Questions 53 through 56 focus specifically on the relationship between the IT organization and the firm as a whole. Question 53 tackles the challenge of defining the attributes that create an effective relationship between an IT organization and the rest of the business. Question 54 addresses the pros and cons of the centralized and decentralized IT organization structures. Question 55 discusses how the capability maturity model (CMM), a software process methodology, can be used to increase the effectiveness of an IT organization's software development and maintenance activities. Question 56 outlines how an IT organization can measure and demonstrate success to the rest of the business.

The last question in this section focuses on IT leadership, an increasingly important topic as the effectiveness of the IT function is becoming a make-or-break issue for company success. Question 57 explores the requirements for successful leadership on the part of CIOs, who have a very difficult and challenging responsibility. Without talent, experience, and business acumen on the part of the CIO, the issues raised in this book are unlikely to be properly addressed. They, above all, need to know the answers to all 100 questions.

The essential point in the "IT and Organization" section is straightforward. Unless an organization's structures, processes, and information technology are aligned, the chances of using IT effectively are slim. If the IT organization has strong, effective leadership that can demonstrably align its interests with those of the business as a whole, success is much more likely.

46. What impact does information technology have on an organization's ability to coordinate and control activities?

GRAHAM R. MCDONALD AND KEVIN OBENCHAIN

Information technology has had an enormous impact on organizations and how they operate since the late 1980s. As the rate of change in many industries accelerated, information technology provided ways to increase the speed and flexibility of an organization's operations by changing the way in which they coordinated and controlled activities. The inability to respond quickly to changing market conditions that plagued companies was largely a result of how organizations gathered, moved, and acted on information. Large organizations coordinated and controlled activities by passing information from person to person, or unit to unit. Information moved up the management hierarchy until it reached the proper level for decisions to be made. Then decisions were passed back down the chain of command for execution. As a result, the bigger the organization, the slower it acted.

In the most fundamental sense, an organization's ability to coordinate and control activities depends on the effectiveness of four key activities:

1. information gathering

2. resource planning

3. communication

4. feedback

Exponential advances in information technology have delivered tools changing these activities in ways that were unimaginable 25 years ago. We will illustrate some of the most important changes IT has made by tracing the history of a fictional high-tech engineering manufacturing company, High Tech, Inc. (HTI), through the eyes of one of its managers.

INFORMATION GATHERING

Welcome to HTI, a high-tech manufacturer that relies heavily on information to get its work done. In 1977, our plans, engineering designs, and reports were all recorded on paper. Finding a vendor meant looking through phone books. Our office staff filed, retrieved, and summarized information for management review. Transmittal of information across the country by mail or courier took days. Market research meant going to the library. Information was out of date and difficult to use. Access to it was slow and costly.

Today, HTI stores all its information digitally, and access to data is measured in microseconds. Managers can resort data with a click of a button, and electronic spreadsheets summarize it. Data and reports are available via a Web interface or e-mail. The company has numerous business intelligence and decision support tools to analyze this huge amount of data efficiently, such as data warehouses (Q20), data mining (Q21), and decision support systems (Q19), along with content and knowledge-management tools (Q51).

Twenty-five years ago, it could take months to sense a change in the market or competition. Today, HTI managers are aware of changes immediately and they react as quickly to external events as they do to information about internal operations, profitability, and risk factors. With the ability to see the big picture as well as the detail, they can quickly coordinate and control responses to changing market conditions.

RESOURCE PLANNING

In the 1970s, having a business plan meant you had a strategy. Detailed resource planning and scheduling was implemented in NASA (National Aeronautics and Space Administration), but not in smaller companies. We used card files for inventory tracking, and updated them manually. Each month we'd try to manually reconcile these to the general ledger transactions. Due to our lead times, reacting to market changes took six months or more. We either carried inventory or paid "expeditors" to fix data errors and poor estimates inherent in our manual systems, and to bypass cumbersome processes for moving parts through the factory. Purchasing—which had no idea of current demand—was often wrong and bought the wrong parts, or the right parts arrived late. Work orders were manually split into labor and material requirements and delivered to supervisors. Significant experience was required to be a supervisor or project manager because of the need to rely on instincts to make proper decisions.

Today, everything regarding projects, production, or engineering is stored digitally. Computer-aided design (CAD) tools eliminate wasteful prototyping, making it easy to share blueprints and specs with our vendors. Our product bill of material and the projected quantity is entered into our enterprise resource planning (Q62) system, which instantly sends orders to purchasing agents or vendors. Through our supply chain management system (Q67), vendors can see our material usage trends and stage their products to meet our tight schedules. Every procurement document is handled electronically instead of on paper. When we need more capacity, our project planning software makes automatic adjustments to reallocate our workforce. Work orders are calculated and displayed to production personnel online so they can make instant changes.

As a result, our lead times are only a week or two, allowing us to react to market changes quickly. Finished goods and work-in-process inventory is dramatically reduced, due to shortened lead times and higher inventory accuracy. We can recalculate our business plan projections, including resources, financials, and bills of material in a few minutes against a variety of business scenarios. These capabilities have enabled a new flexible and customer-focused business strategy, with fewer and less experienced staff.

Communication

Even a generation ago, HTI was on the bleeding-edge of communications technology (Q5). Faxes were our solution to real-time document transmittal with a whole department set up to send and receive them. We had speakerphones for long-distance conference calls. Answering machines, dictating machines, and tape recorders were used extensively by executives. For staff, a major improvement was the invention of "sticky notes." We still traveled for anything that required interactive work with our partners. Most of our correspondence was by letter. Communication to overseas vendors was very difficult, because our suppliers didn't have faxes and often we had translation difficulties. When the CEO communicated to the whole company, we met in the parking lot.

Now, fax and phone survive, but in a different form. Faxes are sent and received via PCs. Our main transaction systems often send faxes automatically, based on events or rules we control. E-mail didn't exist in 1977, but now everyone on staff has it, as well as digital voice mail. We can forward a message at the touch of a button to our Asian supplier. We can schedule a meeting via our groupware application, discuss a subject on our Web discussion board, or use Web conferencing. Any employee, can communicate with the entire company via the intranet or e-mail systems.

Communication has increased in both speed and reach. This speed has generally improved coordination and control because reach has eliminated some layers of our bureaucracy. However, increased reach means that nearly everyone can communicate anything to anybody. This challenges HTI individuals and managers to interpret and manage more frequent direct and time-sensitive communications, risking premature decisions, or ones executed too quickly. Therefore, it's important to find ways to help them categorize, interpret, and manage communication today.

FEEDBACK

HTI used to spend weeks evaluating monthly production data with teams of cost accountants using calculators. Results were typed-up for upper management. By the time we were done, the feedback was too late to make a difference. Our major source of customer feedback was the occasional complaint letter. Employees would sometimes use the suggestion box. Quality control meant that inspectors sat at the end of the production line, weeding out the bad units—they had no feedback on the production process upstream. Basically, we operated according to plan, but changing the plan was difficult.

Today, monitoring systems and feedback/control loops are a major part of every process in our business. We have online measurements for every critical process, and we adjust the process when the system notifies quality assurance that measurements are out of tolerance. Our activity-based cost systems calculate daily unit costs, even for indirect activities like sales calls or help line tickets. All managers have access to the data warehouse, so they can spot trends in performance and drill down to the details for explanations. All production issues and design changes are tracked by workflow systems, which assure closure of such issues. The status of projects is visible to the relevant project managers via our project team's Web site. Our online best-practices discussion boards allow full disclosure of our employees' ideas. Customer feedback is automatically solicited after every sale or comes in daily through our Web site.

This accurate, frequent, and consistent feedback allows the company to serve its customers better, cheaper, and faster. We can resolve process problems and change the plan, based on real-time feedback. Non-value-added activities and bottlenecks don't survive long here, because we provide tools for quality and continuous improvement.

DOES IT ADD UP TO COMPETITIVE ADVANTAGE?

Coordination and control at HTI improved dramatically over 25 years with the adoption of new information technologies. It sounds like a simple story—adopting new IT tools that enabled an organization to increase the speed of its operations and the flexibility of its strategy. These were, in fact, the promises on which much information technology was sold to corporations during the early 1990s. But HTI found that these technology investments did not necessarily improve its competitive position because its competitors were adopting them, too. As a result, these information technologies simply changed the "rules of the game" (Q1).

However, each firm's ability to implement these technologies effectively did make a difference. HTI found that using IT effectively required fundamental changes in its organization and structure—in how it communicated, made decisions, designed jobs, and distributed power. It was these changes, not the information technologies alone, that improved HTI's ability to respond to rapidly changing competitive conditions. And it was these changes that created a whole new set of organizational issues for managers to deal with. These changes and the new problems they created are described in the next answer (**Q47**).

---

47. How does information technology affect communication, decision making, job design, and power within an organization?

GRAHAM R. MCDONALD AND KEVIN OBENCHAIN

The operational speed and strategic flexibility that IT can create for organizations (**Q47**) is as much a result of the changes that take place in an organization's structure and culture as it is of the IT applications (**Q48**). Organizations that use IT to enable fast operations and flexible strategies typically experience radical organizational changes as well. The patterns of communication—who makes decisions—as well as the content and design of jobs, undergo a transformation. Technological and organizational changes eliminate many problems that managers used to face, but new ones are created instead. We continue with the story of High Tech, Inc. (started in **Q46**), as seen through the eyes of one of its managers to show what kinds of changes occur.

COMMUNICATION

In 1977, HTI had three plants located close together to enhance communication. Most communication was by telephone, memo, or a personal visit. My co-worker took a message if I was away from my desk. A secretary typed our memos, checked spelling, and maintained my boss's daily schedule. Clerks filed documents needed for future reference. We mailed or faxed all reports to the plants. Analytical information and announcements were distributed through the rigid hierarchy of our organization. As a middle manager, my job was to train employees and control the flow of information to them. Employees were fed information on a "need-to-know" basis.

Today, HTI's headquarters is in the United States, while our plants are in Mexico and Asia. The primary form of communication is e-mail, occasionally supplemented by Web conferencing. Each employee has a pager, cell phone, PDA, or laptop. With multiple communication channels, our traveling and home-based workers may miss personal contact but they never miss any required business information. Transmittal lag time has decreased to almost zero. If we can't contact each other directly, we can always carry on "conversations" via e-mail, voice mail, or instant messaging. Due to our "democratic" information system, the organization is flatter because fewer middle managers are needed to control the flow of information. Communication is more direct, often crossing functional lines. Customized intranet portals (**Q42**) provide personalized views of job-related information. The secretaries and file clerks we used to have were replaced by online calendars, spell checkers, data warehouses, and direct network access to our digital documents.

These changes increased productivity while creating a new set of challenges. Special tools, such as search engines, filters, and alarms, are required to manage our communication volume. Since it's easy to send things digitally, almost everything gets sent to everyone—whether they need it or not. Security is a much larger problem today; "easy to transmit" is also "easy to lose." Immediate communication, combined with lack of management control, sometimes results in serious errors. Communication has increased the velocity of our successful business, but it can speed us just as quickly toward failure.

DECISION MAKING

HTI used to be an authoritarian culture. Only the higher level managers knew enough to make the right call—particularly involving processes and customer/supplier relations. If we wished to modify a product, we had to gather files, meet with engineers and marketing, prepare presentations for the board, and get a decision weeks later. Individuals were hired for the sole purpose of preparing materials for someone else to make a decision. This inefficient process meant that we couldn't evaluate all scenarios and risks before a decision was needed. Change and adaptation were difficult when all decisions were made by a handful of people.

Now, HTI is an innovative leader in its market segment. Yes, we've changed our culture to empower our employees. But we couldn't have done that without new technology. Some routine decisions, like credit limits, are now embedded into our software logic. Our customer service staff has access to repair records online, giving them authority to decide whether or not to give the customer a refund. Our sales data warehouse (**Q20**) provides historical information, so salespeople can grant discounts to customers with good credit. Since our ERP system (**Q62**) supports customized products, sales personnel can decide independently whether to adjust the product mix each month. Every employee has access to the product knowledge-base (**Q51**) and just-in-time training delivered through our e-learning system (**Q52**). The current business plan and operating results are posted on the intranet (**Q42**). We subscribe to online industry news sources that alert the proper employee when a response is required. Both management and staff benefit from tools such as expert systems, decision support systems (**Q19**), graphical displays of summary data, and automated exception reporting. Every employee makes decisions using a common set of resources.

However, our empowered employees can spin us out of control. Appropriate use of this freedom and decentralization depends on our sophisticated use of IT systems and well-designed, flexible business processes. Employees must understand the "big picture," and their own authority and responsibilities in the context of our business strategy. Therefore, our employees need to be "thinkers," not just "doers," and this is reflected in our recruiting and training strategies (**Q52**). Consequently, HTI is a very flexible and adaptable organization that quickly reacts to competition with focus.

Jobs

In the early days, HTI only used computers for its inventory and shipping systems. Data entry, typing, report preparation, filing, and most other jobs related to manually collecting and analyzing data were specialist positions. Personal knowledge of process was very important, and we depended heavily on our most senior employees to show people how to work correctly and review their output. Since managers were reviewers and decision makers, they didn't need to know how to type, prepare fancy reports, or enter data.

Now, every HTI employee must be computer-literate. Without secretaries and staff, managers must be able to type and use spreadsheets. Electronic content management tasks, such as publishing reports to our intranet or saving files to appropriate places on the network, have eliminated the need for file clerks. We have online training classes and work instructions for the line employees (**Q52**), who make many of their own decisions regarding the details of their processes. Most of our employees view their jobs as learning experiences, preparing them for more complex positions. Our labor productivity and morale are quite high.

Still, we have issues with job content. Our people find themselves doing some mundane clerical work that would previously have been done by assistants. Data and message overload is a common problem. We have trouble supporting the myriad desktop applications and productivity tools used by our employees. Sometimes we design processes to support the software, instead of the business need (**Q56**).

Power

Twenty-five years ago, the most important person at HTI was our CEO. He made the most important decisions, while each level below him had less authority. Information was the currency of power, passed sparingly to our staff for fear it would undermine the formal authority of our management hierarchy. Centralization of decision making meant that the closer you were to the boss, the more powerful you were. Even our CEO's secretary was powerful because she controlled his schedule.

Now, anyone can reach the CEO via e-mail. Most information is immediately published electronically. Information is secured by strict IT processes and access is controlled by company policy, not by an individual manager. If you need something done, it's best to go directly to the process team or a project manager. Due to our delegation of decision making, actual power is often in the hands of the experts doing the task. This often works best for the customer and provides us flexibility.

However, there have been some unintended consequences. For example, our IT organization made the technology selection of our ERP system based on their criteria rather than on whether it helped meet the overall corporate strategy (Q53). As a result, the system is not a particularly good fit for the corporation. Now, the CEO is more careful about defining the decision makers for such important issues. The informality of the power shift has resulted in minor wars between hierarchical authority and other centers of influence. This generates confusion among our teams.

Conclusion

As HTI's experience shows, it is possible to create flexible, adaptable, and lean organizations with the help of information technology. But it also requires significant organizational changes to capture IT's benefits. HTI's experience also shows that the mere application of the latest technologies is not a panacea for core management issues. It simply creates new ones. Life was simpler—and slower—before the information technology revolution, and so were the solutions. Now, every process improvement seems to have "technical issues," people deal with information overload, and what were once clear lines of authority and responsibility are sometimes ambiguous.

Capturing the strategic and operational benefits of new technologies can be difficult because of the organizational transformation required (Q60). These changes can eliminate the problems associated with bureaucracy and the inability to respond to changing market conditions quickly. But they create new organizational issues that managers have to deal with. Many organizations have little choice other than to adapt. If your competitors have adopted these technologies and made the necessary organizational changes, you must make them as well or you will not survive.

---

48. What role does an organization's culture play in determining the benefits gained from new technologies?

RAYMOND F. ZAMMUTO

An often-cited factor in technology implementation failures, or the inability to gain the promised benefits of new technologies (Q46, Q47), is an organization's culture.

The simple answer to the question of how an organization's culture contributes to implementation failure is that new technologies can disrupt existing ways of doing things, many of which are culturally embedded in an organization. As such, the changes required to implement a new technology can trigger resistance. However, the answer isn't that simple and understanding why an organization can or cannot gain the benefits of new technologies also requires an understanding of where the benefits actually come from.

Organization Culture

An organization's culture can be broadly thought of as the shared, implicit rules that govern how people think and act in an organization. These rules reflect underlying values and beliefs about how the world works and how an organization and its members need to act to survive in it. While implicit, these rules manifest themselves in very visible ways—in an organization's structure, its reward system, the distribution of decision-making authority and power, management practices, and the treatment of individuals within it. When a new technology bumps up against these visible cultural manifestations by dictating that something be done differently, the chances for successful implementation decrease.

Research findings on the relationship between organizational culture and technology implementation generally point in the same direction regardless of the model of organizational culture used in the research. These studies show that organizations with cultures emphasizing autonomy, trust, team orientation, information sharing, and individual initiative are more likely to implement new technologies successfully than organizations with cultures emphasizing rule orientation, production focus, hierarchy, and compliance.[1] Their findings are not startling and they are entirely consistent with the broader literature on organizational change. Literally interpreted, they indicate that the more bureaucratic an organization is, the more difficulty it will experience in implementing a new technology and gaining its benefits. However, why this is the case may come as a surprise.

High-Performance Management Practices

There is a small amount of research and anecdotal evidence showing that many of the benefits ascribed to new technologies are realized during the organizational restructuring that occurs prior to installing them. Consider the conclusion that Jeffrey

---

[1] R. F. Zammuto and E. J. O'Connor, "Gaining the Benefits of Advanced Manufacturing Technologies: The Roles of Organization Design and Culture," *Academy of Management Review* 17 (1992): 701–28; K. A. Bates et al., "The Crucial Interrelationship between Manufacturing Strategy and Organizational Culture," *Management Science* 41 (1995): 1565–80.

Pfeffer, a Stanford Business School professor, drew from a review of studies on high-performance management practices:

> What the evidence to be presented here shows—drawing from studies of the survival rates of initial public offerings; studies of profitability and stock prices in large samples of companies from multiple industries; and detailed research in the automobile, apparel, semi-conductor, steel manufacturing, oil refining, and service industries—is this: Substantial gains, on the order of 40 percent or so, can be obtained by implementing high-performance management practices.[2]

Examples of high-performance management practices are:

- self-managed and cross-functional teams,
- autonomy and decentralized decision making,
- performance-based compensation,
- significant investments in employee training and education,
- widely shared information,
- reduced status differences.

These are the same practices that typically precede a successful technology implementation. This indicates that many of the performance gains ascribed to new technologies are actually derived from revamping an organization's culture and its associated structure. In other words, the speed, flexibility, and efficiencies promised by many new technologies are as much characteristics of an organization's work practices and structure as they are of a new technology.

A new technology can leverage the potential already present in an organization, but it cannot in itself provide these benefits. For example, an enterprise resource planning system (Q62) may make it possible for a customer service representative to have access to all the information needed to provide one-stop service to a customer. However, that customer service representative will be unable to provide that service unless he or she is authorized to access the information and empowered to use it, factors that are organizationally determined. In essence, an up-and-running new technology may make increased levels of performance technologically possible, but the benefits will not be realized unless they are culturally and organizationally feasible.

IMPLICATIONS

This characterization of the relationship between organizational culture and technology implementation success has a number of implications for managers. The

---

[2] Jeffrey Pfeffer, *The Human Equation: Building Profits by Putting People First* (Boston: HBSP, 1998), 32.

obvious implications are that the more bureaucratic an organization's culture and structure:

- the less likely that a new technology can be successfully implemented,

- the less likely that many of the promised benefits can be achieved even if the organization gets the technology up-and-running,

- the longer the implementation process will take before a technology's promised benefits can be achieved,

- the greater the soft costs (restructuring, retraining, etc.) vs. the hard costs (acquisition costs of the technology) of implementation (**Q74**).

This analysis also suggests that managers need to conduct a thorough and honest organizational review (**Q60**) in addition to a technology assessment (**Q4**) as part of the planning process. Managers need to seriously question whether a technology is consistent with the way an organization currently operates. If it is not, they should assess the extent to which organizational changes are required prior to introducing a technology, the cost of those changes, and the time it will take to make them.

Look at the organizational assessment carefully. Ask how likely it is that the proposed technology implementation will be successful given the magnitude, cost, and time required for the needed organizational changes. If significant cultural and organizational barriers exist, one option is "green fielding" the technology. Green fielding literally means setting up the technology in a new location or plant where the culture and structure of the organization can be created with the technology in mind, avoiding the resistance likely to be encountered by trying to implement it in the existing organization. If green fielding is not possible, managers should question the wisdom of attempting the technology introduction and seriously consider investing the resources in more traditional organizational change efforts that could make their organization receptive to future technology introductions.

48 ▬▬

49. How will other departments within your organization react to a technology project?

DAVID R. LAUBE

THE PROPOSAL

In a large division of the XYZ Corp., the senior VP of sales walked into the office of the IT director supporting his division. He explained that he needed to open new markets geographically and find alternative sales channels in order to increase the sales of their products. He wanted the IT executive to partner with him on an e-business initiative that would change the way the company would do business. He envisioned a powerful Web site that would attract new customers and allow them to process their orders and obtain customer service online. He wanted to build an electronic bond with his customers for all their relationships—from bill paying to warranty repair. He had discretionary budget available and was willing to fund the IT organization to initiate and complete this project. But, he needed it done quickly.

THE PROJECT BEGINS

The IT executive agreed to undertake the project. Because he did not have available staff for this extra work, he hired a services firm that he knew had successfully completed a similar project. This firm agreed to the budget and timetable only if they could use their own methodology and the software platform and database design with which they were familiar. The project started moving very quickly.

As the project progressed, several other departments in the company began to hear about it. Questions and concerns started to arise and these departments demanded that their issues be considered.

MARKETING

The head of marketing proclaimed that they were in charge of the brand and the corporate image. As such, they demanded that the treatment of the brand on the Web site be consistent with the current branding program. Since they had hired a PR firm to develop a new color scheme for all of the company's collateral marketing materials, they wanted the PR firm to be the ones that did the artistic design of the Web pages. They also insisted that any promotional campaigns that utilized the Web site be coordinated with the campaigns they already had planned.

Finally, they wanted to test the "look and feel" of the Web site to see if it was up to the standards of their competitors. Particularly, they wanted to ensure that any customer could purchase a product in only three clicks, which they had heard was a good Web site design.

OPERATIONS

When the head of operations heard about the project, he immediately demanded a meeting with the IT and sales organizations. He was concerned that the inclusion of the entire product catalog on the Web site would generate sales in products that he no longer stocked in quantity.

Given his outdated product fulfillment system, he was also concerned about promises of rapid delivery that would be made. In fact, he demanded that significant changes be made to modernize his warehousing, inventory, and shipping systems before this Web site was made operational. The implications were that without such modernization, customer service would suffer.

HUMAN RESOURCES

The head of HR quickly voiced her concern. The implications on the skills and quality of the workforce needed to be discussed. Would the move to an e-business channel cause a downsizing of the current customer service workforce? And what about the different training and skills needed for this new approach to business?

FINANCE

When the business unit CFO heard about the project, he was furious. Where was the business case and what was the anticipated ROI and payback for the project? He demanded that a finance representative be placed on the project team and that regular reviews be conducted regarding its costs.

The corporate controller added her concern, wanting to know exactly what sales tax jurisdictions would now be opened up and pointed out to the CFO that this project would subject the entire corporation's revenues to income tax in certain states.

She also questioned the sales and return policies contemplated for the Web site since they would change the accounting treatment for sales and require a financial reserve for returned merchandise. The treasurer wanted to know how sales on the Web site would impact cash collections and wanted the project to pay for the credit card fees incurred when customers paid via that method.

LEGAL

Even the lawyers were concerned. They wanted the opportunity to review any customer contracts that might be embedded in the product sales process. They also pointed out that the company would need to establish a privacy policy and generate controls to ensure that the policy was followed.

They asked for time to review the laws in all the new states where they would now be conducting business to determine if the Web site followed the laws in the areas of warranties and merchandise returns.

INFORMATION TECHNOLOGY

The project then drew criticism from within the IT department. The resource manager pointed out that they had skilled individuals who were just finishing a previous project. Therefore, the outside vendor should not have been hired.

The chief architect said that the software platform and development tools used by the services company were not the standard for the IT organization. Thus, much higher maintenance costs and software license fees would be incurred in the future, which were not included in the project budget.

The data center team demanded to know a precise forecast of the volumes anticipated to hit the Web site and gave a dire prediction of the cost of new servers and data network expenses.

The database management group pointed out that the databases to be used by the project had notoriously dirty data and that cleanup of those data errors would likely be long and costly.

OTHER DIVISIONS

Divisions selling other products joined in the furor. They insisted that their products also be included on the Web site. They also wanted to make sure that their products were featured just as prominently as were those of the sponsoring division.

HYPOTHETICAL OR REALITY?

Is this hypothetical example far fetched? Far from it . . . in fact, portions of this example are encountered every day in corporate life. It just displays one irrevocable fact; a system is rarely an island. Usually its tentacles reach everywhere throughout the organization. Most technology projects will have multiple stakeholders, individuals and groups that have a stake in the outcome of a project because it affects them. They will react to a project based on the way that it affects them and their responsibilities.

In order to have a successful technology project, these broad, company-wide issues must be dealt with. Some suggestions follow.

PROPER STAKEHOLDER IDENTIFICATION

When assigning staff to prepare the project's requirements, choose people who have a broad knowledge of the business *and* technology. Identify all issues that are likely to arise by constructing a "reaction" chart. In the first column, list affected departments based on whose responsibilities it will affect and on whose territory it will intrude. Label the next two columns "positive reactions" and "negative reactions" and identify elements of the project that will evoke positive and negative reactions by each department. At first pass, this exercise can help a project's managers identify likely points of support and resistance and begin surfacing issues that will need to be dealt with.

Then ensure that each organization which is likely to be impacted by the project is given a chance to provide input. That way, all stakeholders can sign on to support the project. Create a steering board (**Q94**, **Q95**) that can provide representative input from affected departments. This may complicate the project's requirements and take more time at the beginning. However, it is worth the effort.

49 ▬

INCLUDE INDIRECT COSTS AND TIME

Be sure to include indirect costs and time in the project's business case and budget (**Q74**). When peripheral impacts start to become more clear, it often leads to identifying costs that will be incurred by organizations outside the directly impacted groups. These are real costs to the corporation and even though they might adversely affect the attractiveness of the business case, if funding for indirect costs is not included, the necessary work might not get done. When that happens, the success of the project is in jeopardy.

RESOLVE ALL INTERNAL ISSUES QUICKLY

Frequently issues like those described arise while the project is in progress. Are these issues valid? They certainly are in the eyes of the group raising them. So deal with them quickly. Otherwise, modifications to the project might be required that cause significant rework, raise the project cost, delay its implementation, or even, if the conflict is serious enough, result in cancellation of the project (**Q100**).

SUMMARY

When a technology project is planned properly within the context of the organization as a whole, then all of the important issues will be addressed. The chances that the project will succeed then rise dramatically.

---

50. Why do customers and suppliers sometimes react negatively to an organization's IT projects?

ALFRED L. STECKLEIN AND BARBARA T. BAUER

Thinking about the recognition he would receive from company executives, Tom sauntered into his office in the phone company's largest warehouse. He had spearheaded the implementation of a new application to provide online procurement, ordering of equipment, warehouse receipt and tracking, and distribution of specialized equipment to the company's largest customers. The conversion occurred over the weekend and he had invited several important customers and suppliers to a demonstration. His reverie stopped abruptly as his IT colleague, Greg, intercepted him in front of his office. "We've got a big problem. Your department dropped the ball. We've had trouble calls all morning from the equipment suppliers who think they're getting duplicate orders, and the parts needed for the new construction downtown haven't shipped. We tested everything, so I know it's not the system."

Tom had worked closely with Greg to make sure the computer center and his own warehouse users had been trained on the system. But as he listened with escalating concern, he realized neither the key customers nor their suppliers had been in the loop. With a sinking feeling, he recognized that there must be significant changes in their systems and work centers as well. Since they were implementing a standard package, he hadn't worried about impacts outside the company. How big a problem did they have, and what could they do to solve it?

He realized the problems were very serious and that his job was probably at stake. As his face reddened with embarrassment, he demanded: "Whose job was it to work with our customers and suppliers?" There was a deafening silence.

ANALYSIS

Is this fictional scenario far fetched and unusual? Unfortunately, no. Is it avoidable? Yes, with effort, attention, and planning. In the world of IT projects, even with the best of intentions, a firm's business customers or business partners all too frequently end up frustrated and unhappy. Why does this happen and what can be done to minimize or eliminate the ill effects? Avoiding the problems described in this scenario, or even subsets of it, requires examining exactly how IT projects affect the total organization, and its suppliers and customers. The fictional scenario is based on a typical inventory project because of the obvious impact to both customers and suppliers, but every project has external stakeholders. While the end users in company work centers and the IT professionals developing the system are the most directly affected, ignoring *any* stakeholder puts the entire effort at risk.

IT projects, including this unfortunate example, start with some desired improvement or objective for the company: reduced cost, improved customer service, or similar objectives. These benefits determine which work centers and internal organizations are affected. Centers directly receiving benefits are among the most important project stakeholders, but all affected operations, including external business partners and customers, must be involved in planning and implementation. The project team must develop appropriate mechanisms to include external stakeholders when identifying requirements and communicating project plan information.

Since many project team meetings need some privacy to get tough issues resolved internally, there usually needs to be a separate forum for external stakeholders. Whichever approach is selected, supplier and customer tasks and requirements must be integrated into the overall project plan. Both supplier and customer end users must be able to approach a new application with confidence, and their information system colleagues need to prepare for the necessary functionality, application robustness, and user support. Any introduction of new information system technology should be accompanied by excellent user training including process flows, and complete explanations of any new hardware, application software, and end user capabilities. Unless users attain appropriate skills and accept the new system as a useful tool, the scenario described is a likely result.

SUPPLIERS

With the increasing use of B2B e-commerce, many previously isolated internal applications now must provide online access to personnel in supplier or partner companies, or to automated systems in these companies. In the opening scenario, inventory suppliers for the warehouses needed to identify their shipments consistently with the new information system prior to shipping. For this to happen, explicit efforts are needed to define these requirements, educate the suppliers, gain their agreement, and develop specific implementation time lines for each unique supplier. These required changes can cause suppliers to balk due to anticipated additional costs, new shipping procedures, and training for their employees, etc. Especially in sophisticated business process applications, the ripple effect of a change in the process can be far reaching, much like a chain of dominoes falling one after the other (**Q68**). Without very careful systems engineering and requirements, and thorough and precise integration and testing, new applications which integrate processes from different companies will result in rude shocks. The visibility of this issue increases with the broader use of XML technology and Web services (**Q14, Q15**). It is easy to overlook differences in the detailed internal definitions of common objects, such as product catalogs, in two different company XML implementations.

CUSTOMERS

At the boundaries of the ripple outward from a new application are the company's customers. In the phone company scenario, customers now receive equipment "just in time" with automatic updates to their respective information systems. As with suppliers, the requirements, implementation agreements, project tasks, and time lines for each customer need to be created and communicated. Done correctly and proactively, this is an opportunity for the company to improve customer loyalty. Done thoughtlessly, it can drive customers to do business with competitors.

Another important step in ensuring customer satisfaction is the early and constant involvement of sales and marketing groups within the company. These groups are the lifeline to the external customer and have the responsibility for the ultimate customer experience. Neither the internal company sponsors nor the IT team itself should approach customers without the full involvement and support of the accountable sales and marketing leaders. The internal project team should spend time in early project meetings to develop an understanding of their project's impact on customers and create plans for eliminating potentially negative effects. (The problems created by a major ERP system implementation that did not adequately address customer impact are discussed elsewhere in this book [**Q87**].)

LESSONS LEARNED

A famous quote from Thomas Merton starts: "No man is an island unto himself . . . ." The intent of this quote should be the mantra of every successful IT project. IT applications are now the lifeblood and heartbeat of business processes and the nerve endings of each project reach many different groups—inside and outside the company. Successful IT and business unit leaders press hard to understand the impact of business process change on their external colleagues and plan how to contain the ripple effect and support all the involved stakeholders.

Fortunately, achieving success and avoiding the painful encounters experienced by Tom and Greg are a "simple matter" of applying appropriate business planning and project management. This "simple matter" requires a team with experience and the program and project processes to ensure adequate stakeholder representation and response. Every project must be examined for impact on external suppliers and customers. Proper methodologies, disciplined project management, and effective communications are the preventive medicine. Implemented correctly, not only are bad reactions from customers and suppliers avoided, but the relationships formed with all groups, especially customers and business partners, can also be deepened and solidified.[1]

51. What is "knowledge management"?

STEVEN WALCZAK AND C. MARLENA FIOL

The XYZ Corporation's eastern sales office submitted a bid on an important job. What they did not realize is that their western office bid on a similar job. The competitors for both bids were the same. The western office lost the bid because of some very aggressive terms offered by one of the competitors. XYZ could have easily matched or beat those terms on the eastern bid. But because their two offices didn't communicate the bid details, the eastern bid was lost as well. This scenario, or some version of it, occurs frequently in today's organizations. Critical business knowledge existed inside the organization, but others either didn't know it existed, or had no means to obtain it. The business framework that serves as the foundation for this issue is often referred to as knowledge management.

Knowledge management (KM) in organizations is concerned with acquiring, creating, distributing, and applying knowledge for competitive advantage. Knowledge is one of an organization's most important strategic assets. Managing this asset is becoming more important and more difficult. The amount of information inside companies is increasing two percent per month.[1] That means that in approximately 35 months, the information available for decision making will double. Consequently everyone's ability to transform information into work is becoming more important

---

[1] We appreciate the assistance of Terry Cheung on an earlier draft of this answer.

[1] Bill Jensen, "Communication or Knowledge Management?" *Communication World* June–July 1998: 44–47.

and more complicated. Maintaining competitiveness in such an environment makes the astute management of knowledge imperative.

Knowledge Management

We begin by dissecting the term *knowledge management* into its component parts, knowledge and its management. Knowledge is an organizational asset. Related terms include *intellectual capital*, *intellectual assets*, and *learning*. Knowledge exists in many different forms. For example, it exists tacitly in the heads of the employees of an organization. In addition to holding this tacit knowledge, people also hold filters for interpreting it and determining appropriate applications. For example, marketing and finance experts within the same organization may have similar knowledge about their firm's service delivery processes but interpret it in very different ways. Finance experts will tend to view their knowledge of service delivery from the perspective of cost and efficiency, while marketing folks will see it in terms of increased sales and improved customer relationships.

Knowledge also exists in more explicit forms as contained in the records of an organization. Such records may be electronic, as in a database of customers for a CRM system; on paper, such as the employee handbook and standard operating procedures; or in any other recordable media (e.g., videotapes of the shareholders meeting). The encoding of information into an explicit record format and subsequent distribution may remove the context that people use implicitly in determining the appropriateness of the knowledge application. Web searches that are performed using standard search engines, such as AltaVista, provide an example of the loss of context suffered when knowledge is encoded into explicit databases. The search term has tacit meaning and context to the individual performing the search, but the search engine does not know the context and hence returns all pages from the Web that contain the specified search terms. It is then up to the search initiator to construct a meaningful context around the new information for determining the application and reuse of the knowledge item.

We turn next to the management component of KM. The enterprise-wide management of knowledge is a process that involves (1) the mapping of knowledge and identification of knowledge gaps, (2) the acquisition of new knowledge to fill the gaps, and (3) the encoding and distribution of that knowledge. Since knowledge is tacitly held by individuals, as well as contained more explicitly in electronic (database) format and other explicit forms of encoding, the management of each of these phases must address both human and technological issues. The interrelated phases are delineated in Figure 51.1.

Figure 51.1 Interrelation of Knowledge Management Processes

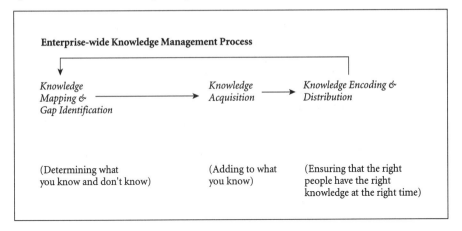

KNOWLEDGE MAPPING AND GAP IDENTIFICATION

Knowledge mapping and gap identification have to do with determining what is known and not known within the organization. This process is critical, given that it drives the remaining phases of knowledge management. But it is often severely neglected. How often have organizational leaders thought that people in their organization had the knowledge to successfully complete a project, when in reality that knowledge was sorely lacking?

Identifying explicitly documented knowledge within your organization is a challenge, but not nearly the challenge of identifying what knowledge resides in people's heads. To come to understand what people tacitly know and don't know, it is important to promote a culture in which it's OK to not have all the answers. When people are not fearful of the consequences of not knowing, they will better ascertain where the knowledge gaps lie and be better able to take actions to fill those gaps. Ideally, an organization wants to create a culture where sharing knowledge to fill gaps is the norm and not the exception.

KNOWLEDGE ACQUISITION

Knowledge acquisition is the process of increasing the knowledge or intellectual capital of an individual or team and consequently the organization as a whole. Businesses that are successful at maintaining high levels of knowledge acquisition have come to be known as *learning organizations*. Increasing knowledge may occur as the result of the creation of entirely new knowledge. More often it is achieved through the transfer and recombination of existing knowledge, such as when a mentor imparts a new framework for solving a specific type of business problem.

Numerous technologies support knowledge acquisition (Q52). Learning management systems (LMS) and content management systems (CMS) come in many forms and are supplied by various providers. But investing in an LMS or CMS system will be a waste of money if it doesn't contain information that is meaningful to users or if people fail to use it as planned. For example, several years ago Texaco's Information Technology group installed Lotus Notes, hoping it would lead to more collaboration and organizational learning. They soon discovered that employees only used Lotus Notes for e-mail. Not until they found an urgent need to collaborate and change the way they worked together, did they use Lotus Notes the way the IT group had envisioned.[2] Information technology can support and reinforce an organization's norms about generating new ideas and information, but it cannot itself create those norms.

KNOWLEDGE ENCODING AND DISTRIBUTION

Knowledge encoding and distribution has to do with ensuring that the right people have the right knowledge at the right time. A common approach to storing and disseminating information is through the implementation of a large database (Q20) or ERP system (Q62). While databases serve to hold vast quantities of information, access to the information in a database may be cumbersome and consequently prevent decision makers from obtaining needed information at the right time. As an example, if an employee needs to navigate through twelve different query screens to access desired information from a performance support database, the database will likely not be utilized. Data warehouses that collect and combine information from different transactional systems (Q18), and group support systems that share information among team members (Q22), can increase the accessibility of information.

E-mail or other electronic communication systems, such as instant messaging or chat rooms, may also facilitate the timely distribution of information resources between individuals or teams. The asynchronous nature of e-mail implies that a business culture must already exist that necessitates the reading and response to e-mail messages.

In addition to ERP, e-mail, and instant messaging, corporate intranets allow employees to create Web pages containing vast amounts of important information that can be easily shared through links or internal search engines. *Blogs* (Weblogs), a new information sharing technology, are like diaries where people can record their information, embed links, and generate a large network of discussion groups and forums

---

[2] Richard McDermott, "Why Information Technology Inspired but Cannot Deliver Knowledge Management," *California Management Review* 41.4 (1999): 103–17.

on topics that may be critical to a business. In fact, a new term, *klogs*, has been coined for *blogs* that are related to knowledge management.[3]

To promote sharing of the tacit knowledge that people carry around in their heads, a knowledge-sharing business culture must exist. What does this mean? We have traditionally rewarded employees for their individual skills, including knowledge, and thus a culture of knowledge hoarding has become pervasive, at least within the United States. We must shift our focus from rewarding individuals to rewarding groups or teams for collaborative decision making to promote a knowledge-sharing culture. AES (American Energy Systems) is an example of a collaborative decision-making culture, where individuals are empowered to make decisions and are held accountable for those decisions. At AES, decision makers are encouraged to gather information from their fellow employees to make the highest quality decisions. This knowledge-sharing atmosphere is a fundamental part of AES's corporate culture.[4] So while information technology is a great facilitator of KM, the users of the technology are the keys to success. If people choose not to share what they know, no amount of technology will make a difference.

Figure 51.1 shows a feedback loop from knowledge encoding and distribution back to knowledge mapping and gap identification processes. The implication is that the process of managing knowledge is never finished. What one learns through knowledge encoding and distribution is a critical input for determining where the gaps may lie.

51

CONCLUSION

While organizations rarely set out to create a knowledge management system or knowledge management friendly culture (Q48), many of them realize the importance of creating, acquiring, and sharing their collective corporate knowledge. When that importance can be expressed in terms of a business benefit (such as winning more contracts, capitalizing on research ideas, sharing cost-saving ideas, etc.), then the organization can support the necessary technology investments and promote the culture required to create that competitive edge in a truly learning organization.

[3] Rebecca Blood, *The Weblog Handbook: Practical Advice On Creating and Maintaining Your Blog* (Cambridge: Perseus, 2002); John Rodzvilla, *We've Got Blog: How Weblogs Are Changing Our Future* (Cambridge: Perseus, 2002); *Blogger Web Site* n.d., 5 Dec. 2002 <http://www.blogger.com>; *Webcrimson Web Site* n.d., 5 Dec. 2002 <http://www.webcrimson.com>.

[4] "AES Values and Principles," *AES Corporate Web Site* n.d., 5 Dec. 2002 <http://www.aesc .com/culture>.

52. Does an e-learning strategy improve a company's training value?

DAYA HAINES HADDOCK

The "new economy's" rapid pace of change creates an environment where a premium is placed on knowledge, skills, and training. Not long ago, the only option for ongoing training occurred infrequently in a classroom for days or weeks at a time. Today, knowledge must continually be created, published, and distributed "just in time." The introduction of e-learning has changed how we access knowledge, how we learn, and how ongoing training is delivered. In this context, adults who have been occasional students become continuous users of knowledge, and they gain control over their own learning and career development. E-learning can enable an organization to keep up with all of these changes.

An e-learning strategy is a new approach to learning, in which organizations must recognize that people learn more effectively in small chunks and not lengthy courses. The corporate culture must support a continuous learning environment and deliver personalized learning based on user skills, experience, and backgrounds. E-learning leverages the power of a networked collaborative community, identifying knowledge experts, and sharing brain trusts, and it is designed to accelerate the speed of learning and knowledge transfer. A company's e-learning strategy involves more than publishing courses online. While most people have used the Internet to gather new information, learn a new skill, maintain certification, or do their jobs, these are just the beginning of a fully formed strategy to support e-learning. A comprehensive e-learning strategy involves:

- building a learning culture to cope with rapid change,

- rethinking the nature and design of learning,

- applying sophisticated software tools such as learning content management systems (LCMSs) or knowledge management systems (KMSs),

- ensuring e-learning generates adequate ROI.

BUILDING A LEARNING CULTURE

Adaptive, fast-paced work teams are the new unit of working and learning in many organizations. These *racehorse teams* are inspired groups working at their best, focused on a goal, equipped to make decisions, initiating, innovating, and delivering. *Racehorse teams* must form and reform continuously in response to new challenges. Two characteristics necessary for their success are the dynamic to learn fast and the ability to collaborate. These characteristics are the essential building blocks of learning organizations.[1]

Highly productive individuals recognize that continuous learning and nurturing of their skills is vital to their productivity and professional satisfaction. Organizations can provide e-learning opportunities to support continuous learning and performance at higher and higher levels. With appropriate learning strategies, companies can build *racehorse organizations*, where more employees are effective in what they are doing and have a passion about their work. E-learning programs accelerate learning and knowledge sharing within organizations and, in turn, organizations can respond and deliver during these fast times.

RETHINKING THE NATURE OF LEARNING

The second characteristic of a learning organization is the ability to capture knowledge and make it easily available to appropriate learners throughout the organization (Q51). However, because each individual's needs are unique, personalization is the key to success—an improvement over traditional classroom courses designed for the *average* learner. Tailoring technology, information, and support to match the unique characteristics of individuals facilitates learning. E-learning has the dynamic and flexible tools to support this need.

The natural power of grouping people with common interests can also be leveraged in a learning organization. E-learning technology enables teams, driven by the demand for new learning, to add to the organization's knowledge pool. An end user may participate as a learner for one topic, a facilitator or coach for another, and a knowledge author or creator on yet a third topic. Users can manage their own training program, progressing at their own pace and convenience. They can also access training materials at any time and learn only as much as they need to know in a "just-in-time" format.

WHAT ARE THE DIFFERENT TYPES
OF E-LEARNING TECHNOLOGIES?

New technologies have emerged to support all of this necessary flexibility and customization. E-learning tools provide both synchronous (learning event at a single

---

[1] Peter Senge, founder of MIT's Society of Organizational Learning, defines organizational learning as "how a group of people collectively enhance their capacities to produce the outcome they really wanted to produce" (from *The Fifth Discipline*, quoted in Web site interview <http://www.solonline.org/organizational_overview>).

Senge also points out that, in addition to being more effective at their job, it is important that students enjoy the learning experience.

point in time with communication and information access in real-time) and asynchronous (learning conducted in a self-paced mode) options. E-learning solutions can be used by Web-browsing software, which is widely available on any platform—Windows, Mac, Unix, OS/2, etc. E-learning programs can be available to users over the Internet or within a corporate intranet without having to create assets for different platforms. Robust software packages now include many features and functions that support collaborative and distance learning, including database repositories for managing content within training courses that can be easily updated and distributed. Tracking and management features are included to support performance monitoring and certification in many industries. These systems interface with ERP (**Q62**) or corporate HR systems and have the ability to manage learning data at the employee level. Content is tagged and considered as reusable objects for learning courses. Collaboration and multimedia delivery options with audio, video, and sophisticated simulation capabilities provide more exciting, interactive, and entertaining "game-style" training than page-turning Microsoft PowerPoint slides. Product categories are shown in Table 52.1.

In each of these groups, available software products vary widely in features, capabilities, and price (from $20K to $1M).[2] Selecting a tool requires the same evaluation and selection processes as for any other tool in the corporate arsenal.

With a corporate e-learning approach, selected tools, and the culture and technology to support e-learning, the last step is to ensure adequate benchmarks to capture your return on investment (ROI).

ACHIEVING E-LEARNING ROI

Return on investment (ROI) is the estimate of the financial benefit (return) on money spent (investment) for a particular initiative over time (**Q75**). Frequently, the costs for an e-learning program are lower than traditional instructor-led training, since travel costs are eliminated and larger numbers of students can be supported. Often, the biggest stumbling blocks are the start-up costs for investment in the technology and the development time. Because the costs associated with e-learning delivery are much lower than for traditional methods, the cost savings will catch management's attention.

An ROI case study from IBM, showcases $395 million saved in 2001 through the use of e-learning, as well as 43 percent of learning hours that were delivered through e-learning.[3] Century 21, the real estate firm, turned off their instructor-led training and offered sales training solely on the Web. Sales agents achieved a 33 percent in-

---

[2] Gartner Group, "The 2002 E-Learning LMS Magic Quadrant: Who Survives?" summarizes the LMS software vendors at <http://www.gartner.com/reprints/pathlore/104389.html>.

[3] An e-learning ROI case study, presented at the ITAA/ASTD Conference, Ted Hoff, VP Learning, IBM, October 12, 2002, ASTD Web site <www.astd.org>.

Table *52.1* E-learning Technologies

Learning Management System (LMS)	Designed to automate administration and track on-line or Web-based training (WBT) and instructor-led training (ILT) classroom learning events; often interfaces with a corporate HR or ERP system, and interoperates with third-party courseware for self-paced tracking.
Knowledge Management System (KMS) **(Q51)**	Collects, stores, and makes information available as knowledge objects; provides a variety of methods for knowledge storage, and sharing, with an emphasis on content creation, reusable object repository, and collaboration.
Learning Content Management System (LCMS)	A hybrid of learning management with training tracking capabilities and content repositories from the content management systems.
Content Management System (CMS)	Single-source content repository with reusable content objects with flexible metadata, and has tight integration with desktop applications to create and publish content. Usually includes intelligent searching, check-in/check-out of content, revision, and version control.
Computer-Based Training (CBT)	A self-contained learning event accessible through a computer interface, typically delivered via a CD-ROM.
Web-Based Training (WBT)	Accessible via Web technologies (such as TCP/IP, http, browsers), is delivered over networks, and is self-paced, often available as third-party courseware.
Virtual Instructor-Led Training (VILT)	Delivered by an instructor, with real-time access to the information and simultaneous communication of participants using Web-based tools and technology.

crease in commissions compared with agents trained traditionally.[4] Another factor in the ROI equation is time and ability to train more users. Krispy Kreme only trained 60 store managers in 1999, then they launched a new Management 101 blended training program including on-line courses, training videos, and classroom with 149 participants in 2001. The management turnover has dropped and Krispy Kreme was able to open eight more stores than planned in 2001.[5] E-learning solutions provide measurable financial paybacks, as well as cost and time savings. A generic ROI template for an e-learning business case is available at www.tiainc.com.[6]

[4] Craig R. Taylor, "E-Learning: The Second Wave," ASTD's online magazine about e-learning <www.learningcircuits.org/2002/oct2002/taylor.html>.

[5] Kim Kiser, "On the Rise," *Online Learning Magazine*, April 2002, page 13.

[6] An e-learning ROI case, "Calculating ROI of Performance Improvement," presented by Daya Haddock and Cindy Gibson, can be found at http://tiainc.com/news/news_archive.html.

E-learning Brings Business Value to the Organization

E-learning provides opportunities to address the following organizational issues:

- the need for a highly skilled workforce to stay competitive,

- the need to distribute information globally to employees, customers, and partners,

- the acknowledgment of new products, changes in technology, and just in time learning requirements,

- the need to keep an eye firmly on the bottom line.

In addition to these benefits, the advantages of implementing an e-learning strategy include substantial savings in travel cost and time. And according to Brandon Hall's report "Return on Investment and Multimedia Training"[7] the actual time required for training by computer averages about half of that required for instructor-led training, lowering costs further.

Summarizing an E-learning Strategy for Your Organization

An e-learning strategy may take more time and money initially, for new software and content development. Like any first-time challenge, learning about and implementing new e-learning technology can take more resources than expected. To reduce risks and improve company satisfaction, companies should start with a prototype course, analyze ROI, and build on success. Remember that the largest costs associated with e-learning are the start-up costs. E-learning programs can be delivered and reused with fewer delivery and distribution costs. And the bottom line for your organization is that e-learning will keep your employees fresh with the rapid pace of change in our new economy.

---

[7] A white paper is available at the Brandon Hall Web site <www.brandonhall.com>.

53. What are the attributes of an effective relationship between an IT organization and the rest of the business?

BARBARA T. BAUER

How many times has an IT organization boasted about a great relationship between itself and the rest of the business? How many times in internal company management meetings has the IT group been commended for contributions to the business? Usually, not very often. Unfortunately, IT organizations and business units often have negative, stressful relationships marked by complaints about missed schedules, poor end user support, budget overruns, and inadequate functionality. This troubled relationship is pervasive and insidious and contributes to the short tenures frequently experienced by CIOs (**Q57**). What accounts for this negativity and what can be done about it?

The good news is there are exceptions to this generally depressing situation. Some IT organizations stand in high regard; they can identify their contributions to the success of the business; and they can also identify the key characteristics of their success. These truly great IT organizations operate within a model of "earned credibility" gained by solid, efficient processes to support their interactions with their business colleagues. While these examples of excellence, when encountered, are easy to identify, their accomplishments are not so easy to achieve.

EARNED CREDIBILITY

Earned credibility is the respect given to IT executives and their organizations by the business when IT demonstrates the ability first to understand the business and then to deliver reliably the critical technology necessary for market success (**Q4**). IT departments must "earn" their way out of the usual atmosphere of skepticism and distrust. There are several minimum requirements necessary to "earn credibility." The first is the personal credibility and effectiveness of the CIO. If the CIO is a valued and respected business partner of other corporate executives, the IT organization has a chance to gain respect. If the CIO does not have this regard, the IT organization is doomed, no matter how effective it is or how hard it tries to improve. Assuming the CIO has this respect, he or she can be an effective leader and communicator of the strategies and priorities of the business, and guide the IT organization toward success.

SUCCESS COMPONENTS: PROCESS AND SCORECARD

After the personal credibility of the CIO, the next requirement is the IT organization's ability to deliver the right features at the right time for the right price, day after day, year after year. This is extremely hard to accomplish and even small missteps can take the credibility quotient back to the starting line. When these missteps occur, they can irrevocably damage the CIO as well as the organization, even after many successful projects. Highly regarded IT organizations have developed professional approaches to providing needed features in a cost effective and timely manner. The most successful approaches include two components:

1. a set of business processes that link IT and the business together on mutual expectations and commitments,

2. a visible scorecard to measure and display progress on these expectations and commitments.

Both of these components are easy to understand in theory, but very hard to implement in practice.

Linked Processes

Expectations and commitments, and the underlying business processes that define these, are the Achilles' heel of the IT world. For decades, IT organizations developed software and operated computer centers in an undisciplined, ad-hoc manner, and some still do. The seductive myth of the gifted, nerdy, independent IT technologist who can pull rabbits out of hats and make miracles happen still exists. A number of the recent dot.com debacles were examples of this undisciplined approach. By contrast, consistent success in IT actually requires discipline, not unlike the discipline of other professions, such as medicine or engineering. Some of the best processes have come from excellent software consulting companies, who base their survival and growth on meeting client expectations. They have employed an approach which utilizes careful software and project management practices on the delivery end (Q55)—while putting significant resources into client and account management skills on the front end. Within the last decade, the truly excellent embedded IT organizations have begun to model their internal company interactions on these consulting company paradigms and are achieving success.

Although many linked processes are important to IT success, meeting commitments and satisfying customers require two fundamental processes:

1. an integrated IT and business strategic planning process,

2. a well-oiled process to prioritize and allocate IT resources and investment.

Strategic Planning Process

The first process, strategic planning, which integrates IT into a comprehensive company strategy, is difficult enough for any company without including the complications of IT. Even companies who have long histories of technical product development or reliance on technology, especially hardware development, fail frequently on integrating IT effectively in strategic plans (Q4). A well-respected CIO is a necessary asset, but many IT organizations do not support their leaders with effective data, insights, and materials for strategic planning. A poorly functioning IT organization does not have the historical data, or even available resources, to prepare for a company strategy session. When operating in this mode, both time and information are in short supply because everyone in IT is usually responding to some crisis. More mature IT organizations, operating at CMM (capability maturity model) Level 2 or higher (Q55), are capable of responding with accurate data, reliable estimates, and forecasts. These organizations are also able to initiate discussions with subunits to ensure that economies of scale and broad technology initiatives can be presented and reviewed effectively.

PRIORITIZATION AND ALLOCATION PROCESS

Assuming the IT organization has sufficient maturity to have collaborated on strategic objectives and the tactical implications of these objectives, the next requirement for a successful relationship is an efficient process to allocate IT investment and resources (Q71, Q76). Multiple business units with high expectations and different requirements can degrade quickly into alley fights over which unit gets the lion's share of the IT pie. This situation is common and a tough one to resolve. The internal organizations that come out on the losing end of budget battles must reset their expectations. If they still expect IT to give them something outside of the official process, these organizations will usually be disappointed and then unfairly blame the IT team.

Similarly, pressure from IT to improve an allocation scheme usually requires fixing much bigger problems internal to the company about how control, authority, and benefit allocations actually occur. An underlying cause, not of IT's making per se, is the fact that many IT capabilities support the general business, not a unique segment or process. This leads to admirable economies of scale and also to the aforementioned conflicts because there is no clear decision authority on these issues across the company. This situation is another true test of CIO survivability, since skillful negotiation and delicate politicking are important to resolve all the contentious issues. Once resolved (including agreement on how to respond to future changes in business conditions), the allocation should lead to detailed project plans and commitments (Q92, Q93). These details are the lifeblood of the last necessity of IT credibility: a balanced scorecard.

BALANCED SCORECARD

The idea of a balanced scorecard can seem trivial, but it represents the same objective as the quarterly and annual reports of a company to its stakeholders. It must

Figure 53.1 Sample Balanced Scorecard for an IT Department

Business Value

- Cycle time as compared to commitments
- Application availability
- Maintenance cost per invoice
- End user satisfaction
- Business unit satisfaction
- Meet IT budget targets

% Metrics Gray, White, Black

	Oct	Nov	Dec
Gray	67%	67%	67%
White	16%	16%	33%
Black	16%	16%	0%

Delivery Excellence

- Schedule variance
- Budget variance
- Percentage of project milestones met on time
- Rework
- Defect density
- Testing stage containment
- Percentage of service level targets met
- Problem resolution time
- Percentage of customer commitments met
- Backlog

% Metrics Gray, White, Black

	Oct	Nov	Dec
Gray	75%	75%	75%
White	25%	25%	25%
Black	0%	0%	0%

Change and Process Excellence

- Transition plan schedule variance
- Percentage of transition goals satisfied
- Percentage of transformation milestones met
- Change readiness
- Percentage of applications with scorecards

% Metrics Gray, White, Black

	Oct	Nov	Dec
Gray	25%	25%	50%
White	50%	50%	50%
Black	25%	25%	0%

Value Our People

- Attrition by performance level
- Employee satisfaction
- Overtime percentage
- Average training hours / FTE
- Percentage of training plans completed
- Staffing mix
- Percentage of positions open

% Metrics Gray, White, Black

	Oct	Nov	Dec
Gray	67%	67%	67%
White	33%	100%	16%
Black	0%	0%	16%

With permission of Accenture LLP.

be stated with the same consistent, conservative, accurate data using language that the business leaders understand and appreciate. Typically, balanced scorecards report progress in four areas: financial performance, customer perspectives, internal process quality, and organizational growth and development. All elements of the IT function must appear on such scorecards or reports: computer center operations, budgets and capital expenses, development progress and completion, maintenance and support, and the distribution of labor costs among all these functions. Many IT practitioners abhor measuring their work in this way, but, when implemented, balanced scorecards can lead to success. It is time-consuming work and must be created as a collaborative project with internal business units to have impact and success. Along with the actual reports, routine meetings between IT and business leaders to review the performance must occur. An example of a balanced scorecard for an IT department is shown in Figure 53.1.

These comments have focused on IT components, processes, and CIO credibility. Equally important and, if missing, equally indicting is the commitment from the top leaders of the company to support the creation and implementation of these processes. Information technology capabilities and expertise are expensive resources and have enormous leverage inside the company. IT needs to run its business as a business, and company executives and business units must collaborate and support the effort. With this support, IT cannot merely earn and maintain credibility; it can be a strategic and successful business asset.

54 ▬▬▬

---

54. Is a centralized or decentralized IT organization better?

BARBARA T. BAUER

How to structure IT organizations has been the topic of many pointed debates. Over the years, different approaches to IT governance have been in vogue. In the early years, the expense involved and the expertise required made a centralized operation the only viable structure. As the cost of computing technology decreased during the 1980s and trained IT personnel became more readily available, individual business units began creating their own IT shops. Client/server hardware and software accelerated this trend. The widespread deployment of desktop computers also made employees desperate for local services. As a result, most companies attempted to decentralize parts of their IT operations, to accommodate business unit needs and reduce the overall tension around IT costs and capabilities.

However, over the last decade the pendulum began to swing back toward the centralized model. This trend was accelerated by work on the Year 2000 (Y2K) systems conversions and by business units that came to appreciate the challenges of cost effective IT procurement and operations. At the same time, new network and database technologies made attractive, high-priority applications possible, but they required centralized IT organizations for development and operation.

Now companies are again asking the fundamental question, "What is the best organizational structure for our IT operations?" Some of the original issues remain—equipment and software is still expensive, and expertise is still difficult to find and manage. There also are new issues—IT is now an essential component of all business processes, and effective use of IT is not just an issue of competitive advantage but also a life-or-death matter for many businesses (**Q1, Q2**). A firm's technology now extends to its customers and suppliers, making its IT organization's performance critical and very visible. As a result, the central issue has evolved from "IT control" to "IT effectiveness." Each of the organizational models has its set of benefits and limitations.

Centralized IT Organizations

In the centralized model, all IT functions—strategy and planning, application development and maintenance, and operations—report directly to a senior executive such as the chief information officer (CIO), chief technical officer (CTO), or sometimes to the chief financial officer (CFO) or an administrative officer. All of the assets—hardware, software, personnel, and the budget—are controlled by this organization. On the surface, this appears to be the most attractive way to manage because there are several obvious benefits. Procurement of hardware and software is possible on the broadest scale within the company, and centralized operations produce substantial economies of scale. For example, centralizing data centers typically results in a 10 to 15 percent cost savings.[1] A centralized staff eliminates redundant functions, such as multiple help desk support groups. A unified approach to architecture and standards reduces integration difficulties and costs for new applications. Clarity of purpose and alignment with overall company strategies improve due to the simpler organizational communications required.

However, there also are potential problems with a centralized structure. As a cost center, IT's large budgets are a constant point of contention, putting it on the defensive within the company. When the costs of these large central IT organizations are allocated back to individual business units, it creates conditions similar to those that led to the Boston Tea Party—central corporate taxation (cost allocation) without representation (control). A fully centralized structure also requires a very effective decision and resource allocation process within the company, since each business unit can have different or conflicting needs for the IT workforce and operations capacity (**Q71,**

---

[1] Thomas Hoffman, "IT Recentralization Efforts Paying Off—With Caveats," *Computerworld* 1 July 2002: 53.

Q76). Also, if the operation of equipment and application support are not excellent, outages in one business unit can cripple the entire company.

The key to a centralized organization's success is its responsiveness. If the big centralized operation can be responsive to the needs of the business, then that approach can make sense. Several companies, such as DaimlerChrysler, Kemper Insurance, and PepsiCo, have migrated back to centralized IT operations after attempts to decentralize them.[2] While each of these companies has a unique approach and reasons for reconsolidation, cost savings and ease of management are two of the most important rationales identified.

DECENTRALIZED IT ORGANIZATIONS

Many companies successfully decentralized IT operations to their business units as they adopted client/server architectures. Many other companies adopted decentralized IT structures during mergers because it was frequently the quickest way to solve the problem of integrating disparate hardware and software infrastructures. The benefits of the decentralized approach in these situations are tangible. Each business unit has complete knowledge and choice over the allocation of IT resources to support business priorities. Costs are fully allocated to business unit initiatives and there is the perception of faster, more flexible responses to necessary changes. IT architects and engineers typically have better access to business information, allowing them to closely tailor their proposed solutions to specific business problems. In decentralized organizational models, the IT organization is typically perceived as a partner in the business unit, and defensive tensions, which can occur in highly centralized models, are reduced.

However, there are challenges to the decentralized model. The company as a whole will have higher total procurement and operations costs due to duplicate data centers and multiple independent procurement and vendor partnerships. New technology can be very difficult and expensive to introduce. Even relatively inexpensive desktop tools, such as e-mail, messaging, and calendar applications, can proliferate widely, producing unnecessary integration expenses and introducing hurdles to the flow of company information. An escalating risk is the potential impact on customers and business partners who need products and services from more than one business unit. With opportunities from new technologies, such as the Internet, increasing the interaction between external partners and internal business processes, the need to have a unified presence for a company increases. This unified presence is nearly impossible to achieve in a completely decentralized organizational model.

Then there is the issue of accountability. Who is responsible for failure—especially of a cross-organizational system? What about accountability for security and its new complexities? There is usually a huge amount of finger pointing that goes on

---

[2] Martin J. Garvey, "Back to the Middle," *InformationWeek* 29 Apr. 1997: 2.

when something goes wrong in IT, and many CEOs don't appreciate it. They prefer a single point of accountability, which is difficult in a decentralized model.

HYBRID OR FEDERATED IT ORGANIZATIONS

Many companies have developed IT structures that keep selected elements of both the centralized and decentralized models. Functions that require consistency across the entire company are centralized, including:

- procurement
- operations
  - data centers
  - data network
  - desktop support
  - help desks
  - common infrastructure such as e-mail and intranets
- architecture
- standards and processes
- development and integration of company-wide ERP applications

Most of these functions have recurring costs that are most easily estimated and budgeted on a central basis, and the centralized IT organization retains these budgets.

Functions that are decentralized to the business units include software application development unique to each unit, planning and management of unit-specific service agreements, and specific BU IT strategy and resource estimates. However, even these unique business unit functions must be rolled up into an overall company plan, so that conflicts or opportunities are visible and actionable. Many hybrid organizations provide business unit budget control over the decentralized functions, but keep the technical resources in the centralized organization, which helps increase both business unit satisfaction and the ability to optimize expensive resources. In this model the IT organization manages the resources on behalf of the business units, which pay specifically for the services they use. This allows for better career planning and development of the technical staff.

The most sophisticated hybrid models separate decisions about organizational centralization from decisions about financial centralization. The corresponding challenge, and possible disadvantage to a federated model, is that it requires strong, collaborative leadership in both headquarters and individual business units. The CIO, in particular, must be an executive that can lead a complex technical organization as well as understand the business needs and strategy of each business unit. It also requires effective strategy, planning, and resource allocation processes in the company (**Q4, Q71, Q76**) so the centralized resources continue to meet the needs of specific business initiatives. Citigroup and YMCA of the United States are examples of this hybrid approach.[3]

Conclusions

IT leaders today face fundamentally different business requirements. In past debates between centralized and decentralized organizations, issues concerning technology evolution, resource abundance or scarcity, and especially control dominated the decisions. Today, "business managers rely on IT to be leaders in identifying and implementing new business-driven applications . . . affecting all levels of operations within a company."[4] There is no single right answer. IT leaders and their colleagues in the company can, and should, choose elements of organizational models that support the company's unique priorities, initiatives, and assets.

---

55. How can the capability maturity model (CMM) be used to improve an IT organization's effectiveness?

55

CRAIG LEWIS

Jokes abound in the software industry about the all-too-familiar delivery, quality, and budget problems of development projects. Producing systems quickly and predictably is very hard to do. Most executives and IT professionals believe that software development projects can have only two of the following three attributes: high quality, low cost, and improved speed to market. Is it possible to build high-quality, reliable systems quickly and inexpensively? The answer could be "yes" if the organization follows a software development model that puts structure around these complex processes.

[3] Hoffman 3.
[4] Aaron Goldberg, "Centralized IT Is Back and Hitting Full Stride," *PC Week* 20 July 1998: 67.

There are several software development models available to software organizations.[1] The most visible model is the capability maturity model (CMM) for software, developed by the Software Engineering Institute (SEI).[2] The CMM is a five-level model:

Level 1: Initial—Software development is ad hoc with few defined processes. Most IT organizations in the United States operate at this level.

Level 2: Repeatable—Fundamental processes for tracking schedule, cost, and effort are in place. Functionality, in the form of requirements, is managed explicitly.

Level 3: Defined—Documented management and engineering processes exist. Software projects utilize organizational processes tailored to meet the specific needs of the project.

Level 4: Managed—Process and product quality are managed quantitatively.

Level 5: Optimizing—Process improvement is a continuous process driven by quantitative measures with an emphasis on defect prevention.

At Level 3 and above, the levels are assessed organizationally. A software development organization operating at Level 3, for example, has established processes and uses them (many organizations have processes but do not use them). The SEI qualifies

---

[1] The CMM is one of several models available to a software organization. Several others exist:

ISO 9001—The International Organization of Standardization (ISO) established a quality management system emphasizing developing a product that meets customer needs. "Quality" is defined as those customer-required features needed in a product.

ISO 12207—Whereas ISO 9001 is a quality system, ISO 12207 is a software life cycle process framework similar to the CMM. The ISO framework spans the entire software life cycle using five primary processes: acquisition, supply, development, maintenance, and operation.

Six Sigma—A quantitative quality system intended to drive defects out of any process. "Six Sigma" is a statistical reference to establishing a deviation of only six standard deviations between a measured average and the specification.

RUP—Rational Software has developed a software engineering process set designed in conjunction with the Rational suite of tools which integrate project management, business modeling, requirements management, analysis and design, testing, and change management into life cycle process.

CMMI—The capability maturity model integration is another product of the SEI that recognizes the fact that software is usually part of a larger technology solution. Intended to consolidate the numerous CMM frameworks, the CMMI integrates software engineering, integrated process and product development, and the software CMM. More readings about these models can be found in the Resources section.

[2] Technically, the CMM for software is referred to as the SW-CMM. The SEI has developed other CMM models for software acquisition, software engineering, integrated product and process development, and individual performance (the Personal CMM).

certain individuals to function as lead assessors, similar to auditors of financial statements, who independently assess maturity levels and ratings. Unlike other standards, such as ISO 9001, software organizations must demonstrate consistent use of their processes. Validation of this use occurs through interviews and the review of software process products, such as peer review forms, requirements documents, etc.

Realistically, most organizations strive for Levels 2 or 3. Level 2 establishes basic project management discipline within each project (Q89). Estimates of project attributes such as cost, size, effort, and schedule are developed at the beginning of the project and tracked throughout its life. Requirements are established and changes to them are managed explicitly throughout the project life cycle. Work subcontracted to a third party is explicitly defined in terms of software processes. Software organizations can expect consistent results in the work efforts because planning and tracking activities are standardized. Successes from one project can be extended to other projects.

Level 3 organizations establish organizational processes for developing and maintaining software that integrates both the development of the software as well as project management. New projects use these standards, apply tailoring rules, and create a set of processes that meet the specific needs of each project. Metrics from the software development process are collected, evaluated, and used to not only determine the status of the project, but to determine where improvements can be made. Key to Level 3 is the establishment of process responsibility at the organization level. Typically, this responsibility is manifested in the form of a software engineering process group that is charged with creating and maintaining a usable set of process assets (including the processes themselves, metrics regarding the use of the processes, and examples of best practices), used throughout the organization. The organizational emphasis also allows for better resource utilization as software professionals can move easily from one project to another, using familiar processes.

At Levels 4 and 5, organizations have institutionalized a rigorous approach to software development, driven by constant monitoring of metrics and automatic corrections of any deviation from the approved processes. Outside of certain industries where software errors must be virtually zero (e.g., defense), large software organizations in the United States have rarely been certified at levels 4 or 5, although software outsourcing organizations strive for these levels.[3]

IMPLICATIONS

If IT leaders can dramatically improve the quality, speed, and cost of their software, why aren't all IT organizations rushing to implement CMM? Several factors must be considered:

[3] "Compiled List of Organizations Who Have Publicly Announced Their Maturity Levels After Having an Appraisal Performed," *Carnegie Mellon Software Engineering Institute Web Site* n.d., 19 Nov. 2002 <http://seir.sei.cmu.edu/pml>.

Implementation Takes Time   To move up the CMM ladder requires that virtually all software developers in an organization be trained in the process. And since more rigor will be put around the development of the customer's requirements, customers must also be trained. Unlike other engineering disciplines, most software engineers do not bring to their IT organizations an inherent engineering process and structure, despite the fact that the size and complexity of most software projects require such discipline. Thus, the training and processes necessary to support professional software engineering appears intrusive to many IT developers. The journey to CMM Levels 2 or 3 can take many months or years depending on the initial organizational maturity and the current IT priorities.

CMM Requires Visible Senior Management Support   As with anything that involves organizational change, vocal, visible commitment to process improvement activities is required. The sponsor of the CMM effort needs to be the senior IT executive in the corporation. Clear communication of the rationale for the move to these processes must be presented and rewards for achieving each level should be offered. Conversely, there will need to be consequences for nonperformance, just as in any organizational change effort.

CMM Implementations Cost Money   In addition to training and assessment costs, there will likely be a period of reduced productivity as software developers learn the new environment. Also, at Level 3, organizational infrastructure is required to maintain the new processes. Success, however, ultimately *reduces* costs as the organization becomes more adept at new processes.

CMM Looks Bureaucratic   To some inside and outside the IT organization, CMM can look cumbersome. Among other things, documented requirements must be obtained from users, good project management techniques must be in place, metrics must be established and followed. But these are all the elements that are likely to make the project successful. Certainly there is some overhead associated with the process, but IT leadership must diligently prevent their teams from getting inappropriately encumbered or complaining unnecessarily. They especially must not allow CMM to be used as an excuse for IT to become less responsive to the business. Contrary to what some critics might say, CMM can even accommodate rapid response projects when they are part of the overall CMM framework.

CMM Must Be Aligned with Corporate Objectives   What does the corporation want from IT (**Q4**)? Better quality? Lower cost? More responsiveness? All three? Any CMM implementation must take these objectives into consideration. The CMM effort should be tailored to deliver results in the desired objective as quickly as possible.

The Payoff

Why go to all this trouble? Perhaps the question should be "Are you satisfied with the performance of the software development organization?" Do they deliver on time, on budget, with high quality and all required functionality? Usually the answer is no, and IT leadership needs to do something to correct that situation (**Q53, Q56**). A perusal of issues discussed in these questions reveals that these issues are the very ones that are addressed in the CMM process. These are the things that make projects succeed.

Recent literature has examples of compelling benefits for successful CMM efforts. A Department of Defense study provides summary results for several typical metrics of improved software capabilities:[4]

- Productivity improvements: 9 to 67% per year, with median improvement of 35%.

- Early defect detection: 6 to 25%, with a median improvement of 22%.

- Development time reduction: 15 to 23%, with median reduction of 19%.

- Postrelease defect reduction: 10 to 94%, with median reduction of 39%.

- IT ROI improvement: 420 to 880%, with median ROI improvement of 500%.

Every IT leader wants results like these. Another study by the Carnegie Mellon Software Institute shows the following metrics from a study of 13 participating organizations:[5]

- Productivity gains: range of 9 to 67%

- Time to market reduction: 15 to 23%

- Defect reduction per year: 10 to 94%

This particular report also includes results from other studies with very positive results. For example, a large aeronautics manufacturer improved productivity by 62 percent, improved cycle time by 36 percent, and improved customer satisfaction by 10 percent.[6]

CMM may not be a panacea for improving software development performance. But whether an organization pursues CMM, ISO, or other approaches, the objective should be to better meet the needs of the business and to gain more control and better insight into the way IT meets those needs. Software engineering is a relatively young, and hence immature, discipline. If it is approached in a rigorous, structured way, it can produce a product that is predictable, reliable, and at lower cost.

---

[4] Thomas McGibbon, *A Business Case for Software Process Improvement Revised*, Department of Defense Data and Analysis Center for Software (DACS), 30 Sept. 1999: 5.

[5] Dave Zubrow, *Software Process Improvement: Just the Facts, Not the Hype*, Carnegie Mellon Software Engineering Institute, n.d.: 11.

[6] Zubrow 32.

56. How can an internal IT organization's success be measured?

MICHAEL S. JACKSON AND DAVID R. LAUBE

Without question, the IT organization is usually one of the most maligned groups in a company. According to a survey of IT executives conducted by *CIO Magazine*, in 70 percent of the companies surveyed, IT is still viewed as a cost center, not a value center.[1] One of the difficulties in changing this view is that it is difficult to properly measure an IT organization's success. One effective mechanism is to use a *balanced scorecard*, which focuses attention on the performance of IT from a variety of viewpoints (Q53). One of the primary areas emphasized by the scorecard is internal process quality.

INTERNAL PROCESS QUALITY

Most IT organizations have internal metrics that they use to evaluate their overall performance. They often consist of things like percentage of systems online, number of network outages, server stability, desktop availability, etc. In certain IT service functions, metrics like these can be effectively used to determine performance, measure improvement, and benchmark against other similar organizations in other companies.

For example, a service desk, often referred to as the help desk, can derive great value from analysis of metrics such as:

- *Average speed of answer (ASA)*—How quickly are customers' calls answered?

- *Abandonment percentage*—How many customers get tired of waiting and disconnect?

- *Average length of call*—How long does it take to resolve problems?

- *First-call/in-house resolution*—What percent of problems are solved on first contact, or without having to assign to another agency or external source?

Typical field IT organizations (those who support the desktop environment) will look at measures such as:

- *Mean-time-to-repair (MTTR)*—The time it takes to resolve a customer's problem, from report of issue to "service restored." Often the benchmark is based on the severity level such as:

    Severity one—less than 4 hours,

[1] "Measuring IT Value," *CIO.com* 21 Feb. 2001, 22 Nov. 2002 <http://www.cio.com/cio/022101_survey.html>.

Severity two—8 hours or less,

Severity three—less than 24 hours.

- *The ratio of technicians to end users*—The more sophisticated the IT organization is in terms of support tools, technology, and practices, the greater the ratio.

- *The number of problems solved per technician*—Measures the efficiency of the staff during a given period of time.

However, while these metrics are valuable for IT leaders to manage their function, they are not particularly valuable to their internal customers who rely on IT to provide them service. A conversation frequently heard coming from a business manager to an IT leader could be, "I don't care if you are up 99.2 percent of the time, when you are down I can't serve ANY customers!" The key to solving this problem is to state the measurement of IT performance in terms of the impact on either their internal customers or the company's revenue-producing customers. Mature companies have moved to a stage of end-to-end measurement, beyond whether individual servers or desktops are working, to evaluate whether or not the end users are impacted. For example, in a company with 2,000 service representatives, the IT organization might have a monthly target of less than 5,000 minutes of cumulative downtime. In other words, an outage that affected every service representative could only be two and one-half minutes long or the objective for the month would be missed.

Targets are typically set for each major functional area (finance, operations, sales, etc.) and are put into internal contracts, called service level agreements (SLAs). These formally document the agreements between IT and the business. They define the targets and the consequences of missing the targets. The most effective SLAs are those that are done in a collaborative manner between each organization and IT, where each side can see a healthy, but achievable stretch objective for all parties. Rewards and incentives can be applied for exceeding hard targets and, in the spirit of continuous improvement, targets can be raised each year.

Improving internal quality can also be measured through traditional quality measures. Among those are:

- *Change control*—This is a process for minimizing disruptions when IT makes changes to a system or business process. The objective in most companies is to drive disruptions to zero.

- *Root cause analysis*—This is the study of chronic or recurring problems with the aim of eliminating them in the future. Companies that succeed in this effort have few repeated systems problems.

In the area of software development and systems implementation, numerous "quality-like" metrics should be instituted by the IT organization in order to improve its software development processes. A common one, for example, would be to track the number of software bugs per systems release (**Q55**). Nevertheless, as described below, they should NOT be used as metrics for purposes of measuring the IT organization's success.

FINANCIAL MEASUREMENTS

The second major way to measure an IT organization's success is through financial measurements. The most common metrics are:

- *Meeting budget*—In many companies, the budget for the IT organization is a significant portion of total corporate spending. So meeting monthly and quarterly budget targets is essential. For individual projects, meeting the project budget is often one of the most highly used measures of performance of an IT organization.

- *Total cost of ownership (TCO)*—This is the cost of information technologies either in total or for specific areas (like desktops or billing) within the company. It includes, but is not limited to hardware, software, IT staff, planning, measurement, administration, downtime, and even opportunity cost. The objective is to drive down TCO over time (**Q74**).

- *Life cycle management*—The threshold set and managed by the company for replacing aged equipment—such as a three-year life span on desktop computers. The concept here is to replace the unit before it breaks or drives up maintenance costs. The objective is to strike that perfect balance between capital expenditures and maintenance that will minimize cash outlays.

- *Return on investment (ROI)*—Measures the time it will take to recoup the cost of a systems expenditure based on the benefits provided. For example, an automated process that could eliminate headcount would be evaluated for its return based on the cost of the project less headcount expenses eliminated (**Q75**). An IT organization that can deliver high ROI on its projects is usually successful.

BENCHMARK THE ORGANIZATION

Many of the internal process and financial measures are common across IT organizations. Consultants have collected this data and can use it to compare one IT organization's performance against another. This information, properly applied, can prove to be invaluable in helping an IT organization understand its strengths and weaknesses. With the popularity of outsourcing (**Q81, Q82, Q83**), some companies periodically invite bids from outsourcers to see if the quality and cost of their internal functions still hold up against those outside services. This provides the ultimate market test to the IT organization.

CUSTOMERS' PERSPECTIVES

An IT organization can do all of the measurements described, hitting its targets and meeting its objectives, and still not be seen as successful. This is because IT success is really about what the users perceive and think of the IT department's performance. It can be influenced by the metrics, but it isn't dominated by them.

In order to understand the customers' perceptions of IT, managers must ask some basic questions:

- Have we asked the customer what they need or want?

- Have we provided counsel and guidance as to the costs and time required for delivery?

- Do we understand their priorities for those requests?

- Have we received a commitment from them to fulfill their end of the project needs (i.e., process changes, skill sets needed, time required to develop requirements)

- Are we following up with the customer to ensure we are still on track? Are we making sure that being "on track" is a shared accountability?

One of the best ways to determine an IT organization's success is to survey the users of its services each year. Areas that would benefit by a large response can be handled by pushing an e-mail out to those from whom a response is desired. But more important, every significant user or client of a software development or implementation project should provide input on IT's performance. This is usually a small number of people and they are the ones whose opinions really count. In particular, the sponsor of an IT-related project should be included (**Q93, Q95**). This survey can consist of a series of questions, or it can simply ask the respondent to grade the IT department's performance on a scale of A–F. The beauty of the latter approach is that traditional quantitative measures such as meeting dates or making the budget get set aside and the person gives one grade encompassing everything they feel about IT. It can be very humbling to read these responses, but it is an important step that can open dialogue and start a course for improvement.

Success in IT terms can be very elusive. But by following the processes described above, an IT organization can get a very good understanding of where it stands through the eyes of its customers.

57. What is the average tenure of a CIO and why?

DAVID R. LAUBE

The position of CIO is one of the most fragile in a company's entire organizational structure. Although studies on CIO turnover have produced varying results over the years, most come to the conclusion that average job tenure is relatively short—as low as two to three years. A study conducted by a consulting firm recently indicated that 36 percent of CIOs in North America had been in the job fewer than two years.[1] It's no wonder that the old adage that the initials CIO stand for "career is over" still resonates within the IT community.

The reasons for this fragility have much to do with the difficulty of the job and the nature of the industry. Perhaps other than the CEO, no other job has as many different and difficult components.[2] It is very hard to handle each element of the job with zero problems, which is the standard to which most CIOs are held.

The difficulty of the job is usually demonstrated through a number of possible failures. Three of these failures are the:

- failure to deliver (**Q85**, **Q86**),

- failure to develop a partnership with the business (**Q4**),

- failure to align technology with business strategy (**Q4**).

FAILURE TO DELIVER

It is a well-known fact that a significant percentage of technology projects are failures in delivery.[3] These failures usually come from three areas:

- *Failure to deliver on time*—Technology projects are notoriously late. This tardiness can be caused by a myriad of things; from bad time estimates to poor project control, to changes to the projects by the customer, to technology that does not work, to staff turnover, etc. It is often a surprise when a project is actually delivered on time. Unfortunately, if the company has built business objectives based on timely delivery, a failure can have major consequences. Business urgencies often push the CIO to make speed a primary objective, but often to no avail.

---

[1] Herbert W. Lovelace, "Where Have All the CIOs Gone?," *InformationWeek* 10 Apr. 2000: 240.
[2] For a light-hearted description of the difficulty of the CIO position, see Rich Karlgaard, "America's Worst C-Title Job," *Forbes* 25 Nov. 2002: 47.
[3] Kim S. Nash, "Companies Don't Learn from Previous IT Snafus," *Computerworld* 30 Oct. 2000: 32.

- *Failure to meet the budget*—Technology projects notoriously overrun their budgets. Sometimes this is due to an expansion in the scope, but it is usually related to many of the same conditions that cause the project to be late. If overruns are significant, companies can miss their financial targets or, as a last resort, simply cancel the project, wasting the entire investment to date. And when CIOs are ordered to reduce their spending without being granted a corresponding reduction in service levels, the seeds are sown for big disappointments.

- *Failure of the technology to do what was promised*—Technology projects notoriously do not meet customers' expectations. Often features are missing or don't work properly, there are bugs in the software, the response time of the system is poor, the vendor's product doesn't work as promised, the project doesn't deliver on the promised savings or efficiencies, the software doesn't work properly with other systems, etc. And by chance, if the software works successfully, the request is often made to rapidly expand the capability throughout the organization. Then if the technology does not scale easily, even a successful project is deemed a failure.

The reasons why these failures are so common is that successful delivery is extremely complex and difficult. The main requirements of successful project delivery include:

- high-quality and highly trained IT staff,
- strong software processes (**Q55**) and project management (**Q89**),
- collaborative relationships with the customers of the system (**Q49**, **Q50**),
- good software and hardware choices (**Q8**).

57 ▬▬▬

Mathematically, if every component necessary for a successful project has as high as a 90 percent probability of success, when you combine a large number of such components, the probability drops to the much lower percentage that is common among typical IT projects. Therefore, the odds are against the CIO from the start. Because frequently there is a lack of understanding of just how difficult it is to meet all three of these expectations, the CIO is easily branded a failure and the job turnover statistics are further enhanced.

FAILURE TO DEVELOP A PARTNERSHIP
WITH THE BUSINESS

A CIO does not work in a vacuum where he or she can just play with technology without considering the internal organizational client. Frequently a CIO is judged as much by whether he or she is a fully functioning member of the management team as by what is actually delivered by the IT group. Other organizational leaders want a CIO who:

- *Understands their business*—The CIO or key members of the IT staff must have strong business as well as IT backgrounds. Unfortunately, many CIOs and their staffs may not know the specific areas of the business as well as their departmental counterpart, and thus have considerable difficulty building credibility.

- *Anticipates their needs*—The CIO is often put into the position of operational strategist, seeing across the spectrum of organizational and business issues and identifying the points of leverage for improvement. However, unless the CIO is trained in business *processes* as well as business *strategy*, and is also given access to the operational details across the organization, it may be difficult to predict in advance where technology projects should be directed or prioritized.

- *Provides them with solutions to their business problems*—The CIO is expected to come up with technological solutions for the business. Unfortunately, technology is often viewed as the panacea for all problems, which is rarely the case.

Handling each of these areas is very difficult since they are more aligned with general business than technology. That is why a current trend among larger organizations is to have a CIO with a strong business background. Nevertheless, when a CIO's peers lose confidence because that business partnership has not been built, another turnover statistic is usually generated.

FAILURE TO ALIGN TECHNOLOGY WITH BUSINESS STRATEGY

Most business executives are not technology experts. Therefore, they want to rely on someone who they trust as a technology expert, usually their CIO, to ensure that technology is leveraged appropriately in their business. For the CIO, this usually means understanding where technology can impact the business, choosing the right technology projects, having the right technology in place at the right time, maintaining technical competitiveness, and spending the right amount on technology.

The Internet revolution has placed a sense of urgency on most businesses to make sure that they are not left behind. For those CIOs who are mere technical experts and not particularly good strategists, these new job demands are sometimes more than they can deliver. When any of these technology strategy areas go awry, it is easy to second-guess the technology choices, the prioritizations that were made, or the dollars that were consumed. Just as sports teams change managers when they lose, businesses change CIOs when technology does not—in hindsight—accomplish what was hoped for.

VOLUNTARY TURNOVER

The many types of failure often result in the involuntary change of a CIO. But statistics also show that voluntary change is almost as large due to the following factors:

- *CIOs experience burnout*—Because the job is so hard, the pressure so high, and the possibility of failure ever present, some CIOs opt to move into other management jobs or into consulting.

- *CIOs see pending failure and leave before it occurs*—Although this is categorized in the statistics as voluntary turnover, it is really related to the failures listed earlier.

- *Successful CIOs leave for greener pastures*—Successful CIOs are in short supply and therefore are in high demand. Therefore, the "free agent" phenomenon is appearing in the marketplace where CIOs with a good track record can move rapidly from job to job at ever increasing compensation levels.

So, the tenure of a CIO seems riveted to a short track. Many join the group of failures and move from job to job. However, the successful ones also move because a successful CIO is an increasingly rare commodity. Either way, companies struggle and will continue to struggle to fill and hold this important position.

57

BARBARA T. BAUER

Heated debates are common inside organizations when the topic is whether technology or business process should be the most important driver for a new project. In years past, there was considerable one-sidedness to the debate—IT professionals argued for the need to let technology dictate the way; clients in the business organizations argued for the need to let business imperatives drive decisions. And, as is always the case, the topic is too complex and the implications too far reaching for a simple answer.

The "IT and Business Processes" section opens with Question 58, which asks "which is more important—business process or technology?" The answer, not surprisingly, is that it all depends. What it depends on is how critical the process is in differentiating a firm from its competitors. Question 59 follows with four business process improvement scenarios. The first three scenarios reflect different balances between the strategic importance of an existing process and the value of the process embedded in a technology. The fourth, unfortunately common, scenario describes the road to process improvement disaster.

Questions 60 and 61 take process improvement from the realm of the strategically abstract to the reality of an organization's capacity for change. Question 60 focuses on how much process transformation is desirable and provides several guidelines that help assess how much process change is feasible. Question 61 describes the situations in which radical changes are needed most and outlines nine key factors for successfully making them.

Questions 62, 63, and 64 focus on what has become the IT backbone in large firms and is quickly becoming more common in smaller firms—enterprise resource planning (ERP) systems. The answer to Question 62 outlines how ERP systems integrate the flow of information across an organization's functional boundaries and the benefits and trade-offs of adopting them. Question 63 discusses the risks that accompany an ERP implementation and the actions that organizations can take to control them. Question 64 then describes the challenges involved in adopting vendor-supplied ERP solutions, including how a firm's orientation toward technology is likely to influence its choices. It also addresses issues of customizing vendor-supplied ERP solutions to fit strategically important processes.

Questions 65 and 66 focus on customer relationship management (CRM) systems. The answer to Question 65 shows how CRM has evolved over the past several years, from a focus on the automation of sales and marketing operations to a focus on better understanding customer needs, opportunities, and contributions to an organization's revenue streams. Question 66 identifies the attributes of a successful CRM system, outlining the capabilities and features that enable CRM to meet the emerging customer-focused vision.

Questions 67 and 68 examine a third major business process technology, supply chain management (SCM). The answer to Question 67 describes the SCM vision—that organizations can reduce costs, increase their flexibility, and decrease time to market by integrating information flows forward and backward through their supply chain. Question 68 explains why effective SCM implementations are so difficult to achieve. In addition to the risks inherent in ERP implementations, SCM implementations add the complexity of integrating a variety of software applications and systems running on different hardware platforms across multiple organizations.

The final answer in this section brings the reader full circle. Question 69 focuses on the tension between the risks of changing an internal business process versus the challenges of customizing a commercially developed application. This answer is a "must-read," since many IT projects fail when they attempt to customize vendor applications. Changing either an existing business process or a commercial application is a daunting proposition, not for the faint of heart or the careless. With the right level of attention to detail and proper change controls, success is possible and significant business benefits realizable.

In short, the "IT and Business Processes" section describes how IT changes the way firms function by integrating the flow of information within and across them. There are significant risks involved in changing business processes and in implementing supporting technologies. However, the benefits of successfully doing so can be a major source of competitive advantage.

58. Which is more important—business process or technology?

RINA DELMONICO AND RAYMOND F. ZAMMUTO

Business transformation became a corporate buzzword in the early 1990s during the "age of reengineering," when companies were urged to reinvent themselves into efficient, responsive organizations from the slow-moving bureaucracies that characterized large businesses.[1] The transformation craze was driven by two factors: (1) perceptions during the 1980s that U.S. corporations had lost their competitive edge, and (2) rapid advances in information technology. Corporations responded by transforming themselves from collections of departmental silos to integrated operations organized by business process.

WHAT IS A BUSINESS PROCESS?

A business process is a workflow, or set of activities (sometimes called methods and procedures), that produces an outcome valued by an internal or external customer.[2] Consider a customer fulfillment process in a typical, fictional firm during the 1980s. Customers would place orders with salespeople, who then entered orders into a stand-alone sales system. A printed order would then be sent to the billing department to be entered into the billing system. Once approved, the order would be sent to a warehouse, where employees using a warehouse inventory system would fill the order (if available), then send the completed order to the shipping department, where the order is entered once more into another unique system. The elapsed time was a few days to a few weeks; the potential for error was large.

---

[1] Michael Hammer and James Champy, *Reengineering the Corporation: A Manifesto for Business Revolution* (New York: HarperBusiness, 1993).

[2] Thomas H. Davenport and James E. Short, "The New Industrial Engineering: Information and Business Process Design," *MIT Sloan Management Review* 31.4 (1990): 11–28.

The activities involved in fulfilling a customer's order crossed many departmental boundaries. Note the absence of communication among the various computer systems. Much of the time needed to complete orders was spent "in transit." Also note that the activities making up this workflow do not by themselves create value. Value is created only if all the sequential activities resulted in a completed order or service.[3]

WHAT IS REENGINEERING?

Reengineering advocates had the fundamental insight that organizations could operate more efficiently and quickly, and be more responsive to customers' needs, if they reorganized along the lines of the workflows that create value. Many organizations began to revamp operations to match business processes. Departmental structures and reporting lines changed, and sets of tasks formerly scattered across different departments were combined into integrated jobs. Process managers instead of functional managers became responsible for outcomes.

Today, in the same fictional firm, order fulfillment processes work very differently than in the 1980s. Customers place orders with a "call center," which is a single point of contact that serves all customer needs—ordering, checking order and bill status, scheduling service, etc.—activities previously located in different departments. Call center employees enter orders into integrated databases and enterprise-wide systems. These applications then check product availability and credit status, update necessary inventory and financial data, and issue packaging and shipping orders. Call center employees, while on the phone with the customer, confirm the order and provide delivery date and time information. Elapsed time is in minutes; the quality is high.

WHY REENGINEERING DIDN'T WORK

Unfortunately, many firms discovered two major barriers to process reengineering. The first barrier is an organization's cultural norms about "how things get done here" (**Q48**). Revamping organizations along process rather than functional lines can dismantle existing status and power hierarchies in most organizations (**Q47**), creating enormous resistance and killing reengineering efforts.[4] This problem still plagues organizations attempting process reengineering.

The second barrier was technical—integrating separate and typically incompatible computer systems so employees supporting integrated processes had access to

---

[3] Michael Hammer, *Beyond Reengineering: How the Process-Centered Organization Is Changing Our Work and Our Lives* (New York: HarperBusiness, 1996) 101–5.

[4] James Champy, *Reengineering Management: The Mandate for New Leadership* (New York: HarperBusiness, 1995).

Thomas Davenport, "The Fad That People Forgot," *FastCompany* November 1995: 70ff.

necessary information. A couple of factors helped ease this problem during the early 1990s: rapid advances in client/server technology (**Q11**) and integrated database applications, which evolved into enterprise resource management (ERP) systems (**Q62**), facilitated the distribution of information. These systems contained modules (e.g., general ledger, sales, inventory, shipping, human resources modules) that replaced individual departmental systems and used a central database. Thus all relevant information is available to employees to support needed process requirements. However, high levels of integration among modules also made systems very complex, making customization difficult. Most organizations had to reorganize their operations to fit the systems, not adapt the systems to fit their operations. The technical problems of implementation, coupled with the resistance accompanying major restructurings, resulted in more failures (**Q63, Q87, Q88**).

Business Process or Technology?

The promise and problems of organizing by business process create dilemmas for organizations seeking transformation. On one hand, installing vendor applications "as is" creates potential problems due to resistance and organizational disruption, but this approach reduces potential technical problems. On the other hand, customizing vendor products (**Q69**) can be expensive and risky, but organizational implementation risks are reduced. In other words, each option has substantial risks. However, each argument has strong benefits as well. The key question managers facing business process transformation must answer is "what should drive the transformation—our business processes or the technology?"

Answering this question depends on a business's strategy.[5] A general rule of thumb applies: if a business process is a critical differentiator, the company should think carefully about the risks of implementing a standardized application that could eliminate points of differentiation (**Q64**). Conversely, if the process does not differentiate, then purchasing an application designed to provide "best in class" performance makes sense.

Understanding this distinction is important. As more organizations within an industry adopt enterprise resource planning (ERP), supply chain management (SCM), customer relationship management (CRM), and other systems to streamline operations, these companies become increasingly similar. That is, they all get better at doing the same things. Unless there are factors that differentiate among them in terms of the unique value they provide customers, the goods and services produced become commodities and the basis for competition shifts to price (**Q2**).[6] Overall margins decrease

[5] Thomas H. Davenport, "Putting the Enterprise into the Enterprise System," *Harvard Business Review* 76.4 (1998): 121–31.

Thomas H. Davenport, *Mission Critical: Realizing the Promise of Enterprise Systems* (Boston: HBSP, 2000) 105–34.

[6] Michael Porter, "What Is Strategy?" *Harvard Business Review* 74.6 (1996): 61–78.

when this happens, which can result in a hypercompetitive environment where only a few, if any, of the industry participants are profitable. This is exactly the situation that the personal computer industry finds itself in today.

If a business process does not create unique value for an organization but is necessary to its operation, then it makes sense to implement a vendor product with "best in class" performance and reorganize the process to fit the technology. "Housekeeping" or back-office functions, like payroll, typically fall into this category. When processes are not strategic differentiators, making processes as efficient as possible and freeing resources to support other areas producing unique value is the right approach.

The following answer (**Q59**) outlines four common scenarios that firms face when making the choice of which is more important—business process or technology.

---

59. Why is it important to consider business process design when implementing a process technology?

PEGGY KENT

A business process and the technology that makes it work are closely intertwined. They must both be considered when making choices to redesign a process or implement a new technology. Issues around the process itself may require new technology or an overall technology change may dictate a change in process. Regardless of the driver, the key question that managers must answer before deciding whether or not to redesign a process while implementing new technology is: "Is this business process truly a differentiator that drives business success?" Stated in technology terms the questions would be "Is it the process that makes customers return and the business profitable, or could the installation of standard industry software drive improved customer service and profit performance?"

A business process is a workflow or set of activities, working inside a corporate culture, that produces an outcome valued by a customer, whether the customer is internal or external (**Q58**). When considering new process technology, it is important to document how the existing process really works, not how the business wants to believe it works. Operating managers must understand the current process to make critical decisions about whether or how to replace it. Because meeting customer needs is the primary driver of most business processes, employees using an existing process will invent "workarounds" for inadequate processes. As a result, most businesses accumulate these informal "fixes" as users find ways to cope with situations that were not considered as part of the original process designs. It is not unusual to find that how work actually gets done is substantially different from how managers think it gets done. It's also not unusual to find that a process, once mapped, is filled with handoffs, dead ends, and other sources of inefficiencies, which can be eliminated during a process redesign. It is essential, then, to understand how the work is being done with manual workarounds and inventive, but undocumented, procedures.

Once a process is mapped, decisions can be made about the approach relative to technology change. Most process/technology redesign efforts fall into one of four scenarios. The first three have desirable outcomes; the fourth is a common disaster to be avoided.

Scenario 1—Business process is not a differentiator and is modified to fit the new technology

Internal back-office processes, such as payroll and accounts payable, typically are not competitive differentiators. Uniqueness is not important for business functions like these and the quickest, most cost-effective solution is to use the best standard software available—as it was designed, with minimal customization (Q69). In today's environment of mergers and business partnerships, implementations like these often arise when companies try to consolidate business processes from multiple divisions or acquired entities.

This scenario is usually the easiest to implement from a systems perspective, but hard to implement from the business perspective. The major work in these implementations is changing internal processes to match standard software. But projects like these should not be undertaken lightly. Without care and attention to detail, the organization and personnel changes involved can sink the project. There are usually enclaves of vocal employees who insist that their specific process is "unique" and not subject to industry standards. The project is, therefore, most successful when a single executive is responsible for its outcome and he or she can dictate to multiple business units the requirement to change their processes to match those embedded in the software. This avoids the potential for endless wrangling and keeps the project from getting derailed. The successful result should be a transformed process modeled after best-in-class examples.

Scenario 2—Business process is a differentiator and new technology is adapted to support the process

In this scenario, business managers recognize that their process is a differentiator in cost, customer service, or revenue. These differentiating processes are frequently refined to:

59

- improve the speed of the transaction,

- provide a better customer experience,

- reduce costs,

- increase the transparency of customer information to better manage that relationship.

Although standardized software can provide much of the desired process support, modifications to include certain important steps or services are key to differentiating the business from its competitors. For example, a catalog company offers online ordering similar to many other companies, but has additional features on their Web site that make it easier for their customers to use than their competitors' sites. To retain these features, a standard call center support application must be modified. The features could include unique ways to list merchandise making it easier to navigate the Web site or, perhaps, a particular representation of their selection of sizes and colors. Similarly, companies who offer complicated discounting arrangements may need to modify standard billing and estimating software modules to accommodate these arrangements.

In these situations, compromises must be reached to maintain the differentiating features while applying proven software to the process. There will be more implementation issues on the technical side with software changes, integration, testing, and so on, but implementation with the users may be easier because existing process steps are preserved. This scenario needs carefully defined requirements and engineering during the implementation in order to avoid eliminating the source of differentiation. Conversely, making extensive changes to standard packages will create larger maintenance and life cycle costs, and add considerable risk to the project itself (Q69).

SCENARIO 3—BUSINESS PROCESS IS A DIFFERENTIATOR AND THE NEW TECHNOLOGY ADEQUATELY SUPPORTS THE PROCESS

A project implementing new technology that supports the existing, differentiating processes provides the best opportunity for success. This scenario usually occurs when a business integrates several standard processes in new, effective ways. Integrating several packages offers substantial benefits if the data elements transferred between standard applications are complete, consistent, and do not require substantial translation. The implementation of new technology provides an opportunity for the business to reexamine their processes and fine-tune them, without making major user-affecting changes. For example, firms engaging in e-commerce can link commercial ordering, billing, fulfillment, and call center software behind customized Web sites to provide unique online experiences for their customers, suppliers, or business partners. Additionally, newer versions of ERP systems, CRM systems, and the like, allow for highly customized configurations that are designed to help preserve a business's differentiated processes without requiring significant modifications of the vendor's software code.

Scenario 4: The death spiral

A "death spiral" scenario occurs when a business process is not changed to match the process contained in a commercial package and when the commercial package is not changed to fit the existing process. This scenario comes about when the differences between the "standard" process embedded in a commercial package and the existing (often undocumented) process are not understood, or where warring user and IT groups refuse to accommodate each other during the project.

Typically, the scenario plays out as follows. A new application is selected without careful analysis of either the "standard" process embedded in the system or the existing process. The application is implemented at significant cost and is (a) used improperly because the existing processes were not updated, (b) worked around and ignored so that promised benefits aren't achieved, or, even worse (c) the new system is subverted by those who work against the new system by refusing to change their existing processes. Productivity decreases or operations grind to a halt as the incompatibilities of the new and old ways of conducting business collide. The system is deemed a failure and terminated, with the investment in time, money, and personnel wasted.

Conclusion

Keeping the right balance between the need for process differentiation and process efficiency is the key to choosing the right scenario and succeeding at the project. Process improvement is the right driver for successful system implementations, and business process owners and IT leaders must partner to analyze, choose, and implement new technology. This partnership between business and IT leaders is critical for the success of technology implementation projects. If either side of this equation attempts to choose or implement a system independently, chances for success drop significantly and the fourth scenario, the death spiral, becomes a reality. Conversely, when the partnership and expertise are in place and working well, the right scenario is obvious, the implementation succeeds, and the business benefits are substantial.

59

60. How much transformation in business processes is needed or desirable?

TOM DEVANE

A major concern facing organizations contemplating technological innovations is the issue of transformation.[1] The question of what is the "right amount" of transformation is one that often keeps CIOs, CEOs, and vice presidents awake at night. It is common industry knowledge that over 70 percent of all transformation efforts fail, this appears to be an appropriate sleep-stopper for those charged with the overall success of an organization.

Successful transformations do not address technology and business processes alone, they also include key performance variables such as strategy, structure, culture, and human resource support. Without these additional factors, we neglect the fact that ultimately people do the work that produces results. No new computer program ever changed deep-seated human beliefs and behavior. No new business process map or automated sales support system ever convinced a person to change how he has been dealing with customers for 20 years.

While there is no simple answer to this question, there is a two-step approach that can help organizations navigate through the often murky waters of transformation planning at the start of a project:

1. Characterize the transformation.

2. Determine the amount of transformation based on key considerations and guidelines.

CHARACTERIZING THE TRANSFORMATION

In this author's view, there are three dimensions to consider when evaluating the amount of transformation needed:

- scale,

- scope,

- magnitude.

---

[1] Definitions of the word "transformation" abound in the business literature today. In this answer transformation is defined as significant changes in how people in an organization think and interact. These new thoughts and interactions may include, but are not necessarily limited to, changes in how they perform business processes, how they conduct themselves in meetings, how they use information technology, how they are structured to accomplish work, and changes in leadership style.

Table 60.1 Examples of Scale Options

Scale Option	Example
The entire organization	Implementation of an ERP system (**Q62**)
Group of departments	Redesign of a new product development process for an electronics assembly operation that includes design engineering, manufacturing, purchasing, and test engineering departments
Single department	Implementation of a computer-aided design (CAD) system in an engineering department for a camera manufacturer
Group within a department	Implementation of an automated sales tool for the field sales group of a global pharmaceutical manufacturer
Spin-off organization	A large, established organization moved 20 people from the IT department to another location to develop an e-business presence

Scale indicates affected parts of the organization. Scale options include those shown in Table 60.1.

Once the target population for the upcoming change has been identified, one can begin to evaluate the transformation using a matrix to address the final two elements, scope and magnitude.

Table 60.2 shows a partially completed characterization matrix for a European-based global pharmaceutical manufacturer. The *scope* of the transformation (appearing across the top) addresses key performance factors that can also be used as change levers to assist in the transformation. The *magnitude* of the transformation (on the left side) helps characterize the amount of change required.

To use this matrix, an organization would gather a group of people—often a group of executives and change agents from several levels in the organization—to complete the cells as in Table 60.2. Though the initial characterizations and cell entries are often subjective, they nevertheless provide an excellent opportunity for healthy dialogue, negotiation, and reconciling expectations about the upcoming major project.

DETERMINING THE AMOUNT OF TRANSFORMATION—
PRACTICAL CONSIDERATIONS AND GUIDELINES

There are four critical considerations useful in determining how much transformation is needed.

1. First consideration—The size of a business performance gap of major concern. Simply stated, an organization needs to determine where it is now, where it wants to

Table 60.2 Example of the Scope and Magnitude of Transformation

Project: *Business Process Excellence (includes process redesign and ERP implementation)*
Scale: *Entire Organization*

Type of Change	Strategy	Process	Culture	Technology	Structure	HR Support
Major change	Company can promise delivery three weeks faster than competitors to retail outlets and hospitals.	New process metrics are used to plan and control work (not previously used department metrics).	Entry of production and warehouse data that impact financial statements made by operations, not financial people. People can no longer hide/hoard department data. Functional silos dissolve.	Departments access other departments' key operating data.	Cross-functional process teams replace individuals within departments as the basic performing unit of work.	
Moderate change		Production personnel enter transactions immediately instead of batching for 3 days.				
Minor change				New system menus require different navigation.		Users are trained in how to develop and deliver technical training.

be, and the gap between these two. An organization may target any number of topics upon which to perform this gap analysis, such as:[2]

- development time for new products (the company's vs. nearest competitor's),

- market share for a target niche (desired vs. actual),

- organizational structure and philosophy (choice of a traditional, functionally organized, bureaucratic structure vs. one composed of multiskilled teams that quickly adapt to changes in the external environment),

- competitive pressures that suggest a greater Internet presence is desirable due to competitors' use of the Internet to minimize overall supply chain costs and compress customer delivery times,

- customer service level (company's current dismal 40% compared to the 94% industry average).

Guideline: In general, the greater the disparity between the target and the actual, the more the need for significant, well-planned transformation. The smaller the disparity, the less there is a need for a major transformation effort. (Note: avoiding an unnecessary major transformation effort is *always* a good thing.)

2. Second consideration—The number of significant changes that will be required of current mind-sets and behaviors to operate in the new environment. Few people initially embrace a change that discards deeply rooted beliefs and assumptions that have been formed over an entire career:[3]

- If a salesperson believes the only effective way of selling products is through personal relationships, she may strongly resist the company's new automated sales force initiative.

- If a vice president's historical behavior was hoarding information because "information is power," then he may try—openly or covertly—to undermine the success of the new enterprise system.

- If a manager's personal identity hinges on his lifelong managerial duties, he may be hesitant to empower teams to assume many of the supervisory tasks he previously performed, even though the team members have the training and information from the new system to do so.

[2] While each would include significant technology support, it is important to state the performance gap in *business* terms, not *technology* terms. This will help keep the focus of the project on proactive solutions, and also help in enlisting support from those outside the IT department.

[3] Samuel Culbert, *Mind-Set Management: The Heart of Leadership* (London: Oxford UP, 1995).

Guideline: Generally speaking, the more mind-set and behavior shifts that are required, the more attentive project planners must be in ensuring that these are addressed in the transformation segment of the project work plan (**Q48**).

3. Third consideration—The leadership team's appetite for improvement vs. their stomach for change. Many grandiose plans for large-scale changes have aggressive timetables and audacious improvement goals. However, without formal leaders actively involving themselves in planning the large-scale change, modeling the new behaviors and technology use, and visibly supporting the change once it is launched, the desired dramatic improvements will not materialize. It is natural to dream of dramatic improvements without having to take dramatic actions; but this rarely, if ever, happens. Huge improvements require a proportional amount of effort from the entire organization, *especially* from the leaders.[4] Key questions to pose include: *Will the formal leaders actively support this effort once it is started? Are they willing to dedicate internal resources, and if needed, fund external resources to succeed? What if senior management needs to be transformed before leading a successful transformation?*

Guideline: If the leadership team's appetite for improvement is significantly greater than the stomach for change, a large-scale transformation is not recommended.

4. Fourth consideration—Congruency of key performance variables. People quickly detect inconsistencies and incongruities in espoused organizational beliefs and actual practices. For example, if an element of the strategy is "empowered, technology-driven teams" and the compensation system rewards individuals, it is unlikely the organization will achieve its desired goals that rely on teamwork. This congruency plays out in two areas in a transformation:

- how congruent the performance variables are now,

- how they are designed to work together in the new environment.

Guideline: If significant incongruence exists now, it's most likely time for a moderate to major transformation.

IMPLICATIONS FOR SENIOR MANAGERS
AND CHANGE AGENTS

As with most complex interactions involving people, technology, and business processes, there is no "silver bullet." However, it is clear that a technology change ef-

---

[4] Peggy Holman and Tom Devane, *The Change Handbook: Group Methods for Shaping the Future* (San Francisco: Berrett-Koehler, 1999).

fort is more likely to succeed if managers who "size" the change keep in mind both the size of the performance gap being addressed and the capacity of the organization for change. The following approach is recommended:

1. Convene a group—ideally senior managers and change agents—to *characterize* the type of change facing the organization.

2. Discuss the *considerations and guidelines* presented.

3. Determine a go-forward strategy.

4. Establish feedback loops to monitor transformation progress and validity of initial assumptions.

5. As the project progresses, evaluate data from the feedback loops.

6. Modify actions as required.

When this is done, the outcome should be a good plan for the right amount of transformation in the organization.

---

61. When are radical changes in processes and technologies more desirable and effective than incremental changes?

TOM DEVANE

61

Senior IT managers are faced with a barrage of decisions at the start of an IT-enabled project. In addition to technical decisions and questions about how the project will link to the company's strategy, senior IT managers also need to consider the impact of change on each organization. The concept of managing change and how people deal with it has received some new, well-deserved attention after recent publicized failures of (**Q63**, **Q87**):

- enterprise systems,

- technology-assisted reengineering efforts,

- CRM systems,

- sales force automation,

- large e-business initiatives.

The main reason cited for most of these failures was the inability to manage the "people component" of a project requiring large-scale organizational change. This chapter addresses three key change-related questions that senior IT managers need to answer:

1. How do we know how much change is needed?

2. What pervasive myths sabotage effective change in technology-enabled projects?

3. How can we design for effective change?

WHEN TO IMPLEMENT RADICAL CHANGES

A first step in any technology-related work plan is to assess the amount of change needed. *Radical changes* tend to be more desirable than *incremental changes* when one or more of the situations shown in Table 61.1 exist.

WHEN TO IMPLEMENT INCREMENTAL CHANGE

In general, *incremental changes* tend to be more desirable when none of the above situations exist. Executives should also seriously consider incremental change when the following "red flag" conditions are present:

- Other radical changes are occurring in the company, and one more could overstress organizational capabilities.

- External regulatory entities can close down a facility if radical change is poorly implemented.

- The risk of change is high from the standpoint of customer satisfaction (**Q50**).

- Senior management is not committed to spending 20 to 75% of their time actively supporting change.

- Management will not support the change effort by engaging change professionals (either internal or external).

Once the amount of change has been decided, IT managers need to be aware of seven common myths that can derail a project and perhaps even a career.

SEVEN MYTHS OF TECHNOLOGY-RELATED IMPLEMENTATIONS

There are seven common myths this author has discovered regarding technology implementations. Consciously or unconsciously adopting these myths leads to im-

Table **61.1** When to Implement Radical Changes

Situation	Example
A large performance gap exists.	Your major competitor gets products to market five times faster than your company.
Organizational inertia is high.	Your company experienced six failed major change efforts in five years. No one believes change is possible, yet the organization must respond quickly to adapt to external changes.
Change must be executed extremely quickly to catch up to or surpass the competition.	Your company has no e-business capabilities. A major competitor now derives 80 percent of their income from e-business and has stolen 35 percent of your customers.
The workforce's existing beliefs and assumptions are completely opposite from marketplace demands.	Long-time workers believe they are entitled to a job for life. Moving slowly is favored over moving quickly, and "good quality" means checking the product eight times before shipment. Three new hungry entrants into your market undercut your costs by 30 percent and introduced products twice as fast.
The new technology will require a significant shift in peoples' responsibilities.	An enterprise system requires that data entry be located as close to a transaction occurrence as possible—requiring operations people to take on responsibilities that were previously accounting's.

plementation problems for both incremental and radical changes. Of course, for radical changes these myths often wreak more havoc because there are more opportunities to impact performance. These myths are:

1. *Technology-enabled change is quick and painless.* For many, a corollary of the big bang theory of the creation of the universe is the big bang theory of IT technology implementations. It is important to resist focusing solely on the computer system and the ease of turning it on.

2. *Everybody starts out with the same assumptions.* It is not uncommon for senior management and the rest of the organization to have entirely different project expectations (**Q49**). Nor is it uncommon to get five months into an implementation and find that the executives all have differing views on what the system will and will not do. Expect executives to hold different assumptions until they convene and mutually agree upon direction and scope.

3. *The initial budget number is the final budget number.* Implementation of IT-enabled projects is a discovery-based process—not an exact science. I have seen

budgets for enterprise system implementations more than triple within as short a time frame as 4 months (**Q99**).

4. *Installation equals implementation.* Installing new software and distributing new log-ins are hardly the sole requirements for success. However, project teams often act that way as the scheduled implementation date looms closer on the horizon. People need to be trained in the operation and use of the new system. They need to understand that new ways of thinking, doing, and managing are required.

5. *People switch painlessly to the new system on the conversion date.* The bigger the change, the more change management is required. However, even the smallest change requires a certain amount of change management planning. There is a natural tendency to revert to old behaviors, manual processes, and workarounds, especially in times of crises.

6. *Since technology is a major cost component of the project, an information systems person needs to run the project.* Business needs should drive the project, and this often means a person from the business side needs to manage the project. If adequate project management skills exist only in IT, then project management responsibilities should be *shared* by business people and IT people (**Q93, Q95**).

7. *Dramatic gains are possible without rocking the current boat.* It is amazing how many organizational leaders passionately say they want "dramatic performance gains" and then in the same sentence continue, ". . . but we don't want to make any radical changes."

Awareness of the above myths and purging them from the organizational consciousness will be sufficient to help implement most incremental changes. However, radical changes typically require an additional set of critical success factors for success.

CRITICAL SUCCESS FACTORS FOR RADICAL CHANGE

Here are nine key factors that enable or allow success to happen on IT projects where radical change is required:

1. A large number of people in the organization have a logical understanding *and* an emotional feeling that the change is necessary.

2. BHAGs (big, hairy, audacious goals) are set. (BHAG is a term coined by Collins and Porras to describe that natural tendency of stretch goals to motivate people toward action.)[1]

3. Effective leadership is in place to set direction and arbitrate resource allocation disputes.

[1] James C. Collins and Jerry I. Porras, *Built to Last* (New York: HarperBusiness, 1997).

4. Cross-functional teams are used to gather diverse perspectives and develop systemic solutions.

5. Middle managers buy in to and actively support the change. (Since their jobs—and often personal identities—usually require the most change, this group *must* actively support the change.)

6. System users are involved early in the process as part of the design team—not just as interviewees (often performing tasks typically thought to be in the solitary domain of IT people, such as creating test conditions, developing test scripts, and developing technical user training).

7. Develop the project implementation plan for sustainability *and* speed; do not make the mistake of deciding between sustainability *or* speed.

8. Include the work plan for change management activities as part of the overall implementation plan; do not separate the effort or when project schedules get tight, change management activities will be jettisoned.

9. Address all—not just some—key business performance levers such as strategy, business processes, technology, culture, and structure. These all need to be planned for, aligned, and monitored during the project.

By considering the amount of change, the common myths, and the radical-change critical success factors, senior IT managers can be off to a great project start.

62. What is an enterprise resource planning (ERP) system?

MARK ENDRY AND TRAVIS WHITE

Enterprise resource planning or ERP is a term coined by Gartner Group to describe a set of software applications that automate the internal processes of an organization. The departments involved typically include finance, manufacturing, distribution (or logistics as it is often called), human resources, and payroll. Some ERP packages may also include maintenance management, asset management, project management, and so on.

Other analyst organizations and commentators have coined other terms to describe essentially the same phenomenon. Other terms include enterprise resource management (ERM) and application programs for the enterprise (APE). A more general term, "enterprise software," is often used as well.

The Origins of ERP

ERP packages originated as independent point solutions, typically in finance, purchasing, and manufacturing. These "high return" departments' operations were often the first to be automated. In the late 1970s and early 1980s, it was typical for a company to buy a general ledger application from one vendor, an accounts receivable application from another vendor, and an accounts payable application from yet another vendor. The company might also develop some of its own in-house or home-grown applications.

In the manufacturing departments, similar stories evolved. Companies often started by automating high-cost processes such as inventory management and bill-of-material processing. Companies developed homegrown applications to address these needs or purchased packaged applications from small vendors. Over time, companies demanded that these applications be integrated with each other to manage a larger portion of the manufacturing process.

The Evolution of ERP

Vendors responded by integrating inventory and bill-of-material applications. These ultimately became known as MRP or manufacturing resource planning applications. MRP applications were among the first "integrated" applications on the market. Seeking to compete with each other, vendors then integrated additional functionality into their MRP packages, typically in the areas of purchasing and sales order management. These packages became known as MRP II applications.

Meanwhile, the financial applications market was also consolidating and integrating point solutions into application suites. Vendors offered "consolidated" financial applications that included, at minimum, general ledger, accounts payable, and accounts receivable. These solutions often included payroll, human resources, international processing (including multicurrency and consolidations), and various different accounting management tools.

By the early 1990s, consolidated financials and MRP were growing together into integrated application suites. It was around this time that Gartner coined the term ERP to describe a suite of applications designed to automate the internal processes of an entire company.

ERP TODAY

ERP vendors seek to distinguish themselves on several different dimensions, including:

- functionality,

- degree of integration,

- architectural flexibility,

- speed of implementation,

- total cost of ownership.

ERP vendors often provide a variety of services as well, including traditional services such as training and implementation support as well as extended services such as business process engineering.

SUMMARY OF TYPICAL ERP SOLUTIONS

Packaged ERP solutions typically help companies rationalize their business operations and reduce their cost. To achieve these advantages, companies need to make a variety of choices. A discussion of these choices follows.

Degree of Customization   Most ERP packages include industry best practices and it is often to the user's advantage to do a "plain vanilla" implementation, adapting the business to the package rather than vice versa. On the other hand, many customers argue that their business is unique and that they need to adapt the software to their practices. Advantages of a "plain vanilla" implementation include lower cost and adherence to best business practices. The disadvantages are that it often takes longer—because you have to change your business—and it gives you no advantage over competitors who implement the same model. A more customized approach often gives a better competitive advantage but tends to cost more and may be more difficult to upgrade and maintain (**Q69**).

Speed of Implementation   Customers often want to implement their ERP software quickly, which produces a set of trade-offs. Faster implementations typically lock customers into preset templates, leaving little opportunity for customization. Faster implementations also tend to skimp on (or eliminate altogether) knowledge transfer from the software vendor to the user. The customer may go live more quickly but without really "owning" the solution. Slower implementations tend to provide more opportunity for customization and greater transfer of knowledge.

Integration vs. Best of Breed   Companies also need to decide the appropriate trade-off between integration and functionality. So-called "best-of-breed" vendors typically offer point solutions that are generally assumed to offer greater functionality within a given application domain (**Q64**). The customer then integrates the various best-of-breed solutions to develop an enterprise-wide solution. For example, a company might select to implement the Human Resources module from one vendor and the Financials module from another vendor. The cost of the integration between the modules that the company is forced to do themselves can be very steep. ERP vendors, on the other hand, offer multiple modules that are preintegrated. It's often assumed that individual modules offer less functionality than their best-of-breed competitors. By contrast, integrated solutions often provide a lower total cost of ownership (**Q74**) and require smaller IT staffs to maintain them. As a general rule of thumb, small and midsize companies tend to prefer integrated solutions. Larger companies, with more specialized needs, are the domain of best-of-breed solutions.

Degree of Flexibility after Implementation   We take it as an axiom that business practices will continue to change. Indeed, the pace of change may well be accelerating. Most ERP solutions are fairly flexible at time of implementation but become less flexible after implementation. The analogy often used is that of pouring cement; wet cement is flexible, dry cement is not. Business practices encased in the original ERP implementation may quickly become out of date. Because of this, customers need to decide on the appropriate balance between initial functionality in a package and the cost of keeping that functionality up to date.

Quality and Timeliness of Releases   Competitive pressures often push vendors to release new functionality and modules as quickly as possible. Industry analysts contribute to this pressure by giving higher marks to vendors who have a particular module and lower marks to vendors who have not yet shipped. At the same time, there is very little standard information available on the quality of the software. Because of this, customers need to do thorough evaluation in deciding the appropriate balance between quality and functionality (**Q79**).

ERP TRENDS

As with any market, the ERP market continues to change. ERP software buyers should be aware of the following trends.

Further Consolidation   Today the Big 4 vendors—SAP, Oracle, J. D. Edwards, and PeopleSoft—account for about half of the ERP software sold worldwide. The remaining half is fragmented among a large number of small vendors. Industry analysts generally predict that further market consolidation is likely.

Further Integration   ERP packages traditionally focused on financial, manufacturing, distribution, and human resources processes. Like an ever-expanding circle, vendors would deliver new functionality with each release and would often incorporate (and sometimes eliminate) point solutions. Two other major strands of software grew up in parallel: supply chain management (SCM) (**Q67**) applications and customer relationship management (CRM) (**Q65**) applications. The challenge for enterprise vendors today is to integrate ERP, SCM, and CRM applications in one coherent offering.

From Introverted to Extraverted   ERP software traditionally focused on automating processes within a company. Today, many companies are interested in exchanging information or sharing business processes with their customers and suppliers. By doing so, they can improve visibility and predictability and can often manage inventory more effectively. Thus, ERP vendors are starting to deliver software that goes beyond the four walls of the enterprise and helps link a company with its partners. This trend is often known as collaborative commerce or c-commerce.

Increased Functionality Unique to an Industry   Originally, ERP packages might have supported "manufacturing" operations. Today, it is increasingly likely that they will support the manufacturing process of, for instance, consumer package goods companies or pharmaceutical companies.

Growing Emphasis on Thin Clients   Today, the emphasis is on providing thin client access to ERP systems because thin clients provide lower cost and easier administration. Today's thin clients typically provide a friendly GUI, often driven by HTML or Java (**Q12**).

62

From Department to Process   ERP packages, and software in general, traditionally targeted specific departments such as finance or purchasing. The result was that different departments automated at a different pace and the company wound up with a patchwork of automated and nonautomated departments. This method of automation also encouraged "silos" within the organization. Today, many customers are thinking about enterprise software in terms of processes rather than departments. For instance, the order-to-cash process ties together many departments in a single, seamless operation. Vendors are responding by repackaging their software as well as their implementation and training deliverables.

63. What risks does an organization face from an ERP implementation?

JUDY SCOTT

The implementation of software in an organization is inherently risky. In fact, many software implementations fail (**Q86**, **Q87**, **Q88**). Because of the complexity of enterprise resource planning (ERP) systems, the number of stakeholders, and the potential impacts on the entire organization, ERP implementation projects are especially prone to risks. Current estimates are that at least 90 percent of ERP implementations end up late or overbudget.[1] ERP risks appear at the project level, the information systems level, the organizational level, as well as outside the organization.[2]

PROJECT RISKS

For ERP projects, customization of purchased packages and the difficulty of interfacing them with existing legacy systems are the major causes of project delays and cost overruns. Many organizations do not accept or understand that "best practices" are embedded in the ERP systems they purchase. Instead, they insist that their own business processes are somehow unique and thus customize the software instead of doing a "plain vanilla" implementation. This increases the risk substantially (**Q69**). Interfaces to legacy systems increase the complexity and risk of the project because the ability of systems to interoperate seamlessly is often not known until the project is well under way. If major problems are encountered late in the project, schedules slip and costs rise. Data conversion is another problematic area because of lack of data integrity. Companies that choose not to clean up their data prior to embarking on the project will pay the price later. For example, Brother Industries wasted time entering data for thousands of obsolete parts for their ERP project.[3]

When project delays and cost overruns become severe, or when the software is a misfit with the organization, some troubled ERP projects are abandoned.[4] Dell aban-

[1] Michael H. Martin, "Smart Managing," *Fortune* 2 Feb. 1998: 149–51.

[2] Judy E. Scott and Iris Vessey, "Toward a Multi-Level Theory of Risks in Enterprise Systems Implementations," Working Paper, 2002, and "Managing Risks in Enterprise Systems Implementations," *Communications of the ACM* 45.4 (2002): 74–81.

[3] Claudia H. Deutsch, "Software That Can Make a Grown Company Cry," *New York Times* 8 Nov. 1998, late ed.

[4] Thomas H. Davenport, "Putting the Enterprise into the Enterprise System," *Harvard Business Review* 76.4 (1998): 121–31; M. Lynne Markus and Cornelis Tanis, "The Enterprise Systems Experience—From Adoption to Success," *Framing the Domains of IT Research: Glimpsing the Future through the Past.* Robert W. Zmud, ed. (Cincinnati: Pinnaflex Educational Resources, 2002).

doned their initial attempt at an ERP system after two years of implementation because it perceived the package's flexibility as inadequate for Dell's growth.[5] Unisource wrote off $168 million three years into a ten-year ERP project because of problems standardizing its 11 service centers and lack of time to meet the Y2K deadline.[6]

All ERP vendors have had vocal discontented customers. However, to keep these reports in perspective, it needs to be noted that the negative impacts of an ERP implementation are often temporary. Most organizations have recovered from a period of decreased productivity immediately following a "go live" ERP implementation and have experienced benefits after a lag time.[7]

Another point to consider is the evolution of ERP implementations. Many of the problematic implementations occurred between 1996 and 1999, when client-server ERP technology was new and expertise was in short supply. Since then however, the shortage of expertise has eased. In recent years, the project risks of ERP systems have been better understood and companies are therefore managing their implementations better.

Information Systems Risks

At the information systems level, the ERP system may run slowly and have performance issues. For example, the ERP system may be poorly configured, have too many queries to be run online, or the hardware may need upgrading. Integration of the ERP system with legacy systems or other packages consumes much of the labor in ERP implementations. For example, multiple vendors, with the need for multiple system interfaces, contributed to problems at Hershey Foods Corporation, Whirlpool, FoxMeyer, and Tri Valley Growers.

Data conversion from legacy systems is complex and often problematic. Because of the risk that data conversion could render the company inoperable, it is extremely important that conversion recovery plans be built (Q99).

63—

Organizational Risks

The impact of a bad ERP implementation can negatively impact a company's operating results. Problems with the ERP system might cause delivery problems, which could affect the organization's financial performance in the short term. Although in the long term the issues are usually resolved, the organization's reputation and

---

[5] Julia King, "Dell Zaps SAP," *Computerworld* 26 May 1997: 2.

[6] Tom Stein, "SAP Installation Scuttled," *InformationWeek* 26 Jan. 1998: 34.

[7] Jeanne W. Ross and Michael R. Vitale, "The ERP Revolution: Surviving vs. Thriving," *Information Systems Frontier* 2.2 (2000): 233–41; *ERP's Second Wave: Maximizing the Value of ERP-Enabled Processes*, Deloitte Consulting, Report, 1998.

relationships with customers are at risk. Hershey Foods reported massive distribution problems associated with its ERP project that caused a third-quarter 12.4 percent sales drop, a 18.6 percent earnings drop, a full year $466 million revenue shortfall, and share price drop of 26 percent.[8] When Whirlpool blamed shipping delays of up to 8 weeks and difficulties in meeting some of its orders on its ERP implementation, its share price fell from well over $70 to below $60.[9] W. W. Grainger reported a 57 percent decline in income in 1999, net earnings for the third quarter were down 18 percent, and service disruptions caused by its transition to its new ERP system accounted for an $11 million reduction in operating earnings.[10] Snap-on reported a $50 million loss in 1998 with its ERP project.[11] Because ERP installations touch virtually every part of an organization, any problems can generate immediate impacts financially, with customers, or with internal business objectives.

EXTERNAL RISKS

At the external level, there have been cases of litigation associated with ERP implementations. The cases are against consultants who implemented the ERP system and ERP vendors. Gore-Tex complained that its consultant promised expert staff for its ERP implementation and delivered incompetent trainees who learned the software at the company's expense.[12] SunLite Casual Furniture accused its consultant of incompetence and overbilling, and charged that the consultant, hoping for years of lucrative fees, maliciously indoctrinated total dependency on its services. Although Tri Valley Growers does not blame its failed consumer packaged goods ERP implementation for its Chapter 11 bankruptcy in 2000, it is suing its ERP vendor for $20 million, claiming that it would have saved more than $5 million per year if the software had worked.[13]

Finally, in one extreme case, an organization did blame its bankruptcy on its ERP implementation. FoxMeyer is suing its vendor and its implementation consultant for

[8] Marc L. Songini, "Halloween Less Haunting for Hershey This Year," *Computerworld* 2 Nov. 2000: 12; Emily Nelson and Evan Ramstad, "Trick or Treat: Hershey's Biggest Dud Has Turned Out to Be Its New Technology," *The Wall Street Journal* 29 Oct. 1999, sec. A: 1; Craig Stedman, "Failed ERP Gamble Haunts Hershey," *Computerworld* 1 Nov. 1999: 1.

[9] Stacy Collett, "SAP: Whirlpool's Rush to Go Live Led to Shipping Snafus," *Computerworld* .com 4 Nov. 1999, 20 Aug. 2002 <http://www.computerworld.com/cwi/story/0,1199,NAV47_STO29365,00.html>.

[10] "Grainger's Net Income Declines 57% On Costs Tied to Software Problems," *The Wall Street Journal* 31 Jan. 2000, interactive ed.

[11] Thomas Hoffman, "Software Snafu Triggers Order Delays, Loss," *Computerworld* 6 July 1998: 6.

[12] Elizabeth MacDonald, "W. L. Gore Alleges PeopleSoft, Deloitte Botched a Costly Software Installation," *The Wall Street Journal* 2 Nov. 1999, sec. B:14.

[13] Christopher Koch, "Why Your Integration Efforts End Up Looking Like This," *CIO* 15 Nov. 2001: 98ff.

$500 million each.[14] Similar to Gore-Tex and SunLite Casual Furniture, FoxMeyer accuses the consultants of incompetence. On the other hand, FoxMeyer apparently used a risky "big bang" strategy, went "live" too soon, cut short testing, had inadequate training, did not monitor the project closely enough, and appeared to have made many of the classic mistakes often seen in large systems installations.

CONTROLLING ERP RISKS

Is there anything that can be done about this very high-risk environment? There is no way to totally eliminate risk, but there are some things that can be done to reduce risk.

- *Project risks*—At the project level, strong project management is extremely important for controlling risk. The project leader should control the project and monitor its progress (**Q89**). Standard project management techniques such as limiting the project scope are critical. Customization should be the exception rather than the rule (**Q69**). A phased implementation is less risky than a "big bang" introduction, although it is more expensive.

- *Information systems risks*—At the information systems level, a "plain vanilla" implementation minimizes performance issues. Transactions may take too long if complex queries are run against the ERP database. To avoid this, some organizations decide to use a data warehouse for reports and queries (**Q20**). Other ways to control risk is to stay away from multivendor implementations with their complex interfaces and to avoid "pushing the envelope" if a new technology is used on the project.

- *Organizational risks*—At the organizational level, one of the most important ways to control ERP implementation risk is training.[15] A Gartner study showed that when a minimum of 10 percent, and more likely 15 percent, of the total project budget is allocated to training, it increased the likelihood of success of the project.[16] Also strong leadership can control risks.[17] A strong leader will ensure that sufficient resources are allocated to the project and that there is cultural alignment to the implementation (**Q48**). The leader will also be sufficiently involved with the project to limit its complexity and inspire employees who otherwise might resist the organizational change. If the organization is reluctant to accept the "best practices" embedded in the ERP, the leader needs to decide whether to enforce a "plain vanilla" implementation or accept the risks of customization (**Q58**).

63 ▬

[14] J. Jesitus, "Broken Promises?" *Industry Week* 3 Nov. 1997: 31–37.

William M. Bulkeley, "Technology: When Things Go Wrong," *The Wall Street Journal* 18 Nov. 1996, sec. R:25; Bruce Caldwell "Andersen Sued On R/3," *InformationWeek* 6 July 1998: 152.

[15] Malcolm Wheatley, "ERP Training Stinks," *CIO* 1 June 2000: 86ff.

[16] Derek Slater, "The Hidden Costs of Enterprise Software," *CIO* 15 Jan. 1998: 123–29.

[17] Leslie P. Willcocks and Richard Sykes, "Enterprise Resource Planning: The Role of the CIO and IT Function in ERP," *Communications of the ACM* 43.4 (2000): 32–38.

- *External risks*—At the external level, effective partnerships with consultants and ERP vendors will ensure that expertise is available. Contracts with consultants should align goals and specify the individuals who will implement the ERP system to avoid problems with incompetence.

All large software projects have risks and ERP projects are especially risky. However, with careful attention to these major elements as well as quality planning and a dedicated and competent staff, there is good reason to be optimistic that an ERP implementation can be successful.

---

64. What are the challenges in using a vendor-supplied ERP system to support redesigned business processes?

MARK ENDRY AND TRAVIS WHITE

In choosing business processes supplied by an ERP vendor, a company must first determine how "standard" its business is. If the business practices and processes are fairly similar to other companies in the same industry, then the company can often implement more-or-less standard processes delivered in software by ERP vendors. As the company's business processes diverge from the industry norm, it becomes increasingly difficult to implement standard processes (Q58).

To address the issue of "standardness," a company must first clarify its objectives regarding the IT function. A simple question that a company should ask itself is, "Do we seek to compete on IT functions or do we see IT mainly as a cost that should be reduced?" Though it seems simple, most companies find it difficult to answer this question clearly. Indeed, many companies wish to answer "yes" to both halves of the question. In reality, the two halves of the question lead to different IT structures, services, and, ultimately, ERP software. Here's a brief summary of the differences:

- *Companies that seek to compete on IT functions* (a.k.a. *competitive*)—These companies tend to be larger than their more cost-conscious cousins, and they typically have significantly larger IT staffs. They tend to be early adopters of new technologies and often have a formal program of testing and evaluating new technologies. They often buy "one of everything." They also have a reasonably high tolerance for failure; they expect some programs to fail but are willing to pay this cost to stay near the leading edge. Similarly, they have a fairly high tolerance for low-quality deliverables from vendors. They want to be early adopters and realize that the quality of leading-edge technologies may not be fully realized. They lean toward best-of-breed solutions and have a large budget for integration. These companies tend to see themselves as ultimately responsible for their own solutions.

- *Companies that see IT as a cost* (a.k.a. *value oriented*)—These companies tend to be smaller and invest a smaller proportion of revenues in technology. They tend not to adapt new technologies aggressively but rather wait to "learn from the mistakes of others." These companies tend to evaluate each program on its projected return; there is relatively little interest in experimental programs. Similarly, they look for a high degree of prepackaged integration and demand relatively high quality from their vendors. Finally, they look for the vendor to take responsibility for the solution and are often looking for a single point of contact in terms of vendor management.

Companies may find it frustrating to debate these questions in the abstract. It is often more useful to do some "self-scouting"—to observe one's own behavior. This may take the form of benchmarking the company's IT functions against industry peers or informal discussions with fellow executives at industry events.

If we think of "competitive oriented" and "value oriented" as two ends of a spectrum, it is likely that most companies will fall somewhere in between—though they will often tend to "tilt" in one direction or another. The degree of tilt may be influenced by a number of factors, including size and age of the company, industry segment, competitive position, and so on (**Q5**). To sort out their ERP software, companies first need to sort out their degree of tilt toward one pole or the other; it is a question of understanding values, spending patterns, and operational behaviors. Once the question is sorted out, the company can then address whether and how it should adapt the business practices that are delivered with ERP software. The two types of companies described above will have very different challenges as they approach the implementation of ERP-based business processes. Table 64.1 on the next page compares the "competitive" company with the "value-oriented" company. Let's look at each in turn.

The "competitive" group consists of those who seek to use IT as a competitive weapon. Companies that tilt toward this pole tend to have business processes that differ from the norm. They do things differently. They also tend to be larger companies and may be able to—or even wish to—support more than one ERP solution. As a matter of policy, some large companies prefer a multi-ERP vendor strategy.

For this reason, the companies in this group must clarify their current business practices. In all likelihood, these processes are not well understood, are not well documented, and vary from operation to operation. However, before the company can automate processes, it needs to understand what they are. It is often useful to divide the processes into two groups (**Q58, Q59**):

1. processes that are basic to the business but do not provide competitive advantage

2. processes that yield a competitive advantage

Table **64.1** Comparison of Competitive vs. Value-Oriented Companies

Competitive Companies	Value-Oriented Companies
Characteristics	
• tend to have business processes that differ from the norm	• tend to have business processes that are fairly standard
• tend to be larger companies with large IT staffs	• tend to be smaller companies with smaller IT staffs
• may be able to support more than one ERP solution	• usually do not support more than one ERP solution
• need ERP software built around an inherently flexible architecture	• need a long-term ERP partner
• adapt the ERP software to their practices	• adapt their practices to the ERP software
• generally better prepared to deal with disruptive or noncontinuous technologies	• look for a vendor that can deliver new technologies transparently, (i.e., in a nondisruptive manner)
• often have a formal program of testing and evaluating new technologies	• look for a high degree of prepackaged integration
• often buy "one of everything"	• tend to evaluate each program on its projected return
• looking for technologies and are willing to take responsibility for their own solution	• looking for solutions for which their vendor will take responsibility
• high tolerance for low-quality deliverables from vendors	• demand relatively high quality from their vendors
• have a large budget for IT integration	• invest a smaller proportion of revenues in technology
• want to be on the leading edge (early adopters)	• want to follow when the path is smoother, learn from others' mistakes
• prepared for revolution	• prefer evolution
Challenges	

• clarify their business processes since they probably:
  are not well understood
  are not well documented
  vary from operation to operation
	• adapt their business processes to the best practices encased in their ERP software:
	  must thoroughly understand the processes embedded in the software being considered for purchase

• finding ERP software that maps to the company's basic processes but is flexible enough to adapt to the company's competitive processes	• finding an ERP vendor who will continue to supply business practices that the company wants to implement
• want to deal with leading-edge technology	• focus their attention on other competitive factors

For processes that do not add competitive advantage, it is often a good idea simply to adopt the best practices that are typically embodied in modern ERP packages. On the other hand, for those processes that yield competitive advantage, competitive-oriented companies will often want to mold the software to the process rather than vice versa. An outside consultant can prove very helpful in this endeavor, as can tools such as process modelers.

Another major challenge for the competitive company is to find ERP software that maps to the company's basic processes but is flexible enough to adapt to the company's competitive processes. The typical challenge is the flexibility of the software. Implementing ERP software is often compared to pouring cement—it is flexible as long as it is new and wet, but extremely inflexible once it sets.

To adapt the ERP software to their processes, competitive companies need ERP software built around an inherently flexible architecture. The key criterion is the amount of code that needs to be written. More code results in greater expense, a longer time to implement, and greater difficulty in upgrading to new releases. More flexible ERP systems can adapt to competitive or changing business processes with minimal changes to code; they adapt by flipping switches, choosing options, and so on.

Meanwhile, value-oriented companies face a completely different set of challenges. These companies are more likely to adapt all of their business processes to the best practices encased in their ERP software. While the competitive companies need to understand their own business practices, the value companies need to understand thoroughly the practices that are embedded in the software they are considering for purchase. Are these the practices that the company wants to implement? Moreover, what are the chances that the ERP vendor will continue to supply business practices that the company wants to implement?

The competitive company is looking to adapt the ERP software to its practices. The value-oriented company is looking to adapt its practices to the ERP software. Thus, while the competitive company is looking primarily for a flexible architecture, the value company is searching mainly for a long-term partner. The value-oriented company is more likely to use only one ERP solution. Thus, it is all the more important to establish a partnership relationship with a vendor that can not only provide rich business processes initially but also update them over time (**Q79**).

The vendor is also likely to be called upon to help the company derive the maximum value from the software. It is very helpful if the vendor provides value-added service such as training, implementation support, and even business process engineering. These services tend to be less important to the competitive IT company.

More subtly, competitive and value-oriented companies will want their technology delivered in different ways. The competitive company understands technology and is able—even willing—to deal with it at the leading edge. The value-oriented company focuses more of its attention on other competitive factors and less on the role of technology. Companies in the former category are generally better prepared to deal with disruptive or noncontinuous technologies. Value-oriented companies, on the other hand, should generally look for a vendor that can deliver new technologies transparently (i.e., in a nondisruptive manner).

The bottom line is that companies that use IT as a competitive weapon are looking for technologies and are willing to take responsibility for their own solution. On the other hand, companies seeking maximum value from IT are looking for vendors who will stand behind their technology solutions. One wants to be on the leading edge; the other wants to follow when the path is smoother. One is prepared for revolution; the other prefers evolution. One seeks technology; the other seeks a long-term partnership. Both can find a solution but they will face different challenges and will often buy from different vendors (Q5).

65. What is a customer relationship management (CRM) system?

RANDY HARRIS

It's impossible to state precisely what customer relationship management (CRM) means to everyone. The term has been applied to almost every element of business that even remotely interacts with a customer. In its infancy, CRM systems were a series of mainframe or server-based applications specific to sales, marketing, and support business functions. The applications were lightweight by today's standards and did little more than capture and file critical data. But as cultural boundaries within organizations weakened, individual fiefdoms of information gave way to sophisticated applications that could span business functions. By doing so, these applications created the vision of a single view of the customer. For the first time, organizations could track and analyze shifting customer needs, link marketing campaigns to sales results, and monitor sales activities for improved forecasting accuracy and manufacturing demand.

CRM's Evolution

CRM has evolved since its earliest incarnation, originally driven by an inside-out focus, through three phases of evolution: technology, integration, and process. Recently have we seen a major leap forward to a fourth phase: customer-driven CRM—an outside-in approach that has intriguing financial promise.

1. *Technology*—In its earliest incarnation, CRM meant applying automation to existing sales, marketing, support, and channel processes as organizations attempted to improve communications, planning, opportunity and campaign management, forecasting, problem solving, and to share best practices. To some degree, it worked. However, automating poorly performing activities or processes rarely improves the quality of the outcome. So, for the most part, the quality of the return on investment (ROI) was meager—if measurable at all. The promise of the technology was there, but few organizations were realizing the pinnacle of performance. The metric of success was increased efficiency in sales, marketing, support, and channel processes.

2. *Integration*—By developing cross-functional integration, supported by data warehousing and shared roles and responsibilities, organizations began to create a customized view of the customer. Support issues, Web hits, sales calls, and marketing inquiries started building a deeper understanding of each customer and allowed aggressive organizations to adapt their tactics to fit individual needs. Integration focused around two primary components:

   –Make it easier to do business with the seller—Instead of operational silos that inhibited superior customer relationships, the organization as a whole took ownership and responsibility for customer satisfaction. With a single view of the customer, it was much easier for anyone to respond to sales opportunities or impending support issues and take appropriate steps. Expected benefits are to improve retention and lower support costs.

   –Predictive modeling—Data mining (**Q21**) of an aggregate of corporate knowledge and the customer contact experience was used to improve operational and sales performance. By applying complex algorithms to a history of purchasing or inquiry characteristics, it became practical to predict the demands of individual customers. Up-selling, cross-selling, even the ability to preempt potential problems, was now possible for all customer-facing representatives. Expected benefits are to have better cross-selling/up-selling and improved product offerings or delivery.

3. *Process*—By rethinking the quality and effectiveness of customer-related processes, many organizations began to eliminate unnecessary activities, improve outdated processes, and redesign activities that had failed to deliver the desired outcomes. Then, by re-creating the process through an understanding of the capabilities of the technology, the outcomes were more predictable and the promises for a meaningful ROI more substantial and realistic. The metrics for success became the improved effectiveness in serving the customer.

Thus far, almost everything about CRM has focused on improving the effectiveness and efficiency of the seller's organization. Organizations have evolved from sales representatives working from paper notebooks, or a card system, to a tightly integrated network that sees movement in sales activity, predicts product demand on manufacturing, and manages the logistics of complex teams to serve the buyer and seller. Marketing, support services, channel management, revenue management, resource allocation/management, forecasting, manufacturing, logistics, and even research and development have all seen the benefits of a well-designed CRM strategy.

However, the past decade of CRM and its associated improvements have been based on three assumptions:

1. The past would be a logical foundation to predict future customer needs and profitability.

2. Demand for traditional value propositions would remain constant.

3. Better customer relationships would deter attrition.

All three of these assumptions have failed—or at least become unstable—in a post–September 11, 2001 environment. Historical purchases or inquiries are not a clear indication of future needs as buyers are rapidly redefining requirements to satisfy their current business, market, or shareholder demands. Value propositions are changing in highly competitive markets as sellers are working aggressively to reestablish structural bonds. And, driven by sensitive financial markets, buyers move to whichever supplier can provide the best aligned, most cost effective solution that promises to stabilize, or improve, their business performance. These factors are driving CRM into a fourth phase.

Customer-Driven CRM—The Fourth Phase

Today, revenue performance has become the central theme for CRM as organizations seek to achieve and maintain expected financial results. Leading executives are asking:

- Which of my customers have the potential for a high-profit, sustainable relationship?

- What defines profitable and unprofitable customer segments?

- What must change to realize that optimal potential?

- Where's my opportunity for growth?

- Where's my risk for loss?

- Am I making the right decisions related to balancing acquisition, cross-selling, and up-selling—and for the right customer groups?

The epiphany isn't in the questions themselves, but in the fact that we're asking them after a decade of CRM investments—investments intended to provide just those very answers.

It is important to understand that a disruptive change has occurred causing large segments of customer organizations to reassess many of their basic needs, values, and assumptions. Research indicates that this event was triggered by the uncertain complexities of the post–September 11th world. Organizations are now challenging everything from how they create value, to how they serve their markets, to how they meet shareholder expectations. It is the answers to these questions that create the framework for phase four CRM. Without a deep understanding of what's going on in the customer's head—specifically what will influence their buying behavior—it is difficult to establish customer strategies that mutually serve the needs and expectations of the buyer and seller communities.

Understanding the Difference

In the past, CRM has followed a basic *balanced scorecard* technique (**Q53**) involving four categories: *customer, financial, operations,* and *people.* From an inside-out perspective, organizations first analyzed the needs and capabilities of *operations* and their *people* to determine what could be delivered to the *customer.* From that, they drew conclusions and predictions to determine the impact on the *financial* category. As this has changed, so have the priorities. Now the focus is first on the customer:

- What will they buy, when, why, and how much?

- What creates value for them, and does this create a structural bond?

- What services can we perform that merits premium margins?

- Can we establish a new market segmentation strategy focused on potential profitability and willingness to purchase?

- Do we understand their business drivers, financial metrics, buying process, and decision criteria?

Customer driven CRM means that organizations first understand the *customer,* then move inward to *operations.* Within the context of the *customer,* the systems and infrastructure capabilities needed to serve those customers and segmentation-based requirements must be reassessed (**Q66**). Next, it's imperative to explore the skills and competency requirements for the *people* component of the CRM design. A decade of CRM has taught us that nothing happens until your *people* interact with the *customer* in a manner consistent with new CRM customer strategies and systems. And, finally, you should be well positioned to apply predictive modeling algorithms to establish a *financial* model with exceptional accuracy. Not an easy task, but case studies are proving financial predictions that can demonstrate account-level forecasting with over 80 percent accuracy.

SUMMARY

Developing a CRM strategy isn't an easy task. Complex organizational design, comprehensive technologies, and ever-changing customer demands are just the beginning. The lessons learned are monumental but we know that the promises of customer driven CRM are worth the journey. Here's a simple framework for fourth generation CRM:

- *Focus on financial results*—Learn how to identify existing profitable customer segments and determine what will establish a profit-based profile for moving forward. Then develop the business requirements to support sustained, and structurally bonded, relationships.

- *Find cost effective alternatives for nonbuyers or low-margin customers*—Not all customer relationships are profitable and very few companies can afford to pay to deliver an equal level of services. Control costs and save your best resources for premium accounts—while working to bring low performers into an acceptable profit portfolio.

---

66. What are the attributes of a good CRM system?

BRETT ANDERSON

Customer relationship management (CRM) is focused on acquiring, developing, and retaining satisfied, loyal customers, in order to achieve profitable growth and create economic value from the corporate brand. Successful implementation involves much more than simply installing packaged software or building a technology solution. It requires the integration of people, processes, and technology to successfully achieve corporate objectives (Q65). Although technology is only the enabler, a good CRM system needs to address and support the following capabilities:

- Customer service

- Multiple channels

- Customer segmentation and insight

- Predictive modeling

- Marketing integration

- Performance measurement

CUSTOMER SERVICE

Successful companies are investing in and delivering higher levels of service to the customers most likely to value, and pay for, such enhanced service. Enhanced services help to build customer trust and loyalty. However, it is very important to understand the makeup of the revenue base. If low value customers make up a greater portion of the revenue base, special perks for high value customers could end up alienating that revenue base. CRM systems need to provide the capability to deliver enhanced customer services. Examples of these capabilities include:

- Online customer order-entry that provides:

  - the benefits of 24×7 operations,

  - the ability to process a greater number of orders more efficiently,

  - a choice of how to interact with the company,

  - a reduction in the time spent by processing representatives during order entry, allowing them to focus their time on meeting the customer's needs.

- Dedicated Web sites and telephone access that can address the needs and concerns of high value users.

- Automated call distribution (ACD) of high value customers (based on the originating telephone number) to call center organizations providing a higher level of service and responsiveness.

- Customer access to billing detail and capability for online customer payment.

MULTIPLE CHANNELS

66 ▬◀

CRM systems need to go beyond just supporting multiple channels (call center, Web portal, e-mail, voice-response, computer telephony integration [CTI]) to serve their customer. The channels need to:

- provide a seamless integrated experience using the same brand look and feel,

- transform the customer experience in a series of "intelligent conversations" that build over time into a long-term, meaningful dialogue.

In order to accomplish this, a system needs to be able to:

- track and analyze every interaction with a customer, from a phone call to a Web click to an angry e-mail complaining of shoddy service,

- integrate data across customer channels and information (e.g., a bank develops a deeper understanding of their high value customers by assimilating data from a customer's use of online, voice, ATM, and walk-up services in order to manage their savings, checking, credit, loan, and investment accounts),

• exchange and act upon this data in real-time to meet the expectations of all parties (e.g., information provided via a Web-based ordering system is made available to a customer representative to deal with a customer who has telephoned with a question).

The objectives are to build brand loyalty and lifetime customer value as well as a lasting and profitable customer relationship.

CUSTOMER SEGMENTATION AND INSIGHT

Customer segmentation is the process of segmenting groups of customers based on like attributes and managing those segments in a way that maximizes both the benefits to customers and the long-term profit potential of the organization. Segmentation is built with various types of customer data. CRM systems need to be able to capture data pertaining to:

• transactions,

• purchased products or services,

• quantities,

• timing,

• promotional purchases,

• demographics,

• lifestyle information.

Today, CRM systems are able to collect, store, manipulate, and distribute large amounts of customer data. The cost of this process is no longer a major issue for most organizations. In order to make effective use of this data, these systems need to include tools for data mining, deep analytics, and a data mart in order to translate this overwhelming amount of data into real insight (**Q20, Q21**). System links to an operational customer database, core information management systems, external marketing information, and/or third-party databases provide additional information to refine the customer segments based on like attributes. By understanding the customer needs and buying behavior, an organization can achieve greater customer satisfaction and, with it, stronger revenue growth and customer retention.

PREDICTIVE MODELING

An organization can use predictive modeling to understand the customer and markets and to drive future customer interaction (**Q21**). A CRM system needs to be able to take information collected from each channel, analyze it, and develop predictions of customer behavior. Such a system should:

- include self-learning and pattern detection software in order to analyze significant transactions and volumes,

- support the development of powerful models capable of predicting customer response to marketing and other treatments and offers,

- take into account the most profitable customer segment that can drive future growth.

An example of predictive modeling is Amazon.com's use of data from prior customer "conversations" and transactions to make book suggestions to its customers. Another example is a call center representative being provided with a pop-up window containing suggested products and services for a customer based on the history of interactions with that customer or, using customer segmentation analyses, other customers who have the same profile characteristics. A customer's history may go beyond the traditional sense of the past transactions and include the makeup of the home (number and type of family members) or other information accumulated during prior transactions and from external sources.

MARKETING INTEGRATION

While companies have used CRM to improve customer sales and service, they have not done an effective job of incorporating marketing into the equation.[1] Integrating marketing into the CRM solution suite can be accomplished using sophisticated tools and methods to understand and respond more effectively to the customer.

Analytical marketing tools and customer insight capabilities provide a CRM system with the ability to:

- identify improvements in marketing programs,

- optimize the overall marketing investment and deliver on brand promise,

- collect information from each customer interaction, and analyze and develop predictions of an individual customer's behavior,

- identify a company's most profitable customer,

[1]John G. Freeland, "The Evolution of CRM: Revitalizing Sales, Service and Marketing," *Defying the Limits Volume 2* (San Francisco: Montgomery Research, 2001) 10.

- personalize interaction and differentiate sales and service across customer segments,

- incorporate automated detection systems that identify sale opportunities and generate leads automatically.

The CRM system needs to be able to apply the insight gained about the customer to support sophisticated marketing, sales, and differentiated service, but in a transparent and easy-to-use manner, consistently and seamlessly across all channels.

PERFORMANCE MEASUREMENT

CRM systems need to be able to track activity and report key customer metrics so that the effectiveness of segment strategies is understood and can be modified when necessary (**Q65**). Metrics need to be easy to collect and timely if improvement decisions are to be made rapidly. The system should:

- contain benchmarks and alerts to monitor and identify what needs attention,

- collect Web site measurements including the number of clicks and click-through rates, response times, and drop-off metrics to help make improvements in customer interactions,

- collect metrics for campaign response rates, sales measurements, and customer satisfaction to help measure the success of products and marketing campaigns,

- collect various call center measurements for customer interaction, transaction volumes, and routing details to identify overall improvements to the CRM systems that support these call centers.

All of these measurements need to be tied to an organization's strategic, financial, and operational objectives in order to gain the maximum value from its CRM systems.

SUMMARY

Effective CRM systems need to:

- integrate marketing, sales, and service across multiple channels to provide seamless marketing, sales, and service to customers,

- support effective customer segmentation and insight to identify, target, and manage customers based on their value to the company,

- provide predictive modeling of customer behaviors to anticipate needs and future customer interactions,

- supply effective performance measurement to track operational performance and identify opportunities for improvement.

Technology enables CRM, but effective CRM also requires strong processes and a powerful commitment from each organization to succeed.

---

67. What are the key attributes of supply chain management (SCM) systems?

JAHANGIR KARIMI

A supply chain refers to the flow of materials, information, and services from raw material suppliers through factories and warehouses to the end customers. Supply chains have three components:

1. an *upstream supply chain*, which includes an organization's first-tier suppliers,

2. an *internal supply chain*, which includes all the processes used by an organization in transforming the inputs of the supplier to outputs,

3. a *downstream supply chain*, which includes all the processes involved in delivery of the product to the final customers.[1]

Physical goods flow sequentially downstream along the supply chain. Information flows upstream from customer orders and downstream from shipping information, and coordinates the operations of the supply chain.[2]

67 ▬▬◀

[1] Efraim Turban, Efraim R. McLean, and James C. Wetherbe, *Information Technology for Management: Making Connections for Strategic Advantage*, 2nd ed. update (New York: Wiley, 2001) 115–16.

[2] For example, the supply chain of a packaged consumer goods manufacturer includes manufacturing, packaging, distribution, warehousing, and retail. Managing this involves the coordination of the materials inventory and production capacity availability across several organizations to produce products that can satisfy forecasted demand in an environment with a high level of uncertainty.

The concept is similar to the value chain; the operation and management are related, but they differ in emphasis. For example, the value-chain stages for a manufacturing company consists of these activities:

1. *Inbound logistics*—for obtaining raw materials, subassemblies, and other input products from the suppliers, warehousing them, and delivering them to the production site

Supply chain management (SCM) is concerned with the coordination of all the components of the supply chain, their processes, and the information flows, so products and services can be brought to the final customer at the right time, cost, and quality. It includes tasks such as purchasing, materials handling, production planning and control, logistics and warehousing inventory control, and distribution and delivery. The goal of modern SCM is to reduce the uncertainty and risks in the supply chain, thereby:

- decreasing inventory levels and cycle time,

- increasing the efficiency of business processes,

- making customer service more effective.

The major source of supply chain uncertainties is the demand forecast, which is influenced by several factors such as competition, prices, weather conditions, technological development, and customers' general confidence.[3] Quality problems with materials and parts may also create production delays. A major symptom of poor SCM is poor customer service, which hinders people getting the product or service when and where needed, or gives them a product of poor quality. Other symptoms are high inventory costs, loss of revenues, extra cost of expediting shipments, and more. Proper SCM requires coordination of all different activities and "links" within the chain.

The rapid flow of information along the supply chains is key to efficient SCM. Today, the Internet offers high-speed communication and tight connectivity; opens new venues for trade, such as electronic marketplaces; and makes channels more accessible. By using these channels, firms can dispose of excess inventory or procure needed inventory and build flexible supply chains (or supply webs). The Internet also facilitates collaboration among parts of a supply chain, and promises to make the dream of virtual integration a reality by providing a centralized optimal solution in a decentralized world.

In recent years, applying technology and automation to supply chain activities has resulted in reduced cost, expedited processing, and reduced errors. Technologies for SCM evolve from inward facing supply chain optimization and planning suites to-

---

2. *Operations*—for transformation of input into finished products

3. *Outbound logistics*—for storing products and delivering them to customers on customer orders

4. *Marketing*—for establishing customer need for the product and assisting the customer in specifying the assortments and quantities

5. *Service*—for after-sale service, including maintenance

[3] Other uncertainties exist in delivery times, which depend on many factors ranging from machine failures to road conditions and traffic jams that may interfere with shipments.

ward outward-facing applications for collaboration. Gartner research suggests four distinct phases in the evolution of SCM software over the past decade:

1. *Stand-alone or "niche" applications*—coordinating parts of the internal supply chain,

2. *Integrated suites*—combinations of niche solutions coordinating across parts of the internal supply chain,

3. *Collaboration*—extensions of SCM suites or enterprise resource planning (ERP) applications (**Q62**) across upstream and downstream components of the supply chain,

4. *Value chain interoperability*[4]—collaborating with supply chain partners, the ability of different value chains to trade data.

Each phase is progressive in terms of increased opportunities to boost return on investment (ROI) (**Q77**). Companies are adopting these technologies at different paces depending on their strategies for collaborative commerce and their level of technology adoption aggressiveness (**Q5**).

As SCM has evolved, there has been more and more integration of information systems. ERP systems, which integrate the transaction processing activities (**Q18**) within a company's value chain, have expanded to include internal suppliers and customers and to incorporate external suppliers and customers in what is known as extended ERP/SCM software. To make SCM more efficient, firms need to integrate SCM with customer relationship management (CRM) (**Q65**) and enterprise resource planning (ERP) capabilities to differentiate the way they treat each and every customer. Integration has been facilitated by the need to streamline operations in order to meet customer demands in the areas of product and service cost, quality, delivery, technology, and cycle time brought by increased global competition. Furthermore, new forms of organizational relationships and Internet technologies have brought SCM to the forefront of management attention.

New Internet technologies for supply chain and customer management have now reached a stage where companies can create *digital loyalty networks* to profitably meet different customer needs with appropriate differential supply chain capabilities. Digital loyalty networks can be in any of the following forms:

• *Loyalty networkers*—companies that leverage their collaborative supply chains with a deep understanding of their loyal customers

• *Market takers*—companies that perform below average on both supply chain collaboration and customer loyalty

[4] Karen Peterson and Ned Frey, *Supply Chain Planning Implementation: Avoiding Failure, Driving Success,* Gartner, Inc., Strategic Analysis Report R-14-2245, 17 Aug. 2001: 2.

- *Collaborators*—companies with strong supply chain collaboration but lackluster customer loyalty

- *Loyalists*—companies that have excelled in building customer loyalty but are not yet collaborating effectively with supply chain partners[5]

Loyalty networkers are estimated to be:

- 70 percent more profitable than *market takers*,

- 54 percent more profitable and up to three times as likely to report exceptional performance on their goals for shareholder value, sales growth, market share, and return on assets compared to *collaborators*,

- 19 percent more profitable than *loyalists*.

As more companies leverage new e-business capabilities, they have discovered that excellence in products, service, and production alone will not be enough to compete in the future. Companies such as Dell and Herman Miller (a leading furniture manufacturer) are tailoring their business processes to sell and service their most important customers, and to streamline their internal processes and their information flow to and from their suppliers and customers around the world. These new capabilities will differentiate products, service, and delivery for customers according to the value they bring to a company. Companies will segment their customer base, measure the lifetime value of their customers, and manage their interactions through tailored Web services (Q15) to offer each customer the most profitable customer service level. As they succeed in integrating customer and supply chain systems, they can further reduce inventories, improve customer responsiveness, and increase customer loyalty and shareholder value.

---

68. What are the key technology issues around SCM implementation?

CHRISTOPHER F. SCHMIDT

As companies rush to reap the benefits of supply chain management (SCM) (Q67), they must understand the key technology issues that contribute to successful or un-

[5] *Digital Loyalty Networks: e-Differentiated Supply Chain and Customer Management*, Deloitte Consulting, Global Manufacturing Study, 2 Sept. 2002: 2.

successful SCM implementations. It is important that SCM implementation be successful because some estimates put the payback on SCM projects to be as few as two years. But, unfortunately, SCM implementations are susceptible to the same risks associated with other technologies, such as transaction processing systems, enterprise resource systems, and customer relationship systems (**Q63, Q87, Q88**). These common risks frequently result in projects that are delivered late, over budget, and without full functionality, or scrapped outright. SCM implementations are uniquely plagued by a higher level of risk. This risk is associated with the complexity of integrating information technologies across multiple organizations that have different hardware and operating systems and incompatible applications. This higher level of technological complexity substantially increases the difficulty of implementing an SCM successfully. As an eye opener, by 2003, Gartner's most likely prediction is that 35 percent of SCM projects in place in 2001 will have to be reimplemented.[1]

SCM implementations can be successful when potential technical issues are addressed properly. But building an SCM solution is as much art as it is science. It is different than implementations of ERP or transaction processing systems, which often are purchased in product suites that are already tightly integrated. Understanding the differences and knowing what to do about them is critical to gaining the benefits of SCM.

KEY TECHNOLOGY ISSUES

These issues are best understood by dividing SCM into two categories and describing the technology issues associated with each.[2]

1. *General supply chain*—General supply chain technology issues are usually characterized by the large number of interfaces among different legacy systems. These legacy systems usually have multiple data sources, often of varying quality, that must be synchronized.

2. *Supply chain planning*—Supply chain planning relies on complex calculation and solver / optimization engines for forecasting and planning that create a unique set of challenges.

68

---

[1] Karen Peterson and Ned Frey, *Supply Chain Planning Implementation: Avoiding Failure, Driving Success*, Gartner, Inc., Strategic Analysis Report R-14-2245, 17 Aug. 2001:1.

[2] James B. Ayers, ed., *Making Supply Chain Management Work: Design, Implementation, Partnerships, Technology, and Profits* (New York: Auerbach, 2001) 25.

GENERAL SUPPLY CHAIN

The critical issues are described below.

Interfaces   SCM tools use data from multiple legacy systems and feed their results to a number of transactional systems (e.g., demand planning takes active sales orders, which ultimately feed raw material requirements and then purchasing systems). These exchanges of data often require complex interfaces to existing legacy systems and transactional systems that use vendor applications, middleware, and different databases to facilitate rapid and accurate flow of information. In a recent project, the SCM tools being implemented (demand planning and production scheduling) required 12 interfaces from 5 legacy systems and several outside sources. This is fairly typical.

Integration   A common SCM solution usually includes several different technologies (e.g., middleware, messaging, alert, databases, work flow, and Web applications) and solution components (e.g., demand planning, demand collaboration, strategic network optimization, production scheduling, transportation planning, and order promising). The SCM solution has the potential to break down at the intersection of any of these technologies or solution components. As the number of technologies or solution components increase, the opportunities for problems increase exponentially. Creating a smooth flow across these intersections is critical for a successful project.

Further complicating the matter is the integration between different technology vendors and modules from different vendors offering the desired SCM functionality. Vendors rarely have a complete solution that can suit all of an enterprise's specific business needs, and therefore the majority of SCM implementations rely on multi-vendor solutions.[3] This means that much of the integration task must be shouldered by the project team, which increases the cost and risk of the project.

Data Quality   The saying "garbage in, garbage out" is well known, and data quality is often a key issue in supply chain implementations. The overall integrity and standardization of data being passed to and from supply chain applications is of monumental importance. Typically, supply chain applications receive much of their data from other applications, so the quality of data from those systems needs to be verified.

Data Integrity   The information exported to the demand forecasting application requires that the various item master records be reviewed for integrity. All the item master records must be analyzed for inconsistent data from the various source systems. Duplicate records, data-formatting issues, outdated records, missing data (not all the

---

[3] Peterson and Frey 11.

information exists to support the hierarchy definition), and extraneous characters (not visible in one operating system, but recognized in another operating system/ database combination) must all be resolved.

Data Standardization   The item master information requires standardized processes to handle inconsistent:

- data field values (hierarchy category code),

- data relationships (item master assigned to customer),

- data definitions (item master number scheme),

- data across legacy systems (item master).

Real-Time Synchronization

In an ideal world, business partners are tightly linked through their supply chain systems. So a change in demand forecast or a sudden up-tick in sales would automatically cascade through a company's supply chain environment and immediately make its way through the company to its suppliers' systems to update inventories and modify future forecasts and the associated procurement of raw materials and the creation of factory and logistics plans.

As a result, SCM tools rely on real-time information (vs. batch processing) to perform tactical and execution activities. For example, for a finished goods inventory, the execution of the category "available and capable to promise" requires a view of system-wide inventory availability and production capacity to calculate promise dates for a customer waiting on the phone. To accomplish this level of real-time synchronization, SCM systems need the interfaces and integration previously discussed to be coupled with sophisticated messaging, alert, exception management, and reporting capabilities to ensure users have accurate knowledge.

Increasingly, companies are linking their systems through data sent in XML format. But since XML standards are being implemented differently (**Q14, Q15**), successfully linking one supplier doesn't always successfully link all suppliers. This makes tight integration in the B2B environment extremely difficult.

Supply Chain Planning

Typically, supply chain planning contains six components:

1. demand forecasting,

2. supply chain planning (multiplant planning),

3. production planning,

4. production scheduling,

5. distribution planning,

6. transportation planning.

Generically, the supply chain planning components employ the use of either complex calculation engines or solver programs. However, supply chain vendors generally use different math techniques within each component. Thus, one key to successful deployment of supply chain planning tools is to understand the algorithms and computational processes. That is because some of these complex algorithms generate answers that are not intuitively obvious. Generally, business people feel it is dangerous to publish mathematically generated information without first validating it and making sure it "makes sense." Forecasts, for example, are ultimately scrutinized by human beings, whether they are the demand planners who are managing the forecasting process itself, or operations personnel who act upon it. This means that they need to understand *how* it was calculated. Without an intuitive feel for where the numbers came from, users:

- eventually take the forecast for granted, and thus miss something that is wrong,

- cannot predict how the forecast will behave in future time periods,

- won't know the degree to which the calculated number needs to be adjusted, even with accompanying accuracy and confidence in it.

Conclusion

While many companies rush to implement SCM solutions to gain quick returns, the risks of project failure are significant because of the inherent technological complexities of SCM systems. By addressing these complexities directly, companies can significantly improve their chances for successful deployments of SCM.

69. What are the issues to consider when deciding to customize a standard vendor application?

GREG ALLEN

Organizations purchasing large vendor applications, such as ERP and CRM systems, often face the question of whether they should customize the system to better fit their specific needs. The general rule is to customize as little as possible, and only as much as necessary to reach maximum value. Decisions about whether to customize, and how much, begin during the vendor selection process (**Q78, Q79**). This is when an organization should consider the degree of customization required to implement a vendor package. Three common reasons why an organization needs to customize a vendor application are:

1. Current business processes do not match the vendor application.

2. Vendor application functionality does not satisfy all of a firm's required business needs.

3. A new vendor application requires integration into an existing environment.

CURRENT BUSINESS PROCESSES

When current business processes do not match vendor application features, an organization must decide what is going to change—its processes or the new application (**Q59**). If these processes are important to building or maintaining a firm's competitive position, it can likely justify the time, expense, and risk of customizing the vendor application. Companies using IT as a competitive advantage (**Q5, Q64**), or applications that are critical to their competitive advantage, usually require more extensive customization. Value-oriented companies can get away with minimal modifications if they do not rely on IT for competitive advantage or for applications not related to core competencies. In this case, a carefully selected vendor application can be implemented as a "vanilla" package and accepted as a "best of breed." For example, a supply chain management (**Q67**) application for a manufacturing company is more likely to be customized than a human resource application for the same company.

There are also three issues to consider when customizing a vendor application to support current business processes:

1. Are internal business practice experts available?

2. Are vendor package experts available, whether yours or others?

3. Is the value of the customization worth more than the cost?

Business practice experts must determine the *value* and *criticality* of the customizations. The vendor package experts must estimate the *cost* of the customization. With value and cost data, it is possible to determine the return on investment (ROI) and the level of customization needed (Q75). Partial customization is one option; phasing-in the customization over time to spread the cost is another. It is critical that the business practice experts work closely with the vendor package experts to implement a system that takes full advantage of the new application.

REQUIRED FUNCTIONALITY

A second reason a company may decide to customize a vendor application is if all of the required functionality is not available in one package. A function point analysis can be performed to identify gaps between the vendor application and the firm's requirements.[1] Function point analysis identifies mismatches between an organization's functionality requirements and the functionality offered in vendor packages. Giving the most important functionality requirements a high weighting factor helps identify the criticality of any missing functionalities. A function point analysis can also identify any overlaps in functionality if multiple packages are being considered. Some packages offer higher levels of functionality in specific areas than other packages, so it is possible that the best overall package may be weak in a critical area. However, it is usually better to create a business process work-around rather than to customize an application for noncritical functionality.

The end users of the new application should answer the following questions before deciding whether customization is needed:

- Is the functionality truly critical?

- Will a source of competitive advantage be lost if the package is not customized?

- What operational changes are needed to offset the missing functionality?

- What is the trade-off between the value obtained from the customization and the amount of time to implement?

Generally, the more an application is customized, the longer it takes to implement and the more expensive it is to maintain. Decisions must be made about whether the value of the customization is worth these delays and costs.

The IT group implementing the application also needs to answer several questions:

- Is there another vendor package that can provide the required (but missing) functionality?

- How will overlaps in functionality be handled?

[1] Lori Holmes, "Evaluating COTS Using Function Fit Analysis," Presentation, *Q/P Management Group, Inc. Web Site* 2002, 22 Nov. 2002 <http://www.qpmg.com/EvalCOTS.pdf>.

- How well documented is the existing system?

- How well defined are the requirements?

Sometimes multiple vendor packages are needed to satisfy an organization's needs, but there may be an overlap in functionality among them. Some of the overlapping functionality may need to be hidden, deleted, or not activated. When doing the functional gap analysis, the documentation of the current system and the requirements that are being compared must be as detailed and accurate as possible for valid conclusions to be reached.

INTEGRATING THE APPLICATION INTO THE CURRENT ENVIRONMENT

The third common reason for customizing vendor applications is integrating the new application into the existing IT environment. Creating interfaces often requires a major effort in time and resources when implementing a vendor package. Large vendor packages will have data elements that must be shared with other existing applications. For example, a human resource application and an IT help desk ticket tracking system can both use employee ID, location, and job code. The more applications that are able to share common data elements, the tighter the data integrity can be controlled.

When integrating vendor applications with all the existing applications, IT groups must consider several issues:

- Will the application fit into current architecture including hardware, network, and operating system software (**Q8**)?

- How many interfaces will be required between the new application and existing applications (**Q13**)?

- Is data conversion needed before loading into the new application?

69

Taking the following precautions can mitigate these issues:

- The more that available equipment and software can be used, the less it will cost to customize vendor applications.

- Keep tight control over the scope of the customization. Adding departments or functionality can quickly cause budget overruns. The cost for additional hardware, network connections, operating systems, middleware, interfaces, and application experts adds up quickly.

- Be careful when using a phased approach to implement a highly integrated package, such as an ERP system. In this situation, implementing only a few modules at a time can dramatically increase the number of interfaces required.

- Keep in mind that historical data conversions are not always straightforward or 100 percent convertible. Alternate solutions may be required.

- Strive to keep all the components of the customized code and all the existing applications consistent for greater maintainability. By making the environment easier to maintain, fewer resources will be required for ongoing maintenance.

- Finally, note that the more a vendor's application is customized, the more difficult it will be to upgrade to a later version of the vendor's product. During the upgrade process, many companies discover that they need to completely rebuild both the customized modules as well as the interfaces because the vendors upgrade has changed so much. In those situations, the upgrade can be almost as costly and disruptive as the initial installation.

CONCLUSION

There are many reasons why an organization will want to customize vendor applications. The decision to customize boils down to the value added compared to the cost, time, and risk associated with the customization. The key to successful implementation and achieving the projected return on investment is planning ahead to anticipate the risks and to allow issues to be resolved quickly.

IT and Resource Allocation

DAVID R. LAUBE

Information technology costs money—usually a lot of money. So decisions about IT spending are among the most difficult and contentious of all corporate spending decisions. This section covers a number of the economic and practical business considerations that organizations should include in their overall decision process.

The discussion starts with the seemingly simple issue of how much a business should spend on IT, which is raised in Question 70. Rather than the time-honored method of picking a number based on prior year's spending, this answer suggests that strategy, competitive comparisons, probable investment returns, and many other factors should really drive the decision. But the fun is just starting. After total IT dollars are allocated, a framework around which individual spending decisions should be built is needed. The answer to Question 71 presents such a framework.

Once inside that framework, the process of evaluating individual projects begins. Question 72 looks at the battle that occurs in many firms between cost-reducing projects and revenue-enhancing projects. Sometimes people try to justify IT projects, not with how much new revenue they will help create, but with how much will be lost if the project isn't done. Whether or not this is a valid approach is the topic of Question 73. Of course, many people considerably underestimate the cost of technology. This is addressed in Question 74 on total cost of ownership and its use as a tool to understand and control costs as well as to compare competitive proposals.

There are a number of ways to financially evaluate IT alternatives, starting with an understanding of the various financial tools commonly used in investment decisions, which are discussed in the answer to Question 75. But financial metrics are only among several factors that are used to rate and rank competitive IT proposals. A methodology that wraps all necessary components together is proposed in Question 76. But with all the energy and arguments that surround the selection of IT projects, it is curious that so little attention is spent on tracking whether the selected projects live up to their promises. The way to apply that discipline is found in the answer to Question 77.

Some of the toughest IT spending decisions surround the issue of whether to do the project "in house" or with an outside firm. The elements of "build-or-buy" decisions are the topic of Question 78. In today's environment, many firms realize that they can't do it all themselves. Since that realization is now such an important component of most IT spending decisions, questions are devoted to issues such as how to select a vendor (Question 79), and whether to use an application service provider (Question 80).

Continuing the theme of leveraging outsiders to achieve IT goals, the topic of outsourcing is discussed in depth. Question 81 examines the different types of outsourcing relationships that businesses can enter, ranging from conventional arrangements for the provision of services to deeper relationships aimed at transforming the firm. Question 82 outlines the situations where businesses are likely to find outsourcing relationships beneficial. Question 83 focuses on the increasingly popular topic of outsourcing to an offshore provider, examining the benefits, drawbacks, and manner in which such relationships should be structured.

Finally, Question 84 focuses on the costly issue of continual hardware and software upgrades with a discussion of the risks and concerns surrounding them.

The intent of this "Resource Allocation" section is to provide a very practical discussion of the major elements of the IT decision-making process. Theoretical evaluations are nice, but in the real world, these hard decisions are the result of a complex matrix of financial analysis, business strategy, and, yes, even company politics. Understanding the answers to the questions in this section will help anyone make the right choices.

70. How does a company know how much it should spend on information technology?

ERIC V. ROBINSON AND DAVID R. LAUBE

The amount of spending on information technology is often the subject of fierce debate in the hallways of most companies. With IT forming the backbone of many company activities, there always seems to be a steady stream of new projects being proposed, more software or hardware that must be upgraded, or new investments in infrastructure that are required. CEOs and CFOs sometimes feel that the IT area is an insatiable creature, devouring all available cash during its constant feedings. Complicating matters is the fact that IT spending decisions are not one-time events. Many of these decisions carry with them significant commitments of resources to cover not only the one-time, up front investment, but also substantial ongoing maintenance and long-term operating costs.

In the face of all this, where does a company draw the line on IT spending? Is there a "right" amount? That decision is a complicated one and must be firmly linked to market, industry, and economic realities. Corporations are looking for technology solutions that address business problems directly, provide a near-term return on invested capital, and improve the customer experience.[1] The power of IT to produce business results will vary depending on several major considerations, which, in turn, are strong factors in driving the total IT spending decision:

1. Technology spending pattern for the industry

2. Rate of industry change

3. Returns on the IT investment

[1] David Kirkpatrick, "Beyond Buzzwords," *Fortune Web Site* 3 Mar. 2002, 3 Dec. 2002 <http://www.fortune.com/fortune/techatwork/articles/0,15114,372270,00.html>.

4. Strategy of the business

5. Status of the IT infrastructure

Technology Spending Pattern for the Industry

Various industries have different technology dependencies and therefore different spending profiles. Why is this relevant? If a company is underspending on technology, it may be missing a competitive advantage that its competition is enjoying.[2] That is, a business may be growing at a very fast pace, but outgrowing its technology capability and thereby leaving the company exposed to its competition. If a company is overspending relative to its industry peers, it may be hurting its cost structure only to realize a diminishing marginal benefit.[3] In this situation, the money might be better spent on advertising, hiring sales associates, etc., or even dropped to the bottom line.

There are reliable guiding principles and metrics in this area. One of the key measures is an enterprise's technology spending as a percentage of total revenue. Table 70.1 shows some approximate percentages by industry:

Table 70.1 IT Spending Percentages by Industry

Industry	% of Revenue Spent on IT
Financial (noninsurance)	8.2%
Insurance	8.0%
Services	5.2%
Distribution	5.1%
Electricity and Gas	4.8%
Retail	4.5%
Primary Production and Supply	4.2%
Technology and Telecom	4.0%
Finished Goods Mfg.	2.7%
Chemicals and Petroleum	2.1%

Source: Data from Tom Pohlmann, Benchmark March 2002 Data Overview, Forrester, Research Inc., Business Technographics Report, March 2002: 3.

[2] Carolyn LeVasseur, "Best Practices for Evaluating, Justifying and Forecasting IT Spending Levels," *Gartner, Inc. Web Site* 3 July 2002, 3 Dec. 2002 <http://www4.gartner.com/4_decision_tools/measurement/measure_it_articles/july01/mit_spending_levels1.html>.

[3] Geoffrey A Moore, *Living on the Fault Line: Managing for Shareholder Value in Any Economy*, Rev. ed. (New York: HarperBusiness. 2002) 76.

It is clear from this chart that different industries have different spending profiles. So the industry itself helps determine at least a broad parameter for IT spending. A caution regarding this benchmark—there is always some IT spending outside of the formal IT organization. So these benchmarks are good for comparisons but probably understate total IT spending. Unless a corporation has a completely centralized IT structure, it is likely to be difficult to accumulate all IT spending, since little pockets of IT activity show up across many operational units. Even the definition of IT spending is rarely common, with items like telecommunications costs, depreciation on buildings and computers, various outsourced functions like procurement or desktop support, etc., all appearing either in or out of the IT category depending on company preferences. Perhaps the best way to determine comparative spending is to undertake a formal benchmarking study led by a firm who specializes in this area. These firms have extensive databases against which companies can compare their total spending as well as the relative efficiency of their IT effort.

RATE OF INDUSTRY CHANGE

One risk in relying on benchmarking to determine the level of IT spending is that those comparisons are backward looking. Many industries are undergoing significant changes, some of which are driven by technology. The whole trend toward e-business capabilities (**Q34**), customer relationship management systems (**Q65**), supply chain systems (**Q67**), and new infrastructures, such as wireless (**Q28, Q29**), influence the amount of investment in IT systems. Perhaps the industry is consolidating into fewer players, requiring more IT investment to harmonize multiple systems across newly acquired companies. It is safe to say that static industries will likely require less IT spending than those where change is rampant.

RETURNS ON THE IT INVESTMENT

An investment in IT is really no different than any other business investment. It needs to have a business case that justifies the reason for the spending (**Q71**). When compared to other investments, if the IT project measures up to the corporate criteria, then a company should feel comfortable in going ahead just as it would with other non-IT projects. For example, if a business unit could cut costs by $10 million by making a $2 million IT investment or generate $20 million in revenues by making a $5 million IT investment, why wouldn't the project be approved? Theoretically, if there is a green field of opportunity through IT spending, then the spending should take place regardless of IT benchmarks or IT spending trends. Tempering this economic analysis, however, is often a deep skepticism that the project will truly generate the promised returns. This is because IT implementation issues are commonplace and project risks become a concern (**Q85**, **Q86**). So IT projects often get "risk adjusted" when compared against other spending alternatives.

STRATEGY OF THE BUSINESS

Often a big factor in total IT spending is the strategic orientation of the business regarding IT (**Q5**). In some companies, IT is viewed as a tool to drive competitive advantage. When IT-driven business opportunities arise, they don't hesitate to approve the expenditures, even when they understand implementation risks. Other companies, particularly those who are concerned about costs, view IT as an overhead expense to be minimized. They are constantly looking for ways to appear on the low end of their industry benchmarks. One possible way to address this dichotomy is to drive the IT organization to "best-in-class" cost performance in areas of computer operations, maintenance, and infrastructure. At the same time, for new IT spending, projects that clearly show a superior return would get approved. Regardless of a business's orientation toward IT, it is important that it develop a business driven technology strategy to guide its investments (**Q4**).

STATUS OF THE IT INFRASTRUCTURE

A large factor in determining the amount of IT spending is the current status of a company's IT infrastructure. Many well-managed firms try to spend a steady amount on infrastructure each year. These firms have a component of their spending that adds to their essential infrastructure of servers, desktops, networks, and storage capacity. Firms that do not include this in their IT investment plans encounter a "spending bubble" when older, obsolete hardware needs to be replaced or networks need expansion. An even greater problem occurs when a company has let its essential business software age. If a billing system, for example, is 20 years old, it likely needs to be replaced, causing a further "bubble" in IT spending.

SUMMARY

The decision regarding the amount of investment in IT is a difficult, but extremely important, one. The proper level of IT investment over time is a significant indicator of the alignment and health of an IT organization relative to the business. By understanding the factors described above, it is possible to make the kind of wise choices about IT investments that will maximize their value to the enterprise.

71. How should a company spend its money on technology?

ERIC V. ROBINSON AND DAVID R. LAUBE

Technology investment has gone through a slow, yet dramatic, change over the last three decades. In earlier years, IT spending was focused on automating repetitious work efforts. Later, it shifted to the development of management information and growing the amount of captured data. Spending on IT reached a crescendo in the late 1990s when e-business investments, ERP and CRM investments, and year 2000 (Y2K) fixes all collided. The current landscape is even more complex because, as a result of the 1990s spending spree, there is now a new level of spending required just to maintain and operate recent investments.

When faced with stunning amounts of IT spending, senior executives started asking the important question, "Why are we spending all of this money and what are we getting for it?" They are demanding value from their IT investments. They are putting proposed new IT investments through the same screening processes as any new investment in plant, marketing, R&D, etc. So today's biggest challenge to IT spending isn't about the technology at all, but about focusing the spending on generating sustained competitive advantage.[1]

IT investments are being viewed as a means to create significant business value. The way a company thinks about that investment and where they invest the limited funds should now reflect that shift in mind-set. CIOs must drive business discussions that not only take into account IT projects, but the *impact of these projects to the enterprise in total* (Q4). The phrase "business investment" has now replaced "IT investment" as the focus of the IT benefits has changed.[2] To achieve the proper conclusion with this new mind-set requires an enterprise to follow a fairly straightforward framework, which is discussed below.

STEP ONE—UNDERSTAND THE TOTAL TECHNOLOGY SPENDING OF AN ENTERPRISE

71 ▬

The first step is to understand all of the technology-related work efforts, projects, and functions that are being performed in the enterprise. This sounds simple, but it is quite difficult. This means not only identifying the centralized IT spending, but also identifying any spending that occurs outside of the centralized IT organization in

---

[1] David Kirkpatrick, "Beyond Buzzwords," *Fortune Web Site* 3 Mar. 2002, 3 Dec. 2002 <http://www.fortune.com/fortune/techatwork/articles/0,15114,372270,00.html>.

[2] Peter Hennigan, "CIOs: Take IT Investment by the Horns," *ZDNet* 30 Sept. 2002, 3 Dec. 2002 <http://www.zdnet.com/techupdate/stories/main/0,14179,2882000,00.html>.

other business entities. Overhead costs, such as facilities, procurement, depreciation, HR support, etc., that are often found in non-IT overhead budgets, should be included to provide a complete picture. This will allow the company to do some benchmarking to see how its spending compares to other comparable companies (Q70). It is also important to know how much of this spending is focused on core capabilities of the business versus noncore support functions. Knowing how much is being spent, where it is being spent, and whether it is supporting active benefit streams is the starting point for decision making.

Step Two—Stratify the Existing Technology Spending into Major Categories

The second step in evaluating IT spending is to stratify or divide the spending into major categories of like activities so a company knows how the money is actually being spent, and can frame the financial information for discussion.[3] Typical categories include:

- *Production and operations*—These are the activities that "keep the lights on." This category represents resources required for the infrastructure supporting the enterprise's applications, including hardware and software platforms in data centers or elsewhere. The costs would include: telecommunications, help desks, license fees for operating systems, infrastructure, etc. These costs have very little flexibility in the short run. In the long run, they can be decreased by operating efficiencies, quality programs, careful attention to low-cost architectures, or perhaps outsourcing noncompetitive activities. Some companies authorize expenditures each year in this area to refresh the technology being used in the business. These expenditures are discretionary in the short run, but if not included on a recurring basis, it will cause a "bubble" of costs when large sections of the computing environment become obsolete.

- *Maintenance*—These are all of the resources required to maintain existing legacy applications. It includes "bug" fixes and modest enhancements to existing systems that can be done quickly (less than 40 hours). Any enhancement activity in excess of that would be treated as a new software project as described below. Also included in this category would be the annual license fees for purchased applications. Costs in this area are generally nondiscretionary and difficult to reduce in the short run. In fact, it is quite difficult to keep spending in this area from increasing rapidly. License fees from vendors tend to rise in excess of the rate of inflation. Maintenance is very people-intensive and their salaries also rise. But more important, all of the IT investments in new projects move into this category once they are completed. Unless the new projects replace old systems which can be retired, the maintenance portfolio continues to grow and these costs continue to rise.

[3] Hennigan.

- *Mandates and legal requirements*—These are the activities required to maintain compliance with legal and governmental laws and regulation, such as conforming with new tax laws, privacy laws, data retention requirements, etc. In this category, companies usually include systems costs related to mergers, changes in corporate strategy, or other major initiatives where systems are just a follow-on requirement of the business activity. For example, opening an overseas subsidiary would require an international telecommunications network and modifications to the corporate financial systems for currency translations, etc. These costs are generally nondiscretionary. For large corporate initiatives in this category, the systems costs are often included in the business cases for the initiative itself, rather than set forth separately as described next.

- *New technology initiatives (projects)*—These are resources required to introduce new technologies and business capabilities. These are the investments that generate significant benefits and competitive advantages to the business. They are often presented in the form of business cases to senior management for approval. These initiatives are generally considered discretionary spending in the short run; however, they deliver the biggest potential benefits to the business once delivered (**Q70**, **Q76**).

STEP THREE—UNDERSTAND THE BUSINESS PRIORITIES AND THE PROBLEM STATEMENT

Once the current category mix of IT spending is known, the business objectives and priorities must be clearly understood in order to create a plan that continuously refocuses the IT investment categories to match the strategic direction for the future (**Q4**). Many executives are shocked to discover that the majority of their IT spending concentrated in the first three categories, leaving little funding for the truly transformational efforts. In such cases, tough decisions need to be made about business priorities and the role IT spending may have in those priorities.

STEP FOUR—CREATE A MULTI-YEAR TECHNOLOGY INVESTMENT PLAN TO MAXIMIZE BENEFITS

71

The final step is to create a multi-year investment plan. This allows the enterprise to migrate more spending from a lower value category (usually operations and maintenance), to higher value, more strategic ones. It intentionally focuses on the alignment of IT with the strategies of the business (**Q4**).[4] Ideally, over a period of time, an organization's IT spending profile should move from the left side of Figure 71.1 to the right side.

[4] Scott Berinato, "Do the Math," *CIO.com* 1 Oct. 2001, 3 Dec. 2002 <http://www.cio.com/archive/100101/math.html>.

Figure *71.1* IT Spending Profile

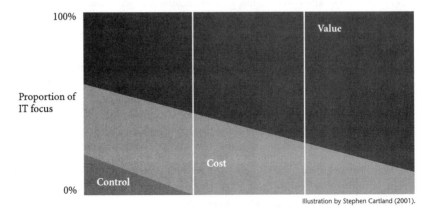

Illustration by Stephen Cartland (2001).

The process of shifting investments from low value to high value categories is a difficult one, but unless it is set as a major corporate objective, with the full cooperation and agreement of both IT and business leaders, it will be hard to achieve. But the payoff for achieving it is huge—an IT investment that is primarily focused on driving value into the business.

72. Is it easier to justify a revenue-enhancing technology investment or one that reduces costs?

DANIEL G. FOX-GLIESSMAN AND DAVID R. LAUBE

IT projects are under extreme scrutiny in the current economic climate. They usually compete for scarce investment dollars with other non-IT projects that promise cost reductions or revenue benefits. A list of IT projects will typically contain projects that focus on both costs and revenues. On the surface, any analysis about the comparative benefits of competing IT projects would seem to drive to an easy answer—chose the project that is the most beneficial. But, unfortunately, it is not that simple. Approving an IT investment usually is not solely about which one has the best financial metric (**Q75, Q76**). There are also a considerable number of subjective factors. So in an environment where subjectivity is present, will a *cost-reduction* project or a *revenue-enhancing* project fare more favorably?

With IT becoming a critical component of any corporate strategy (**Q2, Q4**), it is common to see both types of projects being considered. Cost-reduction activities are usually straightforward. They are focused on reducing headcount through automation of various tasks, improving business processes to abate waste in materials or time, or reducing the payments to suppliers by consolidating purchases across multiple entities. Usually complete blocks of expense are permanently eliminated. In addition, they are attractive because even when a company expects growth, the "cleaned-up" processes and cost structure improvements will benefit the added layer of new revenues, improving the margins on the new business.

Revenue-enhancing projects are more complex since they can be applied to developing or delivering new products and services; identifying, managing, or serving customers; or opening new markets or distribution channels. Each of these types of IT projects has certain characteristics that make them either more attractive or less attractive to those in who are in the position of approving them.

KEY DIFFERENCES

There are several key differences between revenue-enhancing and cost-reduction technology projects that influence how likely a project is to receive approval.

Ability to Calculate the Benefits   Lower costs are a rather straightforward calculation. Determining the reductions in people, vendor savings, maintenance improvements, etc., is a fairly mathematical exercise. If the system will accomplish its promised efficiencies, then the savings are highly precise and reliable. Revenues, on the other hand, are subject to much more estimation. Many factors play into the degree to which revenue flows increase and decrease over time. Are the increased revenues due to the systems improvements or to the skills of the sales team or to the attractiveness of the product? How quickly do better customer relationships or improved service translate into more sales? If revenues stay stable instead of declining in a competitive marketplace, can that "revenue protection" be attributed to the system (**Q73**)? These complications create a fertile ground for disputes over whether the system is paying back its investment.

Characteristics of the Numbers   Every dollar saved in a cost-reduction project (net of investment) goes directly to the bottom line. But from a revenue-generating project, one must not only subtract the cost of the investment, but also the cost of sales. So if a project costs $100,000 and saves $1 million, the benefit is $900,000. If that same project were instead to generate $1 million in sales and the net margin before taxes was 10 percent, the benefit would be zero after the $100,000 investment is deducted. So a revenue-oriented project must leverage itself quite heavily to have the same bottom line impact. On the other hand, a revenue-enhancing project has more potential. Costs can only go down so far, but revenue increases can theoretically be unlimited.

Ability to Find a Sponsor   Every successful IT project needs a sponsor (Q93). Usually this sponsor is the executive that has the most at stake in the success of the project. But accountability always accompanies sponsorship. By sponsoring the project, the executive is usually agreeing that, in exchange for the company's investment in the project, he or she will undergo a modification of their business plan that, in effect, generates accountability for the promised improvements. So budgets are adjusted, sales forecasts are modified, financial plans are improved, etc., all in anticipation that the project will be successful. What executives would want to be "on the hook" for those improvements? Only those who are highly confident that they can deliver the promised results. In addition to being more precise and quantifiable as discussed above, cost-reduction projects also are under the control of the executives managing them. Revenue-enhancing projects, on the other hand, are subject to numerous outside influences such as customer acceptance, competitors' actions, economic conditions, and the like. So the real issue is whether or not a sponsor has control over the result. Since sponsors have more ability to control a cost project, those projects will more easily obtain sponsorship and thus gain better competitive positions in the resource allocation process.

Ability to Assign Accountability   Those making the decision to proceed with an IT investment will always want to hold someone accountable for the results. In addition to the characteristics that generate sponsorship described above, cost and revenue-enhancing projects have an additional differentiating characteristic. Cost projects are usually carried out within a specific organization, department, division, etc. The leader of the portion of the organization can easily be identified and be held accountable for the results. But revenue-enhancing projects are another matter. Unless the accountability is assigned at the highest level of a sales or operating executive, revenues are often the responsibility of a number of teams. The sales forces, the marketing organization, the manufacturing or production groups, the new product release teams, etc., all have an impact on whether revenue targets are achieved. If they are not, who is accountable? Particularly when a system is justified by its revenue promises, everyone will dodge accountability and point fingers if the project's targets are not met. The executives making the investment decisions will factor this well-known and predictable behavior into their decision processes.

Linkage to Company Strategy   Individual company strategy should be the driving force behind technology investment decisions (Q4). So, if a company views its cost structure as its key competitive advantage, it will be relentless in its quest for cost reductions, making IT cost projects attractive. One the other hand, many common strategies focus on revenues. In the pharmaceutical industry, for example, two critical factors are (1) the ability to get new drugs approved and launched into the market quickly, and (2) the broad exposure of the new product to the maximum number of prescribing physicians. Because of high product margins, speed and exposure are more important than costs. So a cost savings project designed to improve the company's supply chain, even if it has a high ROI, might get bypassed in favor of a project to improve a product's time to market.

Economic Environment   When the economy or a specific industry is doing particularly well, revenue-enhancing projects tend to be more attractive. In that expanding environment, strong attention is paid to systems devoted to maintaining or increasing market share. When revenues are rising, profits are also rising and the fact that cost inefficiencies might cause margins to decline slightly tend to become secondary. Everything changes, though, when times become tough. If customers are not buying because of their own economic troubles, IT revenue-enhancing projects are easily dismissed because of a lack of confidence that they will change anything. Costs become a point of focus as companies try to shed expenses. Particularly if an IT cost project can pay back very quickly, (in less than 6 months) it will likely get approved.

CONCLUSION

So does this complicated set of factors point to the unsatisfying conclusion of "it depends"? It is most likely that individual factors will rise in importance at different times. In a perfect world, company strategy should trump other factors. But economic conditions, particularly if they are difficult, tend to overwhelm other influences. The wildcards in this equation could be the issues of sponsorship and accountability. Given projects with equal financial benefits, the project with a strong sponsor who is willing to take accountability for the results may get the nod, regardless of whether it is one that reduces costs or increases revenues.

73

73. Is revenue protection a valid justification for a technology investment?

DAVID R. LAUBE AND ANDREW EISEMAN

The objective of revenue protection is to defend revenue that already exists, rather than letting it slide into competitive decline. It manifests itself in a technology business case when, in addition to revenue increases and/or cost reductions, the amount of revenue that will be "preserved" by an investment is shown as a financial benefit for purposes of determining the project approval (Q75).

Arguing revenue protection in a technology investment business case is difficult to sell for several reasons:

- *Revenue protection does not generate new cash.* When compared to investment options that generate fresh money, a revenue protection proposal that provides no new source of funds to pay for the investment can appear less desirable.

- *Revenue protection proposals appear to have more risk than other investment alternatives.* This is particularly true when such proposals are compared to those that promise to reduce costs. Cost saving proposals, by their very nature, are easier to calculate and measure; their benefits can be seen and tracked (**Q72**). The promise that revenues will not decline does not have that feeling of a "sure thing" that will inspire a skeptical CFO to sign off on the project.

- *It is hard to assign accountability to a revenue protection technology investment.* If a company's revenue streams increase (or do not decrease) over time, everyone lines up to take credit. However, there are so many factors involved with the generation of income, it is hard to determine whether the revenue performance is due to the success of the project or just brilliant sales and marketing. This then manifests itself in a lack of sponsorship when it comes time to step up for accountability for the results in the technology proposal. Without strong sponsorship, projects are rarely approved (**Q93**).

These issues are fundamental in the discussion of a revenue protection investment. If corporate leaders can agree on the identified revenue stream and how it is counted, who plays primary and ancillary roles in the generation and protection of the revenue, and, perhaps most important, how comfortable they are in dealing with less than fully assured results, then a revenue protection project can be considered an investment option.

Despite these issues, the risks of not taking the issue of revenue protection seriously can be seen in British Telecom's experience in the United Kingdom. This company had allowed its service levels to deteriorate under its monopoly franchise. When the government changed regulations allowing competitors, it chose not to defend its customer base. Rather than investing in its existing network and improving customer service, the company chose to go after new markets. In other words, revenue protection took a subordinate priority to revenue growth. The result was that the company quickly lost 20 percent of its customers to competitive telephone and cable companies.[1] Because of the pricing structure in that country, each customer generated a positive margin, so the loss of market share had a significant financial impact.

---

[1] "Consumers' Use of Fixed Telecoms Services," Survey, *Office of Telecommunications (Oftel) Web Site* Feb. 2002, 21 Aug. 2002 <http://www.oftel.gov.uk/publications/research/2002/q8fixr0402.htm>.

Protecting Market Share

The two strategic situations in which corporations should consider revenue protection as a valid justification for technology investments are (1) maintaining market share and (2) protecting important revenue streams. If maintaining market share is a major strategy of the business, revenue protection justifications need to be evaluated within the overall context of that corporate strategy. In particularly competitive industries, it is common to see an objective of the company stated as "maintain market share." If this is a key component of the company's strategy, it usually then spawns a series of plans and programs designed to ensure that this objective is met. In such a corporate environment, a technology program that supports market share (revenue protection) would likely be accepted.

This is the situation many executives faced during the late 1990s as they started to realize the impact that e-business would have on their companies and their industries. One result was a surge in technology spending designed to build e-business capabilities, electronically connect companies with their customers, and modernize their technology infrastructure. The business case for many of these decisions was based not on costs saved or new revenues to be harvested, but strictly on a revenue protection basis. These companies were defensively positioning themselves to compete against the new "Internet only" start-ups that were beginning to attack virtually all markets. Events have subsequently shown that this counterattack was largely effective, blunting the attempts of these new companies to enter established markets.

Protecting Revenue Streams

If revenue protection justifications are being considered because a revenue stream itself is important and technology is the best investment to protect it, managers need to ask two questions: (1) is the revenue stream in real danger of being encroached upon by competitors, and (2) does the revenue come from a highly profitable product or from highly valued customers? If the answers to both of these questions are yes, technology investments based on a revenue protection rationale may make sense.

For example, it is common in the telecommunications industry to segment customers by their value to the firm and their vulnerability to offers from competitors.[2] In recent years, a segment that received particular attention was a group of customers who contributed greatly to the company's profitability, and whom research indicated would switch to another supplier if a credible one were available. In one telecommunications company, this group spent more than did other segments on telecom and entertainment services and was savvy about technology. Since this market segment

[2] Louis Anthony Cox, Jr., "Learning Improved Demand Forecasts for Telecommunications Products from Cross-Sectional Data," Paper, *Cox Associates, Inc. Web Site* n.d., 22 Aug. 2002 <http://www.cox-associates.com/forecst2.doc>.

accounted for a significant portion of this company's cash flow and profitability, its loss would be debilitating. This customer segment, thus, became the target for many potential investments including programs in marketing, sales, public affairs, and technology. The question was not whether to invest, but how much and in what ways. It was entirely appropriate for the revenue from these customers to be included in the business cases because of the high margins embedded in those revenues and the risk that they could disappear at any time.

Similar behavior has been seen in the airline industry. The large, multiline carriers have generated disproportionate margins from their business customers for years. One characteristic of that market segment was a need for short-interval reservations and frequent changes to schedules. The airlines, recognizing the value of these particular customers, made significant investments in technology and in marketing programs designed to maximize the value of that segment. What developed were a complex and fast-changing fare structure, and frequent flyer programs, both of which have proliferated across most competitors. These business initiatives required significant investments in technology, infrastructure, and marketing. Yet, given that they are now common characteristics across the industry, it is likely that these investments have just maintained each company's competitive position and protected the revenue streams they already had.

When to Protect

To answer the initial question directly then, executives must ask a few questions to determine whether revenue protection is a justifiable rationale for a technology investment:

- Can an investment be handled with results that are difficult to measure and to ascribe accountability?

- Is maintaining market share a specific corporate objective?

- What is the specific revenue stream that needs to be protected and how important is it in terms of cash flow and profitability?

- How credible is the threat from competition? Will the technology investment be timely and appropriate to the threat and the revenue?

- What nontechnology investments (marketing, sales, regulatory, etc.) might meet the same revenue protection objective?

If company leadership sufficiently answers each of these questions, then revenue protection is, indeed, a good justification for a technology investment. If the concerns are addressed, then such an investment will enhance the company's competitive position. Moreover, such analyses are likely to help the enterprise more clearly understand and value its existing revenues and customers.

74. Why is total cost of ownership (TCO) important?

JOHN TAYLOR BAILEY AND STEPHEN R. HEIDT

When companies make decisions about their IT investments, one of the most common problems they encounter is the seemingly simple issue of how much does it cost? Most of the time, it is easy to calculate the purchase price of the hardware or the license fees for the vendor's software. IT projects typically include the costs of conversion to the new hardware or software. But when the analysis stops at that point, companies find themselves wondering why, even after successful project implementations, their IT operations, support, and software maintenance costs keep going up. The reason, of course, is that there are many hidden and ongoing costs that frequently are not considered when a project is originally proposed. Because this issue is so pervasive, a discipline and methodology has been developed called *total cost of ownership* (TCO) that is designed to properly state the costs of an IT investment.

WHAT IS TCO?

TCO was originally developed in the late 1980s by the research firm, Gartner, to determine the cost of owning and deploying personal computers. Their initial findings, that PCs cost an enterprise nearly $10,000 per year, caused quite a stir in the technology community and among CFOs. Their methodology was carefully examined and, over the ensuing years, has been accepted as a standard way to evaluate total costs. Simply stated, TCO consists of the costs, direct and indirect, incurred throughout the life cycle of an asset, including acquisition, deployment, operation, support, and retirement.[1]

HOW IS TCO CALCULATED?

The Gartner TCO model utilizes two major categories to organize costs:[2]

74 ▬

- *Direct costs*—These costs generally cover the visible IT- and support-related investments and expenses and include:

  - *Hardware and software*—This typically includes the initial purchase or lease costs. Divide those costs by the expected life of the asset to get an annual figure. The costs

[1] "Lowering TCO: Proven Ways to Reduce Complexity and Total Cost of Ownership in the Data Center," *Sun Microsystems Web Site* n.d., 16 Dec. 2002 <http://www.sun.com/datacenter/feature_articles/tco_tour.html>.

[2] "TCO Manager for Distributed Computing, Chart of Accounts," *Gartner, Inc. Web Site* April 1999, 13 Dec. 2002 <http://www4.gartner.com/4_decision_tools/modeling_tools/costcat.pdf>.

of associated hardware (storage, network equipment, etc.) would be also included. Next add maintenance contracts from vendors, spare systems, and spare parts as well as the annual costs of all supplies and materials.

- *Operations*—This includes all labor costs for technical operations and support as well as the help desk. If personnel such as database administrators or software maintenance staff are required, include their costs. All labor costs should be at rates loaded for all fringe benefits. Operations costs include the fully loaded facilities costs for the appropriate share of the floor space used and furniture purchased specifically for the project. Network costs also fall into this category.

- *Administration*—This includes an appropriate allocation of finance, HR, administration, and procurement department costs. Sometimes IT planning costs are included here, however a significant portion of this category is the training costs required for both the IT and the end user staff.

In order to calculate direct costs, one must have accurate inventory, purchase, vendor, and personnel records. All of the above costs are included even if they are not organizationally part of the IT budget.

- *Indirect costs*—These costs are less visible and usually are dispersed across the business operations organizations and are comprised of:

- *End user operations*—Frequently, an IT investment requires ongoing end user support within the organization. These costs are identified as part of the project or investment and are easily tracked and computed. But there is also a more subtle category of end user costs. These are the costs incurred when individuals gradually evolve to become part of the support structure. They usually do this on a part-time basis in addition to their "regular" job. A shadow support group starts to emerge, consuming considerable time and resources in an unplanned way. This most often manifests itself when self-nominated individuals step up to handle personal computer assistance within a work group. In order to properly calculate TCO, costs of this nature must be identified and captured, a task that is sometimes quite difficult.

- *Downtime*—This occurs when the end user is interrupted from their regular work when things break or something goes wrong with the system. Regular maintenance can also cause downtime when, for example, a software update takes 30 minutes, resulting in 30 minutes of lost productivity.

All of the direct and indirect costs are compiled, computed on an annual basis, and then totaled to provide the total cost of ownership. This exercise can produce some stunning results as studies regularly show that, even in today's world of PCs costing less than $1,000, the TCO of a PC continues to average over $5,000 per year. A $200 printer could easily have an annual cost of over $1,000 when all the supplies and maintenance costs are included. For organizations that want to determine their

TCO for a specific area of IT, there are numerous consultants and vendors who will assist in the task.

What Is the Value of Using TCO?

Over the years, TCO has developed into a valuable tool for companies to use in their management of IT spending.[3]

- *TCO provides a framework for good financial analysis of IT investments.* Not only will the true financial costs of an investment be properly computed, but it also allows solid comparisons of similar alternatives. For example, a Gartner study of the costs of "fat" vs. "thin" clients (**Q12**) showed that the annual cost of a thin client was $5,160 versus $5,360 for a fat "managed" PC.[4] If the initial purchase price differences of the hardware (roughly $500 for each thin client versus $1,200 for a business-class PC) were all that was considered, a company might incorrectly conclude that a thin client was significantly less costly. The Gartner study shows that initial hardware costs are, in reality, a relatively small portion of total costs.

- *TCO sets a baseline for IT costs.* Since TCO is now an accepted industry measurement, IT organizations can determine their TCO of various operating environments. They then can benchmark themselves against other companies and determine areas where they can improve. TCO should typically show up on an IT organization's balanced scorecard (**Q53, Q54**) and targets should be set for regular improvement.

- *TCO generates a widespread understanding that first cost isn't total cost.* As the concept of TCO becomes ingrained in the organization, proposals for IT projects become more realistic. When vendors propose some hardware or software solution, there will be less temptation for the end user to come to IT with the demand to "just put it in" without the careful understanding of how that product could impact the total cost structure.

Like other tools, TCO does not solve all problems. For example, because TCO is a long-term measure, reducing TCO only reduces costs over time. So it is hard to capture a TCO reduction as a specific benefit when budgets need to be cut. Also, TCO does not assess risk or help align technology investments with strategic goals (**Q4**). Nevertheless, TCO is an important tool for the analysis of IT costs and for the management of those costs in an IT organization. With a good understanding of TCO, companies can make proper IT investment decisions and develop solid improvement plans for their overall IT costs.

[3] Other analytical tools are discussed elsewhere in this book (**Q75**).
[4] Peter Lowber, *Thin-Client vs. Fat-Client TCO*, Gartner, Inc., Research Note DF-14-2800, 28 Sept. 2001.

75. Which is more important, the payback period for a project or its return on investment? Are there other financial measures that should be considered in evaluating a project?

DANIEL G. FOX-GLIESSMAN

In some ways, the two measurement metrics, *payback period* and *return on investment (ROI)* are significantly different from one another regarding complexity, sophistication and value to the IT manager, CIO, or CFO. As project management metrics, each represents a theory that has a place in IT management and each has different followings. While ROI has the financial discipline that is often advocated by CFOs, payback period is both more practical and more relevant, especially for the shorter duration projects that are more likely to receive funding in today's economic environment. Other financial measures relevant to measuring the financial feasibility and success of IT projects include:

- Net present value (NPV),

- Internal rate of return (IRR),

- Total cost of ownership (TCO).

PROJECT PAYBACK PERIOD

The *project payback period* is the anticipated length of time it will take a project to pay for itself. It is calculated as follows: Take the initial project investment (in dollars) and divide it by the annual benefit (in dollars). This generates the period of time it will take for the project to pay for itself. The lower the cost and the higher the benefit, the faster the payback. So for example, the equation would look like this:

$$\frac{\text{Initial Investment}}{\text{Annual Net Benefit}} = \text{Payback Period}$$

For a project that had an initial cost or investment amount of $100,000 and the amount of benefit (reduced cost, increased revenue, etc.) each year was $25,000, the payback period would be four years:

$$\frac{\$100,000}{\$25,000} = 4 \text{ Years}$$

This metric is easy to calculate and easily understood by the nonfinancial professional. However, it does not account for the true significance of the payback during the period in question. A 4 year payback on a $20,000 project is much different from a 4 year payback on a $1 million project. Also, for long projects, this method does not consider the time value of money. Despite these limitations, because of its simplicity and for reasons further described below, this method is the one most frequently used as the first level of project evaluation.

What Is Return on Investment (ROI)?

ROI equals the percentage resulting from dividing the benefits of a project by the investment. The benefits can be cost reductions, revenues generated, or revenues protected (Q73). The investment would be the total cost of the project over the measurement period. To take a simple example, assume a 1 year analysis period and a return of $150,000 on a project costing $100,000. The equation would look like this:

$$\frac{\text{Earnings or Savings}}{\text{Investment}} = \text{ROI}$$

or

$$\frac{\$150,000}{\$100,000} = 1.5 \text{ times or } 150\%$$

When the analysis period exceeds a year, an interest rate factor needs to be applied. Often this is the company's cost of capital and is usually determined by the CFO who takes into account inflation expectations, interest rate assumptions, and the company's risk profile. These rates are often in the 10–15 percent range. So, for example, using a 15 percent discount rate, a 3 year depreciation period, and a return of $50,000 per year, the ROI calculation looks like this:

$$\frac{\dfrac{\$50,000}{1.15} + \dfrac{\$50,000}{1.15 \cdot 1.15} + \dfrac{\$50,000}{1.15 \cdot 1.15 \cdot 1.15}}{\$100,000} = 1.14 \text{ or } 114\%$$

This metric can be used to decide between multiple projects of competing priorities. It works best when both the *benefits* and the *investment* can be quantified with high certainty (i.e., when both the ROI and the investment are known). However, there is no adjustment for, or indication of, the magnitude of the project in real dollars. For example, there is a big difference between a $10,000 project with a 120 percent ROI over 3 years and a $1 million project with a 120 percent ROI over 3 years. Also, project risk is not considered as a factor. Finally, when an IT project is strategic to the business, it may be difficult to express its importance in strictly ROI terms.

WHAT IS NET PRESENT VALUE (NPV)?

NPV is the value of the net benefits of the project minus the initial investment. It defines the value of the investment in "today's" dollars by applying a discount rate appropriate for the project or for the company. Assuming a 3 year depreciation and a 15 percent discount rate, the equation looks like this:

$$\frac{\$50,000}{1.15} + \frac{\$50,000}{1.15 \cdot 1.15} + \frac{\$50,000}{1.15 \cdot 1.15 \cdot 1.15} - \$100,000 = \$14,161.26$$

The result is a projection of the total return over the life of the project and is represented in discounted or adjusted dollars. In theory, a project that has a *positive* net present value is worth doing.

NPV includes all cash flows related to the project and considers the time value of money. Projects can be ranked in priority by NPV. However, NPV does not give a meaningful representation of when the returns will be realized. This limits its use in many technology projects.

WHAT IS INTERNAL RATE OF RETURN (IRR)?

IRR represents the economic rate of return of the project. It is the interest rate, when applied to the cost and benefits of a project, which discounts the cash flows to zero. Thus, the equation, again assuming 3 year depreciation is as follows:

$$\$100,000 - \frac{50000}{1.234} + \frac{50000}{1.234 \cdot 1.234} + \frac{50000}{1.234 \cdot 1.234 \cdot 1.234} = 37.4068 \text{ (approximately 0)}$$

In this example, the calculation solved for the IRR, turned out to be a 23.4 percent discount rate. The IRR is often compared to the "hurdle" rate of the corporation, which is usually the corporation's cost of capital. Theoretically, a project with an IRR in excess of the hurdle rate is worth doing.

Projects can be easily ranked by IRR for comparison purposes. If one project has a higher IRR than another, the executive team may choose that project in order to generate better returns for the business. As with NPV, IRR considers all cash flows related to a project and the time value of money. However, as with ROI, this metric is somewhat of an overkill for small projects and does not take into account the total magnitude of the benefit. In fact, IRR is most often applied to large projects with multiple year durations. The nature of the calculation assumes that cash flows are reinvested each year at the IRR rate, which is rarely the case.

TOTAL COST OF OWNERSHIP

Some technology investments are expressed in other financial metrics. One frequently seen is total cost of ownership (TCO) (**Q74**). This metric is usually associated with a specific asset or set of assets. It is designed to consider all costs associated with those assets including the purchase price, training costs, maintenance expense, and support costs. For example, a personal computer with an initial purchase price of $1500 is likely to have a total cost of ownership over its useful life of $6000 or higher. Unlike the other measures described above, TCO focuses mainly on the cost side of the equation and is therefore used for specific technology investment analyses.

WHICH MEASUREMENT IS THE BEST FIT FOR INFORMATION TECHNOLOGY PROJECTS?

As mentioned earlier, the best measure is the one that is correctly scaled to the size of the project and its purpose.

- *Project payback period*—This is the easiest to use and understand and has typically been applied to projects of short duration. Nevertheless, in recent years, it has even been used on larger projects. With so many valuable and competing technology projects in most organizations, companies are requiring their projects to pay back very quickly, usually in less than 18 months. When this becomes the initial screen for project prioritization, the longer projects, where some of the other measures are technically more appropriate, are not even considered. Therefore, project payback has taken a dominating role as the initial yardstick for project approval.

- *Return on investment (ROI)*—This is commonly used and is relatively easy to calculate on an ongoing basis throughout the life of a project.[1] It is most valuable when used to decide between different projects of competing priorities. However, it can be deceiving when used on small projects where the overall dollar impact is small, even if the ROI looks very strong.

- *Net present value (NPV)* and *internal rate of return (IRR)*—These are two sides of the same mathematical calculation and are primarily used for large projects where the time value of money is a big factor, or where the corporation requires such projects to exceed its hurdle rate.

75 ▬

---

[1] Software is now available to guide the calculation of ROI. See "CIOs:ROI Software to the Rescue," Larry Dignan, *ZDNet News*, November 11, 2002 <http://zdnet.com.com/2100-1106-965187.html>.

CRITICAL SUCCESS FACTORS—THE IMPORTANCE
OF FOLLOW-THROUGH

Regardless of the financial metrics used in the project approval phase, it is critically important that projects, once approved, be tracked against their benchmark. IT managers must continually monitor the project's costs and benefits, not only during the project, but after it is in operation (Q77). In fact, it is the responsibility of the CIO and the CFO to make sure that projects are measured on an ongoing basis. When such discipline is applied, companies can track the various metrics and see which one is most appropriate for each specific technology opportunity.

---

76. How do you choose one technology project over another?

ERIC V. ROBINSON AND DAVID R. LAUBE

With the growing importance of technology as a competitive tool, it is common for companies to have multiple technology projects under consideration. The process of choosing the right projects varies widely from company to company. Sometimes the executive with the loudest voice and most clout gets his or her project approved. Other times, executives may cut "side deals" among themselves or with the CFO or CIO to get their pet project approved. But the selection process no longer needs to be this subjective. There are well-tested frameworks that companies can use to evaluate and prioritize technology projects in an orderly and rational manner. These frameworks focus on benefits and the delivery of measurable business results.[1] By selecting only those projects that align with the strategy of the business in a way that produces sustainable competitive advantage, the value of IT and the firm are both enhanced.

A FOCUS ON BENEFITS

Benefits and value have become the focus in how an enterprise addresses the selection of new IT projects.[2] They act as filters through which projects presented to IT for consideration can be evaluated. These filters include:[3]

[1] Scott Berinato, "Do the Math," *CIO.com* 1 Oct. 2001, 3 Dec. 2002 <http://www.cio.com/archive/100101/math.html>.
[2] Berinato.
[3] John Thorpe and DMR's Center for Strategic Leadership. *The Information Paradox: Realizing the Business Benefits of Information Technology* (Toronto: McGraw-Hill Ryerson, 1998) 76.

1. understanding the strategic alignment of the project with the goals of the business,

2. understanding the financial value of the project to the business,

3. understanding the technical risks and risks of achieving the benefits,

4. selecting only the "best" projects that meet these criteria.

These factors must be measured and weighted to provide a relative separation of the proposed IT projects and balanced against the potential returns in other areas of the enterprise. Four filters that can be used to help determine which projects to select are discussed on the following pages.

Executive Sponsorship

The first step in the evaluation process is to obtain the short list (not the "wish list") of serious projects from the leaders of each business unit in the enterprise. Each proposed project should include a description of the project, the estimated one-time and ongoing costs (including depreciation and maintenance), as well as the timing and the expected business benefit to be derived. Those projects for which a benefit is not claimed by the executive sponsor should be dropped from consideration (Q72).

Strategic Alignment

A project must be aligned with a company's strategies and objectives. It is up to the top leaders of a company to define the business strategies. This information is used to evaluate whether a given technology project supports the strategic objectives and may be good investment (Q4). At a minimum, projects must assist a company in progressing toward its strategic objectives in the core areas of the business.

Consider the differences between two projects in an organization: Project A (an expense-reduction project) and Project B (a revenue-generating project). Given three broad strategic objectives of increasing revenues, reducing costs, and speeding the delivery of new products, a matrix can be constructed to test how each of these projects aligns with the objectives.[4]

The scores are based on questions or criteria designed to reveal the degree that the project is aligned with each strategic objective. For example, given the strategic objective of delivering new products, a relevant question for each project is, "does it increase our ability to bring new products to market quickly?" Each project is scored on how well it helps the business meet that objective. The weightings vary depending on management's emphasis on current tactical needs versus longer term strategic needs

[4] Thorpe 113, 115–17.

Table *76.1* Sample Matrix—*Project Alignment with Strategic Objectives*

Strategy	Weight	Score (1–5)		Weighted Score	
		Proj. A	Proj. B	Proj. A	Proj. B
Increase Revenues	25%	2	4	.50	1.00
Reduce Costs	25%	4	2	1.00	.50
Deliver New Products	50%	2	3	1.00	1.50
Total	100%	N/A	N/A	2.50	3.00

for the enterprise. In this example, increasing the ability to bring new products to market quickly is considered more important by the management team than increasing revenues or reducing costs in the short run (Table 76.1).

This step alone usually eliminates a large number of proposed IT projects that do not strongly align with the strategic objectives. For example, a firm would not consider a project to create an external data center hosting business if the firm's core competencies were not around operating data centers and if hosting were a mere sideline to its main strategy. Conversely, a company whose core strategy is to be the best hosting business in the country, might score this same initiative very highly in terms of its alignment with the company's strategy and ability to create a sustainable market advantage. Each company should periodically review its IT spending to see how much of it is aligned with its strategic objectives.[5]

FINANCIAL VALUE

The next filter is financial value. A simple business case no longer is sufficient. The financial evaluation should take into account the costs *and* the expected benefit stream (e.g., sustainable revenue increases, cost savings, cost avoidance, etc.) from implementing the initiative (**Q73, Q75**). The benefits must be measurable (**Q77, Q92**) and have a business sponsor who is willing to achieve those benefits (i.e., in the form of a hard commitment to the business).[6] The sponsor should understand that if the technology investment is made, the CFO will adjust the sponsor's business plan to capture the benefits that have been committed. The financial evaluation should include key financial measures: net present value (NPV), payback period, and internal rate of return (IRR), to name a few (**Q75**). As the financial needs of the business change, each of these measures can be emphasized more or less (i.e., payback period may be relatively more important during a cash crunch). A simple matrix to evaluate the financial value attribute of a project follows (Table 76.2).[7]

[5] Berinato.
[6] Thorpe 76.
[7] Thorpe 113–17.

Table 76.2 Sample Matrix—Evaluate Financial Value of a Project

Financial Measure*	Weight	Score (1–5)*		Weighted Score	
		Proj. A	Proj. B	Proj. A	Proj. B
NPV	30%	3	4	.90	1.20
Payback Period	40%	4	2	1.60	.80
IRR	30%	3	3	.90	.90
Total	100%	N/A	N/A	3.40	2.90

*Higher score is achieved by higher financial value (detail not shown). Note that other measures such as the ratio of economic costs vs. economic benefits or EVA can be used, etc.

Table 76.3 Sample Matrix—Determining Project Risk

Risk	Weight	Score (1–5)*		Weighted Score	
		Proj. A	Proj. B	Proj. A	Proj. B
Org. Support	30%	3	4	.90	1.20
New Technology	30%	2	4	.60	1.20
Complexity	40%	3	3	.90	.90
Total	100%	N/A	N/A	2.40	3.30

*Higher scores indicate lower project risks and a greater likelihood that the project's proposed benefits can be delivered.

RISK

The technological and business risk should be quantified and compared to the risk profile on the other new technology initiatives (**Q85, Q86**). Risk implies the technical risk of being able to deliver the project as well as the risk of realizing the benefits in the sponsor organization. The risk matrix, using targeted questions to reveal the results, could be constructed as shown in Table 76.3.[8]

76 ▬▬

ADDING IT UP

The results of the evaluation of strategic alignment, financial value, and risk can then be weighted and tallied.[9] The result provides a summary evaluation of the

[8] Thorpe 114–17.

[9] Another approach to evaluate IT investments is to treat technology assets and projects more as portfolios much like the financial firms have for many years. Using this approach, a firm's entire

Table 76.4 Sample Matrix—Summary Evaluation of Proposed Projects

Area	Weight	Scores (from above)		Weighted Scores	
		Proj. A	Proj. B	Proj. A	Proj. B
Strategic Alignment	30%	2.50	3.00	.75	.90
Financial Value	40%	3.40	2.90	1.36	1.16
Risk	30%	2.40	3.90	.72	1.17
Total	100%	N/A	N/A	2.83	3.23

proposed projects. As shown in Table 76.4, Project B would deliver the greatest value to the business.

OTHER FACTORS TO CONSIDER

Because of the dynamics within an organization, political and personal preferences can sometimes override the rational project evaluation process. The framework described above works best when evaluating multiple projects across a single business unit or evaluating projects across multiple units when the funding comes from a corporate source. If projects are allowed to be separately funded by business units themselves, the business units will often override the framework because they will view the projects strictly in the context of their own business objectives. Of course, they should use the framework described above to prioritize the projects within their own unit. But if individual business units can make their own technology decisions, this can sometimes alter (and in many cases temporarily suboptimize) the IT project selection process. Even the best ideas must still be compared across the enterprise, as the best IT project may still be worse than the return that can be achieved by investing in another area of the business, such as advertising, new sales offices, or the like. Com-

---

suite of IT investments is collected and controlled as one set of interrelated activities in one place—a portfolio. The cost of IT projects is measured against their potential financial value, risk, and business impact, and budgets can then be allocated to the portfolios with the highest potential returns. In addition to providing a centralized overview of all IT projects, a portfolio approach makes it easier for CIOs to ensure their IT investments are well balanced in terms of size, risk, and projected payoff. Properly executed, it allows for greater visibility of projects that are redundant or too risky, while at the same time, highlighting the opportunities to shift from relatively low value investments to more high value or strategic ones. For more information on qualitative methods of measuring IT value see "A Buyer's Guide to IT Value Methodologies: Qualitative Methods," *CIO.com* 7 July 2002, 16 Dec. 2002 <http://www.cio.com/archive/071502/value_qualitative.html>; Berinato Thomas Hoffman, "IT Investment Model Wins Converts," *Computerworld* 5 Aug. 2002: 3.

panies in this situation may set up a technology review committee, often chaired by the CEO or COO, who makes the final allocations of technology projects across their business units and ensure linkage to overall company strategy (**Q4**).

SUMMARY

IT investments are sometimes huge, often long term, and therefore inherently risky investments. Using the techniques just described to evaluate each project relative to other projects will provide an objective evaluation of the technology ideas in the enterprise and allow selection of only those projects that create the greatest value for the firm. Arguably the decisions will improve, the discussions between IT and business will be more focused, and the chances of realizing the outcomes of the projects will increase. IT investment decisions should not be considered "different" or "special" from a funding selection standpoint. They should operate with the same accountability and responsibility to deliver as the rest of the business.

---

77. How will you know if the assumed benefits of a project have been realized?

CHERYL WHITE AND THOMAS KIEFER

IT investments are generally funded because of their projected contribution to achieving a firm's strategy. As with any other investment, many companies traditionally assess the value of their IT investments against bottom line financial objectives such as return on investment, payback period, and net present value (**Q75**). In practical terms, however, financial indicators represent only one element in a technology project's overall value to an organization. Project objectives may include real but nonfinancial benefits, such as complying with legal mandates, increasing customer satisfaction, or improving employee morale. What is important is that these other outcomes can be measured, are tied to the organization's business strategy, and drive the performance required to achieve expected business goals.[1] In this context, project value is best understood as the degree to which a project aligns with and supports the

[1] Ray McKenzie, *The Relationship-Based Enterprise: Powering Business Success through Customer Relationship Management* (Toronto: McGraw-Hill Ryerson, 2001).

strategic objectives of the organization and/or business unit, and how each project fits into a firm's overall portfolio of technology projects (**Q4**).[2]

Regardless of whether the type of contribution is financial or otherwise, IT executives must have the ability to measure the actual return on their IT investment. This requires an upfront definition of desired benefits or value of a project and a system to track a project's benefits over time. Ironically, most IT project benefits are not tracked, so many organizations have not even developed the ability to measure the realized value of their investments. Because tracking IT investments is hard to do, many companies fail to assess their benefits. For example, one study of CRM (**Q64**) implementations reported that 56 percent of companies implementing CRM programs had no metrics in place and 22 percent had minimal metrics.[3] Another study found that 90 percent of the fifty largest CRM user companies were unable to quantify a return on their CRM investments.[4]

MODELING PROGRAM BENEFITS

Benefits modeling is a technique that can aid IT executives in managing the delivery of benefits from IT projects and in selecting the best potential IT investments (**Q76**). Created at the start of the initiative, a benefits plan is developed to quantify, track, and manage the attainment of project benefits throughout a project's life cycle. The same process that is used to develop the business case for project approval is usually used to define the benefits. But beyond typical project metrics, a scoring and weighting process for risks relative to each metric can be defined and a total risk index developed. The risk index can then be factored into the "value" score for a project and used to establish acceptable parameters for measuring achievements.[5]

The benefits need to be defined at all levels of the technology project. So, for example, they should encompass the linkages to corporate strategy (**Q4**), the organizational impacts (**Q46, Q47**), the tactical benefits as well as the financial results. Beyond the definition of desired benefits, a benefits plan includes specifics related to measurements of benefits, how outcomes will be derived, and who is accountable for each benefit.

[2] John Thorp, *The Information Paradox Realizing the Business Benefits of Information Technology* (Toronto: McGraw-Hill Ryerson, 1998).

[3] Jan Andresen et al., "A Framework for Measuring IT Innovation Benefits," *Electronic Journal of Information Technology in Construction* 5 (2000), 7 Oct. 2002 <http://www.itcon.org/2000/4>; Tom Kaneshige, "DMR Talks CRM," *Line56 Media Web Site* 27 Feb. 2002, 7 Oct. 2002 <http://www.line56.com/articles/default.asp?ArticleID=3419&KeyWords=dmr++AND+talks++AND+crm>.

[4] Jill Dyché, *The CRM Handbook: A Business Guide to Customer Relationship Management* (Boston: Addison-Wesley, 2002).

[5] Thorp.

Once a project's desired outcomes are identified, the next step is to establish the owner of each benefit. A single manager or executive is assigned responsibility for achieving each benefit and is given authority to do what must be done to deliver value (**Q93**). Isolating metrics is the next challenge, and the goal is to define precisely how each benefit will be measured (**Q92**). This step includes describing the source of measurable data and establishing values against which the benefits can be compared. Determining the baseline for the initial metrics is imperative if progress against target objectives is to be meaningfully tracked. For example, if an IT project is targeted to save 20 percent, then the exact calculation of the current cost levels must be made and documented. Otherwise, when the project savings are evaluated, there will be nonproductive debates over whether the savings were off of last period's costs, off of the budgeted costs, off of the current run rate, etc. Sometimes results are expressed in terms of industry or other performance benchmarks; just make sure they can be accurately calculated.

INDEPENDENT ASSESSMENT

One of the issues in developing, assessing, and tracking project value throughout its life cycle is objectivity. While many large companies have people dedicated to developing business cases and program management offices (PMO) that track and maintain the health of multiple programs, these groups often have a vested interest in their projects' outcomes and can be less than objective. The addition of a value management office (VMO) can significantly increase the potential for objective assessment and tracking of the value delivered by project investments.[6] VMOs are typically staffed with individuals who are trained and competent in the concepts of value assessments and who have no vested interest in the success or failure of any project. Sometimes when there are not enough projects to justify a separate team to do assessments, the finance organization will provide an analyst who can be trained to make them. Similarly, an internal audit group sometimes receives this assignment as well.

These individuals work with project teams to objectively assess the relative value, strategic alignment, and risk of each project. Using the benefits plan that was developed during a project's planning stages, the VMO collects the actual benefit metric results, reassesses the status of project risks, and reports the findings to the executive decision board at intervals that suit the needs of the board (**Q95**). Since expected benefits evolve as a greater understanding is gained about the project, the VMO also works with project leadership to set new and different benefit metrics for projects over time.[7] As the value results are reported throughout the life cycle of each project, the

77 ▬

---

[6] Thorp.

[7] Dan Remenyi, "The Elusive Nature of Delivering Benefits from IT Investment," *The Electronic Journal of Information Systems Evaluation* March 2000, 26 Feb. 2002 <http://www.iteva.rug.nl/ejise/vol3/paper1.html>.

decision board is then armed with the data needed to make adjustments to the funded projects and the technology investment portfolio. They then have the ability to understand the value each project has delivered and can hold the appropriate people accountable for successes and failures.

Tracking over Time

Even in organizations where tracking processes are implemented, the discipline usually only lasts until the project is complete. At that point, project measurements are taken, reward or punishment is handed out to the project team for their success or failure, and everyone moves on to the next challenge. But projects usually have a much longer life cycle, and, even though, in big projects, the benefits are expected to last for several years, they are rarely tracked. Project teams sometimes know this so they conveniently push benefits into the outer years, knowing that they'll never be held accountable for those results. Savvy business leaders also are aware of this behavior and they usually look to their CFO to inject some accountability into the future. This is done by driving any promised financial benefits into future budget planning cycles. So, for example, if a technology project's objective was to cut call center costs 20 percent a year for three years, the CFO would automatically drop the call center's budget target by that amount each year. This would ensure that the benefits of the project flow through and that any variations would be explained.

Summary

The way an organization determines whether or not its technology projects are delivering on promised benefits is straightforward. Define those benefits, track them, and do it over time. It requires discipline, careful definitions, and independent assessments. Early efforts will likely be cumbersome and reveal real weaknesses in initial technology business cases. But it is only through tracking results that companies can learn whether their investments are paying off. Future projects will then benefit and companies will improve the way they evaluate, prioritize, and spend on technology projects.[8]

---

[8] We appreciate Jay Bransford's contributions to an early draft of this answer.

78. What are the major components of a "build-or-buy" decision?

BARBARA T. BAUER

Some people only like brand-new houses. For these people, the process of build-ing is thrilling and produces a house perfectly tailored to their habits and idiosyn-crasies. For others, buying an existing house and adapting it to become a special home is just as thrilling, usually with very attractive cost and time benefits. Decisions to build or buy software are similar, and frequently just as personal and emotional. Since many "build-or-buy" decisions are expensive and have a big impact on an organiza-tion, getting emotions under control is important.

HISTORY

Only twenty years ago, "buying" an application wasn't possible. Off-the-shelf ap-plications didn't exist. Automating a business function required developing a brand-new application. Every business with resources and courage commissioned their internal IT shop to write billing systems, payroll systems, inventory management ap-plications, and so on. These were great days for consulting companies who did cus-tom development, and they were traumatic and expensive days for the businesses try-ing to automate processes.

While almost everyone survived these early development projects, there was gen-eral (and vocal) dissatisfaction with the difficulty, expense, and unpredictability of software projects. Two important resources emerged from the early days: (1) con-sulting firms developed substantial staffs of software engineers who knew the "ins" and "outs" of specific business processes, and (2) product companies started building generic applications that could be used by many similar companies. Today, there are thousands of generic software products available. Businesses now face the challenge of determining whether to buy a generic application or build one from "scratch." It is the new house vs. existing house question, but with much more complexity and usu-ally greater impact.

78 ▬▬

IMPORTANT TRENDS

Both time and technology have improved the application products, producing quality and flexibility that frequently weigh the option toward a purchased solution. For example, products that are widely used have embedded "world-class" process efficiency into the software application and its implementation. Configuration flexi-bility and coding sophistication enable a purchased package to appear quite "custom" to the end users (Q69). Finally, time, cost, and risk are almost always reduced in the purchased application, increasing the attractiveness of this solution. These trends are likely to continue, constantly improving the application products, therefore a company must have a very unique situation to assume the higher cost, risk, and time to develop and implement a unique application solution.

DECISION CRITERIA

Although each company and its internal processes are unique, the criteria affecting the decision are common and fairly easy to understand. The keys to reducing bias and emotionalism are evaluating the decision criteria and articulating their characteristics in a business case that has real cost and benefit numbers. Both the product companies and consulting companies can offer experienced help. However, even with help from experts, company leaders need to understand each element that impacts the choice in the context of the total company strategy and structure. The three key decision criteria to evaluate concern:

1. company structure and strategy,

2. features and functions of the off-the-shelf products available,

3. characteristics of the desired implementation.

COMPANY STRATEGY AND STRUCTURE

The company's business strategy and structure influence most strongly the choice of "build vs. buy." If the purpose of the application under consideration is to differentiate a product in the market or to provide more excellent customer service than competitors provide, the correct, and perhaps only, choice is to build a custom application. However, if the purpose of the application is, for example, to improve internal efficiency of typical financial processes such as accounts receivable, accounts payable, or financial journals, the right choice probably is to choose one of the successful, widely used financial packages. It is pretty clear that in today's environment it is only the rare company that embarks on any custom development of standard company infrastructure systems (financial, HR, ERP, etc.) because those systems rarely drive competitive advantage.

Company structure is another important and fairly obvious element to understand. Available packages are built on implicit models of the relationship between different parts of a company and their roles and responsibilities. Some company structures are easily mapped to the generic product, while others may be singularly idiosyncratic, such as highly matrixed multinational companies. The cost advantage of a generic package can disappear if the entire company has to be redesigned to implement the application (**Q58, Q59**). While extreme upheaval is a real "red flag" to a packaged implementation, frequently organizations that are resistant to change put up a formidable facade of concern, when in reality, a packaged approach may not really require structural change at all. Skilled and disciplined analysis of the actual business process and of the potential benefits of a "buy" option are the antidote to "posturing" from different parts of the company in an attempt to derail a "buy" decision.

FEATURES AND FUNCTIONS OF OFF-THE-SHELF APPLICATIONS

Each generic application has defined features and supports a set of business processes. These features and implicit processes must have some level of congruence with the requirements of the company and the existing processes. The work to achieve a clear understanding of the package functionality and the current and new business process can be difficult and time consuming (**Q69**). Resources must be appointed (or acquired) to do this work, and appropriate support and management applied. It is easy to avoid doing this work and fall headfirst into bias, prejudice, and opinion, instead of digging into the nitty-gritty analysis of what the company needs, how it currently works, and how much it is willing to change. Frequently in these situations, subject matter experts from inside the company try to maintain the status quo, rather than apply an impartial analysis. To avoid this, some companies find external impartial experts who won't benefit from the decision. The most important antitoxin is clear direction from upper management, and appropriate levels of review and probing. An example of this behavior is the situation where subject matter experts insist that certain data or processes are matters of law, when, in fact, they are embedded traditions. This is delicate and critically important information to sift out.

A significant risk to many technology projects is that of vague business requirements. Often the business units have a hard time deciding or even agreeing on the features and functionality of a custom system (**Q92**). When the "buy" alternative is exercised, the range of possible systems features narrows quickly, helping to end internal bickering or indecision.

THE DESIRED IMPLEMENTATION

Implementation requirements are the final set of critical elements that generate doom or happiness in the project. In either a build or buy strategy, the skills of both the client business unit and the IT organization will determine success or failure. But there are IT organizations without the ability to develop a major application from scratch. Costs can escalate quickly when consultants are necessary to actually do the development. However, many companies do not have adequate self-reflective skills and dramatically overestimate their ability to build successfully. If there is the least hint that reality and pragmatism are absent, then executives must intervene. If the company has a good grip on its expertise and capability, it will be reasonably straightforward to map the expertise against the needs of the project and determine if outside resources must be added. This option is sometimes necessary in both "build" and "buy" options, but getting it wrong is exceptionally devastating in the build strategy.

Role of Management

The other fundamental element in either strategy is the need for executive leadership (Q93). Whether the business needs to conform to the processes inherent in the commercial package or to simplify to enable a development effort to succeed, ensuring the company's management team is absolutely clear about this and ready to adapt is essential. It is tempting to assume that conformance will occur as implementation begins, but there is no guarantee that it will. Instead, back-sliding, work-arounds, and other creative underground forms of noncompliance frequently surface. The solution for this is superb, insightful, involved management, communicating clearly and evenly with all the participants about the decision, direction, and the benefits of appropriate implementation. Getting all these elements in line is difficult, but rewarding work. The result is a successful project that provides the required functionality and strategic benefits using the best balance of time and resources.

---

79. How do you select a vendor?

DON WENNINGER

Today's IT executive is faced with numerous solicitations every month from well-meaning suppliers of everything from computer peripherals and enterprise application software to consulting services and outsourcing solutions. Unsolicited marketing of even the best of these vendor products through the mail, e-mail, and telephone can become distracting for IT managers due to the sheer volume of such time-consuming contacts. Conversely, some vendors bypass IT management altogether and directly contact companies' business executives to try to market their IT wares. In some cases, company employees may develop preferences for certain vendors and products based on input from magazines, sales people, acquaintances, or conferences. The issue with all of these circumstances is that vendors should not be selected based on relatively random contacts and minimal analysis. Instead, when a company is ready to research vendors to satisfy real, business driven IT requirements, it should proactively:

- search for and narrow down the list of prospective vendors,

- determine which vendors are the most qualified,

- select the best vendor based on structured criteria.

VENDOR IDENTIFICATION

Finding a reliable vendor with cost effective, stable products that both meet the company's business needs and fit with the company's standard architecture and skilled resources can be challenging. The first and most critical step for any organization is to understand what problem it is trying to solve and the objective it is trying to achieve. Solutions to nonexistent problems waste money and speculative purchases rarely yield firm returns.

Once the business needs are understood, the company can proceed to identify vendors of products and services to help meet the needs. If few or no vendors are known, or if a company isn't sure if any known vendors can meet its unique needs, then it may need to advertise or send out a request for information (RFI). Prospective vendors or consultants may respond with information regarding how they think the business needs might be met. Governmental agencies often use this approach to identify potential vendors and gather the latest information to help assemble detailed, comprehensive specifications for what is to be procured.

Alternatively, the company may research prospective vendors and products in published industry sources (or Web sites), sometimes only available for a subscription fee. Some companies, such as Gartner Research, Forrester Research, Inc., and IDC, routinely analyze various vendors and product categories, and make their analyses available for a fee. Subscribers not only see rankings of the leading vendors and products, but may talk to these firms about the details of their findings.

VENDOR QUALIFICATION

Once a list of prospective vendors has been prepared and other research performed, a company can send requests for qualifications (RFQs) to the most promising vendors. After screening the responses, a company will often ask the top few (three or four) vendors to present their qualifications in person, focusing on the vendors' financial stability, key personnel, product architecture, and product features. Specifically, some of the considerations a company needs to investigate at this stage include:

- *Past success*—What successes have the vendor and its customers had that relate to the company's business needs?

- *Size*—A small vendor may provide more individualized service than a large one and may offer so-called best-of-breed software for a specific niche. The downside is that one large customer may monopolize too much of a small vendor's limited financial and personnel resources. A larger company may have a wider variety of integrated solutions and greater resources.

- *Financial stability*—If the prospective vendor is not on solid financial footing, it may not be in business much longer.

- *Length of time in business*—Newer companies may have some start-up problems or "growing pains," especially related to processes such as testing, change control, or customer service. However, an older business may become complacent and not be as innovative as a newer company.

- *Reputation*—What have you heard about this business? What do the trade publications, current reference customers, and research groups such as Gartner say about the vendor?

- *Fit of product or service*—Does the vendor's product architecture fit with the company's standards? Do the vendor's key personnel understand the company's industry, business processes, and systems needs? Are the right resources available?

- *Resources and responsiveness*—Can the vendor deliver what you need in the appropriate time frame? Suppliers of software and hardware often stretch themselves so thin, they lose their ability to deliver. Having a long list of clients that signed up in the last month could mean that this company is stressing its support and development staffs beyond their ability to adequately respond to customer issues. The ability to respond quickly is critical to any enterprise. An IT organization's reputation can rely on the success of a major project, which in turn is heavily dependent on key vendors' resources and responsiveness.

Designating the supplier as a "partner" or "vendor" should be carefully considered. Does the company want the vendor to be a true partner going forward, supplying all the support that partnerships require? Or does the company want this supplier to simply drop off the CD or server and move on? Developing a partnership with a supplier can be problematic if it becomes hard to detach from the supplier, but can also yield significant benefit when the partner shares some accountability (and gets fees) for a project's success.

VENDOR SELECTION

Traditionally, companies have made one of two mistakes in the vendor selection process: either they quickly select a vendor based on insufficient information or analysis, or they spend too much time scoring and trying to exhaustively analyze the results of 100 or more detailed questions. These questions are given to the top few vendors in the form of written requests for proposal (RFPs). RFPs can be one-page statements of the business problem or can expand into 40 pages or more of detailed functional and technical questions (**Q81**).

A good RFP should include one page of the most critical ten or twelve criteria upon which the decision will almost always be made. Any one of these questions may cause a vendor to drop off the list:

- overall fit in terms of architecture and platform of the vendor's solution,

- financial stability of the company,

- scope of the vendor's products or services,

- industry understanding and experience of the vendor,

- references from similar companies,

- customer service, problem escalation, and upgrade practices,

- price and other contractual terms and conditions.

Then the RFP should list the detailed questions needed to assess the degree of detailed functional and technical fit offered by each vendor. This will help the company plan how much the vendor can provide versus internal development or other work required.

Responses to RFPs, if incorporated into the ultimate contracts, can also provide leverage to ensure a vendor doesn't overpromise. In the extreme, this method can ensure a company's ability to sue for nonperformance, although this is a last resort, because it becomes a lose-lose situation for both parties.

Automated Vendor Selection

Beginning in the late 1990s, automated sourcing tools, sometimes referred to as e-sourcing applications, have come to market to assist in the vendor selection process. These products were originally championed by niche software providers, but as the market grows, more mainstream players, such as the large ERP vendors, have entered this space.

Sourcing software can offer a wide range of functionality, supporting requirements such as demand aggregation, RFxs (RFIs, RFQs, and RFPs), reverse auctions, bid analysis, negotiations, and contract development and management. More recent enhancements have been (1) the addition of sophisticated optimization techniques for ensuring that the optimal bid is identified, and (2) better support on the front end as to what's been purchased in the past (spend analysis). Overall, these products

79

leverage the power of the Internet to make the issuing and responding to RFxs more automated. They also increase the overall efficiency of the sourcing process, delivering enough incremental vendor price savings over manual processes to generate a rapid return on the software investment.

CONCLUSION

The final vendor selection can be difficult in today's markets. In the end, once properly accomplished, the single largest issue to face is that the functionality offered must be balanced by the ability of the supplier to perform. It does no good to select a supplier that won't exist tomorrow. Carefully considering all aspects of the requirements and making the viability analysis a firm part of the requirements statements will help ensure the immediate and long-term success of the vendor selection process.

---

80. What are the advantages and disadvantages of using an application service provider?

MARION JENKINS

An application service provider (ASP) is a company that specializes in IT outsourcing by hosting preconfigured software applications in a centralized environment. The customer pays a monthly fee based on the number of users. Conceptually, it is very attractive; theoretically, it improves cash flow, shortens implementation times, and conserves internal IT resources. However, there are some technical and practical limitations. ASP was a very hot concept in the late 1990s, but very few ASPs gained customers and many have gone out of business. There are some notable survivors and it is still an important segment of the industry, although like many other late-1990s business models, it exists today at a fraction of the size envisioned even a few years ago.

BACKGROUND

Typically, IT managers can either build software internally or buy COTS (commercial off-the-shelf) applications. However, even where there is close alignment between the capabilities of COTS applications and the business processes, a certain amount of customization is still necessary.

Regardless of whether the software is purchased or developed internally, the costs of software licensing, custom development and integration, plus the necessary development, test and production environments, and training, can run into tens of millions of dollars for a large corporate project and into millions for a moderate-sized project. Implementation can take months or even years. And, internal IT resources may be completely occupied providing day-to-day support for ongoing operations, making it very difficult to add a new development project to the mix.

Traditionally, companies have used integrators and consultancies to provide additional resources to develop and implement new applications. Ideally, the integrators brought in personnel who had experience with similar implementations. The company didn't have to ramp up their internal staff for a project only to ramp it back down once the project was complete.

In the late 1990s, many hosting companies such as Exodus, Digex, Globix, etc., built large data centers with excellent power, upstream network connectivity and other features needed by large corporate applications. At the same time, the dot.com companies and other new technology firms were increasingly drawing many IT resources away. Experienced legacy technical employees left in droves to join new start-ups. Because time to market was critical, the new start-ups did not want to waste their technical resources in developing and running "utility" software like billing and customer care. They needed their technical resources to develop the specialized applications that THEY were bringing to the market.

Major parts of common enterprise applications are similar—if not identical. A customer relationship management (CRM) **(Q65)** package contains basic common features regardless of the industry. So for example, if a company implemented a major CRM package, it could sell that CRM package "by-the-slice" to multiple companies with only minor customization from one implementation to another.

The ASP Industry Is Born

In this favorable environment, the ASP Industry Consortium (ASPIC) started with approximately 60 members in May 1999. Almost immediately, it became an incredibly lucrative area for both investment and technology activities. Potential customers could gain needed enterprise applications without building them themselves or buying them, and could do it at lower cost in less time. Software vendors saw a new channel for selling large numbers of licenses to a larger number of smaller customers. Infrastructure service providers of all kinds—data center/hosting companies, broadband and backbone network providers—saw an opportunity to add traffic rapidly to their newly built facilities.

The ASPs saw the possibility of gaining large numbers of users, challenging the likes of the large enterprise outsourcing companies like EDS and IBM Global Services, without having to compete directly to take their accounts away from them. Their hope was that there would be many early adopters jumping on the ASP model.

The ASP industry and the players change so rapidly that a list of ASPs would be outdated within a few months. Two ASPs are mentioned here because they were around when the ASPIC was first formed and they were still around in mid-2002. They also represent two different approaches to the ASP model: Corio initially focused primarily on large enterprise financial packages, notably PeopleSoft®. USinternetworking focused on utility services like Microsoft Exchange® and e-commerce platforms; both companies have since branched out to other software suites.

Advantages

The ASP model is not a cure-all for poor project planning. Senior technical management must be every bit as experienced and savvy—perhaps more so—than with an internal project. Many times CFOs and CEOs are looking for a "silver bullet" that will drastically slash time and money from IT projects. An ASP is not an automatic answer to those questions. But an ASP can help a company when there is:

- a shortage of skilled IT workers,

- the need for a 24×7 operation,

- the drive to reduce costs throughout the IT service supply chain,

- the need to reduce time to market,

- an unfavorable cash flow profile of IT investment,

- the need to make applications globally accessible.[1]

By using an ASP, a company saves the cost of:

- recruiting, maintaining, and retaining a large IT/development staff,

- building and maintaining the infrastructure (data center, networks, etc.) needed to support internally hosted applications,

- purchasing the software (by "renting" it).

If the company can implement the ASP configured software "as is," then the project can be completed quickly—possibly sooner than if done internally.

There is substantial evidence—albeit largely supported by the ASPIC and its members—that, under the right circumstances, the ASP model creates a positive and viable ROI for customers. According to the report, "The Financial Impact of ASPs," some customers have reported ROIs percentages in the hundreds.[2]

[1] Lynda M. Applegate, Robert D. Austin, and F. Warren McFarlan, *Creating Business Advantage in the Information Age* (Boston: McGraw-Hill, 2002).

[2] Amy Mizoras, *The Financial Impact of ASPs*, IDC, Web Conference, IDC Doc #25896, Oct. 2001.

DISADVANTAGES FOR BUSINESSES

Even though the ASP model has some huge advantages over either traditional approach of "build internal" or "buy COTS" (**Q78**), there are some real disadvantages for businesses, including:

- *Geographic*—You are an ASP customer and you just acquired a company in Malaysia. You need to provide the same application functionality overseas as in Silicon Valley, where your ASP has its major facility. Your ASP has no ability to support your applications in Malaysia.

- *Customization*—You are an ASP customer using MegaCRM (fictitious software) and need custom development beyond the ability of your ASP to modify the current version of MegaCRM. There is a non-ASP integrator that does the type of customization you need for your business, but you are locked into a service agreement with your ASP and it cannot or will not provide the customization you need.

- *Data security*—Your CFO is adamant that your financial data remain in-house on its own stand-alone servers and storage, and under no circumstances will he/she allow your financial data out of the house, especially to sit in a remote data center where there is a possibility of other companies' data residing on or even near the same platform. You have explained the benefits of outsourcing in general and the ASP model in general, but the CFO wants none of it.

- *Reliability*—Your ASP has a massive outage. Although you have lost 100 percent of your systems, representing thousands of dollars per hour, the ASP is losing millions with bigger customers and therefore is handling its issues first.

DISADVANTAGES FOR ASPs

There are also disadvantages from the ASP standpoint:

- *Version control*—Suppose you are an ASP hosting MegaCRM 8.0. Version 9.0, due out shortly, fixes known bugs and brings new feature/functionality. Many of your ASP customers have already built interfaces to take advantage of 9.0 and are pressuring you to implement 9.0 as soon as possible. Your internal IT staff has identified serious issues with 9.0 and recommends waiting for version 9.1. Other customers have built extensive interfaces with version 8.0, and have not had time to build to 9.0 and want you to delay 9.0 as long as possible. The only alternative that makes all of your customers happy is to support both versions—that significantly increases your overhead. You have to create separate environments and double your support resources.

- *Operational*—You are an ASP and are hosting with BigEdHost (a fictitious carrier/ data center company). They go out of business, or decide to consolidate, and they shut down the data center you are using. The property owner and/or other creditors

80

padlock the doors and hold your equipment for payment. How do you continue to support your ASP customers when your data center is shut down and your equipment locked up?

These disadvantages have tended to slow the adoption of the ASP model in many companies. As a result, many ASPs have struggled or gone out of business. It is likely that there will still be a demand for this particular business model; it is just not yet clear how large the ASP industry will become.

REQUIREMENTS FOR SUCCESS

The requirements for a successful ASP implementation are the same as those for any enterprise IT project:

- clear requirements

- alignment with core business objectives

- strong buy-in at the executive level and from business unit owners and end users

- rigorous project management

- strong oversight by internal IT resources

The application being outsourced to the ASP should be well matched with the ASP's capability and functionality. In addition, the customer must be comfortable with the ASP's experience implementing similar projects, and should check the ASP's references carefully. Finally, a thorough understanding of the contract terms, including service level agreements (SLAs) and remedies, is essential (Q79, Q81).

SUMMARY

The ASP model may offer significant time and financial savings to companies that want to implement standard enterprise applications, especially when the company does not have or does not want to develop the IT infrastructure and expertise internally. As with any integrated implementation, it is necessary to have solid requirements, executive buy-in, and detailed implementation plans. The ASP approach cannot compensate for bad IT management or poorly defined business processes. When ASPs were first conceived, their wide adoption appeared almost certain. However, although there are some examples of successful ASPs, many have not survived beyond the concept stage because of operational and other issues.

81. What purposes do different types of outsourcing relationships serve?

ELLEN BALAGUER

Outsourcing is the transfer of some or all of a company's business processes and/or supporting infrastructure to a service provider in order to achieve certain company objectives. The decision to outsource is driven by business considerations that depend upon the scale, skills, and strategy of the enterprise (**Q82**). Once the decision has been made to outsource, however, the organization must address two key questions, (1) what will be outsourced? and (2) what relationship will exist between the company and its outsourcing provider? Depending on the company objectives, it may be decided to outsource technology, business applications, or even business processes. The form of the outsourcing relationship can range from a conventional one focusing on cost reduction to a collaborative or even transformational one where the two parties work together to achieve and share in business results that neither could achieve alone.

TECHNOLOGY INFRASTRUCTURE OUTSOURCING

Technology infrastructure outsourcing is commonly used by companies that want to focus on core business strategies while the service provider focuses on the technology. Outsourcing arrangements can involve:

- operation of a customer's data servers, network devices, and hardware—everything usually included in a data center,

- management of an organization's internal infrastructure (e.g., networks, office equipment [LAN, desktop], voice and video communications),

- taking responsibility for security and disaster recovery (**Q30**, **Q33**) for all computing and network functions

BUSINESS APPLICATION OUTSOURCING

There are several forms of business application outsourcing that can allow an organization to achieve the benefits of leading-edge application solutions while controlling baseline development costs. Some of these include:

- *Software application management*—This provides support in the areas of:

    -programming of software changes and enhancements

—management and maintenance services for enterprise-wide software applications, such as SAP, PeopleSoft, Oracle, etc.

- *Design-build-run*—This operation has the supplier assume full responsibility for both software development and delivery, and ongoing management and maintenance of software platforms. In this model, in addition to application management (described above), the outsourcer continues to operate the system after implementation.

- *Onshore/Offshore solution centers*—These are foreign locations where an outsourcing provider has concentrated a large, skilled work group with a strong infrastructure of supervision, processes, and technology (**Q83**). They can provide additional cost savings by leveraging their skills and scale and providing proven methods, tools, and techniques for delivery.

BUSINESS PROCESS OUTSOURCING

Business process outsourcing (BPO) involves an organization asking a provider to assume full responsibility for complete business functions. This provider then owns, administers, and manages those functions for an organization. The BPO option delivers management, operation, and continuous improvement of a business's critical processes such as:

- customer relationship management (CRM)

- call centers

- training and e-learning

- supply chain and procurement

- logistics, building management, and maintenance

- finance and/or accounting activities (billing, taxes, accounts payable, etc.)

- human resources functions (benefits management, hiring, etc.)

OUTSOURCING RELATIONSHIPS

The relationship between a company and an outsourcing provider is a complex one. The business agreement that they reach is designed to (1) ensure that the outsourcer provides agreed upon levels of service, and (2) provide a framework for compensation and costs that meet both the company's and the outsourcer's objectives. There are three degrees of outsourcing relationships that can exist between an organization and the supplier:

- *Conventional outsourcing*—a contractual relationship that motivates the outsourcer to achieve specific measurable targets

- *Collaborative outsourcing*—an interactive relationship in which the organization and the outsourcer work jointly to define business outputs that meet current business needs

- *Business transformational outsourcing*—a committed relationship where both parties do what is necessary to achieve dramatic improvements in enterprise-level outcomes

CONVENTIONAL OUTSOURCING

A conventional outsourcing agreement typically involves contracting selected business processes to a service provider whose compensation is based on achieving specific and measurable target metrics. For example, an organization may outsource its IT organization in order to improve reliability and quality of service as well as decrease operational costs. The outsourcer agrees to provide end-to-end integrated IT services including support of operations, incident management, change management, and capacity planning.

Conventional outsourcing usually involves fixed-fee compensation and motivates the outsourcer through additional payments for reaching targeted performance. It usually also provides for cash penalties for missing targets. One challenge to this type of arrangement is that the stream of incremental savings will eventually reach its limit. Once the operation has been tuned, the ability to generate additional cost savings diminishes substantially.

COLLABORATIVE OUTSOURCING

Collaborative outsourcing relationships create value beyond simple cost reductions. For example, the objectives may target an increase in customer satisfaction or operational efficiency. Collaborative deals can motivate the outsourcer to exceed objectives since it will share in the benefits from implemented improvements. In a collaborative outsourcing arrangement, the customer and outsourcer work together to define the relationship. They jointly set target objectives, articulate principles of operations, and share in the benefits.

Challenges to this type of relationship can exist if there are dependencies across the business processes of the organization and the outsourcer. It becomes more difficult to make improvements to complex processes that span multiple organizations. As organizations seek to outsource more complex processes it also becomes more difficult to control and determine accountability. For example, if the business process being outsourced was sales in a call center, the outsourcer may not have any control over sales strategy or new product introductions, yet be expected to achieve certain results in performance. In order to manage these issues and target greater value from an outsourcing model, an organization can expand its relationship into a transformational arrangement as described below. In the example mentioned, the

81

transformational arrangement can allow the outsourcer to directly be part of the sales strategy thereby allowing it to have a better chance at achieving the expected results.

BUSINESS TRANSFORMATIONAL OUTSOURCING

Business transformational outsourcing (BTO) is used to fundamentally reshape an organization and its business. It shares many aspects of the collaborative model, but goes further. BTO arrangements are structured to make the company and the outsourcer *both* directly responsible for the bottom line business outcomes desired. Typically these are revenue-oriented outcomes. Also, where collaborative arrangements reward the outsourcer based on hitting specific performance targets, BTO arrangements often allow the outsourcer to share in the revenues and profits of the outsourced part of the business. To be successful, BTO arrangements typically:

- require a committed relationship between an organization and the outsourcer,
- outsource the hardest aspects of the program to increase chances of success,
- drive dramatic enterprise-level business improvements,
- have multi-year commitments that may have their rewards several years away,
- require joint leadership with long- and short-term decision making at the executive level.

In a BTO arrangement the two parties:

- jointly develop strategic objectives,
- conduct regular board reviews (including the most senior executives in the organization) to ensure achievement of objectives, review metrics, and drive strategy,
- use incentives that include sharing in the benefits of a new business agreement.

Instead of rewarding the meeting of targets such as cost reduction and delivery dates, rewards are typically based on a share of the increased revenue. For example, a company might enter into a BTO arrangement to establish a new sales channel for a new product line. The outsourcing provider and the company will jointly manage this channel and share in the revenues it generates. Business transformational outsourcing is intended to drive big paybacks for both sides of the arrangement.

CONCLUSION

Outsourcing can be an important way for a business to achieve some of its objectives. It is important to recognize that outsourcing can cover a wide range of areas in the business—from a single function like an IT organization to entire business processes. It is equally important to think through the nature of the outsourcing relationship. Depending on the objectives desired and the scope of what is being outsourced, the relationship can be a straightforward cost-oriented one, or it could be a highly transformational one. In the latter case, all aspects of management, execution, and rewards are shared.

82. When should an organization consider outsourcing?

ELLEN BALAGUER

More and more executives are using outsourcing as a means of making an immediate impact on a company's bottom line. Additionally, the right type of outsourcing relationship can drive critical enterprise-level transformations (**Q81**). Companies are taking advantage of the multitude of benefits offered by outsourcing relationships. Worldwide spending in outsourcing services in 1999 totaled $116 billion.[1] Other studies show outsourcing spending in 2000 was $248 billion with projections of $449 billion by 2005.[2] Companies are reporting cost savings that average 50 percent over ten years, as opposed to an average of 20 percent savings reported in the mid 1990s.[3]

In today's competitive landscape, organizations can look to outsourcing relationships to:

- achieve *scale* in their technologies,

- support a *skilled* organization,

- implement their *strategic* objectives,

- move with rapid *speed.*

An outsourcing vendor can provide companies with lower costs, access to competitive skills, and an increased ability to respond to changing business needs.

82 ———

[1] Cynthia Doyle, *Worldwide Outsourcing Market Forecast and Analysis, 1999–2004*, IDC, Report, n.d.

[2] Bruce Caldwell and Michelle Cantara, *IT Professional Services: Forecasts, Growth Rates and Market Share 2001*, Gartner, Inc., Market Statistics ITES-WW-MS-0108, 31 Jan. 2002.

[3] David J. Bryce and Michael Useem, "The Impact of Corporate Outsourcing on Company Value," *European Management Journal* 16. 6 (1998): 635–43.

Many outsourcing decisions are driven by a lack of understanding by senior executives of their cost structure. If a company's size makes it difficult to achieve cost competitiveness in its industry, then an outsourcing relationship may be the solution to drive lower costs. Even in a large company, this can be true at the business process level. For example, a company's data center(s) or call center(s) may be too small to gain the cost profile of a larger operation. An outsourcer generates a very large scale by managing multiple customer relationships on its infrastructure. This allows the outsourcing company to achieve lower costs compared to what their customers can achieve on their own. Particularly in areas where infrastructure must be spread over large volumes, or where large purchasing quantities are necessary to obtain good prices, most organizations will find it difficult to match the economies of scale offered by a large outsourcing vendor.

Scale also allows an outsourcing supplier to make the kind of investments needed to keep its capabilities current. A company lacking this scale will find it a daunting task to keep pace with a technology that changes (on average) every 18 months, let alone build the infrastructure necessary to support new capabilities. These characteristics serve as core competencies for outsourcing organizations.

An organization may find that it is too small to support the infrastructure necessary to achieve its business objectives. In order to implement a cost effective leading-edge technical solution, a U.S. city turned to an outsourcer to help manage the collection of parking violations. The outsourcer was able to deliver a technical solution at a lower cost than could be achieved by the city. The vendor used handheld computers that were networked to a central database and were able to print tickets on the spot. The vendor used its size and scale to obtain the hardware at a much lower price than the city could obtain on its own. The results from outsourcing its parking enforcement activities allowed the city to quadruple the percentage of paid parking tickets.

SKILLS

If a company lacks the human resources necessary to accomplish its business objectives, an outsourcing relationship can provide immediate access to world-class expertise, industry knowledge, and specifically targeted skills. A company may be having difficulty acquiring the right skills to rapidly implement change. Outsourcing vendors often are high-performance support organizations designed to keep pace with industry best practices. Sometimes when the technology in an industry is changing, existing employees are too focused on their existing jobs to be quickly trained in new areas. Outsourcers can provide a company access to a whole set of new skills without the time and cost of retooling their existing workforce.

The employees of an organization may be dissatisfied and unchallenged performing a support function. For example, people responsible for helping fix PC problems might feel that they are not really appreciated by the rest of the IT organization who are trained in the more complex technology platforms. Turnover may be high and it might be difficult to attract quality people to this function. An outsourcer who specializes in this area will have a workforce who knows that their work is mainstream to their employer. This improves motivation and quality of work and allows the outsourcer to attract people with leading skills and experience.

STRATEGY

Strategic considerations for outsourcing fall into two categories: (1) outsourcing nonstrategic functions, and (2) using outsourcing to deliver strategically differentiating capabilities that otherwise could not be done "in-house."

Outsourcing Nonstrategic Functions   Classically, business processes and technologies that do not provide strategic differentiation can always be considered prime candidates for outsourcing (**Q58, Q59**). Outsourcing of nonstrategic components allows the company to devote itself to growing the business and focusing on functions that make them more competitive. Depending on the industry, typical outsourcing arrangements are seen in the area of data center operations, network management, call centers, software development and maintenance, billing, etc. Recently, many companies are reevaluating what they consider "core." If their business processes are not differentiating them from their competitors or are necessary to drive strategic advantage, then they are outsourcing them. Thus there is a trend to outsourcing a large array of general business processes (**Q81**).

A further advantage is that the cost savings achieved by an outsourcing arrangement can be invested in new strategic business objectives and critical applications. To illustrate, the London Stock Exchange was interested in making its day-to-day operations more reliable and cost effective. It also wanted to have its resources focused on new applications and services that could offer greater value. It outsourced its trading operations and was able to reduce its service problems by more than 50 percent and its IT costs by 40 percent. Freeing up its own resources allowed the Exchange to focus on introducing new market capabilities and information services.[4]

Using Outsourcing to Deliver Strategically Differentiating Capabilities   Sometimes organizations may have only part of the capability to build a new business or product line or transform an internal operation. What is lacking can be obtained by partnering with an outsourcer. The combination enables the new organization to achieve re-

[4] "Case Study: London Stock Exchange," Client Case Study, *Accenture Web Site* n.d. 26 Sept. 2002 <http://www.accenture.com/xd/xd.asp?it=enWeb&xd=Industries\Financial\capital\case\cap_londonstockex.xml>.

sults that neither could achieve individually. For example, a major auto manufacturer established a new sales channel teaming with an outsourcer. The outsourcer employed innovative customer insight and analysis strategies and tools that the manufacturer was not able to use in its existing organizations. The outsourcer was empowered to set sales strategies and create and execute sales campaigns. The result was that the new channel had a tenfold improvement in sales versus the company's existing channels. These strategic outsourcing relationships may free the company from internal inertia and organizational constraints by offering new rewards, new processes, and new incentives for performance that cannot be used within the traditional company frameworks. These strategic arrangements are usually set up as collaborative or business transformational outsourcing relationships (**Q81**) depending on the magnitude and complexity of the company's business objectives.

Speed

An organization may find itself in a situation where it needs to move very quickly. Perhaps there are new competitive forces in the industry. Maybe there are business issues that are creating severe financial pressures. Perhaps a large critical project is faring very poorly. Or maybe some component of the business needs to expand very rapidly. The business knows that it must act and must act fast. But many organizations are not in a position to move quickly. There is often organizational inertia and even internal resistance to rapid change (**Q61**). In those situations, the only way to achieve quick results may be to outsource. When companies were scrambling to build e-business capabilities quickly, many of them chose to outsource the creation, maintenance, and operation of their Web sites, simply because they needed to move fast.

Conclusion

The bottom line is that outsourcing can provide significant business value to a company. When thinking about outsourcing, the critical factors are the four *s*'s: scale, skills, strategy, and speed. A company should consider outsourcing any part of its business where there is an outsourcing provider that is able to do those things better than the company can itself.

83. What are the considerations for outsourcing portions of your IT offshore?

CHAN POLLOCK

The IT industry has seen a significant rise in the existence and popularity of off-shore IT service providers. These providers offer a wide variety of IT capabilities from application maintenance to infrastructure services. For this discussion, *offshore* means outside of the United States. India is the most often used location for IT outsourcing services but the Philippines, Russia, and Ireland are recent entrants with other countries developing offerings too. Except for the language and cultural differences that exist between countries, the coordination of any offshore arrangement is largely the same no matter which country is providing the service.

Companies that utilize offshore services have often benefited from a highly educated labor force, an abundance of specialized technical talent, and high-quality work. They have also seen significant labor cost savings due to wage rates reflective of a much lower cost of living. Indian companies, for example, offer hourly rates that are typically one-third to one-sixth of the fully loaded United States rates for employees or contractors. Offshore outsourcing is, however, a complex process to manage and some companies have experienced difficulties with timeliness and quality. These difficulties can be mitigated with an appropriate understanding of how to appropriately manage the offshore process.

SERVICE AVAILABILITY, MATURITY, AND INHERENT RISK

A variety of offshore service offerings are available and it is important to understand the types of services available, the maturity of the offering, and the level of mainstream acceptance in the marketplace. According to Gartner research, offshore services can be classified into 10 generic service offerings and ranked according to their respective maturity levels (see Figure 83.1).[1]

Application maintenance, legacy development, and application migration have the highest degree of maturity. These offerings include ongoing maintenance, monitoring, support, and day-to-day enhancement of back-office applications. In practice, stable mainframe solutions typically provide back-office transaction functionality. Look for applications that rarely break and have a low or predictable rate of software change. Also in this category are projects that require a large amount of routine effort,

83 ▬

---

[1] Maturity level is a blend of service availability, provider capability, and onshore market acceptance. Frances Karamouzis, *Offshore Service Offerings Spectrum*, Gartner, Inc. Research Note M-15-0832, 16 Jan. 2002.

Figure *83.1* Offshore Service Offering Spectrum

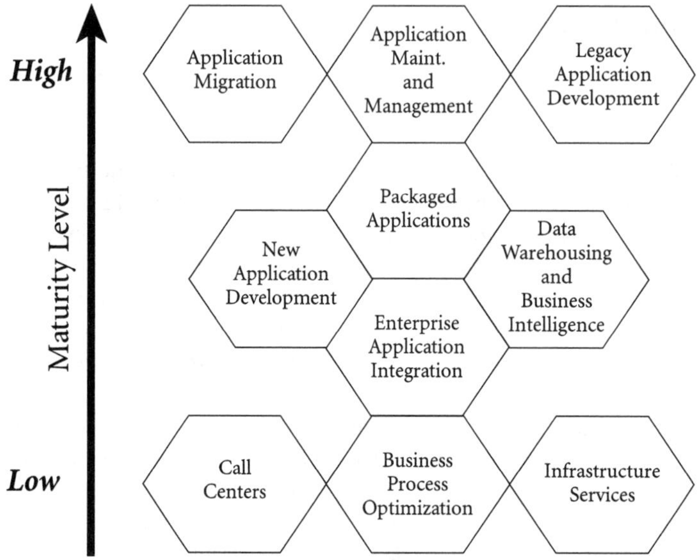

Source: Frances Karamouzis, *Offshore Service Offerings Spectrum*, Gartner, Inc. Research Note M-15-0832, 16 Jan. 2002. With permission of Gartner, Inc.

such as data conversion or the porting of an application from one platform to another. In these situations, there is rarely any contact between the outsourcer and the actual end user of these applications. The interfaces are typically handled by the IT department. For these types of situations, there are many available offshore service providers and a large pool of trained talent. For this category, you will routinely find in place long-term sourcing contracts, staff augmentation arrangements, and project-based contracts.

Call centers, business process outsourcing, and infrastructure services have the lowest levels of offshore maturity but are developing very rapidly. These services are generally long-term sourcing contracts with very strict service requirements. In general, the service provider assumes responsibility for the business process from end-to-end (for example, human resource management or support center problem assistance). The outsourcing of these processes carries high business risk, and cultural acceptance has been low, as companies are somewhat hesitant to outsource critical business processes offshore. Language issues become important since, in this situation, the outsourcer is directly in contact with customers and company employees. Some United States–based companies have built their own facilities or formed joint ventures in offshore locations, hired local workers, and trained them to their specifications to help mitigate this reluctance.

New application development, packaged application implementation, enterprise architecture integration, and data warehousing services fall in the middle of the maturity scale. Although there is a great deal of technical talent for these newer technologies available offshore, many IT organizations try to keep the new tools and technologies for themselves. Contributing factors for this include a higher degree of senior management visibility, providing new opportunities for internal staff, a higher level of end user interaction, and a rapid prototyping cycle requirement. Nonetheless, this market is evolving rapidly and organizations tend to source these services on a project-by-project basis.

Selection, Qualification, Monitoring, and Management

One can be easily motivated to look into offshore IT sourcing of services by cost savings alone. The inherent difficulties and risks, however, can easily outweigh the promised savings when appropriate controls aren't put into place. Because of language, cultural, and time zone differences, it is even more critical to pay attention to the basics when outsourcing to an offshore supplier.

So, how does one go about selecting, qualifying, contracting, and monitoring the service in order to capture the potential savings? During the selection and qualification phase, keep the following tips in mind:

- *Know what needs to be outsourced and why*—As with any outsourcing arrangement, it is very important to have a clear, detailed definition of services provided, roles and responsibilities of all parties, process boundaries and handoffs, etc. It may seem obvious, but many times it isn't until after a great deal of time has been spent on a selection process before someone questions the reasonability of having an external provider manage a core IT service. Do you really want to outsource a core competence (**Q82**)? Also, pay careful attention to the maturity level of the offshore service and align the inherent risk with the criticality to your business process.

- *Use your peer network to find a reputable supplier*—Simply ask others who have done this before for their opinion of suppliers they have used and how the experience has been. There is nothing better than a personal reference from a trusted and respected colleague.

- *Pilot a small low-risk project*—It's usually best to evaluate offshore sourcing with a contained, low-profile project. This helps test capability, quality, and cultural fit. It also helps develop an internal understanding of the types of services and service levels you can build into a longer term contract. You'll also discover that with some offshore cultures (especially India) you will get *exactly* what you ask for. Two-way communication regarding specifications becomes crucial.

- *When you're ready to pursue a large opportunity, get expert help*—A request for proposal (RFP) is usually the most effective way to specify—in detail—your service requirements, expectations, process boundaries, costs, and service rewards or penalties (**Q73**).

Numerous outside firms are available to help guide you through the outsourcing process. This is well worth the expenditure. A small investment up front can help avoid large and costly issues later.

Tips to remember regarding contracting for offshore services are:

- *Validate their capability*— Once you think you've found the right firm for your needs, follow-up on references and be sure to tour their facility in their home location.

- *Create an appropriate contract*—If you went to the trouble to create an RFP, be sure to include the service level expectations, workflow coordination requirements, costs and payment schedules, and consequences for missed service levels in the contract. Of course, you'll need legal assistance and advice. Be ready to deal with questions about what language (English?) will be used for the contract and which country's legal system will be the basis for the contract. Usually, the same external firm that helped with the RFP can easily provide professional negotiation and legal assistance.

- *Investigate visa and special security requirements*—Although most offshore firms take care of appropriate visa provisions for employee visits to the United States, you should check with your HR or legal department regarding special company policies or procedures. You might also have unusual security situations regarding the work that you do, especially if it's related to government activities. Be sure to do a thorough analysis and develop an appropriate plan.

Once the contract is in place:

- *Appoint a full-time "offshore manager"*—Ensuring a single point of contact with the external service provider is crucial for success. The individual should act as the funnel through which all requests and answers flow, and should be given the authority and responsibility to manage the relationship, hire and fire contract resources, and oversee service payments and credits.

- *Maintain an appropriate balance of onshore and offshore resources*—The offshore service provider will be more than willing to bring resources to your facility from their country to "learn your systems." They usually promise to do this for little to no cost (certainly for no more than the offshore rate). Often times, however, they become an onshore sales team and find plenty of other things to do for you. Then, of course, the rate goes up (generally 2.5 to 3× the offshore rate). If you're not careful, you could end up with an improper ratio of onshore to offshore resources. Generally, for every four or five offshore resources, you'll need one at your location.

- *Manage the offshore provider like any other external service provider*—Measure the service levels specified in the contract and hold the provider accountable to them. Service rewards and credits are especially useful for ensuring the highest quality of service.

- *Build "making it work" into the goals of the IT management team*—A good way to build a strong offshore external service and ongoing relationship is to include an offshore effectiveness goal in each affected manager's annual appraisal plan. This can help overcome the natural internal hesitancy and resistance to offshore outsourcing.

Finally:

- *Don't underestimate the significance of time*—Distance and speed play significant roles in offshore outsourcing. Depending on the country, using the time zone differential to your advantage can provide the potential for "around-the-clock" coverage of a business process. Business analysts, for example, can write specifications by day while coders in India program by night, often having results ready for the analysts when they return the next day. Be sure to monitor billable hours carefully. A task done at half the cost but twice the time gains nothing.

- *Develop a relationship with multiple offshore firms*—Once you have experience with one offshore firm, it's generally good to create a competitive atmosphere and introduce a second. The overhead increase necessary to do this is not very significant.

Offshore IT sourcing has great potential to help lower operational and software development costs while improving overall IT quality and throughput. It's nothing to be afraid of. With appropriate selection, management, and monitoring processes, it can be a very rewarding experience that helps your firm retain a competitive advantage.

---

84. When should an organization upgrade its software technologies?

DON WENNINGER

Every CIO (chief information officer) dreads receiving the infamous "we must upgrade our system to the latest version" call from someone in the business. The inevitable first question is "why"? There are many types of upgrades, from enterprise-wide back-office applications such as ERP (enterprise resource planning) or reservations and billing systems, to local desktop applications. Each has a different set of evaluation and management criteria.

84

Enterprise Back-Office Application Upgrades

Upgrading a major back-office system such as packaged ERP software to the most current version poses a major challenge, especially if the package has been significantly modified or customized. In that case, vendor upgrades could replace the customized portions of the software altogether, or cause it to stop working. Every prior change must be analyzed in light of the new vendor version. Many such changes will need to be rewritten or modified before reimplementing in the new version.

A further complication involves the impact of the upgrade on interfaces between the enterprise package and other applications (e.g., CRM or e-business systems) from different vendors. Full system retesting must be performed to ensure the vendor upgrade plus all custom changes and interfaces still work after the upgrade is installed. Furthermore, unless there is a compelling business reason to be the first to use the functionality from a new version, companies should not risk implementing vendor upgrades until the upgrades have been in the marketplace long enough to have stabilized.

Many enterprise application software packages cover nearly every back-office process across the enterprise and are highly integrated. Hence if one area of the business mandates installation of upgrades to obtain desirable new functionality, the entire package must often be upgraded. Numerous employees may be impacted, possibly requiring upgrades to training and other additional implementation costs. If the vendor upgrades are frequent, the lost time and resources can be very disruptive. Consequently, companies must seriously consider how critical the requested upgrades are, and delay such upgrades until the business benefits clearly outweigh the substantial costs and disruption to the business. The timing of such upgrades must also be carefully planned to avoid conflicts with other major business events or projects.

Some ERP vendors and hardware suppliers have initiated forced upgrade policies to minimize their own support costs.[1] These forced upgrades mean that the costs and disruptions come at the convenience of the vendor, rather than through the planning of the company.

Desktop Software Upgrades

Desktop software is another matter. Unfortunately, desktop operating system upgrades often require hardware upgrades to run the new more robust software. Maintaining stability in the enterprise is difficult because of the physical logistics of upgrading or replacing large numbers of desktops, especially when a high percentage of users are located in distributed locations across multiple states or countries. Unless there is a compelling business reason to make the upgrade immediately, businesses

---

[1] Forced upgrades occur when support is dropped for some older versions of software much sooner than others. If the user wants continued software support, an upgrade is necessary.

can sometimes save significant money by delaying such upgrades until absolutely necessary. One caution—by waiting to install new versions of desktop operating systems, an organization may limit its ability to deploy other desktop applications that only work on that new platform. Conversely, some existing desktop applications may not work on the new platforms, and, if those applications are critical, the company may have to wait until the vendors catch up.

Some highly computer-literate end users, especially in fast-paced, high-tech companies, are not sympathetic to these difficulties. They may actually acquire and implement vendor upgrades on their own outside the normal approved procurement process. In these cases, help desk personnel and PC technicians will not yet be trained on the new version and will not be able to easily solve desktop problems. Also, the company will not be able to take advantage of volume discounts on such upgrades. Some CIOs either forbid such maverick spending, or tell such users they will not receive support if they call the help desk. These sorts of logical business controls often brand the IT organization as "nonresponsive" in the eyes of their users. This leads to some of the organizational conflicts surrounding IT that are found in many businesses (**Q53**).

Sometimes, when one division of a company implements desktop upgrades while others do not, intracompany communications suffer because employees cannot easily share files (spreadsheets, documents, etc.). Similarly, this situation happens with business partners who have decided not to upgrade yet, especially when the files are not backwardly compatible with the older versions.

Balancing Need vs. Want

"I *want* this new feature" is sometimes the impetus behind requesting a new software or hardware upgrade. Yet, the business may not experience any practical value from the requested change. This is especially apparent in the cases of operating systems and high-end multimedia applications. The recent hype for online music, video, multimedia capability, and minor convenience interfaces must be balanced with real business needs. It is typical for users to use only 20–30 percent of the current capabilities of a piece of software and still desire the incremental new features. Assessing need is hard to balance against want—even in the most controlled environments.

True business needs fall into three categories:

1. *Compatibility with business-critical applications*—Enterprise software suppliers require certification of other vendor software packages, which work in conjunction with the primary application. Regardless of perceived needs, a company must make sure it doesn't upgrade one package causing it to no longer work with another.

2. *Increased productivity*—Will this upgrade truly increase productivity? Finding a tangible measurement of the benefits is paramount to the upgrade decision (**Q77**).

3. *Discontinued platform support*—Sometimes hardware or software vendors go out of business or inform customers they must migrate to a newer version or lose all vendor support by a specified date. In either case, the company must get off the current platform before the risks of failure become too great.

COSTS AND BENEFITS OF BEING ON THE CUTTING EDGE OF THE UPGRADE CURVE

The primary costs of being on the cutting edge in terms of implementing the latest vendor upgrades include *tangible* costs of implementation projects, reapplying customization changes (**Q69**), and reimplementing interfaces to other products (**Q13**). *Intangible* costs relate to risks that upgrades won't work right away or yield the desired results, or that upgrades will result in extreme disruption of business processes and productivity. Both types of costs can be very substantial.

Benefits may include strategic differentiators such as offering new capabilities to customers, enhancing employee productivity, or reducing operating costs. Incremental revenue is often suggested but rarely proven. Tangible benefits such as reduction in cycle time or transaction time, increased recovery of funds, incremental revenue, or reduction in workforce are valuable measurements and necessary to an effective return on investment (ROI) (**Q72**) calculation.

Since new operating systems often improve the platform's stability and the ability of other applications to work well with the platform, it is possible to estimate the value of reduced calls to the help desk or even the benefit of reduced downtime if the previous platform has had stability problems. Intangible benefits such as improved ease of use, additional functionality, and the ability to integrate are also assessments that carry great value, although they may not show up in the ROI calculation.

CONCLUSION

It would be easy to conclude from the above comments that a business should try to avoid upgrading their software and hardware. But it is a fact that upgrades are eventually necessary and businesses are implementing them every day. The key is that they should be treated like any other business decision—with an eye to the benefit vs. the cost as well as a complete understanding of the accompanying implementation and business risks.

SECTION 7 *IT and Implementation*

RINA DELMONICO

Technology implementation is a difficult art to master. Implementation failure rates are high for technology projects in terms of delivering promised functionality on time and on budget, and they have not changed much over the past thirty years. Failure rates are so high, in fact, that projects delivered on time and on budget with full functionality are akin to miracles. The point of the "IT and Implementation" section is that managers can make miracles a regular occurrence with a lot of forethought and a bit of luck.

The reason for high failure rates is simple—it is an art to combine complex technological systems with complex human systems. Combining complex systems is full of risks, which Questions 85 and 86 outline. Question 85 describes risks that are associated with a project's business model in terms of a project's strategic fit, its objectives, and an organization's capacity to use a new technology. Question 86 focuses on the inherent risks in a project—those related to a project's scale, complexity, and structure—and an organization's experience with a technology. Question 87 presents a case study of an ERP implementation gone wrong, while Question 88 analyzes and shows that the risks identified in Questions 85 and 86 were present and little had been done to control them. Murphy's infamous law—that "if anything can go wrong, it will"—was applied with a vengeance. Instead of a miracle, a disaster occurred.

The next several answers in this section focus on what managers can do to minimize the risks inherent in technology implementations and make miracles occur with regularity. The answer to Question 89 outlines the project management process and provides a concise summary of what a project manager needs to do to successfully manage an implementation. Question 90 examines the types of tools available for project managers for project planning, scheduling, monitoring, reporting, and communicating. Question 91 revisits Brooks's Law—that adding manpower to a late project makes it later—and discusses its implications for project staffing.

The next seven answers focus on the process of managing projects. Question 92 examines the role of measures of performance in making a project's objectives explicit. Question 93 focuses on project sponsorship, identifying multiple sponsorship roles that are often held by different individuals. The responsibilities of these roles are discussed as is the nature of the relationship between the individuals filling them. The answer to Question 94 presents a set of questions that sponsors can use with project managers to monitor progress and provide early warning of problems without micromanaging a project.

Question 95 looks at the role that a steering board can play in the implementation process, particularly with respect to building the support of important stakeholders. Two different steering committee models are discussed. Question 96 focuses on the authorities that a project manager needs to get the job done, including the ability to select and remove team members, assign tasks, and provide consequences for performance.

Question 97 addresses the issue of managing project teams when team members are drawn from different units within an organization and report to multiple managers. The answer identifies several techniques that can reduce the stresses and problems associated with multiple project reporting lines. The answer to Question 98 identifies the top ten things that project managers can do to increase the likelihood that their projects will be successful. Written from the perspective of a project manager, it offers sound advice on how a project manager can increase the chances for a miracle occurring.

The last two answers in this section address issues that arise when it doesn't look like a miracle is about to happen: Should you plan for failure, and when should you kill a project? Question 99 focuses on actions managers can take to protect against failure, including contingency and fallback plans, phasing a project implementation, tracking transactions during project cutover, and emergency communication and escalation systems. Question 100 identifies the conditions under which executives and steering boards need to consider terminating a project. While it can be politically difficult to kill a project, not doing so when necessary wastes time, resources, and opportunities. This answer presents a set guidelines or benchmarks that senior managers can use to determine whether a project is a candidate for termination.

The miracle of successful implementation *can* occur with regularity. What it takes is an understanding of the risks inherent in implementing technologies and close attention to the details of managing projects to minimize those risks. The answers in this section can help project managers and their executive sponsors accomplish that difficult task.

85. What are the risks associated with the business model of a project?

WILLIAM WHITE

A key question that needs to be asked at the beginning of any technology project is "what is the project's business model?" By project business model, we mean the "story" or underlying logic that describes a project's financial and nonfinancial (Q77) objectives and how these objectives are going to be achieved.[1] Three areas of risk that are common in technology project business models are examined. Analyzing these risks at the onset of a project helps identify blind spots—areas where underlying assumptions in a project's business model may be incorrect—and increases the chances for project success.

RISK 1: PROJECT/CORPORATE STRATEGY FIT

The first risk lies in the identification of the value that a project provides to the attainment of a firm's strategic objectives. It seems obvious that projects that don't make a clear contribution to corporate strategic objectives are not likely to be funded, or will be deemed failures if they are funded. However, identifying the fit between a technology project's business model and a corporation's strategy can be challenging because many firms do not have clear and concise strategic objectives. When strategic objectives are unclear, it is common for project teams to define a project business model in terms of existing processes and procedures facilitating locally defined goals and objectives, rather than in relation to the corporate strategic objectives. The risk

---

[1] Joan Magretta, "Why Business Models Matter," *Harvard Business Review* 80.5 (2002): 3–8.

here is that technology projects will be approved that do little to advance a firm toward its strategic objectives.[2]

The justification sections of IT project proposals typically describe how they support the buzzwords in a corporate strategy. Given the broad sweep of the terms embedded in corporate strategy statements, almost every IT project objective can be related to the corporate strategy in some form or another. Consider a firm with a strategic objective of improving profit margins through increased customer retention. The underlying strategic business model assumes that customer retention will improve by increasing customer satisfaction, which is driven by decreasing cycle times in the delivery of its goods and services. The justification section of a typical proposal to develop and install a new order entry system for a call center might state the project's intended outcome as: "*The new order entry project will leverage the technology advancements of the Web to integrate several older generation platforms into a faster, easier GUI interface for our call centers.*" Although this outcome is commendable, where is the linkage to the corporate strategy? In this example, the linkage between the project's business model and the firm's strategy would be improved by stating the project's objectives in terms of decreasing cycle times and increasing customer satisfaction.

The substance of how a project's business model fits with strategic objectives will most often be found in the "what is it" section of the IT project proposal where there is an articulation of the project deliverables. Unfortunately, these deliverables are often stated in technology-centric instead of business terms, such as "the project will be delivered in six months at cost of $1,000,000." These objectives, however, leave unanswered the question of what the project does specifically that will help achieve the firm's strategic objectives. If our hypothetical project team had paid attention to the fit between strategy and the project's business model, the outcome statement would be more like, "The new system will improve customer retention by decreasing order entry time 20 percent." This ties the project back to the higher level corporate objectives.

The risk of a poor fit between a project's business model and corporate strategy are significantly reduced when a firm has developed a business driven technology strategy (Q4). A business driven technology strategy should provide substantive guidance to project teams on how their project's business model is linked to the firm's strategic objectives.

RISK 2: PROJECT OUTCOMES

The second major area of risk in a project business model lies in the assumptions underlying a project's stated outcomes. Much of this risk is associated with one-sided

---

[2] It is important to note that this is as much a problem of poorly developed and unarticulated corporate strategies as it is of project business models. Ambiguous or vacuous corporate strategy

success criteria often found in project plans that don't consider their impact on the entire organization. Simply put, do all the relevant parties agree on the project's objectives? Too often, managers throughout an organization find out after the fact that they have different goals and objectives for a project, many of which are often incompatible (**Q92**). Project success is not just about project delivery, budget management, feature content, and so on, which is the standard content of IT project measurement systems. The risk to a project occurs when its business model lacks a holistic success measurement system. What can appear to be a significant improvement in one area can actually cause a corollary negative impact in others or an event not properly coordinated with the project can put the IT outcomes at risk.

For instance, the project team for our hypothetical order entry system estimated that the new Web interface would allow a 20 percent reduction in order entry time and a corresponding 20 percent reduction in staff. But, unknown to the project team, the company had just introduced a new product line that was more complex to explain and sell. In fact, it consumed all of the planned reductions, resulting in static order entry times and no reduction in staff. The project was then at risk to be deemed a failure because it didn't meet its objectives. The risk to the project's business model was created by the project team assuming: (1) that the current and future states of the business would be the same, and (2) that the objectives of the project were narrowly defined by all the parties involved. This risk can be reduced by asking a few questions:

- Do you know how the introduction of the new technology is going to impact other areas of the business (**Q49**)? Has a corollary impact analysis been performed?

- Have the measures of performance for the project been structured to minimize potential negative effects (**Q92**)?

The use of a project steering board (**Q95**) can minimize the risk of one-sided criteria by ensuring input into project plans by affected parties. It also can play an important role in managing expectations and building consensus around them.

A second area of risk related to project outcomes is that outcomes are time sensitive. Businesses usually need changes faster that IT can deliver results. The risk is that business managers will build business plans that assume delivery of the project faster than can actually occur. The primary cause of this problem is a lack of communication between the business and IT. Not only must the business and IT negotiate a delivery schedule reasonable for both sides, but the risks of trying to deliver even faster must also be understood. If IT agrees to a schedule that can't be met, and the business makes commitments based on that schedule, disappointment surely follows. This risk can be minimized by establishing clear lines of communication between a project's IT sponsor and executive sponsor (**Q93**).

85 ━━

---

statements do not provide much guidance for either a firm's overall technology strategy or for individual technology projects.

In this fast-paced business environment, there is also a companion time-sensitive risk. That is the risk that the strategic objectives supporting a project's strategic rationale may change, eliminating the need for it even if it is already under way. The best managers can do in this situation is to constantly monitor the alignment of each project with shifting strategic priorities and cancel a project when its rationale disappears. Canceling projects quickly as priorities change is an important discipline that comes from a strong focus on the business model (**Q100**).

Risk 3: Organizational Capacity

The third major area of risk in a project's business model lies in its assumptions about an organization's capacity to change in support of a technology project. Technology projects are usually undertaken to do things better, faster, or more efficiently. However, most such technology initiatives require corresponding organizational changes, such as:

- increasing cross-functional cooperation,

- the delegation of more authority to line employees,

- broader access to information,

- upgraded employee skills.

Depending on the organization, its culture (**Q48**), and its track record of success with past technology implementations (**Q60**), there may be significant organizational barriers to project success.[3] Technology projects parachuted into place without careful consideration of the organizational context often fail. If the project team does not understand the culture of the organization and the day-to-day life of the line workers, the risk of implementing changes that will not work or will not provide the improvements desired are greatly increased.

The amount of organizational change required will also have an impact on the timeliness with which results can be delivered. The greater the amount of organizational change needed, the longer it will take to get the expected level of results outlined in a project's business model, which is one of the reasons for the time-sensitive risk mentioned above. Just because the project team delivered the technology, does not mean that 100 percent of the results will happen right away. If significant organizational changes are required to implement a project, there is likely to be a lag time between the time the technology becomes available and the desired results are achieved. The risk for project managers comes when they underestimate the amount of change required on the part of the business to reap the proposed benefits. Has a

[3] T. L. Griffith, R. F. Zammuto, and L. Aiman-Smith, "Why New Technologies Fail: Overcoming the Invisibility of Implementation," *Industrial Management* 43.2 (1999): 29–34.

thorough analysis been done on all elements that need to change in order for successful implementation to occur (**Q60, Q61**)? This type of assessment should include process redefinition, restructuring, evaluation and reward systems, training, and measurement systems to reinforce the change.

SUMMARY

The risk of project failure increases when key assumptions concerning a project's fit with corporate strategy, its objectives, and the organization's capacity for change are not closely examined at the project's outset. On the surface, project failures are related to classic root causes such as schedule overruns, cost overruns, requirements deficiencies, and the like. But in reality, poor assumptions left unexamined by project managers often are the true culprit. Questioning these assumptions and addressing them properly is an important way to turn a pending project failure into a success.

---

86. What are the risks associated with the implementation of a project?

SHIRLEY KOMOTO AND TED SCHAEFER

Grouping risks into categories is one way to better understand project risks and allows for an equal comparison between different projects. Grouping risks also allows companies to identify the overall risk impact at an enterprise level.[1] This grouping approach categorizes risks into four levels (Figure 86.1):

- *Level 4 risks*—Enterprise-level events or initiatives that can impact a project's outcome, such as a merger or acquisition, changing corporate priorities, or changes in leadership.

- *Level 3 risks*—Project dependencies within an organization that can have an influence on the project, such as resources that are shared across various projects or conflicting cross-functional priorities.

[1] "Project Office Methodology, Chapter L-Risk Management," PricewaterhouseCoopers LLP, Internal Document, 2002.

Figure 86.1 Levels of Project Risk

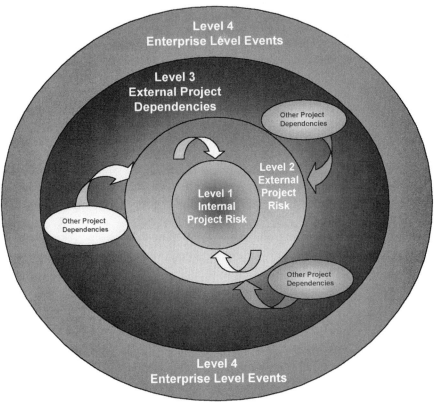

With permission of PricewaterhouseCoopers LLP.

- *Level 2 risks*—External risks affecting the project. An example would be equipment provided by a third-party supplier that must be available at a specific time because a project's success is dependent on the timely arrival and successful commissioning of that equipment.

- *Level 1 risk*—Inherent to a project, these risks are related to aspects of the project that cannot be changed without affecting its scope, such as the *scale* and *complexity* of the project, the team's *experience* with the technology, and the project's *structure*. Simply put, the greater the complexity, size, and uniqueness of the project and the more it relies on unproven technology, the greater its risk.[2] These risks are outlined in the sections that follow.

[2] "BPS Risk Check" PWC Internal Documentation, version 1.0. PricewaterhouseCoopers LLP, Global Risk Management Solutions, July 12, 1999.

PROJECT SCALE AND COMPLEXITY

If the scale of the project is significantly greater than past projects undertaken, project risk increases. Applegate, McFarlan, and McKenney define several attributes that help management assess the size-related risks of technology projects.[3] They include the:

- *Dollar size of the project*—Multimillion-dollar projects are more critical and obviously carry greater risk.

- *Duration*—Projects longer than a year carry more risk.

- *Project size relative to the organization's experience*—A million dollar project being implemented in a unit that routinely handles million dollar projects has less risk compared to a unit that is doing its first million dollar project.

- *Numbers and types of staff and skill sets required*—The more staff, consultants, and skill sets required, the greater a project's risk.

- *Number of departments and functional areas affected*—The more departments and functional areas impacted by a project, the greater its risk.

The risk of implementation failure also increases with the complexity of the technology being implemented. Complex technologies require more changes to an organization's hardware, software, and networks, which increase the risk of failure. The more mature a technology solution is, the fewer the problems during the implementation. This is because anticipated benefits and technical requirements are clearly defined and stable, and customizations and enhancements are more easily controlled.

The maturity of an organization's systems development process can reduce the extent to which these are significant risk factors. A mature development process (Q55) reduces implementation risks generally and enables an organization to take on more complex technology projects successfully. Mature systems development capabilities help a project avoid excessive change orders, costs, and schedule delays.[4]

---

[3] Lynda M. Applegate, F. Warren McFarlan, and James L. McKenney, *Corporate Information Systems Management: Text and Cases*, 5th ed. (Boston: Irwin/McGraw-Hill, 1999).

[4] Steve McConnell, *Software Project Survival Guide* (Redmond: Microsoft Press, 1998); Roger S. Pressman, *Software Engineering: A Practitioner's Approach*, 5th ed. (Boston: McGraw-Hill, 2001); Joc Sanders and Eugene Curran, *Software Quality: A Framework for Success in Software Development and Support* (New York: Addison-Wesley, 1994); Project Management Institute, *A Guide to the Project Management Body of Knowledge (PMBOK Guide)* (Newtown Square: Project Management Institute, 2000).

86 ■

Organizations and IT staff gain experience with technologies as they use them, making implementation of the same or similar technologies easier over time. When IT staff has had experience and training in the technologies and has had prior development and implementation experience, the risk is lower. When a new technology is adopted, the learning curve starts over. As a result, the more dissimilar a project's technology is from what is already in place, the higher the inherent risk.

Changes in a project's technology during the course of its implementation also increase risk. The less the technology solution is likely to change during the project, the lower the risk. Risks also can be reduced when anticipated benefits and technical requirements of a change are clearly defined and stable, customizations and enhancements are controlled (**Q69**), and change control procedures are in place (**Q56**).

Project Structure

A project's risk of failure is higher if:

- standard project management methodology is not used,

- if the project does not have effective executive sponsorship,

- if the project's costs and benefits are not understood or defined,

- if inadequate or inappropriate personnel are assigned to the project,

- if key stakeholders (especially end users) are not included in the team that defines the problem, and designs and implements the solution.

When evaluating a project's management and operations risks, consider the following:

- *Process and capability*—Are standard project management processes used (**Q89**)? Is there a formal process to define, prioritize, and fund projects (**Q76**)? Is there a central project management office overseeing the project, especially for large and complex projects? A central project office can be an important tool in the complicated process of delivering a project because it can detect cross-functional problems earlier, facilitate communication and knowledge transfer, and be an independent channel to elevate difficult problems or decisions for executive action (**Q77**).

- *Sponsorship*—Does the project have effective executive sponsorship? Effective executive sponsorship is critical to success of technology projects because executives set the standards for success and have the authority and influence to make the project happen (**Q93**). How do you get executives on board? To build executive support, the value of the project has to be expressed as a value to the business, from the perspective of the executive whose support is being sought (**Q4, Q72**).

• *Financial*—Are there formal guidelines for estimating projects and accounting for project costs? Have project financial feasibility and return been thoroughly evaluated and has the cost of money been considered (**Q75**)? Are there sufficient project financial controls in place as well as plans for contingencies (**Q99**)?

• *Resources*—Are there sufficient dedicated resources with the right experience to get the job done in the time allowed (**Q91**)? How are project turnover and resource conflicts addressed?

• *Project clients*—Is there involvement and commitment by management and the project's end users? Is there a communication process in place to inform, involve, and seek input and buy-in from project stakeholders (**Q94, Q95**)?

Reviewing the organizational environment in which the project will operate, the capabilities of the project team, management's commitment and support, the level of attention given to determining the project's feasibility and benefits, and the involvement of key stakeholders and end users will provide information about the risks ahead.

SUMMARY

Risks are fundamental to projects. Some risks can be prevented, others controlled. Each project will have its own set of risks, depending on the nature and complexity of the work. Good project management means that risks are identified at the start of a project, assessed for their potential impact and the likelihood of occurrence, and addressed. Defining, monitoring, and addressing the risks inherent in a project can provide early warning as to where problems may arise. Early warning provides room for action and can mean the difference between project success and failure.

---

87. What does technology implementation failure look like?

SHIRLEY KOMOTO

87

Remember the story of High Tech, Inc., a fictional organization that successfully implemented and used information technology to improve its competitive position

(**Q46**, **Q47**)? It became an agile, fleet-of-foot manufacturing firm, using information technology to streamline its operations and increase its ability to sense and rapidly respond to changing market conditions. High Tech, Inc., is fictional for good reason—it portrays a history of widespread, long-term, successful technology implementation. Few organizations can claim this type of implementation track record. As Gartner notes, "More than 80 percent of IS-related projects are late, over budget, lacking in functionality or never delivered." [1] It is not a pretty picture.

What does it look like in the 80 percent of the cases where technology implementations outright failed or did not deliver their promised results? The following example is a composite of several projects. All information, issues, etc., are actual examples of real-life situations. The names of hardware, platforms, and applications have been changed, however, to protect the guilty. [2]

XYZ's ERP Implementation Project

A $2 billion distribution company completed a multimillion dollar, 30 month implementation of an enterprise resource planning (ERP) system and a separate warehouse management system on a new computing platform. This was a completely redesigned version of a well-known ERP application. This was also the first time that this new ERP application had been implemented on this particular architecture. The project was much larger than previous projects undertaken by the company. The company did not have a standard project management approach.

The company has been going through major organizational changes. Seven out of ten of the top executives have been with the company for less than a year, including the project sponsor. Even though they were implementing two new applications (ERP and warehouse management system), end-to-end system testing and user acceptance testing were not performed because they ran out of time.

The implementation was originally scheduled to take 12 months, but slipped to 30 months. The cost of the implementation of the ERP system nearly doubled (and these costs excluded the warehouse system design and implementation). Three months after "Go Live," a consultant was retained to conduct an assessment of the project to determine the reliability and validity of financial information in preparation for year-end close. Parent company management (in Tokyo) requested this review, because of "rumors" of major systems instability, inability to take orders, ship goods, generate bills, or record receipts.

---

[1] Simon Mingay, *A Project Checklist*, Gartner, Inc., May 2000.

[2] Summarized with permission from PricewaterhouseCoopers, LLP, training case for Project Assurance programs, 2001.

THE POSTMORTEM

The CFO disclosed to the consultant in his kick off meeting that he didn't trust the information in the system and had been unable to manage working capital since the system went live, three months ago. The system crashed and could not be brought up for the first 8 days. The next 45 days were seriously unstable with daily crashes and many disconnects and lost orders.

RESULTS OF INTERVIEWS WITH KEY TEAM MEMBERS
AND STAKEHOLDERS

When the consultant met with key team members and stakeholders she found that:

- Instead of implementing best practices provided by the vendor, many customizations were made to accommodate existing practices. In many cases, these customizations degraded controls and performance.

- Data conversion was automated but data was not "cleansed" or deleted prior to conversion. Now inaccurate and obsolete data were complicating the postimplementation clean-up process.

- Marketing and customer service were strategic areas of focus for the ERP system design, but the new system did not meet key marketing and customer requirements (partial deliveries, single invoice with multiple drop ships, etc.). The new system was operating with manual work-around processes in sales order processing, fulfillment, and inventory.

- During the conversion, the system released payments from invoices in error. As a result, a year's worth of unapplied payments were floating around and customers were automatically sent overdue notices for payments already made. This error was discovered when customers called to complain. In addition, correctly applying current and historical payments to invoices would take months to research and apply correctly.

- Order fulfillment staff continued to operate during the crisis. Invoice and sales order data weren't matching and weren't always available, because the system was so erratic. Warehouse staff worked long hours to fulfill orders manually and used their best judgment in shipping orders. As a result, equipment was shipped with mismatched, incorrect, or completely missing invoices. In addition, records of what shipped, to whom, and for what price were not updated in the system, either because the system was not available or because there simply was not enough time to do it.

- Updating sales order and inventory records took more time than before conversion, so workers on the floor stopped doing it. The new warehouse system in Las Vegas

87

automatically reconciled the differences between the inventory in the ERP system and the warehouse system in a manner that left no trail of the differences or the changes made.

- Cost of goods sold was understated by an estimated $3 million during this period, because the system failed to capture direct labor, as it had in the old system.

- Where the old system allowed one invoice with multiple "ship to" locations, the new system did not, but this difference was not accounted for during the requirements, design, implementation, or testing.

- No one could accurately detail the entire process and there were no process flows in evidence. The systems' many manual processes, user decision points (e.g., lack of standard configurations in the sales order process) and many exceptions complicated the process of identifying issues, determining root causes, and devising solutions.

- There was no contingency or business continuity plan done prior to switching over.

- There was a detailed project definition document that described the original project charter, objectives, etc. This document was signed off by the original management team (30 months ago) and had not been updated since. The warehouse system requirements, design, and implementation plans were not documented.

- Minutes of meetings, action items, issues log, risk assessment and log and change control documents existed, but were not consistently updated. The last entry in any project controls documents was 4 months before "go live."

There were so many problems from hardware, applications, data conversion, and user/process errors that it was difficult for the project team to prioritize, research, isolate, and address the most serious causes. The team simply did not know where to start. Burned out from the long hours spent to "go live," they didn't have the physical reserves to move quickly and decisively. This was compounded by the lack of clear lines of authority and leadership, poor communication, and missing contingency plans. A 30-day postimplementation management review also found that the project had ignored a number of critical management and customer requirements. Retrofitting solutions to these requirements would take months and cost significant dollars.

CONCLUSION

This postmortem of implementation failure, while extreme, isn't unusual. It captures the essence of what happens much too often in technology implementations. The steps needed to minimize the risks of failure were ignored. The next answer (**Q88**) explains how XYZ's managers created a situation that was designed to fail by ignoring the risk factors identified in two previous answers (**Q85**, **Q86**).

88. Why do so many technology implementations fail?

SHIRLEY KOMOTO

As business increases its investment in technology, there is an increasing expectation that the business goals of these technology projects will be met. Yet, after over 40 years of IT projects, more projects still fail than succeed. And, of those projects that "succeed," most of them fail to deliver the anticipated business results (**Q87**). An analysis of XYZ Corporation's failed ERP and warehousing systems implementation, described in the previous answer, shows why organizations experience technology project failures if they do not manage the risks of implementation (**Q85, Q86**).

Unclear Objectives and Lack of Sponsorship

Executive sponsorship is essential to a technology project's success because the sponsor provides the resources and political support needed by the project manager. However, getting a sponsor on board depends, in part, on their belief that the project will have important business outcomes since they are putting their reputation (and sometimes career) on the line (**Q72**). If a project's objectives are not stated clearly in business terms to reflect important business outcomes, effective sponsorship is unlikely.

Going back to the example of the XYZ Corporation (**Q87**), the project failed, in part, because the business benefits of the project were not clearly defined and there was not a clear consensus on the objectives of the project (**Q92**). This situation was made worse by the fact that most of the senior executive team, including the project sponsor, had been hired after the implementation began. So there was not clear support for the project, goals were poorly defined, and there was no understanding of how the project would benefit the new managers. Lack of support and undefined goals meant that once the project began to fail, there was no clear direction for the needed corrective actions or anyone willing to accept responsibility for taking them.

Overwhelming Project Scale and Complexity

The greater the project size in terms of (1) dollars, (2) duration, (3) size relative to past projects, (4) numbers and types of staff/skills sets required, and (5) number of departments/functions affected, the greater the risk of implementation failure (**Q61, Q85, Q86**).[1]

88 ━━━━

[1] Lynda M. Applegate, F. Warren McFarland, and James L. McKenney, *Corporate Information Systems Management: Text and Cases*, 5th ed. (Boston: Irwin/McGraw-Hill, 1999).

The scale-related risks of the XYZ's project were significant, but there was little evidence of mitigating actions. Even a simple risk assessment up front would have identified these risk factors and alerted executives. A systematic risk management process (1) could have led the team to adopt technical or software development and project control measures to reduce the risks, and (2) could have provided executives with early warning when risks were not being addressed.

The complexity-related risks of XYZ's project also were immense and many elements of a mature systems development methodology were missing. The implementation was poorly planned and executed, and technical discipline and testing were inadequate. Moreover, extensive customization degraded performance and made the system unstable. As a result, when the new system went live, it immediately crashed; the company was without financial information for eight days; the project team was hard pressed to isolate the root causes; and there were no contingency plans (Q99). These problems could have been avoided if the following elements had been in place:

- a strong technical methodology

- well-researched and constructed technical and business requirements

- a solid testing program

- a cutover plan that involved user acceptance and approval

Inadequate Organizational Capacity for Change

The amount of transformation needed by an organization to implement a new technology is a major implementation risk factor (Q58, Q85). An organization's ability to embrace change depends on many elements (Q60, Q61). Some of these elements are (1) the organization's culture (Q48) and its past experience introducing and managing change, (2) the perceived need for change, and (3) the willingness and support of top management for the change. Simply put, the more organizational change needed, the riskier the project.

In XYZ's case, the amount of transformation needed to implement the technology was high. The new systems required major changes in policies and procedures, lines of authority, departmental structures, and workflows. However, the organization's ability to change was already taxed by other projects that were under way. The additional change requirements imposed by the new ERP and warehouse management systems were overwhelming. Once operational problems began to ripple through the organization, all attention was focused on simply surviving. While these operational problems created a crisis atmosphere, the absence of clear leadership and contingency plans allowed the crisis to grow. Corrective action would have mitigated these problems.

INADEQUATE PROJECT MANAGEMENT METHODOLOGY

The greater the project risk, the more important it is to use a formal project management process (**Q89**). XYZ's implementation effort was a classic case study of poor project management:

- The project definition document was not complete.

- Project objectives were not clear.

- Project requirements were not updated when the warehouse management system was added to the ERP project.

- The organization had little prior experience or knowledge of formal project management methods.

- A project methodology was adopted, but poorly introduced.

- Project staffs were not trained.

- Management did not assure compliance with project management standards.

- There was no control over changes and the changes made were not communicated.

- There was insufficient staff to oversee and control consultants.

- The project plan was inadequate for assessing progress and exerting control over changes.

- The steering committee did not function well.

- Quality controls were missing throughout the project.

The remaining answers in this section address the elements of project management that need to be in place to reduce the risk of implementation failure. Effective project management requires:

- a sound project management methodology (**Q89**),

- clear objectives (**Q92**),

- that the sponsorship roles and responsibilities are defined and executed (**Q93**),

- active oversight of the project by the sponsor and steering board (**Q94**, **Q95**),

- that the project manager has the authority needed to get cross-functional cooperation (**Q96**, **Q97**),

- that contingency plans are in place (**Q99**).

SUMMARY

Implementing technology projects is risky; more IT projects fail than succeed. Management teams can reduce the risks of implementation failure by asking five questions at the outset of a project:

1. Are the project's objectives clearly defined and is there significant executive support and sponsorship for the project?

2. Is the project's scale and complexity something the organization can handle?

3. Is an adequate systems development methodology in place?

4. Does the organization have the capacity for the changes required?

5. Does the organization have the necessary project management skills and clearly defined processes?

Although there are no sure-fire guarantees for project success, understanding the risk factors identified in two earlier questions (Q85, Q86) at the outset of a project and taking actions to minimize them can go a long way to reducing the likelihood of project failure.

89. What are the key components of project management?

RINA DELMONICO

A project is a "one-time, multitask job that has clearly defined starting and ending dates, a specific scope of work to be performed, a budget, and a specified level of performance to be achieved."[1] Project management is defined as the application of knowledge, skill, tools, and techniques to a broad range of activities in order to meet the requirements of a particular project.[2] The steps of the project management methodology can be applied to any project regardless of size, budget, or time lines (e.g., building a bridge, setting up a new e-commerce site, developing a new product, or sending a probe to Mars). Project management is the most important factor in successful delivery of a project.

[1] James P. Lewis, *The Project Managers Desk Reference: A Comprehensive Guide to Project Planning, Scheduling, Evaluation and Systems*, 2nd ed. (New York: McGraw-Hill, 2000) 4.

[2] *Project Management Institute Web Site* <www.pmi.org/projectmanagement/idea.htm> 1.

BASIC COMPONENTS OF PROJECT MANAGEMENT

There are six elements requisite to competent project management:

1. Project Scope (the outcome)

2. Project Sponsorship and Management (the people)

3. Project Management Methodology (the process)

4. Project Reporting (communications)

5. Project Control (the quality)

6. Project Value (business value and technology support)

PROJECT SCOPE (CLEARLY DEFINED
BUSINESS OBJECTIVES)

The first step in any project is defining its outcomes. Why is the project being undertaken? A project's business objectives must be identified in its business case and the expected benefits and results clearly defined. Expected benefits must be clearly specified and broken down into identifiable and measurable elements (Q92).[3] If objectives are not clearly defined, it is difficult to sort out competing priorities during the implementation process or to know whether the project will add value to the organization (Q77).

PROJECT SPONSORSHIP, STAKEHOLDERS,
AND PROJECT MANAGER

There are several roles in the project management process. The first role is that of the project sponsor. Project sponsorship is a critical success factor, especially to cross-functional projects. Much of the project management literature assumes that a project has one sponsor, but there are multiple sponsorship roles and they are often held by different individuals (Q93). Regardless of whether the sponsorship roles are held by one or more persons, it is the project sponsor who orders that a project be done and supports it throughout its life cycle. The project sponsor must be the "champion" of the project, must help in overcoming difficult obstacles, and also must have a vested interest in the outcome of the project.

Project stakeholders are individuals or parts of an organization who have a vested interest in a project because they are affected by its outcomes. It is not unusual for

89 ▬

[3] Richard Murch, *Project Management: Best Practices for IT Professionals* (Upper Saddle River: Prentice Hall, 2001) 10.

project stakeholders to have different and conflicting interests and expectations for a project's outcomes (**Q49**). One of the primary roles of the project sponsor is to ensure that a consensus is reached about project objectives and to work with the stakeholders to develop and maintain their support. One of the tools available to project sponsors and project managers for managing stakeholder expectations is the steering board (**Q95**).

The project manager is the individual responsible for ensuring that the project is completed on time, within budget, within scope, and at the desired performance level. The project manager's ability to demonstrate leadership, empathy, intuition, and vision are critical to project success. These are the qualities that enable project managers to correctly interpret and recognize how and when to apply the methodologies, activities, processes, procedures, and tools used to plan and manage a project. They are also the qualities that enable project managers to proactively identify and address activities and issues before they become risks and reasons for project failure (**Q85**, **Q86**). The project manager is accountable to the project sponsor, and one of the responsibilities of the sponsor is monitoring the activities of the project manager and project team (**Q94**).[4]

Project Management Methodology

Project management methodology refers to the processes, procedures, tools, and techniques required to maintain project control and achieve project success. It effectively outlines the responsibilities of the project manager such as:

- Business benefits and budgets are clearly defined and managed.

- Project scope, changes, and impacts are clearly defined and managed.

- Roles, responsibilities, accountability hierarchies, and escalation processes are defined, providing ownership, authority, and accountability. Successful project teams with the appropriate skills and dynamics are assembled.

- Project planning, time lines, and deliverables are necessary to identify activities and reduce the risk of deliverables being overlooked. Deliverables and activities are reviewed and approved. This includes all phases, milestones, duration, dates, and dependencies between deliverables. Project planning, tracking, status, and plan adjustments are provided.

- Appropriate processes, technologies, and tools (**Q90**) are defined, utilized, streamlined, and shared for repeatability.

- Project documentation and control is provided.

- Risks and issues are identified, escalated, mitigated, and resolved.

[4] Lewis 6–7.

- Workloads and the use of appropriate resources are optimized.

- Subcontractor (vendor) coordination and management is provided.

- Communication between all involved and affected parties is achieved.

- Transition from development to production (support) are defined and managed, including training.

- Appropriate project documentation, wrap-up, closure, and postimplementation activities are clearly defined and completed.

- Lessons learned are captured, shared, and utilized to share knowledge and provide continuous improvement.

PROJECT REPORTING, PROGRESS REPORTING, AND MONITORING

Consistent and accurate reports on a project's progress should be communicated and available to all interested parties on a regular basis. Depending on the project status, reports might be made monthly, weekly, or even daily. Factors to consider when determining the number of meetings and status reports include:

- the current phase of the project and time frame for implementation

- the criticality of the project to the business

- the size of the project and the number of people and sites involved

- the newness of the technology to the organization

- whether the project is running on schedule

For example, if a project is a long-term, lower priority effort, monthly status reports and meetings would be appropriate. If a project is critical, behind schedule, and experiencing significant problems during testing, daily meetings and status reports would be required. These progress reports must provide management and the steering board (**Q95**) with a working understanding of the overall project plan and the progress made against it.[5]

PROJECT CONTROL (QUALITY ASSURANCE)

Effective *quality management, change management,* and *risk management* practices play a key role in ensuring the success of a project. Quality management is the process of ensuring that a project's deliverables are produced:

89 ━━━

[5] www.oit.nsw.gov.au /pages /4.3.21—Project Management pages 2 and 10.

- according to specification and standards

- according to users needs and expectations

- on time

- within budget

- in a manner that is perceived by the business as successful

To achieve these results, the project manager must define and enforce a quality plan, framework, quality measurements, and corrective actions.[6]

Project Value (Benefits Realization)

Identifying and realizing a project's value is too often an overlooked but absolutely vital element of project management. Provision for a structured approach to benefits realization—where objectives are identified, measured, and tracked over the life of a project—is essential to effective project management (Q77). If a project's objectives are not measured and tracked, it is impossible to know when success has been achieved or when failure is imminent. The inability to distinguish between success and failure makes it more likely that projects will fail, resources will be wasted, and unsuccessful projects will be continued because there are no criteria in place to kill them (Q100).

Summary

Although each project has its idiosyncrasies, the overall steps and guidelines for completing projects remain remarkably consistent. While project management tools continue to evolve, project management's key components remain constant. It is about people, processes, and technology working together in a powerful union to do things better, faster, and more efficiently.

[6] www.oit.nsw.gov.au /pages /4.3.21—Project Management page 2.

90. What are the key tools for managing a project?

SUSAN HEINZEROTH

The primary purpose for using project management tools is to support the project management process (**Q89**). Project management tools help managers plan, execute, and control all aspects of a project—resources, tasks, milestones, budgets, etc.—that, in turn, impact its outcome. Project management tools serve many purposes, including:

- ensuring "on-time and on-budget" results,
- facilitating team collaboration,
- enhancing resource efficiency,
- ensuring project scope and delivery,
- monitoring project cost,
- streamlining project communications,
- eliminating duplicate efforts.

Historically, project management tools focused on aiding the managers of individual projects. Today, the focus has expanded to enterprise-wide or portfolio project management. In order to meet corporate objectives, understanding the interrelationships between projects and their prioritization is imperative. This complexity and the need for both micro and macro project information now drive the use of project management tools in most organizations. As executives seek information from both the individual project and the enterprise-wide efforts, project managers turn to project management tools to support many critical aspects of project management including:

- estimating, planning, and tracking,
- assigning and scheduling resources,
- identifying and managing contingencies, interdependencies, and risks,
- reporting and communicating,
- analyzing and organizing.

Table 90.1 lists examples for each function of a project management tool.

Several project management programs are available for IT-centered projects, each having specific strengths. Potential users should appraise these programs by:

90 ▬

Table **90.1** *Project Management Functions and Associated Tools*

PM Function	Example PM Tool Output
Estimating, planning, and tracking	• Project workplan • Task assignments • Project budget • Estimated durations • Gantt charts—Project[1] • % complete reports
Assigning and scheduling resources	• Resources inventory • Resource time & expense reporting • Gantt charts—Personal
Identifying and managing contingencies	• Pert chart[2] • Critical path chart • Project interdependencies chart
Reporting and communicating	• Status reports • Web-based collaboration • Project repository
Analyzing and organizing	• Administrative module • Task calendars • Work breakdown structure • Deadline date reports • Materials reports

[1] *For a definition, see: "Gantt Chart,"* searchSystemsManagment.com *21 Sept. 2002, 8 Oct. 2002 <http:// searchsystemsmanagement.techtarget.com/sDefinition/0,,sid20_gci331397,00.html>.*

[2] *For a definition, see: "PERT Chart,"* searchSystemsManagment.com *6 Sept. 2000, 8 Oct. 2002 <http:// searchsystemsmanagement.techtarget.com/sDefinition/0,,sid20_gci331391,00.html>.*

1. carefully evaluating the products and matching their functions to project requirements,

2. developing an awareness of the software vendor's financial and technical viability along with the vendor's vision for enterprise-wide deployment (**Q79**),

3. selecting the program that suits their needs and goals.

The Standish Group International, an organization focused on primary research for the IT field, identified 10 fundamental features that determine the compatibility of project management tools with an organization's needs.[1] The features are shown in Table 90.2.

[1] "CHAOS: A Recipe for Success," Paper, *Standish Group International Inc. Web Site* 1999, 8 Oct. 2002 <http://www.standishgroup.com/sample_research/chaos1998.pdf>.

Table **90.2** Project Management Tool Features

Feature	Description
Ease of use	Has a quick learning curve, easy implementation, availability in the market, and good product support and documentation.
Adaptability	Is flexible and customizable so as to accommodate "nested" projects and projects with unique plan attributes.
Scalability	Can support small departmental projects, and enterprise-wide, multi-site, multiproject distributed environment initiatives.
Affordability	In the context of project size, tools must be affordable to warrant the initial expenditure.
Interoperability	Project management tools must interface and integrate with other tools used in the organization.
Security	Features such as version control, access management, password protection and field level control; project data is often mission-critical; as such, it should be secure.
Portability	The tool can run independently of the environment, allowing the project manager and team members to work "off-site".
Distribution of data	Distribution of data features include reporting facilities, Web access, online queries, e-mail updates, etc.
Integrity	Features including assurance that the tool will maintain the data as developed and recorded by the project manager and project team.
Rapid response time	The project management tool must rapidly update so that project management, team members, and executives are working with accurate, up-to-the-minute information.

High-end project management tools, for IT-centered projects, include packages such as:

- Artemis Views
- Portfolio Manager
- PlanView
- TeamPlay
- Milestones Professional 2002
- Open Plan

90

Midrange project management tools include products such as:

- Microsoft Project 2002

- Project Office

- RealTime

- Business Engine Network

Niche project management tools include products such as:

- Rational Software

- QSM Inc.

- Software Productivity Research

The functionality of the project management software varies among these options—emphasizing the need to clearly understand the organization's goals and requirements and then compare these requirements with the functionality of each program.

CONCLUSION

It is important to remember that project management tools are valuable for *supporting* implementation efforts. Project management tools are only as effective as the people using them.

---

91. What are the implications of Brooks's Law for staffing a technology project?

BARBARA T. BAUER

Brooks's Law states, "Adding manpower to a late software project makes it later." This quote is from Frederick P. Brooks Jr.'s book, *The Mythical Man-Month*.[1] Written in 1975, the book is considered a classic in the field of software engineering. Since

[1] Frederick P. Brooks Jr. *The Mythical Man-Month: Essays on Software Engineering* (Reading: Addison-Wesley, 1995) 15.

the software industry, and its professional practitioners', boasts that software technology changes so fast it is impossible to keep up, can a book this old still matter? The advances of the last twenty years are indeed impressive: PCs with the capacity of mainframes, Web sites and services galore, Internet access in the most remote reaches of the planet, and technology savvy users of all ages and professions. Can a "law" coined almost thirty years ago, in the dark ages of the software industry, be relevant today?

WHO IS FREDERICK BROOKS?

Frederick P. Brooks Jr. was the "father of the IBM System/360" and is the Kenan Professor of Computer Science at the University of North Carolina. Of all the essays and books published in those early days of massive project delays, system failures, and software quality problems, *The Mythical Man-Month* explained the problems best and created the memorable taglines still popular today in the industry: "conceptual integrity," the "mythical man-month," the "second system effect," and the frequently heard "no silver bullet." Brooks's writing was lucid, humorous, and very well informed. His insight has been part of the wisdom and folklore of software engineering ever since.

Nonetheless, there are many parts of the information technology industry which have dramatically improved since 1975: hardware capacity, speed and costs, architecture, and project management and software development tools. However, thirty years after Brooks's original book, software development and scheduling problems are still not under control. Every year project overruns and cancellations cost companies millions. Even with more sophisticated estimating, better project management techniques, and vastly improved development tools, many software projects still finish late, over budget, and with less functionality than originally planned. This is exactly the "tar-pit" which Brooks described in the introductory chapter of his book.[2]

His assertion then, and now, thirty years later, is that scheduling and estimating are still the root issues; and the most instinctive response when trouble develops is to increase manpower.[3] Brooks identifies two deeply rooted causes of software schedule problems: (1) the assumption that "all will go well,"[4] and (2) the use of the "man-month" unit to estimate and schedule.[5] The "all will go well" assumption is frequently the result of the natural optimism of the individual programmer-developer. While a single talented developer might estimate and schedule correctly, a project team of almost any size has a small probability of experiencing "all will go well." Convincing data that all does *not* go well is provided in recent articles on government software projects, ". . . about $9 billion per year in cost growth associated with estimating and

---

[2] Brooks 4.
[3] Brooks uses "manpower" in the gender generic sense to mean total human resources.
[4] Brooks 15.
[5] Brooks 17–25.

engineering problems, many of which are likely software related."[6] The need to predict that "all will not go well" is discussed elsewhere in this book (Q85, Q86).

Although the "all will go well" issue is insidious and hard to eradicate in large projects, it does not have the devastating consequences of Brooks's Law: "Adding manpower to a late software project makes it later." Anyone who has experienced the gut-wrenching trauma of a major project in schedule trouble will recall the compelling and seductive temptation to add people in hopes of getting back on track. Late at night over drinks at technical forums or project reviews, every experienced development executive will admit to falling for this fallacy and shifting resources around from project to project to shore-up a troubled area.

Brooks gives a clear, readable explanation of the fallacy of using "man-month" as a unit to schedule in the first place, and the ultimate foolishness of trying to resolve a slip in schedule by doubling (or more) the human resources applied to the project. The logic underlying his law is straightforward. When personnel are added to a project, there is not an immediate upsurge in productivity because the new people need to be trained and brought up to speed. In fact, productivity will go down in the short run because current project personnel have to take the time to bring the new people up to speed. His final paragraph says it best:

> the number of months of a project depends upon its sequential constraints. The maximum number of men depends upon the number of independent subtasks. From these two quantities one can derive schedules using fewer men and more months. . . . One cannot, however, get workable schedules using more men and fewer months. More software projects have gone awry for lack of calendar time than for all other causes combined.[7]

How True Is Brooks's Law Today?

A 20th anniversary edition of Brooks's book was published in 1995. In an added chapter, Brooks references some recent studies and includes other helpful strategies including practical advice on training, tools, project communications, and other refinements. Brooks concludes, and experienced developers would agree, that his law in all its bold simplicity is a powerful statement, still true, and ignored at your own risk.

What Are Its Implications for Staffing a Technology Project Today?

The entire book, not just his famous law, should be reread before every major project commits to a schedule. Perhaps the most important insight about staffing a

---

[6] Lloyd K. Mosemann II, "Did We Lose Our Religion?" Paper, Software Technology Conference 2002, Salt Lake City, May 2002.
[7] Brooks 25–26.

project today is the opportunity to reduce cost and risk associated with in-house software development by integrating commercial products (**Q69, Q78**). However, in either "buy" or "build," the basics still apply:

1. Spend the time up front to plan.

2. Always plan and schedule the critical "human" path.

3. Don't succumb to temptation when schedule problems surface.

4. Always revise a schedule when adding staff; put in the real times for training and additional communication.[8]

5. Train quickly and well; avoid the drag of the uninformed project member.

6. Remember the cost of "integrating" independent projects into a system, the cost of integrating systems into a product, and the cost of complexity and maintenance that starts with the first line of code.

7. Plan and schedule the administration and management of the project.

8. Design the project into small chunks of work that can be partitioned as necessary to create flexibility to shift workloads to match resources.[9]

Certainly, the central concerns of software engineering stated in Brooks's original chapter 1 are precisely the central concerns today.[10] Each chapter still offers clear insights about all the necessary aspects of development management: team organization, architecture and implementation distinctions, prototyping, communication and change management, and other topics. So in the dawning of a new century of software sophistication, keep *either* the old or new version of Brooks handy and stay the course.

[8] "Two Little-Known 'Laws' of IT Staffing," *HR Magazine* June 1998: 133.
[9] Don Reinertsen, "Is It Always a Bad Idea to Add Resources to a Late Project?" *Electronic Design* 30 Oct. 2000: 70.
[10] Brooks 288.

92. Why is it important to explicitly state the intended business result of an IT project? How should this be done?

WILLIAM W. CASEY

THE CUSTOMER SERVICE REPRESENTATIVE IMPROVEMENT PROJECT

In the massive IT shop of a Fortune 50 company, five million dollars had been set aside for the customer service representative improvement project. Dozens of cubicle-ensconced developers had labored to help automate the work of hundreds of telephone answerers. After months of muddled effort, the budget was exhausted and there was little to show for the effort. The three client-side vice presidents met to sort out the mess and decide exactly how the IT department should be punished for the failure. However, as they talked, the three executives learned that each had been paying for (and orchestrating) a different version of "automation and improvement." For one, the point had been to reduce headcount. For another, the goal had been to reduce training time for new employees. The third had been hoping to increase sales. It turned out that their mushy business goal, "automate and improve," had led them in circles, and myriad functional and technical requirements had done nothing to resolve and communicate the point of the project. The project was, thus, pointless. On all projects, there is a moment of truth, a time to discuss the project's intended purpose or result. The question is, will it come before or after the dollars are spent?

WHY WE DO IT PROJECTS

IT projects are not conducted because of their functional or technical requirements. They are not conducted because of their scopes. Nor are they conducted because of their budgets or schedules. The point of any IT project is the *result* that it will produce for the enterprise. One way to express this result is the measure of performance (MOP), borrowed from "systems thinking" gurus.[1]

A project's MOP expresses the measurable *result* of the project. The MOP brings clarity to project definition and helps focus a team and stakeholders. MOPs become a basis for declining the countless ad hoc pork-barrel requests to which large budgets are usually subject.

[1] For a typical discussion of the characteristics of a system see: Jeffrey A. Hoffer, Joey F. George, and Joseph S. Valacich, *Modern Systems Analysis and Design*, 3rd ed. (Upper Saddle River: Prentice Hall, 2002) 41. Two of those characteristics are employed in the measure of performance definition offered here.

ANATOMY OF AN MOP

MOPs consist of two parts. The first part is the intended result or *goal*. Some examples of goals are:

• Reduce time to access database to two seconds or less.

• Increase market share to 12% or more.

• Reduce abandoned calls rate to 8% or less. (Abandoned calls are times when telephone callers hang up rather than stay on hold.)

For anyone who has written goals before, none of these examples will seem remarkable. However, a couple of features are noteworthy. First, each example is about the *result* of an effort and does not describe the effort itself. For example, it is not stated whether the project manager will reduce abandoned call rate by adding more phones, adding more employees, installing better equipment, implementing voice menus, or by getting rid of customers. There is not a word about *how*. Second, each goal states a *measurable result*. Using the same example, the goal did not state "improve the customer experience," or "deliver world-class customer service," or any other inspiring statements of general direction. Goals are boringly objective.

Parameters (also called restrictions or constraints) are the second element of MOPs. In contrast to the goal, which states the result to be produced, parameters state the results *not* to be produced. Stating parameters helps prevent unintended consequences and other results of tunnel vision or local optimization.

A properly written MOP essentially takes this form: "Please deliver this result, but don't do these unpleasant things while you're at it." or, "Do this: [goal], subject to these [parameters]." Drawing from earlier examples, here are two complete MOPs (goal + parameter(s)):

Goal:	Reduce time to access database to two seconds or less.
Parameters:	No decrease in the amount of data available.
	No decrease in number of work stations running at one time.

Goal:	Reduce abandoned calls rate to 8% or less.
Parameters:	No increase in number of customers calling back because they have been cut off or because their problem was not satisfactorily resolved.

GOOD MOPS ENABLE STRATEGIC TRADE-OFFS

No doubt, the omission of *schedule* and *budget* from these examples will discomfit some readers. However, the omission of these two critical parameters from MOPs is quite deliberate. Here is why: executives must continually make trade-offs between the project's result (MOP), its schedule, and its budget. (That is to say that they must

92 ▬

*Figure **92.1** Good MOPs Enable Strategic Trade-Offs*

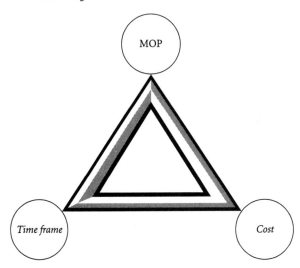

continually decide between good, fast, and cheap!) Consequently, it's unwise to insert budget or schedule *into* the MOP, as it is difficult to balance a thing against itself. It is better to keep each of these three factors separate. In every project environment, one of these factors will tend to trump the other two. However, all three must be clear for the trade-offs to be clear (Figure 92.1).

Of course, executives are not the only ones making trade-offs. At a less strategic level, everyone on a project makes trade-offs throughout the course of the project. MOPs provide the context in which to make those decisions. Even software developers contributing relatively small portions of a project have reported that MOPs help immensely, providing a perspective that scope statements and litanies of requirements do not.

Technology MOPs Are Necessary but Not Sufficient

The MOP of a major program is usually built on the MOPs of subordinate projects; MOPs are hierarchical. Frequently, for example, the MOP of an internal client's program will be fed by an IT project MOP—but it will also be fed by MOPs from other disciplines such as training and process design. For example, the IT department of a bank may install a customer information system to give tellers the information they need to suggest appropriate products to individual customers. However, the intent of the system cannot be achieved without tellers learning how to sell and how to use the system. The tellers' compensation system also may need tweaking and staffing levels may need to be adjusted as tellers spend more time per customer.

When clients understand that the achievement of their MOP is based on the achievement of *several* MOPs, not just the most expensive and obvious one (IT's), their own success is likelier and scapegoating IT is less likely.

MOPs Aren't Always Easy or Popular

For all the benefits of MOPs, there is inevitable resistance to their creation—they are difficult to write. Like a Japanese haiku, which packs volumes into seventeen syllables on three lines, the MOP must do heavy lifting in a few words. One must *really* understand the point of an endeavor to do that successfully.

A paragon of clear thinking and wit, Robert F. Mager has helped many managers weed out what he calls the "fuzzies." Although not aimed specifically at project executives, his book, *Goal Analysis: How to Clarify Your Goals So You Can Actually Achieve Them,* teaches how to write exact and articulate goals. No project management book does as well. Mager does not discuss the "parameters" portion of MOPs, however the precision he applies to goals can just as easily be applied to parameters.[2]

Further, MOPs surface differences of opinion. MOPs force answers to questions such as: what problem are we actually trying to solve, how good is good enough, and what boundaries must we not cross in the process? Such precision provokes arguments and is not for the fainthearted.

For better or worse, MOPs derail "free rides." One IT project manager who had received her MOP midway into her project discovered that better than three-quarters of the project's alleged requirements were obviated by understanding the point of the project. That did not please all the employees who had been attaching requirements to her project.

Summary

Any IT project is conducted in the service of producing a result. The more clearly executives understand and communicate the project's intended purpose the more likely they are to succeed. Although precision at the detailed level of scope and requirements is common, precision at the strategic level of purpose is not. One way to achieve that is through measures of performance, which specify the result the project is intended to produce and the results it is proscribed from producing along the way.

---

[2] Robert F. Mager, *Goal Analysis: How to Clarify Your Goals So You Can Actually Achieve Them,* 3rd ed. (Atlanta: The Center for Effective Performance, June 1997).

93. *What role does a project's sponsor need to play in the technology implementation process?*

WILLIAM W. CASEY

There is no term more confusing than "project sponsor." At times it is used interchangeably with "project owner," "project executive," "senior user," and "primary stakeholder." The accountabilities attributed to this role are often contradictory, such as "holding the purse strings," "appointing the project manager," and "securing resources."[1] These accountabilities are usually held by different individuals. For example, it would be hard to imagine a VP of marketing who is purchasing a CRM implementation also to be the person appointing the IT project team; that role lies outside his or her realm of expertise and authority.

There are two key, sponsorlike roles, each of which is important enough to deserve its own name. First, the *executive client* is the executive on the business side who is trying to achieve a business solution through a project. This role is even more complex when multiple business units are involved (Q95). Second, the *executive provider* is the client's IT counterpart accountable for ensuring that the IT portion of the project is delivered as agreed. Unless the IT department is building something for itself, the provider and the client are not the same person. These people are generally peers in the organizational hierarchy.

A third role—the person who funds the project—may belong to the client, the provider, or a third person, depending on the organization's project funding model. The third role will not be considered here.

The Point of Each Role

The point of the client's role is to achieve a business benefit, not a technological one. So, for example, the VP of marketing isn't attempting to "install a new billing platform." She is trying to increase the speed and flexibility with which new products and pricing plans can be adopted.

The point of the provider's role is delivering the agreed upon system capability, on time and on budget.

Who Is Accountable to Whom?

The relationship between the client and the provider is one of customer and supplier, not boss and subordinate. While neither executive is accountable to the other,

---

[1] John G. Freeland, "The Evolution of CRM: Revitalizing Sales, Service and Marketing," *Defying the Limits Volume 2* (San Francisco: Montgomery Research, 2001).

each executive *is* accountable to his own manager for the quality of the customer-supplier relationship and the fruits of it.

The distinction between an accountability relationship and one of customer-supplier is an important one. If the provider were accountable to the client, then the client could dictate technological solutions that might well solve the immediate problem, but would suboptimize the entire organization's information system. For example, the client might demand equipment or a data structure that is incompatible with the rest of the company. As a supplier rather than a subordinate to the client, the provider must instead work within the constraints laid out by senior management to optimize technological solutions for the entire company, not just for a specific business unit.

The provider will assign an IT project manager to the project. That project manager will be accountable to the provider, either directly or through middle management. (On larger endeavors, the provider may assign a program manager, to whom several IT project managers will be accountable for components of the program.)

The client will (or should) appoint her own project or program manager in a relationship that will parallel the one in IT. Lower down the ladder, the IT project manager will act as supplier or vendor to that client project manager, paralleling the one between the provider and the client.

What Are Their Accountabilities?

Because each executive's success is linked to project success, each of them will naturally work to remove roadblocks and ensure that their respective project managers and project teams do their jobs. In some cases, the work performed in these two roles is similar. In other cases it is strikingly dissimilar.

Setting Context and Ground Rules   There are actually two projects to launch, the total business project, and the IT project, which is a portion of the business project. The executives set context and ground rules for their respective projects during the launch of the project and then throughout the project.

The communication vehicle for the project's context and ground rules is the project kickoff meeting. There are other vehicles, such as video conferencing, Web conferencing, e-mail, or a plain old conference call, but none are as effective as a face-to-face meeting. Each executive's message to the project team and the community of stakeholders needs to include:

- *The importance of the project*—Employees on projects, like employees everywhere, need to know how their effort will contribute to something important. This is especially true on project work. The project's kickoff meeting is the perfect place for each executive to display this essential skill of leadership. It is also something each executive must do throughout each project. In the provider's launch meeting, he will explain the importance of the business project, and will emphasize the importance of IT's contribution to success.

- *The project's measure of performance* (MOP) (**Q92**)—In the client's kickoff meeting, the client will explain the project's MOP. In the provider's kickoff meeting, the provider will explain the MOP for the business project, and the MOP for the IT portion.

- *The project's accountability structure*—A frequent cause of project difficulties is that the players do not know who is accountable to whom for what. The kickoff meeting and a subsequent memo should completely prevent this confusion. Clarity is essential. This is no time to say that "Larry will be working with Mary," when what is meant is that Larry will be working *for* Mary. Such gentle obfuscation will ultimately cause far more pain than it prevents.

- *The project manager's authority*—Again, this is no time for fuzzy talk. It's important to spell out precisely who has what authorities (**Q96**). This announcement must come from the executive. Unskilled executives have been observed telling project managers to announce their own authorities, which is a sure way to turn the usual headaches of project management into real migraines.

Client's Job: Project Implementation   The provider's job is "delivery" (i.e., providing the promised functionality within schedule and budget constraints), but the client's job is to implement what the provider has delivered. Because IT's portion of the expense is so large, clients can sometimes minimize the importance of their own role in the implementation of what IT provides. However, savvy clients will ensure that each of these implementation chores is done, and done well:

- Design new business processes required by the project.

- Participate in requirements sessions with knowledgeable staff.

- Provide timely training on the new system.

- Schedule conversion to the new system.

- Ensure participation in system testing.

- Manage the human side of the change to minimize resistance. This will include high-level stakeholder management, which may require the use of a steering board (**Q95**).

Provider's Job: Make the Client Successful   It would be great for providers if they could just worry about all the gnarly problems of delivery and leave clients to sink or swim on their own. Unfortunately, due to the well-known whipping boy status of most IT departments (**Q57**), providers must do their own jobs and more. Their best defense, as it turns out, is to help the client succeed. A few approaches to doing that include:

- Working with the client to develop a well-articulated MOP.

- Helping the client make strategic trade-off decisions. When funds are cut, for instance, schedules must be lengthened, MOPs curtailed, or higher risk endured. Many clients will try to take a head-in-the-sand approach to these decisions. The provider will need to help the client deal with reality proactively.

- The provider can strongly recommend a contingency fund (**Q99**) for the project that can be drawn from as the client changes or increases project requirements, or as unforeseen technical problems must be solved. The fund operates as a bank from which withdrawals can be made only with executive approval.

- The provider can help clarify roles, such as the client PM and the IT PM, and help build successful relationships among those roles.

Conclusion

The executive's role in project success or failure is overwhelmingly important, and frequently overlooked. As executive clients and executive providers increasingly understand the accountabilities, authorities, and limits of their roles, the likelihood of project success will rise, measure for measure.

---

94. What questions does the project sponsor need to ask a project manager?

WENDI PECK

The *executive provider's* challenge (**Q93**) is to keep thinking at a high level, doing deep dives only where necessary.[1] That's a tough challenge in the IT environment where there is constant pressure to excel at the minutiae of technology. The provider's response to that challenge must be to keep a short mental checklist of the key factors in project success, *and to keep coming back to it*. The list isn't long:

[1] A previous question (**Q93**) explains that "the sponsor" can refer to either of two roles: the *executive client* who will benefit from the technology implementation, or the *executive provider* in IT who will provide executive oversight for the IT portion of the project. Here, we will consider questions that can be asked by the provider; however, most of them could just as easily be asked by the client as well.

94 ∎

1. *Project manager performance*—Examine the performance of that person. Look for what else could be done or provided to make the project manager successful.

2. *Project team dynamics*—Determine if the team members are getting along and focused on the right things.

3. *Project approach and outcomes*—Learn the current results, cost, schedule, and risks—and possible trade-offs between those factors.

4. *Client expectations*—Uncover current client expectations and how to manage them in the face of changing reality. Learn what non-IT issues will make or break the business result of this project, and determine if the executive client (**Q93**) is attending to those issues.

5. *Stakeholder commitment*—Determine the most recent stakeholder issues that need to be resolved or exploited.

Like the circus juggler spinning plates, each of these five areas requires the provider's ongoing attention. The fact that any one factor is proceeding smoothly does not mean that it can be ignored.

The best way for providers to exploit this mental checklist is to keep scanning its five dimensions as context for incisive questions. Questions are surely one of the executive's most potent tools. Questions direct conversation, focus a discussion without monopolizing it, and can unearth information that might otherwise have been forgotten, hidden, or prettified.

For each of the five factors, no single question is always the right one. Within each factor the questions will change based on the project phase and the circumstance. However, the examples that follow indicate a direction of inquiry that generally works. Notice that every area of inquiry offers the opportunity for providers to understand what is needed from *them*.

The emphasis here is on communication between the provider and the project manager. Questions and style of inquiry can be adjusted when the provider is in conversation with someone else.

PROJECT MANAGER PERFORMANCE

One researcher has found a powerful distinction between effective managers and ineffective ones.[2] The effective managers more often engage employees in conversation *about the employee's own performance*. Questions that help the provider do that with the project manager include:

[2] Judith L. Komaki, *Leadership from an Operant Perspective: People and Organizations* (New York: Routledge, 1998).

- How are you feeling about your work on the project?

- What are your biggest challenges right now?

- What are your plans for dealing with those problems?

In addition, the provider should look for opportunities to assist by asking:

- Is there anything I can do to make your job easier?

- What sort of help do you need from me at this point in the project?

If the project manager paints only rosy pictures, the provider can ferret out information with the use of hypothetical questions such as:

- I'm glad things are going so well, but if we were to experience a problem, from what direction do you think it might come?

PROJECT TEAM DYNAMICS

Some "teams" are teams in name only, without much teamwork evident. To discover the health of the team, the provider can ask the project manager questions along these lines:

- How clear are team members about their roles and the roles of those around them?

- How well is the team working together?

- Are any problems between team members creating distractions or slowing progress?

- For those resources that are borrowed from functional areas, are you receiving the level of support needed from their supervisors?

- Did all team members attend the last team meeting? If not, why not?

- Are there any team members who seem not to support recent team decisions?

- How is team morale? Has it changed recently? If so, when and why?

- Is the team enforcing its agreed-upon ground rules?

- What can I do to help in this area?

Team work aside, the team may or may not have enough talent or the right kind of talent. The provider can ask questions such as these to determine resource adequacy:

- Are you satisfied with the capabilities of each of your team members?

- Is each team member meeting your performance expectations? If not, how will it affect the project? What have you already tried to improve performance?

- Are additional or different resources required? If so, help me understand why.

94

PROJECT APPROACH AND OUTCOMES

There are many dimensions to the project work itself. Understanding the effectiveness of the project approach, the real status of the work, and whether or not desired outcomes will be achieved requires inquiry into several areas. The following ideas will start the right conversations:

- *Project Approach*

  −Do you believe our current project approach is still the right one? Why or why not?

  −Were we right about the risks and benefits inherent in this approach? If not, what needs to change?

  −Is the measure of performance we established for this project still appropriate? Achievable? (**Q92**)

- *Results to Date*—The provider will benefit from gaining an understanding of a bit of project management esoterica called "earned value." In a nutshell, it takes the pulse of a project by examining budget, schedule, and work achieved in *relationship to each other*, rather than each separately. It isn't adequate simply to know whether the project is on schedule or within budget. It is better to know:

  −Have we completed the work that needed to be completed by this date in the schedule?

  −Have we spent more or less money completing that work than we planned?

  −It is also helpful to ask: Have you made any financial commitments that aren't yet reflected in the current project financials?

- *Contingency Status*

  −Early in the project: What kind of contingency, in time and dollars, are included in this project? (**Q75, Q99**)

  −Later on: How much of the contingency is left? Knowing what you now know, is it enough?

- *Project Changes*

  −Are there any new changes to scope and features that I don't know about?[3]

  −If so, what is the potential impact of these changes on schedule and budget?

[3] If there is an executive steering committee involved in the project (**Q95**), it will also be important for the provider to inquire about their knowledge of such changes. Sometimes changes that initially seem small and inconsequential evolve into changes that have huge impact. The provider needs to stay in touch with steering board members, maintaining awareness of their issues. That allows the project manager freedom to focus on day-to-day decisions, but prevents undesired scope creep.

- *Project Cutover*

  –What problems do you anticipate with cutover?

  –What are your fallback plans if things go wrong (**Q99**)?

CLIENT EXPECTATIONS

Especially in IT projects, many people "on the client side" are sometimes called "the client." In reality, there is likely only one executive (or a small handful of executives if the project is being shared across business units) who has the authority to determine required outcomes (**Q93**). That person is the real "client." Expectations of that person must be managed first; expectations can then be reset elsewhere, lower down the client organization(s), as necessary. The provider, not the project manager, should manage client expectations and iron out problems with clients at the executive level.

In this area, some starter questions for the provider include:

- Do you detect any problems with the executive client right now? (Problems might include diminished support or participation, discontent with the project team, etc.)

- What inconsistencies are we hearing between what the client expects and what others in their own organization expect?

- Does the client's current expected outcome match ours?

- Have there been any requested changes to scope (by anyone in the client organization)? If so, how have those been handled?

- Are you receiving adequate client support from the individuals who have regular interface with the IT project team?

STAKEHOLDER MANAGEMENT

Stakeholders are individuals who will be (or perceive they will be) affected by a project in some way (**Q49**, **Q50**). They are usually also individuals who can either help the project succeed or help it fail. Knowing who these individuals are is critical to project success. Often, the people who can help the most or do the most damage aren't the people with the biggest titles.

One of the key functions of the provider is to help manage project stakeholders—especially stakeholders for whom positional clout is required. The provider is in the position to help keep the path cleared so that the project team can be successful. A fair amount of formality in this regard is recommended. Specifically, the provider and the project manager should meet initially to determine who—of all the stakeholders—represents the critical mass. In other words, determine who the 12 to 15 individuals

94

are who have the ability to make or break the project. This does not mean all other stakeholders are forgotten. Communication and involvement plans need to exist for all stakeholders. However, those individuals in the critical mass (which may change over the life of the project) obviously must receive more one-on-one attention.

The goal here is to get and maintain enough commitment and support from each stakeholder to ensure project success. Not all stakeholders need to have the same level of commitment to the project. Some stakeholders may simply need not to be roadblocks, while others are needed to actually help sell the project. The provider should work closely with the project manager to determine and manage a strategy appropriate for each. Once stakeholder management strategies are developed, ongoing inquiry might look like this:

- For each stakeholder within the critical mass: Is John Doe's level of commitment where we need it to be at this point in the project? What indicators do you have of this?

- And if not: What can I do to help achieve it?

- Are new stakeholders surfacing that we should be discussing and managing?

Summary

Providers can find themselves awash with project data, but still bereft of information needed for wise strategic control. Meeting that challenge requires frequent, informal conversations with the project manager and others related to the project. The key to success in those conversations is skillful inquiry: use of questions arising from an understanding of the basic factors of project success.

---

95. What role does a project's steering board need to play in the technology implementation process?

WILLIAM W. CASEY AND WENDI PECK

IT projects that reach across the enterprise have many stakeholders—people with a strong interest in the project's approach and outcome (Q50). Those stakeholders may support or subvert the project; their advice and acceptance often drive project success.

Use of a steering board is one way to engage those stakeholders. Steering boards offer practical and political advantages, ensuring that the project receives key strategic input, as well as ensuring that interested parties believe that they have been sufficiently represented.

A project's steering board comprises executives representing the various groups of stakeholders. For example, in a project designed to install an order and billing application, the departments represented might include sales, customer service, finance, distribution, and IT. Therefore, an executive from each area would sit on the board.

The *executive client* chairs the board (**Q93**). Only one person should occupy this position, no matter how many business units are affected by the project. If in doubt about the identity of this *client*, choose the executive representing the business unit with the most at stake in the outcome of the project, or the one paying the largest portion of the project's costs.

Generally, the other board members should occupy positions at the level of the person chairing the board, or slightly below. Board members who rank much lower than the chair may receive scant attention from the chair, or may not speak up. Neither should the chair occupy a lower organizational rung than the other board members, for similar reasons.

To Steer or Not to Steer

Does the steering board actually steer? The answer is either yes or no, depending on which of two steering board models are employed.

It *does* steer in the *committee model*, which sets the steering board at the apex of the project. The chair guides and facilitates, but wields no more authority than the other members. The chair and other steering board members serve as coequals.

This model produces a sense of inclusion among steering board members because of its inherent use of power sharing. Some projects never get off the ground without this political advantage. On the other hand, this model produces the usual pitfalls of committees-in-charge, messages and directives conflict, disagreements drag on, personal agendas exert inordinate weight, and the task of managing multiple bosses devours the project manager's time.

Clear role definition for each steering board member can help mitigate these dangers. By assigning categories of decision making to each member, the board can reduce the number of group decisions that inevitably slow the project's progress. The project manager also plays an important role in this model. As the person the steering board often sees as accountable for project success, the project manager can often force an agenda and obtain decisions from the board that he or she feels are essential for the project to successfully proceed.

The *strong leader model* is the nonsteering alternative to the committee model. In this model, the chair seeks consensus and works mightily for it, but retains the right to decide, if consensus cannot be reached. Steering board members who believe their interests are being trammeled can escalate their concerns to higher management (unless, of course, the steering board chair is the CEO). In most organizations, escalation is not done lightly, but its possibility helps ensure that the chair considers the interests of the whole enterprise, not just his or her own portion of it.

MEMBER ACCOUNTABILITIES

In the strong leader model, the chair is accountable to ensure that the *business purpose* of the project is achieved. In the committee model, the committee members experience shared accountability for project success—along with all the potential hazards of collective responsibility.

All board members have three broad accountabilities: (1) Advise and advocate *on behalf of their constituencies*, to influence favorably the conduct and outcome of the project, (2) advise and advocate *on behalf of the project*, to influence the acceptance and engagement of their constituencies, and (3) ensure the delivery of any element of the project which is due from that member's organization. The third accountability is particularly important when business process changes are significant parts of a project. The board member must make sure that the process redesign, employee training, data conversion, and testing activities that his or her organization has committed to are successfully handled. Board members are accountable to their immediate managers to perform these three accountabilities.

The IT seat on the *client's* steering board possesses those three accountabilities, plus an additional one. The IT executive must ensure, as far as practicable, that technology decisions serve the long-term interest of the total organization, such as conforming to architectural standards and advancing the organization's technology strategy.

Board members are not accountable in any direct way to the chair. The chair is normally in no position to hold the board members accountable and doing so would undermine the checks and balances that are normally built into the steering board structure.

THE BOARD'S BUSINESS

Unless there exists a project portfolio management process that allocates resources across multiple projects (Q76), it is the board's job to accept or reject the business plan that supports the project. This function is most likely to occur when the board is actually a standing committee, such as the CEO's executive committee, and not an ad hoc committee formed to head a particular initiative.

The board also accepts the project plan (or a high-level version of it), including the project's measure of performance and statement of scope, which it must then manage against. As the project unfolds, there will inevitably be unforeseen events that trigger strategic trade-offs between the project's intended results, schedule, and costs (including availability of resources). It is the board's role to plan and control these trade-offs as much as possible—or explicitly accept the increased risk of not doing so. To be able to make the needed strategic trade-offs, the board monitors the project's progress against major milestones and formally accepts its major deliverables.

One important role of the board during the project is to exercise the right to approve any changes in scope—at least above a certain amount. This is particularly important when scope changes have cross-organizational impacts. Scope changes often consume the project's contingency (**Q99**), the use of which should also be controlled by the board. In addition, if the project strays too far off course to correct, the board may be obliged to kill it (**Q100**).

BOARD MEETINGS

Steering boards should meet as often as needed, but monthly meetings are typical. Early in the project, late in the project, and at crisis points, the steering board may meet more often. When the steering board convenes on a regular basis, instead of a reactive basis, the need for hastily assembled crisis control meetings diminishes considerably. The chair leads the meetings using an agenda the project manager has developed with input from each board member. Ideally, supportive information should accompany that agenda in advance of the meeting so that board members can come prepared to contribute. Periodic project updates can occur between meetings if necessary through e-mail or Web-based communication channels.

SUMMARY

Regardless of whether an organization employs the *committee* model or the *strong leader* model, well-structured and well-conducted steering boards offer a dramatic opportunity; they can empower enterprise-wide projects to stay relevant to the organization and to make the right strategic trade-offs along the way. In the end, steering boards ensure that all the stakeholders stay involved, creating the political, organizational, and financial strength so essential for project success.

96. What are the key managerial authorities a project manager needs to succeed?

WILLIAM W. CASEY

A classic bromide of business is that *there can be no accountability without commensurate authority*. The logic is self-evident, but the sticking point for managers has been to translate each side of that equation into clear and actionable terms. An earlier discussion (**Q92**) addressed accountability, showing that a project manager's basic accountability is to achieve the project's measure of performance. Is such a clear statement of managerial authority also possible? This answer attempts to do so after first establishing whether the issue is worth bothering about.

SHOULD PROJECT MANAGERS HAVE AUTHORITY?

Harold Kerzner, a prolific writer on project management, echoes many of his colleagues when he states, "Project managers have very little real authority."[1] He and similar writers do not contend that project managers should not have authority, only that it is a fact that they do not have it. Their resulting prescription is that project managers should learn to deal with it and not expect the situation to change. This thinking is sufficiently prevalent that a small industry of books and seminars has arisen to teach project managers how to influence without authority. Fortunately, Kerzner's statement does not apply everywhere. At many companies project managers do have authority. Indeed, much of their success is credited to it.

One dramatic example of the importance of the authorities possessed by project managers is found in a study comparing two companies, Honda and General Motors. Each company had set out to design a new automotive platform. Honda achieved its goals handily, but General Motors fell spectacularly short, nearly doubling its targeted schedule and costs. Researchers found the pivotal distinction to be in the authority conferred upon the project manager.[2] Honda's project manager had as much authority as any divisional head; General Motors' project manager was practically powerless. Other studies have yielded similar results.[3]

I have conducted informal research on the same topic. In over 200 seminars pre-

---

[1] Harold Kerzner, *Applied Project Management: Best Practices on Implementation* (New York: Wiley, 2000) 310.

[2] James P. Womack, Daniel T. Jones, and Daniel Roos, *The Machine That Changed the World: The Story of Lean Production* (New York: HarperPerennial, 1991) Chapter Five.

[3] Robert J. Graham and Randall L. Englund, *Creating an Environment for Successful Projects: The Quest to Manage Project Management* (San Francisco: Jossey-Bass, 1997) 122, 126.

Figure **96.1** Relationship between Project Manager Authorities and Project Success

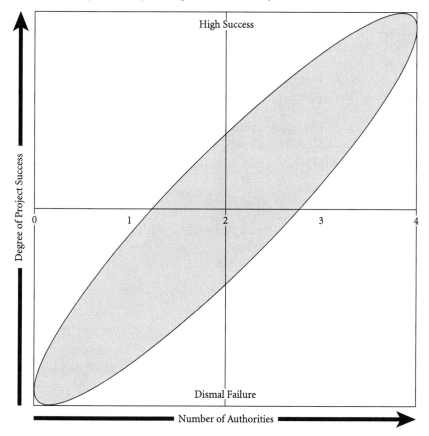

sented to project managers, each seminar participant has been asked to recall two or three projects and represent them as data points on a two-dimensional chart indicating (1) project success (admittedly subjective), and (2) number of authorities granted the project manager—from a list of four to be described in a moment. Data from each seminar participant are then summarized on a single chart for the entire class.

Without exception, the data points have clustered as shown in Figure 96.1, with very few outliers. The conclusion is that a strong correlation exists between the number of authorities possessed by a project manager and the success of the project. A slightly more aggressive conclusion is that the *absence of project manager authority poses a significant risk to project success*. However, it is an atypical project risk: one of the few that can be prevented without additional cost, delays, or compromises.

MANAGERIAL AUTHORITIES

It is apparent that managers require authorities. Some of the authorities required vary, based on the demands of the situation. Authorities to negotiate contracts, control budget, decide the technical approach, etc., are not universally applicable. However, one situational demand does not vary—the accountability for the outputs of others. This is the fundamental managerial accountability.[4] A simple set of managerial authorities may be derived by considering what authorities a project manager (or any manager) might reasonably desire to fulfill that accountability. One researcher calls the four authorities described below the "requisite authorities," as no manager can manage effectively without them.[5]

THE FIRST TWO AUTHORITIES

First, a project manager might say "If you are going to hold me accountable for the output of my team, then let me have some control over who is on that team." In such a case, the manager must be authorized to:

1. Select new team members

2. Remove team members

Of course, these two authorities must exist within the bounds of reality. Just as a department store manager has to work within the constraints of budget, personnel policies, and a limited labor pool, the project manager will have to do the same. If the project needs a C++ programmer and the IT department has only one available, the project manager will probably be forced to choose that programmer. The absence of authority is felt, however, when there is a pool of programmers from which to choose, and the project manager has no say in who is chosen. At a bare minimum, any project manager should be able to veto the appointment of team members.

As with other managers, project managers should be bound by the routine and necessary requirements of coaching, counseling, etc., prior to removing someone from the team. But if coaching and counseling do not result in a performance improvement, a project manager should not be told, "You two work it out!" Enjoining project managers to communicate, to persuade, and to lead is fair enough, but insufficient. Other managers are also thus enjoined, but they are also authorized.

---

[4] Elliott Jaques, *Requisite Organization: A Total System for Effective Managerial Organization and Managerial Leadership for the 21st Century*, 2nd rev. ed. (Arlington: Cason Hall, 1998) 35.
[5] Jaques.

THE LAST TWO AUTHORITIES

Having gained the ability to influence team membership, a project manager might then request to have influence over individual performance. This means the project manager must be authorized to:

1. Assign tasks

2. Provide performance consequences

The third authority may seem obvious, but enough project managers have heard, "You can't tell me what to do," that it is worth stating.

The fourth authority allows project managers to give weight to their assignments literally, to make them matters of consequence. Without this authority, team member commitments may not be realized. In practice, consequence control may mean anything from allocating bonuses or giving time-off to writing a portion of each team member's appraisal.

Instead of consequence control, executives often bestow the authority to tattle, "If you have any problems with your team, let me know about it and I'll take care of it." Although the intended support is commendable, and consequences from executives are certainly better than no consequences at all, this approach generally works less well. One project manager described it as trying to fight a skirmish armed only with nuclear warheads. One exception is that it may make sense to employ "tattle authority" when project team members are of higher rank than the project manager.

The complications encountered when managing cross-functional and matrix situations are discussed in another answer (**Q97**).

REFUSAL TO USE AUTHORITY

What if project managers will not use the authorities they have been granted? This is a common complaint of project executives. Usually, this problem derives from one of two causes:

1. The project manager is not truly being held accountable for project success. When that happens, then the controlling factor will be the project manager's social relationships with members of the project team.

2. The project executive has failed to formally identify the project manager's authorities (**Q93**). The authorities, therefore, exist mainly in that executive's mind.

SUMMARY

Evidence weighs heavily that project managers do indeed succeed more often when accorded ordinary managerial authorities. Authorities requisite to all managers, including project managers, are the authorities to:

1. Select new team members

2. Remove team members

3. Assign tasks

4. Provide rewards (and other performance consequences).

---

97. What are the keys to getting cross-functional work done?

WILLIAM W. CASEY

Adhocracy is the name some management gurus have given to organizations that tackle goals and problems with temporary, fluid structures staffed with a cross-functional team of experts.[1] Tom Peters considers it quite the wave of the future.[2] Most IT organizations, on the other hand, just consider it a way of life, and have no fancy terms for it. Few major IT undertakings can be done in any way other than the *ad hoc* gathering of various business and technical expertise onto the same, temporary, fluid structure: a project team.

However, such cross-functional efforts can give managers and employees an unsettled feeling. Situations where an employee has more than one manager (i.e., cross-functional) can result in a number of difficulties such as:

- *Team members receive conflicting directions from their multiple managers.* If it is not clear which manager is in charge of what (without overlapping accountability), then it is left to the team member to decide which manager to take seriously.

---

[1] James Brian Quinn, Henry Mintzberg, and Robert M. James, *The Strategy Process: Concepts, Contexts and Cases* (Englewood Cliffs: Prentice Hall, 1988); Robert H. Waterman, *Adhocracy: The Power to Change* (New York: Norton, 1993).

[2] Tom Peters, "Introduction," *Adhocracy: The Power to Change*, by Robert H. Waterman (New York: Norton, 1993).

- *Team members have unrealistic demands put on their time.* When two managers each want 80% of a team member's time, it's up to the team member to either burn out or, again, decide which manager to take seriously.

- *Managers (usually project managers) cannot get their work done.* When the project manager assigns work to a "dotted-line" team member, that work competes with assignments from the real manager, the one who performs the team member's performance appraisals.

THREE RULES OF CROSS-FUNCTIONAL MANAGEMENT

Such problems are the norm in many organizations. However, I have interviewed managers in many other cross-functional organizations that perform their resource-sharing feats without a hitch. These successful cross-functional organizations are mostly professional service firms such as law, engineering, and management consultation, but also include the occasional IT shop. The three commonalities among these successful organizations are sufficiently consistent that they might rightly be called rules.

1. *No two managers can make the same assignment to the same team member.* For example, a math teacher does not tell a student how to hold a clarinet and a music teacher does not tell the student how do factorials. Disaster results when a parent and a coach yell instructions to a young soccer player at the same time. Placing two project managers at the helm of the same project, or allowing both the employee's project manager and functional manager to make project assignments will result in a similar disaster.

2. *Each manager must control meaningful performance consequences.* That is what happens when each teacher hands out grades for his or her class. It is interesting to consider what would happen to students' study habits if only one of several teachers handed out grades. That situation would be akin to the results obtained by managers with dotted-line employees. Those managers often wish that they, too, could meaningfully grade the work of their indirect reports, and that it would be treated as more than polite "input."

3. *Resolving work overloads (and underloads) is the accountability of the managers, not the employee.* The employee's accountability is to notify the managers of the problem and assist in its resolution. Without this rule, the resource being allocated (the employee) is, *de facto*, put in charge of resource allocation—not a good idea.

These rules represent no departure from the requisite authorities cited earlier (**Q96**); they serve only as an additional stipulation when employees are accountable to more than one manager.

THE RESOURCE POOL

Some IT departments lean heavily on the resource pool approach to structure; projects draw from resource pools of experts. The resource pools can serve as "home-rooms" for specialized knowledge workers such as programmers, database experts, project managers, technical writers—whatever kind of expertise that benefits from oversight by a manager proficient in that area of knowledge.

Many successful resource pools lean heavily on the first rule cited. The resource pool manager holds employees accountable for the proper exercise of their expertise, while the project manager holds them accountable for agreed-upon outputs. Put more simply, one manager holds employees accountable for the *how;* the other manager holds them accountable for the *what.* In this arrangement, project managers do not have to be experts in every facet of the project. Further, employees get the benefit of ongoing professional development—a keen advantage in retaining technical talent.

THE CUSTOMER-SUPPLIER ARRANGEMENT

Not every contributor on a project team is sufficiently central to the project that the project manager needs to manage that person, with all the authorities implied by the word *manage* (**Q96**). A workable alternative, then, is the *customer-supplier relationship.* In this arrangement, the project manager (the customer) explicitly arranges with the employee *and* that person's manager (the supplier) the nature of the employee's contribution to the project.

The probability of success increases with adherence to several commonsense guidelines outlined below:

- *Spell out the agreement in writing and have it signed by all parties concerned.* This proviso is accepted in some cultures and quite revolutionary in others. As an acceptable compromise to actually signing the agreement, the project manager can treat the written agreement as "meeting minutes" to be e-mailed to all participants after the meeting.

- *Agree to specific supplier outputs, not just time spent.* When the customer specifies the need for, say, a database analyst half-time for 12 weeks, it is not nearly as effective as also specifying the outputs required in that interval.

- *Agree to what is needed of the customer by the supplier.* Usually, the supplier can succeed only with customer support. By specifying the nature of that support in the agreement, success becomes much more likely.

- *Agree to a remedy process, should one party deem the other to have fallen short of the agreement.* This is the customer-supplier equivalent of a prenuptial agreement. It makes conflict less likely to occur, and less rocky if it does occur.

- *The person doing the work* and *that person's manager need to be involved in the discussions with the customer.* Agreements with only the worker risk excluding the resource allocator (the worker's manager) from an important resource allocation agreement. Therefore, the agreement might not receive much support.

SUMMARY

IT project teams frequently consist of members of different organizations, each person accountable to multiple managers, including the project manager. The potential confusion arising from such cross-functional arrangements can be mitigated with these rules, which are extensions of the stipulations cited in another answer (**Q96**):

1. No two managers can make the same assignment to the same team member.

2. Each manager must control meaningful performance consequences.

3. Resolving work overloads (and underloads) is the responsibility of the managers, not the employee—with the employee's assistance.

When the project manager requires less control than that afforded by these guidelines, then a customer-supplier agreement will help ensure that team members receive clear directives and treat project deliverables as priorities.

---

98. What top ten actions can IT project managers take to increase the likelihood of implementation success?

WENDI PECK AND WILLIAM W. CASEY

Most of the answers in the "IT and Implementation" section of this book offer or imply suggestions that project managers will find helpful in ensuring success. Drawing from those ideas and others, here is the top ten list of actions most likely to lead to implementation success.

1. Adopt a proactive mind-set. A significant amount of psychological research has shown that successful people differ from their less successful peers in one overarching way: they see themselves in control of their own success and failure.[1] This is a uniquely beneficial perspective for project managers.

[1] Herbert M. Lefcourt, *Locus of Control: Current Trends in Theory and Research* (Hillsdale: L. Erlbaum, 1982).

Consider that every project problem contains aspects that the project manager can control as well as plenty that are uncontrollable. The more successful project managers adapt *proactively*; they act on the pieces they control while learning how to prevent the problem next time. The less successful ones waste time whining and blaming, and are quick to point out what someone else should do next time to prevent the problem. In the authors' research, project managers who had previously received training in this area attributed much of their current project—and career—success to their learned ability to adopt a proactive mind-set.

2. Establish an effective relationship with the *executive provider*. Project managers do well to quickly establish a relationship with the *executive provider* (**Q93**), the person ultimately accountable for delivering the project. With this executive "guardian angel" on their side, project managers stand a good chance of avoiding some of the project and organizational pitfalls that can cause failure (**Q88**). The *provider* can often grant the project manager appropriate authorities, help remove roadblocks along the way, expedite trade-off decisions and help manage the politics.

Not all *providers* understand the project side of their jobs as thoroughly as they know the other aspects. A wise project manager creates a conversation to clarify roles, communication protocols, and other mutual expectations.

3. Ask for (and exercise) the necessary managerial authorities. Project management resembles any other kind of management: one person is on the hook for the performance of others. But somehow, when the word "management" has "project" in front of it, executives forget to confer the standard managerial authorities they otherwise would. Proactive project managers work with their supervisor at the beginning of the project to secure the needed authorities for the life of the project (**Q96**).

4. Define success before the project starts. Like a politician's promises, fuzzy project goals imply goodies for everyone. But this expediency carries a price. Avoidance of difficult discussions before the project only delays them until after the project—after the opportunities are gone and the money is spent.

The antidote to fuzzy thinking and political pandering is the "measure of performance" (MOP) (**Q92**). The MOP asserts an objective, overarching project result. It states the objective *reason* for the project far better than any statement of scope or list of requirements. In the end, it will be the unambiguous indicator of whether the project achieved what it promised.

A project's MOP (or MOPs, if it is a program) requires the involvement of the *executive provider,* the *executive client,* and central stakeholders. The project manager's job is to coordinate those people's efforts until they reach a satisfactory result.

5. Establish a clear, logical structure up front. Where a camper pitches a tent usually receives less attention than where that same person chooses to live. Temporary structures just don't receive a lot of consideration. That includes projects.

Because projects are temporary organizations, many receive scant attention to their organizational structure: *who is accountable to whom for what,* plus *their authorities.* The understandable inattention to this detail carries severe costs. In most collapsed projects, unclear or illogical structures helped cause the failure. It is exactly because projects are temporary that their structure demands rigor. Project work affords little chance to get the structure right over time; there isn't any time so it must be done at the beginning.

When working with their supervisor and the *executive provider*, project managers must clarify three critical messages:

1. the desired output for each participant,

2. to whom is each participant accountable and for which output,

3. what positive or negative consequences will accrue to each participant based on his or her project performance.

6. Manage stakeholders with a formal plan. Stakeholders are individuals or organizations who are affected by (have a stake in) the project. The good news is they can help a project succeed. The bad news is they can completely derail the project. Savvy project managers work with the executives to analyze the organizational landscape, then create, update, and manage a stakeholder plan. This means knowing what is needed from each stakeholder for the project to be most successful. Some stakeholders simply need to be kept from creating roadblocks. Others, such as those who will be using the project's deliverables, need to play an active role from start to finish (**Q47, Q48**). Caveat: many powerful stakeholders do not possess impressive titles; do not neglect them.

7. Use a project plan and keep it flexible. There exists a sweet spot between obsessive planning and the unfortunate sequence of Ready-Fire-Aim. Skillful project managers occupy that sweet spot, balancing the necessity for immediate action with the necessity for intelligent action. Successful project managers do not neglect planning, nor are they slaves to it.

Successful project managers update their plans for two reasons. First, they get smarter as the project proceeds; as unknowns become known, updated plans are better plans. Second, *clients* get smarter; needs, problems, and opportunities all become clearer. Good project managers help craft updated plans that reflect win-win solutions that serve the client's interests without promising the impossible.

8. Create strict project controls before they're needed. Because most projects don't deliver the original project plan, the project manager must establish mechanisms for controlling change—*up front*. Change causes project failure only if it gets out of control (**Q87**).

Change control comes easiest when its process is documented and agreed upon prior to the need for its use. Often this involves interaction with the project's steering board (**Q95**). Project managers will have much less success if they wait until changes start careening out of control. By then it is too late to put controls in place.

9. Get out from behind the computer screen. Many managers believe that project management *software* skill equates with project management skill. Yes, good project managers understand their tools and wield them effectively. But a person who can use a hammer isn't necessarily a carpenter—and a person who can use project management software isn't necessarily a project manager. Project managers who spend more than 25% of their time hunched over glowing Gantt charts have missed the most important part of the job—communicating with people.

10. Reward good performance and quickly correct bad performance. Irrespective of designated authorities, every project manager can influence performance. They can achieve this influence through their ability to reward the performance they want and correct the performance they don't want. Successful managers of any kind do three things: (1) set clear expectations, (2) monitor performance without micromanaging it, and (3) confer performance consequences for delivery on expectations.[2]

Positive performance consequences may include no more than praise or an inexpensive "thank you" such as tickets to a sports event. Negative consequences may include private, verbal correction or removal from the team. Be advised—ignoring poor performance can have a devastating impact on the project team's performance.[3]

---

99. Should you plan for failure?

DAVID R. LAUBE

Failure. What a dreadful word. It's a word that nobody likes and everybody runs from. It's a word that can attach itself to a person and, once attached, is never eradicated. Failure has no friends. Contemporary philosopher Eric Hoffer once observed, "There is no loneliness greater than the loneliness of a failure."[1] Yes, failure is dreadful.

However, failure is just part of the landscape of technology projects. Because technology projects are inherently risky (**Q85, Q86**), failure is a commonplace occurrence. Veteran technologists have usually experienced failure. Their experiences, often associated with considerable emotional trauma, drive them to avoid those situations again. Their solution—plan for failure. So the question is now not *if* you should plan

[2] Judith L. Komaki, *Leadership from an Operant Perspective: People and Organizations* (New York: Routledge, 1998).

[3] Frank M. J. Lafasto and Carl E. Larson, *When Teams Work Best* (Thousand Oaks: Sage, 2001) 143–44.

[1] Eric Hoffer, Quote, "Thoughts on the Business of Life," *Forbes* 27 May 2002: 184.

for failure, but *how* to plan for it. Below are several suggestions in that regard that will help when the inevitable happens.

Put a Contingency in Your Plan

Failure on many technology projects is defined as a missed target date or an overrun project budget. It is not surprising that this occurs. Estimating a project is a complex matter requiring the complete understanding of:

- all of the business requirements,
- the technology to be employed,
- the interfaces with other systems,
- the network used to connect the systems and users,
- the sources and quality of the data.

Any misunderstanding or miscalculation of any of these items can easily cause a project to get off track.

To help with this common occurrence in a technology project, many projects establish a contingency, both in time and in dollars. The contingency is a cushion placed in the project's financial budget and time estimate that is unallocated at the start of the project. The size of the contingency varies depending on the size, complexity, and risk of the project. A large, multi-year project could have a contingency of as much as 25%. Shorter, smaller projects would have less.

The problem is getting the contingency established. The business unit sponsoring the system usually hates the idea of a contingency, believing that the IT organization is merely padding the project to make it easier. Moreover, the addition of a contingency can sometimes change the economics of the business case making the project harder to be approved. Therefore, the pressure is usually the other direction—estimate the project quickly, make the schedule very aggressive, and assume that everything will go perfectly. Such unrealistic expectations are usually a guaranteed formula for failure and might cause the project team to attempt shortcuts or make counterproductive decisions (**Q91**).

The real way to get the contingency established and accepted by all parties is for it to be jointly administered by the project's steering committee (**Q95**). They would make the decisions to use the contingency when requirements are added, unforeseen problems surface, or business emergencies disturb the plan. Uses of the contingency due to errors or incompetence of the team might still be approved, but not counted in the calculation of incentives to the project team. The team should know from the outset that their rewards are based on hitting project targets *without* using up the contingency. So—bottom line—put in a contingency. You will probably use it, avoiding the project being labeled a failure.

Convert Only Portions of the System at a Time

There is a reason why people committing suicide favor such venues as jumping off the Golden Gate Bridge or the top floor of tall buildings; they are highly likely to be successful. Given the ability of intelligent business professionals to observe this phenomenon, it seems curious that many technology project plans call for the project to "cutover" all at once. So, usually over a weekend, all the data is converted and loaded into the new system, the hardware and network are activated, and on Monday morning users start to work with the new system in a live business environment.

This "cliff cutover" (as in "jump off a cliff") is fraught with danger. With so many moving parts, it only takes a little glitch for problems to erupt, and they frequently mushroom into major issues that will disrupt the operations of the business. In short, it is not the best idea to attempt such a cutover. Instead, assume that some part of the system will fail; would it be better to have failure confined to a single department, geographic region, or division than the entire enterprise? It is best to confine problems to a small area where they can be fixed easily. This will avoid impacting the entire enterprise and having the project labeled as a failure.

Build a "Fall Back" Conversion Plan

It is surprising how many projects can only "fall forward." That is, databases are converted; hardware, network, and systems interfaces are activated; and old equipment or processes are immediately discarded. In those situations, it may be virtually impossible to go back to the original system should major problems arise. It is unwise to build a plan that will only go forward. Always have the ability to go back to the old system. Data in the old format needs to be maintained for a time, old software and hardware should be kept ready to reactivate, and old business processes should remain available. If a big failure occurs, at least you can put the company back into its old operational condition.

Be Able to Track All Transactions

One of the greatest risks with a new system is that somewhere in the conversion process or in the new software, some transaction will be treated differently than expected, or perhaps even lost. Savvy project managers understand that such a situation will cause a project to be labeled a failure. The only way to avoid this is to build a tracking mechanism for all transactions affected by a new system. You should be able to see all transactions go into the system, know where each one is inside that new system and all its interfaces, and see it come out at the end. Without that ability, should something go wrong, you will be unable to assure the business that everything still has been accounted for. Worse yet, if the system is incorrectly modifying or dropping some data midway through the transactions process, you may be unable to find the data and correct the errors. So, make sure you are able to find and track *everything*.

Maintain Open Communication

With the inevitability of project problems, it is imperative that IT and the business units keep communicating about project issues. Perhaps new requirements have arisen or testing is not going well, for example. There should be an established process for such issues to be communicated within the stakeholders. That way, any adjustments to the project will be joint decisions (**Q93**, **Q94**, **Q95**). Blame and failure are harder labels to assign when everyone has had a part in decision making on the project. If a crisis occurs, a preestablished emergency communication and escalation system should be in place to keep everyone informed on progress and problems.

Sometimes, despite all best efforts and good planning, a project will fail. Then the challenge is knowing when to cancel it (**Q100**). However, no one wants to be part of a failure. Therefore, in the world of technology projects, you should ensure that the items discussed above are in place. If so, these preparations will pay large dividends and perhaps avoid the dreadful label called "failure."

---

100. How do you know when to kill a project?

EDWARD F. LUKES, JR.

The primary purpose of any IT project is to better enable an enterprise to achieve its objectives. Any time it is determined this will not happen, a project should be killed (or canceled) as early in its life cycle as possible. Projects that are not terminated promptly result in wasted money, time, and managerial effort. They also can result in business disruption, lost opportunities to focus on high-return projects, and a loss of management good will and credibility.

Enabling an enterprise to achieve its objectives through an IT project requires the definition of measurable results from the project (**Q77**, **Q92**). Measurable results and related accountabilities establish a clear definition of project "success." These objectives must be defined at the project's outset because, as Eric Olsen notes, "what gets measured gets done." [1] These success benchmarks provide the basis for frequent objective and fact-based evaluations of a project's continuation. Without these benchmarks, a project's purpose will never be clear, and the basis for determining if it should be continued becomes subjective and political.

WHEN TO KILL AN IT PROJECT

A project should be killed whenever its success benchmarks cannot be met. Requirements, estimates, and assumptions for measuring a project's success are usually defined at the project's outset or in its early phases, before significant investments are made. As a project progresses, if these factors do not hold true, the project should be killed. Some examples follow.

Development costs or schedule delays increase beyond estimates resulting in not meeting the success benchmarks. This may be due to factors such as:

- *A project gets too complex.* Increasing project complexity leads to greater development cost and longer intervals, as well as more difficult system implementation and support. After a project is approved for development, there is often tremendous pressure from users, as well as technology staff, to put more capabilities into the system and even make changes to a packaged software product. If this ruins the project's value proposition and it cannot be corrected, kill the project.

- *Estimates of cost or benefits become highly inaccurate.* Initial estimates that are the basis for beginning a project are just that, estimates. Funding a project's initial phase allows for the development of (1) a better understanding of the project's value proposition and (2) detailed estimates before significant investments are put at risk. If these detailed estimates reveal an inadequate value proposition for the project, or if the estimates cannot be met, kill the project.[2]

- *Project management mistakes jeopardize the results.* If a project manager does not communicate the status of the schedule, deliverables, and cost status of the project at frequent enough intervals, the executive sponsor (**Q93**) and steering committee (**Q95**) may not have time to correct the course of the project. If this information is not provided regularly, more often than not, the project will be late and over budget. If the course of a project cannot be altered in time to maintain its value proposition, kill it.

[1] Carl W. Stern and George Stalk, eds., *Perspectives on Strategy: From the Boston Consulting Group* (New York: Wiley, 1998).

[2] Peter Weill and Marianne Broadbent, *Leveraging the New Infrastructure: How Market Leaders Capitalize on Information Technology* (Boston: HBSP, 1998).

- *Communications break down between the designers and users.* Poor communications be-tween designers and users often result in significant rework to revise or redevelop part of an application. For example, the designers may not adequately understand the busi-ness or the users may be too busy with daily activities to spend adequate time identify-ing their requirements and communicating them to the designers during the design phase. If communications between designers and users do not lead to a strong design and delivery of planned value, kill the project.

- *Internal organizational conflicts cannot be resolved.* Internal conflict can lead to cumber-some organization decision making. This could make it too difficult or time consuming to resolve design or implementation issues. In this case, kill the project.

The technology chosen may not prove to be reliable or able to meet performance needs. Ideally, an IT organization would not consider using an unproven technology or one where necessary experience was lacking. However, there are cases where use of a new technology is the only way to meet a key business objective (**Q5**). If the use of new technologies is critical for business success, it may be necessary to invest in, or have access to, a lab where dependability can be proven before full-scale implementation. However, if the technology starts to miss its performance metrics once the project is under way, the project should be cancelled.

The skills needed to develop a system or support it after implementation may prove too difficult to obtain, maintain, or afford. Without these skills, the quality of, or the business use of, a system will be at significant risk. Imagine a system that cannot keep up with new products, pricing structure changes, or commission program changes. Under these conditions, the investment will not generate planned returns and the project should be killed.

The cross-functional managers responsible for the project's success are not working as a team. Katzenbach and Smith found that high-performance teams are extremely rare.[3] They also found that companies with strong performance standards seem to spawn more "real teams" than companies that promote teams per se. The IT system may be built, but if lack of teamwork means performance improvement results will not be adequate, kill the project.

The business transformation needed to capture the value from the technology investment is determined to be unachievable, or too costly. This may be because the management focus, commitment, or skills necessary to capture the value after the system is imple-mented prove to be inadequate, perhaps due to higher priorities and competing ini-tiatives (**Q60**). If this occurs, kill the project.

[3] Jon R. Katzenbach and Douglas K. Smith, *The Wisdom of Teams* (New York: HarperBusiness, 1999).

The business parameters of a project change due to factors such as strategy changes, competitive changes, or changing customer needs.   Large, long-term projects are especially susceptible to this development. If this is a possibility, it is especially critical for the project team to fully explore the question with the internal strategic planners while evaluating future strategies and potential external impacts. If the risks of key business parameter changes outweigh the value to be generated, it is time to kill the project.

Conclusion

Ensuring that IT investments add the desired value or canceling them is a significant issue for any enterprise. The "Chaos Report" by the Standish Group International, Inc., found that failed and troubled projects cost U.S. companies and government agencies an estimated $145 billion per year.[4]

The implication is that the IT department and other departmental managers need to astutely position a project for success in its very early stages by addressing many of the potential issues discussed in this answer. Because technology implementation is so risky (Q85, Q86), projects can get into trouble. When that happens, do not be afraid to kill the project, and do not let the culture of the organization prevent an objective assessment of the problem. Yes, there may be internal repercussions, political fallout and financial consequences. But, it is very important to limit the damage. Kill the project, and apply the lessons learned and the resources saved to a new project that can be successful.

[4] Tom Field, "When Bad Things Happen to Good Projects," *CIO* 15 Oct. 1997, 29 Dec. 2002 <http://www.cio.com/archive/101597/bad.html>.

DAWN GREGG

The answers to the 100 questions contained in this book provide valuable IT information for managers. However, they are not meant to be complete treatises on any subject. The resources contained in this section were selected to allow readers to gain more in-depth knowledge of the topics covered in this book. The resources were selected for their content and for their suitability for a managerial audience.

These resources are grouped by question so the reader can locate specific information on a given topic. Each topic contains three types of resources. "Web Resources" are portals that contain links to many articles related to a specific topic. The Web resources are continually being upgraded and are usually the best place to get the most current information. The "Articles" section directs readers to more focused discussions and, sometimes, competing points of view. The "Books" section points to additional resources that can be accessed should broader coverage of the topic be desired.

The resources in this section provide a good starting point for learning more about any of the topics covered in this book. Because of the dynamic nature of the Web, some of the Web-based resources listed in this section may have been upgraded or replaced, and others may no longer be available. All of the hyperlinks listed in this section were active as of April 2003.

──────── SECTION 1. IT AND STRATEGY

Questions 1 and 2: IT and industries

Web Resources

CIO.com: E-business Research Center—Strategy. <http://www.cio.com/research/ec/strategy.html>.

Computerworld.com E-business Knowledge Center. <http://www.computerworld.com/managementtopics/ebusiness>.

Articles

Porter, Michael E. "Strategy and the Internet." *Harvard Business Review* 79.3 (2001): 62–78.

Books

Bradley, Stephen P., Jerry A. Hausman, and Richard L. Nolan, eds. *Globalization, Technology, and Competition: The Fusion of Computers and Telecommunications in the 1990s.* Boston: HBSP, 1993.

D'Aveni, Richard A. *Hypercompetition: Managing the Dynamics of Strategic Maneuvering.* New York: Free Press, 1994.

Kemerer, Chris F., ed. *Information Technology and Industrial Competitiveness: How It Shapes Competition.* Boston: Kluwer Academic Publishers, 1998.

McKenney, James L. *Waves of Change: Business Evolution through Information Technology.* Boston: HBSP, 1995.

Smith, Cooper. *Technology Strategies.* Upper Saddle River: Prentice Hall, 2002.

Tapscott, Don, Alex Lowy, and David Ticoll, eds. *Blueprint to the Digital Economy: Creating Wealth in the Era of E-Business.* New York: McGraw-Hill, 1998.

────────────────────

Question 3: Disruptive change

Web Resources

Business 2.0: Web Guide—Christensen, Clayton. <http://www.business2.com/webguide/0,1660,15514,00.html>.

Articles

Anderson, Phillip, and Michael L. Tushman. "Technological Discontinuities and Dominant Designs: A Cyclical Model of Technological Change." *Administrative Science Quarterly* 35 (1990): 604–33.

Christensen, Clayton M., Michael Raynor, and Matthew Verlinden. "Skate to Where the Money Will Be." *Harvard Business Review* 79.10 (2001): 73–81.

Gilbert, Clark, and Joseph L. Bower. "Disruptive Change: When Trying Harder Is Part of the Problem." *Harvard Business Review* 80.5 (2002): 94–101.

Rafi, Farshad, and Paul J. Kampas. "How to Identify Your Enemies before They Destroy You." *Harvard Business Review* 80.11 (2002): 115–23.

Books

Christensen, Clayton M. *The Innovator's Dilemma: When New Technologies Cause Great Firms to Fail.* Boston: HBSP, 1997.

Grove, Andrew S. *Only the Paranoid Survive: How to Exploit the Crisis Points That Challenge Every Company.* New York: Currency Doubleday, 1996.

R5

Question 4: Business driven technology strategy

Web Resources

Internet.com: IT Management: CIO Strategies. <http://itmanagement.earthweb.com/cio>.
Strategy+Business Web Site. <http://www.strategy-business.com/magazine>.

Articles

Bessant, John, et al. "Developing the Agile Enterprise." *International Journal of Technology Management* 24.5/6 (2002): 484–97.

Mattern, Frank, Stephan Schonwalder, and Wolfram Stein. "Fighting Complexity in IT." *McKinsey Quarterly* 1 (2003): 56–65.

Prahalad, C. K., and M. S. Krishnan. "The Dynamic Synchronization of Strategy and Information Technology." *MIT Sloan Management Review* 43.4 (2002): 24–33.

Ross, Jeanne W., and Peter Weill. "Six IT Decisions Your IT People Shouldn't Make." *Harvard Business Review* 80.11 (2002): 84–91.

Weill, Peter, Mani Subramani, and Marianne Broadbent. "Building IT Infrastructure for Strategic Agility." *MIT Sloan Management Review* 44.1 (2002): 57–65.

Books

Boar, Bernard H. *The Art of Strategic Planning for Information Technology.* 2nd ed. New York: Wiley, 2000.

Devaraj, Sarv, and Rajiv Kohli. *The IT Payoff: Measuring the Business Value of Information Technology Investments.* New York: Financial Times Prentice Hall, 2002.

Pearlson, Keri E. *Managing and Using Information Systems: A Strategic Approach.* New York: Wiley, 2001.

Question 5: Bleeding-, leading-, or following-edge

Web Resources

Internet.com: IT Management—IT Management Trends. <http://itmanagement.earthweb.com/it_mgmt_trends>.

Articles

Huisman, Kuno J. M., and Peter M. Kort. "Strategic Investment in Technological Innovations." *European Journal of Operational Research* 144.1 (2003): 209–23.

Oliver, Richard W. "Compensating for the Zero Sweet Spot." *Journal of Business Strategy* 23.3 (2002): 6–8.

Roberts, Edward B. "Benchmarking Global Strategic Management of Technology," *Research Technology Management* 44.2 (2001): 25–36.

Books

McKenney, James L., Duncan C. Copeland, and Richard O. Mason. *Waves of Change: Business Evolution through Information Technology*. Boston: HBSP, 1995.

Moore, Geoffrey A. *Crossing the Chasm: Marketing and Selling High-Tech Products to Mainstream Customers*. New York: HarperBusiness, 1999.

———. *Inside the Tornado: Marketing Strategies from Silicon Valley's Cutting Edge*. New York: HarperBusiness, 1995.

Rapp, William V. *Information Technology Strategies: How Leading Firms Use It to Gain Advantage*. New York: Oxford UP, 2002.

Weill, Peter, and Marianne Broadbent. *Leveraging the New Infrastructure: How Market Leaders Capitalize on Information Technology*. Boston: HBSP, 1998.

Question 6: Mass customization

Web Resources

TheManager.org: Management—Mass Customization. <http://www.themanager.org/Knowledgebase/Management/Mass.htm>.

Articles

Fitzgerald, Brian. "Mass Customization—At a Profit." *World Class Design to Manufacture* 43.1 (1995): 43–46.

Zipkin, Paul. "The Limits of Mass Customization." *MIT Sloan Management Review* 42.3 (2001): 81–87.

Books

Gilmore, James H., and B. Joseph Pine, eds. *Markets of One: Creating Customer-Unique Value through Mass Customization*. Boston: HBSP, 2000.

McKenna, Regis. *Total Access: Giving Customers What They Want in an Anytime, Anywhere World*. Boston: HBSP, 2002.

Pine, B. Joseph. *Mass Customization: The New Frontier in Business Competition*. Boston: HBSP, 1993.

Question 7: Throwaway systems

Web Resources

Extreme Programming Web Site. <http://www.extremeprogramming.org>.
XProgramming.com. <http://www.xprogramming.com>.

R10

Articles

Bloomberg, Jason. "Software Methodologies on Internet Time." *developer.com* Oct. 1999.
    <http://www.developer.com/java/other/article.php/616711>.
Card, David N. "The RAD Fad: Is Timing Really Everything?" *IEEE Software* Sept. 1995:
    19–22.
Jones, Bradley L. "eXtreme Programming." *developer.com* 2002. <http://www.developer.com/
    tech/article.php/761841>.

Books

Harmon, Paul, Michael Rosen, and Michael Guttman. *Developing E-Business Systems and
    Architectures: A Manager's Guide.* San Diego: Academic Press, 2001.
McConnell, Steve. *Rapid Development: Taming Wild Software Schedules.* Redmond: Microsoft
    Press, 1996.

SECTION 2. INFORMATION TECHNOLOGY

Questions 8, 9, and 10: IT architecture

Web Resources

Carnegie Mellon Software Engineering Institute Web Site. <http://www.sei.cmu.edu/str/
    descriptions/clientserver.html>.
developer.com: Architecture and Design Articles. <http://www.developer.com/design>.
ITPapers.com: Systems Architecture. <http://www.itpapers.com/cgi/SubcatIT.pl?scid=79>.
Java 2 Platform Enterprise Edition Web Site. <http://java.sun.com/j2ee>.
Microsoft .NET Web Site. <http://www.microsoft.com/net>.

Articles

Broadbent, Marianne. "IT Architecture Matters." *CIO.com (Australia)* 9 Oct. 2002. <http://
    www.cio.com.au/idg2.nsf/AllCIO/31BB4ECEAF61DB1CCA256C480004CCCB?
    OpenDocument>.
Hay, Gordon, and Rick Munoz. "Establishing an IT Architecture Strategy." *Information Sys-
    tems Management* 14.3 (1997): 67–69.
Laartz, Jurgen, Ernst Sonderregger, and Johan Vinckier. "The Paris Guide to IT Architec-
    ture." *McKinsey Quarterly* 3 (2000): 118–27.
Mayor, Tracy. "Back to the Drawing Board." *CIO.com* 1 Aug. 2001. <http://www.cio.com/
    archive/080101/board.html>.

Muller, Gerrit. "The System Architecture Process." *Philips Research Extra Web Site* 18 Mar. 2003. <http://www.extra.research.philips.com/natlab/sysarch/SystemArchitectureProcessPaper.pdf>.

Schneider, Polly. "Blueprint for Harmony" *CIO.com* 1 Sept. 1999. <http://www.cio.com/archive/090199/acrimony.html>.

Books

Cook, Melissa A. *Building Enterprise Information Architectures*. Upper Saddle River: Prentice Hall, 1996.

Khanna, R. *Distributed Computing: Implementation and Management Strategies*. Englewood Cliffs: Prentice Hall, 1993.

Strassman, Paul A. *The Politics of Information Management*. New Canaan: Information Economics, 1995.

Question 11: Client/server

Web Resources

Client Server News Web Site. <http://www.g2news.com/clientservernews.html>.
N-Tier.com. <http://www.n-tier.com>.

Articles

"Client/Server Fundamentals." *Network Computing Web Site* 8 Feb. 1999. <http://www.networkcomputing.com/netdesign/1005part1f.html>.

Fabris, Peter. "Client/Server Revisited." *CIO.com* 1 Sept. 1996. <http://www.cio.com/archive/090196_client.html>.

Sadoski, Darleen. "Client/Server Software Architectures—An Overview." *Carnegie Mellon Software Engineering Institute Web Site* 2 Aug. 1997. <http://www.sei.cmu.edu/str/descriptions/clientserver.html>.

Books

Edwards, Jeri. *3-Tier Client/Server at Work*. Rev. ed. New York: Wiley, 1999.

Orfali, Robert, Dan Harkey, and Jeri Edwards. *Client/Server Survival Guide*. 3rd ed. New York: Wiley, 1999.

Question 12: Fat/thin client

Web Resources

Business 2.0: Web Guide—Thin Client Computing. <http://www.business2.com/webguide/0,1660,4098,00.html>.

Giga Information Group Web Site. <http://www.gigaweb.com>.

Articles

Angel, Jonathan. "Decreasing TCO with Thin Clients." *Network Magazine.com* 1 Apr. 2000. <http://www.networkmagazine.com /article/ NMG20000508S0028>.

Crothers, Brooke. "Straight Talk on 'Thin Clients.'" *CNET* 8 Oct. 1996. <http://news.com .com /2100-1001-236247.html?legacy=cnet>.

Halfhill, Tom. "Cheaper Computing—Part 1." *Byte.com* Apr. 1997. <http://www.byte.com/ art /9704/sec6/art1.htm>.

Shankland, Stephen. "Sun Keeps Plugging at Thin Clients." *CNET* 11 Apr. 2002. <http://news .com.com /2100-1001-881467.html>.

Books

Sinclair, Joseph T., and Mark S. Merkow. *Thin Clients Clearly Explained.* San Diego: Morgan Kaufmann, 2000.

R14 ━━

Question 13: Middleware   •

Web Resources

The Data Warehousing Information Center: Middleware Web Site. <http://www.dwinfocenter .org/middlewr.html>.

IEEE Distributed Systems Online: Middleware. <http://dsonline.computer.org/middleware/>.

Internet2: Middleware Web Site. <http://middleware.internet2.edu/>.

Articles

Bray, Mike. "Middleware." *Carnegie Mellon Software Engineering Institute Web Site* 25 June 1997. <http://www.sei.cmu.edu /activities/str/descriptions /middleware_body.html>.

Fontana, John. "Web Services: Where XML and Middleware Converge." *Network World Web Site* 24 Sept. 2001 <http://www.nwfusion.com /buzz2001/webserv>.

"Network Design Manual: What Is Middleware?" *Network Computing Web Site* 15 Nov. 1995. <http://www.networkcomputing.com /netdesign /cdmwdef.htm>.

Radding, Alan. "Middleware Evolution." *InformationWeek.com* 6 July 1998. <http://www .informationweek.com /690/90iumid.htm>.

Books

Myerson, Judith M. *The Complete Book of Middleware.* Boca Raton: Auerbach, 2002.

Question 14: XML

Web Resources

Darwin Executive Guides: XML Web Site. <http://guide.darwinmag.com /technology/ program /xml>.

XML.com: A Technical Introduction to XML. <http://www.xml.com/pub/a/98/10/guide0
.html>.
XMLFiles.com. <http://www.xmlfiles.com/xml>.

Articles

Grunner, Ron. "XML: Harnessing the Power for Your Investor Relations Web Site." *Strategic
Investor Relations* 1.4 (2001): 43–49.
Usdin, Tommie, and Tony Graham. "XML: Not a Silver Bullet, But a Great Pipe Wrench."
Standard View 6.3 (1998): 127–32.

Books

Dick, Kevin. *XML: A Manager's Guide.* Reading: Addison-Wesley, 2002.
Simon, Solomon Hank. *XML: eCommerce Solutions for Business and IT Managers.* New York:
McGraw-Hill, 2001.

Question 15: Web services

Web Resources

Line56.com: EAI and Web Services Topic Center. <http://www.line56.com/topics/default
.asp?TopicID=4>.
ZDNet: Web Services Update. <http://techupdate.zdnet.com/techupdate/filters/itdtoolkit/
0,15209,6024120,00.html>.

Articles

Hagel, John III. "The Strategic Value of Web Services." *The McKinsey Quarterly* Nov. 2002.
<http://www.mckinseyquarterly.com>.
Hagel, John III, and John Seely Brown. "Your Next IT Strategy." *Harvard Business Review* 79.9
(2001): 105–13.
Kalin, Sari. "The Essential Guide to Web Services." *Darwinmag.com* Jan. 2002. <http://www
.darwinmag.com/read/010102/essential.html>.
"The Promise of Web Services." *CIO.com* 15 Apr. 2002. <http://64.28.79.79/sponsors/
041502ws/webservices.pdf>.
TripleTree. "Web Services." *TripleTree Web Site.* Spotlight Report 5:1. 15 Feb. 2002. <http://
www.triple-tree.com/reports/WebServices.pdf>.

Books

Apshankar, Kapil, et al. *Web Services Business Strategies and Architectures.* Birmingham, UK:
Expert Press, 2002.

Question 16: Windows vs. Unix

Web Resources

Internet.com: Hardware and Systems—Systems Software. <http://hardware.earthweb
.com/hsos>.
OS Opinion Web Site. <http://www.osopinion.com/>.

Articles

R17 ▬

LeBlanc, Jon C. *Migrate with Confidence from Microsoft Windows Servers to UNIX/Linux:
Strategic Information for IT Executives and Managers.* White Paper. 8 Dec. 2002
<http://www.cuug.ab.ca/~leblancj/nt_to_unix.html>.
Shankland, Stephen. "Windows Inches Up on Unix." *ZDNet* 10 Sept. 2002. <http://zdnet
.com.com/2100-1104-957226.html>.
Slater, Derek. "Deciding Factors." *CIO.com* 1 Feb. 2000. <http://www.cio.com/archive/
020100/opsys.html>.

Books

Frisch, Æleen. *Complete Windows NT & UNIX System Administration Pack.* 1st ed. Se-
bastopol: O'Reilly, 1999.

Question 17: Unix

Web Resources

Linux Online. <http://www.linux.org>.
LinuxInsider.com. <http://www.linuxinsider.com>.
The Open Group: The Unix System Web Site. <http://www.unix.org>.

Articles

Jahnke, Art. "Is It Time to Start Running Linux?" *CIO.com* 15 Aug. 2002. <http://comment
.cio.com/soundoff/081502.html>.
Stevenson, Cooper. "Blueprint for Linux in the Enterprise." White Paper. *Metasource Tech-
nologies* 23 Feb. 2003. <http://www.metasource.us/linux.pdf>.
Valdés, Ray. "The Perils of Platform Selection." *New Architect* (formerly *Web Techniques*)
Mar. 2000. <http://www.newarchitectmag.com/archives/2000/03/plat/>.

Books

Stallings, William. *Computer Organization and Architecture: Designing for Performance.* 5th ed.
Upper Saddle River: Prentice Hall, 2000.
Vaughn, Larry T. *Client/Server System Design and Implementation.* New York: McGraw-Hill,
1994.

Question 18: Transaction processing systems

Web Resources

ITPapers.com: Transaction Processing. <http://www.itpapers.com/cgi/SubcatIT.pl?scid=78>.
Transaction Processing Performance Council Web Site. <http://www.tpc.org>.

Articles

Allamaraju, Subrahmanyam. "Nuts and Bolts of Transaction Processing." *Subrahmanyam Al-lamaraju Web Site* 2 Mar. 2002. <http://www.subrahmanyam.com/articles/transactions/NutsAndBoltsOfTP.html>.

Frolund, Svend, Fernando Pedone, and Jim Pruyne. "Web e-Transactions." HP Labs Technical Report HP-2001-177. *Hewlett Packard Company Web Site* 7 July 2001. <http://www.hpl.hp.com/techreports/2001/HPL-2001-177.html>.

Sequent. "Online Transaction Processing (OLTP)." *DM Review Web Site* 2002. <http://www.dmreview.com/master.cfm?NavID=61&WhitePaperID=175>.

Books

Gray, Jim, and Andreas Reuter. *Transaction Processing Concepts and Techniques.* San Mateo: Morgan Kaufmann, 1993.

Question 19: Decision support systems

Web Resources

Business 2.0: Web Guide—Corporate Planning: Decision Making. <http://www.business2.com/webguide/0,1660,51942,00.html>.
Decision Support Systems Resources Web Site. <http://dssresources.com>.
Decision Support Systems Web Site. <http://www.elsevier.com/homepage/sae/orms/dss/menu.htm>.

Articles

Power, Daniel J. "What Is a Decision Support System?" *On-line Executive Journal for Data-Intensive Decision Support* 21 Oct. 1997. <http://dssresources.com/papers/whatisadss/index.html>.

Books

Dhar, Vasant, and Roger Stein. *Intelligent Decision Support Methods: The Science of Knowledge.* Upper Saddle River: Prentice Hall, 1997.

Power, Daniel J. *Decision Support Systems: Concepts and Resources for Managers.* Westport: Greenwood Publishing, 2002.

Turban, Efraim. *Decision Support and Expert Systems: Management Support Systems.* 3rd ed. New York: Macmillan, 1993.

Question 20: Data warehouses

Web Resources

The Data Warehousing Information Center Web Site. <http://www.dwinfocenter.org>.
The Data Warehousing Institute: Journal of Data Warehousing Web Site. <http://www.
dw-institute.com/research/display.asp?id=5119>.
DM Review Web Site. <http://www.dmreview.com>.

Articles

R21

"A Practical Guide to Getting Started in Data Warehousing." *IBM Web Site* 1999. <http://
www-3.ibm.com/e-business/doc/content/resource/pdf/26250.pdf>.
Boar, Bernard H. "Understanding Data Warehousing Strategically." *Carleton Australia Web
Site* n.d. <http://www.carleton.com.au/Understanding%20Data%20Warehousing%
20Strategically.htm>.
Gupta, Vivek R. "An Introduction to Data Warehousing." *System Services Corporation Web
Site* Aug. 1997. <http://system-services.com/dwintro.asp>.

Books

Kimball, Ralph. *Data Warehouse Toolkit.* 2nd ed. New York: Wiley, 2002.
Inmon, William H. *Building the Data Warehouse.* 3rd ed. New York: Wiley, 2002.
Inmon, William H., et al. *Corporate Information Factory.* 2nd ed. New York: Wiley, 2000.

Question 21: Data mining

Web Resources

*The Data Management Center: Directory of Data Warehouse, Data Mining and Decision Sup-
port Resources.* <http://www.infogoal.com/dmc/dmcdwh.htm>.
The Data Mine Web Site. <http://www.the-data-mine.com>.
DM Review: Resource Portal—Data Mining Web Site. <http://www.dmreview.com/portal
.cfm?NavID=9&Topic=1&PortalID=9>.

Articles

Schwenk, Helena. "OVUM Evaluates: OLAP." *Ovum Web Site* 2002. <http://www.ovum
.com/go/product/flyer/EI3.htm>.
"What Is Data Mining?" *Megaputer Intelligence, Inc. Web Site* 2002. <http://www.megaputer
.com/dm/dm101.php3>.

Books

Delmater, Rhonda, and Monte Hancock. *Data Mining Explained: A Manager's Guide to
Customer-Centric Business Intelligence.* Boston: Digital Press, 2001.

Groth, Robert. *Data Mining: A Hands-on Approach for Business Professionals*. Upper Saddle River: Prentice Hall, 1998.

Kudyba, Stephan, and Richard Hoptroff. *Data Mining and Business Intelligence: A Guide to Productivity*. Hershey: Idea Group Publishing, 2001.

Question 22: Group support systems

Web Resources

Kluwer Online: Computer Supported Cooperative Work—The Journal of Collaborative Computing. <http://www.kluweronline.com/issn/0925-9724>.

Articles

Burke, Kelly. "E-Collaboration: Working Together, Being Apart." *e-Service Journal* 1.3 (2002): 1–3.

Damian, Daniela. "An Empirical Study of a Multimedia Group Support System for Distributed Software Requirements Meetings." *e-Service Journal* 1.3 (2002): 43–60.

Hoxmeier, John A., and Kenneth A. Kozar. "Electronic Meetings and Subsequent Meeting Behaviour: Systems as Agents of Change." *Journal of Applied Management Studies* 9.2 (2002): 177–95.

Nunamaker, J. F., et al. "Electronic Meeting Systems to Support Group Work." *Communications of the ACM* 34.7 (1991): 40–61.

Parent, Michael, and R. Brent Gallupe. "Knowledge Creation in Focus Groups: Can Group Technologies Help?" *Information & Management* 38.1 (2000): 47–58.

Books

Andriessen, Erik. *Working with Groupware: Understanding and Evaluating Collaboration Technology*. Berlin: Springer Verlag, 2002.

Chaffey, Dave. *Groupware, Workflow and Intranets : Reengineering the Enterprise with Collaborative Software*. Boston: Digital Press, 1999.

Questions 23 and 24: Networks

Web Resources

Computerworld.com Networking Knowledge Center. <http://www.computerworld.com/networkingtopics/networking>.

Internet.com: Networking and Communications—Network Hardware. <http://networking.earthweb.com/nethub>.

ZDNet: Reviews—Networking. <http://www.zdnet.com/products/filter/guide/0,7267,6001332,00.html>.

Articles

"Networking Essentials for Small and Medium-Sized Businesses." *Cisco Web Site* n.d. <http://www.cisco.com/warp/public/779/smbiz/netguide/>.

Slater, Derek. "The Corporate Skeleton." *CIO.com* 15 Dec. 1998/1 Jan. 1999. <http://www.cio.com/archive/010199/fadap.html>.

"Small Business Solutions." *3Com Corporation Web Site* n.d. <http://www.3com.com/solutions/en_US/index.jsp?solutiontype=1000003>.

"What Is Architecture?" White Paper. *The Burton Group Web Site* 2000. <http://www.burtongroup.com/Public/Downloads/Pdf/whatis.PDF>.

Books

Gallo, Michael A., and William M. Hancock. *Networking Explained.* 2nd ed. Boston: Digital Press, 2002.

Held, Gilbert. *Understanding Data Communications.* 7th ed. Boston: Addison-Wesley, 2002.

Tanenbaum, Andrew. *Computer Networks.* 4th ed. Upper Saddle River: Prentice Hall, 2003.

R25 ▬▬

Question 25: Voice vs. data networks

Web Resources

Business Communications Review Web Site. <http://www.bcr.com>.

Business 2.0: Web Guide—Voice Technologies. <http://www.business2.com/webguide/0,1660,208,00.html>.

Articles

Angus, Ian. "Who Put the Con in Convergence?" *Business Communications Review* Mar. 2002: 28–32.

Emmerson, Bob. "Convergence: The Business Case for IP Telephony." White Paper. *Webtorials.Com.* Electronic Words. Mar. 2002. <http://www.webtorials.com/main/resource/papers/emmerson/paper1/convergence.pdf>.

Morris, Noemy, et al. "Voice Over IP: A Primer for Datacom Professionals." *Webtorials.Com.* MCK Communications. 2001. <http://www.webtorials.com/main/resource/papers/mck/paper1/4data/voip4data.pdf>.

Rigney, Steve. "Building an Integrated Network." *Voice 2000: Supplement to Business Communications Review* Sept. 2000: 14+.

Books

Harte, Lawrence. *Voice over Data Networks for Managers.* Bucuresti: Athos, 2003.

Question 26: The Internet

Web Resources

About.com: Internet for Beginners. <http://netforbeginners.about.com/index.htm>.
Internet Society Web Site. <http://www.isoc.org>.
Suite101.com: E-Business Basics. <http://www.suite101.com/welcome.cfm/e_business_
    basics>.
World Wide Web Consortium Web Site. <http://www.w3c.org/>.

Articles

"Internet." *Marketing News* 2 July 2001: 12–13.
Ryan, Jerry, ed. "The Internet and e-Business Opportunities." *ITPapers.com.* Technology
    Guide Series. Jan. 2000. <http://www.itpapers.com/techguide/ebus.pdf>.

Books

Atkins, Derek, et al., eds. *Internet Security Professional Reference.* 2nd ed. Indianapolis: New
    Riders, 1997.
Castells, Manuel. *The Internet Galaxy: Reflections on the Internet, Business, and Society.*
    Oxford: Oxford UP, 2001.

Question 27: Broadband

Web Resources

Broadband Week Online. <http://www.broadbandweek.com>.
Cable Television Laboratories, Inc. Web Site. <http://www.cablelabs.com>.
Federal Communications Commission: Broadband Web Site. <http://www.fcc.gov/
    broadband>.
The Internet Engineering Task Force Web Site. <http://www.ietf.org>.
Nielsen//Netratings Web Site. <http://www.nielsen-netratings.com>.

Articles

Grant, Peter. "Comcast Shows Broadband Is Hitting Its Stride." *Wall Street Journal* 29 Oct.
    2002: A3.
Woolley, Scott. "Bottleneck Breakers." *Forbes* 11 Nov. 2002: 106–8.

Books

Tanenbaum, Andrew. *Computer Networks.* 4th ed. Upper Saddle River: Prentice Hall, 2003.

Questions 28 and 29: Wireless

Web Resources

developer.com: Newest Wireless/Mobile Articles. <http://www.developer.com/ws>.
Wireless NewsFactor Web Site. <http://wirelessnewsfactor.com>.

Articles

Beal, Alex, et al. *The Future of Wireless: Different Than You Think, Bolder Than You Imagine.*
  Accenture Institute for Strategic Change. Report. June 2001.
Kanell, Michael. "Big Network Off Campus." *CIO.com* 15 Mar. 2003. <http://www.cio.com/
  archive/031503/campus.html>.
"The Mobile Computing Market: The Big Picture." *Mobileinfo.com* 2001. <http://www
  .mobileinfo.com/market.htm>.
"Mobile Computing Outlook for 2002." *Mobileinfo.com* Jan. 2002.
  <http://www.mobileinfo.com/Market/market_outlook_2002.htm>.
Srivatsan, Nagaraja. "Making Wireless Work." *CIO* 1 July 2001. <http://www.cio.com/
  archive/070101/expert.html>

Books

Paavilainen, Jouni. *Mobile Business Strategies: Understanding the Technologies and Opportunities.* Boston: Addison-Wesley, 2002.
Sadeh, Norman. *M Commerce: Technologies, Services, and Business Models.* New York: Wiley,
  2002.
Stallings, William. *Wireless Communications & Networks.* Upper Saddle River: Prentice Hall,
  2001.

Question 30: Security

Web Resources

Computer Security Institute Web Site. <http://www.gocsi.com>.
International Information Systems Security Certification Consortium, Inc. Web Site. <http://
  www.isc2.org>.
PricewaterhouseCoopers: Security and Privacy Solutions Web Site. <http://www.pwcglobal
  .com/security>.

Articles

Clarke, Richard A., and Howard A. Schmidt. "National Strategy to Secure Cyberspace." *White
  House Web Site* 18 Sept. 2002. <http://www.whitehouse.gov/pcipb>.
Gregory, Peter H. "Keep IT Managers on Top of Security." *Computerworld.com* 8 Nov. 2002.
  <http://www.computerworld.com/securitytopics/security/story/0,10801,75748,00.html>.

Ross, Jeanne W., and Peter Weill. "Six IT Decisions Your IT People Shouldn't Make." *Harvard Business Review* 80.11 (2002): 84–91.

Books

Krause, Micki, and Harold F. Tipton, eds. *Information Security Management Handbook*. 4th ed. Boca Raton: Auerbach, 2002.

Shipley, Greg. *Maximum Security: A Hacker's Guide to Protecting Your Internet Site and Network*. 3rd ed. Indianapolis: Sams, 2001.

Question 31: Firewalls

Web Resources

Computerworld.com: Security Knowledge Center—Firewall. <http://www.computerworld.com/securitytopics/security/firewall?from=top>.

InfoSysSec: Firewall Security and the Internet Web Site. <http://www.infosyssec.com/infosyssec/firew1.htm>.

Articles

Radcliff, Deborah. "Picking a Winner." *Computerworld.com* 12 Aug. 2002. <http://www.computerworld.com/securitytopics/security/firewall/story/0,10801,73349,00.html>.

Tweney, Dylan. "False Alarms on the Firewall." *Business 2.0 Web Site* 15 Nov. 2002. <http://www.business2.com/articles/web/0,1653,45262,FF.html>.

Books

Cheswick, William R., and Steven M. Bellovin. *Firewalls and Internet Security: Repelling the Wily Hacker*. Boston: Addison-Wesley, 1994.

Shipley, Greg. *Maximum Security: A Hacker's Guide to Protecting Your Internet Site and Network*. 3rd ed. Indianapolis: Sams, 2001.

Zwicky, Elizabeth D., Simon Cooper, and D. Brent Chapman. *Building Internet Firewalls*. 2nd ed. Cambridge: O'Reilly, 2000.

Question 32: Viruses

Web Resources

Edmonton Community Network: FAQ—Viruses, Trojan Horses and Worms. <http://www.freenet.edmonton.ab.ca/helpdesk/FAQ_NOTE/FAQ_VRS.HTM>.

McAfee.com Corporation Web Site. <http://www.mcafee.com>.

PageWise: How Computer Viruses Work Web Site. <http://www.allsands.com/Science/computervirusi_ol_gn.htm>.

Symantec Corporation Web Site. <http://www.symantec.com>.

Articles

Lyman, Jay. "How Computer Worms Work—and Why They Never Die." *NewsFactor Network* 13 Nov. 2001. <http://www.newsfactor.com/perl/story/14733.html>.

Stewart, Bruce. "How to Protect against Computer Viruses." *ZDNet* 12 Feb. 2001. <http://www.zdnet.com/products/stories/reviews/0,4161,2248291-1,00.html>.

Books

PriceWaterhouseCoopers. *Risk Management Forecast 2001: Creating Trust in the E-Business World*. Jersey City: PriceWaterhouseCoopers, 2001.

Shipley, Greg. *Maximum Security: A Hacker's Guide to Protecting Your Internet Site and Network*. 3rd ed. Indianapolis: Sams, 2001.

Question 33: Disaster recovery planning

R34 ◼━━

Web Resources

American Red Cross: Business and Industry Guide Web Site. <http://www.redcross.org/services/disaster/beprepared/busi_industry.html>.

Association of Contingency Planners Web Site. <http://www.acp-international.com/>.

Business 2.0: Web Guide—Disaster Management. <http://www.business2.com/webguide/0,1660,878,00.html>.

Contingency Planning and Management Web Site. <http://www.contingencyplanning.com/>.

Disaster Recovery Journal Web Site. <http://www.drj.com/>.

Articles

Ball, Leslie D. "CIO on Center Stage: 9/11 Changes Everything." *Information Systems Management* 19.2 (2002): 8–11.

Wahle, Thomas, and Gregg Beatty. "Emergency Management Guide for Business and Industry." *FEMA Web Site* n.d. <http://www.fema.gov/library/bizindex.shtm>.

Books

Meyers, Kenneth N. *Manager's Guide to Contingency Planning for Disasters: Protecting Vital Facilities and Critical Operations*. New York: Wiley, 1999.

━━━   SECTION 3. IT AND E-BUSINESS

Question 34: E-business strategy

Web Resources

Line56.com: E-Markets Topic Center. <http://www.line56.com/topics/default.asp?TopicID=8>.

StrategyPortal. <http://www.strategyportal.co.uk>.

Articles

Porter, Michael E. "Strategy and the Internet." *Harvard Business Review* 79.3 (2001): 62–78.

Varon, Elana. "The New Lords of E-biz." *CIO.com* 15 Mar. 2003. <http://www.cio.com/archive/031503/lords.html>.

Books

Barrenechea, Mark. *E-Business or Out of Business*. New York: McGraw-Hill, 2001.

Hamel, Gary. *Leading the Revolution*. Boston: HBSP, 2000.

Kalakota, Ravi, and Andrew Whinston. *Electronic Commerce: A Managers Guide*. Reading: Addison-Wesley, 1997.

Means, Grady, and David Schneider. *MetaCapitalism*. New York: Wiley, 2000.

Tapscott, Don, David Ticoll, and Alex Lowy. *Digital Capital: Harnessing the Power of Business Webs*. Boston: HBSP, 2000.

Questions 35 and 36: E-business revenue and costs

Web Resources

Business 2.0: Web Guide—E-Business Transformation. <http://www.business2.com/webguide/0,1660,34286,00.html>.

CIO.com: IT Value Research Center. <http://www.cio.com/research/itvalue>.

Articles

Barua, Anitesh, et al. "Making E-Business Pay: Eight Key Drivers for Operational Success." *Center for Research in Electronic Commerce at the University of Texas at Austin Web Site*. Nov./Dec. 2000. <http://cism.bus.utexas.edu/works/articles/f6barua.pdf>.

Connolly, P. J. "Top 10 Rules for E-Business Success." *InfoWorld Web Site* 7 Dec. 2000, <http://www.infoworld.com/articles/tc/xml/00/12/11/001211tcrules.xml>.

"Define and Sell." *Economist* 26 Feb. 2000: 6–9.

Hagel, John III, and John Seely Brown. "Your Next IT Strategy." *Harvard Business Review* 79.9 (2001): 105–13.

"How Dell Keeps from Stumbling." *BusinessWeek* 14 May 2001: 38B-39B.

Siekman, Philip. "How a Tighter Supply Chain Extends the Enterprise as Companies Go to the Internet to Cut Costs, the Boundary Is..." *Fortune Web Site* 8 Nov. 1999. <http://www.fortune.com/fortune/articles/0,15114,374363,00.html>.

Slater, Derek. "GM Shifts Gears." *CIO.com* 1 Apr. 2002. <http://www.cio.com/archive/040102/matters.html>.

Books

Shaw, Jack, and Judy Sperry, eds. *Surviving the Digital Jungle: What Every Executive Needs to Know about eCommerce and eBusiness*. Marietta: Electronic Commerce Strategies, 2000.

Questions 37 and 38: E-business models

Web Resources

Business 2.0: Web Guide—E-Commerce. <http://www.business2.com/webguide/0,,122,00.html>.

Managing the Digital Enterprise: Business Models on the Web. <http://digitalenterprise.org/models/models.html>.

Internet.com: ecommerce-guide.com. <http://ecommerce.internet.com>.

Articles

Applegate, Lynda M. *Overview of E-Business Models.* HBSP. Case 9-801-172. 30 Aug. 30, 2000.

Barnes-Vieyra, Pamela, and Cindy Claycomb. "Business-to-Business E-commerce: Models and Managerial Decisions." *Business Horizons* 44.3 (2001): 13–20.

Dubosson-Torbay, Magali, Alexander Osterwalder, and Yves Pigneur. "E-Business Model Design, Classification, and Measurement." *Thunderbird International Business Review* 44.1 (2002): 5–23.

Malhotra, Yogesh. "Enabling Knowledge Exchanges for E-Business Communities." *Information Strategy: The Executives Journal* 18.3 (2002): 26–31.

Trombly, Richard. "E-Business Models." *Computerworld.com* 4 Dec. 2000. <http://www.computerworld.com/industrytopics/retail/story/0,10801,54589,00.html>.

Weill, Peter, and Michael Vitale. "What IT Infrastructure Capabilities Are Needed to Implement eBusiness Models?" *MIS Executive Quarterly* 1.1 (2002): 17–34.

Books

Afuah, Allan, and Christopher L. Tucci. *Internet Business Models and Strategies: Text and Cases.* 2nd ed. Boston: Irwin/McGraw-Hill, 2001.

Kalakota, Ravi, and Marcia Robinson. *e-Business 2.0.* Boston: Addison-Wesley, 2001.

Weill, Peter, and Michael Vitale. *Place to Space: Migrating to eBusiness Models.* Boston: HBSP, 2001.

Question 39: Bricks and clicks

Web Resources

Business 2.0: Web Guide—E-commerce: Clicks and Mortar. <http://www.business2.com/webguide/0,1660,57917,00.html>.

Articles

Grimes, Ann. "What's in Store?" *Wall Street Journal* 15 July 2002, R6.

Teresko, John. "Adding Clicks to Bricks." *IndustryWeek.com* 18 Sept. 2000. <http://www.industryweek.com/CurrentArticles/Asp/articles.asp?ArticleId=901>.

Wingfield, Nick. "Click and . . . Drive?" *Wall Street Journal* 15 July 2002, R11.

Books

Liautaud, B. *E-Business Intelligence: Turning Information into Knowledge into Profit.* New York: McGraw-Hill, 2000.

McKenzie, R. *The Relationship Based Enterprise: Powering Business Success through Customer Relationship Management.* Montreal: McGraw-Hill Ryerson, 2000.

McMahon, E. *Bricks to Clicks: Strategies That Will Transform Your Business.* Toronto: Stoddard, 2000.

Timacheff, S., and D. Rand. *From Bricks to Clicks: 5 Steps to Creating a Durable Online Brand.* New York: McGraw-Hill, 2001.

Question 40: E-business and customers

Web Resources

eCRM Magazine Web Site. <http://www.ecrmmagazine.com>.
eMarket News Web Site. <http://www.emarketnews.com>.

Articles

Fisher, Andrew. "New Ways to Win Over Fickle Clients: In the Battle for Profits, Companies Are Turning to Customer Relationship Management (CRM) Systems." *Financial Times* 17 Oct. 2001: 1.

Levine, Shira. "Clicking on the Customer: Clickstream Analysis Can Improve Website Marketing and Efficiency." *America's Network* 1 Apr. 2000: 86.

Schwartz, Jeffrey. "Webcasts Tapped for More Than Meetings." *Business to Business* 6 May 2002: 1–2.

Books

Barnes, James. *Secrets of Customer Relationship Management.* New York: McGraw-Hill, 2001.

Bergeron, Bryan. *Essentials of CRM: A Guide to Customer Relationship Management.* New York: Wiley, 2002.

Haig, Matt. *The E-Marketing Handbook.* London: Kogan Page, 2001.

Sterne, Jim. *World Wide Web Marketing: Integrating the Web into Your Marketing Strategy.* New York: Wiley, 2001.

Question 41: E-business and privacy

Web Resources

Electronic Privacy Information Center. <http://www.epic.org>.
FTC.gov: Privacy Initiatives. <http://www.ftc.gov/privacy/index.html>.
Online Privacy Alliance. <http://www.privacyalliance.org>.

Privacy & American Business. <http://www.pandab.org>.

U.S. Department of Commerce: Safe Harbor Web Site. <http://www.export.gov/safeharbor>.

Articles

PricewaterhouseCoopers. "E-Privacy: Solving the On-Line Equation." *Global Risk Management Solutions.* Jersey City: PricewaterhouseCoopers, 2001.

Books

Merkow, Mark S., and James Breithaupt. *The E-Privacy Imperative: Protect Your Customers' Internet Privacy and Ensure Your Company's Survival in the Electronic Age.* New York: AMACOM, 2001.

Bentley, Tom. *Safe Computing: How to Protect Your Computer, Your Body, Your Data, Your Money and Your Privacy in the Information Age.* Concord: Untechnical Press, 2000.

Question 42: Intranets, extranets, and portals

Web Resources

CIO.com: Intranet/Extranet Resource Center. <http://www.cio.com/research/intranet>.
Intranet Journal Web Site. <http://www.intranetjournal.com>.
Line56.com: Portals Topic Center. <http://www.line56.com/topics/default.asp?TopicID=7>.

Articles

Bhatt, Anand, and Joe Fenner. "A Portal Odyssey." *Network Computing* 23 July 2001: 38–41.

Stuart, Anne, and Jill Hecht Maxwell. "Inside Story: Special Technology Report." *Inc.* April 2002: 94–99.

Varon, Elana. "Portals (Finally) Get Down to Business." *CIO.com* 1 Dec 2002. <http://www.cio.com/archive/120102/portals.html>.

Books

Collins, Heidi. *Corporate Portals: Revolutionizing Information Access to Increase Productivity and Drive the Bottom Line.* New York: AMACOM, 2000.

Davydov, Mark M. *Corporate Portals and e-Business Integration.* New York: McGraw-Hill, 2001.

Koehler, Jerry W., et al., eds. *The Human Side of Intranets: Content, Style, and Politics.* Boca Raton: St. Lucie Press, 1998.

Question 43: E-business technical elements

Web Resources

Business 2.0: Web Guide—E-Business Transformation. <http://www.business2.com/webguide/0,1660,34286,00.html>.

Articles

"Strategic Directions: E-Business: Payoffs & Partnerships." *CIO.com* July 2002. <http://www
.cio.com /sponsors /061502sd /sdebiz.pdf>.

Vu, John. "The eCommerce Capability Model." A Tutorial for SEPG 2002. *Carnegie Mellon:
Information Technology Services Qualification Center Web Site* Feb. 2002. <http://itsqc
.srv.cs.cmu.edu /eccm /SEI_SEPG_Tutorial_2002.pdf>.

Weill, Peter, and Michael Vitale. "What IT Infrastructure Capabilities Are Needed to Implement eBusiness Models?" *MIS Executive Quarterly* 1.1 (2002).

Books

Deise, Martin V., et al. *Executive's Guide to E-Business from Tactics to Strategy*. New York:
Wiley, 2000.

McKie, Stewart. *E-Business Best Practices*. New York: Wiley, 2001.

Seigel, David. *Futurize Your Enterprise*. New York: Wiley, 1999.

Slywotzky, Adrian J., and David Morrison. *How Digital Is Your Business?* New York: Crown
Business, 2000.

Question 44: Front- and back-end integration

Web Resources

ebizQ Web Site. <http://www.ebizq.net>.

IT Toolbox: EAI Knowledgebase Web Site. <http://eai.ittoolbox.com>.

Articles

Carr, David F. "Mix and Match: Custom Sites from Common Components." *Internet World*
1 Jan. 2001. <http://www.internetworld.com /magazine.php?inc=010101/01.01
.01internettech1.html>.

Fingar, Peter. "The Fourth Tier." *Internet World* 1 Apr. 2002. <http://www.internetworld
.com /magazine.php?inc=040102/04.01.02ebusiness2.html>.

Gonsalves, Antone. "Uniting Front-End Apps with Back /End Systems."
InformationWeek.com 15 Jan. 2002. <http://www.informationweek.com /story/
IWK20020115S0006>.

McKeen, J. D., and H. A. Smith. "New Developments in Practice II: Enterprise Application
Integration." *Communications of the Association for Information Systems* 8 (2002):
451–66.

Books

Fingar, Peter, and Ronald Aronica. *The Death of "e" and the Birth of the New Economy*.
Tampa: Meghan-Kiffer, 2001.

Linthicum, D. S. *B2B Application Integration*. Reading: Addison-Wesley, 2001.

Question 45: Dot.com crash

Web Resources

Business 2.0: Web Guide—Failed Dotcoms. <http://www.business2.com/webguide/
0,,42935,00.html?ref=wgtoc3>.
Harvard Business School Institute for Strategy and Competitiveness Web Site. <http://www
.isc.hbs.edu/index.html>.

Articles

Porter, Michael E. "Strategy and the Internet." *Harvard Business Review* 79.3 (2001): 62–78.
Upton, Molly. "Dot-Coms Feel Cruel Winds." ETrends Newsletter. *IDC Web Site* 23 Nov.
2000. <http://www.idc.com/getdoc.jhtml?containerId=ebt20001123>.
Young, Eric. "B-to-B's Broken Models." *The Industry Standard* 30 Oct. 2000. <http://www
.thestandard.com/article/display/0,1151,19693,00.html>.

Books

Fingar, Peter, and Ronald Aronica. *The Death of "e" and the Birth of the New Economy.*
Tampa: Meghan-Kiffer, 2001.
Shapiro, Carl, and Hal R. Varian. *Information Rules.* Boston: HBSP, 1999.
Turban, Efraim, et al. *Electronic Commerce 2002: A Managerial Perspective.* 2nd ed. New York: R47
Prentice Hall, 2002.

────── SECTION 4. IT AND ORGANIZATION

Questions 46 and 47: IT impact on organizations

Web Resources

Business 2.0: Web Guide—Organizational Behavior. <http://www.business2.com/webguide/
0,1660,69337,00.html>.
CIO.com: CIO Executive Research Center. <http://www.cio.com/research/executive>.

Articles

Borck, James R. "Automating Internal Workflow Drives Good E-Business." *InfoWorld
Web Site* 7 Dec. 2000. <http://www.infoworld.com/articles/tc/xml/00/12/11/
001211tcworkflow.xml>.
Krell, Terence C. "Organizational Longevity and Technological Change." *Journal of Organiza-
tional Change Management* 13.1 (2000): 8–14.
Mathieson, Kieran, and T. J. Wharton. "Are Information Systems a Barrier to Total Quality
Management?" *Journal of Systems Management* 44.9 (1993): 34–38.
Tsai, Wenpin. "Social Structure of 'Coopetition' within a Multiunit Organization: Coordina-
tion, Competition, and Intraorganizational Knowledge Sharing." *Organization Science*
13.2 (2002): 179–90.

Books

Davenport, Thomas H. *Process Innovation: Reengineering Work through Information Technology*. Boston: HBSP, 1993.

Kanter, Rosabeth Moss. *Evolve! Succeeding in the Digital Culture of Tomorrow*. Boston: HBSP, 2001.

Zuboff, Shoshana. *In the Age of the Smart Machine: The Future of Work and Power*. New York: Basic Books, 1988.

Question 48: Culture and IT

Web Resources

Business 2.0: Web Guide—Corporate Culture. <http://www.business2.com/webguide/0,1660,4569,00.html>.

Articles

Harper, G. R., and D. R. Utley. "Organizational Culture and Successful Information Technology Implementation." *Engineering Management Journal* 13.2 (2001): 11–15.

O'Reilly, C. A., J. A. Chatman, and D. F. Caldwell. "People and Organizational Culture: A Profile Comparison Approach to Assessing Person-Organization Fit." *Academy of Management Journal* 34 (1991): 487–516.

Zammuto, R. F., B. Gifford, and E. A. Goodman. "Managerial Ideologies, Organization Culture and the Outcomes of Innovation: A Competing Values Perspective." *The Handbook of Organizational Culture and Climate*. N. Ashkanasy, C. Wilderom, and M. Peterson, eds. 263–80. Thousand Oaks: Sage, 2000.

Zammuto, R. F., and E. J. O'Connor. "Gaining the Benefits of Advanced Manufacturing Technologies: The Roles of Organization Design and Culture." *Academy of Management Review* 17 (1992): 701–28.

Books

Quinn, Robert E. *Beyond Rational Management*. San Francisco: Jossey-Bass, 1988.

Schein, Edgar. *The Corporate Culture Survival Guide*. San Francisco: Jossey-Bass, 1999.

Question 49: Department reactions to IT

Web Resources

Business 2.0: Web Guide—Organizational Behavior. <http://www.business2.com/webguide/0,1660,69337,00.html>.

CIO.com: CIO Executive Research Center. <http://www.cio.com/research/executive>.

Articles

Clifford, Stephanie. "How to Get the Geeks and the Suits to Play Nice." *Business 2.0 Web Site*
    May 2002. <http://www.business2.com/articles/mag/0,1640,39246,FF.html>.
Moles, Cathy. "Organizational Behavior Briefing Book." *Florida State University Business Reference Webrary* n.d. <http://mailer.fsu.edu/~kshelfer/busrefpapers/orgbeh.html>.
Rockart, John F., and James E. Short. "The Networked Organization and the Management of
    Interdependence." *The Corporation of the 1990's*. M. S. Scott-Morton, ed. 189–219. New
    York: Oxford UP, 1991.

Books

Poirier, Charles C., and Michael J. Bauer. *E-Supply Chain: Using the Internet to Revolutionize
    Your Business*. San Francisco: Berrett-Koehler, 2000.

Question 50: IT, customers, and suppliers

Web Resources

BetterManagement.com. <http://www.bettermanagement.com/default.aspx>.
Business 2.0: Web Guide—Value-Chain Management. <http://www.business2.com/webguide/
    0,1660,6525,00.html>.

Articles   R51 ▬

Ange, David P. "Inter-firm Collaboration and Technology Development Partnerships within
    US Manufacturing Industries." *Regional Studies* 36.4 (2002): 333–44.
Belyea, Kathryn. "Pitney Bowes Transforms Itself for E-Business." *Purchasing* 24 Aug. 2000:
    135–37.
Devadas, Arj. "Interactive Business Portals," *Manufacturing Engineering* 125.4 (2000): 64–67.
Rotemberg, Julio J., and Garth Saloner. "Interfirm Competition and Collaboration." *The
    Corporation of the 1990's*. M. S. Scott-Morton, ed. 95–121. New York: Oxford UP, 1991.

Books

Richardson, Tom, Augusto Vidaurreta, and Tom Gorman. *Business Is a Contact Sport: Using
    the 12 Principles of Relationship Asset Management to Build Buy-In, Blast Away Barriers,
    and Boost Your Business*. Indianapolis: Alpha, 2002.

Question 51: Knowledge management

Web Resources

CIO.com: Knowledge Management Research Center. <http://www.cio.com/research/
    knowledge>.

Knowledge Management Network. <http://www.kmnetwork.com>.

Knowledge Management Resource Center Web Site. <http://www.kmresource.com>.

Articles

Alavi, M., and D. E. Leidner. "Knowledge Management and Knowledge Management Systems: Conceptual Foundations and Research Issues." *MIS Quarterly* 25.1 (2001): 107–36.

Jensen, Bill. "Communication or Knowledge Management?" *Communication World* June–July 1998: 44–47.

Kogut, B., and U. Zander. "Knowledge of the Firm, Combinative Capabilities and the Replication of Technology." *Organization Science* 3.3 (1992): 383–97.

McDermott, Richard. "Why Information Technology Inspired but Cannot Deliver Knowledge Management." *California Management Review* 41.4 (1999): 103–17.

Books

Liebowitz, J., ed. *Knowledge Management Handbook.* Boca Raton: CRC Press, 1999.

Question 52: E-learning

Web Resources

CIO.com: E-Learning Research Center. <http://www.cio.com/research/elearning>.

MIT: The Center for Advanced Educational Services (CAES) Web Site. <http://www-caes.mit.edu>.

Articles

Charles, Barrie. "E-Learning under the Spotlight." *IT Training* Oct. 2002: 5–7.

"e-Learning Found to Be Most Effective Way to Control Costs." *Managing Training & Development* 2.10 (2002): 6–7.

Hartigan Shea, Rachel. "E-Learning Today." *U.S. News & World Report* 28 Oct. 2002: 54–56.

Oakes, Kevin. "E-Learning." *T+D* Nov. 2002: 58–60.

Books

Horton, William. *Evaluating E-Learning.* Alexandria: American Society for Training & Development, 2001.

Rosenberg, Marc J. *E-Learning: Strategies for Delivering Knowledge in the Digital Age.* New York: McGraw-Hill, 2001.

Question 53: IT's relationship to the organization

Web Resources

Balanced Scorecard Collaborative, Inc. Web Site. <http://www.bscol.com>.
Business 2.0: Web Guide—Management Style. <http://www.business2.com/webguide/
0,1660,4570,00.html>.

Articles

Clifford, Stephanie. "How to Get the Geeks and the Suits to Play Nice." *Business 2.0 Web Site*
May 2002. <http://www.business2.com/articles/mag/0,1640,39246,FF.html>.

Rockart, John F., and James E. Short. "The Networked Organization and the Management
of Interdependence." *The Corporation of the 1990's.* M. S. Scott-Morton, ed. New York:
Oxford UP, 1991. 189–219.

Books

Harbour, Jerry L. *The Basics of Performance Measurement.* New York: Productivity, 1997.
Kaplan, Robert S., and David P. Norton. *The Balanced Scorecard.* Boston: HBSP, 1996.
Kaplan, Robert S., and David P. Norton. *The Strategy-Focused Organization: How Balanced
Scorecard Companies Thrive in the New Business Environment.* Boston: HBSP, 2000.
Nils-Goran, Olve, Jan Roy, and Magnus Wetter. *The Performance Drivers: A Practical Guide to
Using the Balanced Scorecard.* New York: Wiley, 1999.

R54 ▬

Question 54: Centralized vs. decentralized

Web Resources

CIO.com: Executive Research Center. <http://www.cio.com/research/executive>.

Articles

Andriole, Steve. "IT Management—The Organization of IT." *Internet.com* 7 Dec. 2001.
<http://itmanagement.earthweb.com/columns/bizalign/article/0,,2711_936101,00
.html>.

Berkman, Eric. "Next Stop: Centralization." *CIO.com* 15 Sept. 2001. <http://www.cio.com/
archive/091501/centralization_content.html>.

Champy, Jim. "A New Old Debate." *Computerworld.com* 29 Jan. 2001. <http://www
.computerworld.com/printthis/2001/0,4814,56967,00.html>.

Kontzer, Tony. "Centralization Redux For IT." *InformationWeek.com* 17 Sept. 2001.
<http://www.informationweek.com/story/IWK20010914S0008>.

Schuff, David, and Robert St. Louis. "Centralization vs. decentralization of application software." *Communications of the ACM* 44. 6 (2001): 88–94.

Books

Brown, Carol, and V. V. Sambamurthy. *Repositioning the IT Organization to Enable Business Transformation.* Cincinnati: Pinnaflex Educational Resources, 2000.

Question 55: Capability Maturity Model

Web Resources

Carnegie Mellon Software Engineering Institute: Capability Maturity Model Integration (CMMI) Web Site. <http://www.sei.cmu.edu/str/descriptions/cmmi.html>.

Articles

McGarry, Frank, and Bill Decker. "Attaining Level 5 in CMM Process Maturity," *IEEE Software* 19.6 (2002): 87–96.

McGibbon, Thomas. "A Business Case for Software Process Improvement Revised." Department of Defense Data and Analysis Center for Software (DACS). 30 Sept. 1999.

Phan, Dien D. "Software Quality and Management," *Information Systems Management* 18.1 (2001): 56–67.

Books

Burwick, Diane M. *How to Implement the CMM.* 2nd ed. Leicester, England: BPS Publications, 2001.

Dymond, Kenneth M. *A Guide to the CMM.* Annapolis: Process Transition, 1997.

Humphrey, Watts S. *Managing the Software Process.* Reading: Addison-Wesley, 1990.

Paulk, Mark C., Charles V. Weber, and Bill Curtis. *The Capability Maturity Model: Guidelines for Improving the Software Process.* Reading: Addison-Wesley, 1995.

Question 56: Measuring IT organization's success

Web Resources

Business 2.0: Web Guide—Business Performance Measurement. <http://www.business2.com/webguide/0,1660,51243,00.html>.

Meta Group, Inc. Web Site. <http://www.metagroup.com>.

Articles

Conrad, Kurt. "Measuring the Strategic Value of Information Technology Investments." *The Sagebrush Group Web Site* 1995. <http://www.sagebrushgroup.com/value.htm>.

Jones, Steve, and Jim Hughes. "IS Value and Investment Appraisal: A Case Study of a Local Authority." *The Electronic Journal of Information Systems Evaluation* n.d. <http://www.iteva.rug.nl/ejise/vol2/issue1/paper3/fr_pap.html>.

Shand, Dawne. "Service-Level Agreements." *Computerworld.com* 22 Jan. 2001. <http://www
.computerworld.com/databasetopics/data/datamining/story/0,10801,56572,00.html>.

Books

Devaraj, Sarv, and Rajiv Kohli. *The IT Payoff: Measuring the Business Value of Information
Technology Investments.* Upper Saddle River: Prentice Hall, 2002.

Kaplan, Robert S., and David P. Norton. *The Strategy-Focused Organization: How Balanced
Scorecard Companies Thrive in the New Business Environment.* Boston: HBSP, 2000.

Question 57: CIO tenure

Web Resources

CIO.com: Executive Research Center. <http://www.cio.com/research/executive>.

Internet.com: IT Management—Career and Staffing. <http://itmanagement.earthweb
.com/career>.

Articles

Karimi, Jahangir, Yash P. Gupta, and Toni M. Somers. "The Congruence Between a Firm's
Competitive Strategy and Information Technology Leader's Rank and Role." *Journal of
Management Information Systems* 13.1 (1996): 63–88.

Preston, Robert. "CEO, CIO Turnover Is Just Part of E-Transformation." *Internetweek.com*
8 Dec. 2000. <http://www.internetweek.com/columns00/rob120800.htm>.

Shand, Dawne. "Can This IT Department Deliver?" *Premier 100 IT Leaders 2001: Supplement
to Computerworld* 26 Mar. 2001: 40

R59

Strassman, Paul A. "The Price of Uncertain Leadership." *Computerworld* 10 Nov. 1997: 72.

Streveler, Dennis J. "Pity the Poor CIO." *Healthcare Business* Apr. 1998: 78.

Books

Frenzel, Carroll W. *Management of Information Technology.* Cambridge: Course Technology,
1999.

--- SECTION 5. IT AND BUSINESS PROCESSES

Questions 58 and 59: Business process and technology

Web Resources

BetterManagement.com: Process Management. <http://www.bettermanagement.com/
library/default.aspx?SubjectInitiative=81&Industry=0&MediaType=0&x=37&y=
6&PageControl=Results&CurrentPage=1>.

ITPapers.com: Business Processes. <http://www.itpapers.com/cgi/SubcatIT.pl?scid=83>.

Articles

Boehringer, Robert D. "Process Mapping and Business Process Redesign." *BetterManagement.com* n.d. <http://www.bettermanagement.com/Library/Library.aspx?LibraryID=4317>.

Davenport, Thomas H. "Putting the Enterprise into the Enterprise System." *Harvard Business Review* July–August (1998): 121–31.

Hammer, Michael, and Steven Stanton. "How Process Enterprises *Really* Work." *Harvard Business Review* November–December (1999): 108–18.

Wrenn, Joyce. "The IT Train That Could." *CIO.com* January 15, 2002. <http://www.cio.com/archive/011502/peer_content.html>.

Books

Davenport, Thomas H. *Process Innovation*. Boston: HBSP, 1993.

Fried, Louis. *Managing Information Technology in Turbulent Times*. New York: Wiley, 1995.

Jacka, J. Mike, and Paulette J. Keller. *Business Process Mapping: Improving Customer Satisfaction*. New York: Wiley, 2001.

Keen, Peter G. W. *The Process Edge: Creating Value Where It Counts*. Boston: HBSP, 1999.

Wilson, Ray W., and Paul Harsin. *Process Mastering: How to Establish and Document the Best Known Way to Do a Job*. New York: Productivity Press, 1998.

Question 60: Process transformation

Web Resources

ITPapers.com: Business Processes. <http://www.itpapers.com/cgi/SubcatIT.pl?scid=83>.

Articles

Schein, Edgar. "How Can Organizations Learn Faster? The Challenge of Entering the Green Room." *MIT Sloan Management Review* 34.2 (1993): 85–92.

Venkatramn, N. "IT-Induced Business Reconfiguration." *The Corporation of the 1990's*. M. S. Scott-Morton, ed. New York: Oxford UP, 1991. 122–58.

Books

Albhers Mohrman, Susan, et al. *Tomorrow's Organization: Crafting Winning Capabilities in a Dynamic World*. San Francisco: Jossey-Bass, 1998.

Culbert, Samuel. *Mind-Set Management: The Heart of Leadership*. London: Oxford UP, 1995.

Holman, Peggy, and Tom Devane. *The Change Handbook: Group Methods for Shaping the Future*. San Francisco: Berrett-Koehler, 1999.

Question 61: Radical vs. incremental change

Web Resources

Business 2.0: Web Guide—Organizational Change. <http://www.business2.com/webguide/0,1660,4563,00.html>.

ITPapers.com: Business Processes. <http://www.itpapers.com/cgi/SubcatIT.pl?scid=83>.

Articles

McKersie, Robert B., and Richard Walton. "Organizational Change." *The Corporation of the 1990's.* M. S. Scott-Morton, ed. New York: Oxford UP, 1991. 244–77.

Schein, Edgar. "How Can Organizations Learn Faster? The Challenge of Entering the Green Room." *MIT Sloan Management Review* 34.2 (1993): 85–92.

Stoddard, Donna, and Sirkka Jarvenpaa. "Reengineering Design Is Radical, Reengineering Change Is Not!" HBSP. Case 9-196-037. July 1995.

Books

Holman, Peggy, and Tom Devane. *The Change Handbook: Group Methods for Shaping the Future.* San Francisco: Berrett-Koehler, 1999.

Kotter, John. *Leading Change.* Boston: HBSP, 1996.

Lawler, Edward E., et al. *Strategies for High Performance Organizations—The CEO Report.* San Francisco: Jossey-Bass, 1998.

Question 62 and 63: Enterprise resource planning systems

Web Resources

R63

CIO.com: Enterprise Resource Planning Research Center. <http://www.cio.com/research/erp>.

darwinmag.com: Executive Guide—Enterprise Resource Planning. <http://guide.darwinmag.com/technology/enterprise/erp/index.html>.

Internet.com: IT Management—Enterprise Resource Planning. <http://itmanagement.earthweb.com/erp>.

ZDNet: ERP Update. <http://techupdate.cnet.com/enterprise/0-6119811-724-6733082.html>.

Articles

Cliffe, Sarah. "ERP Implementation: How to Avoid $100 Million Write-Offs." *Harvard Business Review* 77.1 (1999): 16–17.

Hong, Kyung-Kwon, and Young-Gul Kim. "The Critical Success Factors for ERP Implementation: An Organizational Fit Perspective." *Information & Management* 40.1 (2002): 25–40.

Mabert, Vincent A., Ashok Soni, and M. A. Venkataramanan. "Enterprise Resource Planning: Common Myths versus Evolving Reality." *Business Horizons* 44.3 (2001): 69–76.

Osterland, Andrew. "Blaming ERP." *CFO* Jan. 2000: 89–93.

Scott, Judy E., and Iris Vessey. "Managing Risks in Enterprise Systems Implementations." *Communications of the ACM* 45.4 (2002): 74–81.

Sumner, Mary. "Risk Factors in Enterprise-wide/ERP Projects." *Journal of Information Technology* 15.4 (2000): 317–27.

Wheatley, Malcolm. "ERP Disasters: Bet the Company; and Lose." *Financial Director* 1 Mar. 2000: 35.

Books

Davenport, Thomas H. *Mission Critical: Realizing the Promise of Enterprise Systems.* Boston: HBSP, 2000.

Wallace, Thomas F., and Michael H. Kremzar. *ERP: Making It Happen: The Implementers' Guide to Success with Enterprise Resource Planning.* 3rd ed. New York: Wiley, 2001.

Question 64: ERP and business process redesign

Web Resources

Brint.com: Business Process Reengineering. <http://www.brint.com/BPR.htm>.

Business 2.0: Web Guide—ERP (Enterprise Resource Planning). <http://www.business2.com/webguide/0,,774,00.html>.

Outsourcing Center: Outsourcing ERP Web Site. <http://www.outsourcing-erp.com/>.

TOTALsupplychain.com: Enterprise Systems Channel. <http://www.totalsupplychain.com/Channels/ES/ESHome.asp>.

Articles

Davenport, Thomas H. "Putting the Enterprise into the Enterprise System." *Harvard Business Review* 76.4 (1998): 121–31.

"ERP Redefines Itself." *Management Services* 46.10 (2002): 24–28.

Konicki, Steve, et al. "Break Out." *InformationWeek* 18 Dec. 2000: 65–71.

Books

Davenport, Thomas H. *Mission Critical: Realizing the Promise of Enterprise Systems.* Boston: HBSP, 2000.

Questions 65 and 66: Customer relationship management

Web Resources

CIO.com: Customer Relationship Management Research Center. <http://www.cio.com/research/crm>.

CRM-Forum Web Site. <http://www.crm-forum.com>.

CRMGuru.com. <http://www.crmguru.com>.

Montgomery Research, Inc.: CRM Project Web Site. <http://www.crmproject.com>.

ZDNet: CRM Update. <http://techupdate.zdnet.com/techupdate/filters/rc/0,14177,6020476,00.html>.

Articles

Crothers, Bill, and Philip Tamminga. *Looking Through the Customer's Lens.* Accenture. Point of View. n.d. <http://www.accenture.com/xdoc/en/ideas/Outlook/pov/customers_lens_pov_rev.pdf>.

"How Much Are Customer Relationship Management Capabilities Really Worth? What Every CEO Should Know." *Accenture Web Site* 2000. <http://www.accenture.com/xd/xd.asp?it=enWeb&xd=industries\communications\communications\comm_crmstudy.xml>.

Selden, Larry, and Geoffrey Colvin. "Will This Customer Sink Your Stock?" *Fortune* 30 Sept. 2002: 127–30.

Books

Bergeron, Bryan P. *Essentials of CRM: A Guide to Customer Relationship Management.* New York: Wiley, 2002.

Dyche, Jill. *The CRM Handbook: A Business Guide to Customer Relationship Management.* Boston: Addison-Wesley, 2001.

Freeland, John G. *The Ultimate CRM Handbook.* New York: McGraw-Hill, 2003.

McKenna, Regis. *Total Access.* Boston: HBSP, 2002.

Swift, Ronald S. *Accelerating Customer Relationships.* Upper Saddle River: Prentice Hall, October 2000.

R68

Questions 67 and 68: Supply chain management

Web Resources

CIO.com: Supply Chain Management Research Center. <http://www.cio.com/research/scm>.

IT Toolbox: Supply Chain Management Web Site. <http://supplychain.ittoolbox.com>.

Montgomery Research, Inc.: Achieving Supply Chain Excellence through Technology (ASCET) Web Site. <http://www.ascet.com>.

Supply Chain Management Review Web Site. <http://www.manufacturing.net/scm>.

Articles

Kanakamedala, Kishore, Vats Srivatsan, and Glenn Ramsdell. "Getting Supply Chain Software Right." *McKinsey Quarterly* 1 (2003): 78–85.

Koch, Christopher. "Four Strategies." *CIO.com* 1 Oct. 2000. <http://www.cio.com/archive/100100_four.html>.

Mount, Ian, and Brian Caulfield. "The Missing Link: What You Need to Know About Supply-Chain Technology." *Business 2.0 Web Site.* May 2001, 12 Dec. 2001. <http://www.business2.com/articles/mag/0,1640,11253,00.html>.

Siekman, Philip. "How a Tighter Supply Chain Extends the Enterprise as Companies Go to the Internet to Cut Costs, the Boundary Is . . ." *Fortune Web Site* 8 Nov. 1999. <http://www.fortune.com/fortune/articles/0,15114,374363,00.html>.

"Will Your Supply Chain Survive?" Report. Doc #07137. *Advisor.com* 12 Sept. 2000. <http://www.advisor.com/Articles.nsf/aid/LEEDH142>.

Books

Ayers, James B. *Handbook of Supply Chain Management.* Boca Raton: St. Lucie Press, 2001.

Chopra, Sunil, and Peter Meindl. *Supply Chain Management: Strategy, Planning and Operations.* Upper Saddle River: Prentice Hall, 2000.

Question 69: Customizing commercial-off-the-shelf software

Web Resources

ITPapers.com: Business Processes. <http://www.itpapers.com/cgi/SubcatIT.pl?scid=83>.

Articles

Beheshti, Jamshid, and John Dupuis. "Problems with COTS Software: A Case Study." *Proceedings of the 28th Annual Conference of the Canadian Association of Information Science,* May 28–30, 2000. <http://www.slis.ualberta.ca/cais2000/beheshti.htm>.

Hohpe, Gregor. "Stairway to Heaven." *Software Development* May 2002. <http://www.sdmagazine.com/documents/s=7134/sdm0205l/0205l.htm>.

Stephens, Early. "READY, SET, GO! (AGAIN)." *Software Development* July 1998. <http://www.sdmagazine.com/documents/s=769/sdm9807a/9807a.htm>.

Wallnau, Kurt C. "Commercial-Off-The-Shelf (COTS) Software: Five Key Implications for the System Architect." *Software Tech News* 1999. <http://www.dacs.dtic.mil/awareness/newsletters/technews2-3/cots.html>.

Wallnau, Kurt C., David Carney, and Bill Pollak. "How COTS Software Affects the Design of COTS-Intensive Systems." *news@sei interactive Web Site* June 1998. <http://interactive.sei.cmu.edu/Features/1998/June/COTS_Software/Cots_Software.htm>.

Books

Clements, Paul, Rick Kazman, and Mark Klein. *Evaluating Software Architectures: Methods and Case Studies*. Boston: Addison-Wesley, 2002.

———— SECTION 6. IT AND RESOURCE ALLOCATION

Question 70: Technology spending level

Web Resources

CIO.com: IT Value Research Center. <http://www.cio.com/research/itvalue>.
Computerworld.com: Management Knowledge Center—IT Spending Section. <http://www.computerworld.com/managementtopics/management/itspending>.

Articles

Kirkpatrick, David. "Beyond Buzzwords." *Fortune* 18 Mar. 2002: 80–84.
Kumar, K. "Technology for Supporting Supply Chain Management." *Communications of the ACM* 44.6 (2001): 74–79.
Mattern, Frank, Stephan Schonwalder, and Wolfram Stein. "Fighting Complexity in IT." *McKinsey Quarterly* 1 (2003): 56–65.
Ramachandran, Girish, and Sanjay Tiwari. "Challenges in the Air Cargo Supply Chain." *Communications of the ACM* 44. 6 (2001): 80–82.
Ross, Jeanne W., and Peter Weill. "Six IT Decisions Your IT People Shouldn't Make." *Harvard Business Review* 80.11 (2002): 84–91.

Books

Moore, Geoffrey A. *Living on the Fault Line—Managing for Shareholder Value in Any Economy*. Rev. ed. New York: HarperBusiness. 2002.
Stadtler, Hartmut, and Christoph Kilger, eds. *Supply Chain Management and Advanced Planning*. Berlin: Springer Verlag, 2002.

————————————————

R71

Question 71: Resource allocation

Web Resources

CIO.com: IT Value Research Center. <http://www.cio.com/research/itvalue>.
Computerworld.com: Management Knowledge Center—IT Spending Section. <http://www.computerworld.com/managementtopics/management/itspending>.

Articles

Berinato, Scott. "Do the Math." *CIO.com.* 1 Oct. 2001. <http://www.cio.com/archive/100101/math.html>.
Davis, Alan M. "The Art of Requirements Triangle." *Computer* 36. 3 (2003): 42–49.

Hennigan, Peter. "CIOs: Take IT Investment by the Horns." *TechRepublic* 30 Sept. 2002.
    ZDNet <http://www.zdnet.com/techupdate/stories/main/0,14179,2882000,00.html>.
"Make Flexible IT Investments." *Sprint Web Site* May 2002. <http://www.sprint.com/
    whitepapers/IT-Final.pdf>.

Books

Money, Arthur, et al. *The Effective Measurement and Management of IT Costs and Benefits.*
    Oxford: Butterworth-Heinemann, 2000.
Remenyi, Dan. *Measuring and Managing IT: Costs and Benefits.* Boston: Digital Press, 1995.
Sveiby, Karl-Erik. *The New Organizational Wealth: Managing & Measuring Knowledge-Based
    Assets.* San Francisco: Berrett-Koehler, 1997.

Question 72: Revenue enhancement vs. cost reduction

Web Resources

CIO.com: IT Value Research Center. <http://www.cio.com/research/itvalue>.
Computerworld.com: ROI Knowledge Center. <http://www.computerworld.com/
    managementtopics/roi>.

Articles

Joachim, David. "The Fuzzier Side of ROI." *Computerworld.com* 13 May 2002. <http://www
    .computerworld.com/printthis/2002/0,4814,71126,00.html>.
Raghavan, Rajaji. "How to Get Your Budget Approved." *CIO.com* 1 Apr. 2002. <http://www
    .cio.com/archive/040102/perspective.html>.

Books

Bysinger, Bill, and Ken Knight. *Investing in Information Technology: A Decision-Making Guide
    for Business and Technology Managers.* New York: Wiley, 1996.
Keen, Jack M., and Bonita A. Digris. *Making Technology Investments Profitable: Bringing in
    Real ROI.* New York: Wiley, 2002.

Question 73: Revenue protection

Web Resources

CIO.com: IT Value Research Center. <http://www.cio.com/research/itvalue>.
Computerworld.com: ROI Knowledge Center. <http://www.computerworld.com/
    managementtopics/roi>.

Articles

Cox, Louis Anthony, Jr. "Learning Improved Demand Forecasts for Telecommunications Products from Cross-Sectional Data." Paper. *Cox Associates, Inc. Web Site* n.d. <http://www.cox-associates.com/forecst2.doc>.

Hoffman, Thomas. "CIOs Try New Ways to Demonstrate IT's Value." *Computerworld.com* 4 Nov. 2002. <http://www.computerworld.com/printthis/2002/0,4814,75623,00.html>.

Wagner, G. Martin. "An Analytical Framework for Capital Planning and Investment Control for Information Technology." *National Institutes of Health, Center for Information Technology Web Site* 29 Aug. 1996. <http://irm.cit.nih.gov/itmra/caplan1.html>.

Books

Keen, Jack M., and Bonita A. Digris. *Making Technology Investments Profitable: Bringing in Real ROI*. New York: Wiley, 2002.

Money, Arthur, et al. *The Effective Measurement and Management of IT Costs and Benefits*. Oxford: Butterworth-Heinemann, 2000.

Question 74: Total cost of ownership

Web Resources

Compaq: Total Cost of Ownership Web Site. <http://www.compaq.com/tco>.

Articles

David, Julie Smith, David Schuff, and Robert St. Louis. "Managing Your It Total Cost of Ownership." *Communications of the ACM* 45.1 (2002): 101–6.

Hildebrand, Carol. "The PC Price Tag." *CIO.com* 15 Oct. 1997. <http://www.cio.com/archive/enterprise/101597_price.html>.

McKinley, Barton. "Total Cost of Ownership: Behind the Numbers." *Network Magazine* Nov. 2002: 52–55.

Wheatley, Malcolm. "Every Last Dime." *CIO.com* 15 Nov. 2000. <http://www.cio.com/archive/111500/dime.html>.

Books

Hornby, David, and Ken Pepple. *Consolidation in the Data Center: Simplifying IT Environments to Reduce Total Cost of Ownership*. Upper Saddle River: Prentice Hall, 2002.

Question 75: Financial measures for evaluating projects

Web Resources

CIO.com: IT Value Research Center. <http://www.cio.com/research/itvalue>.

Computerworld.com: ROI Knowledge Center. <http://www.computerworld.com/managementtopics/roi>.

Articles

Boehm, Barry, and Li Guo Huang. "Value-Based Software Engineering: A Case Study," *Computer* 36. 3 (2003): 33–41.

Emigh, Jacqueline. "Net Present Value (NPV) and Cost of Capital." *Computerworld.com* 26 July 1999. <http://www.computerworld.com/news/1999/story/0,11280,36470,00.html>.

Mayor, Tracy. "A Buyers Guide to I.T. Value Methodologies." *CIO.com* 15 July 2002. <http://www.cio.com/archive/071502/value.html>.

McCarthy, Jack. "Rethinking ROI." *InfoWorld Web Site* 7 June 2002. <http://www.infoworld.com/articles/ct/xml/02/06/10/020610ctroi.xml>.

Books

Devaraj, Sarv, and Rajiv Kohli. *The IT Payoff: Measuring the Business Value of Information Technology Investments*. New York: Financial Times Prentice Hall, 2002.

Keen, Jack M., and Bonita A. Digris. *Making Technology Investments Profitable: Bringing in Real ROI*. New York: Wiley, 2002.

Question 76: Technology project selection

Web Resources

CIO.com: IT Value Research Center. <http://www.cio.com/research/itvalue>.

Computerworld.com: ROI Knowledge Center. <http://www.computerworld.com/managementtopics/roi>.

Articles

Berinato, Scott. "Do the Math." *CIO.com.* 1 Oct. 2001. <http://www.cio.com/archive/100101/math.html>.

Koch, Christopher. "Your Budget Playbook." *CIO.com* 1 Sept. 2001. <http://www.cio.com/archive/090101/playbook.html>.

Rubin, Howard. "How Do I Link IT Metrics to Business Performance? Building Scorecards to Manage the IT Portfolio." META Group, Inc. 16 Apr. 2002. <http://www.metagroup.com/cgi-bin/inetcgi/jsp/displayArticle.do?oid=30471>.

Solomon, Melissa. "Project Portfolio Management." *Computerworld.com* 18 Mar. 2002. <http://www.computerworld.com/managementtopics/management/story/0,10801,69129,00.html>.

Books

Moore, Geoffrey A. *Living on the Fault Line—Managing for Shareholder Value in Any Economy*. Rev. ed. New York: HarperBusiness. 2002.

Thorp, John. *The Information Paradox Realizing the Business Benefits of Information Technology*. Toronto: McGraw-Hill Ryerson, 1998.

Question 77: Measuring project benefits

Web Resources

American Productivity and Quality Center Web Site. <http://www.apqc.org>.
The Well: Benchmarking Network. <http://www.well.com/user/benchmar/tbnhome.html>.

Articles

Andresen, Jan, et al. "A Framework for Measuring IT Innovation Benefits." *Electronic Journal of Information Technology in Construction* 5 (2000). <http://www.itcon.org/2000/4>.

Mahmood, Mo Adam, and Gary J. Mann. "Special Issue: Impacts of Information Technology Investment on Organizational Performance." *Journal of Management Information Systems* 16.4 (2000): 3–10.

Sveiby, Karl Erik. *The Intangible Assets Monitor.* 20 Dec. 1997. <http://sveiby.konverge.com/articles/companymonitor_nov2001.html>.

Books

Boulton, Richard, Steve Samek, and Barry Libert. *Cracking the Value Code: How Successful Businesses Are Creating Wealth in the New Economy*. New York: HarperBusiness, 2000.

Devaraj, Sarv, and Rajiv Kohli. *The IT Payoff: Measuring the Business Value of Information Technology Investments*. New York: Financial Times Prentice Hall, 2002.

Lucas, Henry C., Jr. *Information Technology and the Productivity Paradox: The Search for Value*. Oxford: Oxford UP, 1999.

Remenyi, Dan, Arthur Money, and Michael Sherwood-Smith. *The Effective Measurement and Management of IT Costs and Benefits*. 2nd ed. Boston: Butterworth-Heinemann, 2000.

Thorp, John. *The Information Paradox Realizing the Business Benefits of Information Technology*. Toronto: McGraw-Hill Ryerson, 1998.

R78

Question 78: Build vs. buy

Web Resources

CIO.com: Research Centers. <http://www.cio.com/research>.
Line56.com: Procurement and Buy Side Topic Center. <http://www.line56.com/topics/default.asp?TopicID=1>.

Articles

Murthi, Sanjay. "Build versus Buy—Making the Right Decision." *developer.com* 2002. <http://www.developer.com/mgmt/article.php/1488331>.

Reed, Brian. "Revisiting Build vs. Buy." *Software Development Times Web Site* 1 June 2001. <http://www.sdtimes.com/opinions/guestview_031.htm>.

Rigby, Rhymer. "B2B Special: To Build or Buy." *Business 2.0 Web Site (UK)* 19 Oct. 2000. <http://www.business2.com/articles/web/0,1653,16258,FF.html>.

Rosen, Joe. "Weighing Options: Build or Buy: A Fresh Look and Other 'Gotchas.'" *Wall Street and Technology* 18 Sept. 2001. <http://www.wallstreetandtech.com/story/WST20010918S0018>.

"Strategic Directions: E-Business: Payoffs & Partnerships." *CIO.com* July 2002. <http://www.cio.com/sponsors/061502sd/sdebiz.pdf>.

Books

Money, Arthur, et al. *The Effective Measurement and Management of IT Costs and Benefits.* Oxford: Butterworth-Heinemann, 2000.

Smith, M. Estellie. *Trade and Trade-offs: Using Resources, Making Choices, and Taking Risks.* Prospect Heights: Waveland Press, 2000.

Question 79: Selecting a vendor

Web Resources

Business 2.0: Web Guide—Choosing an IT Vendor. <http://www.business2.com/webguide/0,1660,59374,00.html>.

Line56.com: Procurement and Buy Side Topic Center. <http://www.line56.com/topics/default.asp?TopicID=1>.

Articles

Berinato, Scott. "Good Stuff, Cheap." *CIO.com* 15 Oct. 2002. <http://www.cio.com/archive/101502/cheap.html>.

Degraeve, Zeger, and Eva Labro. "An Evaluation of Vendor Selection Models from a Total Cost of Ownership Perspective." *European Journal of Operational Research* 125.1 (2000): 34–58.

Perez, Juan Carlos. "CIOs Consolidate IT Spending on Larger Vendors." *Computerworld.com* 4 Oct. 2002. <http://www.computerworld.com/printthis/2002/0,4814,74878,00.html>.

Radcliff, Deborah. "Picking a Winner." *Computerworld.com* 12 Aug. 2002. <http://www.computerworld.com/printthis/2002/0,4814,73349,00.html>.

Sawhney, Mohanbir. "The Problem with Solutions." *CIO.com* 15 Feb. 2003. <http://www.cio.com/archive/021503/gain.html>.

Books

Plotnick, Neil. *The IT Professional's Guide to Managing Systems, Vendors and End Users.* Berkeley: Osborne/McGraw-Hill, 2000.

Verville, Jacques, and Alannah Halingten. *Acquiring Enterprise Software: Beating the Vendors at Their Own Game.* Upper Saddle River: Prentice Hall, 2001.

Question 80: Application service providers

Web Resources

ASP Street Web Portal. <http://www.aspstreet.com/>.

Articles

Blan, Vikki. "Outsourcing the Geek Stuff: But Can ASPs Deliver the Goods." *New Zealand Management* 49.4 (2002): 50–53.

Leibs, Scott. "ASPs: Alive and . . . Well, Alive." *CFO* Oct. 2002: 28.

Mears, Jennifer. "ASP Customers Hail Return on Investment." *Network World* 25 Mar. 2002: 32.

Mizoras, Amy. "The Financial Impact of ASPs." IDC. Web Conference. IDC Doc #25896. Oct. 2001.

Books

Applegate, Lynda M., Robert D. Austin, and F. Warren McFarlan. *Creating Business Advantage in the Information Age.* Boston: McGraw-Hill, 2002.

Questions 81, 82, and 83: Outsourcing

Web Resources

CIO.com: Outsourcing Research Center. <http://www.cio.com/research/outsourcing>.

Computerworld.com Outsourcing News. <http://www.computerworld.com/managementtopics/management/outsourcing>.

Outsourcing Center: Outsourcing BPO Web Site. <http://www.outsourcing-bpo.com>.

Outsourcing Center Web Site. <http://www.outsourcing-center.com>.

Articles   R83 ━━━

Amoribieta, Inigo, Kaushik Bhaumik, Kishore Kanakamedala, and Ajay D. Parkhe. "Programmers Abroad: A Primer on Offshore Software Development." *McKinsey Quarterly* 2 (2001): 128–39.

Doyle, Cynthia, and David Tapper. "Evaluating the Benefits of IT Outsourcing." IDC White Paper. *Clear Cube Web Site* Aug. 2001. <http://www.clearcube.com/whitepapers/downloads/CC-IDCBenefitsofOutsourcingPaper.pdf>.

Dunn, Stephen. "The Coming Sea Change in Offshore IT." *Outsourcing Center: Outsourcing Journal Web Site* Oct. 2002. <http://www.outsourcing-journal.com/issues/oct2002/everest.html>.

Linder, Jane, et al. "Business Transformation Outsourcing: Partnering for Radical Change." White Paper. *Accenture Web Site* 18 July 2001. <http://www.accenture.com/xdoc/en/services/bpm/bto_white_paper.pdf>.

Linder, Jane, Susan Cantrell, and Scott Crist. "Business Process Outsourcing Big Bang: Creating Value in an Expanding Universe." White Paper. *Accenture Web Site* Aug. 2002. <http://www.accenture.com/xdoc/en/services/bpm/bpm_big_bang.pdf>.

McDermott, Michael J. "The Evolution of Outsourcing." *Chief Executive* June 2002: 20–23.

"Outsourcing—A Strategy for Business Transformation." *IBM Web Site* 1999. <http://www-3.ibm.com/e-business/doc/content/resource/pdf/26554.pdf>.

Peterson, Brad L., and Mark Prinsley. "Contracting for International Outsourcing." *Outsourcing Center: Outsourcing Journal Web Site* Oct. 2002. <http://www.outsourcing-journal.com/issues/oct2002/legal.html>.

Books

Bendor-Samuel, Peter. *Turning Lead into Gold: The Demystification of Outsourcing*. Provo: Executive Excellence, 2000.

Bragg, Steven M. *Outsourcing: A Guide to . . . Selecting the Correct Business Unit . . . Negotiating the Contract . . . Maintaining Control of the Process*. New York: Wiley, 1998.

Lacity, Mary Cecelia, and Leslie Willcocks. *Global Information Technology Outsourcing: In Search of Business Advantage*. New York: Wiley, 2001.

Question 84: Software upgrade decision

Web Resources

CIO.com: IT Value Research Center. <http://www.cio.com/research/itvalue>.

Articles

Hoffman, Thomas. "CIOs Try New Ways to Demonstrate IT's Value." *Computerworld.com* 4 Nov. 2002. <http://www.computerworld.com/printthis/2002/0,4814,75623,00.html>.

Ross, Jeanne W., and Peter Weill. "Six IT Decisions Your IT People Shouldn't Make." *Harvard Business Review* 80.11 (2002): 84–91.

Books

Money, Arthur, et al. *The Effective Measurement and Management of IT Costs and Benefits*. Oxford: Butterworth-Heinemann, 2000.

Murphy, Tony. *Achieving Business Value from Technology: A Practical Guide for Today's Executive*. New York: Wiley, 2002.

Smith, M. Estellie. *Trade and Trade-offs: Using Resources, Making Choices, and Taking Risks.* Prospect Heights: Waveland Press, 2000.

───────── SECTION 7. IT AND IMPLEMENTATION

Questions 85 and 86: Determining risks

Web Resources

Business 2.0: Web Guide—Risk Management. <http://www.business2.com/webguide/0,1660,191,00.html>.

ITPapers.com: IT Management—Risk Management. <http://www.itpapers.com/cgi/SubcatIT.pl?scid=88>.

Strategy+Business Web Site. <http://www.strategy-business.com/magazine>.

Articles

Bernstein, Sally. "Project Offices in Practice." *Project Management Journal* 31.4 (2000): 4–6.

Magretta, Joan. "Why Business Models Matter." *Harvard Business Review* 80.5 (2002): 3–8.

Snee, Ronald D., et al. "Improving Team Effectiveness." *Quality Progress* 31.5 (1998): 43–48.

Books

Adams, John R. *Principles of Project Management—Collected Handbooks from the Project Management Institute.* Newtown Square: Project Management Institute, 1997.

Fisher, Kimball. *Leading Self-Directed Work Teams—A Guide to Developing New Team Leadership Skills.* New York: McGraw-Hill, 1993.

Katzenbach, Jon R., and Douglas K. Smith. *The Wisdom of Teams: Creating the High-Performance Organization.* New York: HarperBusiness, 1999.

Kerzner, Harold. *Project Management: A Systems Approach to Planning, Scheduling and Controlling.* 6th ed. New York: Wiley, 1998.

Pearlson, Keri E. *Managing and Using Information Systems: A Strategic Approach.* New York: Wiley, 2001.

Senge, Peter M., et al. *The Fifth Discipline Field Book: Strategies and Tools for Building a Learning Organization.* New York: Doubleday, 1994.

Questions 87 and 88: IT failure

Web Resources

Business 2.0: Web Guide—Risk Management. <http://www.business2.com/webguide/0,1660,191,00.html>.

ITPapers.com: IT Management—Risk Management. <http://www.itpapers.com/cgi/SubcatIT.pl?scid=88>.

R88

Articles

Griffith, T. L., R. F. Zammuto, and L. Aiman-Smith. "Why New Technologies Fail: Overcoming the Invisibility of Implementation." *Industrial Management* 43.2 (1999): 29–34.

Lyytinen, Kalle, and Rudy Hirschheim. "Information Systems Failures: A Survey and Classification of the Empirical Literature." *Oxford Survey in Information Technology.* P. I. Zorkoczy, ed. Vol. 4. Oxford: Oxford UP, 1987. 257–309.

Ribbers, Pieter M. A., and Klaus-Clemens Schoo. "Program Management Complexity of ERP Implementations." *Engineering Management Journal* 14.2 (2002): 45–52.

Umble, Elisabeth J., and M. Michael Umble. "Avoiding ERP Implementation Failure." *Industrial Management* 44.1 (2002): 25–33.

Willcocks, Leslie, and Catherine Griffths. "Predicting Risk of Failure in Large-Scale Information Technology Projects." *Technological Forecasting and Social Change* 47.2 (1994): 205–28.

Books

McCarthy, Jim. *Dynamics of Software Development.* Redmond: Microsoft, 1995.

McConnell, Steve. *Software Project Survival Guide.* Redmond: Microsoft, 1998.

Price Waterhouse Change Integration Team. *The Paradox Principles: How High-Performance Companies Manage Chaos, Complexity, and Contradiction to Achieve Superior Results.* Chicago: Irwin Professional, 1996.

Sanders, Joc, and Eugene Curran. *Software Quality: A Framework for Success in Software Development and Support.* Dublin: Addison-Wesley, 1994.

Questions 89 and 90: Project management

Web Resources

Association for Project Management Web Site. <http://www.apm.org.uk>.
iSixSigma Web Site. <http://www.isixsigma.com>.
The Project Management Institute Web Site. <http://www.pmi.org>.

Articles

"The Capability Maturity Model for Software." *Carnegie Mellon Software Engineering Institute Web Site* 11 Nov. 2002. <http://www.sei.cmu.edu/cmm>.

Caulfield, Brian. "How to Spot Potential Pitfalls Before You Begin That Big IT Project." *Business 2.0 Web Site.* Aug. 2001. <http://www.business2.com/articles/mag/0,1640,16695,FF.html>.

Books

Bothell, Timothy W., G. Lynne Snead, and Jack J. Phillips. *The Project Management Scorecard: Measuring the Success of Project Management Solutions.* Boston: Butterworth-Heinemann, 2002.

Burke, Rory. *Project Management: Planning & Control Techniques.* New York: Wiley, 1999.

Cleland, David I., and Lewis R. Ireland. *Project Management: Strategic Design and Implementation.* 4th ed. New York: McGraw-Hill, 2002.

Kerzner, Harold. *Applied Project Management: Best Practices on Implementation.* New York: Wiley, 2000.

Lewis, James P. *The Project Managers Desk Reference.* 2nd ed. Upper Saddle River: Prentice Hall, 2001.

Murch, Richard. *Project Management, Best Practices for IT Professionals.* Upper Saddle River: Prentice Hall, 2001.

Pressman, Roger S. *Software Engineering: A Practitioner's Approach.* 5th ed. Boston: McGraw-Hill, 2001.

Project Management Institute. *A Guide to the Project Management Body of Knowledge (PMBOK Guide).* Newtown Square: Project Management Institute, 2000.

Question 91: Brooks's Law

Web Resources

Business 2.0: Web Guide—Talent Management. <http://www.business2.com/webguide/0,1660,16063,00.html>.

Workforce Stability Institute Web Site. <http://www.employee.org>.

Articles

Berry, Daniel M. "The Importance of Ignorance in Requirements Engineering: An Earlier Sighting and a Revisitation." *Journal of Systems & Software* 60.1 (2002): 83–85.

Kay, Russell. "It's the Law!" *Computerworld.com* 12 Aug. 2002. <http://www.computerworld.com/managementtopics/management/project/story/0,10801,73338,00.html>.

McConnell, Steve. "Brooks' Law Repealed." *IEEE Software* Nov./Dec. 1999: 6.

Books

Abdel-Hamid, Tarek, and Stuart Madnick. *Software Project Dynamics: An Integrated Approach.* Englewood Cliffs: Prentice Hall, 1991.

Brooks, Frederick J., Jr. *The Mythical Man-Month: Essays on Software Engineering.* Reading: Addison-Wesley, 1995.

Question 92: Stating intended results of a project

Web Resources

CIO.com: Leadership and Management Research Center. <http://www.cio.com/research/leadership>.

R92

Articles

Hartman, Francis, and Rafi A. Ashrafi. "Project Management in the Information Systems and Information Technologies Industries." *Project Management Journal* 33.3 (2002): 5–15.

Hoffman, Thomas. "Biz Units' New Task: Prove Value of IT." *Computerworld.com* 14 Oct. 2002. <http://www.computerworld.com/printthis/2002/0,4814,75105,00.html>.

Knowledge@Wharton and Microsoft. "Back to the Basics: Accounting for IT in Business Performance." *Knowledge@Wharton Web Site* n.d. <http://knowledge.wharton.upenn.edu/microsoft/070302.html>.

Books

Hoffer, Jeffrey A., Joey F. George, and Joseph S. Valacich. *Modern Systems Analysis and Design.* 3rd ed. Upper Saddle River: Prentice Hall, 2002.

Mager, Robert F. *Goal Analysis: How to Clarify Your Goals So You Can Actually Achieve Them.* 3rd ed. Atlanta: Center for Effective Performance, 1997.

Questions 93, 94, and 95: Project sponsor and steering board roles

Web Resources

Business 2.0: Web Guide—Management Style. <http://www.business2.com/webguide/0,1660,4570,00.html>.

CIO.com: Leadership and Management Research Center. <http://www.cio.com/research/leadership>.

Articles

Davenport, Thomas H. "Saving IT's Soul: Human Centered Information Management." *Harvard Business Review on the Business Value of IT.* 1–34. Boston: HBSP, 1999.

Goldfarb, Eric. "The CIO as Coach." *CIO.com* 15 July 2000. <http://www.cio.com/archive/071500_re.html>.

Hartman, Francis, and Rafi A. Ashrafi. "Project Management in the Information Systems and Information Technologies Industries." *Project Management Journal* 33.3 (2002): 5–15.

"Managerial Self Awareness: Even High Performers Don't Know What Is Important." *HRZone Web Site* 1997. <http://www.hrzone.com/articles/managerial_awareness.html>.

Ross, Jeanne W., and Peter Weill. "Six IT Decisions Your IT People Shouldn't Make." *Harvard Business Review* 80.11 (2002): 84–91.

Books

Fleming, Q. W., and J. M. Koppelman. *Earned Value Project Management.* 2nd ed. Newtown Square: Project Management Institute, 2000.

Jaques, E., and S. D. Clement. *Executive Leadership: A Practical Guide to Managing Complexity.* New York: Blackwell, 1991.

Komaki, Judith L. *Leadership from an Operant Perspective: People and Organizations*. London: Routledge, 1998.

Leeds, D. *Smart Questions: The Essential Strategy for Successful Managers*. New York: Berkeley Books, 2000.

Love, N., and J. Brant-Love. *Project Sponsor Guide*. Newtown Square: Project Management Institute, 2000.

Verzuh, E. *The Fast Forward MBA in Project Management: Quick Tips, Speedy Solutions, Cutting-Edge Ideas*. Chapter 3. New York: Wiley, 1999.

Question 96: Key project manager authorities

Web Resources

CIO.com: Leadership and Management Research Center. <http://www.cio.com/research/leadership>.

Articles

Hartman, Francis, and Rafi A. Ashrafi. "Project Management in the Information Systems and Information Technologies Industries." *Project Management Journal* 33.3 (2002): 5–15.

Books

Graham, Robert J., and Randall L. Englund. *Creating an Environment for Successful Projects: The Quest to Manage Project Management*. 124–27. San Francisco: Jossey-Bass, 1997.

Jaques, Elliott. *Requisite Organization: A Total System for Effective Managerial Organization and Managerial Leadership for the 21st Century*. 2nd rev. ed. Arlington: Cason Hall, 1998.

Womack, James P., Daniel T. Jones, and Daniel Roos. *The Machine That Changed the World: The Story of Lean Production*. New York: HarperPerennial, 1991.

Yourdon, Edward. *Death March: The Complete Software Developer's Guide to Surviving Mission Impossible Projects*. Upper Saddle River: Prentice Hall, 1997.

Question 97: Cross-functional work

Web Resources

Business 2.0: Web Guide—Management Style. <http://www.business2.com/webguide/0,1660,4570,00.html>.

Articles

Clifford, Stephanie. "How to Get the Geeks and the Suits to Play Nice." *Business 2.0 Web Site* May 2002. <http://www.business2.com/articles/mag/0,1640,39246,FF.html>.

Graham, Robert J., and Randall L. Englund. *Creating an Environment for Successful Projects: The Quest to Manage Project Management.* 124–27. San Francisco: Jossey-Bass, 1997.

Tesluk, Paul E., and John E. Mathieu. "Overcoming Roadblocks to Effectiveness: Incorporating Management of Performance Barriers into Models of Work Group Effectiveness." *Journal of Applied Psychology* 84.2 (1999): 200–217.

Books

Davis, Stanley M., and Paul R. Lawrence. *Matrix.* Reading: Addison-Wesley, 1977.

Verma, V. K. *Organizing Projects for Success: The Human Aspects of Project Management.* Chapter 6. Newton Square: Project Management Institute, 1995.

Waterman, Robert H. *Adhocracy: The Power to Change.* New York: Norton, 1993.

Question 98: Improving chances for project success

Web Resources

Gantthead Web Site. <http://www.gantthead.com>
PM Boulevard Web Site. <http://www.pmboulevard.com>
TechRepublic Web Site. <http://www.techrepublic.com>

Articles

Caulfield, Brian. "How to Spot Potential Pitfalls Before You Begin That Big IT Project." *Business 2.0 Web Site.* Aug. 2001. <http://www.business2.com/articles/mag/ 0,1640,16695,FF.html>.

Books

Bothell, Timothy W., G. Lynne Snead, and Jack J. Phillips. *The Project Management Scorecard: Measuring the Success of Project Management Solutions.* Boston: Butterworth-Heinemann, 2002.

Cleland, David I., and Lewis R. Ireland. *Project Management: Strategic Design and Implementation.* 4th ed. New York: McGraw-Hill, 2002.

LaFasto, Frank M. J., and Carl E. Larson. *When Teams Work Best.* Thousand Oaks: Sage Publications, 2001.

Questions 99 and 100: Planning for and dealing with failure

Web Resources

Business 2.0: Web Guide—Risk Management. <http://www.business2.com/webguide/ 0,1660,191,00.html>.

Carlstedt Research and Technology: Martin Börjesson—Scenario Planning Resources Web Site. <http://www.crt.se/~mb/scenario>.

ITPapers.com: IT Management—Risk Management. <http://www.itpapers.com/cgi/SubcatIT
.pl?scid=88>.

Articles

Field, Tom. "When Bad Things Happen to Good Projects." *CIO* 15 Oct. 1997. <http://www
.cio.com/archive/101597/bad.html>.

Keil, M. "Pulling the Plug: Software Project Management and the Problem of Project Escalation." *MIS Quarterly* 19.4 (1995): 421–47.

Moss Kanter, Rosabeth. "Managing through the Miserable Middle." *Business 2.0 Web Site*
Nov. 2001, 16 Dec. 2001. <http://www.business2.com/articles/mag/0,1640,17495,FF
.html>.

Stauffer, David. "Five Reasons Why You Still Need Scenario Planning." *Harvard Management
Update* 7.6 (2002): 3–7.

"Strategic Management: Using Scenario Planning as a Weapon Against Uncertainty."
Knowledge@Wharton Web Site 5 Dec. 2001. <http://knowledge.wharton.upenn.edu/
articles.cfm?catid=7&articleid=470&homepage=yes>.

Books

Strassmann, Paul A. *The Business Value of Computers.* New Canaan: Information Economics,
1990.

Strassmann, Paul A. *The Squandered Computer: Evaluating the Business Alignment of Information Technologies.* New Canaan: Information Economics, 1997.

Weill, Peter, and Marianne Broadbent. *Leveraging the New Infrastructure: How Market Leaders
Capitalize on Information Technology.* Boston: HBSP, 1998.

Appendix: Acronyms

ACD	Automatic Call Distribution
ADE	Application Development Environment
ADSL	Asymmetric Digital Subscriber Line
APE	Application Programs for the Enterprise
ASA	Average Speed of Answer
ASP	Application Service Provider
ASPIC	ASP Industry Consortium
B2B	Business-to-Business
B2C	Business-to-Consumer
B2E	Business-to-Employee
BIS	Business Intelligence System
BPO	Business Process Outsourcing
BSP	Business Service Provider
BU	Business Unit
CASE	Computer-Aided Software Engineering
CBT	Computer-Based Training
CDMA	Code Division Multiple Access
CFO	Chief Financial Officer
CIO	Chief Information Officer
CMM	Capability Maturity Model
CMS	Content Management System
CO	Central Office (local telephone switching office)
COM	Component Object Model
COO	Chief Operations Officer
CORBA	Common Object Request Broker Architecture (object-oriented middleware)
CRM	Customer Relationship Management
CTI	Computer Telephony Interface
CTO	Chief Technical Officer
DBMS	Database Management System
DR	Disaster Recovery
DRP	Distribution Requirements Planning
DSL	Digital Subscriber Line
DSS	Decision Support System
EAI	Enterprise Application Integration
EDI	Electronic Data Interchange
EIP	Enterprise Information Portal
EIS	Executive Information System
ERM	Enterprise Resource Management
ERP	Enterprise Resource Planning

FCC	Federal Communications Commission	PBCC	Packet Binary Convolutional Code (trademarked name for Texas Instruments' high rate 802.11b product)
FTP	File Transfer Protocol		
GSM	General System for Mobile Communications		
		PCS	Personal Communications System
GSS	Group Support System (also known as Groupware)		
		PDA	Personal Digital Assistant
GUI	Graphical User Interface	PDC	Primary Domain Controller
HFC	Hybrid Fiber Coax	PLC	Program Logic Controller
HR	Human Resources	PMO	Program Management Office
HTML	Hypertext Markup Language	POS	Point of Sale
HTTP	Hypertext Transfer Protocol	POTS	Plain Old Telephone Service
IDSL	ISDN Digital Subscriber Line	PSTN	Public Switched Telephone Network
ILT	Instructor-Led Training		
IM	Information Management	PVR	Personal Video Recorder
IP	Internet Protocol	RAD	Rapid Application Development
IS	Information Systems or Information Services	RFI	Request for Information
		RFP	Request for Proposal
ISP	Internet Service Provider	RFQ	Request for Qualification
IT	Information Technology	RFx	Collective reference to RFIs RFPs and RFQs
J2EE	Java 2 Platform Enterprise Edition		
		ROI	Return on Investment
KD	Knowledge Discovery	RSVP	ReSerVation Protocol
KM	Knowledge Management	SCM	Supply Chain Management
KMS	Knowledge Management System	SDSL	Symmetric Digital Subscriber Line
KPI	Key Performance Indicators		
LAN	Local Area Network	SEI	Software Engineering Institute
LCMS	Learning Content Management System	SLA	Service Level Agreement
		SMS	Short Messaging Services
LMS	Learning Management System	SNA	Systems Network Architecture
MAN	Metropolitan Area Network	SOAP	Simple Object Access Protocol
MIS	Management Information System	SPC	Statistical Process Control
MOP	Measure of Performance	SWOT	Strengths, Weaknesses, Opportunities, and Threats
MRP	Manufacturing Resource Planning		
MTTR	Mean Time to Repair	TCP	Transmission Control Protocol
NAT	Network Administration Translation	TCP/IP	combination of Transmission Control Protocol and Internet Protocol
NIC	Network Interface Card		
NPV	Net Present Value	TDMA	Time Division Multiple Access
OOP	Object-Oriented Programming	TPS	Transaction Processing System
ORB	Object Request Broker	UDDI	Universal Description, Discovery, and Integration
PAN	Personal Area Network		
		UTP	Unshielded Twisted Pair

VMO	Value Management Office	WPAN	Wireless Personal Area Network
VPN	Virtual Private Network	WSDL	Web Services Description Language
WAN	Wide Area Network		
WAP	Wireless Application Protocol	XBRL	Extensible Business Reporting Language
WBT	Web-Based Training		
WEBINAR	Web (Internet) Based Seminar	XML	eXtensible Markup Language
WiFi	Wireless Fidelity	XP	Xtreme Programming
WLAN	Wireless Local Area Network		

Contributor Biographical Sketches

THE EDITORS

David R. Laube, University of Colorado at Denver, is currently executive in residence at the business school. He also actively consults in the fields of telecommunications and information technology. Prior to July 2000, Dave spent 17 years as a senior executive at US WEST, the regional Bell company. Over his last five years at US WEST, Dave was the vice president and chief information officer, leading the largest information technologies organization in Colorado. In this role, he was responsible for all systems development, computer operations, and systems architecture for the company. Under Laube's leadership, US WEST's 6,000 person IT organization was recognized for its service and cost-effectiveness.

In addition to this role, Laube held a number of leadership positions in technology and finance in the company. He previously served as vice president-controller and treasurer, responsible for all of the accounting, treasury operations, and financial systems development for the communications business of US WEST. He also was chief financial officer of Mountain Bell and US WEST Cellular and the head of information systems for the individual Bell companies.

Before joining US WEST in 1983, Laube was vice president of finance and information systems for the digital telephone division of the Harris Corporation, a manufacturer of telecommunications equipment. He began his career with Arthur Andersen in San Francisco, specializing in high-tech start-up firms.

Laube is a Phi Beta Kappa graduate of the University of Washington with a bachelor of arts in finance, holds an MBA from the Wharton School of Business at the University of Pennsylvania, and is a CPA. He serves on several corporate boards and university advisory boards.

Raymond F. Zammuto, University of Colorado at Denver, is a professor of management who teaches strategic management, technology management, and organization design. He has consulted on and conducted workshops about organization culture, organization redesign, and strategic management for a variety of service and manufacturing organizations, ranging from hospitals and universities to insurance carriers and computer firms.

His research focuses on various aspects of how organizations adapt to changing industry conditions, including studies of how organizations' cultures can impede or enhance their ability to innovate and implement new technologies. He has published two books, *Assessing Organizational Effectiveness: Systems Change, Adaptation, and Strategy* and *Organizations: Theory and Design*, as well as numerous journal articles and book chapters.

Zammuto has served as division chair of the Organization and Management Theory Division of the Academy of Management. He has been a member of several editorial boards including the *Academy of Management Journal, Administrative Science Quarterly*, and *Organization Science* and is a past associate editor of the *Academy of Management Executive*, a journal dedicated to translating academic theory and research into practical information for managers. Zammuto received his doctorate from the University of Illinois.

The Contributors

René J. Aerdts, Electronic Data Systems, is an EDS Fellow and the chief technology officer for the WorldCom Infrastructure Delivery organization. Aerdts helps develop enterprise-wide initiatives that provide technology planning for the mainframe and midrange environments within the WorldCom infrastructure. His organization also creates and delivers technology plans and implementation strategies for major technologies. Before joining EDS in 1986, Aerdts spent almost five years as a scientific assistant at the State University of Utrecht in the Netherlands, teaching, performing research, and publishing articles. Aerdts earned his doctorate in mathematics with a minor in physics from the State University of Utrecht in the Netherlands.

Greg Allen, Electronic Data Systems, has over 20 years experience in software development and integration. Prior to his current assignment as a senior information specialist, Allen was also a developer, a project manager, and a project management consultant, and he has provided applications support. His expertise spans several industries including financial, health care, transportation, manufacturing, and consumer goods. Allen is a certified function point specialist providing structured functional analysis of software systems for multiple EDS clients.

Brett Anderson, Accenture LLP, became the partner in charge of Accenture's western US Communications, Media, and Entertainment (CME) industry customer relationship management (CRM) practice in 1999. His responsibilities include ensuring the growth and development of the western US CME CRM practice, developing and overseeing relationships with strategic CRM ventures and alliances, and serving as a client partner to several communications and high-technology accounts in the Denver market. Anderson has 15 years of CRM experience in the communications industry and over the past three years his western US CME CRM practice has experienced double-digit growth.

Thomas E. Andrews, Ball Corporation, is vice president, information services, packaging operations. He is responsible for management information computing services and technology, including operation, management, and support of business systems and data. Andrews joined Ball Aerospace & Technologies Corporation in 1981 and has been a member of the technical staff, senior programmer database analyst, manager of technical services, and director of technology services. Prior to joining Ball, Andrews worked for Neodata Services. He obtained a bachelor's degree in applied mathematics from Stockton State College in New Jersey in 1978.

Joseph Bagan, Adelphia Communications, is the chief administrative officer and senior vice president responsible for leading Adelphia's CLEC business, directing the logistics and supply chain functions, managing the national billing operations team, and leading the information technology function. Prior to joining Adelphia Communications, he was senior vice president and chief information officer for AT&T Broadband and a partner at Arthur Andersen. He has also taught introductory cost accounting and financial accounting courses at the University of Denver. Bagan holds a BS degree in accounting and a master's of accountancy from the University of Denver. He earned his certified public accountant status in 1988 and is a member of AICPA, CSCPA, and APICS.

John T. Bailey, Electronic Data Systems, is a distributed systems services solutions architect. Bailey has led IT assessment efforts dealing with the functional, technological, and financial aspects of operating IT systems for clients around the world. He has taught assessment, design, and implementation methodologies to EDS teams in North America, Europe, and Asia. John is an active contributor to EDS distributed systems assessment (DSA) and distributed systems design (DSD) practices. He has a bachelor of science degree in computer information systems from Humboldt State University and numerous technical certifications, including certified TCO expert from the Gartner Group.

Ellen Balaguer, Accenture LLP, is a partner with Accenture's communications and high-tech market unit and is the managing partner of Accenture's market maker group within Communications, Media, and Entertainment for the western United States. Balaguer's extensive experience includes large-scale change programs, new business launch efforts, e-business enablement, and value-oriented client relationships. She works primarily with clients in North America, but has international experience as well. Ellen's forté is structuring outsourcing deals with clients, ranging from simple contracts with small start-ups to large, complex contracts with some of the world's largest companies. She has been with Accenture for 19 years.

Denise Barndt, PricewaterhouseCoopers LLP, is a senior manager in San Francisco and has extensive experience designing and facilitating executive-level crisis management simulations. Barndt has over 25 years of experience in business continuity, technology recovery, community and statewide emergency planning, and testing in emergency management. She is also a certified business continuity professional and certified emergency manager. Barndt is a frequent presenter at international and national conferences on business continuity.

Barbara T. Bauer, BTB, Inc., is president of BTB, Inc., a consulting firm providing services to the technology, telecommunications, and education industries. Prior to starting BTB, Inc., she was an executive at US WEST, responsible for a large software development organization. Prior to US WEST, she was the vice president, general manager of the Rides business unit, a subsidiary of Raynet, Inc. Bauer started her career as a systems engineer and software developer in Bell Laboratories. She earned her bachelor's degree in physics from St. Louis University and her master's degree in physics from the University of Kansas. She has also completed the Stanford Summer Executive Program.

William Casey, Executive Leadership Group, is president of ELG and consults on organizational behavior management, specializing in organizational structure design and project management. Casey was recently the topic of an article in the Project Management Institute's *PM Net Magazine* and the coauthor of an article on project management offices for the February 2001 issue. He also coauthors the monthly column, "Managing for Results," in the *Denver Business Journal* and speaks on management-related topics. Casey completed his doctorate in applied behavior analysis at the University of Kansas. His master's degree is in education from the University of Denver where he also serves on the adjunct faculty at the Daniels School of Business.

James D. Collins currently provides consulting services to the communications and high-tech industry. Collins specializes in working with global organizations and start-ups to introduce leading-edge customer relationship management (CRM) and billing capabilities. Collins has over 17 years of CRM and billing experience in the communications industry. Prior to October 2002, James was an associate partner in Accenture's western US Communications, Media, and Entertainment (CME) industry CRM practice. His responsibilities included program management and business case development leadership, customer billing system and process management, large program planning, and working with communications and high-tech client teams worldwide.

Rina Delmonico, REN, Inc., founded REN, an executive IT consulting company in 1997. REN, Inc., was recently named in the top 250 private-owned businesses by *Colorado Biz.* She is also an information management commissioner for the State of Colorado and is the executive director for the University of Colorado at Denver's

Center for IT Innovation (CITI) program. She serves on various educational and corporate boards. She has spent 28 years in IT with various *Fortune* 500 companies; the last 10 years were in a CIO role. Delmonico is a graduate of CU Denver's MBA program and, in 1999, was awarded IT Executive of the Year for the State of Colorado.

Tom Devane, Premier Integration, is an internationally recognized consultant, author, and workshop leader who helps clients integrate business strategy, processes, technology, and human factors in large-scale change efforts. Prior to founding Premier Integration in 1988, Devane held management positions at two Big 5 Consulting firms and an energy company. He coauthored *The Change Handbook: Group Methods for Shaping the Future* and is a contributor to *The Organization Development and Training Sourcebook* series, *The Consultant's Toolkit,* and *Executive Excellence Magazine* on the topics of performance improvement and large-scale change. Devane holds bachelor's and master's degrees in finance from the University of Illinois.

Gary Dodge, Oracle Corporation, has served in various management and technical positions within the sales and consulting divisions of Oracle since 1987. He has been a frequent speaker on database topics at many information technology conferences. He is coauthor of *Oracle8 Data Warehousing,* 1998, and *Essential Oracle8i Data Warehousing,* 2000, both published by John Wiley & Sons. Dodge received his BA in behavioral psychology as a Boettcher scholar at The Colorado College. He served in several board positions, including president, for the Mile High Chapter of the Data Processing Management Association (now the Association of Information Technology Professionals).

Andrew Eiseman, Eiseman Consulting, Inc., is an independent consultant in the field of broadband communication and digital and interactive television. He has assisted cable and telephone companies in Europe, Asia, and the United States in development and deployment of advanced broadband, digital television, and interactive television services. Prior to establishing his current business, Eiseman was with US WEST and US WEST Advanced Technologies, where he worked with Bellcore on some of the fundamental technologies used in today's digital television and DSL industries. Andrew has a BA from the University of Rochester and an MBA from the University of Denver.

Mark Endry, J. D. Edwards, is senior vice president and chief information officer of J. D. Edwards, a provider of open-system collaborative commerce solutions. Mark is heavily involved in the development of J. D. Edwards' products, services, and business strategies. Endry was named 2000 Colorado CIO of the Year, and *ComputerWorld* Premier 100 IT Leader. He joined J. D. Edwards in 1995 as director of infrastructure services. Endry serves on the CITI board and on the board of ITU Ventures. He is also a member of the HyperSpace Communications, Inc., advisory board.

C. Marlena Fiol, University of Colorado at Denver, is a professor of strategy with over 25 years of experience in strategic management. She has helped small and large companies identify their core competencies, clarify market demands, develop strategic directions, and implement the tactics required to compete successfully in changing markets. She has extensive experience in the areas of cross-cultural relations and globalization, with particular emphasis on Latin American business practices.

Fiol has authored numerous research articles, book chapters, and papers on topics related to strategic thinking, organizational learning, and change management. She is a frequent international, national, and regional speaker. She received her doctorate from the University of Illinois.

Daniel G. Fox-Gliessman, Statera, is currently principal and vice president IT outsourcing with Statera, an IT consulting firm in Denver, Colorado. In addition to leading the IT outsourcing practice at Statera, he also leads CIO Assist, a service targeted to companies needing assistance at the IT leadership level. Fox-Gliessman has also held executive positions such as vice president, CIO, and IT consultant at Relera, Inc., Boston Market, Coopers and Lybrand, BDM Technologies, and Raymond James. He holds a BA from San Diego State University and an MA (international economics and econometrics) from the University of Denver.

Dawn Gregg, University of Colorado at Denver, is an assistant professor of information systems. Prior to her doctoral studies, she was employed for nine years as a research and development engineer. Her current research focuses on how to organize and maintain Web-based content so that it can be used to better meet business needs. Her work has been published in *Communications of the ACM, Information Systems Frontiers*, and *Decision Support Systems*. She received her PhD in computer information systems from Arizona State University, her MBA from Arizona State University West, and her BS in mechanical engineering from the University of California at Irvine.

Daya Haines Haddock, Technical Information Associates, Inc. (TIA), is chief operations officer and oversees TIA's professional services providing knowledge management, training, online learning, and documentation programs. She has 18 years of experience building entrepreneurial businesses focused on knowledge sharing, managing corporate content, implementing marketing and branding strategies, and delivering Web-based solutions. Her intranet work at US WEST was profiled in *CIO Magazine*. She is a frequent speaker on knowledge management and e-learning at national conferences. She holds a BA from The Colorado College. Haddock served in several board positions, including president, for the Mile High Chapter of the Data Processing Management Association (now the Association of Information Technology Professionals).

Mike Hager, Oppenheimer Funds, Inc., is currently the vice president of network security and disaster recovery. He has over 30 years of experience in the areas of computer security, counterintelligence, investigation, information security, and telecommunications security for both private industry and the federal government. Hager has numerous certifications in the area of computer security, information security, and counterintelligence. He is also an experienced speaker recently presenting for Microsoft, Computer Associates, ISACA, ICSA, as well as for ICM and Marcus Evans. Hager was selected by *Computer World* magazine as one of the Top 100 Professional IT Leaders for 2002.

Randy Harris, Executive Intelligence, Inc., is a managing partner of Executive Intelligence, Inc., an international research and analytics company that turns current and evolving business-drivers into highly predictable sales and marketing execution strategies for complex B2B selling organizations. Harris has a multidiscipline background in customer research, process and capacity evaluation and design, multichannel delivery, performance-based major-account design strategies, supply chain performance, and transition management for technology integration. Harris speaks at over 40 major conferences a year. He has been published by many publications, including *Harvard Business Review*, *Strategy & Leadership*, *Microsoft*, *1-to-1 Marketing*, and is often cited as an expert resource.

Stephen R. Heidt, Electronic Data Systems, is president, Business Process Outsourcing Global Delivery, and is a member of the EDS operations council. Heidt is responsible for a best-in-class global delivery organization that provides customer relationship management, financial process management, human resources, finance and accounting services, and procurement services to EDS clients around the globe. Before assuming his current role, Heidt served as president, EDS distributed systems services, leading the world's largest provider of desktop services. Previously, Heidt spent several years in London where he served as president, Europe, Middle East, and Africa delivery for information solutions. Leading more than 28,000 technical personnel, Heidt's organization delivered a full range of technical services to clients in more than 20 countries.

Susan Heinzeroth, SageRiver Consulting, Inc., is founder and director of SageRiver Consulting, Inc., a firm that crafts business architectures for clients to provide blueprints for organizational change. Prior to starting SageRiver, she was a partner with Cornerstone Consulting Group, and before that she was a consultant with Coopers & Lybrand Consulting. Heinzeroth received an MBA in management and finance from the University of Colorado at Denver. She completed her undergraduate studies at Luther College obtaining degrees in both business administration and sociology with a minor in accounting.

Stan Hume, Johns Manville, has 25 years experience in IT ranging from software engineering to defining architecture and implementing ERP systems. Early in his career, he cowrote the BASIC interpreter for Texas Instruments, and wrote control software for Honeywell. As an IT manager, he has led business process reengineering efforts, ERP implementations, major system consolidations, and IT strategy and architecture definitions. He is currently responsible for the overall IT architecture, standards, system integration, database, and IT security areas at Johns Manville. Hume serves as a faculty member at the University of Phoenix, teaching various IT management, software engineering, and project management courses.

Michael S. Jackson has been a senior business analyst for IT operations at AT&T Broadband where he was the head of technology for the Central Division of TCI, and the total cost of ownership manager. He has developed an exceptional array of creative business, marketing, technical, and analytical expertise through 15 years of information technology experience. His extensive technical past ranges from end user support to technical-financial management and consulting. Jackson has been instrumental in the development and implementation of business and marketing strategies for small start-up companies as well as the direction of marketing, media, accounting, technology, and public relations for international associations.

Marion K. Jenkins, QSE Technologies, Inc., is the founder and CEO of QSE Technologies, which provides *Fortune* 500–type technology services for small and medium businesses. He has held many strategic executive positions, including CIO, CTO, and COO, in the technology and communications industries, including: NAREX, FirstWorld Communications, Qwest Communications, LCI International, USLD Communications, American Telco, Inc., and Exxon Production Research. Jenkins received his BS in mechanical engineering from Utah State University and his MS and PhD in mechanical engineering from Stanford University.

Jahangir Karimi, University of Colorado at Denver, is professor of information systems and serves as the director of information systems program. He has been published in many engineering and management information systems publications and a number of conference proceedings. Karimi is on the editorial board of *International Journal of Electronic Commerce* and *IEEE Transactions on Engineering Management* journals. He is also a member of the Association for Computing Machinery, the Computing Society, and the Society for Information Management. Karimi received his PhD in management information systems from the University of Arizona.

Peggy Kent has focused her career on managing large organizations and improving their use of good business processes. For a number of years, she was vice president, billing services, for US WEST, the regional Bell telephone company, where she also led process improvement efforts in the finance organization. Most recently, she was vice president, information technologies, for MediaOne Corporation, now part of Comcast. Kent received her bachelor of science in business from City University in Seattle, Washington.

Thomas Kiefer, Fujitsu Consulting, is a senior vice president who joined Fujitsu Consulting in 1996. He is currently responsible for telecommunications business development for the western United States and his primary customers are Qwest, Sprint, and AT&T Broadband. Prior to joining Fujitsu Consulting, Kiefer worked at IBM where he was responsible for development of a new billing system for British Telcom. He started his career at US WEST (now Qwest) and held various IT management positions. Kiefer received his BS/BA and MBA at Creighton University in Omaha, Nebraska, and a certificate in project management from Denver University.

Steve Kiel, Oracle Corporation, is a practice director and leads the Northwest Business Intelligence and warehouse practice for Oracle's consulting organization. Kiel has over 15 years of experience managing a wide variety of information systems implementation projects. He worked as a programmer for the Department of Energy and as a consultant for Anderson Consulting. As an expert in the data warehousing field, Kiel has helped corporations across the United States improve their information management capabilities and their bottom line. He obtained his bachelor's degree in computer information systems from Arizona State University.

Shirley Komoto, PricewaterhouseCoopers LLP, is a consultant specializing in helping clients improve the way they work. She has 25 years of experience in business process improvement, project management, and organizational development in corporate and government settings. Prior to PwC, she led business planning and worked in theme park development and construction finance and scheduling, facilitated large product brainstorming groups, ran leadership and team building exercises, led merger integration and organizational effectiveness efforts, and conducted project management training. Komoto holds an MBA from the University of Southern California and an MPA from California State University at Long Beach. She is a certified project management professional.

Mark L. Labovitz, Regis University, has 22 years of experience with analytics and database marketing. Mark is an affiliated faculty member at Regis University teaching in the e-commerce and database concentration in the MSCIT program. Other recent positions include chief operating officer for Baetis, a company focused on providing CRM and direct marketing services to insurance agencies; a second-generation founder of NextAction, a company that developed new patentable analytics methodology that went beyond conventional data mining; and GM/VP of customer intelligence and GM database marketing/analytics for mainstream service providers. Labovitz's background includes CRM, customer intelligence, data mining and analytics, and information technology.

Craig Lewis, Science Applications International Corporation, is a corporate vice president and division manager with SAIC. He serves as the general manager for SAIC's telecommunications and information technology consulting practice where he oversees all aspects of the business operations. Under his leadership, SAIC has developed multiple consulting practice areas including information technology support to telecommunications companies and an industry recognized practice software process improvement (SPI). Lewis earned his bachelor's degree in mathematics from the University of Maryland. He also holds a master's degree in computer science from the Johns Hopkins University and an MBA from the University of Colorado.

Cheri Linden, a former partner of Accenture, is a business/consulting executive with 14 years of experience in leading sales/account teams, business architecture strategy and execution, program management, and information systems solutions.

She has developed and led strategic, process, and technology solutions in different industries primarily focusing on telecommunications. Linden has an MBA from the University of Texas at Austin and a bachelor of science degree in finance from the University of Colorado at Boulder. She is a cofounder of the Accenture Leadership Seminar and the E-Commerce Center of Excellence with the University of Colorado at Boulder.

Kirk Lowery, Oracle Corporation, is vice president of e-business solution architecture at Oracle where he leads a team of business architects that help executives improve the profitability and competitiveness of their businesses through e-business innovation. Lowery has extensive experience in implementing large-scale information systems in the public and private sector. He currently teaches professional education programs in technology strategy and architecture and program management, and has served as an instructor in the Graduate School of Business at the University of Colorado. Lowery is a certified public accountant and a frequent author and speaker on e-business and technology management topics.

Edward F. Lukes Jr. is a consultant for senior executives and boards of directors. He has been helping companies improve their profitability and the development, alignment, and execution of their business and information technology strategies for over 35 years. His previous positions include president and chief operating officer of Solant, Inc.; president of SHL Systemhouse, Europe; partner, McKinsey & Co.; director and cofounder, The Information Consulting Group; and senior partner, Andersen Consulting. Lukes received his BS in industrial management and his MS in industrial administration and operations research at Purdue University. He served on Purdue's Krannert School of Management Dean's Advisory Council for 10 years. He also serves on the board of governors for Opportunity International.

Graham R. McDonald, Great-West Life & Annuity Insurance Company, is vice president, corporate finance and investment operations. He is responsible for a variety of functions, including: the company's Corporate IT Division, investment operations, corporate properties, headquarter services, and procurement. The corporate IT division manages over 500 NT and Unix servers, 1481 mips of mainframe capacity, 25 terabytes of storage, and 8,000 TCP/IP network nodes. Great-West Life & Annuity Insurance Company specializes in life, health, disability insurance, and 401(k) products. McDonald is a Fellow of the Society of Actuaries and a member of the American Academy of Actuaries.

Chuck McGrath, Accenture LLP, is the partner in charge of Accenture's western US Communications, Media, and Entertainment (CME) industry network service line practice where his responsibilities include supporting the growth of the network practice across his region, developing assets related to network operations issues, and developing network professionals. Additionally, he serves as the lead partner for several communications and high-technology companies in Colorado. With 16 years of experience in the communications industry, McGrath specializes in working with global organizations and emerging next-generation network carriers to quickly and effectively improve network operations capabilities. He joined Accenture in 1986 and was admitted to the partnership in 1998.

Jeffrey R. Nystrom, University of Colorado at Denver, is an instructor of management teaching undergraduate and graduate courses in strategic management and organization theory. Nystrom began his career as an educator in 1995 and spent five years on the faculty at College America at Denver where he taught courses in management and served as the program director of the management department. He also held a number of sales and management positions in industry while earning his academic credentials. Jeffrey earned his BS degree in business administration and MS degree in management and organization from the University of Colorado at Denver.

Kevin Obenchain, Great-West Life & Annuity Insurance Company, is manager, investment systems. He has held financial and IT management positions in the high-technology industry over the past 20 years. In 1991, he cofounded Gold Systems, Inc., and served as both CFO and board member. He has served as an ERP consultant, as well as a CPA in public practice, while advising numerous high-tech start-ups on business strategy and financing. Obenchain received his MBA in accounting from the University of Colorado, and his bachelor's in international relations from Michigan State University. He is a member of the American Institute of CPAs.

Jacky Oorloff, PricewaterhouseCoopers LLP, is a manager in the security and privacy practice within PwC's Global Risk Management Solutions, where she specializes in assisting large companies manage their privacy exposures. Oorloff's specific area of focus is international and domestic privacy law; she also has extensive experience in privacy best practices across a range of industries, with an online focus. She has delivered training in, spoken about, and authored several articles and white papers on privacy-related topics. Prior to specializing in privacy compliance, Oorloff spent considerable time in both financial audit and information systems risk management, including assessing IT infrastructures, controls, systems, and processes.

Wendi Peck, Executive Leadership Group, Inc., is the CEO and cofounder of ELG where she consults on strategy implementation. Peck specializes in implementing and managing large-scale programs, developing measurable representations of strategy, and aligning organizational components to them. She has over 20 years experience directing large programs and driving successful organizational change. Peck writes and speaks on management-related topics. In addition to occasional writing projects, she coauthors the monthly column, "Managing for Results" in the *Denver Business Journal*. She received an MBA from the University of Denver and a master's in project management from George Washington University.

William H. Phifer, Electronic Data Systems, is an EDS Fellow. He directs the EDS capability maturity model (CMM) assessments program and provides enterprise CMM strategies. Phifer is also president of the Delaware Valley Science Council, and a member of the International Association of Professional Lead Appraisers, Institute of Electrical and Electronics Engineers (IEEE), and the Philadelphia Software Process Improvement Network (SPIN). He has delivered technical papers at numerous National and International Software Engineering Process Group (SEPG) conferences. Phifer earned his bachelor's degree in mathematics from Lebanon Valley College. He achieved fellow status from the Life Management Institute in 1980.

Chan Pollock, Johns Manville, is vice president of information systems and chief information officer. He has been responsible for Johns Manville's global information systems since 1998. Pollock's 26-plus years of systems and technology experience include positions such as: CIO for StorageTek and director of IT for Network Systems in Minneapolis, Minnesota. In addition, he has held various technology management and software development positions for Network Systems and Control Data. Pollock holds a BS in computer science from Michigan Technological University and an MBA from the University of Minnesota.

Eric V. Robinson, Limited Brands, Inc., is the director of finance. Prior to joining Limited Brands Technology Services, Inc., Robinson was the director of Customer Support and Planning for Qwest Information Technologies, Inc. He worked in various capacities for Qwest and US WEST over a 17-year span with responsibilities in finance, cost accounting, network planning, internal audit, and IT. He holds a CPA and is a member of the AICPA and Colorado Society of CPAs. Robinson received his MBA from the University of Nebraska and his BS in accounting from the University of South Dakota.

Rob Rudloff, PricewaterhouseCoopers LLP, is a senior manager at PwC where he focuses on end-to-end security solutions including security strategy, architecture, planning, design, implementation, and review. His work experience includes information systems and information security covering a variety of commercial, government, and military work, ranging from e-business initiatives to security assessments to full-scale enterprise security architecture. He regularly speaks on end-to-end security strategy and is regarded as a leader in end-to-end security architecture. Rudloff is a certified CISA, CISSP, and PMP. He has a master's degree in information and telecommunications management from Capitol College, Laurel, Maryland, and a bachelor's degree in physics from the University of Colorado at Boulder.

Ted V. Schaefer, PricewaterhouseCoopers LLP, is a partner in PwC's Global Risk Management Solutions group. He specializes in system and operational risk, process improvement, and internal control services to his clients. Schaefer primarily serves the technology, telecommunications, and cable industries. He earned a bachelor of business administration, emphasis in management information systems, from the University of Iowa and a master's of business administration from the University of Colorado at Denver. He is a certified information systems auditor and serves as a board member for the University of Colorado at Denver's Center for Information Technology Innovation.

Christopher F. Schmidt, Deloitte & Touche LLP, is a senior manager with Deloitte & Touche's Management Solutions and Services group (Solutions) in Denver, Colorado. Schmidt leads the Solutions IT consulting practice in Denver and has consulted in the areas of strategic information systems planning, systems implementations, and has helped clients deal with difficult transition periods as an interim CIO. He has twelve years of experience with systems implementations and specializes in global ERP and supply chain management software implementations. Schmidt has worked with many entities across the high-tech manufacturing and consumer business industries. He holds a bachelor's degree in accounting from Colorado State University and a master's in business administration from the University of Colorado at Denver.

Judy Scott, University of Colorado at Denver, is an assistant professor of information systems and was previously on the faculty of the University of Texas at Austin. Her teaching and research interests are in the area of ERP systems, business-to-business e-commerce, information technology, and organizational learning and knowledge management. Her publications appear in journals such as the *Journal of Management Information Systems, Journal of Computer-Mediated Communications, Decision Support Systems, Information and Management,* and *Information Systems Frontiers.* She received an undergraduate degree in science from Sydney University, Australia, and an MBA and PhD from the University of California at Irvine.

Carlos E. C. Silva, Electronic Data Systems, is a consultant architect. As a member of EDS's Colorado Solutions Center, he consults in all aspects of an application's development life cycle. In the last five years he has focused on the mobile computing space, designing and implementing wireless-enabled projects for major companies in the automobile, construction, and agricultural industries. His projects have included General Motors' OnStar and Case New Holland's FleetLink. Silva completed his master's degree in computer sciences and undergraduate degree in electrical engineering at the State University in Rio de Janeiro, Brazil.

Mary Lee Stansifer, University of Colorado at Denver, has been teaching at the University of Colorado at Denver since January 1996. She teaches international marketing, introduction to marketing, marketing in Spain, and marketing research at the undergraduate and graduate levels. Stansifer previously taught at the University of Colorado at Boulder, Regis University, and the University of Denver. International consumer behavior is Stansifer's major research interest. She received her PhD in international marketing from Northwestern University, an MBA from Indiana University in marketing, and a BA with Distinction in Spanish, political science, and Latin American area studies from the University of Kansas.

Alfred L. Stecklein, Gates Rubber Company, is group president, Worldwide Aftermarket Division at Gates, and is responsible for the sales, marketing, and distribution of automotive aftermarket products manufactured by Gates worldwide. In his

33 years at Gates, Stecklein has held a number of international executive positions. In 1999, he was named to the board of directors of the Rubber Manufacturers Association (RMA) and was elected to the board of directors of the Motor and Equipment Manufacturers Association (MEMA). He received a bachelor's degree in mechanical engineering from Kansas State University and a master's in business administration from the University of Colorado at Denver.

Steven Walczak, University of Colorado at Denver, is an associate professor of information systems. Before joining academia in 1991, Walczak worked for the Department of Defense and for government contractors. His research interests are in applied artificial intelligence, object-oriented systems development, and knowledge management. Walczak is widely published in journals such as the *Journal of Management Information Systems*, *Decision Support Systems*, and leading national and international conference proceedings. He received his PhD in computer information sciences from the University of Florida and his MS in computer science and BS in mathematics from Johns Hopkins University and Pennsylvania State University, respectively.

Randy Weldon, Weldon IT Consulting, is an independent consultant focusing on e-business, strategic IT planning, and program/project management processes for companies such as Ball Corporation. He has filled the roles of: CIO, director of application development, and management consultant for Geneva Pharmaceuticals, Storage Technology Corporation, and Andersen Consulting. Weldon received his MBA in international business from the University of Colorado at Denver, and his undergraduate degree in business with a concentration in management science from Colorado State University. He was selected as the global e-business champion for the generic drug sector of Novartis Corporation, the parent company for Geneva Pharmaceuticals.

Donald P. Wenninger, MCDATA, is vice president and chief information officer and is responsible for MCDATA's global IT strategy and infrastructure. Wenninger has over 14 years of experience in managing IT departments at Vixel Corporation, Intermec, Boeing, and IBM. He also has experience in establishing and building storage area network infrastructures. Wenninger has been a member of Gartner's CIO best practice group for the past eight years and is a current member of Colorado's CITI council and Tampa Bay's CIO council. He is frequently quoted and published in *SW Magazine*, *IndustryWeek*, *InformationWeek*, and *Profit* magazines. Wenninger holds a BS in business technology and MBAs in engineering and information technology.

Cheryl White, Fujitsu Consulting, is a director with Fujitsu. She is an executive coach and business architect specializing in the design and implementation of organization change. White writes articles periodically for the trade press and was a contributing author to *The Relationship Based Enterprise: Powering Business Success Through Customer Relationship Management*. She received her master's of science in business from Regis University.

Travis White is an independent analyst in the software industry who specializes in topics associated with company strategy, product planning, and technology marketing. White has held strategy and marketing positions with companies including J. D. Edwards, Solbourne Computer, and NBI, Inc. He has also taught at a variety of colleges and universities, including the University of Denver, and institutions in Mexico, Venezuela, Colombia, and Ecuador. White holds a bachelor's degree from the University of Delaware and a master's degree and a PhD from the University of Denver.

William White, Citigroup Diner's Club International, is executive vice president and CIO and has over 20 years of experience in the communications and computing industries. He is responsible for the North American and international Diner's Club Franchise base, with operations in 57 countries. White was previously the chief technology officer for US WEST Information Technologies, Inc., and was a member of President Clinton's Y2K Task Force. He has served on the technical advisory boards of Hewlett-Packard and Sequent Computers. He developed and managed software products and systems at NCR Corporation, Teradata, Digital Equipment Corporation, and the Boeing Corporation. White received a bachelor of computer science degree from Colorado State University.

Patricia M. Wilkey, Electronic Data Systems, is vice president of the Communications, Entertainment, and Media global industry group for EDS. Wilkey is active in global personal communications that range from wireline to wireless to infotainment. She is responsible for creating strategic alliances, developing strategic plans, and leading new business opportunities. Wilkey is a frequent guest speaker at Cellular Telecommunication & Internet Association (CTIA), IEC Supercomm, New Jersey Business Association, and various communication trade events. She received a BS degree from Nazareth College of Rochester, New York, with a double major in business and Spanish. She also attended the American Institute of Spanish Studies in Valencia, Spain, and the Université de Haute Bretagne in Rennes, France.

Philip Winterburn was responsible for AT&T Broadband's Internet, extranet, and intranet development teams as senior director. After joining AT&T Broadband (then TCI) in 1996, he was responsible for implementing Oracle Financials' accounts payable, delivering an enterprise reporting and decision support platform, and leading the IT department supporting engineering, finance, rate and regulatory matters, risk management, and revenue accounting. Recently, Winterburn led a team that delivered a CRM strategy and implementation road map for AT&T Broadband. Prior to joining AT&T Broadband, Winterburn worked in software development project management for over 10 years with Ernst & Young and EDS.

Index

Page numbers in italics refer to diagrams, tables, and figures.

A La Zing, 157

access points, 103

accountability, 235, 314, 316, 334, 396–99, 406

ACD (automated call distribution), 113, 287

ACID properties of transaction processing, 80n1

adapter. *See* network interface card (NIC)

addressing in networks, 106

adhocracy, 412

ADSL (asymmetric digital subscriber line), 119

advertising, 196. *See also* marketing

advertising model of B2C e-commerce, 167–68

AES (American Energy Systems), 223

affiliate model of B2C e-commerce, 170

airline industry, 4, 5, 6, 9, 27, 160, 173, 318

airports, 127

Albertsons, 173–74

always-on connection to Internet, 120

Amazon.com, 157, 167, 173, 195

America Online (AOL), 114, 116, 168

American Airlines, 4, 5, 6

American Energy Systems (AES), 223

American Express, 146

AMR, 4

analog cellular networks, 122

Analysis of Variance/Design of Experiments (ANOVA/DOE), 92

ANOVA/DOE (Analysis of Variance/Design of Experiments), 92

antivirus software, 141, 142

Any^6 concept, 187, 187n2

AOL, 114, 116, 168

APE (application programs for the enterprise), 269. *See also* ERP (enterprise resource planning) systems

Apollo reservation system, 4

Apple, 51

application integration middleware, 58n2, 60–61, *61*

application programs for the enterprise (APE), 269. *See also* enterprise resource planning (ERP) systems

application service provider (ASP): advantages and disadvantages of, 342–46; compared with business service provider (BSP), 189; and group support system (GSS), 97; and hype cycle, 66n1; and mass customization, 27; and return on investment (ROI), 344
architectures. See information technology (IT) architectures
Ariba, 165
ARPANET, 114
Artemis Views, 387
ASA (average speed of answer), 242
ASP (application service provider): advantages and disadvantages of, 342–46; compared with Business Service Provider (BSP), 189; and group support system (GSS), 97; and hype cycle, 66n1; and mass customization, 27; and return on investment (ROI), 344
ASP Industry Consortium (ASPIC), 343–44
ASPIC (ASP Industry Consortium), 343–44
assessment. See evaluation
asymmetric digital subscriber line (ADSL), 119
Asynchronous Transport Mode (ATM), 109
AT&T, 114, 116
ATM (Asynchronous Transport Mode), 109
ATM financial transactions, 9, 127, 288
auctions, 67–68, 167, 195
automated call distribution (ACD), 113, 287
automated vendor selection, 341–42
automobile industry, 26, 68, 157, 159–61, 166
average speed of answer (ASA), 242

B2B (business-to-business) e-commerce: definition of, 163; and dot.com crash, 197; models of, 163–66; and pricing on purchased goods and services, 159–60; private exchange or portal models of, 165–66; public marketplace and exchange models of, 164–65; and revenue opportunities, 155–56; supply chain integration models of, 166; and transaction processing system (TPS), 82; and web services, 67–68; and wireless technology, 126. See also e-business
B2C (business-to-consumer) e-commerce: advertising model of, 167–68; affiliate model of, 170; and bricks and clicks model, 169, 171–74, 173, 196, 197; brokerage model of, 169; manufacturer model of, 170; and margin opportunity, 167–70; merchant model of, 168–69; models of, 167–71; and revenue opportunities, 155–56; and revenue streams, 167–70; and sales and service cycle time, 128; subscription model of, 168; and web services, 67–68; and wireless technology, 126. See also e-business
B2E (business-to-employee) process, 126, 128, 183. See also intranets
Baan manufacturing system, 61
back-end systems, 189, 190–93
balanced scorecard, 231, 232, 242, 285
banking industry, 8–10, 287–88
banner ads, 196
Barnes & Noble, 177
benchmarking, 244, 307, 422–23
benefits modeling, 332–33
Best Buy, 174
BHAGs (big, hairy, audacious goals), 268
BIS (business intelligence system), 90, 92, 92n1
bizrate.com, 170
bleeding-edge technology, 22–25, 23
blogs (weblogs), 222–23
Bluetooth, 12–13, 120, 125
BPO (business process outsourcing), 348
brand awareness, 171–72, 195, 196, 197
Brandon Hall, 228
bricks and clicks model, 169, 171–74, 173, 196, 197
bridges, 103, 111
British Telecom, 316

broadband technologies: cable, 118; characteristics of broadband Internet access, 120–22; definition of, 117–18; delivery mechanisms for, 118–20; direction connection, 120; as disruptive, 12; DSL, 119; satellite, 119; wireless, 119–20
broadcast network architecture, 108
Broadvision, 176
brokerage model of B2C e-commerce, 169
Brooks, Frederick P., Jr., 388–91
Brooks's Law for staffing, 388–91
Brown, Dick, 127
browsers. *See* Web browsers
BSP (business service provider), 189–90
BTO (business transformational outsourcing), 349, 350
BU (business unit), 236
buddy system, *144*
"build-or-buy" decision, 335–38
bus networks, 107, *108*
business application outsourcing, 347–48
business continuity plan, 143
business-driven technology strategy: bottom-up input for, 16; and business knowledge, 15–16; characteristics of, 15; CIO's role in, 248; and IT architecture plan, 48; and managers, 20–21; need for, 10, 14–15; and organization culture, 211; process for development of, 15–20; project/corporate strategy fit, 365–66; and resource allocation, 308; and revenue enhancing versus cost reduction projects, 314–15; strategic technology vision for, 17, *18*; tactical implementation plan for, 17, 19–20, *19, 20*; top-down direction for, 16–17
business engine network, 388
business intelligence system (BIS), 90, 92, 92n1
business investment, 309. *See also* resource allocation
business models, 196–97, *198*, 365–69
business process outsourcing (BPO), 348
business processes: challenges in using

vendor-supplied ERP system to support redesigned business processes, 278–82, *280*; and customization of standard vendor applications, 299–302; definition of, 253–54, 256; and implementation of process technology, 256–59; integration of, by IT, 5–6; overview of, 251–52; radical versus incremental changes in, 265–69, *267*; and reengineering, 254–55; technology versus, 253–56; transformation in, 208, 260–69, *261, 262,* 423; and wireless technology, 126–29. *See also names of specific processes*
business service provider (BSP), 189–90
business-to-business (B2B) e-commerce. *See* B2B (business-to-business) e-commerce
business-to-consumer (B2C) e-commerce. *See* B2C (business-to-consumer) e-commerce
business-to-employee (B2E) process, 126, 128, 183. *See also* intranets
business transformational outsourcing (BTO), 349, 350
business unit (BU), 236
businesses. *See* e-business; organizations; *names of specific companies and organizations*

cable, 118
cabling for networks, 103–5, *103*
CAD (computer-aided design), 202, *261*
call centers, 254, 334, 356
cancellation of technology project, 215
capability maturity model (CMM), 230, 237–41, 238n2
capability maturity model integration (CMMI), 238n1
Carnegie Mellon Software Institute, 241
CASE (computer-aided software engineering), 66n1
casino gambling, 158
CBT (computer-based training), *227*
c-commerce, 273

CDMA2000 Phase 2, 123n2

CDMA (code division multiple access), 122, 122n1, 123

CDnow, 191

cell sites, 122

cellular telephony, 121–23

Center for Rural Studies, 96n3

central office (CO), 110

centralization of IT organization, 233–37

Century 21, 227

CEO (chief executive officer): and accountability, 235–36; and ASP model, 344; power of, 207–8; and spending for information technology, 305; and technology review committee, 17, 331; and transformation in business processes, 260

CFO (chief financial officer): and accountability, 334; and ASP model, 344; in centralized IT organization, 234; and cost of personal computers (PCs), 319; and financial measures of IT projects, 322; reaction of, to technology project, 213; and selection of IT projects, 326, 328; and spending for information technology, 305

change agents, 264–65

change control, 243, 417

change management, 260–69, 383–84

chat rooms, 222

chemicals and petroleum industry, 306

chief executive officer. *See* CEO (chief executive officer)

chief financial officer. *See* CFO (chief financial officer)

chief information officer. *See* CIO (chief information officer)

chief operations officer. *See* COO (chief operations officer)

chief technical officer. *See* CTO (chief technical officer)

Christensen, Clayton, 10–12

CIO (chief information officer): and centralized IT organization, 234; and failure to

align technology with business strategy, 248; and failure to deliver, 246–47; and failure to develop partnership with business, 247–48; and financial measures of IT projects, 322, 326; and hybrid or federated IT organization, 236–37; and portfolio evaluation of IT projects, 329–30n9; and reactions of other departments to technology project, 212; and relationship between IT organization and rest of the business, 229, 231, 242, 247–48; relationship of CTO to, 15n1; and resource allocation, 309, 329–30n9; and software upgrades, 359, 361; and strategic technology vision, 17; tenure of, 246–49; and transformation in business processes, 260; voluntary turnover of, 249; and Web services, 68–70

circuit-based networks, 108

Circuit City, 174

circuit-switched technology, 110

circuit switching, 110

Cisco, 82, 154

Citigroup, 237

clicks and bricks model, 169, 171–74, *173*, 196, 197

clickstream analysis, 176, 189

client: definition of, 52; fat versus thin clients, 54–57, 273, 321

client/server technology: advantages of, 53–54; architecture for, 40–41, *40*, 51–54, 108; and business processes, 255; definition of "client" and "server," 52; evolution of, 52; examples of, 53; and personal computers (PCs), 54–55; two- and three-tier architectures for, 40–41, *40*, 53

clients. *See* customers

cliff cutover, 403, 420

CMM (capability maturity model), 230, 237–41, 238n2

CMMI (capability maturity model integration), 238n1

CMS (content management system), *19*, 221, *226*

cnet.com, 170

CO (central office), 110

coaxial cable, *103*, 104

code division multiple access (CDMA), 122, 122n1, 123

Code Red, 139

Cohen, Fred, 139

cold site, *144*

collaborative commerce, 273

collaborative computing, 95, 95n1

collaborative decision making, 222–23

collaborative outsourcing, 349–50

Collins, Jerry C., 268

Colorado Department of Agriculture, 68

COM (component object model), *61*

Comergent, 176

CommerceOne, 165

commercial off-the-shelf (COTS) applications, 335–38, 342

committee model for steering board, 405

Common Object Request Broker Architecture (CORBA), 59, *61*

communication in organizations, 203, 205–6, 367, 421, 423

companies. *See* organizations; *names of specific companies*

Compaq, 11

competition: and business processes, 255; changes in, within industries, 4–10; and consumer bargaining power, 9–10; and ERP systems, 7, 278–82, *280*; intensity of rivalry, 7–8; new entrant and substitution threats, 8–9; restructuring supplier relationships by IT, 8

component-object model (COM), *61*

component-oriented middleware, 59, *61*

computer-aided design (CAD), 202, *261*

computer aided software engineering (CASE), 66n1

computer-based training (CBT), *226*

computer industry: and mass customization, 27; minicomputer, 11, 51; personal computer (PC), 11, 12, 13, 51, 54–55, 319. *See also names of specific companies*

computer technology. *See* information technology (IT)

computer telephony integration (CTI), 46, 287–88

computer viruses. *See* viruses

consultancies, 343

consumer bargaining power, 9–10

consumer trust, 179–80

consumers. *See* B2C (business-to-consumer) e-commerce; customers

content filtering, 141

content management system (CMS), *19*, 222, *227*

conventional outsourcing, 348, 349

convergence, 111–13

COO (chief operations officer), 17, 331

cookies, 181

CORBA (Common Object Request Broker Architecture), 59, *61*

Corio, 344

cost: of bleeding-edge technology, 23–24; of capital equipment for IT, 3; of CMM (capability maturity model), 240; of customer service, 162; of customization, 300; of data mining, 94; design cost, 77; of e-learning software, 226; of failed and troubled IT projects, 424; of fat versus thin clients, 56–57; of government software projects, 389–90; implementation cost, 77; intangible costs, 362; maintenance cost, 77; of operating systems, 73; of outsourcing, 351; of personal computers (PCs), 319; purchase cost, 77; of software upgrades, 362; tangible costs, 362; total cost of ownership (TCO), 77, 244, 319–21, 325; of Unix platform, 76–77; of viruses, 139. *See also* cost reductions; resource allocation cost reduction projects, 312–15

cost reductions: and CMM (capability maturity model), 240; and competition, 4–6, 7; in customer service, 162; and e-business, 9, 154–55, 159–62, 172–73; and e-learning, 227, 228; and e-marketing, 177; in information technology (IT), 161–62; and offshore outsourcing, 355; and resource allocation on information technology, 312–15; and Web services, 69; and wireless technology, 128–29. *See also* cost; resource allocation

COTS (commercial off-the-shelf) applications, 335–38, 342

Covisint, 159–60, 166

credibility, earned, 229

crisis management, 142

CRM (customer relationship management) systems: attributes and capabilities of, 286–91; and balanced scorecard, 285; and business processes, 255, 258–59; and business-driven technology strategy, 16, *19*; common features of, 343; customer-driven CRM, 284–85; and customer segmentation and insight, 288; customer service in, 287; customization of, 299; description of, 282–86; and e-business, 157, 174–78, 189; and e-marketing, 174, 176, 177; evolution of, 282–84; integration of, with ERP and SCM systems, 272–73, 293; and Internet, 116, 157; and marketing integration, 289–90; and mass customization, 28, 29; multiple channels in, 287–88; and performance measurement, 290; and predictive modeling, 289; and productivity, 6; and return on investment (ROI), 283, 332

cross-functional management, 412–15, 423

cross-selling, 176–77

CTI (computer telephony integration), 46, 287–88

CTO (chief technical officer), 15, 15n1, 17, 69, 234

culture of organization, 28–29, 208–11, 223, 368

customer-driven CRM, 284–85

customer relationship management (CRM) systems: attributes and capabilities of, 286–91; and balanced scorecard, 285; and business processes, 255, 258–59; and business-driven technology strategy, 16, *19*; common features of, 343; customer-driven CRM, 284–85; and customer segmentation and insight, 288; customer service in, 287; customization of, 299; description of, 282–86; and e-business, 157, 174–78, 189; and e-marketing, 174, 176, 177; evolution of, 282–84; integration of, with ERP and SCM systems, 272–73, 293; and Internet, 116, 157; and marketing integration, 289–90; and mass customization, 28, 29; multiple channels in, 287–88; and performance measurement, 290; and predictive modeling, 289; and productivity, 6; and return on investment (ROI), 283, 332

customer segmentation and insight, 288

customer service, 162, 287, 292, 392

customers: bargaining power of, 9–10; better knowledge and targeting of, 6; and e-business, 153, 156–58, 172, *173*, 174–78, 195–96; and e-marketing, 174–78; evaluation of IT organization by, 245; feedback by, 204; and mass customization, 28; needs and habits of, 176; negative reaction to IT projects by, 216–19; and privacy issues, 178–82; profiling of, 189; satisfaction and loyalty of, 127, 293–94; trust of, 179–80; and wireless technology, 127. *See also other entries beginning with* "customer"

customization: and ASP (application service provider), 345; cost of, 300; and e-business, 154; of ERP systems, 271; and integration of application into current environment, 301–2; and required functionality, 300–301; of standard vendor applications, 299–302; versus mass customization, 26. *See also* mass customization

cutover, 403, 420

DaimlerChrysler, 161, 235
DARPA (Defense Advanced Research Projects Agency), 114
data conversion, 274, 275
data integrity, 296–97
data marts, 89, 92, 288
data mining, 10, 90, 91–95, 157, 175, 202, 283, 288
data networks, 105–13. *See also* networks
data quality, 296
data standardization, 297
data storage recovery strategy, 145
data warehouses, 83, 87–90, 92, 175, 202
database gateways, 60–61
database management system (DBMS), 40
Davis, Stan, 25
DBMS (database management system), 40
DEC, 11
decentralization, 146–47, 206–7, 233–37
decision making in organizations, 206–8, 222–23
decision support systems (DSS): applications, 84–85; benefits and challenges of, 85–86; characteristics of, 83–84; compared with transaction processing system (TPS), 84; and competition, 7; definition of, 83; development of, 86; example of uses of, 206; and information gathering, 202; and IT architecture, 40
deep analytics, 288
Defense Advanced Research Projects Agency (DARPA), 114
Defense Department, 241
Dell Computer Corp., 13, 27, 160, 170, 274–75, 294
design-build-run, 348
desktop software upgrades, 360–61

Deutsche Bank, 147
dial-up speed, 117–18n1
Digex, 343
digital content and services, 158
digital data transmission, 124
Digital Equipment Corporation (DEC), 11
digital loyalty networks, 293–94
digital technologies, 122
digital voice mail, 203, 206
disaster recovery (DR) plan, 142–47, *144*, 189
disruptive technology, 10–14
distributed computing, 40–41, 53. *See also* client/server technology
distributed headquarters, 146–47
distribution channels, 6
dot.com crash, 159, 194–98
downstream supply chain, 291
DR (disaster recovery) plan, 142–47, *144*, 189
DSL, 119
DSS (decision support systems): applications, 84–85; characteristics of, 83–84; compared with transaction processing system (TPS), 84; and competition, 7; definition of, 83; example of uses of, 206; and information gathering, 202; and IT architecture, 40
dumb terminals, definition of, 54

E*Trade, 175
EAI (enterprise application integration), *19*, *59*, 61, *61*, 192–93
earned credibility, 229
Eastman Kodak, 158, 181
eBay, 82, 167, 169, 195, 196
e-business: and access to customers, 56–57; assumptions of, 194–98; B2C (business-to-consumer) e-commerce, 67, 68, 126, 128, 155–56; B2E (business-to-employee) process, 126, 128, 183; and brand awareness, 171–72, 195, 196, 197; and bricks and clicks model, 169, 171–74, *173*, 196,

e-business (*continued*)
197; business model assumptions of,
196–97; business-to-business (B2B)
e-commerce, 67–68, 82, 126, 141, 155–
56, 159–60, 163–66, 197; and client relationships, 172, *173*; components of
e-business strategy, 151–55, *152*; consumer acceptance assumptions of, 195–
96; and cost reduction, 9, 154–55, 159–
62, 172–73; and customer service costs,
162; and customer value, 153; and customized services, 154; dot.com crash, 159,
194–98; economic assumptions of, 194–
95; and electronically enabled products,
158; and elimination of middleman, 160;
and e-marketing, 174–78; financial assumptions of, 194; and front-end/back-
end integration, 189, 190–93, 196; and
geographic reach, 156–57; and hackers,
136; and infrastructure investments, 162;
introduction to, 149–50; and leveraging
core competencies, 154; and new customer segments, 157; and new sales channels, 156; and pricing on purchased goods
and services, 159–60; privacy issues in,
178–82, 189; revenue opportunities created by, 155–58; and sales to existing customers, 157–58; and security, 187, 189;
and streamlining business infrastructure,
154–55; technical elements for implementation of, 186–90; and technology
standards, 155, 192; and virtual fulfillment
networks, 154
e-commerce. *See* e-business
EDGE, 123n2
EDI (electronic data interchange), 8, 60, 63–
64, 64n6, 163
EDS, 127, 187nn. 1–2, 343
education of employees. *See* e-learning; employee training
802.11a standard, 125
802.11b standard, 125

802.11g standard, 125
EIP (enterprise information portals), 183.
See also extranets
EIS (executive information system), 85
e-learning, 185, 206, 207, 224–28, 225n1,
227
electronic data interchange (EDI), 8, 60, 63–
64, 64n6, 163
electronic vaulting, 145
e-mail: and connectionless networks, 105;
and firewalls, 137; as Internet service, 116;
and knowledge encoding and distribution,
222; Lotus Notes for, 222; and marketing,
175–76; as message-oriented middleware,
60; Microsoft's Hotmail, 67; protocol for,
116; uses of, 203, 206, 222; viruses and
e-mail attachments, 141
e-marketing, 174–78
emergency management, 142
employee portals. *See* intranets
employee training, 140–41, 185, 206, 207,
224–28, *227*
encryption, 117, 138
enterprise application integration (EAI), *19*,
59, 61, *61*, 192–93
enterprise information portals (EIP), 183
Enterprise Java Beans, 42
enterprise portals. *See* intranets
enterprise resource management (ERM),
269. *See also* enterprise resource planning
(ERP) systems
enterprise resource planning (ERP) systems:
and business processes, 255, 258–59; and
business-driven technology strategy, 16,
19; challenges in using vendor-supplied
ERP system to support redesigned business processes, 278–82, *280*; and Cisco,
82; and collaborative commerce, 273; and
competitive versus value-oriented companies, 7, 278–82, *280*; customization
of, 271, 299; and decision making, 206;
definition of, 269; dimensions of, 270–

71; and e-learning, 226; evolution of, 270; external risks for implementation of, 276–77, 278; and extranet, 183; failure in implementation of, 373–76; flexibility of, after implementation, 272; and front-end/back-end integration, 190–93; and high performance management practices, 210; implementation of, 218, *261*, 271, 274–78, 373–76; information system risks in implementation of, 275, 277; integration of, with CRM and SCM, 272–73, 293; integration versus best-of-breed, 271–72; and knowledge encoding and distribution, 222; and mass customization, 28, 29; organizational risks in implementation of, 275–76, 277; origins of, 270; and productivity, 5; project risks in implementation of, 274–75, 277; quality and timeliness of releases, 272; risks of implementation of, 274–78; selection of, 208; trends in, 272–73; typical ERP solutions, 271–72; upgrading of, 359–60; use of, 202–3

enterprise software, 269. *See also* ERP (enterprise resource planning) systems

Epicentric, 183

e-procurement, 22, 23

Ericsson, 12–13

ERM (enterprise resource management), 269. *See also* ERP (enterprise resource planning) systems

ERP (enterprise resource planning) systems: and business processes, 255, 258–59; and business-driven technology strategy, 16, *19*; challenges in using vendor-supplied ERP system to support redesigned business processes, 278–82, *280*; and Cisco, 82; and collaborative commerce, 273; and competitive versus value-oriented companies, 7, 278–82, *280*; customization of, 271, 299; and decision making, 206; definition of, 269; dimensions of, 270–71; and e-learning, 226; evolution of, 270;

external risks for implementation of, 276–77, 278; and extranet, 183; failure in implementation of, 373–76; flexibility of, after implementation, 272; and front-end/back-end integration, 190–93; and high performance management practices, 210; implementation of, 218, *261*, 271, 274–78, 373–76; information system risks in implementation of, 275, 277; integration of, with CRM and SCM, 272–73, 293; integration versus best-of-breed, 271–72; and knowledge encoding and distribution, 222; and mass customization, 28, 29; organizational risks in implementation of, 275–76, 277; origins of, 270; and productivity, 5; project risks in implementation of, 274–75, 277; quality and timeliness of releases, 272; risks of implementation of, 274–78; selection of, 208; trends in, 272–73; typical ERP solutions, 271–72; upgrading of, 359–60; use of, 202–3

ESNET, 114

Ethernet, 52, 103, 104–5, *104*, 109, 111

Ethertalk, 101

evaluation: benchmarking, 244, 307, 422–23; and benefits modeling, 332–33; of choice of one IT project over another, 326–31, *328*, *329*, *330*; customers' perspectives on IT organization, 245; of data mining software, 93; of disaster recovery plan, 146; financial measures of IT organizations and projects, 244, 322–26, 328, *329*; independent assessment of IT projects, 333–34; internal process quality of IT organization, 242–44; of IT organizations, 242–45; measure of performance (MOP), 392–95, *394*, 398–99, 416, 421–22; of transaction processing system (TPS), 81

executive clients, 396–99, 405, 416

executive information system (EIS), 85

executive providers, 396–404, 399–400n1, 402n3, 416, 417, 422

Exodus, 343

Extended Business Reporting Language (XBRL), 63

eXtensible Markup Language (XML), 60–66, *61*, *63*, 69–70, 188, 189, 297

eXtensible Stylesheet Language (XSL), 64n8

extranets: definition of, 183; partner portal uses of, 185–86; and security, 183; uses of, 183, 185–86; virus protection for, 141; and Web architecture, 41

failure of technology implementation, 373–80, 418–21

fall back conversion plan, 420

Fast Ethernet, 103, 104, *104*

fat versus thin clients, 54–57, 273, 321

faxes, 203

FCC (Federal Communications Commission), 13, 118

FDDI (Fiber Distributed Data Interface), *104*, 105

Federal Communications Commission (FCC), 13, 118

Federal Trade Commission (FTC), 178, 180

FedEx (Federal Express), 4, 6, 126–27

feedback, 204, *221*, 223. *See also* evaluation

Fiber Distributed Data Interface (FDDI), *104*, 105

fiber optics, *103*, 104–5

Fidesic, 67

file server, 53

File Transfer Protocol (FTP), 116, 137

finance department, 213

financial analysis and reporting, 84–85

financial measures of organizations and projects, 244, 322–26

financial services industry, 8–10, 13, 287–88, *306*

firewall, 67–69, 135–38, 141, 191

first-mover advantage, 195, 197

fixed wireless services, 120

Flash animations, 115

following-edge technology, 21, *23*

food industry, 157, 275, 276

Ford, Henry, 26

Ford Motor Company, 26

fork-lift upgrades, 53

Forrester Research, Inc., 17, 339

forums. *See* newsgroups

FoxMeyer, 275, 276–77

frame relay networks, 109

FreeMarkets, Inc., 166

front-end/back-end integration, 189, 190–93, 196

front-end systems, 189, 190–93

FTC (Federal Trade Commission), 178, 180

FTP (File Transfer Protocol), 116, 137

function point analysis, 300

functional recovery, 143

gambling, 120, 158

Gartner Group, 17, 58n2, 67, 68n7, 165, 269, 293, 319, 321, 339, 355

Gates, Bill, 57

gateways, 103, 111

GDSS (group decision support system), 95n1

General Electric, 160

General Motors, 68, 154, 159–61

General System for Mobile Communications (GSM), 122, 122n1, 123

geo-fence, 128

Geographic Information Systems (GIS), 92

Gigabit Ethernet, 104–5, *104*, 109

GIS (Geographic Information Systems), 92

Globix, 343

Goldman Sachs, 146

Gore-Tex, 276, 277

GPS, 127

Grainger, 165, 276

granularity, 88–89

graphical system interface (GUI), 72, 273

green fielding, 211

group decision support system (GDSS), 95n1

group support system (GSS), 95–99

GroupSystems, 98n6

groupware, 96, 96n4, 98n6, 203

Grove, Andrew, 13

GSM (General System for Mobile Communications), 122, 122n1, 123

GSS (group support system), 95–99

GUI (graphical system interface), 72, 273

hacker signatures, 137

hackers, 136, 141

hard tokens, 132

hazardous materials companies, 127–28

help desk, 242–43, 362

Herman Miller furniture manufacturer, 294

Hershey Foods Corporation, 275, 276

Hewlett Packard, 181

HFC (hybrid fiber coax) plants, 118

high bandwidth for Internet access, 120–21

high-performance management practices, 209–10

high-performance teams, 423

Home Depot, 68

"honey pots," 137

Hopper, Max, 6

hot site, *144*

Hotel Gatti, 157

Hotmail, 67

HTML (Hypertext Markup Language), *61*, 62, 115, 273

HTTP (Hypertext Transfer Protocol), 105, 115

hubs, 102, 107, *108*, 111

human resources department, 213

hurdle rate, 324

hybrid fiber coax (HFC) plants, 118

hyperlinks, 115

Hypertext Markup Language (HTML), *61*, 62, 115, 273

Hypertext Transfer Protocol (HTTP), 105, 115

IBM, 4, 11, 13, 51, 181, 227

IBM Global Services, 343

IBM MQSeries, 60

IBM PC, 12, 51

IBM System / 360, 3, 389

IDC, 339

IDSL (ISDN Digital Subscriber Line), 119

implementation: Brooks's Law for staffing, 388–91; and "build or buy" decision, 337–38; of business-driven technology strategy, 17, 19–20, *19*, *20*; and business process design, 256–59; and CMM (capability maturity model), 239–40; cost of Unix platform, 77; costs of, 77, 240; and cross-functional management, 412–15, 423; of ERP systems, 218, *261*, 271, 274–78, 373–76; failure of, 373–80, 418–21; and managerial authority, 408–12, *409*, 416; measure of performance (MOP) in, 392–95, *394*, 398, 416, 421–22; myths of technology-related implementations, 266–68; overview of, 363–64; and project management, 379–88, 399–404, 408–18, 422; and project manager, 382, 398, 399–404, 408–12, *409*, 413, 415–18; of radical versus incremental changes, 265–69, *267*; risks of, 369–73, *370*; risks of business model of project, 365–69; risks of ERP implementation, 274–78; risks of SCM implementation, 295; risks of throwaway systems, 31; and sponsors of projects, 19, 245, 314, 327, 367, 372–73, 377, 381, 382, 396–404, 416, 422; and steering board for technology projects, 215, 376, 402n3, 404–7, 422; strategies for success, 415–18; of supply chain management (SCM) system, 294–98; technical elements for e-business implementation, 168–90; termination of IT project, 421–24

incremental changes in business processes, 265–69

industries. *See names of specific industries and companies*

information gathering, 202

information technology (IT): bleeding-edge, leading-edge, or following-edge technology, 21–25; business-driven technology strategy, 10, 14–21, 211; as disruptive technology, 10–14; history of computer technology, 5, 51–52, 54–55; impact of, on industries generally, 1–6, 204; survey on companies' approach to, 25, *25*; throwaway systems, 30–33. *See also* e-business; Internet; networks; *names of specific applications; other entries beginning with "information technology"*

information technology (IT) architectures: client/server architecture, 40–41, *40*, 51–54, 108; components and use of, 39, 43; considerations for choice of, 42–46; definition of, 43; development of, 44; for e-business, 187, 188; levels of, 46; mainframe architecture, 39, *40*; for networks, 107–8; and organization structure, 44; overview of, 35–36, *40*; plan for, 47–51, *49*; principles for, 43–44; and technological change, 46; three-tier client/server architecture, *40*, 41; and throwaway systems, 31; two-tier client/server architecture, 40, *40*; and Web architecture, 41–42

information technology (IT) organizations: balanced scorecard for, 231–33, *232*, 242; and benchmarking the organization, 244; budget of, 244, 247; and capability maturity model (CMM), 237–41; centralized or decentralized organization of, 233–37; customers' perspectives on, 245; and earned credibility, 229; financial measures of, 244; hybrid or federated organization of, 236–37; internal process quality of, 242–44; linked processes for,

230–31; measurement of success of, 242–45; prioritization and allocation proces for, 231; reactions of IT department to technology project, 214; relationship between rest of the business and, 229–33, 242, 247–48; strategic planning process for, 230–31; success components for, 229–233, *232*; tenure of CIO in, 246–49

information technology (IT) projects: approach to, 402–3; and authorities of project manager, 408–12, *409*, 416; benefits of, 326–27, 331–34, 384, 422; Brooks's Law for staffing, 388–91; and "build-or-buy" decision, 335–38; changes in, 402–3, 402n3; choice of one project over another, 326–31, *328*, *329*, *330*; and client expectations, 403; and cliff cutover, 403, 420; and communication, 367, 421, 423; contingency for, 402, 419–20; and cross-functional management, 412–15, 423; and customer-supplier relationship, 414–15; definition of, 380; failure in implementation of, 373–80, 418–21; fall back conversion plan for, 420; financial measures for, 322–26, 328, *329*; financial value of, 328–29, *329*, *330*; independent assessment of, 333–34; management of, 379–88, 399–404, 408–18, 422; management tools for, 385–88, *386*, *387*; monitoring of, 383, 418; and MOP (measure of performance), 392–95, *394*, 398, 416, 421–22; and organizational capacity, 368–69, 378; outcomes of, 366–68, 381, 402–3; plan for, 417, 418–21; portfolio evaluation of, 329–30n9; project manager of, 382, 398, 399–404, 408–12, 413, 415–18; reporting on, 383; resource pools of experts for, 414; risk matrix for, 329, *330*; risks of business model of, 365–69; risks of implementation of, 369–73, *370*; scale and complexity of, 371, 377–78, 422;

scope of, 381; sponsors of, 19, 245, 314, 327, 367, 372–73, 377, 381, 382, 396–404, 416, 422; and staff experience with technology, 372; and staff performance, 418; and stakeholders, 381–82, 403–7, 416, 417; steering board for, 215, 367, 402n3, 404–7, 422; strategic alignment of, 327–28, *328*, *330*; structure of, 372–73, 416–17; successful implementation of, 415–18; team members of, 401, 412–13, 423; termination of, 421–24; tracking mechanism for, 420–21; value of and benefits realization for, 384, 422. *See also* implementation; resource allocation

insiders, 131

instant messaging, 206, 222

Instinet, 147

Institute of Electrical and Electronics Engineers, 124

intangible costs, 362

integration: of business operations, 5–6; CTI (computer telephony integration), 46, 287–88; and customer relationship management (CRM) system, 283; and customization of standard vendor applications, 301–2; of ERP, SCM, and CRM applications, 272–73, 293; of front-end and back-end systems, 190–93; marketing integration, 289–90; and supply chain management (SCM), 296

integration brokers, 61

integrators, 343

Intel, 13

internal process quality of IT organization, 242–44

internal rate of return (IRR), 324, 325, 328, *329*

internal supply chain, 291

International Organization of Standardization (ISO) 9001, 237n1

International Organization of Standardization (ISO) 12207, 237n1

Internet: access to, 116–17; and airline industry, 9; auction sites, 67–68, 167, 195; and banking industry, 9–10; and broadband technologies, 117–21; business uses of generally, 116–17; communication with customers by, 6; compared with World Wide Web (WWW), 115; and competition within industries, 7; and consumer bargaining power, 9–10; definition of, 114; and delivery of digital content, 158; description of, 114–16, *115*; and discount brokerages, 13; and e-marketing, 176–77; gaming on, 120, 158; history of, 114; and middleware, 58; and new entrant and substitution threats, 8–9; number of users of, 116; and privacy issues, 179–82; protocols, 12, 111, 115, 116; services of, 115, 116; supply technologies based on, 8; and telecommuting, 121; and video conferencing, 121; and viruses, 141; and Web architecture, 41; Web services, 8, 32. *See also* e-business; Web services

Internet advertising, 196

Internet Protocol (IP), 12, 111, 115

Internet service provider (ISP), 114, *115*, 116–17, 120, 124

interoperability of networks, 106

intranets: and business-driven technology strategy, *19*; and cost reduction for IT, 161; definition of, 182–83; employee portal uses of, 183–84, 206; example of use of, 203; and integration with back-office applications, 185; and knowledge encoding and distribution, 222–23; and knowledge management, 185; and tools for employees' management of work lives, 184–85; uses of, 183–85, 206; and viruses, 141; and Web architecture, 41

intrusion detection systems, 137

investment in technology. *See* resource allocation

IP (Internet Protocol), 111, 112, 115

IRR (internal rate of return), 324, 325, 328, *329*

ISDN Digital Subscriber Line (IDSL), 119

ISO (International Organization of Standardization) 9001, 237n1

ISO (International Organization of Standardization) 12207, 237n1

ISP (Internet service provider), 114, *115*, 116–17, 120, 124

IT. *See* information technology (IT)

IT organizations. *See* information technology (IT) organizations

IT projects. *See* information technology (IT) projects

J2EE (Java 2 Enterprise Edition), 41–42, 59, *61*, 67

J. Crew, 156

J. D. Edwards, 183–84, 272

Java, 188, 273

Java applets, 115

Java 2 Enterprise Edition (J2EE), 41–42, 59, *61*, 67

JavaScript, 115

Katzenbach, Jon R., 423

KBkids.com, 191

KD (Knowledge Discovery), 92

Kemper Insurance, 235

Kerzner, Harold, 408

key performance indicators (KPIs), 85

klogs, 223

KM. *See* knowledge management (KM)

KMS (knowledge management system), 224, 227

Knowledge Discovery (KD), 92

knowledge encoding and distribution, 222–23

Knowledge Garden, 184

knowledge management (KM): and competition, 7; and data warehouses, 88; and decision making, 206; definition of, 219–20; and information gathering, 202; and intranets, 185; and knowledge acquisition, 221–22; knowledge component of, 219–20, *221*; and knowledge encoding and distribution, 222–23; and knowledge mapping and gap identification, 221; management component of, 220, *221*. *See also* e-learning

knowledge management system (KMS), 224, *227*

knowledge mapping and gap identification, 221

Kodak, 158, 181

KPIs (key performance indicators), 85

Krispy Kreme, 227

LAN (Local Area Network): and ATM, 109; and Bluetooth technology, 120; combined data and voice networks, 112; description of, 106, *107*; and Ethernet, 52, 109; and frame relay, 109; and routers, 103; switches for multiple LANs, 106, *107*; wireless LANs, 122, 124–25

LCMS (learning content management system), 224, *227*

lead generation in marketing, 176

leading-edge technology, 22, *23*

learning content management system (LCMS), 224, *227*

learning management system (LMS), 222, *227*

learning organizations, 221–22, 224–28. *See also* e-learning

learning plans, 91–92

Learning Space, 96n3

legal department, 214

Level3, 116

Liberty Alliance, 67

licensing of software, 343

life-cycle management, 244

Linux, 73–77, *75*, 101

living.com, 196

LMS (learning management system), 222, *227*

Local Area Network (LAN): and Bluetooth technology, 120; combined data and voice networks, 112; description of, 106, *107*; and Ethernet, 52, 109; and frame relay, 109; and routers, 103; switches for multiple LANs, 106, *107*; wireless LANs, 122, 124–25

logic bombs, 140

"logical" partitions, 53

Lotus Notes, 96n3, 222

loyalty of customers, 127, 293–94

Lucent Technologies, 13

Macintosh operating system, 51, 101, 226

Mager, Robert F., 395

mail server, 53

mainframes, 39, *40*, 51

mainstream technology, 22, *23*

maintenance: cost of, 77; of disaster recovery (DR) plan, 146; resource allocation for, 310

MAN (Metropolitan Area Network), 106

man-month units, 388–91

management practices: authorities of project manager, 408–12, *409*, 416; and "build or buy" decision, 338; and business-driven technology strategy, 20–21; and CMM (capability maturity model), 240; cross-functional management, 412–15, 423; high performance management practices, 209–10; project management, 379–88, 399–404, 408–12, 422; quality management, 383–84; and transformation in business processes, 260, 264–65, 423

management support systems (MSS), 36–37

management tools, 385–88, *386*, *387*

managerial authority, 408–12, *409*, 416

manufacturer model of B2C e-commerce, 170

manufacturing industries: and enterprise application integration (EAI), 61; and ERP systems, 270, 373–76; IT architecture for, 44; IT architecture plan for, *49*; and mass customization, 27; technology spending pattern of, *306*

manufacturing resource planning (MRP), 270

margin opportunity, 167–70

market analysis, 175

market share protection, 317

marketing: access to marketing collateral and other documentation, 177; and clickstream analysis, 176, 189; cost reduction for, 177; and CRM systems, 289–90; cross-selling and up-selling, 176–77; and customer needs and habits, 176; and e-marketing, 174–78; lead generation in, 176; market analysis, 175; personalization and customization in, 175–76; targeted marketing, 175

marketing department, 212–13

Marsh & McLennan, 146

mass customization, 6, 25–29

McDonalds, 124

McKenna, Regis, 25–26

McKenzie, Ray, 173

mean time to repair (MTTR), 242

measure of performance (MOP), 392–95, *394*, 398, 416, 421–22

medical profession, 128

merchant model of B2C e-commerce, 168–69

Merrill Lynch, 69

Merton, Thomas, 218

mesh networks, 107, *108*

message boards. *See* newsgroups

message queuing, 60, *61*

message-oriented middleware, 59–60, *61*

meter reading job, 129

Metropolitan Area Network (MAN), 106

micromarketing databases, 175

Microsoft, 13, 181

Microsoft .NET, 41, 42, 59, *61*, 67

Microsoft Exchange, 344

Microsoft Hotmail, 67

Microsoft NetMeeting, 98n5

Microsoft Network (MSN), 114, 116, 168

Microsoft Power Point, 226

Microsoft Project 2002, 388

Microsoft Windows, 41, 51, 70–73, 101

middleman, elimination of, 160

middleware: application integration middleware, 60–61, *61*; benefits of, 58; categories of, 59–62, *59*, *61*; and client/server,
53; definition of, 53, 58; for e-business,
188; and intranets, 185; and IT architecture, 41, 42; market for, 58n2; message-
oriented middleware, 59–60, *61*; object-
and component-oriented middleware, 59,
61; objective of, 57–58, 161; Web-based
middleware, 60, *61*

Milestones Professional 2002, 387

minicomputer, 11, 51

mobile site, *144*

mobile telephony technologies, 121–23

mobile wireless services, 119, 122–23

model, 92

MOP (measure of performance), 392–95,
394, 398, 416, 421–22

Morgan Stanley, 146

Motorola, 13

MQSeries, 60

MRP (manufacturing resource planning),
270

MS-DOS, 51

MSN (Microsoft Network), 16, 114, 168

MSS (management support systems), 36–37

MTTR (mean time to repair), 242

multicast network architecture, 108

NASA (National Aeronautics and Space Administration), 202

National Aeronautics and Space Administration (NASA), 202

.NET Application Architecture, 41, 42, 59,
61, 67

net present value (NPV), 20, 324, 325, 328,
329

Netscape Collabra Server, 98n5

network architecture, 107–8

network interface card (NIC), 101, 102,
104–5, 140–41

network protocols, 101, 105, 111, 115, 116

network wiring, 103–5, *103*

networks: access points, 103; addressing,
106; architecture of, 107–8; bridges, 103,
111; cabling for, 103–5, *103*; combined
data and voice networks, 111–12; data
networks, 105–13; definition of, 101;
dimensions of, 105–6; and firewall,
135–38, 141; gateways, 103, 111; hardware elements of, 101–5; hubs/repeaters,
102, 107, *108*, 111; interface cards for,
101, 102; logical topology of, 108–9;
MAN (Metropolitan Area Network),
106; overview of, 37; PAN (Personal
Area Network), 106, 122, 124–25; physical topology of, 107, *108*; protocols for,
101, 105, 111, 115, 116; routers, 102–3,
106, 111; signaling method of, 108–9;
standards for, 106; switches, 102, 106,
110–11; voice networks, 110–13. *See
also* extranets; intranets; LAN (Local
Area Network); WAN (Wide Area
Network)

newsgroups, 116

NIC (network interface card), 101, 102,
104–5, 140–41

niche retailers, 169

NIMDA, 139

928 International, 157

Nokia, 13

nonvolatile data, 88

NORDUNET, 114

Novell GroupWise, 98n5

Novell network protocol, 101

NPV (net present value), 20, 324, 325, 328, *329*

NSFNET, 114

NSINET, 114

object-oriented middleware, 59, *61*

Object-Oriented Programming (OOP), 66n1

Object Request Broker (ORB), 59, *61*

OEM (Original Equipment Manufacturer) Insurance, *144*

offshore IT service providers, 348, 355–59, *356*

off-site data storage, 145

Olsen, Eric, 422

OLTP (On Line Transaction Processing), 92

On Line Transaction Processing (OLTP), 92

OOP (Object-Oriented Programming), 66n1

Open Plan, 387

operating systems: choice of Unix platform, 74–77, *75*; cost of, 73; reliability of, 72; scalability of, 71–72; selection of, 71–73; and system management, 72–73; upgrades of, 362; Windows versus Unix, 70–73

operations department, 213

Oracle, 82, 185, 272

ORB (Object Request Broker), 59, *61*

Orbitz, 9, 169

organizational review, 211

organizations: and capability maturity model (CMM), 237–41; centralized or decentralized organization of IT organization, 233–37; communication in, 203, 205–6, 367, 421, 423; competitive versus value-oriented companies, 278–82, *280*; coordination and control of activities by, 201–5; culture of, 28–29, 208–11, 223, 368; decision making in, 206–8; e-learning strategy in, 224–28, *227*; IT organization's relationship with rest of the business, 229–33, 242, 247–48; job content in, 207; learning organizations, 221–22, 224–28, *227*; mea-

surement of success of IT organization, 242–45; negative reactions by customers and suppliers to IT projects of, 216–19; overview of, 199–200; power in, 207–8; racehorse organizations, 225; reactions of departments within, to technology project, 212–16; steering board for technology projects in, 215, 367, 402n3, 404–7, 422. *See also* information technology (IT) organizations; information technology (IT) projects; *names of specific companies*

Original Equipment Manufacturer (OEM) Insurance, *144*

OS/2, 226

outsourcing: and ASP (application service provider), 342–46; business application outsourcing, 347–48; business process outsourcing, 348; business transformational outsourcing (BTO), 349, 350; and business-driven technology strategy, 20; collaborative outsourcing, 349–50; considerations on decisions about, 351–54; conventional outsourcing, 348, 349; expenditures on, 351; and IT organization, 244; and needed skills, 352–53; of nonstrategic functions, 353; and offshore IT service providers, 348, 355–59, *356*; purposes of different types of, 347–51; relationships in, 348–49; and scale, 352; and speed, 354; strategic considerations for, 353–54; technology infrastructure outsourcing, 347

packet-switched networks, 109, 110, 111

Palm company, 156

PAN (Personal Area Network), 106, 122, 124–25

parameters, 393, 424

partner portals. *See* extranets

payback period, 322–23, 325, 328, *329*

PBX (Private Branch Exchange), 110–11, 113

PC (personal computer), 11, 12, 13, 51, 54–55, 319

PCS (personal communication system), 122–23

PDA (personal digital assistant), 124

PDC (primary domain controller), 53

peer-to-peer network architecture, 107

PeopleSoft, 185, 272, 344

PepsiCo, 235

permanent virtual circuits (PVCs), 109

Personal Area Network (PAN), 106, 122, 124–25

personal communication system (PCS), 122–23

personal computer (PC), 11, 12, 13, 51, 54–55, 319

personal digital assistant (PDA), 124

personal video recorders (PVR), 121

Peters, Tom, 412

Pfeffer, Jeffrey, 209–10

pharmaceutical industry, 261, *262*

plain old telephone service (POTS), 119

planning: business continuity plan, 143; disaster recovery (DR) plan, 142–47, *144*; enterprise resource planning (ERP) system, 5, 7, 16, *19*, 28, 29, 82, 183, 269–82; fall back conversion plan, 420; IT architecture plan, 47–51, *49*; for IT projects, 417, 418–21; learning plans, 91–92; manufacturing resource planning (MRP), 270; multi-year technology investment plan, 311–12, *312*; and organizational review, 211; resource planning, 202–3; strategic planning process, 230–31; supply chain planning, 295, 297–98

PlanView, 387

Plumtree, 176, 183

PMO (Program Management Office), 333

point-of-sale (POS) system, 68

porn sites, 141

Porras, Jerry I., 268

portable media, 138

portals: definition of, 183; and e-business, 189; employee portal uses of intranets, 183–84, 206; and GSS (group support system), 97; market for, 58n2; partner portal uses of extranets, 185–86; private versus public portals, 183; software for, 176

Porter, Michael, 7, 9, 26

Porter 5-Forces Matrix, 17, *18*

portfolio evaluation of IT projects, 329–30n9

Portfolio Manager, 387

POS (point-of-sale) system, 68

POTS (plain old telephone service), 119

power in organizations, 207–8

Power Point, 226

predictive modeling, 283, 289

Priceline, 169

pricing on purchased goods and services, 159–60

primary domain controller (PDC), 53

print server, 53

prioritization and allocation process, 231

privacy issues, 178–82, 189

Private Branch Exchange (PBX), 110–11, 113

private exchange or portal models of B2B e-commerce, 165–66

private exchanges, 186. *See also* extranets

private portals, 183

process losses of working in groups, 97, 97n5

Proctor & Gamble, 181

productivity: and CMM (capability maturity model), 241; increases in, based on IT, 4–6; and software upgrades, 361; and wireless technology, 126–27

Program Management Office (PMO), 333

progress reporting, 383

project business model, 365–69

project control, 383–84, 417

project management, 379–88, 399–404, 422

project management tools, 385–88, *386*, *387*

project manager, 382, 398, 399–404, 408–12, 413, 415–18

Project Office, 388

project payback period, 322–23, 325, 328, *329*

project reporting, 383

project sponsors. *See* sponsors of IT projects

projects. *See* information technology (IT) projects

protocols: definition of, 101; for e-mail, 116; FTP (File Transfer Protocol), 116, 137; HTTP (Hypertext Transfer Protocol), 105, 115; for Internet, 12, 111, 115, 116; RSVP (ReSerVation Protocol), 113; SOAP (Simple Object Access Protocol), 64, 66; WAP (Wireless Application Protocol), 124

prototyping, 32

PSTN (public switched telephone network), 110–11

public exchanges, 186

public marketplace and exchange models of B2B e-commerce, 164–65

public portals, 183

public switched telephone network (PSTN), 110–11

public voice network, 110–11

publish and subscribe systems, 59–60, *61*

pull system, 29

push system, 29

PVCs (permanent virtual circuits), 109

PVR (personal video recorders), 121

QoS (Quality of Service), 112–13

QSM, Inc., 388

quality assurance/control, 204, 242–56, 383–84. *See also* evaluation

quality management, 383–84

Quality of Service (QoS), 112–13

queuing systems, 60, *61*

quick ship, *144*

Qwest, 116

racehorse organizations, 225

racehorse teams, 224–25

RAD (Rapid Application Development), 32, 66n1

radical changes in business processes, 265–69, *267*

Rapid Application Development (RAD), 32, 66n1

rapid prototyping, 32

Rappa, Michael, 167n1

Rational Software, 238n1, 388

"reaction" chart, 215

real-time synchronization, 297

RealTime, 388

reciprocal site, *144*

recovery plan. *See* disaster recovery (DR) plan

reengineering, 254–55

reliability: and ASP (application service provider), 345; of networks, 106; of operating systems, 72

repeaters, 102

Request for Information (RFI), 339

Request for Proposal (RFP), 341, 357–58

Request for Qualifications (RFQ), 339–40

ReSerVation Protocol (RSVP), 113

resource allocation: amount of spending on information technology (IT), 305–8, *306*; and ASP (application service provider), 342–46; and benefits modeling, 332–33; and benefits of IT projects, 326–27, 331–34; and "build or buy" decision, 335–38; and business investment, 309; and business-driven technology strategy, 308; choice of one IT project over another, 326–31, *328, 329, 330*; decisions on how to spend money on technology, 309–12, *312*; and financial measures of IT projects, 322–26, 328, *329*; and multi-year technology investment plan, 311–12, *312*; and outsourcing, 342–59; overview of, 303–4; and rate of industry change, 307;

resource allocation (*continued*)
revenue-enhancing versus cost-reduction projects, 312–15; and revenue protection, 315–18; software upgrades, 24, 359–62; and spending bubble, 308; and status of IT infrastructure, 308; technology spending pattern for industry, 306–7, *306*; and total cost of ownership (TCO), 319–21, 325; and vendor selection, 338–42. *See also* cost; cost reductions
resource planning, 202–3
resource pools of experts, 414
retail sales, *306*
retail sales online, 156, 167–74, 191, 194–98. *See also* e-business
return on investment (ROI): and ASP (application service provider), 344; and business-driven technology strategy, 20; calculation of, 323, 325; and capability maturity model (CMM), 241; and customer relationship management (CRM) system, 283, 332; of customization of standard vendor applications, 300; definition of, 244; in e-learning, 224, 226–28; and information technology (IT) investment, 307–8; and IT organization, 244; payback period compared with, 322–23, 325; software for, 325n1; and software upgrades, 362; and supply chain management (SCM), 293
revenue enhancing projects, 312–15
revenue protection, 315–18
revenue stream protection, 317–18
revenue streams and B2C e-commerce, 167–70
RFI (Request for Information), 339
RFP (Request for Proposal), 341, 357–58
RFQ (Request for Qualifications), 339–40
Right[6] concept, 187, 187n1
ring networks, 107, *108*
risk management, 383–84
risks: of business model of project, 365–69;

of ERP implementation, 274–78; of information technology (IT) projects, 329, 329–30, *330*; of project implementation, 369–73, *370*; of SCM implementation, 295; of throwaway systems, 31
ROI (return on investment): and ASP (application service provider), 344; and business-driven technology strategy, 20; calculation of, 323, 325; and capability maturity model (CMM), 241; and customer relationship management (CRM) system, 283, 332; of customization of standard vendor applications, 300; definition of, 244; in e-learning, 224, 226–28; and information technology (IT) investment, 307–8; and IT organization, 244; payback period compared with, 322–23, 325; software for, 325n1; and software upgrades, 362; and supply chain management (SCM), 293
root cause analysis, 243
routers, 102–3, 106, 111
routing table, 102
RSVP (ReSerVation Protocol), 113
RUP, 238n1

SABRE system, 4, 6
sales and service, *20*, 128–29, 156, 156–58, 167–74, 191, 194–98, 214, *306*
SAP, 61, 165, 185, 272
satellite broadband technology, 119
scalability, 71–72, 90
scanner, 137
Schwab, 169
SCM (supply chain management): attributes and capabilities of, 291–94; and business processes, 255; and business-driven technology strategy, 16; and competition, 8; and data integrity, 296–97; and data quality, 296; and data standardization, 297; and e-business, 160; evolution of, 293; and integration, 296; integration of, with ERP

and CRM systems, 272–73, 293; and interfaces, 296; and mass customization, 29; and productivity, 6; and real time synchronization, 297; and supply chain planning, 295, 297–98; technology issues in implementation of, 294–98; and transaction processing system (TPS), 82; use of, 203

scorecard. *See* balanced scorecard

screen scraping, 60

SDSL (symmetric digital subscriber line), 119

Sears, 126–27, 174

security: as component for e-business, 187, 189; components of security architecture, 132–34, *133*; decision drivers for, 132–33, *133*; and encryption, 117, 138; and extranets, 183; and firewall, 135–38, 141; and front-end/back-end integration, 192; goal of, 134–35; importance of, 131–32; internal security, 138; and Internet, 117; of networks, 106; operations, *133*, 134; overview of, 37–38; policies, standards, and procedures for, 132, *133*, 134, 140; standard approach to authentication, 132; support framework for, 132, *133*; and viruses, 138–42; and Web services, 69; and WiFi (Wireless Fidelity), 124–25; and wireless technology, 124–25, 127–28

segmentation marketing, 175, 288

SEI (Software Engineering Institute), 238, 238n2

Senge, Peter, 225n1

server, 52. *See also* client/server technology

service customization, 27

service desk, 242–43

service level agreement (SLA), 113, 243, 346

Short Messaging Service (SMS), 123

Simple Mail Transfer Protocol (SMTP), 116

Simple Object Access Protocol (SOAP), 64, 66

SirCam, 139

Six Sigma, 238n1

SLA (service level agreement), 113, 243, 346

smart cards, 127

Smith, Douglas K., 423

SMS (Short Messaging Service), 123

SMTP (Simple Mail Transfer Protocol), 116

SNA (Systems Network Architecture), 101

SOAP (Simple Object Access Protocol), 64, 66

software: antivirus software, 141, 142; and CMM (capability maturity model), 237–41; desktop software, 161; desktop software upgrades, 360–61; early adopters of upgrades, 24, 359–62; for e-business, 187; for e-learning, 225–26, *227*; forced upgrades for, 360, 360n1; licensing of, 343; portal software, 176; quality measures for development of, 243–44; for ROI (return on investment), 325n1; and Unix platform, 76. *See also specific business processes*

software application management, 347–48

Software Engineering Institute (SEI), 238, 238n2

Software Productivity Research, 388

Sony, 156

SOPs (standard operating procedures), *19*

spending bubble, 308

sponsors of IT projects: and business-driven technology strategy, 19; and choice of technology project, 327; and client expectations, 403; and evaluation of project risks, 372–73; feedback by, on IT organization's performance, 245; lack of, and project failure, 377; and project approach and outcomes, 402–3; and project manager, 382, 399–404, 416; and project team dynamics, 401; questions asked by, 399–404; questions on, 372–73; of revenue-enhancing versus cost-reduction projects, 314; and risks of business model of project, 367; roles of, 381, 382, 396–99; and

sponsors of IT projects (*continued*)
stakeholder management, 403–4; and termination of projects, 422
Sprint, 116
SQL, 60–61
staffing of technology projects, 388–91, 418
stakeholders, 215, 381–82, 403–7, 416, 417
standard operating procedures (SOPs), *19*
standards: and e-business, 155, 192; for Internet, 155; for networks, 106; for security,
134; for Web services, 66, 69; WiFi standards, 125; for wireless technology, 123
Standish Group International, 386, 424
star networks, 107, *108*
Starbucks, 124
statistical analysis, 92
steering board for technology projects, 215,
376, 402n3, 404–7, 422
strategic inflection points, 13
strategic planning process, 230–31
strong leader model for steering board,
405–6
subscription model of B2C e-commerce, 168
Sun Microsystems, 41–42, 59, 67
SunLite Casual Furniture, 276, 277
Sun's Java 2 Enterprise Edition (J2EE), 41–
42, 59, *61*, 67
suppliers. *See* vendors
supply chain, 29, 291–92, 291n2, 295
supply chain integration models of B2B
e-commerce, 166
supply chain management (SCM): attributes
and capabilities of, 291–94; and business
processes, 255; and business-driven technology strategy, 16; and competition, 8;
and data integrity, 296–97; and data quality, 296; and data standardization, 297;
and e-business, 160; evolution of, 293; and
integration, 296; integration of, with ERP
and CRM systems, 272–73; and interfaces, 296; and mass customization, 29;
and productivity, 6; and real time syn-

chronization, 297; and supply chain planning, 295, 297–98; technology issues in
implementation of, 294–98; and transaction processing system (TPS), 82; use
of, 203
supply chain planning, 295, 297–98
switches, 102, 106, 110–11
SWOT (strengths, weaknesses, opportunities, and threats) analysis, 17, *18*
symmetric digital subscriber line (SDSL),
119
system management, 72–73
Systems Network Architecture (SNA), 101

tangible costs, 362
Target, 172
targeted marketing, 175
TCO (total cost of ownership), 77, 244, 319–
21, 325
TCP (Transmission Control Protocol), 115
TCP/IP, 101, 105, 115, 116
TDMA (Time Division Multiple Access),
122, 122n1, 123
team members of technology projects, 401,
412–13, 423
TeamPlay, 387
technology. *See information technology (IT)
entries*
technology assessment, 14–21, 211
technology infrastructure outsourcing, 347
technology investment. *See* resource
allocation
technology projects. *See* information technology (IT) projects
technology review committee, 17, 331
telecommunications industry, 27, 110, 121–
23, 316, 317–18
telecommuting, 121, 147
telephone companies and services, 110, 121–
23
10Base-2 cable, *103*, 104
10Base-5 cable, *103*, 104

10Base-T wiring, 103–4, *103*

tenure of CIO, 246–49

termination of IT projects, 421–24

Texaco, 222

theory of network externalities, 194–95

thin versus fat clients, 54–57, 273, 321

3Com, 13

3G technologies, 122, 123, 129

3M Corporation, 96n3

3M Meeting Network, 96n3

throwaway systems, 30–33

time bombs, 140

Time Division Multiple Access (TDMA), 122, 122n1, 123

time value of money, 323, 324, 325

Toshiba, 13

total cost of ownership (TCO), 77, 244, 319–21, 325

Toysrus.com, 191

TP (transaction processing) monitors, 81

TPS (transaction processing system): and business intelligence system (BIS), 92, 92n1; compared with decision support system, 84; as data source for decision support system, 83; and data warehouse, 87; definition of, 79; features of, 80; future of, 82; importance of, 81–82; measurement of performance and accuracy of, 81; uses of, 79

tracking mechanism, 420–21

training of employees. *See* employee training

Transaction Performance Council, 71

transaction processing system (TPS), 79–84; and business intelligence system (BIS), 92, 92n1; compared with decision support system, 84; as data source for decision support system, 83; and data warehouse, 87; definition of, 79; features of, 80; future of, 82; importance of, 81–82; measurement of performance and accuracy of, 81; uses of, 79

transaction processing (TP) monitors, 81

transformation in business processes, 208, 260–69, *261*, *262*, 423

transit systems, 127

Transmission Control Protocol (TCP), 115

Tri Valley Growers, 275, 276

trojan horse, 140

twisted pair wiring, 103–4, *103*

2G technologies, 122

2.5G technology, 122–23

Ubid.com, 67–68

UDDI (Universal Description, Discovery, and Integration), 66

UMTS / WCDMA, 123n2

unicast network architecture, 108

Unisource, 275

United Air Lines, 4

United Parcel Service (UPS), 6, 82, 126–27, 154

Universal Description, Discovery, and Integration (UDDI), 66

universities, 44

Unix operating system, 70–77, *75*, 101, 225

unshielded twisted pair wiring, 103–4, *103*

upgrades for software, 24, 359–62

UPS (United Parcel Service), 6, 82, 126–27, 154

up-selling, 176–77

upstream supply chain, 291

Usenet, 116

user-defined tags, 62–63, *63*

USinternetworking, 344

UTP Category 3 wiring, 103–4

UTP Category 5 wiring, 104

value-adding services, 27

value chain, 291–92n2

Value Management Office (VMO), 333–34

value network, 12–13

value-oriented companies, 278–82, *280*

vendors: automated vendor selection, 341–42; and forced software upgrades, 360,

vendors (*continued*)
  360n1; identification of, 339; importance of relationships with, 24; negative reactions of, to IT projects, 216–19; qualification of, 339–40; selection of, 338–42
VerticalNet, Inc., 166
video conferencing, 121
vILT (virtual instructor-led training), *227*
virtual applications, 189
virtual instructor-led training (vILT), *227*
virtual private network (VPN), 141
viruses, 138–42
VMO (Value Management Office), 333–34
voice networks, 110–13. *See also* networks
Voice over IP (VoIP), 112, 113
VoIP (Voice over IP), 112, 113
VPN (virtual private network), 141

W. W. Grainger, 276
Walgreen's, 173–74
Wal-Mart, 4, 156, 172
WAN (Wide Area Network): combined data and voice networks, 112; description of, 106, *107*; and Ethernet, 52; and extranet, 183; and routers, 103
Wang, 11
WAP (Wireless Application Protocol), 124
warm site, *144*
WBT (Web-based training), *227*
Web architecture, 41–42
Web-based middleware, 60, *61*
Web-based training (WBT), *227*
Web browsers, 60, *61*
Web bugs, 180–81
Web conferencing, 203
Web discussion board, 203
Web pages, 222–23
Web servers, 60, *61*
Web services: and airline industry, 9; B2C and B2B transactions, 67–68; benefits of, 67–69; as commercial offerings, 67; and

cost reductions in IT, 161–62; definition of, 66; and front-end/back-end integration, 193; and group support system (GSS), 97; internal systems of, 68–69, 68n7; and intranets, 185; problems of, 69–70; prognosis on, 70; and security, 69; standards for, 66, 69; and supplier relationships, 8; and throwaway systems, 32; and XML, 69–70. *See also* Internet
Web Services Description Language (WSDL), 66
Web site personalization, 181
weblogs (blogs), 222–23
Webvan, 195, 196
Whirlpool, 275, 276
Wide Area Network (WAN): combined data and voice networks, 112; description of, 106, *107*; and Ethernet, 52; and extranet, 183; and routers, 103
WiFi (Wireless Fidelity), 13, 120, 124–25
Windows operating system, 41, 51, 70–73, 101, 226
Wireless Application Protocol (WAP), 124
Wireless Fidelity (WiFi), 13, 120, 124–25
wireless LAN (WLAN), 122, 124–25
wireless Personal Area Network (WPAN), 122, 124–25
wireless technology: benefits of, for businesses, 126–29; and Bluetooth, 125; business applications of, 126; and cost reduction, 128–29; and customer satisfaction and loyalty, 127; as delivery mechanism for broadband, 119–20; digital data transmission, 124; as disruptive, 12–13; fixed wireless, 120; and hype cycle, 66n1; mobile telephony technologies, 121–23; mobile wireless, 119, 122–23; platforms for, 121–25; and productivity, 126–27; and sales and service, 128–29; and security, 124–25, 127–28; Short Messaging Service (SMS), 123; standards for, 123; WiFi

(Wireless Fidelity), 13, 120, 124–25;
WLAN (wireless LAN), 122, 124–25;
WPAN (wireless PAN), 122, 124–25
wiring for networks, 103–5, *103*
WLAN (wireless LAN), 122, 124–25
workgroups, 95–96, 95–96n2
World Wide Web (WWW), 115
worms, 140
WPAN (wireless PAN), 122, 124–25
WPAN (wireless Personal Area Network),
122, 124–25
WSDL (Web Services Description Lan-
guage), 66
WWW (World Wide Web), 115

XBRL (Extended Business Reporting Lan-
guage), 63
Xerox, 51–52
XML (Extensible Markup Language), 60–
66, *61*, *63*, 69–70, 188, 189, 297
XML Web Services, 41
XP (Xtreme Programming), 32
XSL (eXtensible Stylesheet Language), 64n8
Xtreme Programming (XP), 32

YMCA of the United States, 237